CONTEMPORARY ART

FROM CRESCENT MOON PUBLISHING

The Art of Andy Goldsworthy
by William Malpas

The Art of Andy Goldsworthy
by William Malpas

Andy Goldsworthy: Touching Nature
by William Malpas

Richard Long: Pocket Guide
by William Malpas

Constantin Brancusi: Sculpting the Essence of Things
by James Pearson

Alison Wilding: The Embrace of Sculpture
by Susan Quinnell

Eric Gill: Nuptials of God
by Anthony Hoyland

The Erotic Object: Sexuality in Sculpture From Prehistory to the Present Day
by Susan Quinnell

Minimal Art and Artists in the 1960s and After
by Laura Garrard

Land Art, Earthworks, Installations, Environments, Sculpture
by William Malpas

Land Art: A Complete Guide to Landscape, Environmental, Earthworks, Nature, Sculpture and Installation Art
by William Malpas

Andy Goldsworthy In Close-Up
by William Malpas

Land Art In Close-Up
by William Malpas

Colorfield Painting: Minimal, Cool, Hard Edge, Serial and Post-Painterly Abstract Art From the Sixties to the Present
by Laura Garrard

Mark Rothko: The Art of Transcendence
by Julia Davis

Jasper Johns
by L.M. Poole

Brice Marden
by Laura Garrard

Frank Stella: American Abstract Artist: Special Edition
by James Pearson

Maurice Sendak and the Art of Children's Book Illustration
by L.M. Poole

*The Erotic Object In Close-Up: Sexuality in Sculpture
From Prehistory to the Present Day*
By Susan Quinnell

Sacred Gardens: The Garden in Myth, Religion and Art
by Jeremy Robinson

Sex in Art: Pornography and Pleasure in Painting and Sculpture
by Cassidy Hughes

Postwar Art
by George Knighton

The Art of
Richard Long

The Art of Richard Long

William Malpas

Crescent Moon Publishing

First published 2005. Second edition 2005. Third edition 2008. Fourth edition 2012.
Reprinted 2018.
© William Malpas 2005, 2008, 2012, 2018.

Printed and bound in the U.S.A.
Set in Helvetica Neue Condensed 9 on 14pt, Helvetica, and Gill Sans.
Designed by Radiance Graphics.

The right of William Malpas to be identified as the author of *The Art of Richard Long*
has been asserted generally in accordance with sections 77 and 78 of the Copyright,
Designs and Patents Act 1988.

British Library Cataloguing in Publication data

Malpas, William
The Art of Richard Long: Complete Works: Special Edition (Sculptors Series)
1. Long, Richard, 1945- – Criticism and interpretation
2. Sculpture, Modern – 20th century
3. Sculpture, Modern – 20th century – Great Britain
I. Title

709.2

ISBN-13 9781861713490 (Hbk)
ISBN-13 9781861713285 (Pbk)
ISBN-13 978186176729 (Pbk)
ISBN-13 978186177504 (Pbk)

CRESCENT MOON PUBLISHING
P.O. Box 1312,, Maidstone,
Kent, ME14 5XU,
Great Britain
www.crmoon.com

Contents

Acknowledgements   *11*
Abbreviations   *13*
Illustrations   *15*
Introduction   *19*

Part One

1   Sculpture in the Contemporary Era   *25*
2   Sculpture and Gender   *47*
3   Spirit and Matter: Land Art   *59*
4   Land Artists in Britain, Europe and America   *125*

Part Two

5   Richard Long: The Art of Walking   *213*
6   Circles, Lines, Rows, Splashes and Other Forms
    in Richard Long's Art   *259*
7   Idea/ Text/ Desire: Textworks   *287*
8   From Photography to Installations   *311*
9   'A Place of Regeneration': Dartmoor   *321*
10 Walking As Ecstasy   *329*

Illustrations   *339*
Notes   *375*
List of Works   *397*
Bibliography   *403*

Acknowledgements

Thanks to Anthony d'Offay Gallery, London; Sperone Westwater, New York; Verlag der Buchhandlung Walther König, Köln; Thames & Hudson, London; Coracle Press, London; Karsten Schubert, London; Konrad Fischer Galerie, Düsseldorf; Hayward Gallery, London; MW Press, Noordwijk, Holland; Musée d'Art Moderne de la Ville de Paris; Center for Contemporary Arts, Santa Fe, New Mexico; Phaidon Press, London; Tate Gallery, London; Tate Publishing.

Illustrations: photographs are by Jeremy Robinson.

Poetry quotations: University of California Press, Berkeley. Routledge, London. Methuen, London. Faber & Faber, London.

Abbreviations

RICHARD LONG

IC 1/2   *Richard Long: In Conversation*, Parts 1 & 2
FS   *Five, Six, Pick Up Sticks*
OW   *Old World New World*
WC   *Walking in Circles*
MW   *Mountains and Water*
SF   *An Interview with Richard Long*, 1994
RC   *An Interview with Richard Long,* by R. Cork
RL   *Richard Long*, text by R. Fuchs, 1986
WAF   *Words After the Fact*
FC   *Fragments of a Conversation I-VI*
GL   Interview with G. Lobacheff
1994b   *No Where*, interview, 1994
1995a   "Question For Richard Long", 1995
WL   *Richard Long: Walking the Line*
SS   interview, *Stepping Stones*
2003a   "I am just passing through the world", interview, 2003
2004b   "Still walking, after all these years", interview, 2004

ROBERT SMITHSON

RS   *Selected Writings*

ANDY GOLDSWORTHY

S   *Andy Goldsworthy: Stone*
HE   *Hand to Earth: Andy Goldsworthy, Sculpture, 1976-1990*

Do you make art your life, that which always comes first and occupies every moment, the last problem before sleep and the first awaking vision? ...How do you spend your time? More talking about art than making it? How do you spend your money? On art materials first – or do you start to pinch here? ...How much of the work day or the work week do you devote to your profession – that which will be your identity for life?

David Smith

Dartmoor, England.
One of Richard Long's favourite places for making art.

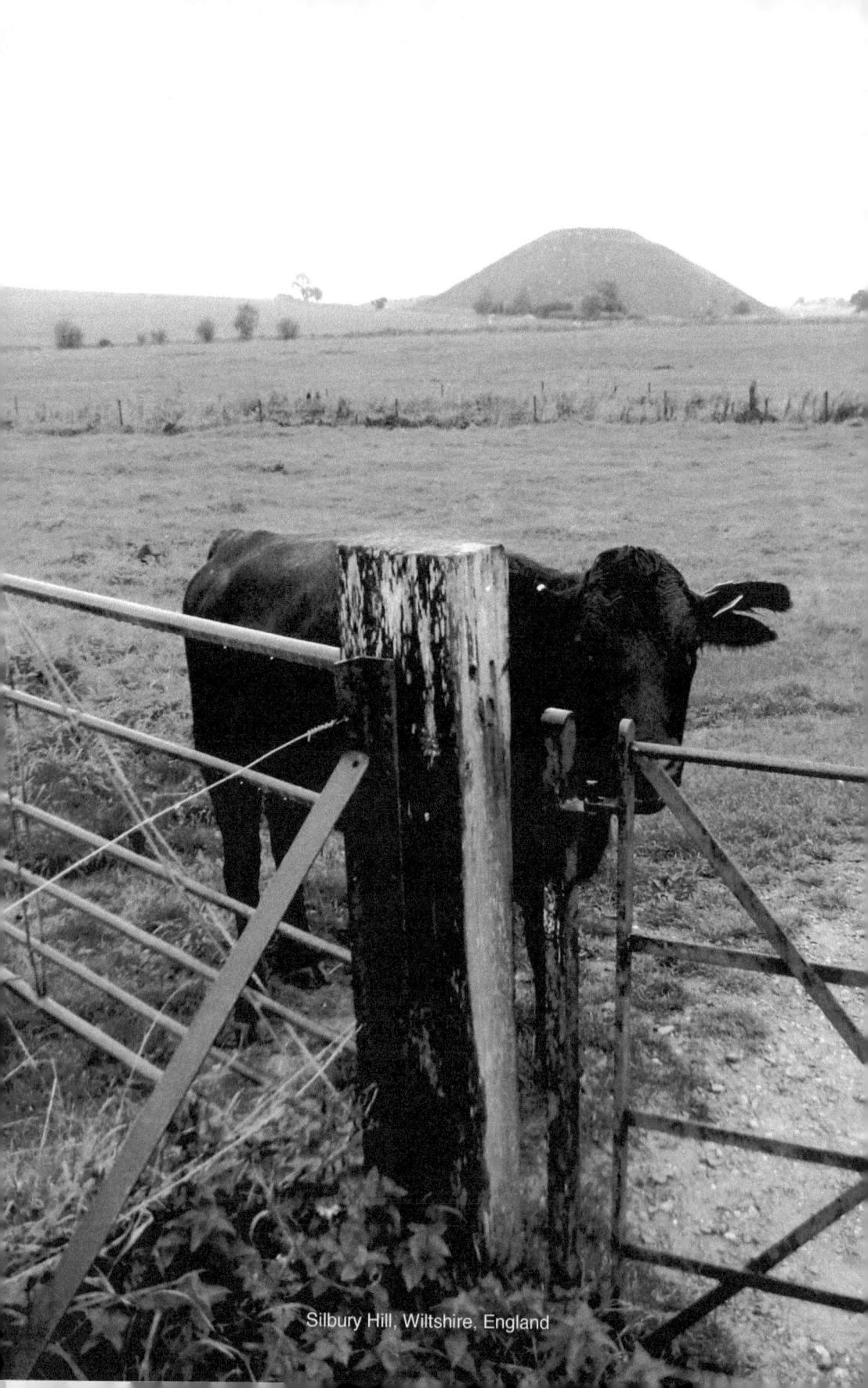
Silbury Hill, Wiltshire, England

Introduction

This study looks at a contemporary artist, Richard Long. It uses some of the material in an earlier monograph on Richard Long (1995 and 1998), and my companion books on Andy Goldsworthy (1995, 1998, 2004) and land and environmental art (1996, 1998 and 2004).[1] This second edition adds some corrections, new material, and new illustrations.

Before the chapters on Richard Long I consider topics such as contemporary and postwar art and sculpture; Long's contemporaries, including fellow British sculptors; and land art. Throughout the study I make comparisons between Long and Andy Goldsworthy, another land artist/ sculptor, eleven years younger than Long. Goldsworthy and Long are similar artists, and I discuss their differences as well as their similarities (and also the artist closest to Long in many respects, Hamish Fulton).

Richard Long is sometimes termed a 'Romantic' sculptor, and part of this book relates his art to British Romanticism, as found in the literature of William Wordsworth, Percy Bysshe Shelley, John Keats and others, and the British landscape tradition, as in J.M.W. Turner, John Constable, Thomas Girtin and other landscape painters. Aspects of British Romantic culture in 20th century and 21st century art also considered (such as the 'New Ruralists', 'New Romantics', 'New Arcadians' and 'Neo-Romantics', such as David Inshaw, Graham Ovenden, Edward Steel Harper, Ann Arnold, etc). I also explore some of the aspects of Romantic culture in Europe as well as Britain.

The British novelist John Cowper Powys (1872-1963) and the British poet Peter

Redgrove (1932-2003) are used as reference points for a lyrical or linguistic equivalent of earthwork art and nature mysticism. Powys's and Redgrove's works evoke a sensitivity which is close to the art of Richard Long (Powys and Redgrove are also idiosyncratic choices on my part – Ruskin, Pater, Wordsworth, Coleridge, Shelley, D.H. Lawrence and Edward Thomas might be more obvious ones).

In the course of this book I make references to Richard Long's contemporary British sculptors (Tony Cragg, Bill Woodrow, David Nash, Barry Flanagan, Alison Wilding, Shirazeh Houshiary, Michael Craig-Martin, Ian Hamilton Finlay, Richard Wentworth, Boyd Webb, Hamish Fulton, Edward Allington, Richard Deacon, Stephen Cox, Philip King, Anthony Caro, Rachel Whiteread, Tim Head, William Tucker, Anish Kapoor, Anthony Gormley, David Mach, Tim Scott, Peter Randall-Page, Nicholas Pope and Gilbert & George). I realize that much more could, and should, be said about these artists and their relation to Richard Long's art. Of those artists, I discuss mainly the ones that have most affinities with Long's art, such as Hamish Fulton, first and foremost, and David Nash, Chris Drury, Andy Goldsworthy, Tony Cragg and Alison Wilding).

Further chapters include: one on women, feminist, body art and performance sculptors, as a comparison with Richard Long's art, which has a strong component of performance (even if it's nearly always private). Also, a consideration of gendered sculpture and art. In the chapter on Minimal, Conceptual, Process and other 1960s and post-1960s art and artists, I'm interested in the artists (primarily European and American) who have most in common with Richard Long's art: the great Minimal and land artists, such as Donald Judd, Robert Morris, Carl Andre, Sol LeWitt, Dennis Oppenheim, James Turrell and Robert Ryman, and the important Conceptual artists, such as Hans Haacke, Bruce Nauman, Yves Klein and Lawrence Weiner.

The 'new British sculpture' and 'New Generation' of the 1960s are also discussed (Long was part of this culture, although he soon moved out into the international scene in the 1970s). The 'Young British Artists', 'Brit-art', *Sensation* and *Freeze* crowd of the Nineties and after are only noted in passing: Tracey Emin, Damien Hirst, Mark Wallinger, Sarah Lucas, the Chapmans, etc. Long's art is diametrically opposed to the kind of art of the YBAs and Brit-artists, not least in its determined attention-seeking, its cultivation of celebrity and stars, its love of camp, ironic, playful, insincere poses, and its emphasis on the immediate and the easily digested.

The chapter on the most celebrated works of land artists (mainly in the US and

Europe) is probably the most pertinent to an exploration of Richard Long's art. No book on Richard Long's *œuvre* would be complete without references to Robert Smithson (still probably the most revered of all land artists), Walter de Maria, Michael Heizer, Alice Aycock, Mary Miss, Nancy Holt, Dennis Oppenheim, Christo and James Turrell. Among British land artists – Goldsworthy, Nash, Fulton, Drury, Harris, Cooper, Martin – Long is among the most famous and perhaps the most important (at least in the international frame).

In discussing land art and land artists, I have focussed on some of the more well-known land artists, such as Roberts Smithson and Morris, Christo, Walter de Maria, Michael Heizer, David Nash, Hamish Fulton, Nancy Holt, Alice Aycock, Mary Miss, Carl Andre, Dennis Oppenheim and James Turrell. There are, of course, many more artists working with place, site, landscape and the environment. They include Robert Adzema, Vijali, Ana Mendieta, Jan Norman, Jane Balsgaard, Jussi Heikkilä, Tom Van Sant, Sherry Wiggins, Charles Jencks, Roger Ackling, Gordon Matta-Clark, Kazuo Shiraga, Bonnie Sherk, Charles Simonds, Isamu Noguchi, Richard Serra, Tony Smith, Daniel Buren, Hans Haacke, Jørn Rønnau, Helge Røed, Nils Udo, Giuliano Mauri, Bror Westman, Debbie Duffin, Gloria Carlos, Phyllidia Barlow, Richard Fleischner, Michelangelo Pistoletto, Hiroshi Teshigahara, Vong Phaephanit, Herman de Vries, Joseph Beuys, Betty Beaumont, Betsy Damon, Keith Arnatt, Herbert Bayer, Newton Harrison, Helen Myer Harrison, Charles Ross, Peter Erskine, Juan Geuer, Jody Pinto, John Baldessari, Donna Henes, Phyllis Yampolsky, William Furlong, Art & Language, Peter Fend, Christian Philip Müller, Cildo Meireles, Harriet Feigenbaum, Ian Hamilton Finlay, Meg Webster, Jan Dibbets, Toshikatsu Endo, Mark Dion, Guo-Qiang Cai, Peter Hutchinson, Lothar Baumgarten, Maya Lin, Douglas Huebler, Bruce McLean, Avital Geva, Barry Flanagan, Mierle Laderman Ukeles, Viet Ngo, Mel Chin, Agnes Denes, William Jackson Maxwell, Constance DeJong, Doris Bloom, Reiko Goto, Michelle Oka Doner, Buster Simpson, Martha Schwartz, Peter Richards, Douglas Hollis, Patrick Zentz, Othello Anderson, Fern Shaffer, Lynne Hull, Patricia Johanson, Karen McCoy, Dominique Mazeaud and Alan Sonfist. What is written here about the more well-known land artists also applies to the other artists cited above, plus many others.

When it comes to performance art – an area Richard Log's art is related to – the field is vast. Performance, live art, happenings and action art has many links with land, environmental, nature and installation art. There isn't space here to consider them all (there are plenty of other studies). There are artists who talk to dead hares in their arms (Joseph Beuys), sculptors who stood and sang in suits (Gilbert & George, contemporaries of Richard Long's at St Martin's art school), artists who carry out weird post-Catholic rituals or cut up sheep carcasses (Hermann Nitsch), artists who perform nude with film, video and installations (Carolee Schneemann), artists who sat in rooms and menstruated (Catherine Elwes), artists who examined their genitals and masturbated before an audience (Annie Sprinkle), artists who had themselves bound and gagged in a gallery, holding a pig's heart (Tania Bruguera), artists who replayed the physical martyrdom of saints (Ron Athey), artists who re-enact car crashes at a happening (Jim Dine and Judy Tersch), artists who douse themselves in water (Nam June Paik), artists who draw on their bodies (while naked, of course), artists who stand against trees (nude, of course), covered in mud and plants (Ana Mendieta), artists who set themselves on fire (Tomas Ruller), or ignite gunpowder charges (Roman Signer), groups who threw paint and food over each other while singing vaudeville songs (the Kipper Kids), artists who painted gallery floors with their long hair (Janine Antoni), artists who (while naked, of course) masturbate with cuddly toys (Mike Kelly), artists who meditate, chant, sing and play music (Caryle Reedy), groups who burn US flags and protest against war while naked on Brooklyn Bridge (Yayoi Kusama), artists who hid under wooden ramps in galleries and masturbated while speaking to visitors (Vito Acconci), artists who hung between bridges (Dennis Oppenheim), artists who shoot guns at paint-filled balloons (Niki de Sant Phalle), artists who burn books (John Latham, a one-time teacher at St Martin's college when Long was there), groups who stage a protest 'blood bath' in a New York street (Guerrilla Art Action Group), artists who sat on horses in galleries (Jannis Kounellis), performers who locked themselves in rooms for six days while covered in paint (Stuart Brisley), artists who hung them- selves upside-down in galleries (Jill Orr), creative couples who walk and bump into each other for an hour (while naked, of course), artists who scrubbed cow bones (Marina Abramovic), groups who sit naked in healing baths (Cai Guo Qiang), per- formers who have their clothes cut off by the audience (Yoko Ono), artists who signed semi-nude women as 'living sculptures' (Piero Manzoni), and artists who crucified themselves on the roof of a Volkeswagen (Chris Burden).

By comparison with most of these performance, political, Conceptual, body, action, happening and installation artists in the era from the Fifties onwards, Richard Long is distinctly mellow and calm and unobtrusive. But his art remains inspiring, and some of the reasons for its enduring spirit are explored in this book.

William Malpas
London, England

Part One

1

Sculpture in the Contemporary Era

Richard Long is a land artist and sculptor (sometimes he's also called an earth artist, earthworks artist, nature artist, landscape artist or environmental artist. I should note that the term 'land art' is used here as a shorthand to refer to many kinds of art, including landscape art, earth art, earthworks, nature art, green or ecological art, and installations. In a way, almost all major contemporary art made nowadays is some kind of 'installation art').

Richard Long works with and in the natural world, but also with and within the highly sophisticated, artificial and humanmade world of art and culture. 'I too wanted to make nature the subject of my work,' Long explained of his early work, 'but in new ways. I started working outside using natural materials like grass and water, and this evolved into the idea of making a sculpture by walking'. Long's sculpture developed out of late modernism, High Modernism, Minimal art, Process art, Conceptual art and, in particular, the culture of 1960s art, the era of late Henry Moore, Robert Morris, Robert Smithson, Yves Klein, Lawrence Weiner, Anthony Caro, William Tucker, Tony Smith and Carl Andre. It was the 1960s-70s era of what Rosalind Krauss called 'expanded field' sculpture, the High Renaissance of land art.[1] Krauss's 'expanded field' sculptors included Robert Irwin, Michael Heizer, Richard Serra, Walter de Maria, Sol LeWitt, Bruce Nauman, Alice Aycock, Mary Miss, Dennis Oppenheim, Nancy Holt,

George Trakis, Hamish Fulton, Christo, Joel Shapiro and Long. It is worth going back a little to look at postwar and contemporary sculpture for a while, to see where Long's art fits in.

THE SCULPTURE OF ARROGANCE: BIG, BIG, BIG

The awareness of scale is a function of the comparison made between that constant, one's body size, and the object. Space between the subject and the object is implied in such a comparison.

Robert Morris (1966, 21)

However exciting a painting by, say, Julian Schnabel, Robert Longo, or David Salle may be, sculptures by artists such as Tony Smith, Nancy Graves, Rebecca Horn, Mark di Suvero, Eva Hesse, Louise Nevelson, Tony Cragg and Richard Long have the edge over the painters. While Renaissance painting may represent the apotheosis of 'high art', and ancient Greek sculpture may be the height of 'high sculpture', contemporary sculpture really is some of the most startling in the history of art (and Richard Long's art is close to the core of contemporary sculpture).

Part of the reason is, of course, *scale*. Postwar and contemporary artists, of all kinds, have made massive art. David Smith's *Wagon I* and *Cubi* (1965) sculptures, the Christos' wrapped buildings, Michael Heizer's *Effigy Tumuli* and Richard Serra's steel leaning slabs and props are huge, heavy, chunky, truly colossal pieces which dominate their surroundings. Donald Judd wrote: '[t]his scale is one of the most important developments in 20th century art'.[1] Richard Long's sculpture is not 'monolithic' in scale, usually – but his works can stretch over many miles, far longer than even the Christos' fences, valley curtains or wrapped coasts.

The Abstract Expressionist artists, such as Helen Frankenthaler, Mark Rothko, Franz Kline and Barnett Newman, produced huge paintings, which swallow up the spectator when s/he approaches them. One can move into the same space as a Morris Louis or Sam Francis painting and be enveloped by it (creating a sense of intimacy was one of the chief motives for large-scale, as Rothko asserted, a sense of a personal relationship between the viewer and the artwork).[2]

Similarly, postwar and contemporary sculptors have made massive works (though perhaps 'intimacy' is not many visitors' first reactions). Artists such as Christo created pieces that were 24 miles long, while some of the earthworks of Robert Morris, Herbert Bayer, James Pierce and Alice Aycock cover acres of land. Even medium-sized examples of contemporary sculpture, such as Donald Judd's wooden or concrete hollow Minimal boxes or an Isamu Noguchi cube, are sometimes seen as monumental. A critic on *The New York Times* called Donald Judd's 1977 installation at the Heiner Friedrich Gallery a 'majestic and finely measured presence'.3 There's no doubt that, when it comes to land art, bigger is often seen as better.

On scale, Carl Andre remarked:

In sculpture, there's quite a concrete relationship between one's size as a person and/ or mass as a person and the mass of a piece of sculpture. (1970, 57)

Sometimes, however, the new sense of scale was paradoxical: many of Judd's boxes, for instance, seemed heavy and solid, but were in fact hollow. Similarly, Tony Smith's black-painted Minimal cubes and polyhedra appeared forbidding and mono-lithic, but they were hollow too (and constructed from plywood).

Lucy Lippard (one of the best – and most prolific – American art critics) described scale not just as something mathematical, optical, *seen*:

Most discussions of scale consider it a strictly optical experience... But a sense of scale is also a *sense* proper. Scale is *felt* and cannot be communicated either by photographic reproduction or by description.4

The bombastic, 'monumental', massive and brash examples of late 20th century sculpture were not made exclusively by male artists, though. Land artists Mary Miss, Nancy Holt, Sherry Wiggins, Donna Henes, Lynne Hull, Patricia Johanson, Alice Aycock and Agnes Denes have all made large-scale land art (some of it requiring machines, diggers, trucks, helpers, backers and finance). Mary Miss created a 5 acre scale work in Illinois,5 while Nancy Holt produced gigantic concrete *Sun Tunnels in the desert.*6 Holt's art, with its large, heavy landscaping gestures (such as her *Dark Star Park*, 1979-84), is comparable with the male land artists' output. The globes and pools of water in *Dark Star Park*, though, could be viewed as more 'feminine', less aggressive or obviously patriarchal art.

Helen Escobedo built some huge concrete and steel sculptures which 'attempt to fuse hard-edge geometric forms with nature's organic manifestations', as she put it.

Escobedo's works, such as *Snake* (1980-81), rise impressively from the Earth, celebrating the flux and movement of organic forms. Beverly Pepper's large, curving mirrored slabs of wood buried in sandy beaches (*Sand Dunes*, 1985) might be seen as a type of 'Earth Mother art', art which worships and works with the Earth, rather than, as in some of male land art, cutting or penetrating it, phallically (as Michael Heizer, Robert Smithson and Walter de Maria did in America's deserts).

Although land art and big outdoor sculpture is not a male preserve, many of the celebrated products of postwar and contemporary environmental art and sculpture, however, have been made by male artists: Donald Judd's 'specific objects', blocks of aluminium and Plexiglas that 'climb' gallery walls;[7] Tony Smith's monumental cubes with their *thereness* (the primacy of presence, not subject, effect not content);[8] Dan Flavin's mesmeric, flickering fluorescent tubes in empty rooms, a sculpture of light and space;[9] Sol LeWitt's Conceptual cubes like scientific models of mathematical permutations, and wall drawings like enormous graphs; Richard Serra's huge walls or slabs of Cor-Ten steel leaning or propped together;[10] and Carl Andre's plates of interlocked steel, copper and zinc laid on the floor.[11]

One of the most exciting developments in contemporary sculpture and art has been the installation, where artists take over a whole space or environment – the floor, walls, windows, doors, ceiling and fittings of an art gallery, as in Rebecca Horn's *Ballet of the Woodpecker* (1986-87), a room full of mirrors, or Sylvia Stone's *Crystal Palace*. Indeed, pretty much every contemporary artist these days (since the early Nineties) is also an installation artist. Or, if not an installation artist, they often create more at their exhibitions than just paintings on gallery walls. (Perhaps artists have always been environmental and installation artists – a room full of paintings or sculptures can create a whole environment. A room of Fra Angelico or Gustave Moreau paintings creates a powerful environment, decades or centuries before virtual reality and cyberspace. The Fra Angelico frescoes in San Marco are a good example, or the amazing Moreau Museum in Paris).

Richard Long's art, like many land artists' works, is clearly part of the art installation culture: it's an art of environments, where even the relatively small addition of a stack of stones forming a stone ring can set alive the surrounding landscape. One sees the landscape in a new way: context is all-important.

KINETIC SCULPTURE

Time is central to Richard Long's sculptures, which move back and forth in time, much as Alexander Calder's mobiles, no matter what the scale, extend far beyond themselves, by virtue of their construction and motion. Like optical and light sculptures (such as those of Dan Flavin, Robert Irwin, Michael Asher or James Turrell), Alexander Calder's mobiles create spaces around themselves which act on the viewer in a palpable manner, quite distinct from the relatively staid and stolid approach to sculpture of, say, Antonio Canova or Luca della Robbia (not precisely a fair comparison, of course: some of the most kinetic sculptures have been immobile marble or bronze statues).[1]

The (overly) kinetic dimension would be out of place in the sombre religiosity of Barnett Newman's or Constantin Brancusi's sculptures. There are some sculptors' work which just seems to be static and rock solid. Indeed if Michelangelo's statues of *Moses* (1513-16) or the *Pièta* (1498-99) were mobile, it would be utterly out of keeping with the tone and theme of these solemn, awe-inspiring sculptures (like adding neon tubing which buzzes on and off to Catholic church sculpture. However, some Catholic art approaches that kind of kitsch).

Other sculptors though (especially from the modernist, Constructivist, Cubist and Dadaist eras onwards), actively developed motion in sculpture: Naum Gabo with his *Kinetic Construction* (1920), with its oscillating rod; Len Lye's magnetized steel *Loop* (1963) and his *Fountain* (1959), which wafts from side to side; Marcel Duchamp with his *Rotorelief* (1920, Yale University Art Gallery), which span around, creating an optical circle; Andy Warhol with his room full of silver balloon-pillows, which drifted about (*Clouds*, 1966, Leo Castelli Gallery, New York); and George Rickey with his swaying rods of steel, as in *Peristyle III* (1966, Washington, DC).

The master of kinetic sculpture must be the rebellious, idiosyncratic modern artist Jean Tinguely, whose motorized sculptures gleefully and mischievously create chaos. Once encountered, a Tinguely machine in full flight is never forgotten. (Rebecca Horn's sculptures give Tinguely a run for his money, though, adding a vicious, parodic streak to kinetic sculpture). Tinguely's sculptures don't just move – in all directions – they are very noisy, with clatterings, bangs, pants, grinds and wheezes. The most famous, *Hommage à New York* of 1960, was a sculpture 'created for self-destruction'.[2] The sculpture was intended to perform many bizarre actions, many of which didn't materialize.[3]

SUGARMAN, NOGUCHI, POMODORO, SAMARAS

Continuing this consideration of modern and contemporary sculpture: George Sugarman's flowing, sinuous sculptures asserted the eroticism of the art object. Like Lynda Benglis's or Gio Pomodoro's sculptures, Sugarman's works were twisting, entwined shapes painted in red, white, green and yellow (the classic primary hues of modernist sculpture from the 1960s onwards). Sugarman created a series of objects, interlinked spatially and thematically, set end to end, a chain of mystery. Sugarman's seemingly disparate clusters of objects were united in part by his use of colour. Taking his cue from Stuart Davis, Sugarman used colour spatially. In Sugarman's sculpture, the flat colour – all-over red, or yellow, or green – tended to suppress the irregularity of his peculiar shapes. This use of colour to flatten things giving a collection of objects a unity is found also in Tony Cragg's *New Stones* (1978), a typical Cragg post-industrial piece, where all the components (the kitchen utensils, household items, children's toys and bits and pieces culled from God knows where) were painted with the colours of the spectrum in a uniform manner, going from red through yellow to blue.

When bright, primary colours are employed in sculpture (which Richard Long eschews, preferring cool blacks, whites, greys, off-whites or terracottas), as in the grand examples of Minimal sculpture – such as in Isamu Noguchi's huge *Red Cube* (1969) – the result has a formal purity that borders on the childlike. The sunny and bold colours seem so obvious and 'right', when combined with the simplicity, self-confidence and exactness of fundamental (Classical) geometric shapes such as cubes, spheres, cones or pyramids. One might see this indulgence in purity and precision combined with vivid colouration as an erotic pleasure. One finds this simplicity of colour and formal purity in Philip King's orange and green painted blocks (*Call*, 1967), the powder colour on Anish Kapoor's semi-organic shapes (*Half*, (1984), Joan Miro's later works, and the green lacquer on John McCracken's *Untitled* (1967). However Minimal and Conceptual sculptors such as Sol LeWitt only permitted themselves white (like Robert Ryman and Jo Baer among Minimal painters).

Gio Pomodoro's sculptures comprised crumpled sheets of fibreglass which directly recalled the fields of unbroken colour of the Abstract Expressionists, in particular Barnett Newman, Franz Kline and Mark Rothko. Lucas Samaras's works were the flipside of Sugarman's sensual forms. Samaras deliberately subverted the eroticism of sculpture by furnishing his sculptures and assemblages with pins, nails, razor blades, knives and scissors, as in his vicious *Book 4* (1962), which is stuffed with knives, nails and razor blades. For Samaras, as for so many (male) Western artists from Dante through the Marquis de Sade to Georges Bataille and William Burroughs, sex (or pleasure) is intermixed with death. Or, as Samaras put it: 'I cannot separate beauty from pain.'[1] It was an art that celebrated sadomasochism and psycho-sexuality (and a world away from Richard Long).

BARNETT NEWMAN AND ALEXANDER CALDER

The affinities between Alexander Calder's mobiles and Richard Long's sculptures include a delicacy of touch, spontaneity, a response to the environment, an actualization of time and motion, and the exploration of spaces. Alexander Calder's constructions are delicate filaments of wire, with the distinctive Calderian 'leaf' or circle shapes at the end of each tendril. The facture of the mobiles is dazzling in itself. In *Thirteen Spines* (1940, Cologne), Calder fixed one wire to another, near the end, forming a chain of spines rather like the quills of some mechanical armadillo. Calder's mobiles mystify with their extraordinary balancing acts.

The mobile, as a form, is taken for granted now, so obvious does its composition seem. One sees mobiles everywhere, with teddy bears, whales, fairies, clowns, stars, moons, cars, trains and Pierrots hanging from them. Yet, before Alexander Calder, there were no mobiles – not in the form they're known today. Sculptors before Calder had employed balance in sculpture, but not quite in his way. When an object balances it sets up an immediate, physical tension. The spectator moves into the same space as a Calder mobile, and is able to react directly to its motion, and also perhaps effect it themselves.

What is most exciting about Alexander Calder's skeletal mobiles, though, is their motion, or their potential to move. Calder's mobiles drift slowly, each arm moving at different speeds (and directions) from the others. They are powered by the random, natural energy of the breeze, heating systems, air conditioning. Thus, they could be seen as environmental artworks, because they are dependent for part of their impact on natural (and humanmade) forces such as wind, temperature and air pressure.

The balancing acts of Alexander Calder's mobiles are playful – the sculptures set alight the space around them with their gravity-shaping design and movement. All sculpture exists in a space, whether virtual, imaginary, artificial or actual. Norbert Kricke created sculptures which looked like frozen lightning strikes, all spikey and angular, the thin rods of steel being set at different angles to each other.1 Calder does not have a monopoly on thin, spindly sculptures made of steel: David Smith, Hans Uhlmann, Eduardo Chillida, Nancy Graves, Jean Tinguely, Alberto Giacometti and Kricke all produced sculptures in this manner, with Giacometti in particular making that kind of sculpture his primary form. (As well as indoor mobiles, Calder has constructed many public sculptures outdoors – such as *La Grande Vitesse* [1969, Grand Rapids] and *Four Arches* in downtown L.A.).

Barnett Newman is an important influence on Minimal art and ethics (and therefore on Richard Long, if not directly). Like Richard Long, Newman emphasized religious awe in art. He traded on the enigmatic, gravity-defying aspect of sculpture in his *Broken Obelisk* (1963-67), which is a pillar balancing on the tip of a pyramid. The balancing of the steel pillar is a technical *tour-de-force*, a piece of bravado that seems macho partly because Newman conceived of the two forms as masculine and feminine. Guess which one is on top: the male. In a similar way, Constantin Brancusi conceived his *Adam and Eve* sculpture (1916-21) as one form on top of the other. Guess which one was on top. In Newman's and Brancusi's sculpture, the male element is nearer the sky, it is spiritual, transcendent, ascendant, superior. The feminine element is underneath, close to the earth, a squat, nurturing figure which holds up the male's balancing act – an unquestioned hierarchy which enshrines the patriarchal powerbase.

Like so many of Barnett Newman's paintings, his *Broken Obelisk* is conceived as an act of faith, a flame in the darkness. Newman's sculpture aims (like Brancusi's *Birds in Space*) to soar heavenward in some ultimate act of earthly transcendence. The religious aspect of Barnett Newman's *Broken Obelisk* is a part of his overall religious sensibility: in his *œuvre* he used elements of the *Qabbalah*, he created a *Stations of the Cross* series, and his famous monochrome paintings have titles such as *Vir Heroicus Sublimis*, *Cathedra* and *Onement*.2

LESS IS MORE: ARTE POVERA

Richard Long's art has affinities with the Italian Arte Povera ('poor art') movement, with its insistence on simple, organic materials (soil, grass, fire, wood, wax) and a simple, direct method of art-making. (The Arte Povera connection has been emphasized by Long himself in interviews). The Arte Povera artists (Jannis Kounellis, Mario Merz, Michelangelo Pistoletto, Luciano Fabro and Giovanni Anselmo) brought unadorned (though not unmanipulated) 'natural' materials into the gallery, which produced a different sort of æsthetic shock: fluffy, unworked cotton packed into a Donald Judd-like steel enclosure; an igloo made from broken glass, slate, clay, wax and branches; a piece of lettuce bound to a chunk of granite. Like Walter de Maria filling a gallery with soil, Jannis Kounellis brought nature – some horses – into a gallery in Rome. The horses stabled in the white, modern gallery provided a striking contrast between nature and culture, the animal and the humanmade worlds. Of his Italian horse piece, Kounellis said the aim was to increase awareness of the 'basic nature of a gallery, of its bourgeois origin', its economic and ideological aspects.[1] Long made similar statements about the dichotomies of indoors/ outdoors, culture/ nature, artificial/ natural when he brought River Avon mud and blocks of slate into the art gallery (though Long has always tended to avoid economic, political or ideological discourses in his art).

HYPERREALIST SCULPTURE

Land artists work with 'real' objects – Dennis Oppenheim with snow, Alan Sonfist and Herman de Vries with trees, Walter de Maria with soil, and Richard Long with his stones, mud and water. There is a different kind of 'reality' in the human figures of realist or hyperrealist sculpture (usually lumped together with the Superrealist or photorealist painters, such as Richard Estes, Chuck Close, Audrey Flack and William Beckman). One sees people frozen in sometimes bizarre attitudes and poses, as in Duane Hanson's *The Tourists* (1970), *Woman With Dog* (1977) and other works. The strangeness comes from the absolute stillness of these near-waxworks, and their unnervingly penetrating mimicry of 'real' people. Hanson's life-size figures are technically dazzling impersonations of 'real' life; they are pure Baudrillardian simulcra. Hanson's sculptures of apparently regular people, so familiar now, are vicious and ironic, while George Segal's figures explore the alienation of 'modern life'. Anthony Donaldson produced a truly horrible *Girl Sculpture* (1970), a plastic red and gold model of a woman – naked, of course – set in a 'streamlined' mould, rather like those 3-D logos beloved of entertainment organizations, where the letters are drawn in exaggerated perspective. Donaldson's sculpture is the diametric opposite of Richard Long's art: this kind of bitter satire on materialism and popular kitsch is not Long's form of art at all.

John De Andrea also explored 'the resignation, emptiness and loneliness' (as he called it)[1] of postwar, contemporary life, that emotional territory of Middle America that Raymond Carver so successfully explored in his short stories. But De Andrea's photorealist nude sculptures turn out to be just as pornographic as other 'high art' nudes. De Andrea's *Reclining Woman* (1970) is a Superrealist version of the 'high art' 'reclining nude', a life-size and seemingly 'life-like' rendition of a person, which recalls the blow-up doll of pornography, a vicious form of erotic objectification and demater-ialization of women.

Reg Butler's bronzes of naked women (such as *Girl On Red Base*, 1968-72) are 'exquisitely crafted', to use terms typical of art criticism,[2] but in fact turn out to be very sexist representations of women. The direct confrontation in hyperrealist sculpt-ure with humanity, with the human form, with the rigours and ironies of con-temporary life, is not Richard Long's way of making art. Long preferred methods that were more considered, or distanced, or contemplative, than the sceptical Photorealism of De Andrea, Hanson, Butler, Donaldson *et al*.

CONSTANTIN BRANCUSI AND LAND ART

The influence of Constantin Brancusi is apparent in Minimal, Arte Povera and Post-minimal sculpture. Robert Morris, Donald Judd, Carl Andre, Dan Flavin, Barbara Hepworth, Scott Burton, Chris Drury and Andy Goldsworthy have acknowledged Brancusi's art, in particular his *Endless Column* (1918). Andre's early work *Last Ladder* (1959, London) is something like Brancusi's *Endless Column* (putting Brancusi along the ground, as Andre remarked). And Andre wasn't the only postwar sculptor to have his/ her Brancusi phase.

Constantin Brancusi was a 'sculptor's sculptor' (like Rodin or Canova or the god of all sculptors, Michelangelo). And Brancusi meant more to the Minimal and 1960s sculptors (the sculptors of Richard Long's formative years) than Auguste Rodin, Pablo Picasso, Marcel Duchamp, Naum Gabo, Henri Gaudier-Brzeska, or even Henry Moore (the king of British sculpture after WW2). Of course the Constructivists (Tatlin, Gabo, Pevsner) were hugely influential, as were the Dadaists and Surrealists (Duchamp, Ernst. Arp), but Brancusi's art's important because of its independence (it carves its own cultural niche), its sculptural project of radical simplification. its emphasis on the object in its space (and the exhibition context), its redevelopment of the pedestal, and its committment to abstraction. And, not least: how it hasn't dated at all, how it still looks completely contemporary.

It was Brancusi's project to strip away the detritus that had accumulated around sculpture, Henry Moore said, and to offer the pure, simple shape. What Brancusi did was 'to concentrate on very simple shapes, to keep his sculpture, as it were, one-cylindered, to refine and polish a single shape to a degree almost too precious.'[1] This is what many contemporary sculptors have done, keeping their shapes simple and purified: Alison Wilding, Richard Deacon, Stephen Cox, David Nash, Richard Serra, Donald Judd and Robert Smithson.

The Brancusian ethics, of simplicity, purity, smoothness, interiority and organic form, are found in the Minimal sculptors (including Richard Long), as well as the Constructivist notion of working with materials in a 'natural' way, so that the material dictates the form one creates with it (Brancusi spoke of the search for the Platonic Ideal Form that resided somewhere in the material). Barry Flanagan commented that sculpture works directly with materials: '[t]he convention of painting has always bothered me. There always seemed to be a *way* of painting. With sculpture, you seemed to be working directly, with materials and with the physical world inventing your own organizations'.2

Also pertinent to Richard Long's art is Brancusi's attitude towards his materials, in particular his reverence for stones (few artists have made stones as pivotal to their art as Long). Fellow Romanian Mircea Eliade remarked:

> Brancusi addressed himself to certain stones with the awed and ecstatic reverence of someone for whom such an object was the manifestation of a sacred power and was thus, in itself, a sacred mystery. (1984, 196)

Some artists make a virtue of simplicity and ease: Jan Dibbets said he liked projects that anyone could do. For example, he chose four sites at random on a Netherlands map and went to each place and took a photo. It was '[q]uite stupid. Anybody can do that', Dibbets admitted. But Dibbets said he enjoyed searching for the places and photographing what was there. It was also silly for people to buy such works: 'it's stupid for other people to do it, or to buy it from me. What matters is the feeling'. And the feeling of the artist was something that couldn't be bought (1970).

Some contemporary artists have deployed one structure or form over and over again and refining it over years and decades: Ad Reinhardt with his square black cruciform canvases, Barnett Newman with his 'zip' on monochrome expanses, Donald Judd with his hollow boxes and stacks, Dan Flavin with his fluorescent tubes, and Long with his circles, textworks and rows.

Quite a few artists (not all of them sculptors) have expressed admiration for Brancusi's photographs, the way he would set up his sculptures in his studio and photograph them at particular times of day, when the lighting was just right. Andy Goldsworthy said he admired how Brancusi created the conditions in his studio so that his work 'comes alive at a particular time of day as the light momentarily touches it'.3 Somehow, it wasn't quite the same when they were displayed in modern art museums (such as the Pompidou Centre in Paris or the Museum of Modern Art in Gotham).

JASPER JOHNS AND LAND ART

Land artists work in a similar manner to the very sculptural painter (or painter-sculptor) Jasper Johns, unquestionably one of the two or three most important painters of the 1960s in the USA (along with Robert Rauschenberg and Andy Warhol). Johns worked very closely with his paintings, becoming absorbed totally in the surfaces, as a critic wrote: 'when he is working, Jasper is totally concentrated on those surfaces. He lives in those surfaces. The surfaces are his whole world, they are everything. He loses himself in them. They are everything.'[1] The same could be said of Richard Long, David Nash or Wolfgang Laib: when they are working, the absorption is complete (Long has often commented on the immersion and contemplation that the art of walking produces).

Like a land artist or a sculptor, Jasper Johns wanted his materials to respond instantly to his touch: he did not want the days-long drying time of oil paint. Johns' tactile surfaces were built up using wax – the thick impasto of oil and wax was one of the keys to his textures, for when the wax cools, one can paint on top of it very soon, instead of waiting for the paint to dry.[2] Land art too often requires a rapid response, as well as works which celebrate the process of making them. Johns used encaustic and oil because he wanted evidence of the gestures he made *before* and *after;* that is, a finished painting which would reveal its making. He said:

> It was very simple. I wanted to show what had gone before in a picture, and what was done after. But if you put on a heavy brushstroke in paint, and then add another stroke, the second smears the first under the paint unless the paint is dry. And paint takes too long to dry. I didn't know what to do. Then someone suggested wax. It worked very well as soon as the wax was cool I could put on another stroke, and it would not alter the first.[3]

These are the seemingly simple and obvious techniques and stratagems that concern artists, this dealing with such simple but important processes like drying times for paint. Artists are, typically, humble, and Johns here says it 'was very simple', yet it is also crucial. Land artists speak in similar terms, of keeping things simple and direct. Richard Long, for instance, produces mud works for indoor installations partly because water dries too quickly, and when it does, it disappears. So the reason for Long choosing mud is practical (but he regards the mud pieces as much water works as mud works, because they are mostly water [2003a]).

Contemporary with Jasper Johns' paintings in the 1960s was Samuel Beckett's exploration of self-referential fiction. Richard Long doesn't feel an affinity with many travel writers, but has cited Beckett as a literary parallel. Like Johns (like any artist), Beckett plundered his back catalogue. Starting from the statement that there is 'nothing to express' and 'nothing with which to express', together with 'the obligation to express', Beckett wrote the short, condensed text pieces which he called 'fizzles', which have similarities with Johns' mirror games and Minimalism's radical reductionism. Beckett's short fictions (*Ping, Lessness, All Strange Away* and *Still*), with their mathematical descriptions of boxes, rotundas and cylinders, seem to be poetic equivalents of the smooth, rigid volumes of Minimal sculpture (Donald Judd, Robert Morris, Carl Andre, Dan Flavin, etc). Like Johns, Beckett often employed the Minimal artists' use of seriality, of doing one thing then another, in sequence. Artists such as Brice Marden, Sol LeWitt, Donald Judd and Carl Andre based some of their artworks on series of numbers or patterns. Minimal ethics can produce some extremes of mathematics and seriality.

Long's art is also an art of numbers, of sequences, systems and series, of counting. Long said he sometimes produced walkworks specifically to illustrate or embody a simple idea, which could involve adding up or subtracting numbers (or hours, or stones, or days). Don't forget that pretty much all of Long's works contain numbers as well as letters and words (even if it's the date or the year of making the work).

Like Samuel Beckett and the Minimal artists, Jasper Johns moved calmly and methodically from one thing to another. For Sol LeWitt, perhaps the most extreme of the Minimal artists ('extreme' because all his work is done in the planning stage, and he has no special love of objects) believed that Johns used numbers, but not necessarily mathematics: not just 'anyone uses mathematics *per se*' wrote LeWitt, 'They use *numbers*. It's just like Jasper Johns using, 1, 2, 3, 4, 5, 6, 7, 8, 9, 0. I use numbers only as a way of drawing something.'[4]

THE WORLD OF MINIMAL AND POSTMINIMAL ART

Sixties Minimal and Postminimal sculpture in the late Sixties and into the Seventies was marked by its extremely hard edges, creating angular and linear forms: lines, rows, corners, rectangles, triangles, octagons, polyhedra, pyramids. It was a blocky, rectilinear art movement, characterized by white, black and grey smooth planes of plastic, glass, aluminium, wood and steel. The cube and box was one of the most highly favoured forms. Suzi Gablik wrote of the Minimal artists: '[c]onjugating the cube to infinity, they conveyed an impression of perfect equilibrium, and produced a visual symmetry that never deviates from its own rigidly plotted field'.1 Symmetrical, unadorned, industrial.

The world of Minimal art was clean, calm, devoid of unruliness, violence, even ambiguity. Something like an airport: white, spotless, spacious. Or a new shopping mall. A row of pristine supermarket shelves, stacked high with new cans of fruit, the labels all turned face-out (while Pop Art celebrated brand names and logos, Minimal art erased them in favour of an all-pervading blankness). Minimal art was an art for the 1960s, an era of mass commodification on a global scale (a vast increase in the sheer number and variety of objects being produced), and the rising affluence in the Western world after the austerity of the 1950s and the immediate postwar period, where mass production created a uniformity to the appearances of so much of street, home, personal, medical, industrial, transport and educational furniture (especially in Europe and America). Minimal sculpture, Barbara Rose remarked, looked 'machine-made, industrial, standardized, materialized or stamped out as a whole'.2 Other aspects of Minimal sculpture include the multiplicity of sculptural material (fluorescent lights, Plexiglas, fibreglass, Formica, chrome, plastic), simplicity (Brancusian reduction to 'essences'), surface (no depth), hollowness (no weight), and the insistence on the environment and contextual space (the surrounding space becomes as important as the sculpture within it).

Minimal sculptures are not set on pedestals or daises, like Renaissance or Greek sculpture; they sit on the floor, or lean against walls (as in Robert Morris's *Floor Piece*, or Carl Andre's *Cedar Piece*). The new sculptural space must have 'three, not two coordinates' said Morris. 'The ground plane, not the wall, is the necessary support for the maximum awareness of the object'.3 Minimal sculptures exist in the same space, on the same plane (the floor) as the viewer. They are, as Morris said, in an in-between cultural space, somewhere between being monuments and being ornaments, between being architecture and jewellery.4 Richard Long's sculptures are wholly within this Minimal/ Postminimal tradition of dispensing with the pedestal.

> I'm fed up with objects on pedestals [said Anthony Caro]. I'd like to break down the graspability of sculpture. Sculpture is terrifically tangible, but a painting, however concrete, is partly in the realm of illusion.

In Minimal sculpture, surfaces were, typically, utterly smooth and 'pure'. Undecorated, unadorned, unmarked (the Minimal artists liked new materials, preferrably machine-made or built by professionals, if they could afford it). Simplicity, repetition, seriality, process, and flatness were exalted (as well as volume and space). The many materials were flattened out and depersonalized. Gestures, so important to certain kinds of sculpture, such as traditional figuration, were suppressed. Indeed, the flatness, blankness and smoothness of the surfaces, whether in the sculpture of Robert Morris, Donald Judd, Dan Flavin, Carl Andre, Ronald Bladen or Tony Smith, was crucial in Minimal art, and consequently some commentators called Minimal sculpture 'boring'.5 They couldn't get on with it, it didn't seem to be 'about' anything, it was too abstract, too severe and ascetic. There wasn't enough to look at. For Peter Fuller, there was nothing 'spiritual' about Minimal art: he spoke of 'the numbing vacuity of works by artists such as Carl Andre, Agnes Martin, Ellsworth Kelly or Brice Marden').6 The boringness, though, becomes a part of the metaphysics of Minimal sculpture, so that Lucy Lippard wrote: '[t]he exciting thing about... the "cool" artists is their daring challenge of the concepts of boredom, monotony and repetition... their demonstration that intensity does not have to be melodramatic.'7 Andy Warhol, patron saint of artistic vacuity, said 'I like boring things. I like things to be exactly the same over and over again'.8 And Donald Judd said about the charge of reductionism, a term which demeaned Minimal art:

> I object to the whole reduction idea. If my work is reductionist, it's because it doesn't have the elements that people thought should be there. But it has other elements that I like.9

Boring art for some is exhilarating art for others, just as erotic art for some is pornography for others. Thus, James Mellow wrote that a Donald Judd show was 'one of the most provocative of the season',10 while Barbara Rose described Judd's art as 'our most radical sculpture, if not perhaps our fullest'.11 Certainly Judd's wall reliefs, his crenellations, his rows of boxes, his 'stacks', are beautiful, sensuous, luscious, sexy – whether constructed from traditional materials such as wood or brass or copper or newer materials such as Plexiglas and red automotive lacquer. Judd combined the eroticism of industrial materials with cool geometric patterns. Judd, like other Minimal sculptors, combined austerity with sensuality, producing 'minimal forms at the service of glamorous, hedonistic effects of light' (Hilton Kramer).12 Judd's sculptures were, paradoxically, far more engaging than most other sculpture being produced at the time, even though the other stuff was more approachable, and figurative. One could see what was going on in it. Judd's art was more austere, and completely abstract. Yet it was the most compelling art of the 1960s. As Barbara Haskell wrote:

> By coupling these luxurious materials with spare forms, he exploited their inherent "language". The opposition between the inert and rigorous geometry of his forms, and the opulent hedonism and shimmering colour effects of his surfaces accounted for the unexpectedly exultant lyricism of his work.13

Minimal artists such as Donald Judd, John McCracken, Carl Andre, Sol LeWitt and Robert Morris explored notions of 'boringness' and 'interestingness' (or, rather, taking something blank and monochrome, an object flat and rectilinear, to extremes). 'Boring art is interesting art', wrote Frances Colpitt in her excellent book on Minimalism (1990, 121). Judd (chief explicator of Minimal æsthetics) wrote: 'I can't see how any good work can be boring or monotonous in the usual sense of those words', adding: '[a]nd no one has developed an unusual sense of them'.14 Clearly, the Minimal sculptors thought they were making 'interesting' art. Or at least, *they* were interested in it. If art's good, it can't be 'boring', said Judd, claiming that 'a work needs only to be interesting'. The discussion of discourses such as 'interesting', 'boring' and 'value' becomes a quagmire of semantics and the metaphysics of meaning. Language soon fails to describe the kinds of intentions that artists have, and the kind of responses that critics and viewers have to works. Robert Mangold commented, 'I certainly know whether I'm interested in the work or whether I'm not interested in the work'.15

Much of sculpture in the decades after WW2 consisted of hard-edged cubes or rectangular slabs (and some of it still does). Whether this use of such stark mathematical forms like cubes and polyhedra is rational or intuitive, it takes a scientific, numerical approach to art to extremes. The idea, Donald Judd wrote, is to simply do 'the next thing'... 'one thing after another'. It is a strategy that is not called a strategy, a systemless system. Of Frank Stella's paintings, Judd wrote that the 'order is not rationalistic and underlying, but is simply order, like that of continuity, one thing after another'.16

The basic tenets of Minimal art – seriality, succession, progression, repetition, permutation – have been around for a long time. Artists have always worked like that. Leonardo da Vinci, one might say, painted the same picture in different ways, often abandoning projects before completion, while J.M.W. Turner seemed to be painting the same sky and sunset, attacking it from thousands of different viewpoints and different locations, from every coastline of Britain, France, Switzerland, Italy and Germany. Turner, one could say, was haunted by one particular format of composition in his paintings and drawings (the landscape was placed in the lower third on the frame, in the Classical manner of composition, a tree or building was situated on the left or right, pointing into the sky, with the sky dominating the image, and the sun in the upper third, in the centre, shining straight at the viewer.) Similarly, Judd had his favourite formats – the wall-hung 'stacks', the smaller wall crenellations, the hollow boxes in rows on the wall or the floor – which he explored in every permutation of material, size, scale, series and sequence.

But – whether the 'system' is serial or modular, whether there is progression or simply repetition – the notion of Donald Judd's of 'doing the next thing', 'one thing after another' – explains so much of Minimal art. It explains so much of Judd's work, for instance, those 'ladders' or 'stacks' of forms ascending to the ceiling in bronze or plastic, and those long lines of crenellations set on a wall. It also describes how artists simply go on making work, as variations, or repetitions, or progressions, like Mark Rothko with his many canvases that explore different combinations of purple or yellow clouds floating on oceans of red or blue, or Ad Reinhardt's seemingly repetitious but actually methodical explorations of five foot square black abstract canvases. Or Richard Long making one stone circle after another, or walking across the same stretch of Dartmoor in Devon time after time. Minimal ethics can produce some extremes of mathematics and seriality.

Minimal sculpture is certainly austere – 'cool', as some critics called it (the word 'cool' seems to have slipped out of art discourse). It is very 'cool', ascetic, restrained, flat, exact, with its smooth, polished, manufactured surfaces and precise square edges and angles. The body seems to have been erased from this 'cool' Minimal art. There seems to be no space left for the body, and the spectator also seems to be 'erased', in some way. The ruthless asceticism of Minimal art denies the body, like early Christian theology or Catholic mediæval saints.17

One of the triumphs of Minimal art was to make seemingly dead and uninteresting materials such as steel and Formica sensual, to take the post-industrial æsthetic and revive it with a rigorous formalism. On 'boringness', Robert Morris wrote that sculpture was found 'boring' by those who desire 'specialness':

> Such work which has the feel and look of openness, extendibility, accessibility, publicness, repeatability, equanimity, directness, immediacy, and has been formed by clear decision rather than groping craft would seem to have a few social implications, none of which are negative. Such work would undoubtedly be boring to those who long for access to an exclusive specialness, the experience of which reassures their superior perception.[18]

Some might see this kind of Minimal, Conceptual or mathematical art as too abstract, too unreal, too dry and clinical. But critics such as Robert Rosenblum claimed that Conceptual art can be 'awesome'. Of Sol LeWitt's art, Rosenblum remarked that it 'elicits…an immediate awe that… has to be translated by the same feeble words – beautiful, elegant, exhilarating – that we use to register similar experiences with earlier art.'[19] One might see Minimal sculpture as so 'cool' it's lifeless, a kind of death of sculpture. Yet, despite the profusion of smooth white surfaces, which evoke clinics, malls and hospitals, there is much sensuality in Minimal sculpture.

Sol LeWitt explained his view thus:

> I wouldn't say that I wanted to like uninteresting things or to dislike interesting things. I think that's one way that you measure your response, if it interests you. 'Interests' means that it somehow makes a bridge between you and it, you and the object, you and the art object. If it hits home, it means that it's of interest. (ib., 121)

Robert Ryman's white-on-white paintings (or Jo Baer's) could be seen as unsensual, flat, 'boring'. In fact, Ryman's paintings are very sensual, intriguing, even erotic. As Ad Reinhardt painted black-on-black squares, and Brice Marden and Gerhard Richter took on gray squares, so Ryman explored the mysticality of white, whiteness, white-on-white, as Kasimir Malevich had done. Paintings of Ryman's such *Untitled,* a small painting by postwar standards (53.5 inches square), or the very small *Untitled* of 1961 (12 inches square), displayed a sense of the tactile to rival Jasper Johns. The surfaces themselves were highly poetic, but Ryman also moved towards the state of sculpture, like Frank Stella or Robert Rauschenberg, with his use of many different materials, from wood to steel, from fibreglass to Plexiglas, from cardboard to copper.[20]

Similarly, the archetypal Minimal painter, Agnes Martin, might appear to be quite 'uninteresting'. Her paintings, though, were deeply poetic. They were, like Ryman's, Baer's and Reinhardt's, flat squares in a human-scale (six foot square, for instance). They have lyrical titles: *Mountain II, Drift of Summer, Stone, Leaf* and *Night Sea*. Agnes Martin's (near) white paintings were not all they seemed at first, as with Ryman's work. They were in fact covered with a faint but strictly controlled grid, usually made with a pencil or india ink. *Night Sea* (1963, London) was, unusually in Martin's *œuvre*, a pale blue background, hinting at nature, at skies and seas. Martin's painterly reductionism seems austere, but in fact poeticizes the world, as with Ryman or Marden. Martin wrote: '[m]y paintings have neither objects, nor space, nor time, not anything – no forms. They are light, lightness, about merging, about formlessness, breaking down forms.'[21] Martin's paintings went beyond being simply graphs made in graphite or ink on oil paint; they shimmered, phosphoresced; they were, as Martin said, about lightness and formlessness. They embraced a physicality of light and were not 'abstract' in the sense of being 'unreal'. Rather, they were grounded in reality, in nature, as with the oil and wax panels of Marden. Like many Minimalists, Martin limited herself to one format – 72 inch square paintings, with pale monochrome backgrounds and lightly pencilled grids. But within that format, Martin could explore all sorts of possibilities. The limitations were actually necessary for the artist.

By limiting himself to white, Robert Ryman freed himself up for an exploration of different media, because he painted in white on many kinds of material: canvas, linen, cotton, wood, paper, steel, copper, aluminium, mylar, fibreglass, Plexiglas, cardboard, etc, and with various sorts of media: oil, baked enamel, paper, glue, shellac, vinyl acetate emulsion and so on. As Ryman said, typically of so many late 20th century artists: '[t]here is never a question of what to paint, but only how to paint'.[22] In the same way, Long took up the Minimal and Postminimal use of simple geometric forms – circles, rows, lines, columns – which would give his pieces a structure upon which he could explore other things.

By contrast with the Minimal artists, Richard Long has not excised as much from his art as Minimal painters such as Marden, Ryman, Martin, Baer, Mangold and Kelly did in the 1960s: Long has held onto things like landscapes, the movement of objects in the sky, and the sensuality of walking. He has not gone the whole way into abstraction, and produced radically emptied works such as the canvases of Stella, Marden or Ryman.

It would be hard to see Sol LeWitt's cuboid, mathematical, Conceptual sculpture as sensual (LeWitt has been an influence on Richard Long's art). LeWitt's angular objects – the frames or skeletons of cubes painted white, for instance – seem to be the antithesis of what would be conventionally dubbed sensuous art.[23] LeWitt's art was all about ideas – the initial idea, the conception, was everything. As LeWitt commented: 'all of the planning and decisions are made beforehand and the execution is a perfunctory affair. The idea becomes a machine that makes the art.'[24] In the same way, Alfred Hitchcock used to remark that by the script stage he had already made the movie in his head, and shooting it was a mundane chore (but Hitch wasn't conceptual enough to just write the scripts or storyboards – he still had to make the damn thing).

Minimal art had its limits, argued Dennis Oppenheim, which was why artists wanted to go beyond it, using phenomenology. 'We know that Minimalism quickly lifted off into phenomenology via the work of Bruce Nauman and Turrell and the writings of Robert Morris'.[25]

Like the Minimal artists, Richard Long was much concerned with seriality, processes, mapping, permutations and variations. Long was very fond of numbers and number systems, and of measuring his walks: he walked so many miles for so many hours on such and such a day, for instance. His walkworks record the everyday events of a walk, as well as the number systems and measurements. Long made walks based on number systems. Many of his walks are repetitions of the same basic idea, just as the Minimalists would take one format and reproduce it many different ways. In fact, as a walker, Long was in love with repetition, because a walk is basically one step then another… then another. The walk's basic unit is the step. Similarly, Minimal artists like Carl Andre constructed larger works from simple, small units (in Andre's case, the metal tile).

THE ART OF SPACE AND LIGHT

Numerous sculptors, installation artists and land artists have worked with light and lighting: James Turrell with his 'skyspaces', Robert Irwin's reworked gallery spaces, Dan Flavin and his fluorescent tubes, Bruce Nauman, who made very narrow corridors lit by green fluorescents, Maria Nordman's extensions to studio exteriors, Nancy Holt's

Sun Tunnels, Eric Orr's sound and light environments, and DeWain Valentine's acrylic tubes hanging alone from gallery ceilings. (Others include Douglas Wheeler, Hap Tivey, Susan Kaiser Vogel, Stephen Antonakos, Keith Sonnier and Larry Bell).

Eric Orr constructed a *Silence and the Ion Wind* installation (1980), a series of dark rooms culminating in the *Golden Room*, 'an allusive structure for an elusive experience', approached by the visitor passing through an ion wind.[1] In pieces such as *Wall Shadow, Sky Lights, Sound Tunnel, Zero Mass, Sunrise, Blood Shadow, The Stone Snake, Prime Matter* and *Blue Void,* Orr deployed sound, light, wind, sand, ice and shadow. In *Prime Matter* (1981), Orr created fog and flames from a twenty foot tall metal column (a larger version was constructed outside the Mitsui Fudosan Building in L.A. in 1991). Orr has fired xenon lasers up into the sky on top of skyscrapers in Long Beach, CA (a permanent installation, *Landmark Lumière*, 1991).

Many artists have taken gallery spaces and reworked them, adding walls or scrims, or curtains, or false ceilings, or doorways, or new windows. Often these light and sound spaces look (at first) like empty gallery rooms: Eric Orr (*Light Space*, 1985), Hap Tivey's *Sodium Exchange* (1976), Susan Kaiser Vogel's *Point Conception* (1980), DeWain Valentine's *Curved Wall Spectrum* (1974), Larry Bell's *Leaning Room II* (1988), Bruce Nauman's *Yellow Triangular Room* (1973), Douglas Wheeler's *All Gray Graduating Light* (1976), Maria Nordman's *6/ 21/ 79 One Day Only* (1979), James Turrell's *Second Meeting* (1988), and Robert Irwin's Kansas *Installation* (1979). The forerunners of these light spaces include Yves Klein's *Le Vide*.

Some artists made the reconstituted gallery interior one of their trademarks. For example, Robert Irwin has constructed *Fractured Light – Partial Scrim Ceiling – Eye-level Wire* (1971), *Acrylic Column* (1970), *Eye-level Room Division* (1973), *Soft Wall* (1973), *Scrim Veil* (1975), *Wall Division – Portal* (1974), *Window Room* (1973), *Black-Line Volume* (1976), *Scrim Veil – Black Rectangle – Natural Light* (1977) and *Untitled (Three Triangulated Light Planes)* (1979). Richard Long has used lighting effects in his works, though not in the manner of many of the light artists noted above. For instance, there are many Long walks based around sunrises and sunsets, or full moons, or eclipses. Many of the indoor sculptures of Long – the stone circles, the mud and wall installations – require fairly standard gallery lighting. Long does not create special indoor environments like Robert Irwin or James Turrell in which the lighting plays a major role.

2

Sculpture and Gender

Sculpture is a three dimensional projection of primitive feeling: touch, texture, size and scale, hardness and warmth, evocation and compulsion to move, live and love.

Barbara Hepworth[1]

EROTICISM IN SCULPTURE

Richard Long's art is not the most obviously 'feminine' among 20th and 21st century artists. His art doesn't appear to address issues that preoccupy feminists or female artists (for instance, identity, the body, equal rights, labour, pregnancy, healthcare, exploitation of women, and so on. But Long also isn't particularly interested in addressing political issues in general, whether gendered or not). Yet the forms of Long's art – the circles, ovals and stones – can be seen as 'feminine' forms, while his intuitive, poetic approach, though not without its 'masculine', mathematical and logical elements, can be seen as a 'feminized' æsthetic methodology. In this chapter I consider some female sculptors and women artists, including performance and action artists, whose works and philosophies have some parallels with Richard Long's art.

Many women sculptors have explored 'feminine' imagery and 'feminine' concerns, including the body, its functions, body image, social identity and the cultural, techno-logical body. Louise Bourgeois – rightly regarded as one of the key female voices in the modernist and postmodernist eras – explored in her art the complex relations between form and eroticism, volume and psychology, shape and nature. Her forms nearly always dealt with eroticism in some shape or other – her *Nature Study* (1984), for instance, featured the bulbous volumes which are practically her trademark, echoing breasts, clitorises, vulvas, buttocks, heads, hands, knees, tongues, all the parts of the sexualized body.

The sexuality of sculpture is everywhere affirmed in 'high art', and in 'high art' cultural criticism. This has to do primarily with the eroticism of the nude human form, which thousands of sculptors have explored and exploited (nudes, while expected in performance art and body art, are lacking in any of Richard Long's work). Renaissance sculptors – Luca della Robbia, Lorenzo Ghiberti, Andrea del Verrocchio, Pietro Lom-bardo, Benvenuto Cellini – systematically exaggerated (drew attention to) the sexuality of the body. Donatello's famous *David* (1440-42) for instance, is a highly camp, homoerotic boy, an icon of stylized homoeroticism. (A similar eroticization occurs in Verrocchio's *David*, Cellini's *Perseus* and Giovanni Bologna's *Mercury*). This Ren-aissance sexualizaton of the human form finds its apotheosis in, of course, Michel-angelo (history's premier sculptor) – his *Dawn*, *David*, early and late *Pietàs*, and possibly the most voluptuous of all figurative statues in the history of Western art, the *Dying Slave*. The heroic, homoerotic style of Michelangelo's sculpture continued to be developed throughout post-Renaissance sculpture. In, for instance, the bombast and masculine power of Antonio Canova's *Hercules and Lichas*, or Gianlorenzo Bernini's *David*.

The famous (hetero)sexist depictions of people in modern sculpture are well-known. They include Alberto Giacometti's *Spoon Woman* (1926), a view of woman as Earth Mother, a totemic figure; Gaston Lachaise's *Standing Woman* (1912-27), one of those smooth, curvy Goddess types, also favoured by Aristide Maillol; Hans Bellmer's bizarre *Dolls* (1936), where the slit of a vulva is where the head would be, and set amidst exaggerated, bulbous forms; Henri Gaudier-Brzeska's *Red Stone Dancer* (1914), though it attempts a new way of depicting gesture and posture in space, is still sexist; Elie Nadelman's *Dancer* (1918) (like Paul Manship's *Dancer and Gazelles* [1916] and Edgar Degas' *Dancer* sculptures), is also sexist; and Ludwig Kirchner's *Standing Nude* (1908-12) is pornography masquerading as art, but then, many of Kirchner's depictions of women are pornography.

Ad Reinhardt:

> I remember I wanted to get to non-art, non connotative, non anthropomorphic, non geometric, non, nothing, everything, but of another kind, vision, sort. From a total other reference point. Is it possible? I have learned anything is possible.[5]

Sometimes loosely hanging, finding their own form, at other times Hesse's sculptures were bound with wire, as if 'making psychic models', as Robert Smithson said (isn't all art at least a psychic model?).[6] Hesse's sculptures have endured as some of the most intriguing examples of contemporary art, wholly individual, existing in a world all their own. The sculptures are semi-organic enough to suggest all sorts of meanings or purposes, but abstract enough too to remain mysterious and ambiguous.

Jackie Winsor took the cube as one of her major forms, but she manufactured her cubes from 'natural' materials, such as twine, hemp and wood. Winsor's cubes take the Minimal cube only as a starting point, because her series of cube sculptures were explorations of the mysteries of ontology. Some of Winsor's works changed or decayed: the *Burnt Piece* (1977-78) cube burnt away, alchemically, when the artist fired its interior. As with the land artists, Winsor said: 'I was unable to see how the piece would look until the moment of completion'.[7] In *Exploded Piece* (1980-82), Winsor blew up one of her solid cubes with dynamite (inside it Winsor packed layers of paint, gold lea and plaster).

Louise Nevelson produced huge reliefs or structures which were like Cubist or Constructivist altarpieces, full of objects, various articles made of wood, all painted in one colour, black, white or gold: chair legs, railings, door knobs. Her sculptures were like magical cupboards, vertical dreamscapes made of boxes stacked on top of each other. Rebecca Horn's sculptures are based, like Barbara Hepworth's, on natural forms, but also on movement, dance, time and environments. Horn's wonderful *Peacock Machine* (1982) is an exuberant activator of space, one of those pieces that aims for the essence of a natural form and captures it: a peacock's magnificent tail.[8] Horn's sculptures playfully and satirically play with the borderlands between figuration and abstraction, the organism and the machine.

Barbara Hepworth's organic forms, as with Constantin Brancusi's, hovered between subjectivity and objectivity, between natural form and æsthetic abstraction (as in her *Two Forms*, for example). Like Brancusi, Hepworth maintained that she always returned to nature, and took her inspiration from nature (Long has also maintained that he takes his inspiration first from nature). For Hepworth, nature meant the landscape (in particular, the Cornish landscape where she lived), and the human body. 'We return always to the human form – the human form in landscape' she said (the 'human form in landscape' also describes Long's art). Hepworth loved the white granite rounded stones of West Penwith, and scattered them around her studio in St Ives. It's easy to see how some of Hepworth's sculptures took some of their inspiration from the beautiful granite boulders of Cornwall. Her sculpture stems from emotion and expression, from feeling: 'I rarely draw what I see – I draw what I feel in my body' she said. [9] Hepworth's distinctive forms, with their smooth curves and holes, are clearly sensual objects. Hepworth acknowledged the sensuality of sculptural forms (but what sculptor doesn't?). Hepworth said that the natural setting was 'the most tremendously inspiring one to me'. Driving around Cornwall, Hepworth found that it was her personal (bodily) response to particular landscapes that mattered. [10]

Alison Wilding directly embraced the potential for sculpture to be supremely sensual. Wilding's (usually wholly) abstract forms hint at alchemical transformations, intimate experiences, investigations of sexuality and the relations between space, imagination, fantasy and the body. [11] Wilding's *Hemlock III* (1986), for example, was, like her *Blueblack* (1984), a wooden dish containing hemlock, lead, lime and beeswax, allusive of arcane experiments. The dish with its dangerous substances was a kind of womb, a motif or experience that appears in much of modern sculpture, from Judy Chicago's *Dinner Party* (1979) to the womb interiors of Louise Bourgeoise and others.

Alison Wilding's sculpture often featured two elements, one was usually large, the other, small. These two elements are luscious and mysterious, part way beyond interpretation, though some critics interpret them as masculine and feminine elements, the twin poles of heterosexuality, which are involved in some arcane dance or dalliance. [12] Wilding herself stressed the enigmatic nature of her work: '[t]he obverse of making is looking, not telling' [13] and she emphasized, as so many artists do, the making of the sculpture: '[t]he making and doing processes…[are] always the mainspring of the work'. [14] Wilding, David Nash and Bill Woodrow iterated the making of sculpture, its actual construction, with real (and sometimes organic, living) materials. In some artists, the material employed also has a symbolic or added meaning, as in Joseph Beuys' *Fettecke* or 'fat corner', a sculpture with powerful autobiographical and semiotic associations. Shirazeh Houshiary, who exhibited with Wilding at Kettle's Yard Gallery in the early 1980s, also stressed the poetic, metaphoric nature of sculpture. 'My quest is to unfix the image,' Houshiary said, 'to go beyond the materiality of things.' [15]

Niki de Sant-Phalle, who, like Louise Bourgeois and Frida Kahlo, is a key modern female artist, produced exuberant Goddesses, such as her *Black Venus* (1967, Whitney Museum), or her marvellous *Pink Childbirth* (1964, Moderner Museet, Stockholm), a Great Mother Goddess made from dolls, toys, tissues and various articles collected together like a totem of the prehistoric world. Sant-Phalle's *Un Ensemble de "Les Nanas"* (1965, New York) was an effervescent – and multicoloured – representation of female forms, dancing, cavorting, balancing.16 Among non-figurative, abstract or partially-figurative artists, women such as Nancy Graves are astonishing, with her superb multi-media fabrications. Graves' skeletal, fossil-like works combine fantasy and natural forms in 'one exuberantly open-form, polychrome, freestanding construction after another'.18 Lila Katzen set alive public spaces with her flowing, curling forms (such as *Guardian*, 1979).

Alice Aycock, using science as her Muse, produced some wonderfully fantastical machines, such as *The Angels Continue Turning the Wheels of the Universe,* or the marvellous, massive piece *The Miraculous Machine in the Garden (Tower of the Winds)* (1983), which features 268 antenna and bells ringing in a vacuum. Some of Aycock's most intriguing pieces are her underground sculptures, environmental works which invite spectators to climb down into them to experience them firsthand (there is more on Alice Aycock in the chapter on land artists).

Miriam Schapiro took up materials branded 'feminine' by patriarchal culture (cotton, taffeta, burlap, wool, sequins, buttons, thread) and created artworks (she called them 'femmages') that dealt with notions of the home, feminist iconography, abstraction and the æsthetics of Pattern and Decoration. Schapiro remarked: 'I wanted to explore and express a part of my life which I had always dismissed – my homemaking, my nesting'.19 A number of male contemporary artists have explored traditionally 'feminine' notions of pattern, decoration and colour, among them Robert Zakanitch, Lucas Samaras, Robert Kushner, Rodney Ripps, Kim MacConnel, Frank Stella and Ned Smyth. But it is female artists who make the most flamboyant and intricate artworks in these areas, such as Joyce Kozloff and Valerie Jaudon.

The 'traditional' 'women's' arts and crafts – textiles, pattern, sewing, decoration, pottery, etc – are bound up, for feminist art critics, with the economies of labour, ethnicity, class, identity, patriarchy, politics and money. They are modes of production and art that continue to be regarded as secondary or inferior by patriarchal culture and masculinist criticism, and are not seen as 'high art', such as the traditional arts of painting or sculpture. The economics of artistic production are shot through with patriarchal slants, just as much as the images themselves. A piece of textiles, a decorative tile, a ceramic pot, are objects that in the patriarchal cultural system speak of their second-rate mode of production. As Catherine King wrote, '[m]edia associated with 'male-stream' codes, like bronze, marble, or oil, have been regarded with suspicion' by women artists.[20] Although Richard Long's art employs impermanent and even intangible materials (thrown stones, splashed water, the memory of a walk), he also uses traditional, 'masculine' media such as stone. This helps his art to be regarded as 'high', 'serious' art.

CONTEMPORARY SCULPTURE AND THE BODY

One can see the body written into, say, Richard Long's smeared Avon mud circles, or Constantin Brancusi's extraordinary egg shapes, but not, perhaps, in the giganticism of Michael Heizer's *Double Negative* (1969-70). Yet, even here, the human body is present – if only by the way it is violently dwarfed by the scale of Heizer's earthwork (but the best way to see *Double Negative* is to experience it firsthand, by walking around it). The body, in short, can never be totally erased. Much of land art is vast. As Carl Andre remarked:

> I once described the change in sculpture in the 20th century as moving in its concerns from form to structure and now having a concern with place... I believe now you can make sculpture you can enter.[1]

Much of sculpture in the modern era has been thoroughly traditional (conservative), and patriarchal, in its orientation and expression. Take Henry Moore, one of the most celebrated of Western sculptors, and one of the big names of modern British art (especially in the mid-century period before Richard Long became a student in Bristol and London). Moore's nudes, though, are no different from the conventional female nude, found in so much of 'high art' from the Renaissance onwards. Moore's polished wood and bronze surfaces, so softly rounded and enigmatic, seem so enchanting. But, despite his formal innovation, Moore is as sexist and reactionary a sculptor as Francis Bacon is as a painter. Postwar figurative sculpture (not only made by men) has rarely escaped the usual confines of patriarchal art (perhaps all art made in a patriarchal culture must be made in relation to patriarchy, even violently opposing it means being in relationship with patriarchy in some way). David Smith's bronze sculpture *The Rape* depicted a woman being raped by a canon, a phallic gun which climbs over her. It is meant to be a savage and ironic comment on violation, but it isn't ironic enough, as with Aristide Maillol's relief of a man assaulting a woman, entitled – what else? – *Desire* (1903-05, Paris). Edward Kienholz's quasi-Surrealist *Back Seat of a '38 Dodge* (1964, the Kleiner Foundation, Los Angeles) is a reassembled car with all manner of bits added to it and inside it – what else? – two people make the beast with two backs. It's meant to be satirical and ironic, but it also indulges in the issues it condemns.

But when sexuality is addressed, postwar and contemporary (male) sculptors have rarely been ironic. Usually, the norms and dualities of male/ female, active/ passive, culture/ nature, good/ evil are exalted. The 'great' or celebrated names in postwar sculpture – Alberto Giacometti, Henry Moore, David Smith, David Hare, Eduardo Chillida, Pablo Picasso, Isamu Noguchi, Mark Di Suvero, Jean Tinguely – rarely tackled notions of sexuality in major works of sculpture. When Picasso incorporated eroticism, it was invariably heterosexist, as in his *Bust* (1932, estate of the artist) with its gigantic breasts, echoing the "Stone Venuses" of yore. The 'great' works of contemporary sculpture – David Smith's *Cubi XXVII* (1965, Guggenheim Museum, New York), Alexander Calder's mobiles, Richard Serra's props of metal, Claes Oldenburg's giant soft sculptures, John Chamberlain's squashed cars (1961, Art Institute, Chicago) – seem to eschew issues of sexuality. Not much of mainstream or 'malestream' contemporary sculpture concerns itself with eroticism without pain or violence, and hardly ever feminism.

In Yves Klein's 'body-paintings' (*Anthropometries*), the intriguing thing was the manufacture of the painting (other artists have printed directly with the body). In Klein's case, this involved women (nude, of course) being doused with blue paint (International Klein Blue, naturally) and writhing around on a huge canvas stretched on the floor. Klein's *Anthropometries of the Blue Period* were *avant garde*, self-conscious, ironic art happenings, accompanied by a string chamber orchestra (playing Klein's *Monotone Symphony*, naturally).2 All very French, bohemian, cool.

Kazuo Shiraga made works of art with his body, such as smearing mud on pieces of paper with his feet, or 'fighting' in the mud (1955). His body art (made a few years before the high tide of body and performance art) was called 'the art of committing the whole self with the body'.3 The Austrian performance painter who enacted 'symbolic 'self-mutilations' and sado-masochistic actions', Günter Brus, said: '[m]y body is the intention, my body is the event, my body is the result'.4

The body features occasionally in the art of Richard Long. One sees the grass rubbed flat or stones kicked by Long's feet. Handprints smear mud on walls. And Long very occasionally appears in photographs, beside his work. But there is nothing in Long's work that is as ferocious as feminist and women's body art and performance art and happenings.

Feminist artists use the body to explore political, erotic, pornographic, æsthetic and philosophical discourses. As Lisa Tickner wrote: '[l]iving *in* a female body is different from looking *at* it, as a man. Even the Venus of Urbino menstruated, as women know and men forget'.5 The female nude, for so long the model and image and object of lust in so many 'high art' paintings, has usurped the power relation between artist and art object, and between artwork and spectator. The woman is no longer content to be looked at and lusted after: she is making her own art, employing her body in a radical, challenging way. The 'Old Master/ *Playboy* tradition', as Tickner called it, has been smashed.6

Chila Kumari Burman made 'body prints'. Carolee Schneemann pulled a scroll from her vagina and read from it.7 Karen Finley poured 'a can of yams over her naked buttocks'. She was called 'a frightening and rare presence'.8 In her *Cut Off Balls* Finley castrated Wall Street bankers.9 Mary Duffy displayed her disabled body in perform-ance art and photographic sequences;10 Jo Spence has photographed the 'unhealthy and ageing female body'.11 Feminist happenings, action art, body art and performance art was a way of repossessing the body, sexuality, identity and power; it was a way of 'rewriting the body', in the terminology of French and postmodern feminist philo-sophy. It can be an act of transgression and subversion, which usurps the power relation between spectator and artwork, so that the (male) viewer's 'cloak of invisibility has been stripped away and his spectatorship becomes an issue within the work' as Catherine Elwes put it.12

By contrast with these dynamic and sometimes infamous and legendary happen-ings and performances, the performance element in Richard Long's art is far quieter and more contemplative. No naked women covered in paint *à la* Yves Klein's *Anthro-pometries* for him, or writhing around in mud on the ground as in Kazuo Shiraga's performances, no dressing up as fantasy creatures *à la* Matthew Barney, no having his clothes cut off his body by an audience like Yoko Ono, or the crazy antics of Allan Kaprow's New York 'happenings', or the 'lovemaking with paint brushes' of Carolee

Schneeman's *Meat Joy*. Long's art is essentially just a guy walking, or placing stones in a circle, or smearing mud on walls.

One aspect of 'feminist' or 'women's' art was (is) embodied by the figure of the Goddess, the ancient and primæval Great Mother, celebrated then – and now – as Isis, Ishtar, Demeter, Kali, Cerridwen and so on. The Goddess for feminist and female artists embodied aspects of the 'feminine' – love, motherhood, purity, nobility, sacrifice, beauty, hunting, and so on. Since the 1960s, the Goddess has been variously interpreted as fact, experience, idea, æsthetic, cult, religion, pagan emblem and many other things by women artists and writers. There are a host of artists who pursue what one might call 'Goddess art', art that employs the figure of the Goddess as an embodiment of female being or experience: Judy Chicago, Mary Beth Edelson, Miriam Schapiro, Niki de Sant-Phalle, Louis Bourgeois and Helen Chadwick.

Mary Beth Edelson engaged in the resurgence of interest in the Goddess in her *Great Goddess* series (1975). Edelson has also produced a piece on menstruation, entitled, appropriately, *Blood Mysteries* (1973). In a performance piece, Catherine Elwes sat in an enclosed studio space and menstruated.[13] Judy Chicago looked to the flowers of Georgia O'Keeffe, which, she said, 'stand for femininity' (Chicago produced a familiar kind of Seventies eroticized feminist art, where associations were evoked between flowers, vulvas, sexuality, women's bodies and feminine identity).[14]

One could see Richard Long's circles or Robert Smithson's spirals and circles as a kind of Goddess art, because circles so clearly evoke Goddess themes such as time, cycles, (Moon) phases, dance, transformation, ritual, initiation, astronomy, and so on. The circle is also a profound shape for alchemists; as the mediæval alchemical tract *Rosarium Philosophorum* has it: 'make a round circle and you will have the stone of the philosophers'.[15] Long created, in his favourite stamping ground of Ireland, an ancient maze form out of small stones set on grass (*Connemara Sculpture*, 1971), and returned to similar forms in *North South East West Circles* (Switzerland, 2000). Robert Morris has also made a labyrinth (*Labyrinth*, 1974). The shape of Long's and Morris's labyrinths directly recall the Cretan labyrinth of initiation and ritual, and the spirals at the entrance to Newgrange in Co. Meath, a huge passage grave some 4,500 years old.

Herman de Vries created a circular walled *Sanctuarium* (1997) in Westfalen, Germany. Alan Sonfist planted a maze from oak trees at TICKON in 1993. In Dennis Oppenheim's *Maze* (1970), cattle are lab rats running after corn in a field. Dan Graham combined hedges and mirrors in his *Two-Way Mirror Hedge Labyrinth* (1989). Chris Drury has made circular mazes (some of which are reworked dew ponds). Drury also carved a maze from snow on a Sussex hill (1999). Bill Vazan has fashioned a number of earthworks on the ground, including a *Stone Maze* (1975-76, reminiscent of Richard Long's Connemara labyrinth) and Richard Fleischner, Michelangelo Pistoletto, Hiroshi Teshigahara, and Vong Phaephanit have also created maze structures (Fleischner built a maze from turf in 1974 at Newport, Rhode Island, and one from a chain link fence in 1978). A number of (land) artists have made miniature labyrinths – maze models: Charles Simonds, Terry Fox and Patrick Ireland. Michelangelo Pistoletto created an interior maze from large pieces of corrugated cardboard laid out across the whole gallery (*Labyrinth,* 1991). In *Monumental Ikebana* (1990) Hiroshi Teshigahara made a giant arched path from bamboo in a gallery space. For Vong Phaephanit's bamboo installation (*What Falls to the Ground Cannot Be Eaten*, 1991), a forest of bamboo sticks was hung from the ceiling of the London gallery, approached through a monumental black doorway.[16]

3

Spirit and Matter: Land Art

SPIRIT OF PLACE

Ah! hills so early loved! in fancy still
I breathe your pure keen air, and still behold
Those widely spreading views, mocking alike
The poet and the painter's utmost art.

Charlotte Smith, from 'Beachy Head'[1]

The whole planet is potentially an artist's studio for the land artist (perhaps even the whole cosmos: if art can be anything, there can be no limits either). The land artist ranges over the whole globe. A desert, a beach, a field, a piece of waste ground can become a studio (and has been, countless times). A forest becomes a place of creative activity. The landscape itself is crucial in land art: everything about a landscape, every detail, the very texture and colour and shape and dampness and springiness and strength and size of grass, for instance. Or a crevice in a rock formation. Pine cones, closed-up. Fallen apples. A small dewpond on an empty hillside. Flowers turning sunward in the late afternoon. The history of a place, its social uses, the layers of human interaction. These are the things land artists deal with in making art. These are the actualities that artists employ when they create artworks. To fully appreciate land art, then, one has to look really closely, to grasp the details, as well as the overall conception. This is true of Richard Long's sculptures, as well as the larger American earthworks of Alice Aycock, Mary Miss and Robert Smithson. For David Nash, 'land art' is 'close-up', not distanced:

> The term "landscape" is like "portrait". It is an expression of a distancing: here I am and there it is. But what has been happening in the last twenty years or so is that artists have been getting right in there. Saying no, it is not out there. It is here. We want to make our images with what is here – here. That is why it is called land art rather than landscape art, "scape" denoting distancing.[2]

For David Nash, land art is about getting as near as possible to nature: the land artist does not paint nature, from way off, with a paintbrush or watercolour block in front of her/ him. The sketchpad or easel is a wall between artist and world. The land artist, rather, dives in, 'gets right in there', as Nash says. The land artist does not use oil or pastel or ink to 'represent' nature. Rather, s/he works directly with nature, getting her/ his fingers dirty with mud, snow, sheep shit, stone, ferns, wood.

It is exactly the same with poetry. Poets have long written of nature in close-up, of the minutiæ that go to make up an accurate description of the natural world. Land art can be seen as the sculptural equivalent, in one sense, of nature poetry, so that Long, Irwin, Fulton, Pierce, Sonfist, Sanborn and Aycock are the inheritors of William Words-worth, Matsuo Basho, Francesco Petrarch, Emily Dickinson, Rainer Maria Rilke and Aleksandr Pushkin. The nature poem itself is a piece of land art, a work evoking or representing or describing or situated in particular places. ('The sculpture that I do,' says David Nash, 'is appropriate to a particular place and it stays in that place. It is made from and for that place.')[3]

William Wordsworth's poetic pantheism is fairly representative of this kind of Romantic relationship with the natural world which land art continues to feed from. As Wordsworth wrote in 'Lines Composed a Few Miles Above Tintern Abbey': 'nature never did betray / The heart that loved her'. One of the classic instances of Words-worthian pantheism is in the same poem:

<pre>
            And I have felt
A presence that disturbs me with the joy
Of elevated thoughts; a sense sublime
Of something far more deeply interfused,
Whose dwelling is the light of the setting sun,
And the round ocean and the living air,
And the blue sky, and in the mind of man:
</pre>

A motion and a spirit, that impels
All thinking things, all objects of all thought,
And rolls through all things.[4]

'Land art' is a term that includes a wide variety of artistic forms, like the term 'garden'. Gardens are not a single form with a single set of characteristics. Gardens can be so various that some critics have suggested that the word 'garden' is as broad and vague as words such as 'art'.[5] If art can be just about anything in modern times, then perhaps a garden can also be anything.[6] Gardens can be very small or very large (can there be a limit on size?); they can be flat or terraced; they can be situated anywhere; they can be organized around a 'natural' plan or a strict geometric plan; they can be 'wild' or 'tamed'; they can be enclosed or open; they can contain lakes, ponds, streams, fountains, statues, trees, lawns, shrubs, rocks, walls, fences, benches, flowers, stones, follies, ruins, grottoes, temples, paths, boardwalks, arches and many kinds of environmental art.

A Japanese Zen garden, with its stones and sand raked into patterns (a favourite of Richard Long's), is quite different from an English kitchen garden. Gardens can be vast displays of state and regal power, such as the gardens at Versailles, or modest attempts at cultivating food in a yard. Gardens have been made for many reasons: in the pursuit of decoration, finance, medicine, religion, contemplation, play, sport and food. Isamu Noguchi thought of gardens as the 'sculpturing of space: a beginning, and a groping to another level of sculptural experience and use: a total sculpture space experience beyond individual sculptures. A man may enter such a space: it is in scale with him; it is real' (1968). For some critics, the most interesting aspect of land art is its connection with gardening and landscape design.[5] If there can be 'found art', can there be 'found gardens'? Perhaps an artist, working in the Conceptual and environmental art mode, could simply claim any piece of land as their 'found garden', just as artists such as Marcel Duchamp, Kurt Schwitters and Robert Rauschenberg took found objects and exhibited them as art. Andy Goldsworthy said that even farming could be regarded as a 'very sculptural activity', so that an act like making haystacks could be 'one of the biggest acts of Minimalism you've ever seen', and planting a row of potatoes could be an installation (*Wall*, 14-15). Land art's premier artist – Robert Smithson – took a dim view of gardening: art degenerates as it approaches gardening, he said.[8] Richard Long's art may not have obvious affinities with gardens or gardening, but the stones, the patterns, reinvention of the landscape in his art is very much central to gardening (and Long's works have been exhibited in gardens and sculpture parks).

When does a garden start becoming a garden? Is a blade of grass a garden? Is two plants on a window ledge a garden? Or five plants, or ten plants, clustered together in pots? Is an overgrown path a garden? Or an allotment dedicated to growing tomatoes and runner beans? Is a patch of grass behind an abandoned gas station a garden? Is a municipal park, consisting only of children's swings and slides on grass a garden? Is a farmer's field a garden? And when does a garden stop being a garden? Is a garden of a hundred years ago that can barely be seen amidst piles of refuse still a garden? How much of the human touch is required to make a piece of land a garden? If sand raked into a pattern can be a garden for the Japanese Zen Buddhist, is *any* piece of raked sand a garden? (Jan Dibbets raked up a beach in Holland with a tractor for a tide sculpture shown on TV in 1969). Are the patterns made in the sand by the receding tide a garden? Is the sea making gardens with every tide (each one unique)? Or the wind, or erosion, or earthquakes or other natural forces?

Environmental art or land art or garden art can include American earthworks (such as those by James Turrell and Mel Chin); ephemeral interventions in the environment (such as those by Richard Long, Hans Haacke and Michael Singer); architectural installations (such as those by Alice Aycock, Mary Miss and Nancy Holt); land art as performance art (Hamish Fulton, Christo), even if the artist is the only audience; land art that involves landscaping and garden art (such as Alan Sonfist, Patricia Johanson, Robert Irwin and Ian Hamilton Finlay); and sculpture or art parks. There are 'video gardens', too, such as Matthew McCaslin's *Bloomer* installation (St Louis Art Museum): 12 TV monitors played tapes of flowers blooming in time-lapse. The TV sets were arranged in groups like plants, with the cables tangled on the floor).

The rise in popularity of Richard Long's has parallels perhaps with the developments and trends in gardening and garden art in Britain and elsewhere. The popularity of Richard Long's art is in tune in the UK with the rise in gardening shows on TV (and those shows' links with programmes on houses, food, vacations, tourism and interior design); the spread of out-of-town household stores, and rural gardening centres; more and more gardens are open to the public (including many more private gardens in the *Yellow Book* scheme); the increasing interest in ecological and environmental politics (for instance, Friends of the Earth, Greenpeace, World Wildlife Fund, saving rainforests, whales, dolphins, elephants, rhinos, tigers, endangered species and habitats); anti-pollution and recycling drives; anxiety about ozone, global warming, car owning and pollution; and the increase of New Age and mind/ body/

spirit pursuits (such as *feng shui*). Some of the things that fuel this revived (or new) interest in gardens, art and the environment include an increase in leisure time, more money for entertainment and travel, low-cost tourism, a bigger ageing population (which also lives longer), new technologies, and new distribution and consumption networks.

Key land art shows include *Earth Art* (Andrew Dickson White Museum of Art, Cornell University, 1969), which showed Dibbets, Long, Smithson, Oppenheim and Morris, *Land Art* (Hanover, 1970), *Earthworks* (Dwan Gallery, 1968), *The New Sculpture, 1965-75* (Whitney, 1990), *Qu'est-ce que la sculpture moderne?* (Paris, 1986), *Virginia Dwan, Art Minimal, Art Conceptuel, Earthworks* (Paris, 1991), *Earthworks* (Seattle, 1979), *Conceptual Art, Arte Povera, Land Art* (Turin, 1971), and many of the Documenta exhibitions at Kassel. At *Earth, Air, Fire, Water* (Boston, 1971), Haacke, Christo, Smithson, Oppenheim, Long, Sonfist, Huebler, Hutchinson, Warhol and Heizer showed works. Some of the key writers on land art include Rosalind Krauss, Lucy Lippard, Michael Fried, Kenneth Baker, John Beardsley, Lawrence Alloway, John Coplans, Diane Waldman, Harold Rosenberg, Stephanie Ross, Robert Hobbs, David Bourdon, Mel Gooding, Germano Celant, Alan Sonfist, Baile Oakes, Jeffrey Kastner, Andrew Causey, and Gilles Tiberghien.

ART AND LIFE

Land artists, like nature poets and nature mystics, are inspired by particular places. Richard Long said 'places gives me the energy for ideas' (FC VI, 6). Nature poets, like religious mystics or land artists (or all artists), can be described as 'following their bliss' (Joseph Campbell's term). When you follow your bliss 'you come to bliss'.[1] Campbell used the model or metaphor of following the 'pollen path' of the Navaho Indians. As Campbell defined it:

> The Navaho have that wonderful image of what they call the pollen path. Pollen is the life source. The pollen path is the path to the centre. The Navaho say, "Oh, beauty before me, beauty behind me, beauty to the right of me, beauty to the left of me, beauty above me, beauty below me, I'm on the pollen path".[2]

This is one way of imagining the creative journey – towards the centre, the life source. Paradise, the Golden Age, Eden, was not back there then, but it is now. 'Eden is…this is it, this is Eden' Campbell stressed (ib.). It's *now*, and can only be 'now'. There is no other time it could possibly be. The journey, whether physical (as in Richard Long's case) or psychic, spiritual or imaginary, is along the *feng shui,* the 'dragon lines', or along the 'lines of song' or 'dream tracks' of the Australian aborigines, the primrose paths, the 'fairy paths' of Celtic mythology, or the 'pollen paths' of the Navaho Indians.3 Long has been walking the pollen path for most of his artistic career. In *Heaven and Earth* (2001) Long talks of the 'the walk as a true path' (WL, 180). There are millions of paths, but each one is individual, as well as being identical with all the others. When Long's walked one path, he's walked them all.

Like Chris Drury, Hamish Fulton and Richard Long, British author Bruce Chatwin spoke lovingly of walking, of wandering, of nomads and wildernesses. In *The Songlines*, Chatwin made notes upon Australian dreamtime and 'songlines', the lines that crisscross the landscape. Britain has its own version of this *feng shui* or earth magic: ley lines ('discovered' by Alfred Watkins).4 Richard Long's maps often look like those of a New Age ley line hunter, crisscrossed with ink lines. Oppenheim, Fulton and Long produced their own versions of 'songlines', whether in powdered snow, drips of water, or words. As in the work of Bruce Chatwin, Paul Theroux, Jonathan Raban, Iain Sinclair, Colin Thubron and other travel writers, there is a deep sense of motion and travelling in the art of Fulton, Drury and Long. Theirs is an art born out of travels, even if the journeys are nothing more than morning walks out from the studio. These journeys don't have to be weeks long, crossing the Sahara on foot or over the Poles by sled; they can be made on an afternoon stroll (although Long has travelled the globe far more than many land artists).

Where people live is both local and universal, both particular to the individual and particular to everyone. The path snaking around the hill outside that town in Peru or India, where one walked in childhood, say, is both a very particular place, with its own kinds of shadows, lights, sounds, stones and plants, and also a universal path, like all other paths.

Mircea Eliade (who was another Jungian, like Joseph Campbell) wrote of regaining what he called the 'mythic centre', which is the spiritual core of one's life. For Eliade, the recovery of this mythic centre is spatial. That is, it pivots around certain places: in *Ordeal By Labyrinth*, Eliade wrote:

Wherever one is, there is a center of the world. As long as you are in that center, you are at home, you are truly in the real self and at the center of the cosmos. Exile helps you to understand that the world is never foreign to you once you have a central stance in it... (100)

For Mircea Eliade, sacred acts create a 'mythic centre'. As art is a sacred act, the creation of an artwork can be seen as the creation of a sacred place or mythic centre. A piece of land art (the boulder, hole, pillar, stone circle) is an obvious form of a mythic centre. Making land art (or any art) can be seen as a sacramental experience – essentially one of a sacralization of life and living things. It is like the Australian Bushmen's *alchuringa* experience, mythic dreamtime and mystical participation with the earth and with life. In the *alchuringa* of the Australian aborigines the world is sung into existence (a notion also found in Western occultism, in the 'music of the spheres' of hermetic philosophy).5 As the poet Rainer Maria Rilke put it, 'song is existence' ('Gesang ist Dasein') where art is life itself, and making art is not a commentary 'about' life, but is life itself.6 This notion of art = life is certainly the foundation of Richard Long's art. It would be difficult for the outsider (and perhaps for the artist too) to separate the art from the life.

As Barry Flanagan put it: '[m]y work isn't centred in experience. The making of it is itself the experience'.7 James Turrell said (in 1987) that the goal was not to turn an experience into art, but 'to set up a situation to which I take you and let you see. It becomes your experience... not taking from nature as much as placing you in contact with it'.8 Turrell's structures were built so that the visitor to his skyspaces could have their own experiences. The visitors would be nudged and encouraged by the artist, but the experiences would be their own.

Germano Celant, one of the key theorists of Arte Povera, likened the sculptor and land artist to an alchemist:

The artist-alchemist organizes living and vegetable matter into magic things, working to discover the root of things, in order to re-find them and extol them... What interests him... is the discovery, the exposition, the insurrection of the magic and marvellous value of natural elements.9

The Arte Povera-type artist-alchemist uses simple, natural elements, said Celant: copper, zinc, earth, water, snow, fire, grass, air, stone, gravity, growth. S/he re-discovers the magic of the world, its composition, growth, precariousness, falseness, reality (1969). 'At the same time he rediscovers his interest in himself. He abandons linguistic intervention in order to live hazardously in an uncertain space... his availability to all is total. He accumulates continuously desire and lack of desire, choice and lack of choice' (1969).

The Arte Povera artist works with life, within life, Celant asserted, discovering the 'finite and infinite moments of life', art as life, 'the explosion of the individual dimension as an æsthetic and feeling communion with nature'; making art becomes identical with living: '[t]o create art, then, one identifies with life and to exist takes on the meaning of reinventing at every moment a new fantasy, pattern of behavior, æstheticism, etc. of one's own life'. Celant quoted from John Cage (one of Richard Long's influences): '[a]rt comes from a kind of experimental condition in which one experiments with the living'. What counts is to live the work, Celant said, to be open to the world, 'to be available to all the facts of life (death, illogic, madness, casualness, nature, infinite, real, unreal, symbiosis)' (1969).

The 'sacred' or 'mythic' element does not have to be extraordinary. Ordinary things can be the sources of sacrality, the mythical and ecstatic. Things such as moss on a wall, or the feel of wood, or the colour of a particular patch of sky. Artists such as Leonardo da Vinci show the viewer that the 'ordinary' is really extraordinary (think of Leonardo's fabulous drawings of a sprig of oak, a lily, a rain storm). The poet Peter Redgrove told me:

....this 'strangeness' is 'strange' because reality is so fucking extraordinary, and strange too because most of us try to live without strangeness, and construct something called the 'ordinary' which never existed. Actually, the strangeness is so ordinary as to be quite natural. The strangeness is wonder and what is wondered at is so wonderful that it is strange we do not wonder more.[10]

What happens is that these tiny sensations and feelings are sidelined, displaced, buried, forgotten, suppressed and ignored by society, by the media. Hardly anyone speaks of such minute feelings, because they seem to be 'unimportant'. Poets such as Marina Tsvetayeva, Louise Labé, Novalis, John Skelton and Bernard de Ventadour show that these sensualities are important. They don't seem to add up to much, as John Cowper Powys said in his *Autobiography,* yet they are crucial to poetic living.

Marcel Proust knew that a ray of sunshine could lift the spirits, and for John Cowper Powys, simply by seeing the sun on a wall one could have a 'Beatific Vision'.[11] Nature poetry (and similarly land art) veers between the sensualism of the pastoral view of life, as created in the ancient bucolic poetry of Theocritus and Virgil, and a more intense pantheism as found in mystics such as Meister Eckhart, Jacob Boehme and

Henry Vaughan. The Elizabethan and Renaissance poets (Edmund Spenser, William Shakespeare, Michael Drayton, Samuel Daniel and others) were particularly fervent about nature. Sir Philip Sidney wrote:

O sweet woods, the delight of solitariness,
O how much I do like your solitariness![12]

Unlike the world of bucolic verse, land art is not populated with images of satyrs, sylphs, Pan-figures, shepherds and shepherdesses and magicians. But there is same reverence for the natural world, the same deep and long-lasting immersion in nature, that one finds in nature poetry.

Robert Herrick, the Cavalier poet (1591-1674), wrote some of the loveliest verse about the British landscape, about laurels, roses, rainbows, blossom, violets, sycamores and seasons. Herrick lived in and wrote about Devonshire, a place beloved of Richard Long. Indeed, Herrick could be called the best writer on Devon. This is from 'To Meddowes':

Ye have been fresh and green,
     Ye have been fill'd with flower:
And ye the Walks have been
     Where Maids have spent their houres.

You have beheld, how they
     With *Wicker Arks* did come
To kisse, and beare away
     The richer Couslips home.[13]

SPIRIT OF PLACE IN LITERATURE

Of the many writers who have explored the 'spirit of place', two of the most interesting were Lawrence Durrell and D.H. Lawrence, British 20th century authors. Lawrence Durrell's notion of landscape or 'spirit of place' was defined by the writer thus: 'I firmly believe in the theory that landscape shapes people and behaviour patterns'.[1] For Durrell, landscape was one of guiding principles or forces that humans must respond to.2 For Durrell, 'man is only an extension of the spirit of place'.3 In Durrell's most famous work, *The Alexandria Quartet* (1956-58), the narratives (and to some extent the characters) are controlled by the city, so that the narrator says '[w]e are the children of our landscape; it dictates our behaviour and even thought'.4 (Sometimes Long acts like a child *in* the landscape: skimming stones on a river, kicking stones, throwing stones, and building cairns).

Lawrence Durrell developed D.H. Lawrence's 'spirit of place',5 mixing it with Sigmund Freud and Oswald Spengler, folklore, and anthropology. D.H. Lawrence employed landscape as a setting and a symbol: he did not choose landscapes simply for their 'beauty'. The settings of Lawrence's fictions add much to their meanings and values. The snowy countryside of the short story "Wintry Peacock", for instance, is central to its theme; the environs of Eastwood in Nottinghamshire, lovingly evoked in *Sons and Lovers* and *The Rainbow,* form so much of the impact of Lawrence's novels. As with *Wuthering Heights, War and Peace* or *Tess of the d'Urbervilles*, one couldn't take away the settings without altering much of the meaning. Lawrence Durrell wrote:

> As a poet of historic consciousness I suppose I am bound to see landscape as a field dominated by the human wish – tortured into farms and hamlets, ploughed into cities. A landscape scribbled with the signatures of men and epochs. Now, however, I am beginning to believe that the wish is inherited from the site; that man depends for the furniture of the will upon his location in place, tenant of fruitful acres or a perverted wood.6

Land art gains much of its power from particular places. Many land artists, for instance, work away from built-up, urban areas (though they choose *urban* zones far more than *sub*urban realms if they have to – partly because the art galleries and museums who fund or exhibit their work tend to be based in cities rather than the suburbs). Some, like Michael Heizer, Nancy Holt and Walter de Maria, work in what are regarded as 'exotic' locations – deserts and mountains. The 'glamour' of the locations enhances the sculptures. Some land art is overpowered by the Romantic settings. Some of Richard Long's stone circles, for instance, look feeble in their desert or snowscape locations.

The fiction of Lawrence Durrell, V.S. Naipaul, Bruce Chatwin, Toni Morrison and others is set in – and is an expression of – what is now called the 'post-colonial' world. It's an epoch in which 'ethnic', 'national' and 'racial' 'boundaries' are dissolving, producing uncertainty and anxiety. The upside of this post-colonial world is the ease with which land artists such as Long, Christo, Andre and others jet around the world.

Land art is very much the product of the privileged, relatively wealthy First World, a world in which the Northern hemisphere is dominant politically and economically over the Southern; American-Eurocentric ethics prevail; bourgeois/ 'imperialist' politics predominate; and the racial 'colour' of the art is not black, brown, red or yellow, but definitely white. Though 'post-colonial', land art is distinctly not 'politically correct' when it comes to issues of ethnicity or economy (although there is a strain of land art that engages with political, financial and ecological issues).

Any number of (travel) writers (Bruce Chatwin, Paul Theroux, Julia Kristeva, V.S. Naipaul, Colin Thubron) have explored the dislocation of a postwar, post-colonial world. The narrators of their fictions, like land artists themselves, are exiles, ex-pats, colonials, 'castaways', 'displaced persons' and migrants. While land art is about 'centring' oneself in a particular place, in postwar fiction the sense of displacement is paramount.

In a key text, the essay "Landscape and Character", Lawrence Durrell spoke of being a 'residence writer', that is, someone who lives in a place not as a tourist or visitor.[7] This is the opposite of Richard Long's desire, which is to pass through the world 'invisibly', to create ephemeral artworks, and not make a lasting mark on the world, but Long does also get to know an environment over many years (such as Scotland, Somerset and Dartmoor).

THE ALCHEMY OF MATTER

There is no habitation between our road and the Schroon river four miles cross country. I enjoy the phenomenon of nature, the sounds, the Northern lights, stars, animal calls, as I did the harbor lights, tugboat whistles, buoy clanks, the yelling of men on barges around the T.I.W. in Brooklyn. I sit up there and dream of the city as I used to dream of the mountains when I sat on the dock in Brooklyn. I like my solitude, black coffee, and daydreams. I like the changes of nature; no two days or nights are the same.

David Smith (1951)[1]

Nature poetry is an ancient form of poetry – from Greek bucolic verse and Classical mythology onwards poets have written of nature. Land art and land artists seem to have much in common in literature with Romantic art and Romantic artists. The marks of late 18th / early 19th century European Romanticism included: exalting nature; going to extremes; the cult of solitude; the Gothic and macabre; the predominance of subjectivity, and so on. Late 20th century artists (such as Mark Rothko, Robert Smithson, David Inshaw, Anish Kapoor and Thérèse Oulton) express, as does Richard Long, some of the marks of Romanticism cited above. The cult of solitude, for instance – as found in writers like Ralph Waldo Emerson, Johann Wolfgang von Goethe, Henry Thoreau (sometimes cited in relation to Long), Jean-Jacques Rousseau and Friedrich Hölderlin – is a part of contemporary art (Long makes most of his works alone). Postwar and contemporary art exalts the subjectivity and sovereignty of the artist creating on her/ his own. R.W. Emerson wrote of the ecstasy of being alone in nature:

> The lover of nature is he whose inward and outward senses are still truly adjusted to each other... His intercourse with heaven and earth becomes part of his daily food. In the presence of nature a wild delight runs through the man in spite of real sorrows.[2]

Land art in its grander moments echoes the gestures of High Romanticism – the Blakean, Wordsworthian, Hölderlinian, Turnerian gestures – which have become so familiar in Western art. One of the apotheoses of High Romanticism is Johann Wolfgang von Goethe's novel *The Sorrows of Young Werther,* where the soul alone actualizes the myriad things of nature. In this passage from Goethe one can see similarities with the more opulent (sublime) moments in the art of Richard Long, Robert Smithson and James Turrell:

> Ah, to view this vast landscape from there! Oh, distance is like the future: before our souls lies an entire and dusky vastness which overwhelms our feelings as it overwhelms our eyes, and ah! we long to surrender the whole of our being, and be filled with all the joy of one single, immense, magnificent emotion.[3]

The 'Land Art Sublime' (*pace* Robert Rosenblum's coining of the term 'Abstract Sublime' to describe Barnett Newman's and Mark Rothko's paintings) might include the snow and stone circles made in the wildernesses of Scotland, Nepal and Peru of Richard Long; Dennis Oppenheim borderland snow circles, the stone circles of Nancy Holt; Christo's islands surrounded with pink polypropylene; and of course Smithson's *Spiral Jetty.*

There are links between land art and the theory of the (Romantic) sublime in the history of art. These are useful to consider. Art critic Christopher Hussey defined (in 1927) seven aspects of the sublime, derived from the philosopher Edmund Burke's *Philosophical Enquiry Into the Origin of Our Ideas of the Sublime and Beautiful* (1757): *(1)* obscurity (physical and intellectual); *(2)* power; *(3)* privations (such as darkness, solitude, silence); *(4)* vastness (vertical or horizontal); *(5)* infinity; *(6)* succession; and *(7)* uniformity (the last two suggest limitless progression).[4] These tenets can be applied to land art, especially that of Turrell, Pierce, Irwin, Smithson *et al* (again linking the art of Long to the British Romantic nature tradition).

The nature poet uses the same emotional/ cultural stuff as the land artist: the human relationship with the natural world. Whatever the poet writes about or the land artist sculpts, it is the *feeling* for nature that is important, the relation between self and nature, that is employed by both poet and land artist. As Clement Greenberg, the foremost critic of postwar art in America, wrote: '[a]rt is a matter strictly of experience, not of principles', a statement which chimes with the views of Long, Drury, Turrell and other land artists, for whom experience is primary.[5] For Long, subjectivity is primary: his art must please himself first, before anyone else. 'I just make art in the way that gives meaning, purpose and pleasure for myself. If it is any good I think it will naturally resonate in all manner of ways for other people.'[6] The Arte Povera artist, said Germano Celant, has 'chosen to live within direct experience, no longer the representative... he aspires to live, not to see' (1969).

Poets regard poems themselves as physical things that affect people, just as land art is a physical thing (a stone, soil, leaves) that affects people. When Walter de Maria filled a gallery with soil, the sensual aspects of the piece (smell/ taste/ touch/ sight/ sound) were crucial. Similarly, when Herrick, Plath, Santoka Teneda, Whitman or Brontë describe a place (even its soil, perhaps), they employ synæsthetic means, in order to make the poem itself a physiological experience. As Ted Hughes wrote:

> The value of [some] poems is that they are better, in some ways, than actual landscapes. The feelings that come over us confusedly and fleetingly when we are actually in the places, are concentrated and purified and intensified in these poems. (80)

Among novelists, it is British author John Cowper Powys who has captured most accurately the synæsthetic experiences of life, where so many tiny and seemingly ordinary and inconsequential sensations fuse into illumination. Powys writes about landscape in a way wholly in tune with land artists such as Long, Nash, Fulton, Turrell and Aycock. One extract from Powys's *Autobiography,* which is one long record of ecstasies and sensations, serves to introduce his highly charged, eidetic, pellucid way of seeing. The author has been out walking and is returning to Cambridge with his walking stick:

> What I am revealing to you now is the deepest and most essential secret of my life. My thoughts were lost in my sensations; and my sensations were of a kind so difficult to describe that I could write a volume upon them and still not really have put them down. But the field-dung upon my boots, the ditch-mud plastered thick, with little bits of dead grass in it, against the turned-up ends of my trousers, the feel of my oak-stick "Sacred" whose every indentation and corrugation and curve I knew as well as those on my hand, the salty taste of half-dried sweat upon my lips, the delicious swollenness of my fingers, the sullen sweet weariness of my legs, the indescribable happiness of my calm, dazed, lulled, wind-drugged, air-drunk spirit, were all, after their kind, a sort of thinking, though of exactly what, it would be very hard for me to explain.7

Powys was a walker *par excellence*, one of the great walker-writers, one might say (others include Thoreau and Hölderlin), (as Richard Long is one of the great walker-artists). Certainly, no one can top Powys when he's in full flow writing about a walk.

The attention to the minute, detailed qualities of nature that land art rejoices in is mirrored in Romantic and nature poetry. John Cowper Powys, for instance, could get excited by nothing more 'spectacular' than a patch of moss on a wall. In his *Autobiography* (1934), Powys wrote: 'I am looking at a patch of moss on a greenish marbly rock and I am aware of a deep sensual pleasure' (41). And in Cambridge, on one of his many walks around the outskirts of the city, Powys remarked that 'certain patches of grass and green moss transported me into a sort of Seventh Heaven' (199).

In his much-neglected fiction John Cowper Powys described the ecstasies that (land) artists have when interacting with nature. Powys's characters, like those in William Wordsworth, Goethe, George Seferis, Maria Tsvetayeva or Victor Hugo, are nature mystics, just as land artists such as Long, Nash, Randall-Page, Holt, Drury and Smithson are in part nature mystics. Sam Dekker, in Powys's truly epic nature mysticism novel *A Glastonbury Romance* (1932), experiences a *participation mystique* with the planet: '[w]hat he felt was a strange and singular reciprocity between his soul and every little fragment of masonry, of stony ground, of mossy ground...'8 And Dud No-Man in the last of the Wessex quartet books, *Maiden Castle* (1936), when he comes 'on a patch of green moss on a grey wall' gets 'a sensation that's more important than what you call 'love', or anything else, nearer the secret of things too!'9

Constantin Brancusi, Bill Woodrow, Shirazeh Houshiary and many sculptors have spoken of the importance of materials in their work, how they learn from their materials, and 'follow' their materials. Tony Cragg spoke of 'works in which I learnt from the materials'.9 A stone is not merely a stone for land artists: it has its own essence, its own form and presence. For Richard Long, stones are one of the primary fetish objects.

> Nothing could convince Brancusi that a rock was only a fragment of inert matter [remarked Mircea Eliade]; like his Carpathian ancestors, like all neolithic men, he sensed a presence in the rock, a power, an "intention" that one can only call "sacred."10

The land artist has a special, fetishistic relation with her/ his materials: they are not simply bits of matter to be wielded in a particular way. They are treated with respect. Wolfgang Laib dusts the Earth with pollen, to form an enormous square layer of brilliant yellow. The delicacy – and potency – of the sculpture is immediately apparent. This is the sort of sculpture that exerts a synæsthetic power over the gallery goer: the pollen affects not only the visual sense with its incandescent hues, but also affects smell, taste and touch. 'I believe that the impossible, the invisible and visions can become reality if one really wants to make the effort' said Laib.11 Another of Laib's installations is *The Passageway* (1988-93), comprising huge panels of beeswax.

Anya Gallaccio made large installations using flowers: thousands of red roses in *Red On Green* (1992), 101 sunflowers in *Preserve Sunflower* (1991) and 1,600 zinnias in *Untitled* (1992). Gallaccio's flower-pieces emphasized beauty and decay, sensuality and death. Goldsworthy, Laib and Drury collect leaves, berries, pollen, honey and other natural elements and weave sensuous artifacts that are ephemeral and intricate. Dennis Oppenheim worked with snow and circles in his *Annual Rings*, a series of concentric circles that straddled the Canadian/ American border, and with burning circles onto grass in his *Branded Mountain*. In fact, Oppenheim was the first land artist to work with snow on a grand scale (in the late Sixties).

'TRUE CAPITALIST ART'?: THE ECONOMICS OF LAND ART

Not all but much of land art is very expensive. That is, it is expensive moving tons of earth around or building enormous structures. Taking a motorbike out into the desert and drawing lines with it is one thing (as Michael Heizer had done in *Circular Surface Displacement* [1968], North of Las Vegas), but making a 40 mile 18 foot high fence (Christo) is another. Much of land art requires patrons, sponsors, co-ordination with galleries, lawyers, public administrators, helpers and industry. (The costliness of land art may help to explain why much of it is American).[1] Land art requires investment with no immediate return. Patrons are crucial to land art. In American earthworks the key patrons were the Dia Art Foundation, Robert C. Scull and Virginia Dwan, director of the Dwan Gallery between 1966 and 1971.

Richard Long voiced a common view (perhaps) among many British sculptors when he wrote of his aversion to American earthwork art:

> In the sixties there was a feeling that art need not be a production line of more objects to fill the world. My interest was in a more thoughtful view of art and nature, making art both visible and invisible, using ideas, walking, stones, tracks, water, time, etc, in a flexible way... It was the antithesis of so-called American "Land Art," where an artist needed money to be an artist, to buy real estate to claim possession of the land, and to wield machinery. True capitalist art.[2]

Although Richard Long (and other Brits) may despise the amounts of money spent by the American earthwork artists, aren't they also part of the system of 'true capitalist art'? Don't they also (partly or wholly) live off their art? Doesn't Long just wander around the planet on his sacred 'walks', putting a few stones into a pile, and taking a photo of his efforts? Aren't Richard Long, David Nash, Shirazeh Houshiary, Rachel Whiteread, Richard Wentworth, Bill Woodrow, Helen Chadwick, Alison Wilding, Hamish Fulton and Richard Deacon (among British artists) also a part of the 'capitalist' art world? Don't their artworks sell for lots of money, a lot more money than the materials plus a little profit cost? Aren't (British) artists being hypocritical when they criticize the bombastic aspects of American land art when they benefit from the hugely over-priced art gallery system, where even mundane art it seems (such as artists' prints) are sold for 'silly prices'?[3] Long himself produces artists' books, postcards, and posters (many of these items are limited editions, sold on websites, via catalogues, or tele sales, or book-stores, by publishers, distributors, museums).

It's easy to view Christo's wrapped buildings or Walter de Maria's $500,000 *Vertical*

Earth Kilometer as expensive, apparently pointless art. This sort of land art may be 'true capitalist art', as Richard Long says, an art of excessive cost and excessive waste, but then, art has been full of silly amounts of money for ages. What about Christo's wrappings? They cost a bomb, for sure, but, as Christo says, he pays for it himself, with money made from selling smaller works. Christo's *Running Fence* cost $2.5 million; *The Umbrellas* cost $26,000,000. Christo says his art 'has to do with things that are very simple'.4 This definition can also apply to other land artists, including Richard Long: they, too, transform ordinary things.

When these transformations of the ordinary cost so much, and require 200 rock climbers, as Christo's covering of the Reichstag in Berlin needed, then commentators wonder about the 'importance' of such artistic productions. There's something cynical and obscene, perhaps, about Michael Heizer or Walter de Maria carving great gashes in the American desert, or Christo making artworks that cost 26 million dollars yet only last for two weeks. Detractors could find better ways to spend that kind of money (a hospital? Or feeding needy communities?) Surely artworks that cost millions of dollars but only 'benefit' a (relatively) tiny number of people are wasteful?5 When artists spend such vast amounts of money on art, it's no wonder some people find this gross. But then, if spending millions of dollars on art were outlawed, there'd be no Hollywood, no music industry, no television, no entertainment industry, no leisure industry, no grand projects (for some, that might be a good thing). These are the hypocrisies and ambiguities that surround art. How can one 'justify' a $26,000,000 Christo wrapping? Or a typical Hollywood feature film (cost: $45 million, with a typical advertizing budget of $5-15 million)?6

Although it may appear that land artists tour the whole globe making art, they actually stick to a small number of countries (tending towards the Northern hemisphere, and the Western world). For instance, there are few major land artists who have made significant work in Africa, or large parts of South America, or mainland China, or Russia (Richard Long, though, has worked in South America and Africa). There are few Western land artworks in Egypt, for instance (perhaps because the competition is pretty fierce there from some of the most wonderful structures humans have ever made – the tombs, temples, cities and pyramids of ancient Egyptians. Of course, there are also social, political, cultural and ideological reasons for the lack of major land art in Islamic and Middle Eastern territories. And even more after 9/11, the Gulf War, and the Iraq war).

Europe's a favourite location, but not Eastern Europe. Favoured places tend to be

North America and Western Europe, obviously, and Japan, and occasionally Australia. Infrequently, also India (if it's that part of the globe, it's usually the scenic parts to the North, in Nepal, or Tibet or the Himalayas, where Long had walked). But even in America, birthplace and chief centre of land art, artworks tend to be clustered around the East (New York, Washington, DC, Chicago), the South-West (New Mexico, Arizona), the Mid-West (Colorado), or California.

THE OBJECT IN LAND ART AND MINIMAL ART

With the development of Minimal, 'Process, Arte Povera and Conceptual art in the 1960s, sculpture became all 'object'.[1] Sculpture was (just) an object, in amongst millions of other objects. 'Objecthood' (Michael Fried's term) became crucial, the 'thing-in-itself', as Existential philosophers such as Jean-Paul Sartre and Edmund Husserl put it.[2] Inner and outer space became one, objects were simply what they are/ were, without referring to anything outside themselves. No sense of illusion, or allusion, which art had been founded upon for millennia. Subject and object became one; no subject any more, just the object. The object was the subject. There was no secret, inner meaning to be uncovered. The subject, the content, was all on the outside. Barbara Rose wrote that the 'thing... is not supposed to be suggestive of anything other than itself'.[3]

It was the American abstract painter Frank Stella who had emphasized the object-in-itself of art, and the objecthood of his paintings in particular. His canvases (and his compatriots such as Kenneth Noland, Robert Ryman and Ellsworth Kelly) were objects which displayed openly their 'objecthood' (such as Stella's *Ophir* [1960-61], one of his shaped canvases, a zigzag shape with striped paint). 'What you see is what you get' Stella said, and his thinking influenced many of the key artists (including – and perhaps especially – the sculptors) of the 1960s: Donald Judd, Carl Andre, Sol LeWitt and Robert Morris. Stella was an important artist in the art world of 1960s Minimal, Postminimal and Process sculpture and painting: '[t]he idea that a painting is primarily a thing-in-itself has been around for a long time', wrote artist and critic Mel Bochner, 'But before Frank Stella not much was done about it'.[4] Stella developed the notion of Barnett Newman's of the unity or 'all-overness' of an artwork, so that it strikes the observer all at once, every part at the same time. No part had precedence over any others. All of the parts had the same weight. It was non-hierarchical painting. Stella said of his 'black paintings':

> I had to do something about relational painting, i.e. the balancing of the various parts of the painting with and against each other. The obvious answer was symmetry – make it the same all over.5

This all-overness or instantaneity certainly applies to Richard Long's stone circles: one sees them all at once, without frames, without being 'led', illusionistically, into the work (although there are plenty of pictorial elements in some of Long's works: Long uses Renaissance illusion, artificial three dimensionality, Renaissance perspective, frontality, figure-ground relations, framing, negative space, selective viewpoint, *chiaroscuro*, silhouettes, outlines, and Classical proportions). All of Long's art is founded, like most of Western art, on familiar Renaissance principles about visual representation and visual perception. Although elements of Long's art are postmodern and conceptual and part of the contemporary art world, most of it is grounded in Classical and Renaissance art.

In Minimal sculpture, the object and its 'objecthood' is primary. As William Tucker wrote: '[it] is the matter-of-fact 'objectness' of sculpture that has become in recent years its prime feature'.6 The notion of 'objecthood' is problematic, theoretically and artistically, for the world is full of objects, it is a continuum of objects (and by the 1960s, there were more objects than ever, as well as more people than ever). As critics have noted, much of what makes sculpture sculpture is that the object is contextualized, physically as well as æsthetically and psychologically, as a sculpture. Context is crucial, as Julia Kristeva said, for context carries so much meaning. The *response*, affected by so much of culture, socialization, physical context, education, and so on, makes objects sculptures. In 1970, Heizer said that the old kind of sculpture had been replaced – 'destroyed, subverted, put down' (170).

Artists of the modern era have explored this area between 'everyday' or 'ordinary' 'objects', and the 'art object' – Marcel Duchamp with his readymades, Kurt Schwitters' multimedia pieces, and, later, Jasper Johns and Robert Rauschenberg, who stuck objects onto their paintings and further explored the blurred region between painting and sculpture.

LAND ART AND CONCEPTUAL ART

Land art is related to, or a part of, Conceptual art.[1] For much land art exists only in photographs, memories, words, various texts which are not the land art itself. Works that can be seen and those that are hidden or 'invisible' have the same importance for the artist. 'Seen and unseen works have equal importance' said Richard Long (IC 1, 5). That's an insightful observation. One of the hallmarks of the 'ideal Conceptual work', as Mel Bochner opined, is 'an exact linguistic correlative, that is, it could be described and experienced in its data and it could be infinitely repeatable'.[2] Land art is often Conceptual art: Dennis Oppenheim's *Whirlpool Eye of Storm* (a jet trail in the sky), Hans Haacke's balloons floating over Central Park, Robert Morris's steam pieces, and many of Andy Goldsworthy's leaf, stone, snow, mud and clay sculptures, exist now only as photographs, memories and criticism. (Although Long will, if one commissions him, come round and smear mud on your living room wall for you: how long it would last, though is another matter, open to dispute).

By contrast, James Turrell wanted to place the viewer right in the midst of his artworks, so they could experience directly the subject of his art (light, the sky, celestial events) for themselves. It was important for Turrell that his art wasn't a record or a photograph of something that happened elsewhere, that the viewer hadn't seen or couldn't see for themselves. Thus, at Roden Crater, Turrell constructed spaces that the spectator could enter physically, to experience light and the sky directly.

The pictorial or visual aspect of land art was over-emphasized by critics and viewers, Dennis Oppenheim argued in 1992. It was 'basically the *idea* of earthworks, the idea of the salt flats' that was important, not the visual element; '[t]he visual quotient is not as strenuous as you think'. Many land artworks were conceptual, mental, not visual or even physical. 'In other words,' said Oppenheim, talking about Robert Smithson's *Spiral Jetty*, 'it's about the salt, submersions, the jetty, what is around the salt flats. In the end it's about mental configurations' (1992).

This presents a problem, because most land artworks are known primarily in a visual form – in photographs. It'd be great if all land artworks were visited or directly experienced, as Dennis Oppenheim and others intended, but they aren't. For Richard Serra, the 'focus of art for me is the experience of living through the pieces', but the actual work itself, the physical object, was not the whole point, or the whole pleasure, of making art: 'that experience may have very little to do with the physical facts of the work of art'.[3]

One of pluses of Conceptual art was that art could be just ideas, and the artist wouldn't have to carry around masses of materials. Dennis Oppenheim wrote:

In 1968 and 1969 I lived in an apartment. I didn't need a studio. Everything that I had done as an artist was contained in one small case of slides. And it accounted for two of the most strenuous years of work in my whole life. [4]

While much Richard Long's output could be collected into a small space – the slides, the cans of film, the textworks which could be summarized in notebooks, and the Avon river mud in a bag – plenty of it is pretty big and hefty (the circles and ellipses and rows of stone, bone, slate and wood).

Land art is meta-art, art about art, art that relies on other art to 'exist'. Land art exists for a brief moment, then becomes myth, gossip, photography and words (and most often criticism and journalism). Many of Richard Long's works are simply collections of words, printed in capitals, in Eric Gill's font, Gill Sans, on large pieces of paper. Part of the text of one of Long's works can be printed here, and this text here will approximate to a Richard Long artwork in itself (although he likes them printed larger). Thus:

A LINE OF GROUND 94 MILES LONG

ROAD STONY TRACK ROAD GRASS FIELD
ROAD BARE ROCK LANE ROAD STONY PATH
HEATHER BURNT MOOR STONY PATH ROAD
ROUGH GRASSLAND RIVERBED SHEEPTRACKS EARTH WALL
ROUGH GRASSLAND GRASS FIELDS BRAMBLES GRASS FIELD
PATH ROAD DUSTY LANE

Well, that's part of a Richard Long artwork. Is that it? Yes.
Here's another one:

GRANITE LINE

SCATTERED ALONG A STRAIGHT 9 MILE LINE
223 STONES PLACED ON DARTMOOR

ENGLAND 1980

It seems as if Richard Long has nothing much to 'say'. Well, he is a sculptor, so he wouldn't have to be so good at writing or speaking. Wrong. He's a land artist and Conceptual artist (though he dislikes the term 'land art'), and land and Conceptual artists are always much concerned with writing and written texts. A Richard Long exhibition, for instance, features written texts on display, and photographs, as well as installation works and sculptures (like most land artists, Long won't let go of real objects. He likes to include sculpted objects in his exhibitions, not only Conceptual photoworks or textworks).

The texts of land and Conceptual artists also draw on poetry, on what's sometimes called concrete or 'visual poetry' or typewriter art. Richard Long, for instance, prints his laconic texts in circles (*Full Moon Circle of Ground*, Dartmoor, 1983), in concentric circles (*Three Moors, Three Circles*, Liskeard to Porlock, 1982), in vertical lines, as in trendy style magazines (*The Isle of Wight as Six Walks*, 1982), and in curved swathes of text (*A Moved Line in Japan*, 1983). *A Moved Line In Japan* was a textwork with short phrases printed in a gentle curve ('shell to crab / crab to feather / feather to fish', and so on.

Sixties Conceptual artist Lawrence Weiner produced text works, capital letters on a wall or in a book (Barbara Kruger, the Art & Language group and Michael Craig-Martin and Long have also made post-Conceptualist wall works of words). Weiner's solution to making sculpture was that a sculpture on a plinth has to be 'translated' into language, so that people can understand it. Sculpture is language, and words are language, therefore, Weiner reckons, words can be sculpture:

> when you see a piece of wood lying on the ground with a piece of stone on top of it, you must translate that in your own head into language. What I try to do is present language itself as a key to what sculpture is about... It is a presentation of a piece of sculpture in language.5

Like John Baldessari and Sophie Calle, and like Richard Long's own text pieces, Weiner produces capital letters in short phrases which are about a viewer's relationship with an object. The words are a means or the expression of a relationship with something.

THINGS PUSHED DOWN TO THE BOTTOM AND
PUSHED UP AGAIN

This is a typical Lawrence Weiner artwork. This is another one, shown at Leo Castelli's gallery in 1974:

UP ON (IN) THE AIR
DOWN ON [IN] THE GROUND
BEING WITHIN THE CONTEXT OF [A]
REACTION

BEING WITHIN THE CONTEXT OF
REACTION.
UP ON (IN) THE AIR
DOWN ON [IN] THE GROUND

Richard Long commented that '[t]he discovery [Weiner] made that art does not necessarily have to be made, that was a great breakthrough'.6 Weiner is right, of course: words alone can be sculpture, for poets have long known that language is an *experience*, not simply abstractions or concepts. Language really does affect people – otherwise why would they spend so much time consuming, expressing, thinking about and living inside language? That is, they consume 20-30 hours of broadcasting per week (on average in the UK) – that's over a day and a half spent consuming television and radio per week. So the words on a gallery wall of Weiner, Calle, Baldessari, Haacke and Fulton don't seem at first to be 'art'. They are not sensual and graspable in the physical realm, like a marble statue. Yet those words, whether photocopied on cheap paper or printed in high quality typography on deluxe paper, or stencilled onto the wall, are 'art', they are communication, language – even sculpture.

MAPS

Richard Long's walks are often based on maps: one of Long's biggest debts must be to the mapmakers and publishers of the world (in the UK, that's Ordnance Survey, based in Southampton. Their Outdoor Leisure maps, Explorer maps and Landranger maps must have been used by Long countless times. The Outdoor Leisure series includes many areas favoured by Long for his walks: Dartmoor, Snowdonia and the Cairngorms. Britain may not have quite the deserts, mountains and wildernesses of the Magreb, Andes or Central Asia, but it does have beautiful cartography. 'One reason I make mapworks in Britain is because you can get good maps' said Long [1985, 2, 15]).

Some of Richard Long's artworks are just maps, sometimes maps with a photograph added (as in the Cerne Abbas work), sometimes with text explaining the work, which is usually a walk. The mapworks are usually 'completely planned beforehand' Long remarked.[1] The text that accompanies the Cerne Abbas walk (1975) anchors the meaning of the work firmly (RL, 85).

A SIX DAY WALK OVER ALL ROADS, LANES AND DOUBLE TRACKS INSIDE A SIX MILE WIDE CIRCLE CENTRED ON THE GIANT OF CERNE ABBAS

The Cerne Abbas walk is a mass of its black lines drawn on the map, the postcard image of the prominently ithyphallic Cerne Giant, and the intricacy and delicacy of the Ordnance Survey cartography. It's a work rich in allusions. For walkers, Ordnance Survey maps themselves are treasured items, with their familiar green blocks of colour indicating woods, the red A roads (highways), the brown B roads (country roads), the black railway lines (so familiar to me from so many train journeys across this part of the U.K. – through stations such as Maiden Newton, Dorchester South, Upwey and Wool). Maps, for walkers and geographers, have their own special poetry, a graphic style that is cherished.

The idea with the early map walkworks, Richard Long said, was to create 'a new art which was also a new way of walking: walking as art' (WL, 68). In 1994 Long described maps as important aids to making walking art, walking as art: maps were layers of information and history (personal and social), they showed the time and space of a walk, the distances traversed, the campsites, the route, the time taken, and were useful aides in planning a walkwork. A map is an 'artistic and poetic combination of image and language' (WL, 84).

Richard Long's maps, then, are pictorial records/ representations/ descriptions of his walks. The maps are 'inner landscapes'.[2] Long writes that a 'map of inner land-scape is an important step towards understanding and self-knowledge.'[3] In black pen he traces his routes along the riverbeds on Dartmoor, across the summits of the Scottish Highlands, in Chinese mountains, in County Mayo, Ireland, etc. A *Dartmoor Walk* (1987) is a large piece of paper with the squiggly lines of Long's movements across the granite tableland set above the usual piece of Long's text which describes some of the aspects of the walk:

**DEEP BREATHING TO GRIMPSOUND TO BENNETT'S CROSS TO
MIDGES TO A NEW BORN CALF
TO GREAT KNEESET TO A LARK ON A BOULDER TO COTTON
GRASS TO THINKING TO A FOX SMELL
TO GREAT LINKS TOR TO RIVER FROTH TO DOZING TO
SWEATING TO YES TOR** (OW, 44)

The work is that curious collection of elements, of graphics and text, which constitute, Richard Long asserted, a record of an 8 day Dartmoor walk:

> It was about the experience of being alone in a place of nature, the topography, the weather, the naming of places, real time, autobiography, imagination. Each new walk carries with it memories of all the others. For me Dartmoor is a place of regeneration, knowledge, history and continuity.[4]

Mapping relates again to Minimal art, for the dominant structure in modern painting is the grid,[9] which is found everywhere (in Agnes Martin's pencilled grids, in Sol LeWitt, Stella, Noland, Marden, Mangold, Andre, etc). Laid over Long's walks is the grid of the map. Minimal and Conceptual art created a 'museum of language', a gallery space made up of... words, ideas, concepts, intangible notions. It is an imaginary space, this new museum of art, for it requires the imagination to make it work. It is something like Jorge Luis Borges' infinite library, existing in the imagination, wholly reliant on the imagination to make it come alive.

The maps in Conceptual art and land art constituted a new landscape of the soul, as Robert Smithson wrote in 1968:

> A cartography of uninhabitable places seems to be developing – complete with decoy diagrams, abstract grid systems made of stone and tape (Carl Andre and Sol LeWitt), and electronic "mosaic" photomaps from NASA. (1968, 26)

Just about every land artist used maps in their work. Not just in the obvious sense of mapping (and finding) future sites for artworks, but as key elements in the artworks themselves. Jan Dibbets chose places on a map at random, visited them and took a photograph. Dennis Oppenheim made maps a central ingredient in his 2-D Conceptual works, which combined maps, text, photos and sketches. Robert Smithson made many mapworks, including map games, folded maps, aerial maps, and cut-up circular maps (*Untitled Circular Map* [*c.* 1968-70] and *Entropic Pole* [1967]). Tom Van Sant collaged satellite maps. John Baldessari spelt out 'California' using maps in *The California Map Project* (1969). Charles Ross made star maps (1975-86). Jasper Johns painted a large map collage painting (1966-71). Nancy Holt buried poems (written for Carl Andre, John Perrault, Robert Smithson, Michael Heizer and Philip Leider) in remote locations, with a map marking the burial site (1969-71).

Chris Drury cut up and wove maps together (a development of his love of basket-weaving). Like Richard Long, Drury often used maps in his work. An off-shoot of Drury's penchant for weaving is the physical interlacing of maps (something Long hasn't done: he prefers to display maps with routes drawn on them). Thus, Drury has inter-woven a map of Manhattan with one of the Hebrides (1996) and West Cork with New Mexico (1995). Like Tony Cragg, Drury has collated found objects into patterns (such as *Tidelines*, 1985, made from pieces of plastic, metal, rubber, driftwood and feathers).

Richard Long said he planned out his walks using maps, examining maps very closely to look out for possible routes, and potential obstacles. Maps are used to ensure there aren't any cliffs, bogs, rivers or other snags along the route. For the mapworks, Richard Long tended to draw the lines first, and follow the route when he made the walk. The idea comes first, then the map and the lines, then the walk (1995b).

LAND ART AND PHOTOGRAPHY

In land art photographs, the viewer is not offered a *range* of viewpoints of a work, although land artists clearly take more than one shot of each work they make. No artist takes just *one* photo out of a 36 exposure 35mm film, or one frame out of a twelve shot 120mm format film, or one digital shot out of hundreds. No, an artist, like an photographer, takes a range of shots, at different, bracketed exposures, from different view-points (much as the trendy advertizing film director of today shoots twelve hours of footage for just one thirty second advert).[1] Andy Goldsworthy, for example, typically takes two viewpoints or shots: a close-up, which is about the artist's subjective relationship with his work – taken from just a few feet away. Then there is a second, more 'objective' view, showing the sculpture as the independent observer might see it. This second photograph shows the work in its environment, which is crucial. Goldsworthy's photos are a mix of these two viewpoints, the subjective and objective: often the most powerful shots are not the close-up images, showing the detail in the sculpture, but the distant views.

Very likely Richard Long would try out a number of viewpoints, and would shoot a number of photos of the work, to give him more possibilities later (although it's apparent that Long has sometimes selected the viewpoint for his photograph *before* he builds his outdoor sculptures. The sculptures are made *for* or *because of* the viewpoint: an interesting range of hills as a background, for example). Due to the size of many of Long's indoor and outdoor stone circles and lines, and the scale of the landscapes he makes work in, most of Long's photographs are taken standing back, using standard or wide angle lenses. To include the whole artwork and the surrounding landscape, Richard Long needs to be positioned some way back. Long also liked to include the background scenery. His sculptures are often constructed for one particular viewpoint, and that's the one that gets into the photograph. Some of Long's work is about visual alignments – between the viewer, the sculpture, the landscape and the horizon (WL, 147). Thus, Long uses far fewer close-up shots of his land art than some land artists. In *Evolution Circle* (1995), made in the High Sierra, the open circle is framed against the distant hills, rocks and a lake. *Cotopaxi Circle* (1998) follows the same principle, with a snowy mountain as the backdrop to the open stone circle (the photograph recalls countless images of Mount Fuji in Japanese art).

In terms of framing and viewpoint Richard Long favours, for the indoor floor works, a high angle, looking down the work. Often Long shoots his floor sculptures from ordinary head height, but also sometimes from higher up. The wall drawings are usually shot head-on, from a right angle to the centre of the artwork. Long also likes to frame two works in the same photo – typically a mud wall drawing and a floor stone circle. Very occasionally, Long plays visual tricks, such as shooting the indoor sculpture *Atlantic Lava Line* (1995) end-on, so the loops of stones on the floor looked like a solid block of stones. But most of the photography is simple and straightforward, using traditional notions of Renaissance space, perspective, proportion and illusion. For the outdoor works, Richard Long prefers Classical proportions to his compositions, usually with the landscape taking up the lower two-thirds of the frame. Again, Long is often tilting his camera down slightly from head height, to include the whole of the sculpture and its surroundings.

Each land artist, then, must select this or that viewpoint, behind this bush or next to that tree. The land artist is therefore also a photographer, selecting views, reframing their works, making choices about lighting, angles, lenses, film stock, etc. Land artists will make decisions about exactly *when* to photograph their work. Some works are ephemeral, and last only moments, so the photograph must be taken immediately (but even when a work lasts only a few seconds or minutes, there are still choices about which moment to capture). Other works, such as the stone circles of Richard Long, or Nancy Holt's *Star-Crossed* (1981), last longer. The land artist as photographer can therefore wait for a certain combination of sunlight and clouds. This is particularly crucial in cloudy places like Britain, where lighting can vary so dramatically over a few minutes. As anyone who has been in, say, Dartmoor or the Peak District in the UK will know, the sunlight can burst through the clouds at one moment, then a moment later there'll be dark, sombre clouds, looking as if it's going to rain. A moment later, it *will* rain, and afterwards, facing away from the sun, one might see a rainbow. Much of the world's weather is this changeable, so every land art photograph is always at least a highly selective and subjective view of a particular place (there are many other factors apart from weather conditions and lighting to consider).

Another critical aspect of photographing land art is not only deciding what to *include*, but choosing what to *exclude* from the composition. Visiting a land artwork in the flesh, one can see it from all sorts of angles, with all sorts of backgrounds, in all sorts of conditions (though *very* few people will have seen an outdoor Richard Long artwork *in situ*). Knowing a land artwork only from a photograph, one knows only *that* particular viewpoint, and no others. The land artist will take great care in framing the images, to show the artwork from the best vantage points. Many aspects of the surr-oundings might be elided from the final published photographs – an apartment block, a row of cars, trash, people, power lines, and so on.

Land artists must also oversee the journey of the films they've shot from develop-ment through printing to framing. As anyone who has taken a photo will know, all manner of details can affect how one reads a photograph: how it is printed, light, dark, soft, hard, cropped, full frame, more red, more blue, burnt in, dodged, touched up, glossy or matt paper, and so on. The size of the photo affects it very much, as does the frame. Go into any framer's store and one'll see a plethora of different types of frame. All these things the viewer might take in at one glance in a gallery, but the artist has to make decisions all the time about all these matters, and many more. Land artists and sculptors, then, must be accomplished photographers. Their work must be high standard, for it is exhibited in 'high art' locations, such as the city gallery, or glossy coffee table art books or limited edition artists' books.

In land art, the commentary, the written records, the obsessive documentation, is just as important as the artwork itself. Often, it *is* the artwork. The land artist's life becomes part of the artwork. The American sculptor David Smith spoke of this consuming aspect of sculpture, where the artist lives and breathes art. In a series of questions to students, Smith described the committed artist's stance:

> Do you make art your life, that which always comes first and occupies every moment, the last problem before sleep and the first awaking vision? …How do you spend your time? More talking about art than making it? How do you spend your money? On art materials first – or do you start to pinch here? …How much of the work day or the work week do you devote to your profession – that which will be your identity for life?[2]

Brilliant late 1960s sculptor Eva Hesse spoke in Romantic, emotional terms of her art, employing words such as 'essence' and 'soul'. She spoke of wanting to emphasize 'soul or presence or whatever you want to call it.' These words of Hesse's could apply, with some minor revisions, to land artists: 'I think art is a total thing. A total person giving a contribution. It is an essence, a soul… In my soul art and life are inseparable.'[3]

Andy Goldsworthy has written two short statements on the relation between photography and his sculpture (both entitled "The Photograph" – in *Hand To Earth*, 9, and *Stone*, 120). Both mini-essays reveal a confusion and ambiguity regarding photography and art. Firstly, Goldsworthy states that the photograph simply records the work, in a direct, clear, routine fashion. His idea is to 'capture' (document) the work of art, which may change at every minute or moment. The photograph, Goldsworthy said, is the *outcome* of his art, not the initial reason for it. He quoted Yves Klein, one of his gurus, discussing his monochrome pictures: '[t]hey are the leftovers from the creative process, the ashes. My pictures, after all, are only the title deeds to my property which I have to produce when I am asked to prove that I am a proprietor' (*Hand To Earth*, 9). The photograph is necessary for Goldsworthy because it brings an outdoor experience into the context of the indoor gallery. The photograph, Goldsworthy says, is necessary to communicate something of the outdoor work in an indoor context, even though '[m]uch of the energy is lost' (ib., 9).

This is all very well, this view that Goldsworthy propounds of the photograph as a necessary record of the outdoor work. In *Stone*'s "The Photograph" essay, the urge to 'capture' the sculpture out of doors becomes much more anxious. For example, if the film goes wrong, Goldsworthy says he feels disappointed – the photograph is needed to 'confirm the success or failure' of the work (similarly, if the film is ruined when Richard Long photographs his outdoor sculptures, those sculptures cannot be exhibited as photos, and cease to exist for the general public). Goldsworthy acknowledged in *Wood* that in making balanced columns of stones there were 'inevitably more failures than successes' (23). Throughout his career Goldsworthy must have known hundreds of failed artworks, and must have thousands of photographs of sculptures that didn't work. If the film doesn't come out, Goldsworthy continued, then the sculpture becomes 'dislocated – like a half-forgotten memory'. This statement demonstrates just how important photography is for Goldsworthy. He is, like Richard Long, not only a sculptor or land artist: he is also very much a photographer. The photograph is needed by Goldsworthy to keep the piece alive – for himself, in his memory: it 'completes' the work, rounds it off. And, crucially, photography shows the work to others. Photography is Goldsworthy's main means of displaying his outdoor work (Long relies heavily on photos too, but also has text pieces and mapworks and more graphical pieces, such as the lines which illustrate walking routes). Rarely are the general public invited to see Goldsworthy making a work of art (never with Richard Long): 'I am not a performer' he says (*Stone*, 120). The ephemeral, outdoor sculpture 'lies at the core of my art and its making must be kept private' (ib.). Similarly, Long never wanted his outdoor sculptures to be visited; that would disturb or destroy the spirit of the work, Long asserted.

Goldsworthy's biggest confusion concerning photography, however, is about that age-old chestnut, the 'reality' of the image, photography's troubled relationship with 'the real'. Ever since photography was invented, in the early/ mid-19th century, critics have pondered on how 'real' photography is (famous explorations of the thorny subject include Roland Barthes, Susan Sontag and John Berger). Goldsworthy's confusion on this point is illustrated by his last words in *Stone*: '[i]f the photograph were to become so real that it overpowered and replaced the work outside, then it would have no purpose or meaning in my art' (*Stone*, 120). Aren't photographs already 'real' then? Or are they mere 'illusions'? Surely the photograph is 'real' already, because Goldsworthy admits it is a 'record' of the work, needed to confirm the work? What does he mean, about photography becoming 'so real'? Isn't photography or the image already 'so real', like film and television are 'so real'? Film/ TV/ photo images are 'so real', in fact, they are consumed as 'real', believed as 'true': the average Briton, for instance, spends around 85 continuous days per year of watching television. Is that not 'real' too, in Goldsworthy's æsthetics? What about other forms of technological recording; are these, too, not yet 'so real'? What about virtual reality, or the 'cyberspace' of the internet, or the 'hyperspace' of telephone conversations? Are these, too, still lodged in an archaic argument of being mere 'illusion'? No.

Jan Dibbets said that documenting the work wasn't important: 'I've done lots of works without taking photographs'.4 But most land artists record their activities (e.g.: 'walk this morning; made a snow sculpture; it wasn't successful; back home for lunch'). Ultimately, *any* activity can be land art. Going to the shops can be a piece of art. One might drop a stone on the path as one goes, or perhaps not. Either way, you've just made a work of art. Is, then, walking to Gilmor's corner store for a pint of milk and a pack of cigarettes a fully accomplished and thoroughly authentic work of art, like Richard Long's *A Straight Northward Walk Across Dartmoor*? Where does authenticity end and artifice begin? Or, rather, where does life end and art begin? Clearly, they are a continuum in land art.

Richard Long said that '[n]ot all walking is art'; that is, a walk becomes art when it is conceived as art. The conception of the walk, made before the walk, is crucial, even if there is no 'reason' at all for the walk. 'A walk, and place, can be chosen for any reason'.5 Long also said, though, that '[a]nything an artist makes, is art', but adds '[n]ot everyone is an artist.'6

The relation between outdoor and indoor works, between stone circles in some remote zone and a stone circle in a Western gallery, is resolved simply in much of land art by being regarded by the artist as a continuum. One can see how for Richard Long both inside and outside works are one, i.e., part of the same thing. (For Long, all of the forms his art takes are part of the same thing. 'The photos, the walks, the sculptures, the text works, they're all just formal variations, just different ways of sort of doing the same thing all the time' (SS, 309).) But the viewer might see them as separate, because the viewer (usually) can't see Long's outdoor pieces (Long likes to keep his locations secret and anonymous).7 The artist is also focussed on her/ his work, it's part of her/ his life, it's what s/he does. But the spectator is doing all sorts of other things in her/ his life, not just consuming art.

The viewer only knows Richard Long's outdoor pieces from his photos, textworks and documentation. So it's always an odd relationship with Long's work for the viewer.

For the artist, it's great, because the big photos and writings relate to his own experiences, of working outdoors. He knows the work inside out: *he lived it*. The viewer, though, gets a different experience: s/he sees odd phrases, titles, dates, measurements. Odd snippets of info. Or photos. Or a zigzag line. Or fingerprints or footprints on the floor. So people love Long's work (and land art) not because they love the photographs, or his writing. They love it, perhaps, because of *what it suggests*. Long's work, and land art in general, persuades people to look outwards, away from cities, towards the landscape, towards stones and water and all the rest of it. Perhaps that's why people love it, and other land art, and nature poetry, and all things to do with nature, from gardening to walking the dog to vacations in wildernesses. As Hamish Fulton put it, 'I walk on the land to be woven into nature' (1995). For Chris Drury, there is no indoor—outdoor divide, because the artist, like all people, is part of nature.

The outdoor work itself, the *walk itself*, isn't present in Richard Long's text pieces or photos. The work isn't 'in' the gallery. No, the work is *elsewhere*, and it is to that *elsewhere place* that people want to go (and the indoor art points to those places). Land art creates *desire* in people, as the work of J.M.W. Turner or Aleksandr Blok creates desire – for travel, for other places. Long spoke in the Santa Fe interview of feeling refreshed and renewed after a good walk: that's the experience, perhaps, that viewers wish to gain from land art, from all art.

Land art, then, whether by Aycock, Shiraga, Drury, Christo or Richard Long, is part of a postmodern trend in self-reflexivity, the *mise-en-âbyme* commentary so familiar now. Art about (the artist's) life. It's found not only in the postmodern literature of the 1960s and 1970s (Alain Robbe-Grillet, Thomas Pynchon, Lawrence Durrell), but also in the fiction of, say, André Gide. The novel *The Counterfeiters*, which Gide published in 1925, is a key text in this respect: the main character is, of course, a novelist (equivalent to any kind of artist). But Edouard is more interested not in the novel he's trying to write, but in his book about the writing of his novel. Thus, the diary/ journal of the making of the work becomes more important than the work itself; and the act of *writing about* the art becomes more important than *making* the artwork itself. Indeed, so crucial was the 'making of' the book *The Counterfeiters* to Gide that he published a book after *The Counterfeiters*, called precisely that, *The Journal of The Counterfeiters* (although he swore he'd never do that, despising artists 'explaining' their works). Land artists, like Conceptual and Process artists, also tend to steer clear of 'explaining' their works (i.e., the work should be self-explanatory, or its own explanation).

André Gide's concerns are also those of the land artists – because, as he lived his life, Gide was conscious of *how he would write it up later*. When something extraordinary occurred, Gide would be thinking about it as an account in his journal. After living, for Gide, comes making art (and Gide was conscious of the two happening at the same time). Similarly, Long has made walks which he knows will work well when they're turned into text or mapworks. Like the readymades of Marcel Duchamp, Gide's *The Counterfeiters* destroys the diegetic effect of fiction, its naturalism and suspension of disbelief. Like Jean-Luc Godard's movies, Bertholt Brecht's theatre and Jasper Johns's paintings, Gide's art is self-reflexive art, a Pop Art æsthetic forty years before Pop Art.

Modernist self-reflexivity or *mise-en-âbyme* occurred in painting and sculpture most famously in the early years of the 20th century, in Dada, Surrealism and Cubism, among other places. When Marcel Duchamp and Kurt Schwitters put 'real' objects into the gallery, they did so because it seemed a logical thing to do. Schwitters explained how he came to do it:

> I simply could not see any reason why old streetcar tickets, driftwood, coat checks, wire and wheel parts, buttons, junk from the attic and heaps of refuse should not be used as material for paintings, any less than colours made in a factory.[8]

It's the same with land artists: why not, they say, have an art made out of found (or real) objects, stones found on a remote path, or leaves, or household bricks. The use of ordinary objects in (land) art ushers in a new sense of the object in sculpture, a new way of looking at art. The 'real' objects and readymades of Duchamp and Schwitters were developed by the mixed media and assemblages paintings of Robert Rauschenberg and Jasper Johns, among others. The objects stuck onto the paintings of Rauschenberg and Johns transform their art into something more than paintings, closer to sculpture. It's a transformation of æsthetics, where illusion and artifice are replaced with real things (at the same time, their paintings still retain notions of depth, 3-D illusions, frontality, Renaissance space, and figure-ground relationships). Easy to see how Rauschenberg's and Johns' thinking applies directly to land art: Nash, Smithson, Morris and Long also like what they see to be real, to be the object in and of itself (the 'thing-in-itself' of Existentialism, or Rainer Maria Rilke's *Kunstding*, 'thing of art'). They too dislike illusionism. For land artists, their sculpture doesn't symbolize or represent nature, it *is* nature, a part of nature. As Jasper Johns remarked:

My thinking is perhaps dependent on a realization of a thing as being the real thing... I like what I see to be real, or to be my idea of what is real. And I think I have a kind of resentment against illusion when I can recognize it. Also, a large part of my work has been involved with the painting as object, as real thing in itself. And in the face of that 'tragedy,' so far, my general development... has moved in the direction of using real things as painting. That is to say I find it more interesting to use a real fork as painting than it is to use painting as a real fork.[9]

Similarly, one can see how, for Richard Long, Patricia Johanson, James Pierce, Michelle Stuart and other land artists, it's much more interesting to use a stone as a stone rather than as a representation of something else. Stones in Long's art are always stones, perhaps only ever stones, perhaps never more than stones. 'I am interested in showing real sculpture in galleries and museums as well as just photographs', Long said (1994b). Robert Smithson's definition of an earthwork is pertinent here: 'instead of putting a work of art on some land, some land is put into a work of art').[10] Smithson's ethic can be applied directly to Long's art.

INTERIOR AND EXTERIOR ART

Sometimes it's odd to see land art in a gallery, because the mound of soil, the cairn of stones, the slate circle, the living tree, demands the viewer to look outwards, to nature, to the wildernesses, to the supposed origins of this kind of art. The viewer is always aware of the place of origin of land artworks (sometimes also the time and season of origin), and how uncanny and disruptive they can look indoors.[1] The leaves and stalks and mud smears and slate slabs are tiny parts of the natural world, bits extracted, rearranged, as all art is nature chopped up and reformed according to the artist's æsthetics. Land art creates an ambiguous continuity with the world of nature that exists outside the gallery (but also inside, and inside the spectator, too). Sometimes this ambiguity works against the art on show in the gallery space.

Land art sites, in the first wave of land art (late 1960s/ early 1970s – by common agreement land art's 'golden age' – tended to be wildernesses, deserts, post-industrial spaces, waste grounds, quarries and dumps. One of the reasons for going far from the gallery, the city and pretty countryside spots was because land artists wanted to avoid the 'pastoral' and the 'picturesque' at all costs.[2] It didn't want beauty for the sake of beauty. Land artists, asserted Dennis Oppenheim, wished to go beyond the picturesque (while British land artists, such as Richard Long, had some relationship with the picturesque, Oppenheim added [ibid.]).

David Nash discussed the (seemingly unavoidable) tension between indoor and outdoor art in a 1978 interview:

> An object made indoors diminishes in scale and stature when placed outside. The reverse happens when an object made outside is brought inside, it seems to grow in stature and presence. It brings the outside in with it. The object outside has to contend with unlimited space, uneven ground and the weather. The sculpture I show inside is meant to be seen inside, it relates to the limited space, the peculiar scale, and the still air.[3]

The indoor-outdoor dialectic much concerned Robert Smithson (every land artist has to consider it at some time), who said 'I don't think you're freer artistically in the desert than you are inside a room'.[4] In fact, Smithson said he 'liked the artificial limits that the gallery presents' (ib.). For David Nash and Andy Goldsworthy, artistic work was simply usually more engaged and more interesting out of doors. In interior spaces, elements were 'neutralised, passive, controlled, time is paused', Nash explained. 'Outside, on and in and over the land, they are active, making space alive and potent with the movement of time. I look for ways of engaging with the life of this space'.[5]

Andy Goldsworthy always speaks of the significance of the surrounding environment in his works. His sculptures are as much about the surroundings in which they are situated, as about the 'sculptures themselves. An exhibition inside, in a gallery, is always going to be a problem, then. The contemporary gallery, with its sparse settings, whitewashed walls, its lists of works of art for sale, and trendy magazines and postcards, is a powerfully *cultural* (and primarily commercial-cultural) environment. The contemporary gallery is not 'natural' at all, it is not 'nature', it is not a place of mist, wind, skies and soil. No wonder, then, that land artists such as Walter de Maria wanted to fill a whole gallery with dark soil, to bring nature into the contemporary gallery in a big way.

Ephemeral, land art aims for an eternity in one place: the soul. As Lawrence Weiner, the Conceptual/ Process artist who exhibited 'statements' (texts on a wall), said: '[o]nce you know about a work of mine, you own it. There's no way I can climb into somebody's head and remove it.'[6] Thus, much of land art exists in that socio-cultural space which is actually inside people's heads (the 'cultural imaginary' as postmodernists like to call it). Thus, anyone can 'own' land art – simply by thinking about it. Once thought about, land art, Conceptual art or Process art is 'possessed' by the viewer, in Weiner's system. Indeed, some Conceptual art requires the existence of the viewer to make the work work at all. The viewer brings the piece alive. (Long, though, requires a physical manifestation of a work, a realization, if it is going to work fully. 'My work is not conceptual in the sense it can be an idea only' (IC 1, 7).)

LAND ART AND CHANGE

Crucial in land art is the concept and reality of change, time and decay, for these works in wood, snow, ice, leaves, water, slate, grass, and so on, do not stay around. They are not 'permanent', in the way that, say, bronze, marble, steel or stone can be (the *concept* of change is as significant as the reality). The soil in Walter de Maria's *Earth Room* dries out and alters (requiring maintenance); Robert Morris's steam works and Hans Haacke's fog and ice sculptures disappear on the breeze; Christo's plastic wraps stay on for two weeks. (Richard Long says he 'stands the stones down' after making a stone sculpture outdoors).

Richard Long has made many sculptures using water only: he has poured water in a line over stony ground, so the water darkens the stones. Typical Long water-sculptures include *Water Lines in Ladakh* (1984), where, near a river and crossing point, Long poured water from his flask in a line then photographed the result. Similar waterlines occur in *Sea Level Waterline* (Death Valley, 1982) and *Footpath Waterline* (197, Mexico). A waterline was made on a wooden bridge in the Piemonte Alps in 1989. In *Water Walk* (1999) Long poured water from one river (in England and Wales) into the next one (i.e., from the River Teme into the River Severn, from the River Severn into the River Arrow, and so on). In *Continuum Walk* (1998) Long carried water from the mouth to the source of the River Dart. Often he throws water at a wall (in Nepal), or over the ground (in Lappland and Spain), or over rocks, as in Switzerland (in 1991), which makes dark stains. These 'sculptures' do not last very long. They have a 'natural' lifespan, which is in keeping with the Conceptual artists' emphasis on simplicity and not interfering too much with the natural order of things (or letting the material dictate the work). Water, Long acknowledged in 1997, was a 'very important theme and idea in my work' (WL, 147). Long said he used water on its own outside, but in a gallery it was better to use mud, because water disappeared when it dried. Talking about water recalls that wonderful Taoist phrase, 'the sound of water says what I think'. In the *Tao Te Ching*, Lao-tzu states 'highest good is like water' (VIII).

Richard Long has also made waterline sculptures in the gallery: *Waterline* (1989), installed in Long's New York dealer (Sperone Westwater), was a long line of white splashes on a black backing. *Footprint Line* (1989, Turin) was a long floor-piece comprising Long's footprints in white paint on black cloth. *Muddy Feet Line* (1990) was a wide line of white footprints, made with paint, on the floor of the Musée d'Art Contemporain de Bordeaux, snaking through the gallery space in square zigzags. To make the splashes and trails of liquid show up, Long uses white paint or mud against a black background, in either floor or wall pieces.

Joseph Beuys emphasized process, evolution, change: his sculpture, he said, was not 'fixed and finished. Processes continue in most of them: chemical reactions, fermentations, colour changes, decay, drying up. Everything is in a *state of change*'.[1] Some land artists (Richard Long included) enjoy the impermanence of (their) art, and exploit it. As politicians know, words such as 'permanent' are difficult to define, and even more difficult to maintain. Artists with a large vision of life know that nothing on Earth will be truly 'permanent'. After all, 'civilized' humanity is only 10,000 years old, or 40,000, or two or three million (depending on how one views 'civilized'). And the planet itself will not last forever: millions more years (maybe), but not forever. As Long said in an interview:

> The planet is full of unbelievably permanent things, like rock strata and tides, and yet full of impermanences like butterflies or the seaweed on the beach, which is in a new pattern every day for thousands of years. I would like to think that my work reflects that beautiful complexity and reality.[2]

Some environmental/ action/ Conceptual artworks had a built-in impermanence, such as Allan Kaprow's *Fluids* (1967, Pasadena, California), large structures made from blocks of ice, which were left to melt (ice is a favourite land art medium). Long's clusters of stones on remote mountainsides will probably endure, but not the splashes of water. Barry Flanagan's *Hole in the Sea* (1969) was a cylinder embedded in a beach: Flanagan filmed the water covering the hole as the tide came in. An installation by Paul

Kos, *The Sound of Ice Melting* (1970, San Francisco), had blocks of ice surrounded by a cluster of microphones on stands.

Hans Haacke produced some of the most compelling works about impermanence in the late 1960s and early 1970s, such as ice freezing around an element.[3] Haacke wrote of an artwork which would be as majestic and as transient as birds gathering in the sky: 'I would like to lure 1000 seagulls to a certain spot (in the air) by some delicious food so as to construct an air sculpture from this combined mass.' In "Natural Phenomena as Public Monuments" (1968), land artist Alan Sonfist suggested building 'museums of air' in cities, which would 'recapture the smells of earth, trees and vegetation different seasons and at different historical times, so that people would be able to experience what has been lost' (1978). Sonfist also suggested monument-alizing the natural world with sounds: '[c]ontinuous loops of natural sounds at the natural level of volume can be placed on historic sites' (ibid.). Museums of natural history already have continuous loops of the sounds of rainforests, say, or ice caps, or animals playing throughout the day (museums of geology, natural history or science often have far more sophisticated and engaging displays than many land and install-ation artists).

There are bronze and marble sculptures still looking remarkable from the Græco-Roman period, and stone figurines from the Palæolithic period have survived well. Michael Heizer's cuts in remote South-West American deserts will endure, but not Hans Haacke's *Grass Grows* (1969), which was a mound of grass growing in a gallery. Indeed, ephemerality, transiency and change are key components in land art. As Barry Flanagan wrote:

> Truly sculpture is always going on. With proper physical circumstances and the visual invitation, one simply joins in and makes the work…there is a never-ending stream of materials and configurations to be seen, both natural and man-made, that have visual strength but not object or function apart from this. It is as if they existed for just this physical, visual purpose – to be seen.[4]

LAND ART AS RELIGION

It's no surprise that the American form of earth art and the British land art of Richard Long and Fulton should be sympathetic to Oriental mysticism: Zen and Taoist religion were in the air (like pot smoke or tear gas) and particularly prevalent in 1960s culture (in the Beats, the 'dharma bums' and the West Coast hippies, for example). It was an inevitable cultural development, it seems, from Parisian Existentialism to Californian Zen Buddhism, from the Old World philosophies based on Classical ideals to the New World's appropriation of the even older Oriental philosophies. Many of the chief precepts of Taoism, Confucianism, Hinduism, Shinto and Zen Buddhism chime with those of land art, not only the American earthworks, but also the British form of land art of Long, Drury, Fulton, Nash and others. Matsuo Basho, an important Oriental poet, wrote:

> Go to the pine if you want to learn about the pine, or to the bamboo if you want to learn about the bamboo. And in doing so, you must leave your subjective pre-occupation with yourself.[1]

That's straight out of an art school manual. Makoto Ueda explained Basho's tenet thus: '[f]or learn means to enter into the object, perceive its delicate life and feel its feelings.'[2] These notions of searching for the 'essence' are absolutely in tune with the æsthetics of Richard Long, Brancusi, Andre, and Judd. Minimal art pursued the oft-used maxim that 'less is more', a radical reductionism and simplification. Or as Carl Andre put it, "minimal' means to me only the greatest economy in attaining the greatest ends'.[3] Michael Heizer confessed he preferred to see art more as a religion than a recreational activity: 'if you consider art as activity then it becomes like recreation. I guess I'd like to see art become more of a religion'.[4]

John White, discussing Oriental art's surface and void in his great book on space in painting, made points which can apply to land art:

> In Chinese art the surface emphasis is negative rather than positive. It is in close accordance with the calm acceptance, the contemplative natural mysticism, which reached its highest flowering in Taoism. The surface is left undisturbed. Colours are few, and soft. Ink, and delicate monotone washes are the characteristic media. Spiritual and decorative qualities are valued high above imitative naturalism, the evocative above the representational... The unmarked silk, or paper, is at once the atmosphere, the space, and the inviolate decorative surface.[5]

The relation between land art and Oriental mysticism – in particular, Taoism, Shinto, Confucianism and Zen Buddhism – has been noted by many commentators. Zen and Taoism, for instance, speak of *(1)* the 'here and now', *(2)* spontaneity, *(3)* *satori* or enlightenment, *(4)* intuition, *(5)* nature, *(6)* emptiness, *(7)* change, *(8)* meditation, *(9)* cosmic unity, *(10)* animism, *(11)* nostalgia and ancestors – all these qualities can be applied to land art, and are sometimes elucidated by land artists. Taking these attributes one by one:

(1) The Zen Buddhist notion of the 'eternal now' or 'now-streaming' (*nunc fluens*) as Alan Watts called it. Zen philosophy makes the present moment primary, the only true reality, and land artists too work in the present. Sculptors continually evoke the transient nature of sculpture: Hans Haacke's fog pieces; Chris Drury's fires; Ana Mendieta's snow and mud body prints; Wolfgang Laib's pollen.

(2) Spontaneity: this is as crucial in land art as it is in Zen Buddhism and Taoism. The land artist works with whatever materials are to hand; changes in weather must be accommodated into the artwork. Richard Long makes stone circles and Drury makes cairns from whatever material are at hand, rather than transporting material to the site.

(3) The experience of viewing land art is not quite Zen *satori*, in the strict definition of *satori* or enlightenment (insight and intuition beyond logic and reason), but certainly land artists aim for an 'epiphany', as James Joyce called the æsthetic shock, however brief it may be. In land art as object, there are 'no strings attached', i.e., 'what you see is what you get', as Frank Stella put it. One sees the whole thing there, and that is everything you get. This instantaneous aspect of land art, as also in contemporary painting, is a Zen-like notion. *Satori*, too, has affinities with the descriptions of land art/ sculpture that some land artists have given (Morris's objecthood, for example). Hui-Neng, the 8th century mystic, said that *satori* was 'seeing into one's own nature'. Some land artists have written of art as a journey towards some inner essence. D.T. Suzuki termed Zen *satori* an 'insight into the Unconscious' (Suzuki identified eight attributes of Zen *satori*: irrationality, intuitive insight, authoritativeness, affirmation, sense of the beyond, impersonal tone, feeling of exaltation and momentariness).

(4) Most land artists value intuition highly, as do most poets and artists. The land artist trusts her/ his instincts, and works grow organically. Systems are adhered to, but land artists often veer off into intuitive areas.

(5) Nature dominates Zen Buddhism and Taoism (as image, metaphor, theme, value), as it does in land art. One is always encouraged in Taoism and Zen to 'follow

one's nature', and to co-operate with the universe. Nature is the teacher in Zen and Taoism, as it is in land art.

(6) Easy to see the lure of the void of religions in land art, in those wildernesses beloved of Long, Heizer, de Maria, Turrell and Oppenheim. (In Taoism, it's called *wu wei* ['without action']). Voids are found in much of postwar culture, from Samuel Beckett's sparse texts and 'fizzles', which painstakingly describe near-voids (the stone circle, so like a piece of land sculpture, in *Ill Seen Ill Said*, the sun setting over the hills in *Still* and the ruthless white 'inscape' of *Ping*), to Ad Reinhardt, Robert Rauschenberg and Robert Ryman painting all-black or all-white canvases.

In the paradoxical bliss of Oriental mysticism, emptiness is also fullness, and to 'have' nothing is to 'have' everything. Zen Buddhist, Hindu and Taoist philosophy thrive on paradox, on the 'not-this-not-that' dialectic of philosophy, as a way of getting at the unsayableness of the essence. As Anne Seymour says of Richard Long, his 'approach also corresponds with the Zen view, which recognises human nature as one with objective nature, in the sense that nature inhabits us and we nature' (OW, 54).

The imagery of Zen Buddhism and Taoism is also that of land art and Richard Long's art: stones, mountains, rivers, water, flowers. China has a long tradition of landscape painting, and it is easy to see the many connections between the contemplative aspects of Chinese landscape painting and land art.

(7) Change, time, transience is central to land art: all land art occurs within a changing landscape, whether it be the artificial (humanmade) changes in the gallery, or the natural changes of erosion, weather, water, light, season, and so on. Land art thrives on mutability, and many land artists have deliberately exploited time and change in their works, from Nancy Holt with her *Sun Tunnels*, which change as the sunlight pours through the holes in the concrete tubes, to the transience of Richard Long's *Mountain, Lake, Powder Snow* (1988), which the elements will swiftly erase.

In Taoism, everything changes, the *yin* and *yang* energies or principles create change, yet the Great Whole remains the same. In nature, everything is changing, transforming into something else, yet the Earth remains whole. Flow is crucial – so land art steps away from Western art, which stops life in snapshots or 'still life' paintings, and produces transmuting art, art which has change built into its design. In the West, there is much anxiety when artworks change (when paintings decay, for instance). On the one hand, there is the desire to keep everything 'natural', without being interferred with; on the other hand, museums and galleries constantly intervene with art – 'restoring' paintings, putting things behind glass, behind ropes, and so on.

The very nature of 'preserving' art is controversial – witness the anger surrounding the 'restoration' of Michelangelo's Sistine Chapel and Leonardo's *Last Supper*. Land artists, though, relish such changes and decay in artworks.

(8) Meditation is clearly not a goal of land artists – they make no pompous claims concerning mysticism and meditation. Yet, clearly, meditation is a part of their work, as it is a part of all artists' work. Making land art often involves a mild form of meditation. Richard Long's walks, for instance, are meditations of a kind.

(9) Land art is close to Taoism in its worldview: like Taoists, land artists believe in a holistic view of things, where each part affects the rest. This interconnected worldview (sometimes called 'Gaia-consciousness') is also the philosophy of ecology and the offshoots of the ecological/ green movement: eco-feminism, Goddess religion, animal rights, eco-paganism, direct action, road activism, anti-hunting lobbies, alternative medicine, and so on. Art now has a world consciousness, said Isamu Noguchi (1968). In the Taoist view, inner and outer commingle, the individual and the mass interconnect.

(10) Animism is another affinity between land art and Japanese and Chinese religion: it's a fundamental element in those religions (animism being the origin of all religions). This manifests itself, for instance, in the notion that spirits can reside in inanimate objects (stones, for example).

(11) Both Oriental religion and land art valorize (the spirits of the) ancestors, and the layering of history in a place. Both Oriental religion and land art are haunted by the past; particular places have their own ghosts (part of the 'spirit of the place'). When Richard Long walks in certain favourite spots, for instance, he's walking with ghosts: the ghosts of people long dead (some he's known, thousands he hasn't), wading through the multiple layers of history, and also walking with the incarnations of his former (younger) selves (Mircea Eliade's concept of 'joyful nostalgia', and the *Tao Te Ching*'s 'returning to one's roots is known as stillness' [XVI]).

Like many land artists, Richard Long is ecologically-friendly, and is careful to make sure his artworks do not scar the landscape. There is no litter in the land artists' photographs of their artworks. Long speaks of wanting to 'pass through life without leaving a trace'.6 They are ecologically and societally conscientious artists. Long said that his art is about finding a harmony between the human and the natural world, between the abstractions of humanity and the reality of nature. As Long put it, his work is 'a balance between the patterns of nature and the formalism of human abstract ideas like lines and circles.'[7] 'Above all,' wrote Irving Sandler, 'Long's art has been a countercultural dialogue with the earth, bringing humankind close to untamed nature, glorifying it, and pointing up ecological concerns' (1996, 64). (I think the eco-friendly aspect of Long's art has been overdone by critics: there are many more things that Long is concerned with in making his art before you get down to green issues).

In *Being and Circumstance,* Robert Irwin proposed four types of land art: 'site dominant', such as monuments and murals; 'site adjusted', in which some considerations are made towards the site, but it's still studio-made; 'site specific', in which steps are made towards integrating the work into the site; and 'site conditioned', work which responds to its surroundings. The 'site determined' category is the one Irwin (and Richard Long) preferred. Irwin defined 'site conditioned' work as an 'intimate, hands-on reading of the site', which results from 'sitting, watching, and walking through the site'; it means being aware of water, weather, sound, surface, movement, history, and so on. Such considerations determine whether the response 'should be monumental or ephemeral, aggressive or gentle, useful or useless, sculptural, architectural, or simply the planting of a tree, or maybe even doing nothing at all' (1985).

The land artist orients her/ himself in terms of post-Renaissance space and time. The Neoplatonic, magical, neo-pagan view of the world in the Renaissance saw humanity at the centre of the cosmos: humans were the microcosm reflecting the make-up of the macrocosm (the 'as above, so below' philosophy of Hermes Trismegistus, occultists and the alchemists). In the view of Christianity, however, God was at the centre (as in Dante's extraordinary vision of a mechanical universe in which God is at the centre of the surrounding nine hierarchies of angels, with the rest of humanity around the edges). During the Renaissance, one sees so clearly the crumbling of the hegemony of mediæval culture, where there was an unambiguous system of good and evil, God and 'man', us and them. In the Renaissance, this worldview falls apart, moving towards an emphasis on the individual, on the Existential sense of beingness and being alone in the universe. It's where Western culture has been ever since.

Because his body exists in space, any man orients himself by the four horizons and stands between above and below [wrote Mircea Eliade]. He is naturally the center. Any culture is always built on existential experience.[8]

This is what the land artist does: s/he orients her/ himself to the four horizons, and to post-Renaissance time. The human level becomes the spiritual centre. Land art – in

Long, Nash, Erskine, Lipkis, Holt – puts people, not God or deities, at the centre of the cosmos (it would be impossible for humans to *really* do otherwise than have themselves at the heart of everything. Even when they're talking about, praying to or sacrificing to gods or God, they're always dealing with themselves. As Weston La Barre, it's *people*, not deities, who create religion).

Land art, then, can be seen on one level as the reaffirmation of 'home', a re-instatement of the notion of 'homeland'. The 'homeland', though, is not primarily a physical place, but a cultural and spiritual space. Homeland is a state of mind as much as a landscape (and it's continually contested, socially, politically, ideologically, eco-nomically, psychologically). Land art may be the manifestation of a spiritual re-orientation. In land art, the 'mythic centre' of one's life is reaffirmed.

Richard Long and other land artists always affirm the 'livingness' of their art, that they *live* their art. Their art, they claim, is not intellectually dissected (or dessicated) or made at a critical distance. Rather, the artist is right in the middle of her/ his art, living it. There is no separation of art and life. Land art is a way of mythicizing one's sense of being-in-the-world, a way of making presence visible, tactile, *there*. 'Presentness is grace' wrote Michael Fried in his influential essay "Art and Objecthood".[9]

Making land art is a religious activity because simply being in the world is religious. Land art, like all art, replays the primordial myth of Creation: each land sculpture reaffirms the Creation. 'Once the center has been reached, we are enriched, our consciousness is broadened and deepened, so that everything becomes clear, mean-ingful' wrote Mircea Eliade.[10]

In archaic societies, through symbol, meditation, prayer and ritual, sites would become 'sacred'.[11] For postwar, postmodern, post-everything people, any site can become 'sacred' if one thinks of it as sacred. If one thinks of this junk yard next to the car lot as a sacred space, why, then it is a sacred space. All that sacred spaces need is human consciousness. It is the level of *desire* and intention that makes a place sacred. In olden times, one might have required a god or a government to have the 'authority' to make something sacred. In the postwar, post-everything world, the individual is her/ his own government and God. If s/he says a place is holy, then it's holy.

Consecration of a sacred space may include any number of rites. The simple act of drawing out a circle in the sand on a beach isolates a sacred space in amongst profane space (Long must have drawn hundreds of circles in his career on the floors of galleries around the world, on beaches, deserts, mountains and forest floors. For this simple but also sacred act, he uses string). By drawing the circle, one marks out a sanctuary or sacred zone. Magicians add to the glamour of creating a magic circle by drawing it with a special knife, making it nine feet in diameter, and placing candles or some ritual object at the four cardinal points. The magician's circle is simply a stylized, ritualized version of the land artist's circle (magicians always have to be flashy and show off). The religionist or magician has the weight of religion or a tradition of hermetic magic behind her/ him; the modern artist has the weight of art behind her/ him. One can't say that a church or a magic circle is 'holier' than a circle made with a stick by a someone on a sandy beach. Cathedrals or temples simply have the 'authority' of paternal figures and governments behind them (able to lay down the law if necessary through physical force). The individual making a sand circle doesn't seem to have the same 'authority', the same tradition of sombre theology and religious *gravitas*. Yet the individual on a beach, or the land artist in a forest, is making a sacred space out of profane space.

Land artists do not think in these terms: or they may do, but they rarely admit it publicly. For the land artist, as for any artist, it is perhaps embarrassing to admit that much of art is about 'childlike' feelings; that is, the 'simple' pleasures of making a line out of stones, or skimming stones on a river, or walking at dawn, or filling a room with soil, or writhing around in mud (if a kid plays with mud, it's called messing about, but if some *avant garde* group like the Gutai Art Association in Japan do it, it's seen as art). These are the basic pleasures of art, which both artist and viewer (and children) enjoy. They are, on one level, 'childlike', even 'infantile', psychologically. Sure. But many other grave, time-honoured institutions are founded on childish impulses: marriage, Catholicism, pop music, the advertizing industry, tourism, and the insurance industry.

The land artwork, then, remakes the sacred in a profane world: 'the manifestation of the Sacred in any space whatsoever implies for one who believes in the authenticity of this hierophany the presence of transcendent reality' remarked Mircea Eliade.12 Not only, then, do land artists make sacred spaces, as all artists do, they also create a sense of the 'real', a sense of beingness, a reaffirmation of the transcendent.

The Sacred is that something altogether other to the Profane. Consequently, it does not belong to the profane world, it comes from somewhere else, it transcends this world. It is for this reason that the Sacred is the real par excellence. A manifestation of the Sacred is always a revelation of being.13

For Eliade, each act of artistic creation echoes (replays) the original act of Creation, which birthed the world.

A creation implies a superabundance of reality... an eruption of the Sacred into the world. It follows that all construction or fabrication has the cosmogony as an exemplary model. The creation of the world became the archetype of each creative human activity, whatever its plane of reference. (1988, 112)

And Eliade asserts that art and architecture are partly about creating centres of the world, centres of being. 'Home', even if it is a modest building, embodies this orientation between the individual and the cosmos. Home is a cosmic relationship.

...every human establishment includes the fixing of a center and the projection of horizons, that is to say the "cosmocization" of a territory, its transformation into a "universe", a replica of the exemplary Universe, created and inhabited by the gods. Every human installation, whether it is a matter of taking possession of an entire country or of the building of a simple dwelling, thus repeats the cosmogony. (1988, 119)

In Richard Long's art, the act of establishment and installation is clear to see. A good deal of Long's walking art is precisely about mapping and measuring territories, traversing terrain, orientating oneself to the horizon and the cardinal points (N, S, E and W), having the right relationship with the natural world (in the American Indian sense of harmony, but also in the Buddhist sense of 'right action'). And it's about creating individual structures (stone circles and rows) or performing ritual acts (pouring water, carrying stones) which celebrate finding the centre (the spiritual centre can be anywhere: it is wherever the artist is – it is wherever you are). In Long's art the process of reconnection with the sacred is made visible. The textworks break it down into stages and strategies. The sacred is something wholly other; it might be called, at various times, the walk, the landscape, nature, the self, the moon, a sunrise, a mountain, or time itself. But it's all fundamentally about the same thing.

What's great about Mircea Eliade's philosophy of the sacred is that it doesn't have to take place in the grand temples, palaces, churches, synagogues and cathedrals of organized, institutionalized religion. It doesn't have to be Notre Dame in Paris, or Lhasa in Tibet, or Barabudur temple in Java, St Peters in Rome, Mecca or Jerusalem or wherever. It can be something as modest as an artwork, or someone's home.

For the land artist, most, if not all, of the world is not just potential art material, but beautiful. Land artists, declining to admit to being romantic or emotional, nevertheless create art that is Earth-loving, nature-loving, ecologically-friendly; that is, in short, full of emotion. The walks of Richard Long can be regarded then as a means of re-establishing a connection with 'the real', with what is meaningful or valuable for the artist. As Eliade wrote, 'the sacred is always the revelation of the real, an encounter with that which saves us by giving meaning to our existence' (1984, 162).

Aspects of Richard Long's sculpture can be related to a primal (ancient) animistic response to the natural. Animism, the 'belief in spiritual beings', as anthropologists and psychoanalysts emphasize, is the origin of all religion. There is an affinity, then, between Long's (and any contemporary artist's or viewer's) response to rocks and sculptures and the so-called 'primitive' or ancient people's response to certain stones, or hilltops, or rivers, and statues, icons, totem poles, standing stones, and so on. For ancient peoples, rivers became goddesses and trees were spirits. Long's stone circles and linear paths made by boots are not much different from the primæval response to the 'energies' in nature of ancient religions and cults. The spiritual aspect of Long's art is not too far from the responses of ancient communities calling a river a Goddess, or regarding the buffalo as holy, or speaking of the Earth-Goddess Demeter and her daughter Persephone who was taken by Pluto into the Underworld for half the year and relating it to the seasonal cycle of agriculture and crops.

Uncomfortable as they are with notions of 'spirituality' or 'mysticism', land artists such as David Nash, Chris Drury and Robert Smithson are religious artists, sensitive to the emanations of particular places. Richard Long, for instance, concedes that 'art is magical', as of course it is (IC 2, 17). Art has been deeply associated with magic and religion for at least 40,000 years, and probably millennia more. Land art, like all art, is full of deep emotions. These emotions collect in clusters around certain places. It is understandable, then, that critics and the public see these emotions as potentially religious.

> Well, sacred I suppose has particular religious meanings and my work is not about religion [Long said]. Probably a special place would be a better word. I suppose, sacred really means a place of intense feelings. If you think of religion as being about intense feelings and emotions, art can be close to religion. (IC 2, 17)

STONE CIRCLES (LAND ART AND PREHISTORIC ART)

God is a circle whose centre is everywhere and whose circumference is nowhere.

Empedocles

The circle motif, one of the primæval symbols of eternity, cycles, time, rebirth, and so on, is employed throughout the work of much of land art. Circles in land art are made from slate, timber, snow, flowers or by walking in a circle; they seem to be gentler, more eco-friendly kinds of sculpture. The circle shape itself speaks of organic forms, and, in some religions, evokes the 'feminine', the maternal realm and the Goddess. Not a few sculptors and land artists have made the circle crucial to their works: Alison Wilding, Richard Deacon, Stephen Cox, Mary Miss, Anish Kapoor, Peter Randall-Page, Robert Morris and Dennis Oppenheim. And Richard Long.

There's a nice remark by Joseph Campbell about circles and squares: the circle is of the body and nature, the square is the head and the mind. Circular thinking is about the body, square thinking is the mind (order, mathematics). Campbell related it to New York City – the grid, the rectangular structure, a place of the mind. But when the moon rises over the concrete canyons, it's a reminder of the body, of nature. of biology and the country. As Campbell said, the link to the natural world is essential: 'in wilderness is salvation'.[1] Richard Long would agree with that.

The circle (and ellipse and spiral) is an organic, even gentle shape, seemingly in tune with 'earth energies'. Circular structures (igloos, huts, stone circles, tombs, earthworks, pools) seem to be in harmony with nature, echoing the circle shapes of the planet itself, or suns, eyes, blood cells, orifices, orbits. The circular structures suggest primitive, archaic, more 'authentic' ethics (the 'back to nature' syndrome). There is, then, not only a mystical side to land art, to Long, Nash, Smithson, Oppenheim, Bayer, but also a nostalgic element (nostalgia is a key element in any religion). Looking *back* to the land, land artists also look *back* to a former (even ancient) era which appeared to be, patently, better (to a golden age which is and was imaginary, which never existed, which never could have existed).[2] This is the hidden subtext in the writings of the land artists, this nostalgia for the imagined better times of archaic cultures, when people lived 'in harmony' with the earth. This is, of course, a wide-spread nostalgia, but not backed up by the evidence, which is that for ancient and prehistoric peoples life was as hard, if not harder, than it is now. (Some commentators have offered contrary views. That, for example, ancient people did not spend as much time working as modern day folk do. Once the basics had been found – food, shelter, warmth, clothing – ancient peoples had much more leisure time. They were not work-aholics).

Land art based on circles includes Vijali's *World Wheel* (1987), Alan Sonfist's *Circles of Life* (1987) and *Pool of Virgin Earth* (1975), Adam Purple's *The Garden of Eden* (1975), Charles Jencks' *Snail Mound* (1992-94), Michael Heizer's *Circular Surface Planar Displacement Drawing* (1970), Stan Herd's *The Circle* (1992), and Mel Chin's *Revival Field* (1993). Many of Nancy Holt's works are circular: *Annual Ring* (1981), *30 Below* (1980), and *Sun Tunnels* (1976).

Donald Judd produced two circular steel bands, 180 inches in diameter, as well as a concrete circular 'wall'. Robert Morris made gigantic circular works, such as his *Observatory* (1971), which was a huge earthwork recalling the megalithic structures of ancient times, such as Avebury stone circle. His *Labyrinth* (1974) was a maze-size sculpture, the kind of maze one finds in theme parks and country houses, except that Morris's *Labyrinth* used the ancient pattern of the Cretan labyrinth, itself a motif some see as distinctly feminine, speaking of Goddess mysteries. Herbert Bayer's *Mill Creek Canyon Earthworks* (1979-82) was a series of earthworks recalling ancient monu-ments. Robert Smithson's *Closed Mirror Square* was like an Aztec ziggurat, while his *Amarillo Ramp* recalled the massive embankments found at Neolithic earthworks in the UK such as Maiden Castle, or Iron Age hill forts such as British Camp on the Malvern Hills.3

Some artists have produced stone circles which look very much like Stonehenge, such as Nancy Holt's monumental *Stone Enclosure: Rock Rings* or Alan Wood's *Ranch-enge* (1983), a wooden Mid-West American version of Stonehenge. Vida Freeman's *Installation* (1981) in an L.A. gallery comprised white porcelain and stoneware stones with white pillars emerging from them. Michelle Stuart constructed cairns and circles in *Stone Alignments/ Solstice Cairns* (1979). Margaret Hicks fashioned three con-centric circles from oak and sandstone in Texas (*Hicks Mandala*, 1975), intended for a 'Ritual of Giving'. David Harding cast his *Henge* (1972) from nine foot tall slabs of concrete, while Donna Myars' *Dream Stones* (1979) were cast and carved from cement. Michael McCafferty built his *Stone Circles* (1977) on a beach in Oregon, where they were flooded at high tide. Marlene Creates' interventions on prehistoric earthworks included laying rows of paper over them (*Paper Over the Turlough Hill Cairn*, 1981).

Many land artists have made mounds which recall prehistoric burial mounds (apart from the ones cited above) including Judy Varga's *Geometry of Echoes Converge* (1980), Maya Lin's *Wave Field* (1995), Peter Walker's *Turf Mountain* (1993) and James Pierce (*Burial Mound*). These (Minimal and Postminimal) sculptures are ambivalently related to ancient monuments, however, as Samuel Wagstaff remarked of Tony Smith's works: '[t]hey are related to early cultures intentionally or through sympathy – menhirs, earth mounds, cairns... [and] to this culture with equal sympathy – smoke-stacks, gas tanks, dump trucks, poured concrete ramps.'[4]

Land artists, then, consciously or slyly invoke ancient, prehistoric monuments. Heizer, Smithson, Gormley, Morris and Holt make references to ancient earthworks. Anthony Gormley likened the *Angel of the North* site to a burial mound. (What separated Haacke's earth mound from gardening? By its *intent*, Haacke replied.) The famous *Serpent Mound* in Adams County, Ohio, dating from the 10th century AD, is an obvious ancestor of landscaped art by Heizer, Bayer, Morris and others.

Some land artists work in megalith-rich landscapes (such as Richard Long in the South-West of Britain). There are over nine hundred stone circles in the British Isles, a fact which surprised Long when I told him ('900...? That's an amazing fact I did not know').[5] Long too makes connections with prehistoric art in terms of manufacture: the cave paintings at Lascaux, Long said, were made by people's hands on the rock. 'And my work is just the same as that. It is very positive, very exciting that I am part of the continuation of... Art itself can be a circle' (IC 2, 24).

Long has made references to some of the key sacred/ religious/ prehistoric sites of Britain: to Silbury Hill, apparently the largest humanmade mound in Europe, so the textbooks say; to the ithyphallic Cerne Giant in Dorset; to Glastonbury Tor, mecca for hippies, occultists and 'New Age' travellers (like Avebury and Silbury Hill); to Windmill Hill, and so on. (Interestingly, although Long has referred to Silbury Hill, Stonehenge and Glastonbury Tor often, he rarely includes Avebury stone circle in his works. Long seems to prefer Stonehenge, even though Avebury is a superior site in many respects).

In Rome Richard Long made a reference to mythology in his *Romulus Circle and Remus Circle* (1994). Long even put a picture of himself with a rucksack in Africa right next to one of the famous ancient hill figures of England, the so-called 'Long Man of Wilmington', 231 foot tall, in Sussex. This is one of those prehistoric sites that some see as being an alien, or St Paul, or King Harold, or a Roman soldier (some reckon is much more recent than prehistoric). Richard Long ironically compares himself here with another 'Long' Man.[6]

Locations such as Silbury Hill, Stonehenge and Glastonbury have long been revered by the faithful as holy sites, 'places of power' as they are called. Land artists capitalize on the mystery of such places. One of Richard Long's works is a walk between two prime magical centres of Britain, Stonehenge and Glastonbury, both deeply associated with prehistoric astronomy, ancient priesthoods, Arthurian legend, Merlin the Magician, the Age of Aquarius, ley lines, Druids, geomancy, and a million other Outta Sight Ideas:

ON MIDSUMMER'S DAY
A WESTWARD WALK
FROM STONEHENGE AT SUNRISE
TO GLASTONBURY BY SUNSET
FORTY FIVE MILES FOLLOWING THE DAY[7]

The photograph that Richard Long puts with this textwork is the sort of picture postcard view one finds in newsagents and heritage centres around the UK: Glastonbury Tor in a dreamy sunset. Like St Paul's, the Tower of London, Big Ben, Buckingham Palace, Beefeaters, the changing of the guard, red buses and red telephone boxes, this is one of the archetypal images of tourist Britain. And, typically, it is Glastonbury Tor that Long chooses to photograph, not the shops nearby, the electricity pylons, the junk yard behind the highways, the rows of garages, the housing estates.

Note that Richard Long walked from Stonehenge to Glastonbury, very New Age. To mark the solar eclipse in Britain in 1999 (which was a big event in popular culture in the UK), Long walked from Stonehenge (where else?) to Cornwall, like some latter-day shaman or a high priest of some obscure cult (the Cult of the Art-Walk, perhaps, or a long-lost sect called the Ecstatic Taoist Walkers of Dartmoor).

Land artists' stone circles — including Richard Long's — often recall prehistoric stone circles. While they may deny it verbally, Nancy Holt's *Stone Enclosure*, Robert Morris's *Observatory* and Long's circle sculptures evoke the great circles of Britain: the Rollright Stones in Oxfordshire, Boscawen-Ûn and the Merry Maidens in West Penwith, Cornwall, Castlerigg in Cumberland, Stanton Drew in Somerset (a huge and little-known set of circles, and the nearest large ancient circle to Long'o homo in Failand, Bristol), and of course the mother of all stone circles, Avebury in Wiltshire (also not far from Bristol). Another link to circles are the 'fairy rings' of folklore and

Celtic mythology. And the many rituals of dancing in circles, of course (with Matisse's famous painting *Dance* as one of the best renditions of this ecstatic theme, though Emil Nolde also made some memorable images of wild dancers).

There are many circles in Richard Long's repertoire: *Touchstones*, made in Iceland in 1982, which features long stones, some two feet high, arranged upright in a circle, *Circle of Standing Sandstones* (Düsseldorf, 1983), *Elterwater Stone Ring* (Kendal, 1985), *Stones and Suilven* (Scotland, 1981), *Stones In Switzerland* (1974), *Summit Stones* (the Swiss Alps, 2000), *Stones in Iceland* (1974), *Stones On Inishmore* (1975), *Stones in Nepal* (1975) and *Stones In Ladakh* (India, 1984). Obviously, Long has to work with what's there, at the location. If there's only long, thin slabs of stone, then that's what he has to use, if he's going to make a sculpture (he could import stones, but that's not his methodology for outdoor art made on walks). Arranged flat, these slabs of stone might not stand out against the rocky ground underneath them. Long does often employ flat slabs of stone, but often in indoor sculptures, such as the *White Marble Circle* (Ottawa) or *Helsinki Circle* (both 1983). Standing upright, the stones make more of a mark, as the builders of stone circles knew well. In *Orcadian Circle* (Cambridge, 1992), irregular slabs of stone are piled against each other, raising the circle a couple of feet off the ground in Jesus College's quad. In *Muir Pass Stones* (1995), the stones are chosen so they stand easily upright, their pointed ends skyward.

Some land artists, such as Richard Long, maintain that their stone rings are subjective, private, individual works, quite different from the public, social art of the prehistoric stones circles. The ancient stone rings were made by a group of people, a society constructed, perhaps, according to the architectural plans devised by a priestly élite (but they might have been made by workers for an exclusive few in a community, like a millionaire commissioning a fashionable new garden design for one of her/ his homes). Land art circles are (nearly always) the work of one person, but a major contemporary artist is no less a member of the cultural, æsthetic élite.

Prehistoric stone circles may have been built for religious rituals, perhaps connected with the position of celestial bodies. The circles in stone, snow, dandelions, trees and concrete of contemporary land art are made for private consumption, for the artist alone, or for an onlooker who wanders into a gallery or a space then out again, back into the chaos of the city. Yet the ancient sacred sites and land art/ Postminimal/ Arte Povera/ earthworks have much in common, because art and religion join at so many points. (And contemporary artists have their own rituals: for instance, to make

Footprint Circle [1989, Italy], Long trudged around in a small circle, turning snow into sludge and forming a small open circle.)

Land artists benefit from the allusions to ancient monuments, because the atmosphere and magic of prehistoric stones rubs off on their own work. In stressing the importance of megaliths, the land artists not-so-subtly imply a continuity between themselves and these pre-Dark Age relics. The æsthetic continuity that's emphasized also implies religious affinities. Thus, the land artist is the contemporary equivalent of the priests and hieratic sects who created Stonehenge, the Nazca lines in Peru, the Egyptian Pyramids, and Australian aborigine 'songlines'. A spirituality is affirmed in land art, which only a few land artists actually speak about. But this religious feeling is definitely there, definitely a part of the discourse of Long, Turrell, Smithson, Fulton, Morris and Holt.

TREES

Many sculptors and land artists have worked with trees: David Nash, Guiseppi Penone, William Jackson Maxwell, Robert Irwin, Jackie Winsor, Daniel Buren, Alan Sonfist, Harvey Fite, Peter Walker, Giuliano Mauri, Nils Udo, Luc Wolff, Maria Nordman, Sjoerd Buisman, Cosima von Bonin, Stefan Banz, Vito Acconci, Jørn Rønnau, Buster Simpson, Jan Dibbets, Helge Røed, Lars Vilks, Andy Lipkis, Herman de Vries and Mel Chin.

> And the larch that is only a column, it goes up too tall to see:
> and the balsam pines that are blue with the grey-blue blueness of
>   things from the sea,
> and the young copper beech, its leaves red-rosy at the ends
> how still they are together, they stand so still
> in the thunder air, all strangers to one another
> as the great grass glows upwards, strangers in the silent garden.

> D.H. Lawrence, from 'Trees in the Garden'[1]

Using trees means working within a long and celebrated religious and cultural tradition.[2] For example, trees have since time immemorial been associated with spirits and religions. The Greeks believed that trees had spirits; there were the apples of immortality and trees of eternal life; Daphne turned into a tree when pursued by Zeus; Actæon was transformed into a stag in the forest when he spied Diana bathing nude; deities such as Athena, Artemis, Dionysus, Apollo, Orpheus and Cybele are associated with trees and woods. The Celts worshipped trees, and the Germanic tribes had a mystical attitude trees. The Druids revered the oak, the royal tree of ancient England, and had rituals that involved oaks and mistletoe (traces of these rites persist in Christmas culture in the West). The oak was sacred to Jupiter, Hercules, the Dagda, Thor, Jehovah, Allah and other gods in their 'thunder-god' mode.

Trees were associated with secret languages and religious symbolism. Fire festivals in particular are linked with trees – burning wood is central to many land artworks: there were the bonfires at the Celtic fire festivals (such as Samhain, or Hallowe'en, a fire festival inaugurating the beginning of the Celtic year which transferred in the UK to Bonfire Night); on Midsummer Day fires are lit, traditionally with oakwood; Midsummer was also the time of the sacrifice of the oak-king of Nemi. The willow is deeply associated with witchcraft (the words 'witch' and 'wicked' are derived from the same ancient word for 'willow', *wicca*); the laurel is linked with poetry – the reward for great poetic endeavour was the laurel ('Daphne', in Greek, is associated with Apollo's pursuit of the Goddess Daphne); laurel was also an intoxicant – the leaves were chewed to induce a frenzy – and the poet Francesco Petrarch revered the laurel tree, linking it with his beloved, the eternal and eternally unavailable Laura, and the notion of poetic immortality which the laurel symbolized and Petrarch longed for desperately.

Particular trees have been mythologized: there was the 'holy thorn' that, as legend has it, sprang from Joseph of Arimathea's staff as he planted it in the sacred ground of Glastonbury; the wood of the Sacred Tree of Creevna, at Killura, had healing properties; naked children were passed through gaps in pollard ashes before dawn as a cure for rupture; Yygdrasill was the sacred ash tree of the god Woden – he used it as his steed; in secular times trees still play a mythic role: there are the trees that hid figures such as Robin Hood and Charles I from their foes.

In fairy tales, forests are places of enchantment, initiation and trial, where strange beasts are encountered, spells are undertaken. The 'dark forest' or *selva oscura* occurs at the opening of the great poem of European culture, Dante's *Divine Comedy*, where the first thing the poet-pilgrim does is enter the 'dark forest'.

When land artists pick up a bit of wood, then, or use a branch in their work, they are activating a mass of associations in the fields of symbolism, legend, myth, magic and religion. Every tree and type of wood has its symbolic associations: oak, beech, laurel, willow, sycamore, ash, larch, hawthorn, holly, vine, hazel, ivy, elder, rowan, alder and birch.

One of the most ancient religious functions of the tree was the World Tree of shamanism, the oldest of all religions. The World Tree was the mythic centre of the world of the community, it was the *axis mundi*, *omphalos*, the pivot of time and space. The archaic shaman had many tasks: one of them was to travel to the Other World, to bring back news of what happened there, and to guide the souls of the departed to the Land of the Dead. The shaman did this by climbing up the Cosmic Tree: the shaman's magical flight to the Other World was linked with climbing the World Tree.

What has all this to do with 20th century land art? A lot. Constantin Brancusi, more influential on land art than Picasso, Arp, Giacometti, Rodin, Matisse or Maillol, worked notions of shamanic flight into his *Birds in Space* sculptures, and most especially in his *Endless Column*, which is cited by many key sculptors (Judd, Andre, Morris, Burton) as an important inspiration. Brancusi's *Birds in Space* aimed to express the essence of flight, the moment when a quivering verticality is released from the chains of gravity and flies upward. One only has to look at David Nash's *Tripods*, Barnett Newman's *Broken Obelisk*, or Donald Judd's stacks, to see how important Brancusi's sculptures were, with their shamanic, World Tree associations.

Planting trees has become a favourite with land and environmental artists: Alan Sonfist created various solid circles and rings of trees (*Circles of Life* [1986], *Circles of Time* [1987]); Mel Chin planted trees and plants on a landfill site in St Paul, Minnesota (*Revival Field*); Joseph Beuys led the planting of oak trees at Documenta 7 in Kassel in 1982; Andy Lipkis planted trees in urban areas (such as Tinseltown), and organized fund-raising marathon runs for trees (1979); Guiseppe Penone placed a long white crystal in tree trunks (*Light Traps*, 1994); Vito Acconci constructed a tower of trees (1996), one above the other, all of the trees upside-down; Robert Irwin installed nine plum trees in Seattle, Washington (1983), separated by blue screens; Buster Simpson planted willow trees in drinking fountains (1993). In *Wood To Wood* (2001, a walkwork through some of England's loveliest forests – Puddletown Forest, Cranborne Chase and the New Forest), Richard Long performed a classic land art act: planting something in the ground (in this case, a nut from each forest).

Guiseppe Penone's tree sculptures include *I Wove Together Three Trees* (1968), made in the Maritime Alps. Jan Dibbets produced a tree-work, *Construction of a Wood*, in 1969. Jackie Winsor's 1971 piece *30 to 1 Bound Trees* was a group of tree trunks tied together. Here, the binding of the trees, as in much of Winsor's work, relates to autobiographical, childhood experiences, often painful, as well as the formal aspects of density, weight and repetition.[3]

Daniel Buren constructed one of the most compelling of all treeworks: an olive tree standing atop a huge cube of soil in a gallery (*Untitled*, 1999), a truly spectacular (and enigmatic) work, with the tree and earth in proportion, quietly dominating the ornate room at Castello di Rivoli. Trees are, in short, the 'architecture of the planet'.[4]

LIVING PLANTS

Many land artists, and many contemporary artists, have used living plants as material for making art. Some artists have installed trees upside-down (Vito Acconci) and plants upside-down in galleries (Michael Blazy, Henrik Håkansson, Sam Kunce). Some artists have forced plants into vacu-formed moulds (Laura Stein) and rubber foam (Ingo Vetter, Annette Weisser). Some artists have lined rooms with cages of bay leaves to produce an aromatic environment (Guiseppe Penone). Some artists have planted seeds on their naked bodies (Teresa Murak). Some artists have planted clover fields in galleries (Nikolaj Recke) and made couches from grass (Daniel Spoerri). Some artists have trained plants to grow at odd angles (Hans Haacke, Cartsen Höller). Some artists have built parks running up the sides of buildings (Vito Acconci); some have made enclosed indoor gardens (Knut Åsdam). Other artists have created portable orchards (the Harrisons); portable indoor vegetable gardens (N55); and crammed hothouses (Lothar Baumgarten). And some have let roses run riot over cars (Silvie Fleury).

Plenty of land artists and sculptors have used real flowers to make works: Herman de Vries (who spread thousands of lavender flowers on a gallery floor in 1998); Wolfgang Laib with his pollen floor spreads; Jenny Holzer's *Black Garden*, a war memorial garden of very dark plants and flowers (1994); Anya Gallaccio used roses (1992), sunflowers (1991) and zinnias (1992); Gary Rieveschl, who planted *Heart Wave,* a line of 12,000 red tulips, in 1980; Peter Hutchinson, who planted 'thrown ropes' of flowers (1996); and Richard Long pressed flowers flat in a field in *Brough of Birsay Circle* (1994). Others include: Annette Wehrmann, Shelagh Wakely, Mark Dion, Meg Webster, Carsten Höller, Paula Hayes, Peter Fischl, David Weiss, Tobias Rehberger, Lothar Baumgarten, Brigitte Raabe, and Olaf Nicolai.

One of the most famous of contemporary sculptures using living flowers was Jeff Koons' giant dog (*Puppy*, 1992), constructed in Arolsen with 17,000 flowers, and standing 11.5 metres tall. 'I decided I wanted to make an image that communicated warmth and love to people. A very spiritual piece. It just came to me to make the *Puppy* out of live flowers'.[1] Although Koons' art was known for its postmodern, camp, trashy chic (it's ideologically and spiritually the opposite of Long's art), Koons likened the interior of the *Puppy* to a church: 'I wanted the piece to deal with the human condition, and this condition in relation to God. I wanted it to be a contemporary Sacred Heart of Jesus' (ibid.).

LAND ART AND CONTEMPORARY SCULPTURE IN BRITAIN

Sculptors in the UK, whether of Richard Long's *alma mater* St Martin's School of Art, the 'New Generation', the 'New British Sculptors' and others, benefited from the influence of openness and freedom of American sculpture (at least in the 1960s and 1970s). 'America made me see that there are no barriers and no regulations' wrote Anthony Caro, the influential British sculptor and teacher at St Martin's when Long was there (although Long was part of the other group).[1] Caro had visited the US and been impressed by the new art (such as Kenneth Noland's paintings). According to William Tucker, postwar or 'modern', post-Cubist sculpture 'could be made from anything, about anything.'[2] (Tucker, though, in a TV documentary on 1960s sculpture, didn't regard Long's walks as sculpture). Caro described a mood that was common in the æsthetics of the 1960s, in painting as much as in sculpture: the idea that sculpture should not be on pedestals, but on the floor; that there are no barriers between the spectator and the work.[3]

The big (and little) statements in sculpture in Britain of the 1960s and after included (here's a brief reminder):

• Anthony Caro's welded steel constructions, which were abstract but also emotional (for instance his *Veduggio Sound* [1973], or *Early One Morning*, [1962], one of his most famous pieces). Like David Smith's work, Caro's sculptures are heavy, chunky, and they are distinctly modernist, like Rodin and Brancusi (Caro's late work drew on ancient mythology in a similar way to literary modernists such as Joyce, Pound, Cavafy, Rilke and Graves);

• Philip King's flamboyant steel and fibreglass pieces, such as his *Genghis Khan* (1963, Tate Modern, London), which speak of a direct apprehension of the object in itself, in the manner of Constantin Brancusi's and Frank Stella's art;

• William Tucker's hard-edged and organic forms, which aim for maximum 'visibility' and physicality (such as *Okeanos* [1988] or *Memphis* [1966]);

• Tim Scott's segments of circles in glass, perspex and acrylic sheets (such as *Quinquereme* [1966] or *Wine* [1968]);

• Stephen Cox's Kleinian, post-Renaissance reliefs;

• Anish Kapoor's erotic, mysterious painted objects, which are bizarre yet wholly believable departures from (variations on) natural forms – a pitted surface like that of a blackcurrant (*Half*, 1984), interfolding petals like those of a rose, multi-part spirals, cones made of shapes like the folds in robes – but the most startling thing about Kapoor's forms are their colours, powdery blues, lemon yellow and scarlet, at once seductive and unreal, simultaneously, like all sculpture, inviting touch and repelling it, perhaps by being indifferent to it;

• Richard Deacon's poetic, open-form sculptures which are 'drawn in space' (such as *Turning a Blind Eye No. 2* [1984-85] or *Listening To Reason* [1986]), allusions to ears, eyes, noses, mouths and genitals, setting space alive in a Rilkean manner, as in the Rilkean sense of space being deep and alive, and in the poet's 'song' (the poem) activating space (it was like, Rainer Maria Rilke said, fruit filling your mouth), where the song, and breathing, is equated, in Orphic fashion, with life itself (see the famous sonnet on the *Archaic Torso of Apollo* by Rilke, where the statue comes alive, though not in the manner of Pygmalion and his statue, or Hermione at the end of Shake-speare's *The Winter's Tale*, where Leontes takes the reborn Hermione's hand and gasps 'o, she's warm! / If this be magic, let it be an art / Lawful as eating');

• Tim Head's *State of the Art* (1984) is a collection of phallic objects, stacked up like a Louis Nevelson wall of sculpture: Head placed a host of dildoes and vibrators next to electronic calculators, model aircraft, tape players, computers, computer games, deodorants, hair sprays, all the panoply of consumerist items;

- Barry Flanagan's witty, seemingly naive semi-figurative works, such as his bronze hares, or his *Soprano* (1981), which is a bronze bird, mouth wide open, singing like an opera diva, with a gilded arrow through her breast;
- David Nash's environmentally-friendly interactions with nature, the elemental stoves, the tree domes and wooden boulders (see below);
- Tony Cragg, one of the consistently intriguing British sculptors (see below);
- And Bill Woodrow's wonderful remaking and remingling of everyday found objects – a post-industrial sculpture (like David Mach's or Anthony Gormley's) with a lot of humour – for instance, structures such as flowers of branches sprouting from the smashed car door of a Porsche 928 (*Trivial Pursuits*, 1985), and *A Passing Car, A Caring Word* (1982), another car door, this time fixed against a decayed double bed base, with a cross on the floor made by tearing the bed's cloth, while in front of the car door is a 'microphone' on a stand, connected by a ribbon of steel torn from the door, with a gun linked to the door, lying on the floor; the resulting sculpture is a meditation, perhaps on violence, oppression, and death. Bill Woodrow's sculpture has an aggressive, satirical or political edge to it, too, unlike Long's relatively non-political sculpture. Woodrow's *English Heritage – Humpty Fucking Dumpty* (1987) is, Robert Hewison wrote:

> made out of a dismembered school vaulting horse, cut up pieces of a hot-water tank, electric circuitry and a nuclear warning symbol [and] plays with the tradition of the equestrian state as a glorification of authority and the nursery rhyme view of politics, to express his anger at the charade of contemporary pomp and circumstance. (118)

1960s British sculpture was connected with the art schools (St Martin's, Chelsea, Slade, RCA); with teachers and modernists such as Anthony Caro, Philip King, Hans Haacke, Lawrence Weiner, Joseph Beuys and Henry Moore; with American Minimalism and Conceptual Art; with New Realism; and with Italian Arte Povera. Richard Long was on the Vocational (Advanced) Sculpture Course at St Martin's School of Art, and was part of the more loose, experimental, Conceptual group (which included teachers such as Peter Atkins and Frank Martin). The other group was headed by Anthony Caro (and included William Tucker), and was associated with welded, modernist New Generation sculpture.

Famously, Richard Long and Fulton were among those art students who organized group walks as artistic statements: one in 1967 involved the students meeting in central London on the corner of Greek Street and Old Compton Street and walking to St

Martin's entrance on Charing Cross Road, while roped together. In another walk work, students walked from St Martin's into the countryside.

The student days of artists such as Bruce McLean, Jan Dibbets, Hamish Fulton and Richard Long at St Martin's were summarized by David Lee:

> [at] St Martin's School of Art... the definition of sculpture was all-inclusively expanded to embrace a hike in the Hindu Kush, a sing song, an OS map with felt tip graffiti, a collection of empty bottles or a stack of horse blankets. Anything, in fact, providing it did not resemble in the smallest particular anything that sculpture had either used or made before.[4]

Richard Long said he thought in the late Sixties that art could be more than constructing sculptures from metal: even the 'new sculpture' (the reference was probably to Caro) was traditional:

> I had a very strong feeling that art could embrace so many more things than it was at the time, that it could be about things like grass and clouds and water, natural phenomena, rather than just the slightly sterile academic, almost mannerism of welding bits of metal together, or using plaster, or the general kind of studio work at that time. (1994b)

The 'new' British sculpture was loved and loathed passionately. Amazingly, art critic David Sylvester reckoned that Richard Long 'has too many admirers'. What did Sylvester mean? That people uncritically adore Richard Long's works? Or that there is too much criticism written about him? Can an artist become too popular? Peter Fuller targetted Bill Woodrow's work as an example of what he hated most in (postmodern) New Art.[5] Peter Fuller loved artists who make 'beautiful' things, things that may be difficult or challenging, but which are also 'beautiful' (his faves included Maggie Hambling, Eric Gill, J.M.W. Turner and Paul Nash). But Woodrow's sculpture, like Tony Cragg's, Jean-Luc Vilmouth's and David Mach's, destroys the traditional notions of the 'beauty' of an art object. Stable (modernist) notions of 'purity' or 'meaning' or 'value' in art are refuted by sculptors such as Cragg, Mach, Woodrow *et al*. Fuller's critique of such (post-Conceptual) sculptors argued that their work lacked craft skills, that it was gimmicky.[6] It's a familiar (and pointless) dart that's thrown at contemporary art from time to time (on a slow news day): 'anyone could do that!'[7] But it doesn't matter at all. The question in postmodern, post-Conceptual art is not: 'what does it mean?', but 'what does it feel like?'... 'what is the experience?'

It doesn't matter if there is no 'craft skill' (or any skill at all) or special techniques used in sculpture if there are a host of other things going on in it. As Donald Judd said, a work *only has to be interesting*. Richard Long claimed his photographs are not made with great skill, but it doesn't affect the value they have as artworks. Similarly, Andy Warhol showed that an artist didn't have to be as skilled as a Leonardo da Vinci to be able to produce 'great art'. One needed to be a good publicist, good with mass mechanical production techniques, good at organizing other people. (Though Warhol was of course highly skilled).

Tony Cragg was known for his coloured spreads of found objects arranged in lines on the floor (such as his *New Stones,* 1978). Cragg's sculptures were constructed from all manner of found objects, each given the same status, in a non-hierarchical fashion, laid out on the floor (anti-hierarchical structures being one of the marks of postmodernism). Cragg's 1980 sculpture *Black and White Stack* contained bicycle tyres, tin cans, car radiator grills, the side of a child's crib and an ironing board. *Instinctive Reactions* (1987) was a group of cast steel vessels and pipes, like the remnants of some long-forgotten alchemical experiment. Tony Cragg has spoken of having 'an erotic response to the external world', something which, it seems, all artists have, or have to have, to be truly 'great' artists.[8] Cragg is not a land or environmental artist, but much more of a traditional sort of sculptor (in the sense of creating objects rather than installations or environments or Conceptual pieces). Cragg is, along with Kapoor and Deacon, one of the most accomplished contemporary sculptors working in Albion.

Kate Blacker discussed Richard Long and Tony Cragg:

> When Cragg made *New Stones, Newton's Tones* in 1978 he was responding directly to Long. The absence you detect in Long is there to the same extent in Cragg but it is caused by the distance between the status of his material as rubbish and as 'art'. Unlike Long, Cragg is not seeking to present spiritual experience.[9]

Tony Cragg's sculptures, like Bill Woodrow's and David Mach's, are not simply sensual modernist objects but ironic, postmodernist commentaries on the social and political uses of commodities (their work is sometimes dubbed 'post-industrial'). In Cragg, Mach and Woodrow familiar consumer durables and industrial materials are represented in an ironic, metaphoric and parodying manner.[10] Cragg, and other sculptors who trawl the dumpsters and junk yards of urban landscapes (Nash, Pope, Gormley, Woodrow), make ironic comments on scavenging and ecological recycling. Cragg was not interested, he said, 'in romanticizing an epoch in the distant past', but questioning the massive amount of commodity consumption in a late capitalist epoch:

> We consume, populating our environment with more and more objects, with no chance of understanding the making processes because we specialize in the production, but not in the consumption.11

The humour, scepticism, pathos and irony in Cragg, Woodrow, Mach, Gormley *et al* makes their post-industrial, post-Conceptualist sculpture automatically disruptive. They evade categorization and easy definitions. It is this sense of shifting meanings and ambiguity in flux that makes much of 'New Sculpture' of the Sixties and late modernist work disliked by some critics, because the work won't *keep still*. It won't be nailed down as an object of High Modernism, such as a family group by Henry Moore or a Picasso nude.

As pop guru/ svengali Malcolm McLaren and his Sex Pistols' scam showed, what counts is a 'great idea', or, rather, an idea properly presented and processed through the mass media and entertainment distribution networks. It doesn't matter if the pop act one's promoting can't play music: one can always get someone else to do the boring bit of playing the musical instruments.12 It didn't matter if the Sex Pistols couldn't display traditional values and examples of musicianship and expertise, it mattered that they were marketed in the right way, with the right image, sound bites, attitude, etc. (In fact, the Sex Pistols were accomplished in what they did, musically, as anyone listening to *Pretty Vacant* or *Anarchy in the UK* will find).13

Artists who come on humble and claim there isn't much 'skill' or 'talent' in what they do are in fact highly skilled, skilled at the manipulation of images, meanings, contexts, scenarios and ideologies. Andy Warhol claimed that anyone could have produced his screenprints of Marilyn Monroe, Elvis Presley and Jackie Onassis. This is true in only one sense (the most uninteresting), the mechanical production technique of screenprinting. In every other respect, the screenprints are Warhol's own, and no one else could have done them. Or, rather, no one *did* do them. It wasn't that 'anyone could do them', it was that Warhol *did* them. And Warhol, acting cool and self-deprecatory in interviews (in the film *Painters Painting*, for example), was in fact a determined and canny self-publicist, and a very skilled artist.

The vehemence that much of postmodern or Conceptual or post-Conceptual art engenders is understandable. Walking into one of the big, white-walled brightly-lit modern gallery spaces in the Western hemisphere (in Frisco, Barcelona, Amsterdam, Milan or Gotham), the viewer is often confronted by a series of baffling photographs, or 'found objects' placed in a line against a wall, or photocopies, or a bank of video monitors playing banal, fuzzy images in slo-mo (TV sets are practically the most common kind of installation art). These shows seem full of worthless, everyday objects, things anyone can find. There seems to be nothing *special* about the objects in Tony Cragg's *New Stones* or Bill Woodrow's dumpster works, or Lawrence Weiner's printed 'wall statements' or the deconstructionist projects of the Art and Language group. Why, the exasperated art lover fresh from a blockbuster show (of, say, Rembrandt, Duccio or Matisse) at the Met in NYC or the Kunsthalle in Hamburg might complain, 'there's no *skill* here, no *talent'*. How many times has that most common criticism of 'modern' art been voiced or overheard in art galleries: *anyone could do that!* Yes, it does seem, at first, as if 'anyone could make' Andy Warhol's screenprints, Tony Cragg's spreads of found objects or Tim Head's arrangement vibrators and tape recorders. But no, art's not like that, it doesn't work that way. The argument that 'anyone could do that', such a common complaint, also lies behind Peter Fuller's 'high art' criticism and the tabloids' 'low brow' mud-slinging. But it is such a simplistic view, revealing such a naïve understanding of what art is, what it does, and how and why it is produced. (In the UK, the Turner Prize, who Richard Long won in 1989, is routinely lambasted in the press).

Postmodern and post-Conceptual art ignites many important questions, such as: how does one gauge the 'authenticity' or 'originality' of something when it is mediated by the mass media? How does one know something is 'the real thing', when all that's known of it is through images and sounds on radio, television and the press? Does it matter if the 'original' artwork is fake when the mediated product has such 'truth', such apparent presence? Is an artwork that consists of photographs that refer to an idea or object or experience that exists elsewhere (like Richard Long's *Thirty Seven Campfires* [1987], or *A Trail of Water Circles* [2000], or Lawrence Weiner's printed words 'wall statement' *Sometimes Found*) as 'authentic' as a bronze sculpture by Degas or Donatello? Is an artwork that is an 'idea' as sensual or compelling as one made out of marble or oil? The 'new' British sculpture, with its scavenged objects and seemingly 'ordinary' objects displayed on the floor, disrupts modernist/ traditional notions of 'beauty', 'purity', 'tradition', 'objecthood', 'presence', 'value' and 'meaning'.

THE BRITISH LANDSCAPE TRADITION

I actually believe in Modernism, in the excitement of new ideas. Art is anyway beautiful if the idea is beautiful, if it has clarity and truth. A lot of the history of land- scape art has been to reveal the beauty of nature, a sort of religious celebration. All that beauty is still there and can be overwhelming, but I was always interested to develop landscape art in new ways.

Richard Long (interview, April, 1985)[1]

American/ New York/ Abstract Expressionist/ Minimal/ Arte Povera influences con- stitute a number of influences in contemporary sculpture in the UK, but another is the 'British' art tradition, and yet another is the British landscape itself. Landscape art in the UK is bound up with notions of Romanticism. For Robert Rosenblum, the Abstract Expressionists (in particular Mark Rothko) were the last in a long line of Romantic artists. Speaking of his influential book *Modern Painting and the Northern Romantic Tradition*, Rosenblum said

> were I to write a supplementary chapter to it – I stopped with Rothko and Abstract Expressionism – I would probably include earthworks of the late 1960s and 1970s. Those seem in some way to be the last gasp of that tradition of trying to find some sort of connection with the Great Beyond or the Void.[2]

Certainly the works of Fulton, Drury, Nash, Long *et al*, are part of this Romantic tradition, as expressed in British landscape art. (Associated with land art were the groups of British artists variously dubbed the New Romantics/ Neo-Romantics/ New Ruralists/ New Arcadians.)

The influence of the landscape in the UK on British sculpture is apparent in many, but by no means all, of British sculptors. Specifically *British* landscape, as opposed to other kinds of landscape, occur in David Nash, Hamish Fulton, David Tremlett, Chris Drury, Roger Ackling and Long, as one might expect. It was Carl Andre who noted, quite rightly, that the British landscape is 'one vast earthwork'.[3] Long has spent much of his life walking all over this giant earthwork, mapping it, measuring it, photo- graphing it, writing about it and building sculptures with it. (*The Sierra Madre*, a 5 day walk in Mexico in 1979, was about 'walking on rock', 'lighting fires on rock', 'sleeping on stones', 'throwing stones' and 'placing stones').

Long, Fulton, Nash, Drury and Goldsworthy, in particular, evoke the British land- scape tradition in art, the tradition of the pastoral, the sublime, the Arcadian. Long,

Fulton, Goldsworthy, Drury and Nash are Romantic, in the sense of British Romantic poetry (Blake, Wordsworth, Keats, Shelley, Coleridge); in the sense of the British Romantic painters (Turner, Constable, Girtin, Cotman, Wilson); and in the sense of the Romantic attitudes and aspirations of infinity, nostalgia, mythology, soul, magic, nature and the Gothic. In sculptors such as Tony Cragg, Nash, Fulton, Shirazeh Houshiary, Anish Kapoor, Richard Wentworth, Bill Woodrow, Barry Flanagan, Ian Hamilton Finlay, Anthony Caro and William Tucker, one can see the elements of British Romantic literature (as well as the Neo-Romanticism of the 1930s and 1940s): the anarchic idealism of Shelley, the luscious sensuality of Keats, the epic nature poetry of Wordsworth, the angelic visions of Blake and the synæsthetic poesie of Coleridge. Romantic culture in other countries should be cited here too: German Romanticism for example (Novalis, Friedrich Hölderlin, Casper David Friedrich, Philipp Otto Runge, Friedrich Schiller, Ludwig Tieck, Heinrich Heine, the Schlegel brothers, and Johann Wolfgang von Goethe). The Romantic ethics of taking things to extremes, of going to the infinite and the eternal, of solitude, of the individual's experience, of the sacred, are very much to the fore in land art, which is an art which quite definitely sustains Romantic myths and tenets.[4] For Stephen Bann, the precursor of Long's formalism is not the Romantic mimesis of J.M.W. Turner, but the cut and paste techniques of the Cubists.

Land art is the sculptural companion of nature poetry. The connections between poetry and painting are ancient: Chinese landscape painters produced the voids found in *haiku* poetry; J.M.W. Turner and John Martin drew on Romantic poetry for their imagery; Renaissance painters looked to Classical poetry (such as Ovid and Homer) in their depictions of myths such as Diana and Actæon, or Leda and the Swan (Jupiter). While poetry and painting are often aligned in art history, poetry and sculpture are rarely mentioned. The importance of British landscape in both poetry and painting has long been noted. Its significance in sculpture is not often acknowledged by art critics.

The relation between poetry and landscape is vividly described by Ted Hughes in his book *Poetry in the Making*. Hughes's poetry has many affinities with land artists, particularly the British ones: Hughes, and other British nature poets (Tony Harrison, Seamus Heaney, Alan Bold), celebrate rainy, grim, Northern landscapes, as beloved of Wordsworth, Clare and Coleridge.[5] Hughes used Gerard Manley Hopkins as an example of first-rate, visionary British landscape:

In this... poem there is much more of what we might call straightforward description, but the vivid details are all aiming one way: it is a scene in sharp focus: all gloom and brilliance, the exhilaration and uneasy sunniness of a bleak, rather lonely place. It is the closest thing to a conventional beauty spot that I know of in poetry. And it is so clean and right that whenever I see anything like it in actual scenery I think – "It's almost as good as Inversnaid" which is the title of this poem by Gerald Manly Hopkins:

This darksome burn, horseback brown,
His rollrock highroad roaring down,
In coop and in comb the fleece of his foam
Flutes and low to the lake falls home.

A windpuff-bonnet of fawn-froth
Turns and twindles over the broth
Of a pool so pitchblack, fell-frowning,
It rounds and rounds Despair to drowning.

Degged with dew, dappled with dew
Are the groins of the braes that the brook treads through,
Wiry heathpacks, flitches of fern,
And the beadbonny ash that sits over the burn.

What would the world be, once bereft
Of wet and of wildness? Let them be left,
O let them be left, wildness and wet;
Long live the weeds and the wilderness yet.6

Some of Richard Long's photographs and textworks are reminiscent of this kind of eidetic imagery. In a way, what Hughes is talking about, and Hopkins is expressing, is the sense of heightened awareness which Long aims for on his walks (something like the enhanced perception which mountaineers sometimes experience). There are many ways of achieving it (drugs, sex, music, yoga, meditation, sleep deprivation), but for Richard Long, it's walking.

4

Land Artists in Britain, Europe and America

ROBERT SMITHSON

Instead of putting a work of art on some land, some land is put into a work of art.

Robert Smithson[1]

Robert Smithson was the chief mouthpiece of American land art/ earth/ site æsthetics, and is probably the most important theoretician among all land artists (he is also the premier land artist by common consent among critics and fans of land art). Robert Smithson's theoretical statements were published in three important essays. In "The Crystal Land" Smithson recounted a trip he made to a quarry with Donald Judd, the key Minimal artist (this sort of trip was a favourite Smithson activity). Smithson evoked the decayed nature of the quarry in his article, those aspects of entropy which would feature in his own work ('cracked broken shattered earth, of fragmentation, corrosion, decomposition, disintegration, rock crisis, debris slides, mud flow avalanche' [RS, 20]). In the second essay, "Entropy and the New Monuments" (1966), Smithson discussed the important Minimal show *Primary Structures* at the Jewish Museum.

Robert Smithson's themes were entropy in nature and art; he used the science of crystals and minerals as paradigms of the new art. Smithson had collected crystals and rocks as a child. Crystallography, for Smithson, offered 'a way of dealing with nature without falling into the old trap of the biological metaphor'.2 No wonder, then, that when Smithson saw Donald Judd's pink plastic boxes he compared them to 'giant crystals from another planet' (RS, 19). The dissolution of crystals also provided Smithson with another analogy for his theory of natural entropy. The third piece, "A Sedimentation of the Mind: Earth Projects" (1968), concerned notions of time and place. While sculptors such as Anthony Caro and his ilk still clung to the old-fashioned ideas of beauty, Smithson spoke warmly of artists such as Walter de Maria, Carl Andre, Michael Heizer, Dennis Oppenheim, Tony Smith and Douglas Huebler (RS, 85).

Robert Smithson was also interested in science fiction: the poetic elements of his art thus form a continuum: between the industrial wastelands he visited for his 'non-site' sculptures and the desolate planets of science fiction; between chaos theory and the New Physics and its exploration in postmodern science fiction; between the forms of crystals and those of Minimal sculptures, and so on. Smithson's exaltation of lonely post-industrial sites was echoed in the speculative fictions of writers who evoked post- or near-holocaust worlds. J.G. Ballard, for example, wrote of post-industrial desert lands and run-down townscapes (in *The Drought, Vermilion Sands, High-Rise* and *Low-Flying Aircraft*). J.G. Ballard, as one would expect, took an eccentric view of Smithson's earthworks: Ballard mused on what kind of cargo might have been berthed at Smithson's *Spiral Jetty* and *Broken Circle*. Ballard wondered if the cargo was a 'very special kind of clock... so many of Smithson's monuments seem to be a potent amalgam of clock, labyrinth and cargo terminal'.3

In the essay "Tour of the Monuments of Passaic" (itself a sci-fi sort of title), Smithson wrote about 'great pipes, sand boxes, bridges with wooden sidewalks, all standing for the irreversibility of eternity. Under the dead light of the Passaic afternoon, the desert becomes a land of infinite disintegration and forgetfulness' (RS, 56). This sort of apocalyptic imagery is echoed in William Burroughs, J.G. Ballard, Tom Disch and other speculative fiction writers. It's the desolate wasteland imagery of Andrei Tark-ovsky's film *Stalker* (1979) and other post-apocalyptic visions.4

J.G. Ballard wrote of Robert Smithson:

The Amarillo Ramp I take to be both jetty and runway, a proto-labyrinth that Smith-son hoped would launch him from the cramping limits of time and space into a richer and more complex realm... I see Smithson's monuments [as] artifacts intended to serve as machines that will suddenly switch themselves on and begin to generate a more complex time and space. All his structures seem to be analogues of advanced neurological processes that have yet to articulate themselves.[5]

For Smithson, Andre, de Maria, Heizer, Oppenheim and Tony Smith were 'the more compelling artists today, concerned with 'Place' or 'Site''.[6] Smithson was impressed by Tony Smith's vision of the mysterious aspects of a dark unfinished road and called Smith 'the agent of endlessness'. Smith's æsthetic became part of Smithson's view of art as a complete 'site', not simply an æsthetic of sculptural objects. Smithson was not inspired by ancient religious sculpture, by burial mounds for example, so much as by decayed industrial sites. He visited some in the mid-1960s that were 'in some way disrupted or pulverized'. He said he was looking for a 'denaturalization rather than built up scenic beauty.'[7] (But he also travelled to prehistoric monuments, including some in Albion).

Robert Smithson asserted that he was concerned, like many land (and postwar) artists with the thing in itself, not its image, its effect, its critical significance: 'I am for an art that takes into account the direct effect of the elements as they exist from day to day apart from representation' he asserted (RS, 133). Smithson's theory of the 'non-site' was based on 'absence, a very ponderous, weighty absence'.[9] Smithson proposed a theory of a dialectic between absence and presence, in which the 'non-site' and 'site' are both interacting. In the 'non-site' work, presence and absence are there simultaneously. 'The land or ground from the Site is placed in the art (Non-Site) rather than the art is placed on the ground. The Non-Site is a container within another container – the room' (RS, 115).

Robert Smithson proposed a schema for 'non-site' art in his essay "Dialectic of Site and Non-Site" which ran thus:

Site	Non-Site
1. Open limits	Closed limits
2. A series of points	An array of Matter
3. Outer coordinates	Inner coordinates
4. Subtraction	Addition
5. Indeterminate certainty	Dominate uncertainty
6. Scattered information	Contained information
7. Reflection	Mirror
8. Edge	Center
9. Some place (physical)	No place (abstract)
10. Many	One (RS, 115)

The 'non-site' works were permanent, gallery-based works. Robert Smithson's *Mirror Displacements* (1968) consisted of putting some mirrors in various settings and taking photographs of them before moving them somewhere else. *Mirror Displacements* was documented in Smithson's *Artforum* article "Incidents of Mirror Travel in the Yucatan" (1969; *Artforum* was one of the key magazines of the period, along with *Art In America, Avalalanche* and *Arts Magazine*). Sometimes Smithson put soil on top of the mirrors, to dirty them up, to sabotage 'the perfect reflections of the sky'. Smithson liked dirt, gravel, sand, sludge and sediment – indeterminate, malleable substances. Land artists often sabotaged the clinical nature of much of art – putting soil or grass or slate or horses in the clean, white gallery space.

Some of Robert Smithson's other projects of the time included putting raw, natural materials into Minimal spaces, creating a tension of dialectic between 'site and non-site', as he called it. *Ziggurat Mirror* was completed by the use of mirrors. The sculpture needed the mirrors to work properly. Using the mirrors to create repetition, Smithson pointed to the delimited nature of the sculpture: with the right use of mirrors, a sculpture could be extended infinitely. Endless repetition was central to Minimal and 1960s art (Warhol, LeWitt, Andre, Morris, Judd, Stella and others took a simple unit and endlessly repeated it. Richard Long's basic units – the walk, the footstep, the handprint, the circle – have also been repeated endlessly).

Before he made the famous *Spiral Jetty* (his signature work), Robert Smithson had already been considering the scientific notions of rotation and equilibrium. His sculpture *Gyrostasis* (1968) was a 75 by 57 by 40 inch painted steel structure based on the spiral. Smithson explained that *Gyrostasis*, as the title implied, was about how rotating bodies maintain their equilibrium. 'The work is a standing triangulated spiral. When I made the sculpture I was thinking of mapping procedures that refer to the planet Earth' (RS, 37).

Robert Smithson's much-reproduced *Spiral Jetty* is a 'monumental' earthwork, though the use of the spiral motif has connotations with the ancient symbols of the Goddess.[10] Of his *Spiral Jetty*, Smithson wrote:

As I looked at the site, it reverberated out to the horizons only to suggest an immobile cyclone while flickering light made the entire landscape appear to quake. A dormant earthquake spread into an immense roundness. From that gyrating space emerged the possibility of the Spiral Jetty. No idea, no concepts, no systems, no structures, no abstractions could hold themselves together in the actuality of that phenomenological evidence.[11]

Robert Smithson was impressed by the characteristics of the Great Salt Lake site, the pinkish mud, the faintly violet water surrounded by limestone hills, and the 'crushing light' of the sun (salt flats were a favourite with other land artists – as with the desert, they liked the abstract qualities of the landscape. The emptiness also meant a lack of competition for their interventions). Smithson had been reading about salt lakes in Bolivia, where bacteria turned the water red to match the colour of the flamingos. Smithson found out that the Utah salt lakes were also red and pink due to algæ and mineral waste. Smithson and his wife, land artist Nancy Holt, surveyed the area and chose a lake at Rozel Point in Utah, which had a number of cracks in the mud under the shallow water. Smithson began building it in April, 1970, excavating 6,650 tons. *Spiral Jetty* was made from rocks, water, mud and precipitated salt crystals. It was 1,500 ft long and 15 ft wide. Smithson was aided by Virginia Dwan and the Ace Gallery of Vancouver. As with many other projects of the time a film was made of the construction of *Spiral Jetty*. Smithson related the work to spiral nebulæ, to salt crystals and microscopic organisms. Smithson thought in terms of eons of time, and mused on how entropy would overtake the site.12

Robert Smithson utilized one of the primary forms of land art, the circle, in many works, combining it with ideas taken from science (such as *Gyrostasis*, which, said Smithson, 'refers to a branch of physics that deals with rotating bodies' [ib., 37]). Smithson was not adverse to religious feelings about art: when he visited the site of his *Spiral Jetty*, in the Utah salt flats, he experienced a feeling of 'a rotary that enclosed itself in an immense roundness' (ib., 111). The two elements – rational, mathematical, scientific precision and intuitive, emotional, religious feeling – are two of the chief characteristics of land art. On the one hand, land artists talk about measurements, practical details, materials, maps and spatial data. On the other hand, they hint at religious awe, spiritual feelings, prehistoric art and the influx of the numinous into modern art.

Robert Smithson also identified his *Spiral Jetty* with a mythic whirlpool that sprang up from a tunnel connected to the Pacific Ocean. His *Spiral Jetty* was an 'immobile cyclone', it spiralled inwards from the outside: the track leaves the shore and twists round and round to the centre. *Spiral Jetty* was also linked with notions of decay in nature. In "A Sedimentation of the Mind: Earth Projects" Smithson had written '[e]very object, if it is art, is charged with the rush of time, even though it is static' (RS, 90). Ironically, Smithson's *Spiral Jetty* was itself subject to natural entropy: the water level rose and *Spiral Jetty* was submerged under water (in Summer it is usually exposed). It was ironic too that Smithson died in a plane crash while he was flying over and inspecting a site in Texas (one of the biggest losses in contemporary art).

Robert Smithson's 1971 *Broken Circle* was another large earthwork using circular motifs that was situated adjacent to the land and extended out into a lake. Smithson chose a quarry site near Emmen, Holland. Again, the site had an interesting geological aspect, which was in keeping with Smithson's love of rocks and minerals (though North-West Europe hasn't quite got the equivalent of the US's deserts and salt flats, so a quarry would have to do). Glacial action had formed unusual layers of soil.

Unlike *Spiral Jetty*, which is often submerged, *Broken Circle* remains close to Robert Smithson's conception. It is maintained by local funds. It is a 140 foot circle comprising one half of soil and one half of water, with a twelve foot wide canal cutting round the earth section of the circle, forming a semicircle. At the centre of *Broken Circle* is a very large glacial boulder. It was supposedly one of the largest in the Netherlands. Significantly, Smithson allowed nothing at the centre of *Spiral Jetty*: the spectator walked round the inward-turning spiral to find no obvious endpoint or marker. Smithson was exasperated by the prehistoric stone at the centre of his *Broken Circle*, but he let this 'accidental center' stay there, commenting 'it became a dark spot of exasperation, a geological gangrene on the sandy expanse'.13

Robert Smithson's last major work, before his untimely death, was *Amarillo Ramp* (1973), one of many land artworks conceived as an observation structure. Nancy Holt worked with one of the major American sculptors of the era, Richard Serra, to complete Smithson's plans. *Amarillo Ramp*, 15 miles North-west of Amarillo in the Texas Panhandle, is a huge inclined ramp or road, made from quarried rocks. The summit of *Amarillo Ramp* is a viewing point.14

Taken together, Robert Smithson's three large-scale earthworks, *Spiral Jetty*, *Broken Circle* and *Amarillo Ramp*, all revolve around circular or spiral motifs, a sense of temporality, of decay and transience and each uses primitive, mythic forms and gestures in a monumental manner. Two of them are set in wilderness spaces, where the marks of humanity are at their weakest. Yet each earthwork of course speaks acutely of the mark of humanity upon the Earth, and a very particular kind of mark: that of late 20th century American highly educated, expensive, high culture art-making. Robert Smithson's influence on land art has been immense. All subsequent land artists owe a debt to him in some way or other.

CARL ANDRE

Carl Andre is an important figure in a discussion of Richard Long. Apart from the fact that they are good friends, and have had exhibitions together, Andre's ideas on art, and the kind of art he produces, have many affinities with Long's view of art and the work he creates. Andre, like Robert Smithson and Morris, has been among the most lucid of Sixties theorists among artists.[1] Andre has many pertinent things to say about sculpture. His mid-1960s summary of the history of sculpture applies directly to land art:

> The course of development
>> Sculpture as form
>> Sculpture as structure
>> Sculpture as place.[2]

Carl Andre's biography is routinely cited in accounts of his art. He worked on the railways, as a freight conductor and brakeman (in Newark, at the Pennsylvania Railroad) from 1960-64, and this is used to explain Andre's use of modules and units which join together to form a work. Like Sol LeWitt and Donald Judd, Andre took one unit and multiplied them until he had a line or a square. Before working on the railroad, Andre was 'a wood-carving disciple of Brancusi', carving chunks out of wood beams. For a long time the shadow of Brancusi lay over Andre's art, so much that sometimes Andre seems to out-Brancusi Brancusi himself. When he came to explain his floor-standing works, such as *Lever*, a line of firebricks, Andre said he was

> putting Brancusi's *Endless Column* on the ground instead of in the sky... Most sculpture is priapic with the male organ in the air. In my work, Priapus is down on the floor. The engaged position is to run along the earth.[3]

The sexualization of sculpture in Carl Andre's remark is no accident: Andre has spoken in interviews that the best creative work is erotic. In a 1970 radio discussion (with Lucy Lippard, Douglas Huebler, Dan Graham and Jan Dibbets on WBAI FM), Andre said desires, not ideas, were important. 'I have very few ideas, but I have strong desires.... I agree with Dr Guillotine that all ideas are the same except in execution... You can't cut off desires except painfully'.[4] Nature was also crucial: Andre said he disliked Conceptual art because it was cut off from nature. Andre maintained that his art 'has never been conceptual in any way'.[5]

While he was in New Hampshire in 1965, canoeing on a lake, Carl Andre (so the story goes) realized that sculpture ought to be level, like water. After this, most of his sculpture was floor-standing and flat. Lines of bricks or squares made from plates of metal were typical Andre works. Andre's use of materials was not 'poetic' or 'spiritual' in the usual sense of the words. In works such as *Cedar Piece* (1959/ 64), *Pyre* (1971, S. & C. Gilman), *Herm* (1976, Guggenheim), *Stile* (1975) and *Well* (1964), which were made out of wood, Andre was using materials as themselves, but 'not to evoke nature'.[6] Andre did not intend his materials to refer to other things, to be allusive in the art historical or lyrical sense. His Styrofoam planks were not alluding to marble, as some viewers mistakenly thought.[7]

Carl Andre's notion of the 'dematerialization' of sculpture was central to his art, and also to land art. When they were not being exhibited, Andre's sculptures simply disappeared. They were not objects on permanent display, but were made, like Long's gallery sculptures, specially for each occasion and space. Most land art is like this. Andre's works outside of shows exist as ideas, photographs, descriptions, memories, and so on, but not as actual works. Much of land art is also this ephemeral, made for a particular occasion then dismantled (Christo, Drury, Morris. Many of Long's indoor works disappear after the exhibition. The mud drawings, for instance, are not portable, but Long has also produced art on paper and wood. As Mel Bochner noted, wallworks could not be held, but only seen). This emphasis on the materiality and dematerialization of his works led Andre to regard his art as non-spiritual. He said:

> My work is atheistic, materialistic, and communistic. It's atheistic because it's without transcendent form, without spiritual or intellectual quality. Materialistic because it's made out of its own materials without pretension to other materials. And communistic because the form is equally accessible to all men. (in ib., 107)

This is a humble, self-effacing view of his own art. It is this aspect of his art that annoyed people when the Tate Gallery in the UK bought, with public money, one of his piles of bricks. The form (a low oblong shape) and the material of the work (brick) seemed available to anyone who visited a household supply store and bought a few hundred bricks and arranged them in a certain way. Yet Andre's art is of course not as simple as that, and not as easy to produce as that.

Carl Andre explored the relation between real and represented objects with his controversial pile of bricks. The sculpture was 'controversial' because the general public (whoever they are) perceived, via the media, that Andre had simply stuck some bricks into a gallery (the debate occurred largely in the mass media, in particular in tabloid newspapers which in Britain take potshots at contemporary art when they're bored). Or rather, that taxpayer's money had been used to purchase Andre's bricks (in the 1970s, the Tate Gallery was partly funded by public money). A pile of bricks on a building site is... a pile of bricks. A pile of bricks in an art gallery is... sculpture. Context is everything here. This is what Carl Andre explored, whether consciously or not: the *response*, affected by so much of culture, socialization, physical context, education, and so on, makes objects sculptures. People make art. A leaf simply exists, but if someone puts it in a gallery or an art book, it becomes art (as well as remaining a leaf). If people think something is art, then it's art, as Donald Judd said. As Garth Evans wrote:

> What happens to a sculpture is determined largely by factors outside of itself. The fact of its being thought of as a sculpture is more critical to its existence, its life, than any other facts about it. This is a fundamental distinction between objects and sculpture.[8]

Carl Andre's *37 Pieces of Work* is a good example of Minimal æsthetic permutations taken to extremes. It is a sculpture that is typical of Andre's art (though its much larger than many of Andre's floor-pieces):

> Taken as a whole *37 Pieces of Work* consists of 1,296 plates, 216 each of aluminium, copper, steel, magnesium, lead and zinc. Each metal appears alone in individual six-foot square plains. Then alternates with another, checkerboard fashion, in every possible permutation. Since each of the six metals in the large piece was laid out in the alphabetical order of its chemical symbol, alternating successively with the others, there are two versions of each combination.[9]

Many of Carl Andre's floor-pieces are similar: the spectator is aware of the material first and foremost: the colour, mass, weight, size and texture of the metals. *37 Pieces of Work* is a 432 inch wide 'floor-hugging' square, in which the colours of the copper, aluminium, lead, steel, zinc and magnesium is beautifully foregrounded.

Carl Andre's *Element* series consisted of wood-carved beams that recalled Brancusi; Andre's *Equivalents* were floor-hugging sculptures shown in 1966. The magnet pieces, which preceded the metal squares, also hugged the floor, so much so that the third dimension was nearly expunged. The floor-pieces neatly rid the sculptor of dealing with pedestals. They became 'place-markers'.[10] They have no space, according to one critic, they have 'no appearance of inside or center. Rather they seem to be coextensive with the very floor on which the viewer stands'.11 Place, not space or sky, became what matters for Andre. (The pedestal was one aspect of Brancusi's art which Andre didn't take up. But Andre's sculptures could be seen as developments of Brancusi's pedestals: Andre's *Element* series and wooden sculptures in particular are very reminiscent of Brancusi's supports).

Carl Andre's floor-pieces are viewer-friendly, too: the viewer is invited to (or allowed to) walk over them. Like Judd, Andre wanted his sculptures to be seen from a variety of viewpoints. Instead of a single viewpoint, one could have a number of angles; he compared viewing his sculptures to walking on roads: '[t]hey cause you to make your way along them or around them or to move...over them' (1970, 57). Andre's works seem to be slight, almost insubstantial, but, simultaneously, 'their matter-of-factness that makes them in a multiple sense *present*'.12

Carl Andre's works are extremely sensuous, with their shiny or dull surfaces of copper, zinc, steel or aluminium. Andre's *Sixteenth Copper Cardinal*, sixteen square copper slabs, is a work that could be described as luscious. People are used to marble and stone being beautiful, and also certain metals – bronze, silver and gold in particular have been central to sculpture for millennia. Why not zinc and copper, too? Carl Andre, like other Minimal sculptors, introduces the viewer to the sensuality of copper, bronze and zinc shaped into nothing more than... a simple shape, like a slab, put on the floor. Andre's tiles are not 'narrative', allusive, literal or anthropomorphic; they do not 'depict' animals or gods or people; but they are no less beautiful, as objects in their own right. Spectators are invited to walk on his sculptures, offering a new relation with the work.

Carl Andre commented:

> The materiality, the presence of the work of sculpture in the world, essentially independent of any single individual, but rather the residue of many individuals and the dream, the experience of the sea, the trees and the stones – I'm interested in that kind of essential thing.13

Carl Andre's *Stone Field* (1977) was one of his site-specific works of the 1970s, consisting of 26 very large glacial boulders, a work more obviously land artish. It was an imposing piece, introducing the idiosyncratic, organic shapes of nature into the 'geometric wilderness' (D.M. Thomas's term) of the city (in this case, Hartford, Connecticut). Andre created a line of hay bales, placed end to end, in a field in Vermont (*Joint*, 1968).14 It was a line like Richard Long's stone rows, or Tony Cragg's floor spreads. 'Many of the activities in farm work are sculptural: stacking the hay bales, ploughing fields, feeding animals; also the marks left behind by the animals or made by farmworkers, tractors... the texture of the land' Andy Goldsworthy remarked in *Time* (180). Andre made one of his floor-pieces of slabs of metal deliberately so it would be altered by being outside. It was called *Small Weathering Piece* (1971), and contained a large number of metals (large for an Andre sculpture): lead, zinc, aluminium, copper, steel and magnesium.

One of Carl Andre's most intriguing theoretical statements is this: 'my ideal piece of sculpture is a road'.[15] This applies not only to Andre's lines of bricks or hay bales, but to Richard Long's lines of stones and walks along roads, to Christo's *Running Fence*, to other land artworks. Andre's notion of the ultimate earthwork as a road has a parallel with the famous anecdote of US artist Tony Smith who, when driving along the New Jersey turnpike, was impressed by the 'dark pavements moving through the landscape of the flats, rimmed in the distance, but punctuated by stacks, towers, fumes, and coloured lights'.[16] Something in such a long stretch of empty roads, as with airstrips (and, more dubiously, a drill ground at Nuremberg) impressed Tony Smith, who wrote '[i]t seemed that there had been a reality there that had not had any expression in art' (ib., 131). Roads are not 'art', not wholly functional either – they have an aura or mystery which Smith tried to explain. Richard Long emphasizes the functional or workaday aspect of his walks. He sees his walks as hard work; roads, in the Tony Smith view, are also for and about labour and functionality. The road, for the Minimal, serial or Process artist, in the Carl Andre manner, embodies materially the sense of a sequence or process. One unit (the foot or brick or slab of tarmac or concrete) is placed next to another, forming a road. Artists such as Carl Andre (and LeWitt and Judd) did exactly the same, putting one unit next to another, creating a line or sequence of units.

The road also may have no obvious end: endlessness was crucial to Minimal, Process and Conceptual art, as it is to land art. Many land artists emphasize art that goes on and on. Christo's fence, for example, goes on and on for 26 miles. One imagines that Christo would love a fence that could run across a whole country, or, even better, a whole continent. Similarly, Long's walks could extend far beyond their limits (his art could be regarded as one very long walk), and the modular art of Judd, Morris, Bladen and LeWitt could expand indefinitely, once the basic pattern had been established. The seriality or endless process of art was identified by Judd as the idea of 'one thing after another'.[17] Andre's concept of the road as the ideal artwork fits in with this urge towards endless process and seriality. The road motif also fits in well with stereotypical American culture, with its love of the 'open road', photography (Robert Frank), road movies (*Easy Rider, Duel, Natural Born Killers, Bonnie & Clyde*), the frontier spirit (in the Western literary and movie genre), the drifter, wanderer or nomad character, and in hippy and beatnik culture (Jack Kerouac's *On the Road*, Allen Ginsberg and the hippies).

DONALD JUDD

Donald Judd is not strictly a land artist, but as one of the most influential 3-D artists of the postwar and contemporary era, he cannot be ignored. Judd was the quintessential Minimal artist, probably the most important Minimal artist, and certainly one of the ten most important international artists between 1960 and 2000. Many of Donald Judd's best Minimal works are housed in his permanent installation in Marfa, Texas, run by the Chinati Foundation. Long has work there (along with Oldenberg, Chamberlain, Bell, Wesley and Kruger. Some of the works are displayed at Judd's home, 60 miles from Marfa). Like many artists before and since, Judd was attracted to the South-West of the US. Judd's Marfa is the culmination and greatest achievement of Minimal art.

Marfa was a former military base (Fort Russell), which Donald Judd completely redesigned. He installed his sculptures in the artillery sheds and the fields, as well as creating exhibition spaces for other artists' work (the army base contained 29 buildings and 340 acres). The Arena reworked the gym to produce an installation of concrete and gravel. One of the main works by Judd at Marfa is the epic *Untitled* (1980-86), one hundred large (41 x 51 x 72 inch) mill-aluminium boxes, each one apparently the same, yet each one different. Like Donald Judd's other hollow Minimal boxes, some of them were open at the side, some on top). The other impressive Judd sculpture at Marfa was a row of enormous hollow concrete boxes (*Untitled*, 1981), separated into groups, and installed in the fields near the artillery sheds. Each module was eight feet high, some eight feet wide and some 16 feet wide. This was Juddian Minimal box permutations on the grandest scale.

DENNIS OPPENHEIM

Like Robert Smithson and James Turrell, Dennis Oppenheim was one of the most interesting of US land artists. Oppenheim produced an amazing body of work. It's significant, for instance, that Oppenheim was the first American land artist to work with snow on a grand scale. Oppenheim began making snowworks in the late Sixties (Long had made a snow trail in the mid-1960s). The only other important environmental artist who regularly used snow and ice, really, was Hans Haacke. But, more than any of the other first generation land artists, Oppenheim made snow one of his primary media.

Dennis Oppenheim's *Annual Rings* (1968), a series of concentric circles that straddled the Canadian/ American border, was created with snow (one of Oppenheim's recurring motifs was the border zone; margins and thresholds in time and space and concept). Richard Long of course has made concentric circles on the ground one of his chief motifs. Oppenheim has drawn a number of snowworks with a snowmobile: *One Hour Run* (1968) was a continuous track made in the snow in Maine (a snowy version of the cuts and tracks de Maria and Heizer created in the desert with motorcycles). Two tracks, side by side, were carved in the snow between Fort Kent, Maine and Clair, New Brunswick, Canada, in 1968, for *Time Line*, a work which explored the different time zones. Oppenheim's *Negative Board* (1968) was a dark cut in the snow and ice in Maine.

Dennis Oppenheim burnt circles onto grass in *Branded Mountain*. 1969's *Accumulation Cut* was made at Cornell University: a hundred foot long cut made in the ice, running away from a waterfall. Also at Cornell, Oppenheim took the floor outline of gallery 4 of the Andrew Dickson White Museum of Art and drew it into the snow and ice outside (1969). Another *Gallery Transplant* was produced that same year, transplanting the floor plan of a gallery in the Stedelijk Museum in Amsterdam to a snowy hillside in New Jersey.

Dennis Oppenheim's *Whirlpool Eye of Storm* (1973) was an ephemeral piece of land art in the Hans Haacke vein: a jet trail created in the sky by a plane flying above the desert at El Mirage Dry Lake in California. *Directed Seeding* (1969) parodied action painting by harvesting a wheat field. In *Cancelled Crop* (1969) Oppenheim cut a giant 'X' in a field in the Netherlands, and kept the grain, as if he were preventing the material he'd cultivated for his art from becoming the raw material for other (illusionistic) art: 'isolating this grain from further processing becomes like stopping raw pigment from becoming an illusionistic force on canvas'.1 Another 'X' was laid onto the landscape at El Mirage Dry Lake out of asphalt primer (covering an area 610 metres square), entitled *Relocated Burial Ground* (1978). (The 'X' shape, as Lucy Lippard noted, was a favourite motif with male land artists (and Minimal artists): Chris Burden, Richard Long, Ronald Bladen and Robert Smithson also created 'Xs').2

Many of Dennis Oppenheim's artworks are conceptual pieces in the tradition of Sixties Conceptual art. That is, many are works made to be exhibited in galleries, on walls. They comprise, like Long's gallery pieces, photographs, drawings and maps, with Oppenheim's typewritten captions and explanations: *Three Downward Blows* (1977), *Salt Flat* (1969), *Boundary Split* (1968), and *Negative Board* (1968) (maps were central to both Oppenheim's and Long's art). Many of Oppenheim's land artworks also existed as framed photo-text-sketch-map works, and many of Oppenheim's photo, map and textworks recall Long's – or vice versa (they were developing the form around the same time). Oppenheim's map-text-photo pieces include as *Accumulation Cut, Boundary Split, One Hour Run* and *Time Pocket*).

One of Dennis Oppenheim's specialities was to impose humanmade geometries, symbols and ideas onto the landscape: to transpose map contours, for instance, or the rings of a tree trunk onto snow (in *Annual Rings*), or the International Date Line in snow (*Time Pocket*). Robert Smithson remarked that Oppenheim was 'transforming a terrestrial site into a map'.3 Generally, Oppenheim tended to enlarge symbols or ideas or images, and recreate them on a colossal scale in the landscape (similarly, Richard Long drew circles or lines on maps and followed them on the real terrain).

In *Time Pocket* (1968) Dennis Oppenheim 'drew' the International Date Line with a diesel-powered skidder in the snow in Maine. In *Boundary Split* (1968) Oppenheim carved lines perpendicular to the Time Boundary between Canada and the US. *Star Skid* (1977) was Oppenheim's proposal for a series of concrete and glass stars that would look from the air as if they had landed on Earth and skidded to a halt.

In *Salt Flat* (1969) Dennis Oppenheim created a 'salt flat' in New York City, with a thousand pounds of salt (salt flats were a favourite environment for land artists to make work in the US). The rectangle of salt was recreated in the sea in the Bahamas, and in the Salt Lake Desert. In *Directed Harvest* (1969) Oppenheim carved up fields of crops. Oppenheim set off underground explosions in *Three Downward Blows (Knuckle Marks)* in Montana in 1977.

In *Ground Mutations – Shoe Prints* (1969), Dennis Oppenheim created shoe print works over the course of three Winter months (by wearing shoes with a 1/4 inch groove

cut in the sole and heel): 'I was connecting the patterns of thousands of individuals…
My thoughts were filled with marching diagrams'. The use of shoes and prints links to
Richard Long's walks. Like many land artists, Oppenheim produced a maze (in 1970).
But Oppenheim's *Maze* was just a little different: it was the design of a maze used in a
scientific laboratory for rats transposed onto a large field, with cows as the rats, lured
around the maze by the promise of food.

Speaking in 1970, Dennis Oppenheim opined that art was now 'more concerned
with the location of material and with speculation' (i.e., locations or ideas). Now, art
was meant to be visited (location) or 'abstracted from a photograph' (conceptualized).[4]
Oppenheim moved towards a kind of art that would be discovered or visited by the
spectator, rather than 'made' in the old, traditional manner (this was part of the
'dematerialization' of the art object in Sixties art). Oppenheim moved away from the
idea of the special, unique art object, towards found objects, and utilizing existing
sites. Oppenheim was replacing objects with locations.

The *Site Markers* series (1967) comprised posts in locations which were documented with texts, maps and photos. The maps and photos explained where the posts
were situated, so that the location, rather than the object, became the centre of the
piece. As Dennis Oppenheim explained, the *Site Markers* works were intended to be
about the sites themselves, rather than the manipulation or replication of an object:
'beginning with the site-markers started in a sense a journey: art is travel'.[5]

One of Dennis Oppenheim's more Conceptual pieces (*Sound Enclosed Land Area*,
1969) comprised four tape recorders buried in cages in Paris enclosing an area 500
by 800 metres. Each machine played a tape loop which had a voice repeating its
position (North, South, East or West). *Contour Lines Scribed in Swamp Grass* (1968)
transposed contour lines on a map in two different locations (a swamp and a
mountain). The use of aluminium filings poured onto grass in concentric circles
recalled Richard Long's stone circles.

The contours of Dennis Oppenheim's own thumbprints were the basis for *Identity
Stretch* (1970-75), where a truck sprayed white paint on the ground, using the
thumbprint (which Oppenheim had elongated) as a guide, within a grid. In 1970
Oppenheim created a performance piece, entitled *Parallel Stress*, made between a
collapsed concrete pier and a wall at Manhattan and Brooklyn bridges. Oppenheim
stretched his body between the wall and the pier, echoing the New York bridges
nearby. The same body position was recreated at an abandoned sump in Long Island.

Dennis Oppenheim continued his post-Conceptual, Postminimal explorations of the art object into the 1980s and 1990s and beyond. Oppenheim's later sculptures feature a bewildering selection materials (such as electric motors, animal masks, time delay relays, electric blowers, plugs, hot plates, plastic toys, electric drills, buffing tools, mirrors, timers, fireworks, flares, phase shifters, TVs and stereo amps). They were large, multi-media sculptures, post-industrial assemblages, reminiscent of Jean Tinguely, with movement as a key ingredient. *Impersonation Station* (1988), for instance, was a huge outdoor sculpture in steel, glass and concrete, with large rotating elements.

Many aspects of Dennis Oppenheim's art chime with those of Richard Long's: the dematerialization of the art object; the emphasis on location (though Long doesn't make works to be visited outdoors); the emphasis on concepts; enlarging simple geometric patterns and projecting them onto the real landscape; forms such as circles, shoe prints and mazes; borderlands; and the photo, map and text pieces.

ROBERT MORRIS

Robert Morris was one of the most eloquent theorists of Sixties, Minimal and Post-minimal sculpture (along with Donald Judd and Carl Andre). Morris had, like Judd (and many others), begun working in painting, but moved on to sculpture. He was part of the Fluxus school, alongside Yoko Ono, Simone Forte, Walter de Maria and Henry Flynt.[1]

Robert Morris wrote many artistic statements, the most famous probably being the articles published in *Artforum* entitled "Notes on Sculpture". For Morris, one of the things that was new about 1960s sculpture was the object's relationship with the viewer. Before then, Morris argued, the viewer related to the object as something separate; the new æsthetic put the viewer into the same space as the object. 'One is more aware than before that he himself is establishing relationships as he apprehends the object from various positions and under varying conditions of light and spatial context.'[2] This is a crucial concept in Minimal art, which is nearly always viewed in an object-spectator continuous space.

Robert Morris's concept of 'objecthood' was central to his notion of sculpture.

'Morris wants to achieve presence through objecthood, which requires a certain largeness of scale, rather than through size alone' wrote Michael Fried (1967). Just as important as the object itself was the sense of space around it, the spatial context in which it was displayed. Morris wanted to emphasize that 'things are in a space with oneself', rather than the notion that 'one is in a space surrounded by things' (ib., 127). The whole context of the object in its space ('the entire situation') was important to Morris's notion of the new sculpture. One might say the new, 1960s sculpture, like land art, was about the 'thing-in-itself', a notion borrowed from Existentialism, but also about the 'thing in its space'. Although Morris denied being an 'environmental' artist, the context was important to his art.[3] For one critic, Morris's sculpture 'redirect[s] the entire environmental experience'.[4] Referring to Donald Judd's "Specific Objects" article, Morris said he did not separate the two, he did not think that something must be either an object or an environment.[5]

As he moved towards Postminimalism and Process art, Robert Morris advocated doing away with a figure-ground relationship; instead, heterogeneous 'stuff' should be used, an 'accumulation of things or stuff'.[6] In 1975, Morris wrote "Aligned with Nazca" (an article in *Artforum*) which related earthwork art with ancient art such as the Nazca lines (a favourite spot with Long and Fulton). However, such connections with ancient art had already been made by artists and critics of land art (and most eloquently summarized by Lucy Lippard in his excellent study *Overlay: Contemporary Art and the Art of Prehistory*).

Robert Morris's sculptures were often simple polyhedrons, such as cubes, circles, ovals and beams. They were modular and serial. 'Unitary Objects' he termed them, recalling Judd's 'Specific Objects'. They appeared to be 'simple'; as with Judd's sculptures, Morris's did not seem to be hiding anything. Yet just because they appeared 'simple' did not mean that their effects were simple: 'simplicity of shape does not necessarily equate with simplicity of experience' wrote Morris,[7] and Minimal art proved him right. Morris's art was by turns ironic, blank, unambiguously clear and frustratingly amorphous.

Robert Morris's *Battered Cubes* (1965/ 88, Margo Leaven Gallery, Los Angeles) comprised four boxes of painted steel that were set near each other. Each unit had a gently sloping outside face. Morris's Unitary Objects were made in materials such as wood, concrete, wire mesh, aluminium and granite. Morris also fabricated felt works which could not be arranged the same each time, which determinedly refused to be locked into the Minimal æsthetic of straight edges and regularity. The felt was partly haphazard, relying on gravity, but it was also stiff enough to stay roughly where it was put. It was not final, but malleable.

Among Robert Morris's stranger concepts was his 'mobile' mausoleum: in an aluminium tunnel 3 miles long a coffin made from iron and suspended from pulleys would be moved intermittently. An attendant with a magnet would shift the coffin from above. By the entrance to the tube would be swooning maidens in marble, carved in the style of Antonio Canova.8 'If something is still capable of moving, is it dead?' Morris wondered.9

In *Pace and Progress*, Robert Morris made a work by walking a horse back and forth over a piece of grass until a path had been worn. The action of walking the horse rubbed down the grass. One of Morris's largest commissions was the *Grand Rapids Project*, in Michigan (1973-74), consisting of huge ramps leading up to a plateau. Another large Morris sitework was created in King County, Washington (1979), a series of oval terraces recalling Iron Age hillforts.

Robert Morris produced some works of a highly 'ephemeral' nature, such as his 'steam piece' (*Untitled*, 1968-69), which was made out of doors on a patch of grass. How the work turned out was dependent upon physicalities such as humidity, air pressure, wind speed and direction, and temperature. Clouds of steam drifted over the grass. A number of (land) artists have worked with clouds: Chris Drury, James Turrell, Alice Aycock, Dennis Oppenheim, Hans Haacke and Peter Hutchinson.

Peter Hutchinson made a cloud piece (*Dissolving Clouds*, 1970) using Hatha yoga meditation techniques, trying to dissolve clouds through thought. The work consisted of a sequence of 6 photographs of clouds. Another British artist, Rose Finn-Kelcey, has produced a steam work: her *Untitled* (1992, London) comprised water placed on a sheet metal base, with an extractor hood hung above it. In between the two was a cloud of steam, made dramatic by the lighting. Some of Hans Haacke's most intriguing works were with ephemeral natural events such as steam, ice, condensation, fog and flooding. Alice Aycock made a *Cloud Piece* (1971), photographs of cumulus clouds which melted after a few minutes. (Richard Long has a series of photoworks on clouds). In a series of works, Robert Barry allowed inert gas to escape from a gas tank into the air.

Robert Morris's *Box With the Sound of Its Own Making* (1961) was precisely that: inside the box was a tape lasting 3 hours which replayed the sound of the box being constructed. The past history of the box and the processes which went towards its construction became available to the viewer – a new way of displaying self-reflexivity.

Morris's *Box With the Sound of Its Own Making* combined the personal touch valued by modernism (the sound of the carpentry and hand saw); an emphasis on the process of manufacture, important for Sixties art (process, materiality); and the use of technology (the tape recorder), valued by Pop Art. *Box With the Sound of Its Own Making* was also a kind of performance art, and it was also the primary structure of Minimal art, the cube. For Frank Stella, the artist was a privileged participant in the making of art: the 'audience' or viewer is always one step away, was always 'after the fact': '[t]he sensation is one that the artist experiences as the first and only necessary viewer' (1986, 127). Morris's *I-Box* (1962) was a jokey comment on Sixties art, on Constructivism and Minimalism. Morris's *I-Box* featured an I-shaped door which revealed a photo of Robert Morris in the nude, smiling. The Duchampian nature of Morris's *I-Box* recalled those paintings of Jasper Johns' which included bits of human anatomy (an arm, a pair of testicles) in amongst otherwise abstract works. The *I-Box* also recalled Johns' *Target* which put male genitals in a little niche above the target.

Robert Morris's *Untitled* (1968) was a pile of cotton waste and mirrors.[10] The mirrors were seen sticking up in the cotton. An *Untitled* of 1969 comprised of little trees in soil set in rectangular boxes of steel; above the trees hung fluorescent 'grow' lamps. These works interfused the human or 'artificial' (the lamps and mirrors) with the 'natural' or organic (the cotton and trees). A number of Morris's works were what appeared to be piles of concrete and wool, large oblong blocks piled up on top of each other. Morris produced both indoor and outdoor versions of these sprawls of oblong blocks. Sometimes they looked like the stacks of timber at a wood merchant's yard on the outskirts of a town, or the detritus that's thrown into heaps beside sidings at railway stations. Morris's later works (in the Nineties) included wall drawings made blindfolded, and felt works, where an element of randomness and chance dictated how the felt strips would hang.

MICHAEL HEIZER

Land art has proved to be among the most domineering and patriarchal of contemporary art projects.1 Christo works on a gigantic scale, wrapping buildings or stretching curtains across valleys or surrounding islands. Some of the most imposing works of land art are by Michael Heizer. In *Double Negative* (1969-70), 80 miles outside Vegas, his most famous work, he took two chunks out of the Earth.2 Heizer claimed *Double Negative* was 'the smallest piece I've done in relation to the size of the site'.3 But an artwork would have to be immense to compete with the deserts of the South-West States. Heizer gouged out 240,000 tons of earth from the site at Mormon Mesa in Nevada with bulldozers. The 30 foot wide cuts are ramps, going down 50 feet through the cliff of the canyon. The spectator can walk down them. The overall dimensions of *Double Negative* are 1,500 x 42 feet. Heizer is very much concerned with *scale*, as well as other formal characteristics of a work. Heizer said he liked working outside because of the scale; he could work large. He also said that '[m]an will never really create anything large in relation to the world.'4

Michael Heizer's *Double Negative* is a widely celebrated example of land art. Photographs of it have been reproduced in many art history books. *Double Negative* appeals to trendy 1960s notions of Zen Buddhism, Existentialism, negativity and emptiness. The point about *Double Negative* was its sense of symmetry and relationship, the one cut reflecting the other across the Nevada canyon. Some viewers saw Heizer's enterprise as combining the sublime grandeur of Abstract Expressionism with the emblematic forms of Minimalism. American earthworks art rejuvenated the myth of the sublime West.5 Mary Miss was not convinced. When she looked at the work of Michael Heizer or Robert Smithson, 'there's always been an aspect which impedes my relating to it... It's like a mark on the earth' (1981, 6-7). Heizer was one of the artists that Long criticized for being capitalist.

Michael Heizer went on archæological digs as a child with his father. He started out with the ambition to be a painter, which he studied in San Francisco. He made his first earthwork in 1967, and accompanied Smithson on geological expeditions. In 1968, Heizer collaborated with Smithson and Nancy Holt on a Super-8 film, *Mono-Lake*. (Heizer had invited Holt and Smithson to his parents' house at Lake Tahoe). Heizer's motorbike earthwork was entitled *Circular Surface Displacement*; it was made at Mono Lake. 'My work is closely tied up with my own experiences; for instance, my personal associations with dirt are very real. I really like it, I really like to lie in the dirt'.6

Michael Heizer's other works include gouging huge holes in the ground and putting great chunks of rock in them. *Nine Nevada Depressions* (1968) was 5 cuts in the Blackrock desert, each one twelve feet long in an area 50 by 50 feet. *Munich Depression* (1969) was another cut, a line 15 feet deep. *North, East, South, West* was a stainless steel sculpture in downtown Los Angeles. Heizer's *Complex One* (1972) was one of Heizer's major works (his follow-up to *Double Negative*): a huge bunker-like mass of earth built with the aid of two assistants in Nevada. It was 23.5 feet high and 140 feet long. Each end of the hill had a cut-off triangle of reinforced concrete like giant book-ends. Over the work were cantilevered concrete beams. '*Complex One* is a magnificent spectacle. Even its minatory look, suggesting a bunker, seems proper to the site – the edge of the Nevada nuclear proving-ground' commented Robert Hughes.[7] Long has said that he wants 'to do away with nuclear weapons, not make art that can withstand them', a obvious reference to Heizer's kind of art.

There are irreconcilable differences between Richard Long and Heizer, which Long has drawn attention to (including economics, funding, scale, æsthetics). They do share, though, a love of deserts and wildernesses (in particular the South-West United States, where they have both made works). And they both love to work with stones and dirt.

JAMES TURRELL

One of the largest land art projects is James Turrell's *Roden Crater Project,* a series of tunnels and chambers in an extinct volcano near Flagstaff, Arizona. Begun in 1974, it was funded by many different sources and administered by the Skystone Foundation.[1] The first stage of Turrell's on-going *Roden Crater* project involved bulldozing 200,000 cubic yards of earth from the volcano's rim, 'so as to shape the sky'. Turrell planned tunnels, pools and viewing chambers at *Roden Crater.* There were spaces where clouds were projected onto the floor during the day, which at night were related to the procession of equinoxes. Many of the spaces planned at *Roden Crater* were built around celestial events, such as full moons, solstices, equinoxes, the movement of the sun, or just being able to view the stars and some planets. The connection with the heavens was important for Turrell: most of his works have openings to the sky, and the relationship with the sky is the centrepiece of the works. It's important for Turrell, in short, to see the stars.

The *Roden Crater* work was about the relationship between the viewer and the elements, in particular the sky, celestial events, and light. James Turrell said '[m]y art is made for one person. I like the solitary experience. Standing alone at night, perceiving the Roden Crater and the moon and stars, you really feel the vastness of the universe and yourself entering into it'.2 The environment was a volcano, relating to geological time, ancient time. 'The work I do intensifies the experience of light by isolating it and occluding all other light. Each space essentially looks to a different portion of sky and accepts a limited number of events' Turrell explained (1995, 67). Thus, each environment at *Roden Crater* was designed to highlight a particular celestial event. The subject of some spaces was the vaulting of the sky, and the curvature of the Earth. Some were about daily occurrences, such as sunrises and sunsets, or the movement of the stars.

The North section of *Roden Crater* is about looking North, the North Star, the rotation of the Earth, changing light, and includes a *camera obscura* (which projects whatever is overhead onto a white sand floor), and a seat for viewing Polaris. The Eastern space is for witnessing sunrise, and a 'skyspace' overhead. *Bath Space* projects a magnified image of the sky above onto a white sand floor, using a water bath above a large sphere as a lens. The *Sun and Moon Room* was constructed around the furthest South moonset (every 18.61 years), the furthest North sunrise and the Summer solstice.

Tso Kiva is a hemispherical space in the centre of the volcano, for observing light, shadows, shapes and the horizon. The *South Space* is an astronomical observatory and star chart. The *West Space*, as one would expect, is for the sunset, and the 'twilight arch', the projection of the Earth's shadow into the atmosphere at nightfall. Turrell said he didn't want Roden Crater to be 'a mark upon Nature, but to be enfolded in Nature in such a way that light from the Sun, Moon, and stars empowered the spaces' (1995, 66).

James Turrell's creative task as he saw it was not to impose his own vision or æsthetics on the viewer, but to encourage them to see things for themselves, to create the situation in which they could have their own experience. These were æsthetics common in much of land art. As he said in 1987, the goal was not to turn an experience into art, but 'to set up a situation to which I take you and let you see. It becomes your experience... not taking from nature as much as placing you in contact with it'.3 Turrell regarded his art as a 'seeing aid', as showing the observer something that was already there but that they might not have noticed.

Richard Long's æsthetics are not the same as James Turrell's: Long takes experiences he's had on his walks and presents them to the viewer, in his photoworks and text pieces. Rather than Turrell's notion of leading the spectator towards their own experience of a particular place, Long takes what he regards as the significant aspects of the location and presents them, packaged as he wants them (edited, reworked, framed), to the viewer. The biggest difference between Turrell and Long of course is that Turrell invites viewers to visit his structures and experience them firsthand – they can visit *Roden Crater* or the other skyspaces around the world. Indeed, it's the only way to truly understand what Turrell is trying to do. By contrast, the spectator is never invited to see the places of Long's walks. When William Furlong asked Richard Long whether he thought of the sites in the wildernesses where he took photographs as places people should visit, in order to experience the work directly, Long replied 'definitely not': 'he ruled it out as being in no sense relevant to the experience. The photograph was the thing'.4

On the indoor-outdoor debate, which exercised so many land artists, James Turrell said that, instead of bringing nature into the museum, he wanted to 'bring culture to the natural surround as if designing a garden or tending a landscape' (1995, 66). The artwork became something to visit in itself, rather than one of many artworks in a museum to see. The viewer travelled specially to see the artwork, as they visited Heizer's *Double Negative,* or Donald Judd's Marfa site in Texas, or Robert Smithson's earthworks.

James Turrell's primary material was not earth or stone or the usual stuff of land art, but light itself, what he called 'light in the space itself'. Turrell wanted to use light as a thing-in-itself, which had presence, just as the sculptor used a physical object which had presence. He achieved this, he said, by setting limits on the space in which light manifested itself: 'I give light thingness by putting limits on it in a formal manner. I do not create an object, only objectified perception' (1995, 65). Turrell was attempting to create spaces in which viewers could perceive the subject of his works, light itself, and celestial events.

It was important also for James Turrell that the viewer was able to enter those spaces physically, not virtually. Turrell's art was not about creating illusions or artificial scenarios or a record of the artwork. Turrell called it 'non-vicarious seeing': '[t]he subject of my work is your nonvicarious seeing. You are not looking at a record of my seeing' (1995, 64). Thus, Turrell's art was not about recording some event that took place elsewhere, or taking photographs of his art, or writing down what happened, as in some land art. Rather, James Turrell wanted to place the viewer right into the artwork, to have them able to walk into and around the artwork, and to experience the artwork for themselves. (By contrast, the viewer in Long's art is always looking at a record of Long's seeing).

Many of James Turrell's artworks were about working with not just light, but with the sky. The archetypal Turrell space was an enclosed area (a 'skyspace') which had an opening above onto the sky. Turrell spoke of the vaulting of the sky, how the sky looked when the viewer was standing up, or sitting down, or lying down. Some of Turrell's 'skyspaces' – indoor rooms or spaces which are open to the sky above – include *Space That Sees* (1992) in Jerusalem, *Heavy Water* (1992, Poitier) and *Razor* (1991, London). *Razor* was an empty blue room, using a mix of artificial and natural light. James Turrell said he was influenced by painters such as Mark Rothko, Claude Monet and Paul Cézanne, who explored light. *Kielder Skyspace* is open to the public, situated outside the village of Kielder near the Scottish border. Turrell has also constructed pools of water which combine water and light: in these works (at *Roden Crater*, and Poitier, France), the viewer is invited to dive under the water to reach a space beyond which's open to the sky (a curious combination of swimming pool and environmental artwork).

James Turrell emphasized the spiritual aspects of light in his land art. 'I am interested in light because of my interest in our spiritual nature and the things that empower us. My art deals with light itself, the bearer of revelation, but as revelation itself' (1995, 64). The kind of effect that Turrell was after in his light works he compared to staring into a fire, a kind of meditation or daydreaming. Turrell encouraged the viewer to sit or lie down and contemplate light itself, and the effects of light in a particular space. Thus, the spaces that Turrell constructed were furnished with viewing platforms, or benches, or places to lie down and look up at the sky. Situating the spectator in relation to the subject of the artwork (light itself) was Turrell's goal.

As well as drifting off by looking at a fire, James Turrell also often spoke of the experience of flight, of being in a plane and rising into new zones of light, different kinds of light. Turrell also spoke of the curvature of the Earth when seen from a plane (and how, between 600 and 3,000 feet, the Earth seems to curve the wrong way). The Roden volcano was chosen partly because of its relation at that particular place in the

Painted Desert to the curvature of the Earth. The low mound of the volcano and its relation to the curvature of the Earth and the sky above had the right mixture of components Turrell was seeking.

NANCY HOLT

Two of the most important land artists were husband and wife: Nancy Holt married the key earthwork artist, Robert Smithson, in 1963. She worked with him on his non-site projects, including the famous *Spiral Jetty* and *Amarillo Ramp*. Nancy Holt's art, with its large, heavy landscaping gestures, is comparable with male land art (such as her *Dark Star Park,* 1979-84). Holt's art concerned the movements of the heavens. Her sculptures focus the viewer on the motions of the earth, moon, sun and stars. Holt's art is about time, in particular geological time, the relation between time and the Earth. Holt was impressed by the desert when she visited it in the late 1960s with Robert Smithson and Michael Heizer.

> Time is not just a mental concept or a mathematical abstraction in the desert. The rocks in the distance are ageless; they have been deposited in layers over hundreds of thousands of years. Time takes on a physical presence.[1]

Nancy Holt said she was interested in 'conjuring up a sense of time that is longer than the built-in obsolescence we have all around us.' Hence she used long-lasting materials, such as steel and rocks. Using enduring materials does not stem from a sense of vanity, of wanting one's works to last forever, but rather because Holt wanted to create a sense of time that extends beyond the human lifespan.[2]

While working on Robert Smithson's enormous *Amarillo Ramp* after his death in a plane crash, Nancy Holt developed the idea for the gigantic *Sun Tunnels*, 18 foot long pipes that were 9 feet high with many holes punched in the side, to let light in.[3] She searched for a suitable site – a desert floor surrounded by low hills. The site she chose (and bought) was in the Great Basin Desert of Utah. *Sun Tunnels* was finished in 1976, with holes in the side of each concrete tube 7, 8, 9 and 10 inches diameter. The holes corresponded with star constellations (Capricorn, Draco, Columba and Perseus), as with *Hydra's Head*. During the day the sun creates points of light on the bottom of the tunnels that move. The moon also shines through the holes by night. *Sun Tunnels* links together the movements of celestial objects and the viewer on the planet.

Nancy Holt said she had the idea for *Sun Tunnels* while being out in the desert and watching the sun rising and setting. The flat desert area evoked 'a sense of being on this planet, rotating in space, in universal time' (1977). It is a cosmological piece of land art, a form of an observatory, like the Bronze Age stone circles of Europe. 'I wanted to bring the vast space of desert back to human scale' (1977). The astronomical observatory has been an enduring theme in land art. Robert Morris, Michael Archer and Julia Barton have also made viewing sites.

Nancy Holt's *Hydra's Head* (1975) also concerned the relation between the heavens and earth. Next to the Niagra River at Art Park, Lewiston, New York, Holt sank 6 concrete tubes into the soil. Each three foot pipe was filled with water, so they formed circular mirrors flush with the ground. Again, Holt based the position of the concrete pits on a constellation (Hydra). *Hydra's Head* combined the presence and noise of the rushing Niagara River with the reflections of the sky, stars and moon. Holt's concrete pipe sculptures used the prime symbol of change and all things cosmic, the circle. The *Sun Tunnels* were like enormous telescopes or astrolabes, while *Hydra's Head* evoked six fallen stars, the circles of water reflecting the sky and stars.

Nancy Holt's romantic evocations of stellar, cosmological themes in concrete and soil flourished again with *Stone Enclosure: Rock Rings* (1977-78), constructed at Western Washington University, Bellingham. Holt's *Stone Enclosure* directly recalled, even emulated, prehistoric stone circles, in particular Stonehenge (a favourite Richard Long site). Holt used ancient schist rocks, between 200 and 230 million years old (known as brown mountain stone) to construct two concentric rings 10 feet high. In each wall of stone Holt made 4 arches, each 8 feet high, and 12 'portholes'. It was not a large stone ring, in terms of diameter (the outer diameter was 40 feet), but being ten feet high it was much taller than most Bronze Age stone circles (in the UK at least). The arches and holes provided views to the cardinal points, and to NE, SW, EW, NW-SE.

Nancy Holt's *Stone Enclosure* made the connections with ancient astronomy and stone circle building explicit, not slyly implied, as in much of land art. Holt was clear that she was dealing with the ancient astronomical realities of weather, seasons, cycles, stars and time. Another work, *30 Below* (1980), a tower with arches facing the points of the compass, was positioned around the North Star. The still point in the heavens, the Pole Star, was also one of the keys to *Stone Enclosure*, which, Holt said, related to a true North, a dead centre.4 (The North Star was the land artists' favourite star, appearing in works by James Turrell and Charles Ross, among others. It links to the Cosmic Tree, the centre of the world, of shamanism; the tent pole in some cultures is related to the Pole Star and is called the Pillar of the Sky).5

Nancy Holt's *Thirty Below* (1980) was a brick tower built near Lake Placid, with slotlike windows allowing light in. *Annual Ring* (1980-81) was an 'open hemi-dome' of steel bars, 30 feet in diameter and 15 feet high, constructed in Saginaw, Michigan. Again, Holt built the dome to highlight celestial events: the sun at the Summer solstice, the equinoxes, and the North Star. One of Holt's biggest projects was the *Sky Mound*, begun in the late 1980s (the first phase cost $11 million). Situated in amongst Amtrack and NJ Transit train tracks, highways, bridges, the Pulaski Skyway, the New Jersey turnpike, and metropolitan New Jersey and New York, with views over Newark and Manhattan, *Sky Mound* was a converted landfill site which Holt turned into an observatory to mark solstices, equinoxes, and the stars Vega and Sirius. Long hasn't made so many walks or works based on stars or constellations, but he has employed solstices, sunrises, sunsets and eclipses in his art.

ALICE AYCOCK

Alice Aycock's land artworks are much more ambiguous and deliberately prob- lematic than Nancy Holt's or Carl Andre's constructions. Many of Aycock's land sculptures involve underground passages and spaces. In 1972 she fabricated a series of underground spaces in *Low Building Made with Dirt Roof (For Mary)* in Penn- sylvania. The visitor entered the 20 by 12 feet work through a doorway thirty inches high. The work was experienced by crawling through it. Aycock's intention was to evoke an experience of claustrophia, of being in a cellar. Aycock's works have titles such as *The Machine That Makes the World* (1979), *A Theory of Universal Causality* (1983) and *How to Catch and Manufacture Ghosts* (1979) – Aycock is brilliant with titles. Aycock's sculpture explored the rationality of machines and technology, and the irrationality of ghosts and magic.1

Alice Aycock's 1972 *Maze* had direct parallels with the observatories and labyrinths of Robert Morris, Nancy Holt, Julia Barton and Michael Dan Archer. *Maze* consisted of 5 concentric wooden rings, each six feet high, forming a 12-sided labyrinth. Essentially it was a fence maze, the kind that can be seen at zoos, theme parks and country houses around the globe. However, Aycock's *Maze* (in New Kingston, Pennsylvania) was intended to be a labyrinth of the ancient type, a structure in which one is meant to get lost, to psychologically as well as physically descend to different realms. Aycock stated that she wanted 'to create a moment of absolute panic – when the only thing that mattered was to get out.'2 Aycock's intentions, then, were quite different from, say, Nancy Holt's, who wished to infuse a sense of celestial contemplation, or James Turrell's, who wanted to instil awe at light, the sky and revelation.

Alice Aycock hoped that viewers would be confused, even frightened, by her underground passages and mazes. Aycock did not want the viewer to be able to get out of her labyrinth easily (it was partially based on a circular Egyptian labyrinth (designed as a prison), the Zulu *kraal* and the Amerindian stockade. Aycock also cited a circular Greek temple at Epidarus, a 'Place of Sacrifice').

Alice Aycock has spoken of the relations between her art and her own childhood dreams and fears. Her works recreate disturbing moments from her childhood, such as when she was trapped in a revolving barrel at an amusement park. Aycock's works deal with such moments of fear, confusion, strangeness and risk. Aycock also remarked that her structures were inspired by visits to the Pyramids in 1970 and the Greek tombs at Mycenae, and fantasies of being buried alive. The strong autobiographical component coupled with the evocations of disturbing childhood experiences of fear and entrapment, place Aycock's art in a very different zone from most land art, Long's art included.

Alice Aycock's *A Simple Network of Underground Walls and Tunnels* (1975) was made in a corn field at Far Hills, New Jersey. It consisted of six square wells in two rows of three excavated out of a 20 by 50 foot area. Two of the wells had seven foot ladders that enabled the spectator to climb down and explore the dark connecting tunnels. Some of the wells were capped, others were open. The effect was a series of spaces that recalled 'ominous historical precedents, caves, catacombs, dungeons and bee-hive tombs' wrote Roberta Smith.3

Another group of underground spaces was created at the Documenta 6 exhibition in 1977: *Project Entitled "The Beginnings of a Complex.* Alice Aycock's 1974's *Walled-Trench/ Earth Platform/ Center Pit* was a series of three concentric walls built from concrete blocks. A platform of earth was made between the inner two walls: it was possible to jump onto this platform over the outer pit. Only when the spectator is standing on the inner platform does another aspect of *Walled-Trench/ Earth Platform/ Center Pit* become visible: a tunnel which leads into a dark inner chamber.

The fear and fantasy elements in Alice Aycock's land and site work found a new level of ambiguity in her 1976 *Circular Building with Narrow Ledge for Walking*. Again, the spectator was invited to explore this artwork physically (and psychologically). *Circular Building with Narrow Ledge for Walking* was a round structure thirteen feet high. Inside the well were three concentric ledges, only 8 inches wide. The wall went 7 feet into the ground, and was 'no more perilous or threatening than a treacherous cliff' the artist said, reassuringly.4 Again, the spectator was invited to investigate the work in person by climbing a ladder outside the building, then edging her/ his way along the ledges. Indeed, the only way to fully appreciate *Circular Building with Narrow Ledge for Walking,* as with Aycock's other works, was to experience it directly by entering it. Aycock experimented with installing guillotines and motorized blade machines in works such as *The Machine That Makes the World* (1979) and later pieces, such as *A Salutation To the Wonderful Pig of Knowledge (Jelly Fish, Water, Spouter...), There's a Hole In My Bucket, There's a Hole In My Head, There's a Hole In My Dream* (1984).

The structure *From the Series Entitled How To Catch and Manufacture Ghosts* (1980) was a much larger development of the earlier *How to Catch and Manufacture Ghosts.* It was a combination of steel, pipes, spheres and galvanized drums that drew inspiration from early experiments with electricity and magnetism, Marcel Duchamp's *Bachelor Apparatus*, Montgolfier's balloon launch pad, and an oil refinery on the New Jersey turnpike. A later work, *Tree of Life Fantasy: Synopsis of the Book of Questions Concerning the World Order and/ or the Order of Worlds* (1990-92), drew on influences from Renaissance illustrations of people walking into the sky to Heaven, DNA helices, ancient Indian observatories, and Walter Gropius's designs for theatres.

With Alice Aycock's bewildering and unsettling catacombs and mazes one had to move 'one's body through them', a process which also involved descending back through time and memory.5 Confronted with the subterranean passage or the *Circular Building with Narrow Ledge for Walking* it is soon apparent to the spectator that one is not dealing simply with an art object to be admired for its formal characteristics alone. Aycock wanted the spectator to become physically involved in the sculpture; the physical actions of climbing and scrabbling over and through the sculpture trigger an exploration of one's own psychology and memory.6 The physicality of the body as a tool for exploration in Aycock's works soon becomes a pretext or an inspiration for an exploration of personal psychology. Spectators are invited to risk themselves in exploring her works. Her land/ site art offers seductive as well as potentially dangerous spaces. Aycock encouraged the spectator to enter, but then confronted her with a door that opened onto a wall, or a tiny passage to crawl through, or a ledge over a precipice, or a pit to vault over. Such devices go straight back to childhood, to acts of dare and bravado (such as walking along a high brick wall, egged on by other children).

MARY MISS

Early works of Mary Miss's included a 'water-line': at Fountain Creek in Colorado, Miss suspended a double knot of hemp rope 100 feet over a dry riverbed; every twenty feet were lines of rope.1 At War's Island in New York Miss threw 15 foot long wooden stakes into the water which were weighted with rocks. In the middle of a wood in Connecticut in 1974 Miss made *Sunken Pool*: it was a circular wooden structure, 10 feet tall, filled with one foot of water in a galvanized steel interior. *Sunken Pool* was sunken because Miss set it in a hole three feet deep and twenty feet across. As with the large site work of Alice Aycock and Robert Smithson, the spectator was invited to explore Miss's *Sunken Pool* physically, either by stepping into the water, or by climbing up the outer part of the wooden structure and looking over the top. Like Aycock's underground caverns, Miss's *Sunken Pool* was secretive, hiding away in a dense wood, with tall wooden sides. It seemed to speak, like Aycock's works, of childhood memories and half-remembered spaces.

Mary Miss's 1978 *Perimeters/ Pavilion/ Decoys* was created in Roslyn, New York, in a field that was part of the Nassau County Museum's ground. *Perimeters/ Pavilion/ Decoys* comprised three wooden towers, which looked like tree houses with four platforms on stilts, two mounds of earth, and an underground space which was accessed by a ladder. The wooden towers were not for climbing on, but for viewing. The tallest was 18 by 10 by 10 feet. The subterranean atrium was for exploring. It was a pit sixteen feet square with a seven foot hole acting as an entrance; visitors climbed down a ladder to explore the various underground spaces, some with wooden walls, others with soil walls. *Perimeters/ Pavilion/ Decoys* was related to Pueblo Indian structures, Pompeiian and Mexican courtyards, and Mesopotamian brick complexes. The site explored the physical and psychological aspects of 'inside/ outside, above/ below, light/ dark, open/ closed, nature/ artifice'.[2] Miss's works were often large, spreading over a wide area of ground. In Illinois she created a 5-acre scale work.[3]

WALTER DE MARIA

Walter de Maria made a dramatic land art gesture when he cut a 4.5 mile-long 6 foot-wide drawing in the desert in Nevada with a bulldozer (*Las Vegas Piece*, 1969). It was a classic piece of land art in the Michael Heizer or Robert Smithson mode (de Maria embarked on art-making excursions with both). Detractors have spoken of this cut as a 'wound' or 'scar' on the Earth. The ultimate in macho, 'look at me!' male land art must be de Maria's *Vertical Earth Kilometer*. At a cost of $500,000, de Maria sunk a one kilometre brass rod into the planet. Nothing can be seen of it except a two inch brass disc on the ground. The making of de Maria's work is perhaps far more interesting than the artwork itself. It must be the ultimate art statement/ non-statement. *Vertical Earth Kilometer* remains practically invisible. It neatly melds two Sixties æsthetic movements: Conceptualism (wow, what an idea, sticking a kilometre of solid brass into the Earth!) and Minimalism (there's nothing to see of it except… a two-inch brass disc!). A kilometre-long piece of metal stuck into the ground with nothing of it showing except a tiny disc was, in Richard Long's words, '[t]rue capitalist art', an art of excessive cost, and maybe excessive waste (it took 79 days to bore the shaft).[1] Shown at Kassel Documenta 6 in 1977, Walter de Maria's *Vertical Earth Kilometer* irritated British artist Stuart Brisley so much he made *Survival in Alien Circumstances*. This was a hole in the earth dug with his bare hands, which Brisley lived in for 2 weeks, intending to mock de Maria's overblown American earthwork (Long has often commented upon other artists, but I don't think he's undertaken a political protest like Brisley's about de Maria). But then, art has been full of idiotic amounts of money and out-size projects for eons. In 1979 de Maria exhibited *The*

Broken Kilometer: 500 brass rods each two metres long arranged in rows on the floor of a New York gallery.

Walter de Maria started out as a musician rather than, like many land artists, as a painter or sculptor. He played drums with the rock act Velvet Underground, dark angel darlings of the New York music scene. One of de Maria's early ideas (1962) for an earthwork was a mile-long pair of walls that would be 12 feet high and 12 feet apart. De Maria said that 'when you walk between, you can look up and see the sky'.[2] Bruce Nauman would later make corridors one of his chief environmental motifs. After the bulldozer square cut in the Earth, de Maria made a chalk drawing in the desert.

Walter de Maria's *Earth Room* was a gallery full of dark earth made in 1968 in Munich and later in Gotham (*The New York Earth Room*, SoHo Gallery, 1977). This was a vivid (and aromatic) example of bringing the outside inside, one of land art's key projects. The contrasts were immediate, between the flat, clean, white, controlled gallery space and the 1,600 cubic feet of uneven, 'dirty', dark, organic soil. Roberta Smith said it was a 'shock' to see the soil taking up the interior space usually reserved for things such as furniture and people. 'The dirt carried its own absence, was somehow a living substance'.[3] A related work, *5 Continents Sculpture* (1987-88), comprised white rocks filling an area 42 by 77 feet in a Stuttgart gallery. De Maria's *Bed of Spikes* (1969) was called 'a piece of Dadaist Sadism' by Harold Rosenberg.[4] *Bed of Spikes*, an installation at the Dwan Gallery, comprised 153 metal spikes set in five planks on the floor. Interestingly, spectators were asked to sign a release form that exempted the gallery for being responsible for any accidents on viewing the installation. *Bed of Spikes* looked forward to *Lightning Field*.

Critic Kenneth Baker called Walter de Maria's most famous work, the *Lightning Field,* the 'grandest Minimal work of the 1970s' and 'the closest thing to a masterpiece to come out of Minimalism'.[5] Walter de Maria's first *Lightning Field* was sited 40 miles from Flagstaff in Arizona, consisting of 2 inch diameter steel poles, 18 feet tall, 30 feet apart, in five rows of seven. The second, larger *Lightning Field* is a grid of 400 stainless steel poles, each about 20 feet high, 16 along the width, 25 along the length, each about 20 feet high, set in the New Mexico desert.[6] The site was chosen for its flatness, isolation and lightning activity. Most lightning activity occurs during May-September; there are about 60 days when thunder and lightning can be seen from *Lightning Field*.[7] *Lightning Field* is about a mile by a kilometre in size. The poles were set in concrete, one foot below ground, able to withstand winds of 110 mph. The poles in *Lightning Field* stand alone, about 220 feet apart. Nothing remains on the ground of the work needed to set them there. The tips of the poles define a plane in space parallel to sea level: the length of each pole varies according to the contours of the landscape.

The *Lightning Field* is an exact, mathematically-precise human site laid onto nature, where the poles are tiny mirrors which mark out and calibrate the landscape. The site looks like a scientific or industrial project – like a radio telescope site, say, or a military communications centre. *Lightning Field* is spectacular, with masculine and phallic connotations (lightning is related in symbolism to male creativity, sperm, fire, power and shamanism).

Lightning Field is ambiguously associated with the Dia Art Foundation, which financed its construction. The site recalls technological experiments, while the poles themselves evoke Brancusi's *Birds in Space*, and his *Endless Column*.8 de Maria's *Lightning Field* attracts lightning, and a storm is one of the most awe-inspiring phenomena in the natural world.9 And during the peak season for great storms in the area, sometimes 'two or three a week cross this field of poles'.10 Joseph Beuys produced a startling piece entitled *Lightning* (1982-85, Tate, London) a gigantic chunk of bronze, narrow at the top, splaying out towards the bottom, as if he was trying to make manifest the bolt of energy leaping down to the Earth. Ronald Bladen's lightning bolt sculpture *Black Lightning* was installed in central Seattle. Justin Holland too used lightning in artworks; he collaborated with Westinghouse Electric, making human-made lightning, and 'seeded' clouds to produce storms.11

SOME OTHER AMERICAN LAND ARTISTS

Some other American land artists include James Pierce, who created a series of earthworks at Pratt Farm in central Maine in the 1970s: there was a triangular turf maze; a small earth *Observatory*; a *Serpent* made from large rocks; a *Stone Ship*; a *Burial Mound*; a stone *Altar* (in the shape of male genitals); and various figures built out of grass and soil: *Earthwoman* and *Suntreeman*. Pierce's *Earthwoman* (1976-77) was a recumbent female shape, with prominent buttocks, evoking the erotic gardens of the 18th century (which featured earth art and monuments in the form of eroticized figures), and the links between prehistoric earth mounds, fertility and femininity.

Herbert Bayer created earthworks which directly evoked prehistoric structures: Bayer's *Earth Mound* (1955) in Aspen, Colorado, contained the familiar motifs of ancient religions and cultures: a circular rampart enclosing a small mound; a standing stone and a hollow were placed beside the mound. In Kent, Washington (a suburb of Seattle), Bayer built a series of earthworks (*Mill Creek Canyon Earthworks*, 1979-82) which featured circular ramparts, circular moats, mounds surmounted by walkways, and circular ramparts split by a path. At a quarry in upstate New York William Bennett fashioned a *Wedge (Stone Boat)* (1976), an 80 foot long smooth-sided channel in the limestone.

Donna Dennis took the vernacular architecture of New York City as her starting-point in her 1970s works: *Tunnel Tower* was based on the entrance building to the Holland Tunnel. Later, nostalgic works, such as *Deep Station* (1981-85), recreated the shadowy recesses of subway stations. Christine Oatman lit a fire on a frozen lake in the centre of a circle of tall icicles in *Icicle Circle and Fire* (1973). Elyn Zimmerman constructed large-scale ecological land art, such as her *Keystone Island* (1989), a 50-foot wide artificial island built on a lagoon in a mangrove swamp. Patricia Johanson's best known work is probably the large water park she fashioned in Dallas, Texas, between 1981 and 1986. *Fair Park Lagoon* comprised a series of interlacing walkways above the pool in an 'organic', Gaudiesque manner, and cost over $2 million.

Gordon Matta-Clark transformed buildings by knocking enormous holes in them (*Conical Intersect,* 1975), or cutting a house in New Jersey in half (*Splitting,* 1974). But these were not sculpted spaces or physical gestures so much as Conceptual reorganizations of a structure. It's easy to discern the influence of Matta-Clark's interventions in houses and buildings (which he called 'unbuilding') on Andy Goldsworthy's holes and Rachel Whiteread's works.

Gordon Matta-Clark bought up pieces of land in the borough of Queens (in 1973), in another Conceptual piece; none of them were big enough for housing or for anything else (some were only 2 by 3 feet). *Reality Positions, Fake Estates* explored the notion of land ownership. Matta-Clark explained:

One or two of the prize ones were a foot strip down somebody's driveway and a square foot of sidewalk. And the others were kerbstone and gutterspace. What I basically wanted to do was to designate spaces that wouldn't be seen and certainly not occupied. Buying them was my own take on the strangeness of existing property demarcation lines. Property is so all-pervasive.[1]

Ana Mendieta (who was married to Carl Andre) covered herself in mud (while nude, of course) and stood against a tree (for *The Tree of Life* series, 1977, made in Old Man's Creek, Iowa), a combination of Goddess art, feminist art, performance art and environmental art. In *The Tree of Life* series, Mendieta left the outline of her body in leaves on a tree trunk (most of Mendieta's art was based around her body and its shape and form). Some of Mendieta's performance works include: the *Silueta* series (1979), where Mendieta imprinted her body in the snow in Amana, Iowa, and in mud on a riverbank, or set the form on fire in the earth, or made a silhouette from flowers. Mendieta's art has an undisguised ideological, spiritual and ecological agenda. Unlike much of land art; some of Mendieta's works are explicit performance explorations of rapes, and Mendieta was also exploring her Cuban and Latin American heritage.

In some pieces Mendieta remodelled the entrance of a cave and a ravine into her Goddess shape. She also buried herself under turf – a literal Earth-Goddess mound, and had herself photographed in an ancient Mexican stone grave.[2] Mendieta also lit fires in her sculptures (such as *Volcano*, 1979), like Chris Drury and David Nash, and lit candles and fireworks in the shape of a woman. Teresa Murak covered her naked body with cress seeds, while lying in a bath (*Seed*, 1989). 'They sprout, swell and begin after a few hours to grow right on my body' she said.[3]

Charles Ross constructed a large observatory, *Star Axis* (1989), which recalled the celestial viewing spaces of Turrell, Holt and Morris. It was designed for viewing the North Star. Charles Simonds made an *Abandoned Observatory* (1976), in model form. Juan Geuer has also worked with the sky: he mounted four pairs of large mirrors in the National Gallery of Canada in order to reflect the sky in the glass cupola above (*Karonhia*, 1989).

Douglas Hollis constructed 'sound gardens' – a series of wind organ pipes mounted on towers beside the shore in Seattle, WA (1980). Hollis's *Field of Vision* (1980) comprised 900 wind vanes at Lake Placid, NY, to 'explore the choreography between windscape and landscape'.[4] In the Seventies Hollis experimented with sending up kites that emitted sound (*Sky Soundings*, 1975).

CHRISTO

Christo is one of the most famous land artists – perhaps the most well-known in contemporary art today. Certainly no other land artist has his international profile. (Christo creates art with his wife, Jeanne-Claude, so his art is often referred to as by the Christos). The Christos make huge, very public gestures: tarpaulin and plastic shrouded buildings, the wrapped Pont Neuf and Reichstag, and curtains hanging across Colorado valleys. Their art is not 'invisible' like Walter de Maria's kilometre-long brass rod which only reveals a brass disc on the ground, or created in a secluded vale.

Born in 1935, in Bulgaria, Christo (Christo Javacheff) attended the Fine Arts Academy in Sofia. One of his early activities as a student involved tidying up the Orient Express route through Bulgaria by covering old farm machinery and haystacks with tarpaulin. At Prague Christo studied set design, and one of his mid-1960s works in New York was making replicas of shopfronts, like a stage set, but the windows were covered with cloth or paper. In his early works, Christo wrapped up items such as books, bottles, tins and boxes. Other assemblages or *empaquetages* (assemblages as packages) included nude models, cars, chairs and motorbikes.

Christo's most famous assemblage, though, was on a larger scale, the *Wall of Oil Barrels – Iron Curtain* (1962). This was a pile of barrels stacked across and blocking one of Paris's oldest streets, Rue Visconti. *Wall of Oil Barrels – Iron Curtain* parodied the Berlin Wall, which had recently been constructed. The sculpture annoyed the locals, and the Christos' large-scale works have been upsetting neighbours (and bureaucrats and politicians) ever since.

The Christos' first large-scale wrapping was to cover the Museum of Contemporary Art in Chicago with 10,000 ft^2 of brown tarpaulin. The Christos' wrapping of the museum made it the focus of attention in the neighbourhood – some people hadn't realized the museum was there until it had been wrapped. The museum's director reckoned the Christos had parodied 'all the associations a museum evokes: a mausoleum, a repository for precious contents, an intent to wrap up all of art history'.[1] Inside the museum was the *Wrapped Floor*, consisting of 2,000 square feet of rented drop cloths.

In 1969 the Christos wrapped a mile-long section of the Australian coastline. The use of open weave cloth (1 million square feet) meant that wildlife would not be affected. *Wrapped Coast*, at Little Bay near Sydney, stayed up for 4 weeks. It was a dramatic land art gesture, difficult to ignore.

Valley Curtain (1972), at Rifle Pass in Colorado, did not last so long. It was blown down. The huge bright orange curtain hung across the valley, providing a passageway as well as a visual block to what was beyond.

> When I was doing Valley Curtain everybody knew that this is a huge curtain crossing a valley. Now everybody knew what it is that is behind the valley. The thing that is behind is not so important...only that motion, the passing through.2

The use of orange, as with the pink in *Surrounded Islands*, gave *Valley Curtain* a new æsthetic, more attuned to Matisse and Monet, quite different from the dull brown tarpaulin of the *Wrapped Museum*.

Many of the Christos' large-scale wrappings took place next to water: *Running Fence* plunged into the sea; *Wrapped Coast* was submerged by the tides; *Surrounded Islands* floated on the ocean; *Pont-Neuf* stretched over the Seine. *Surrounded Islands* (1980-83) was one of the Christos' largest works. Not a wrapping this time, but still involving masses of fabric (6 million square feet of it). With a budget of $3.5 million, 4 engineers, 2 ornithologists, a marine biologist, 2 attorneys and 430 helpers, the Christos surrounded 11 little islands for 2 weeks in May, 1983. The choice of brilliant pink meant the enclosed islands stood out vividly against the green sea at Biscayne Bay in Florida. The pink-enclosed islands looked like flowers floating on the sea, recalling the Japanese Buddhist ceremony of setting flowers afloat. Or, more in tune with Western art history, evoking Claude Monet's waterlilies.

Running Fence (1972-76) consisted of 2,050 18 foot panels of white nylon attached to steel poles, running across Marin and Sonoma counties in California. As with the Christos' other mammoth projects, there was much opposition to *Running Fence*. A committee designed to 'stop Running Fence' brought the subject to the Superior Court of the State of California 3 times. The subsequent report on the environmental impact of the *Running Fence* project found that there were no endangered species in the region, except for the Brown Pelican, and virtually no wildlife would be affected by it. *Running Fence* went ahead, and remained there for two weeks.3 When it was taken down, nothing remained of it in the area: the holes were filled in, and bare parts of soil were reseeded. As with other Christos' projects, when it was taken away some locals were dismayed: the work had helped them realize the beauty of the area.

Christo said his art was

about displacement. Basically even today I am a displaced person. And this is why I make art that does not last. Of course, it will stay for ever in the minds of people.4

Christo here espouses the fundamental Romanticism in land art: that it will live on in the memories of people. The Christos' large-scale projects – *Running Fence, Surrounded Islands, Wrapped Coast* – were spectacular works, part of the land art tradition which moved towards the sublime in landscape art (which has affinities with the Abstract Expressionism of Mark Rothko, Barnett Newman and Robert Motherwell). The ocean end of *Running Fence* was particularly impressive: at Bodega Bay the *Fence* extended gracefully into the Pacific, 558 feet, descending from a height of 18 feet on land to 2 feet at the section which was anchored to the bottom of the sea. The *Umbrellas* stretched for 12 miles in Japan and 18 miles in California.

The Christos' large-scale works are expensive: *Running Fence* cost over $3 million, *Surrounded Islands* cost $3.5 million, and *The Umbrellas* in Japan and California cost $26 million. Denigrators of the Christos' work have noted the expense of the projects, but Christo says they pay for them from their own funds, by selling photos, drawings, lithographs, collages, models and plans and other works, and by collaborating with industry. But the Christos were keen to remind viewers that their sculptures were not funded by sponsors.

HANS HAACKE

The German artist Hans Haacke has produced some of the most intriguing land artworks (although Haacke is more usually linked with Arte Povera, Conceptual and Process art, than land art). Many of Haacke's early works explored natural or organic systems. Later, Haacke moved on to social, economic and political systems (what Haacke called 'real-time systems'). Haacke's 1965 artistic statements included: 'make something that lives in time and makes the "spectator" experience time... articulate something natural'.1 One of Haacke's tenets was 'the simpler the better'.

Grass Grows (1966 and 1969) was a mound of soil with grass growing out of it. Hans Haacke later fashioned a row of beans growing along string suspended at an angle, in soil mounted on glass on the gallery floor (*Directed Growth*, 1972), and in tropical plants growing on a circular area of soil, *Rye in the Tropics* (1972). *Condensation Cube* (1963-65) was a Plexiglas cube (a metre on each side) with water inside which condensed on the clear sides of the box, an exploration of process. 'It is changing freely, bound only by statistical limits' remarked Haacke of his 'Weather Box'.

In *Sky Line* (1967) Hans Haacke released white helium balloons over Central Park. Hans Haacke commented that

> in spite of my environmental and monumental thinking I am still fascinated by the nearly magic, self-contained quality of objects. My water levels, waves and condensation boxes are unthinkable without this physical separation from their surroundings.[2]

Many of Hans Haacke's most compelling artworks were made to explore the ephemeral qualities of ice, snow, fog, steam, smoke and water. *Fog, Flooding, Erosion* (1969) employed a sprinkler system to turn a lawn in Seattle (WA) into mud. *Fog Dripping From or Freezing On Exposed Surfaces* (Boston, 1971) and *Spray of Ithaca: Falls Freezing and Melting On Rope* (1969) explored water and fog freezing on waterfalls and trees.

One of Hans Haacke's air and wind constructions comprised a fan blowing a seven by seven foot chiffon sail hung parallel to the gallery floor. Another air sculpture was a balloon balanced above an air jet (a favourite with science and natural history museums). He had proposals for monumental-sized windmills and sails, all naturally powered by the winds. Haacke preferred to use unmechanical sources of energy.

In *Rhine-Water Purification Plant* (1972), the process of purifying polluted river water was examined. Via a series of acrylic containers, filters, hoses and pools, the spectator could follow the process of the purification of the contaminated Krefeld sewage water. The final destination of the water flow was a square pool containing goldfish. *Rhine-Water Purification Plant* recalled the 3-D displays in science and natural history museums that explained the processes of nature and science.

In Hans Haacke's piece *Ten Turtles Set Free* (1970), the animals were released in a forest near St Paul-de-Vence (France), a symbolic gesture about humanity's relationship with the natural world and its inhabitants. Haacke photographed seagulls feeding on bread scattered on a lake in *Live Airborne System* (1965/ 68).

Hans Haacke later considered economic systems in works such as *Shapolsky et al, Manhattan Real Estate Holdings, a Real-Time Social System* (1971). For the *Inform-*

ation show at Gotham's MOMA (in 1971), Haacke exhibited a poll about Governor Rockerfeller running for election, inviting visitors to vote. Haacke took on cultural institutions such as museums, landlords, and politicians such as President Reagan and British PM Margaret Thatcher. On a few occasions Haacke's proposals were negated by the authorities of the Guggenheim, Wallraf-Richartz and Metropolitan museums, with works and shows being cancelled as a result. Other artists (such as Daniel Buren) protested in support of Haacke. Richard Long has rarely addressed the sorts of economic, political or social issues tackled by Haacke.

DAVID NASH

One of the most intriguing and sensual of land artists working in the British Isles is David Nash (born in the same year as Richard Long, 1945), with whom Andy Goldsworthy worked early in his career. David Nash's æsthetics chime with those of Long, Goldsworthy and Nicholas Pope among British artists.1 Critic Hugh Adams saw David Nash as a kind of 'fixed abode Richard Long', working from one place (North Wales), while Long travels the globe, regarding the whole world as his studio, as material for making art. Hugh Adams wrote:

> Nash is Long in microcosm: the sensibility is the same but, whereas Long travels the world, making, marking, and recording, in distant places, Nash is more sedentary, and content to do the same thing where he has made his home.2

David Nash built a number of 'stoves' and 'hearths', out of natural materials – snow, slate, wood. These structures burn away – fire as 'living' sculpture (like Chris Drury's cairns or Ana Mendieta's *Volcano*). *Snow Stove,* made in Japan in 1982, burnt beautifully – a snow pyramid, fusing those two eternal mysteries – fire and snow, fire and ice. Nash also made a *Wood Stove* (1979), a *Slate Stove* (1981) and also a *Sea Hearth.*3 Anyone who's lit a fire right next to the ocean will know what a magical experience it can be, and Nash's *Sea Hearth* is certainly rich in magic. Nash set his fire built of large stones inches from the waves, to accentuate the contrast between the two elements. Nash's stoves and hearths are thick with alchemical and elemental allusions: they are a poetry of elements, the basic elements out of which everything is made. (William Jackson Maxwell has made burnt tree stumps, like Nash).4

David Nash loves working with wood (and love isn't too strong a word here): his *Wooden Boulder* (1978) was exactly that – a huge, near-spherical chunk of oak. Nash tipped the boulder into a stream near his studio at Blaenau Ffestiniog, North Wales. His idea was for the sculpture to make its way to the ocean. Instead, it stayed put in a pool, and now it interacts continually with the environment (Nash later recorded that the boulder moved about seven times in 22 years, eventually reached an estuary, and looked 'more and more like a stone').

Those delicious Welsh streams, with their chilly, clear water, mossy boulders and constant noise, are one of the most poetic environments Britain possesses. Ramblers are aware of streams and rivers, not only because they have to cross them somehow, but also because they are crucial sources of drinking water. David Nash's art, like Smithson's and Long's, is respectful of water and the landscape. His art is gentle and based firmly in a reverence for nature.

In the Forest of Dean, David Nash made a circular mound of larch poles charred at the end. He spent two weeks charring nine hundred pieces of wood, which were then stuck together in a 'wide circular hole in the ground'.5 Nash wanted to have his *Black Dome* as a mound of nothing but charcoal, but realized it would not last long enough for the public to see it. He wanted to use charcoal because it was a part of the industry of the forest. It was important too that Nash's large sculpture would decay away and become integrated into the forest again. Nash envisaged his *Black Dome* 'gradually reintegrating with its environment, rotting down gradually – fungus, leaf-mould, plants adding to its process of 'return'' (ib., 66).

David Nash constructs fascinating pieces, works which are instantly appealing, partly because of the materials, the natural materials which urban-based cultures are so thirsty for: wood, stone, water, fire. These are the elements not found in cities. Well, one sees trees, stones, skies and wood in cities, but it's not the same somehow: land artists reawaken the viewer, making them aware, again, of nature, of natural materials. One of Herman de Vries's aims was to 'make visible that which people don't see anymore', to draw attention to things happening in the 'primary reality' (nature) that people have forgotten about.6

It's refreshing, after being encased in grey concrete and a maze of straight lines in the city, to imbibe these works of artists such as Long, Nash, Drury and Nicholas Pope. For instance, David Nash's marvellous *Fletched Over Ash Dome*.7 This is a circular group of trees in Wales which Nash planted in 1977: it is a 'living' sculpture, which, over thirty years, will be trained into a dome. It will be not only a circle of trees, but a dome of trees. Nash wrote:

> A circle of young ash trees fletched and woven into a thirty foot dome fletched three times at ten year intervals then left alone. A silver sculpture in winter, a green canopy space in summer, a volcano of growing energy. (1978)

While Robert Morris and Hans Haacke used steam, and Nancy Holt assembled stone, David Nash's deployment of living trees (such as in his *Fire Engine Sweep*, planted in 1980) created, a new form of sculpture, a sculpture which is alive, which changes over decades, rather than seconds. Morris's and Haacke's steam and fog works last mere moments, while Nash's, Mendieta's, Winsor's and Drury's fires last a few hours. *Fletched Over Ash Trees*, though, is a sculpture that will endure for decades, and will change year in year out. Nash's trees will grow and develop for a long time before they decay, which will make them a particularly exciting type of sculpture. Nash spoke of 'observing trees: how they enter and survive in the particular space of their location. Their form being the balance of continual change in the elements and the seasons'.[8]

Some more of David Nash's works include: *Vessel and Volume II* (1988, General Mills), a hollow boat form in black, next to a similarly-shaped boat, as if one could fit inside the other. *Serpentine Vessels* were also boat shapes (1989, collection: the artist), but their prows and sterns were tilted up, away from the floor. These were large objects, basically two slabs of wood fixed together. *Three Longboats* (1986, in oak) were hollow boat-forms, set on pieces of wood (Chris Drury has also made groups of boat forms). These are not boats that will float; they are bottomless. *Descending Vessel* (1988, collection: the artist) was another boat-form, again hollow, set upright on top of a wooden plinth-wall, more like a tower. The end of the vessel was slid into a crack in the top of the tower.

Quite a few of David Nash's sculptures consisted of two objects seen in tandem, one above the other. Like *Descending Vessel, Comet Ball* (1989, Trans Art, Cologne) was one object above the other – a tall curving piece of wood was stuck into a near-spherical globe of wood. Like *Descending Vessel, Comet Ball* recalled Constantin Brancusi – *Descending Vessel* was particularly reminiscent of *Birds in Space*. To emphasize the inspiration for the 1990 *Comet Ball*, Nash built a fire under it. Nash has also made waterfalls and streams from hollowed-out tree trunks, entitled *Wooden*

Waterways (1978, Grizedale, and 1982, Japan), in which water from a stream was diverted along the trunks of a fallen oak tree, an ash, a sycamore, and onto more troughs.

Other vertical or tower-like works include *Oak Spoon* (1988, collection: the artist), and *Red Throne* (1989, collection: the artist). *Started Beech* (1989, collection: Eric Franck, Switzerland) was a tree trunk split into a series of thin planks, still connected at one end to the end of the beech tree trunk. The ends of the planks fanned outward slightly, creating the 'skirt effect'. At Grizedale David Nash's *Horned Tripod* (1977) was a tall tripod made from straight trees, a large-scale work. *Crack and Warp Column* (1989, collection: the artist) was a tower made from thin squares of wood, piled on top of each other. Nash's *Crack and Warp Column* was irregular; each slab of wood bends slightly. In *Crack and Warp Column,* the warped slabs were more severely bent, but the size and shape of each slab was still controlled. The now-destroyed column of 1970 was one of the most Brancusi-like of Nash's sculptures: it was fashioned in sections, one tapering into the next. The tall, vertical Nash sculptures recall not only Brancusi's *Endless Column* but also Barnett Newman's *Broken Obelisk* and notions of growing upwards, skywards, verticality, and are related to Nash's idea of a tree as a fountain of energy.

David Nash has produced giant-size versions of common, domestic forms (a regular device in contemporary sculpture), such as *Ancient Table, Table with Cubes, Oak Spoon, Branch Chair* and *Bowl and Platter*. *Ancient Table* (1983, collection: Capel Rhiw), which has huge weathered trunks for the table's legs; *Table with Cubes* (1971, Cardiff) has a variety of sizes of cubes on it; *Elm Bowl (*1988, collection: the artist) was a large, thin bowl, irregular, the outside smooth, the inside showing the marks of a chisel on top of a chunky wooden pedestal; *Bowl and Platter* (1988, collection: the artist) set the oversize objects on a large, thick table. Other large-scale versions of everyday objects included *Big Ladder* (1984, Japan), *Branch Chair* (1976) and *Standing Frame* (1987, Walker Arts Center).

David Nash took a common, everyday, domestic form, put it into wood, roughed up the outlines and textures, and enlarged the forms. Some of his most intriguing works were spindly, expanded versions of regular, household items. *Branch Chair*, for example, was a recognisable chair, but with twigs and branches poking out of it; *Branch Cube* (1982, private collection) was recognisably a cube, but with twigs and branches sprouting out of it, making it a much larger sculpture than it would be if it was just a cube.

Some of David Nash's sculptures were slotted together, extended forms, one form expanding outwards to produce a series of forms, as in *Extended Cube* (1986, collection: the artist), where the cube spilled out over the floor, in ever-decreasing sizes. *Slot Table* (1979, collection: the artist) was a tree trunk with a large slot cut in it, and displaced slightly. *Extended Length* (1980, Rijksmuseum Kroller Muller) was a large oblong which was dissected, so that the inner part slides out, showing its internal perspectives. *Nature to Nature* (1987, Walker Arts Center) took three simple forms – globe, cube and pyramid – and made them out of solid wood. Nash put the three solids together in a row and built a fire under them. The blackened solids were shown in a gallery, with charcoal drawings of them on the wall behind.

In *Sod Swap* (1983), David Nash took sods of grass from Caen-y-Coed in North Wales to Kensington Gardens (and vice versa), planting the grass in a circle. Later works of Nash's included charred wooden sculptures based on the yew hedge 'twmps' which Nash had seen at Powis Castle, one of the great gardens of Cymru (such as *Beak Twmp*, 2000). Nash's show at the Tate Gallery in St Ives (Cornwall) in 2004 was one of the most refreshing land art shows for some time in the UK.

ANDY GOLDSWORTHY

Andrew Charles Goldsworthy was born in Sale Moor, Cheshire, in 1956. As a young art student, Andy Goldsworthy spent much of his time outside college, working on the beaches at Morecambe and Heysham. Goldsworthy preferred to learn by direct experience, finding out about leaves, mud, stone, rivers and tides by living amongst them. Goldsworthy would go into college for one or two days a week, for the art history classes. This was not enough for the lecturers, who suggested that he spend more time in college, including attending life drawing classes. Little did Goldsworthy's lecturers know – that their errant student, who spent hours clambering around the muddy reaches of Heysham Head and Morecambe Bay instead of dutifully attending college classes, would one day become an artist of international renown, with exhibitions and commissions around the world. At the time (*circa* late-1970s), Goldsworthy must have seemed just another crazy art student, pursuing his own wacky ideas

(British art schools contain plenty of kooky folk – not all of them students). Hearing of his beach-mud-stone-tide antics, Goldsworthy's tutors must have sighed heavily and put another stroke through the 'absent' column on his attendance record. Amazing to think that this artist-in-the-making would one day be exhibiting at the one of the most prestigious museums in the world (the British Museum), designing Royal Mail stamps, and making a Holocaust memorial in New York. For Goldsworthy, the time spent working at Grove House Farm and the Lancashire beaches was as critical as his art education: '[t]he energy and unpredictability of art outside the studio and gallery were important to me. Going outside art college felt so much more raw, and that's what interested me' (*Time*, 180).

'My art', Andy Goldsworthy noted in *Time*, 'is rooted in the British landscape, and this is the source to which I must return' (*Time*, 7). In 1986 Goldsworthy moved from Yorkshire and Cumbria, where he'd spent most of his life, to Penpont in Dumfriesshire, where he has remained ever since. This's Goldsworthy Central, the HQ where Goldsworthy produces most of his work. A nearby 2 1/2 acre piece of land (dubbed Stone Wood by the artist) was leased from the Bucclech estate in the late 1980s. The River Scaur, one of Goldsworthy's most beloved spots, is on one side. Goldsworthy's first *Wall,* and numerous other works, were made at Stone Wood.

Many of Andy Goldsworthy's site-specific works and commissions have been in (and about) the North of Britain: the giant maze and *Lambton Earthwork* (at County Durham, 1988-89), the Grizedale Forest site works (1984 onwards), residencies at Yorkshire Sculpture Park (1987-88), the Lake District National Park (1988), and St Louis Arts Festival (1986), *Sheepfolds* (1996-) and so on. Large Northern commissions included *Sidewinder* (1985) and *Seven Spires* (1984), *The Wall That Went For a Walk* (1991) at Grizedale, Cumbria, *Lambton Earthwork* and *Maze* in Durham (1988), *Stone Gathering* at Northumberland (1993) and *Enclosure* in Edinburgh (1990).

It's Andy Goldsworthy's contemporary, though, Anthony Gormley, who has made the sculpture in Northern Britain that has bedded itself in the public consciousness since the late Nineties: the *Angel of the North, a* 65 foot tall steel figure at Gateshead (1998). For many, especially those who drive past *Angel of the North* regularly, Gormley will be a name known to them via this hard-to-miss work, while Richard Long will still be largely unknown. It's ironic, because Long has been on the international art scene much longer than Gormley. However, Long has chosen to accept the kind of commission Gormley undertook for *Angel of the North* (what would he make? A giant stone circle or line perhaps?).

Andy Goldsworthy has created land art in Grise Fiord, the North Pole, in Japan, upstate New York, California, Castres, Digne, La Rochelle and Sidobre in France, the Australian outback, and in Haarlem, Holland. Goldsworthy has wound up in many of the same spots as Richard Long: Japan, California, and Australia, all favourite countries among international land artists, and has also exhibited in some of the same museums.

The first work that Andy Goldsworthy sold was a bunch of photographs to the Arts Council (via Andrew Causey at North West Arts). He has had one-man shows in France, Japan, Holland, the US and the UK, and participated in groups shows in Italy, Germany, and the US. A major retrospective, *Hand To Earth: Andy Goldsworthy: Sculpture: 1976-1990*, was held at the Henry Moore Centre for the Study of Sculpture, Leeds City Art Gallery: the show also travelled to the Royal Botanic Gardens in Edinburgh, Stedelijke Musea, Gouda and Centre Regional d'Art Contemporain Midi-Pyrénées in Toulouse. This show also produced the most useful and detailed publication to date on Goldsworthy's art (*Hand To Earth*, later reprinted, with 2000's *Time* as a handy update).

In the 1990s, Andy Goldsworthy's art began to rise in popularity: the glossy coffee table book *Stone* became a bestseller (bear in mind it was priced at £35 or about 55 bucks). In 1994 Goldsworthy took over some West End galleries with a large one-man show, *Stone* (this included *Herd of Arches*, also made for the Hathill Sculpture Foundation at Goodwood in Sussex, and ultimately finding a permanent home in Cornwall).[1] In 1995 he took part in an intriguing group show, *Time Machine: Ancient Egypt and Contemporary Art,* at the British Museum in London and Museo Egizio, Turin, creating sculptures, along with Richard Deacon, Peter Randall-Page and others, in amongst the monumental statuary of the famous Egyptian Hall. Also in 1995, Goldsworthy designed a set of Royal Mail stamps (and again in 2003). As well as commissions, installations, TV and radio programmes, and books, Goldsworthy has also produced (like Long) limited edition prints (the pictures of cairns were made with Eyestorm, in editions of 500, priced at $720 each).

Other Andy Goldsworthy shows and projects of the 1990s and after included a clay installation (a hole) in La-La Land (at the Getty Center for the Arts, 1997; later destroyed by a burst pipe); 'ice houses' and stick lines made in Alaska (1995); a slate cone and chamber for British Airways at their West Drayton HQ in 1998; cairns and 'refuges' at Digne les Bains in 1998; new groups of work at the National Museum of Scotland in Edinburgh (1998); the new *Wall* at Storm King (1998); another wall at

Storm King (*Folded Wall*, 1999); a large stone arch in Montréal (1998); *Snowballs in Summer* in London (2000); *Garden of Stone*, a memorial for victims and survivors of the Holocaust, sited in Manhattan (2003), and *Stone Houses* at the Gotham's Met (2004).

Andy Goldsworthy continues to work in countries such as Japan, Australia, Canada, North America and France, but his home ground of Dumfriesshire in Scotland remains (at) the heart of his work. (From the mid-Nineties, Goldsworthy worked increasingly frequently at Digne in South France; it became one of the most valuable places for the sculptor outside of his home in Scotland, and was the site of a major commission, *Réfuges d'Art*).2

It's significant, I think, that Andy Goldsworthy worked as a gardener for the first half of the Eighties. Goldsworthy's art parallels developments and trends in gardening in Britain and elsewhere. For instance, the use of stones and pebbles in the gardens as ornaments or sculptures (a little bit of *feng shui* or Japanese garden design).

Andy Goldsworthy has not created art everywhere. There are plenty of places Goldsworthy has not visited for making art (he is not nearly as well-travelled as Long). Even in the British Isles, Goldsworthy has not made much art in Cornwall or Devon or the South-West (Long's stamping ground), or the East (Norfolk, Suffolk, the fens), not much in the English Midlands, only a few works in Wales, and hardly any in Ireland. If Goldsworthy makes work in the UK, it's usually Scotland, Northern Britain (Cumbria and Yorkshire, but not so much the North-East), or London. By contrast, Long has made many pieces in Scotland, but not so many in the Northern counties of Britain. Southern Britain, though, is Richard Long Central.

Around the world, Andy Goldsworthy has concentrated on Westernized territories: on America, of course (it's the centre of land art), Western Europe, Australia and Japan (with the odd excursion to exotic spots, such as the North Pole). Goldsworthy has not made much art in Eastern Europe, in Russia, in mainland China, in India, in Africa or South America. (Goldsworthy did visit Russia in 1991, but 'administration difficulties' prevented the intended work in Siberia).3 Visits to India, Africa, China and so on will probably come. By contrast, Long has art-walked in all of those territories (though not so much in Russia).

Andy Goldsworthy works with the natural world, and within nature. He uses natural materials in (apparently) natural shapes and forms set in natural contexts. Goldsworthy takes his cue from nature: as Jan Dibbets put it in 1969: 'I realized that if you want to use nature, you have to derive the appropriate structure from nature too'.4

Goldsworthy seems to be a particularly gentle, modest and sensitive artist, compared to many sculptors and land artists: he stitches together leaves to form lines (which're often placed in water, or over branches), or makes circular slabs of snow, or entwines twigs in an arc. He creates a delicate spiral of chestnut leaves, called *Autumn Horn* (1986); he pins bright yellow dandelions on willowherb stalks in a circle, on bluebells (1987); he makes lines and cairns of pebbles; a horizontal line of red sumach leaves was pinned to a willow (at Storm King in 1998); he rubs red stones to stain rockpools; he pins leaves to tree trunks; he makes hollow, circular structures, recalling igloos, from slate, leaves, driftwood and bracken; he makes long wavy ridges in Arizonan and Australian desert sand; he throws sand and sticks in the air and photographs the moment; he makes arches, globes, hollow spheres, slabs, spires, spirals and star-shapes out of snow and ice. Very impressive it all is. The sculptures made of sticks, for instance, stuck together in an arch, or a line, reflected in the mirror-like water of Derwent Water in Cumbria in 1988, are indeed wonderful. The sculptures exude tranquillity, an early morning calm (quite the opposite of another water work, Klaus Rinke's *Water Sculpture*, where a water canon blasted water over visitors as they approached a gallery, or Jim Sanborn's 1995 *Coastline*, which employed a wave generator to simulate waves in a Maryland garden). Then there's the globe made from oak leaves in various states of autumnal decay, superb (Dumfriesshire, 1985). Or the globe of sticks made in Fairfax, California (1995), set next to a sheltering tree. Or the sand serpent in the British Museum (1994). Or the globe made out of snow, and perched amidst some young trees (1980), or the slabs of snow, set up in a line with slits cut in them (1988).

Andy Goldsworthy said: 'I want an intimate physical involvement with the earth. I must touch'.[5] Touching is 'deeply important' for Goldsworthy.[6] Only touching gives the artist the deep understanding of his materials and nature, he asserted.[7] The eroticism of Andy Goldsworthy's sculpture is readily apparent, but the sensuality of Goldsworthy's art is non-human; there are no 'human' figures in his work, though there are vaginal openings, phallic rocks, mounds like breasts or pregnant bellies, and stalks that bend gracefully like ballet dancers: if one wants to anthropomorphize and sexualize Goldsworthy's art, it's easy. Goldsworthy himself anthropomorphizes his work. He says the cones on a hillside are like sentinels or a group of people.[8] Goldsworthy spoke of stones and seeds in terms of phallic tumescence and orgasmic release: 'I found an energy in stone that can best be described as a seed that becomes taut as it ripens – often needing only the slightest of touch to make it explode and scatter its parts' (*Wood*, 23).

Andy Goldsworthy has made more 'traditional' forms of art in galleries: his bracken, fern and horse chestnut stalk works, for instance, were created by pinning the materials onto white gallery walls. These works – *Bracken fronds* (Ecology Centre, London, 1985), *Reeds, bracken and horse chestnut stalks* (Centre d'Art Contemporain, Castres, and Galerie Aline Vidal, Paris, 1989) and *Reed line drawing* (Paris, 1990) – were essentially free, open wall drawings, often employing basic motifs such as the circle and open curve. Goldsworthy's works inside art galleries are much more like Richard Long's: not installations very often, Goldsworthy and Long tend to produce individual pieces that are then arranged inside the gallery space to work together.

Andy Goldsworthy's shows are something of a disappointment, in one way, because the works have to breathe without their usual natural surroundings. Goldsworthy did emulate Walter de Maria in a direct way: in November, 1992, he covered the interior of the London gallery of his agent with clay (*Hard earth – Dorset clay smoothed out, left to dry*). The exhibit began as a smooth creamy-white expanse of wet clay/ earth. It looked as if the gallery was empty, said Goldsworthy (*Stone,* 64), recalling Yves Klein's gallery show of nothingness (*Le Vide,* of 1958). *Hard earth* directly re-echoed de Maria's *New York Earth Room*: the natural world was present in the gallery in both works in force: in de Maria's *New York Earth Room* (1977) the dark soil had a solemn, weighty, fecund presence; in Goldsworthy's *Hard earth* time and transformation played a part: gradually, the clay dried and cracked, allowing the Goldsworthyan vision of the dark energies of nature to well up: nature was erupting into the gallery space.

Andy Goldsworthy's writings are sometimes simple, matter-of-fact, and sometimes blunt – in a stubborn, Northern fashion. Goldsworthy comes across a rugged man of the wild, a 'whole earth man', ecologically sensitive, someone 'in touch' with nature, working with his bare hands, in boots, hat and an anorak, often in Winter. There is a macho posturing to this (no doubt unintentional), in which the relationship with nature is 'fundamental', 'raw', 'violent', 'intense'. Goldsworthy sees working in the hard cond- tions of Winter a challenge, a 'test of my commitment to the landscape'.[9] Goldsworthy has spoken about being 'shocked' by small-scale natural events, about work suddenly becoming 'intense', about the 'raw energy' of colours. Goldsworthy's writings are marked by words such as 'powerful', 'wildness', 'deeper', 'rooted', 'flesh and bone', 'feeling', 'essential', 'sense', 'energy', 'touching' and 'essence' (these words are taken from one page of Goldsworthyan philosophy, in *Stone*, 6).

All this talk of raw, powerful essence in nature suggests one poet in particular – Ted

Hughes, the sombre Yorkshireman and former Poet Laureate whose books (*River, Hawk in the Rain, Lupercal, Wodwo, Elmet*) are full of post-Hopkinsian evocations of wild shingle beaches, desolate moorland, ancient forests and craggy heights. If ever there a poetic equivalent of Goldsworthy's boulders, melting snowballs, slate cairns and red mud 'throws', it is Ted Hughes' verse.[10]

Of a cairn made out of scrap steel which was placed next to an old foundry, Andy Goldsworthy said that the cairn 'touches the nature of an urban environment' (*Stone*, 35). Does it 'touch the nature' of the place? What is the nature of the place? How can a human 'touch the nature' of the place? What is the quality of this touching? What kind of touching is it? And what is the nature of 'the nature of an urban environment'? How does the artist know he's touched it? Simple: he believes wholeheartedly in his subjective, intuitive feelings. Of steel, for example, the artist stated: 'I can feel its source' (ibid.). What does this 'source' 'feel' like? And what is the 'source' of steel? The Earth? The energies that formed it? The people that dug the source material out of the ground and shaped it? How, too, does the viewer know about this feeling for the source of a material? Is it expressed in the work? How can the audience test the authenticity of the artist's feelings? These are questions which one can (and should) fire at any artist. Goldsworthy's art is often unsure about the answers. It knows it is about nature, ecology, place, organic form, and so on, but its views on these matters, and its relation to them is often confused, ambiguous, bland.

A flower sculpture such as *Dandelions* (1993)[11] highlights the recurring problems with Andy Goldsworthy's art: it has instant appeal: brilliant yellow dandelions are set in a mossy, pitted rock next to a stream. The work seems to emphasize the relative beauty of both the flowers and the setting: the 'organic', individual shape of the rock pool, the contrasts in brightness and colour in nature (grey and green rock, yellow dandelions), the transience of nature (the dandelions' colour will fade; the flowers will be pummelled by the next rain, or swept away when the river rises). Yet the sceptical viewer might also say, well *anyone* could make that work (or many other Goldsworthy sculptures). There is little 'technique' or skill involved: one simply places dandelions in a pool (or rocks on top of each other, or wraps boulders in clay, or rubs the bark off twigs, or cracks open pebbles, and so on).

Dandelions seems so simple, so easy, like so many of Andy Goldsworthy's sculptures (*Beech leaves, Balanced stone, Balanced rocks, Two Scaur Water snowballs, Red river rock pools, River rock, Peat, Clay-covered rocks, Torn stones, Red sand thrown into a blue sky, Orange stones* and *Yellow elm leaves*, to cite some works from *Stone*). Hang on, the sceptic might claim, the guy has simply stuck some flowers in a pool! That can't be 'art'! Easy to see how Goldsworthy's art can seem a sham, like Carl Andre's bricks, or Yves Klein's leap, or Andy Warhol's six hour film of someone sleeping. *Come on*, the sceptic'll say, this can't be *serious*. But this view never lasts very long, and soon even sceptics will realize there's a lot more going on in Goldsworthy's work, as with Long's walks.

For Richard Long, Andy Goldsworthy is a 'second generation' artist, and is 'decorative (!)'.12 That's a put-down, by the way. Many critics, though, have been extremely praiseworthy of Goldsworthy's art. Goldsworthy sculptures such as *Yellow elm leaves, Red maple leaves, Beech leaves, Red river rock pools* and other riverside works seem so simple, so easily put together. But Constantin Brancusi's eggs and fish and heads are also very 'simple' shapes and forms: he reduced and rationalized natural forms until he reduced them to an 'essence' (the 'essence' of a fish, of a head, of a bird in flight). Yet Brancusi does not get accusations of superficially and banality thrown at him (well, not so much nowadays). Indeed, his sculpture is really powerful precisely because he radically simplified it. (What the viewer doesn't see in the gallery, of course, are the hundreds of failed attempts, the mistakes, and the years of research and refinement that Brancusi took to get to that stage, Similarly with Goldsworthy's sculptures: there are hundreds of failures which don't make it into the books, prints, and exhibitions).

With Andy Goldsworthy's art, though, the simplicity is of a different order: is the confusion and criticism of Goldsworthy's work because he is using the *actual* material of nature? An actual leaf, rock, petal or ice sheet, not an imitation or image of them? Is it that anti-Goldsworthy critics see a rock covered with real leaves, not a mock-up made in an artist's studio, or a bronze or marble interpretation? Is it that Goldsworthy is getting so 'close' to nature that he is using the very materials of nature themselves, without altering them much at all? Goldsworthy doesn't seem to *do* much with his materials: he wraps them round a rock, sticks them in a pool, builds a mini tower out of 'em, takes a photo, and then it's 'art'. Is it that his art does not do anything more than this?

Light is one of the key formal elements that Andy Goldsworthy explores in his sculpture, as in much of land art. Critics have spoken of Goldsworthy's 'stunning effects of light and atmosphere' 13 The two leafworks of October, 1997, at Storm King (orange and yellow leaves stuck onto a rock), were made specifically to catch the morning sunlight.14 Another shield, *Horse chestnut leaves* (Yorkshire, 1987) was deliberately made for darkness, hanging in amongst some rhododendron bushes. The Getty Institute clay hole was positioned so that the sun would shine on it once a year, at Midsummer. Some of Goldsworthy's *Réfuges d'Art* were constructed to take advantage of certain lighting effects (such as the rising sun at certain times of the year). 15

Because place is so important,16 light (and colour) becomes a primary tool. Some Andy Goldsworthy works pivot very much on luminosity and opacity, not just the leaf shields, but some of the snow walls, the holes in sand, and so on, so that without the right sort of lighting, they do not work properly. Other sculptures are seen in a variety of lighting conditions – stormlight, snowlight, misty skies (the snow wall at Blencathra in Cumbria, is an obvious instance). Some sculptures are created in response to certain lighting conditions – the stick sculpture in the Lake District (1988), made in the pale, liquid light of dawn, for example. 'When I work with the land I work with the sky. When I work with water I am working with the clouds' Goldsworthy stated.17

Andy Goldsworthy's photographs present an idealized world, veritably the pastoral world of ancient times. Goldsworthy's Arcadia, though, is definitely a Northern European pastoral realm, not the Southern, Mediterranean paradise of satyrs, shepherdesses, gods and wild animals of Classical mythology. Goldsworthy's 'pastoral sublime' (to use the phrase applied to a category of J.M.W. Turner's works), is a Northern European realm, very much in the tradition of Turner's paintings of the Alps, with lowering, gloomy skies, raging wind, snow-capped mountains and mossy riverbanks. John Martin, Thomas Girtin, John Sell Cotman, John Constable and J.M.W. Turner made many paintings of the landscapes Goldsworthy works in. Apart from Australia and Japan, Goldsworthy's art centres around cold, rain-sodden, Northern landscapes. True, there is much sunlight in his photographs of Australia, photographs that evoke the colonial view of the outback as a rugged, inhospitable place where the white people sit around camp fires. (Sunshine plays a bigger part in Goldsworthy's more recent sculpture, which has been based in South France. Goldsworthy's Japan is a more sublime, rarefied place, though it is still rough and distinctly non-human.

Andy Goldsworthy photographs his sculptures often looking down on them, so the surrounding landscape is not seen. He edits out unsightly buildings or roads, but art has always involved much more editing than many artists would admit. Goldsworthy knows that what one leaves out of a work is as important as what one puts in. Goldsworthy said that photographs were 'very important to me as a working record', and that he had a record of nearly everything he'd made, which he could look on and use.[18] 'A good work is the result of being in the right place at the right time with the right material' said Goldsworthy.[19]

Much of Andy Goldsworthy's art is about and made from ice and snow. Other artists who have worked with snow include Dennis Oppenheim, Joseph Beuys and Hans Haacke. Goldsworthy is distinctly a 'Northern' artist, who makes work in landscapes that come out of the 'Celtic fringe', out of the sort of landscapes that Celtic culture exalts: misty, craggy moors and hill-scapes; sodden Autumnal forest floors knee-deep with leaves (last year's leaves, decades of dead leaves); wild snowscapes; cold, clear streams banked with large mossy boulders; and still lakes in frosty dawns. Goldsworthy's landscapes could have mythical figures such as the Lady of Shallot, Lancelot or King Arthur or Gandalf riding through them without altering anything. They are the landscapes of Merlin, Taleissin and Morgan Le Fay, of Welsh legends such as *The Mabinogion*, of historical events shrouded in mists, of historical (now legendary) figures such as Robert the Bruce, Owen Glendower, King Edward and Boadiccea. The places associated with Goldsworthy – his studio at Penpont, Scaur Water in Dumfriesshire, Carlisle, Yorkshire Sculpture Park, Grizedale in Cumbria, Leeds, Leadgate in Durham – are all Northern British sites. And the stereotypes of Britain's North – grimy towns, rain, bleak moors, gloomy skies, grim humour, down to Earth and no-nonsense attitudes – all chime with Goldsworthy's sculpture.

One wonders whether Andy Goldsworthy would like to work in snow and ice more than in any other medium. His notes and titles record many frustrations stemming from working with snow. In temperate snowlands, though, one feels Goldsworthy is very much at home. Snow has the right sort of qualities Goldsworthy looks for in a material: it is malleable, it melts and changes, its whiteness makes for good, contrasty imagery, and it seasonally alters the landscape, and later dissolves into it. In Goldsworthy's snowworks one senses also the sheer fun of working with snow. For people in most of Britain, snow is not a definite event each year, as it is in, say, Northern Russia or Alaska.

For children, snow can be an exciting event (while British adults usually gripe about it). Snow was a perennial delight and 'shock' for Andy Goldsworthy. In *Midsummer Snowballs* he wrote that '[e]ven in winter each snowfall is a shock, unpredictable and unexpected'.[20] Goldsworthy retained the child-like enjoyment of snow falling in Britain throughout his life. While much of the UK grinds to a halt at the sight of a snowflake, Goldsworthy has the child's joy when it snows (school's cancelled, snowball fights, ice skating, sledging, and making snowmen and snowballs). One of Richard Long early works was a *Snowball Track* (1964), reminiscent of the snowball trails adults and children alike make, by rolling a snowball over snow.

The biting cold maybe gives Andy Goldsworthy a sense of heroism, for suffering invariably enhances a work (as in, 'this work was difficult, made under adverse conditions'). After all, Goldsworthy is not an artist who makes work in the 'comfort' of a home or studio (working indoors doesn't feel 'real' to him). No: he goes out into the wilderness, where it can be uncomfortable and challenging.

Andy Goldsworthy claims to know the landscape around his studio in Penpont, Scotland, very well, so that the snow does not hide the world: 'I know what lies under the snow – I know the earth beneath' (HE). Always Goldsworthy stresses the intimate relationship he has with nature. Part of this intimacy comes from returning to the same patch of land again and again. Through successive visits, layers of touch and meaning in the landscape are uncovered by the artist. The artist returning to the same space always works in time as well as space, because s/he creates a personal history of that place. S/he works with her former selves, as well as in the present – with the artist she was and ideas she had two years ago, ten years ago, twenty years ago. 'Some places I return to over and over again, going deeper – a relationship, made in layers over a long time'.[21] It's an inevitable consequence for land artists who return to the same sites to make work, this successive layering and repetition.

The personal dimension is important in Andy Goldsworthy's work. His work is not 'impersonal' in the sense that it could be made 'anywhere'. It is, like most land art, always a product of a relationship between an artist and a particular place. Making the art itself, the doing of it, is important for Goldsworthy. So that when people ask the eternal question, *but is it art?*, he retorts, well, he doesn't know and doesn't care, but 'it is important and necessary for me as a person.'[22] (Artists always leave it up to others to decide whether something is 'art' or not).

Sceptics can claim that many of Andy Goldsworthy's sculptures gain much of their fire, like Richard Long's, from their situation in wilderness landscapes. They would be right. Although Goldsworthy states that many of his sculptures are made in built-up areas, areas of dense population and human activity, a glance through any Goldsworthy book or a visit to a Goldsworthy show will reveal the large proportion of wilderness or rural landscapes in his art. He expunges all the trash, houses, telegraph poles, apartment blocks, cars and roads from his photographs, and presents lush streams, moorland, forests and hillsides. There are no people at all in his art, except Goldsworthy himself, who is sometimes seen, with his beard, sweater and jeans, making a piece of art (his assistants are hardly ever seen, while his wife Judith disappears entirely). In this sense, Goldsworthy's work is not at all figurative – but neither is it 'abstract', in the Mark Rothko or Piet Mondrian sense, because real, recognisable objects appear in his work. This is one of the reasons for the growing popularity of his work, and Richard Long's art: apart from the Eighties ecological/ green movement, and the accessible, decorative quality of his work, it is thoroughly countrified and rural, quite in keeping with primæval desires for escape into the country, that nostalgia for nature that lies behind the pastoral and landscape tradition in Britain.

Andy Goldsworthy's skill is not just to 'touch nature' (whatever that means) but to touch the chords of desire for nature in people. Goldsworthy's art is popular partly because of this powerful desire among Western audiences for contact with the natural world, an appetite which is manifested in natural history programmes on television, in jaunts to zoos, gardens, windswept hillside car lots, in Constable, van Gogh and Monet posters and prints, in gardening magazines and gardening centres and plants in the house, in the popularity of English rural novels by George Eliot, Thomas Hardy and Emily Brontë. The eco/ green movement (and its associated movements in pagan/ New Age/ road, anti-capitalist, anarchist and animal activism) taps into this nostalgic love of an urban-centric culture for all things 'natural'.[23] The natural world seems to be green and life-giving and untarnished by the complexities of modern life. The natural world, which is Goldsworthy's preferred world, is a place of leaves, rivers, animals and stones, a place seemingly devoid of people, the ones who fuck things up, who complicate things, who introduce the concepts and realities of neurosis, confusion, waste, violence, consumption and politics into the 'pure' natural world.[24] It's not like that at all, but these ecological feelings are powerful. Goldsworthy's art, like the pastoral novels of Eliot and Hardy, like green politics or the money-spinning popularity of van Gogh and Impressionism, trades on the desires for an earlier, ancient Paradise, a time when things were simpler, richer, deeper. This is the 'green world' of childhood (as Robert Graves called it), a time of playfulness and living close to the Earth, enjoying the seasons passionately but also freely, in a relaxed manner. In mythology, it is the 'Golden Age', *il illo tempore, ab origine*, in the Creation era, at the origin of the world, before the Fall of Adam and Eve into sin, a time before œdipal anxiety and patriarchal psychosis, a Gaia time, a whole earth time, all 'natural' and recycled and vegetarian, a holistic time, a time of social unity, when everyone felt as one in communities and loved each other, a time of maternal bliss, when women were nurturing Mother Goddesses and men could be sweetly dreaming babies without feeling embarrassed. It's a world and a time that never existed, but the myth persists ('myth' and 'mythology' is employed here in its proper sense, as a sacred story, not the way 'myth' is used by politicians, to suggest a lie).

Andy Goldsworthy's art books, commissions and shows, like Richard Long's, trade on this pastoral imagery and nostalgic desire: they allow stressed, confused, over-worked and neurotic city dwellers time out from staring at the control screens (TV, computers, ATMs, cel phones) of the megavisual world, encouraging a little day-dreaming into the soft greens and greys of wild moorlands. Goldsworthy's and Long's art may be increasingly successful because it reminds people that, yes, one does love nature after all: one came from it, one'll go back into it, in the end, in death.

Andy Goldsworthy's art, and Richard Long's, may hit home because it does *not* bombard people with telephones, computers, cars, factories, radios, TVs, microwaves, washing machines, hoovers, irons, faxes, and all those machines and devices that connote *labour*, that are the symbols and mechanisms of working life. In Goldsworthy's and Long's green world, all is natural, untechnological, with artifacts that evoke a return to basics: stone, wood, leaves, ice.

Snowballs In Summer (a.k.a. *Midsummer Snowballs,* 2000) was one of Golds-worthy's larger, more complex installations. Fourteen snowballs were gathered from the snowfields of Dumfriesshire and Perthshire in 1999 and 2000, kept in storage, transported to London and exhibited on the streets of the City of London. This, coupled with the show *Time*, at the Barbican Centre (in August-October), made 2000 the most prominent display of Goldsworthyania for some years in the UK. Goldsworthy liked the idea of the snowballs appearing in the middle of Summer in an urban setting. The snowballs were not 'made for people. They are about people'.25

One of the problems Andy Goldsworthy's art addresses head on is the age-old tension between the 'real world' and art, between objects as they are in the everyday world, and objects as they are represented in art. Goldsworthy, like Richard Long, encourages the viewer to look again at the natural world: not just at the beauty of it, but at the multitudinous variety of forms in nature. The snowballs in the *Snowballs* installations (1989 and 2000) were not plastic or concrete masquerading as snowballs, but real snowballs. Similarly, the twigs and stalks and needles and pebbles folded into the snowballs are real. What's amazing is the actuality of nature: the variety of forms (the way the branches twist, for instance).

Andy Goldsworthy's sculptures (like Richard Long's) used all the tricks and devices of post-Renaissance illusion and representation, including figure-ground relationships, negative space, perspective, selective viewpoint, *chiaroscuro*, silhouettes, outlines, and so on. A good example of the strong pictorial element in Goldsworthy's art are the sculptures that use negative space to create the illusion of continuous form: these sculptures typically have loops of ice or sand on two sides of a rock or a tree. In, for instance, *Reconstructed refrozen icicles* (1999).26

Andy Goldsworthy's ethics are those of Long, Chris Drury, Hamish Fulton, David Nash (he has worked at Nash's Blaenau-Ffestiniog studio) and other British land artists: a mystical feeling for the landscape, expressed by an exquisite sensitivity of *touch*, that all-important component in the eroticism of sculpture. As Goldsworthy affirmed, he *must* touch. A world in which he would not be allowed to touch would be hateful. A world in which the trees had 'DO NOT TOUCH' signs on them would be horrendous. Significantly, Goldsworthy works mainly in areas in which the ownership of the land is not contested. He operates in landscapes where he has been given permission to work. No 'DO NOT TOUCH' signs for him.

Indeed, when it comes to drawing on the sand on a beach, Andy Goldsworthy will not use a stick, as many folks would. Instead, he uses his hands. His *Dark dry sand drawing* is worked by hand, dribbled onto the sand on the Isle of Wight (1987). The result, all swirls and curves, comes directly from Jackson Pollock. Goldsworthy has also drawn lines on frozen water (Nova Scotia, 1999). A lot of the work Goldsworthy has done in deserts has been with carved sand (in New Mexico, Arizona, California and Australia). In a way, these drawings and sculptures of sand (in the shape of spirals, snakes, zigzags and boulders) are basically developments of the work with sand on the beaches of Northern England Goldsworthy undertook in the late 1970s.

Land artists such as Andy Goldsworthy use their hands, primarily, as their means of making art. Goldsworthy does not go out into the landscape with anything, except a knife.27 Perhaps he should, to be really purist, make do without even a knife? Anyway, he *does* really go out into the landscape with 'tools' – the camera not least among them (also spare film too, maybe an extra lens filter or two, and a tripod). Without that camera, the viewer wouldn't know about many of his works. Ditto with all land artists. Without the camera, their work is 'lost'. That is, not really 'lost', but the camera means the viewer too can share in the work. Without the camera, the viewer would have to rely on written texts, perhaps, as a means of 'recording' artworks. Photography is also 'a way of communicating' Goldsworthy told an interviewer, 'and we wouldn't be sitting here if I didn't take the photographs.'28 Here Goldsworthy admits that without the photographs there would be not much communicating going on with his art: it needs photography to work. But, as one can see, Goldsworthy and most other land artists are not writers. Indeed, their writings are, well, often in note form, designed as a 'record' for themselves, or as notes towards an artwork. While there have been any number of painters and sculptors who were also good writers who provided many insights – Leonardo da Vinci, Ad Reinhardt, Vincent van Gogh, Donald Judd – Goldsworthy is not among them (the writings of Smithson, Judd, Morris and Andre are far superior). So, relying on photographs, the viewer gets to find out about many works of land art that might otherwise have never known. The camera is thus an essential 'tool' for the land artist.

Andy Goldsworthy also goes out with many other invisible tools of his craft – his awareness of land art, his education, his knowledge of other sculptors and art history, his memory of previous works, and so on. No artist works alone, culturally. Goldsworthy's art, like all land art, like all art, works within a culture and tradition and history of postwar and contemporary art. Tracing the links with Minimalism, Arte Povera and Conceptualism, for instance, is only one way of looking at Goldsworthy's art.

Andy Goldsworthy's sculptures are marked by a number of elements familiar in land art: transience, domination, penetration, circular forms (globes, circles, spirals, snakes, cones) and nature mysticism. The ephemerality of the pieces, for instance, is a key component (time is perhaps the dominant theme in Goldsworthy's art). Snow and ice will melt away, leaves will disintegrate, stones will be blown over. Each Goldsworthy sculpture has a date printed with its title. Not just a year, as in the usual artwork, but a specific day.

Thus, one of Andy Goldsworthy's best pieces, the delicious poppy covered boulder, has the title: *Poppy petals wrapped around a boulder held with water*, with the time and place inscribed as: Sibobre, France, June 6, 1989. The petal-covered rock, with its brilliant red colour, nestled in some mossy boulders, looks very much like one of Constantin Brancusi's 'cosmic eggs' (egg-shaped sculptures which Brancusi titled *The Beginning of the World*). The red colour revealed the rock's shape, size and form, its position amongst and relation to other rocks. Not wishing to disturb or move the rock (it's not that small really), Goldsworthy's act of covering it in wet poppy petals drew attention to this particular egg-shaped rock, *this* one and *not* the others (although the surrounding boulders also became the subject of the sculpture: attention was drawn to them as well as to the red rock). In *Poppy petals wrapped around a boulder held with water,* then, the place becomes as crucial as the centrepiece, the red rock.

The largest section of Andy Goldsworthy's book *Wood* (1996) is devoted to the *Capenoch Tree* series of works, made between 1994 and 1996 in Dumfriesshire in the UK. The 'Capenoch tree' was an old oak tree standing slightly apart from other trees on private land. Goldsworthy concentrated not on the whole tree, its trunk or its branches (as he often did), but on one particular branch that grew sideways out from the tree, horizontally, a few feet above the grass. 'The long branch that has grown horizontal to the ground has taught me that the tree is the land', Goldsworthy explained. 'The branch is like the landscape' (*Time*, 195). So Goldsworthy treated the branch as a landscape in miniature, a small-scale setting for a range of sculptures which represent all of Goldsworthy's work in microcosm.

In a way, the *Capenoch Tree* series offered a summary of all of Andy Goldsworthy's land art techniques: there were leaves pinned along the branch; wood and snow cairns and globes placed next to the tree; snowballs set in the tree; arches made out of ice and stone on the branch; screens of willowherb and rosebay; walls of snow (some serpentine, some holed); lines of dandelions; and holes in the ground.

Andy Goldsworthy, like Turrell, Aycock and Smithson, has made some huge pieces, such as the long 'snake' and the 'pool' or maze, in Country Durham, large works which take up a lot of space, and certainly dominate the surrounding landscape. Goldsworthy's large-format outside works often use the serpent coil as a fundamental form. Goldsworthy maintained, however, that his 'snake-like' or serpent-shaped sculptures does not refer directly to snakes.[29] Instead, he preferred to call one of his favourite motifs a 'river of earth', or a tree root, or a river.[30]

Whatever the artistic intention, however, it is impossible to limit readings of sculptures such as *Sidewinder, Lambton Earthwork* or the serpentine shapes in the British Museum's Egyptian Hall to responses to the environment.

The serpent as symbol connotes time, change, seasons, birth-and-death-and-rebirth, eternity, sexuality, evil, the cosmos, and so on (like 'moon' or 'circle', 'serpent' can symbolize virtually anything). Goldsworthy might wish to determine how viewers read his serpent-shaped forms, and emphasize the response he makes to the natural environment, but consumers of art will make any interpretation they like, and some artists might wish to suppress (snakes also connote dirt – they slide on the dust; and excrement; the alimentary canal; eating and defecating; poison; reptile life, and so on).

While Andy Goldsworthy insisted that he wasn't interested in the symbolic associations of the snake, or in the snake as an animal, he did link his use of the snake to Brancusi's birds and fish (Brancusi sculpted radically simplified, abstract versions of birds and fish). For Goldsworthy, the serpent wasn't a totemic or symbolic creature, but a form that expressed 'the energy of movement' (ib, 113).

Andy Goldsworthy's large-scale works, like Turrell's, Holt's or Bayer's, are monumental works, which sprawl across the landscape. *Sidewinder* and *Seven Spires*, at Grizedale, U.K. (a Forestry Commission site between Windermere and Coniston Water in Northern Britain), are trunks of trees stripped of their branches, and pinned together. In *Sidewinder*, the curved trunks were placed on the ground, to form a long snake-like sculpture: the form rests on the ground then curves into the air. The impression was of sliding, arching kinetic energy. In other words: a huge serpent slithering along the forest floor.

In *Seven Spires* the trees were pined together to form tall spires. The result was a series of enormous edifices made of wood in amongst other trees. Andy Goldsworthy wanted to harness the sense of the 'almost desperate growth and energy driving upward' in the pine wood, and to evoke a cathedral-like atmosphere, with the spires stretching skyward with the brown gloom underneath.[30] It is, at first, not clear which is a tree and which is sculpture. Both, of course, are made of wood: Goldsworthy has simply drawn together the surrounding trees, it seems, but in doing so, he re-defines the surrounding forest. *Seven Spires* looks at first to be a gentle sculpture, blending in with the surrounding forest. 'In avoiding monumentality, however, Goldsworthy's sculptures do not forego grandeur' wrote Andrew Causey (1990, 128). Yet they do stand out, really, they are distinctly works of art, existing in a paradoxical relationship with the environment. A 'collaboration' is a polite way of saying what Goldsworthy's *Seven Spires* is about: a 'collaboration with nature', a phrase used about much of his art. Other spires, made at the same time, include *Bracken Spires* (1983) and *Stone Spire* (1983).

Commissioned by Sustrans and Northern Arts, *Lambton Earthwork* (1988) was a quarter-mile long bank which coiled along the ground near Chester-le-Street in County Durham. The site was associated with railways and industry, but Andy Goldsworthy turned it into something wholly concerned with æsthetic and religious themes. The long spiralling banks of earth clearly derived from the earthwork sculptures of Robert Smithson and American earth art (Goldsworthy said he is wary of using the 'overblown spiral', the too-obvious spiral as a shape).[31] Goldsworthy spoke of the serpentine shape as being like a river winding through a valley, or the root of a tree.[32]

The other Durham earthwork (*Maze,* 1989, at Leadgate) also used ancient mythology and symbolism, this time the labyrinth. Like *Lambton Earthwork* (but unlike most of Andy Goldsworthy's works), *Maze* was intended to be used by the general public. Both *Maze* and *Lambton Earthwork* were about responses to the energies in nature – thus the public was invited to explore similar things as they physically walked around the earthworks. The usual experiences of the maze were apparent in Goldsworthy's *Maze* – not being able to see the whole plan from above; being enclosed by high banks; a bewildering series of turns and paths. The interwoven series of embankments also recalled Iron Age forts (of which there are many in Britain), such as the complex (and enormous) array of defences at Maiden Castle in Dorset. The comparison between Goldsworthy's sculpture and Iron Age hillforts, though, is not quite fair: Iron Age earthworks were not made by bourgeois contemporary artists for the purposes of providing an interesting æsthetic experience, but were made to protect small, tough communities who wouldn't hesitate to stab the enemy in the heart if attacked (Maiden Castle witnessed some bloody battles – especially when the Romans conquered the site).

Other large-scale Andy Goldsworthy works include the installations *Slate Wall* and *Clay Wall* (1998, Edinburgh), *Clay Wall* (1996, San Francisco) and *Clay Wall* (2000, London). The installation work *Stone sky* in Brussels (1992) comprised flat pieces of slate covered the entire floor of the large space, with a whitish circle in the centre, made by scratching the slate. The circle recalled Richard Long's slate circles, but the title, *Stone sky*, referred directly to nature: the circle could be read as the sun, the moon, the sphere of the heavens, the orbits of planets, and so on. One or two of Andy Goldsworthy's works directly recall those of Richard Long: Goldsworthy's *Burnt sticks* (1995), for example, is reminiscent of some of Long's and Nash's installations which form circles from stone slabs on gallery floors. *Burnt sticks* consisted of sticks charred at one end, the blackened parts of the sticks were put together to form a circle on the gallery floor. The *Fall Creek* installation, at the Herbert F. Johnson Museum of Art at Cornell University (in 2000), comprised a group of low holed mounds fashioned from hundreds of branches on the floor. Goldsworthy has worked at Cornell a number of times: the university has a long history of land art links: one of the important land exhibitions, *Earth Art,* took place in 1969 (it featured Long, Oppenheim, Smithson, Morris and Heizer).

One of the most important of Andy Goldsworthy's later commissions was the installation *Garden of Stone* (2003) at the Museum of Jewish Heritage in Lower Manhattan. *Garden of Stone: A Living Memorial* cost a million dollars (the Public Art fund collaborated with the museum), making it easily Goldsworthy's most expensive commission to date. *Garden of Stone* was made as a memorial for the victims and survivors of the Holocaust. Goldsworthy was an unusual choice, perhaps, for an artist to tackle such a massive political and ideological issue. Goldsworthy has not been known for addressing issues such as the Holocaust in his art. Certainly he could not be described as a high profile political artist. He has also not had much of a connection with Jewish culture or history. At the Metropolitan Museum in NYC Goldsworthy produced two *Stones Houses* (2004) for the roof terrace, another high profile commission.

Many of Andy Goldsworthy's cairns are fabricated from slate (such as *Slate cone*, 1987, 1988); others from branches (*Oak branches*, 1990); or sandstone (*Sandstone*, 1990). Others are put into groups (such as the proposals for stone cone groups at Vassivière, Newcastle and Penpont). Two later cairns include the commissions *Logie Cairn* (1999) in Aberdeenshire and *Hollister Cairn* (1999) in California. The first cairn Goldsworthy made (in Cumbria) he related to the rock formations in that part of North-West England (called the Nine Standards). For Goldsworthy, that pile of stones on the hills were guardians – and the idea of sentinels watching over the landscape has remained with the sculptor ever since, becoming the fundamental interpretation of all his cairns and cones. As well as 'sentinels', guardians of a place, the cairns were also memorials to a place, or a people (Goldsworthy has linked stone cairns to burial mounds),33 or monuments that crown a summit.

'Cone' is perhaps not quite the right term for an image or expression of fullness and ripeness: Andy Goldsworthy's 'cones' look more like fruit. The imagery of fruit would accord with Goldsworthy's ripeness discourse. 'Cairn' is also not quite the right word either, though some of the 'cones' on rocky mountainsides (such as *Cone to mark day becoming night* at Glenleith Fell, and *Cone to mark night becoming day*, Scaur Glen, both 1991) have affinities with natural cairns and outcrops of rock. Some of the cairns were built at night, to be seen at night, as hymns to the night, or the dawn, or the sunset. Like the mulga tree branches edged with red sand to catch the setting sun, these stone cairns were made for particular lighting conditions: the orange-coloured stones made into a cairn were associated with (and completed by) the setting sun. The stone cairns were the sculptural equivalent of lighting a fire in order to celebrate Midsummer or sunset; or erecting a little shrine for a minor deity. They were small-scale celebrations of the daily festivals of dawn, moonlight, noon and sunset, sacred moments that occur every day, but which are no less holy for their common recurrence. Here Goldsworthy is working 'with the sky', with large-scale events such as nightfall and moonlight.

One of Andy Goldsworthy's favourite structures is the stone wall. The wall he made (his first) between his land and a neighbouring farmer's at Stone Wood, Penpont, in Scotland, was a snake-like sculpture (*The Wall*, 1989). *The Wall* was a 'monument to walls',[34] a neat way of creating, on Goldsworthy's side of the wall, a sculpture, and on the farmer's side, a sheepfold. Goldsworthy's walls have a dual purpose: practical, and aesthetic. The walls are boundaries or sheepfolds as well as artistic objects. Their aesthetic derives from their practical applications (*Stone,* 106). While later walls (such as *Room* or *The wall that went for a walk* or the *Storm King Wall*) did not have a 'practical' or agricultural function, Goldsworthy still related them to the practicalities of stonewalling. Goldsworthy spoke proudly and sentimentally of the practice of stone-walling: he talked in terms of 'tradition', 'history', and 'years of experience' (*Stone,* 106).

The wall that went for a walk (1990, Grizedale) was a 150-yard long wall that literally snaked through the forest. The serpentine form of *The wall that went for a walk* related to *Lambton Earthwork* and *Sidewinder* (another Grizedale sculpture). *The wall that went for a walk* has no 'proper' function – i.e., no 'practical' function. It weaves between the trees and follows the lay of the land. Instead of ploughing through trees or rocks, Andy Goldsworthy's curving wall assiduously avoids them. At 2,278 feet long, the *Storm King Wall* was not only Goldsworthy's biggest wall, it was one of Goldsworthy's most significant works. Other artists who had work at the Storm King Art Center included Richard Serra, Louise Nevelson, David Smith, Mark di Suvero, Isamu Noguchi, Alice Aycock and Alexander Calder.

In the mid-1990s, Andy Goldsworthy developed the *Sheepfolds* project: building or renewing a hundred sheepfolds in the North of Blighty. The *100 Sheepfolds* project was funded by public money from the National Lottery (who contributed a grant of £340,000 or about $680,000). The project included exhibitions in Cumbria, St Albans and London, TV documentaries, and books by Goldsworthy (*Sheepfolds, Arch*).

The *Sheepfolds* project – Andy Goldsworthy's largest undertaking to date – revolved around sheep farming, the herding, washing, cleaning, branding, breeding, rearing, and shearing of sheep. Goldsworthy saw the *Sheepfolds* project as a 'monument to agriculture' (*Sheepfolds*, 16).[35]

Andy Goldsworthy has continued to build arches: it has become one of his most distinctive motifs. No other land artist had employed the arch so often as a key structure in their *œuvre*. Goldsworthy's arch sculptures include the offshoot of the *Sheepfolds* project, the *Arch* project of 1996-97; a number of 'herds' of stone arches (such as *Herd of Arches* and *A Clearing of Arches*);36 arches exhibited in Montréal (1998); a private commission made near the Storm King Art Center, *Eleven Arches* (1997); and some large commissioned arches: a stone arch sited in Montréal (1999) and Rainscombe Park, Oare, Wiltshire (2000), both constructed from red Scottish sandstone. Of the *Montréal Arch*, commissioned by Cirque du Soleil for its HQ, Goldsworthy remarked: '[t]he arch is heavy and strong, expressing permanence, but it is in fact about change, movement and journey' (*Time*, 60).

In July, 1995, Andy Goldsworthy constructed a multilayered cairn within sight of Mont St Vincent (in the river Bès valley). The cairn began as a mound of yellow stones, on top of which Goldsworthy placed a different layer of material over a series of days: grey stones, different coloured stones (brown, yellow, white), then blue and yellow stones, then stalks with charred ends, then grey stones, then mud, which Goldsworthy wet, then a layer of sticks around the whole cairn, followed by more grey stones, and finally a 'house' of sticks with a large round hole. The form of the cairn echoed the mountain in the distance, while the changing state of the cairn each day evoked the constant processes of growth and decay in nature.

The cairn was built in South France, at Digne les Bains, which became one of Andy Goldsworthy's favourite spots (which he has returned to nearly every year since). The rocky, wooded hills and icy, rushing rivers of this beautiful area of South France became a kind of Mediterranean version of Goldsworthy's homeground of Dumfriesshire in Scotland: it had the rivers, the valleys, the forests and the hills which Goldsworthy loved, but lit by a Mediterranean sky (and quite a bit warmer than Scotland, too – in fact, Goldsworthy found the heat a little uncomfortable, and took to working early in the morning and late in the afternoon. Keeping Mediterranean hours, in other words). And Digne offered a Southern, Mediterranean culture to Goldsworthy's usual stamping ground of Northern European culture.37

Mysticism is emphasized in Andy Goldsworthy's writing, as also in the 'enigmatic' statements of Robert Smithson, David Nash, Hamish Fulton and Walter de Maria. Goldsworthy's æsthetics, like Richard Long's, are those of a neo-pagan, shamanic, American Indian, Maori, pantheistic, nature worshipping kind, the sort of beliefs that some people call Goddess worship, and others kinda pagan or 'New Age'. Goldsworthy evokes the earth's energies and atmospheres. His talk of 'earth energies' recalls ley lines, and the so-called 'dragon lines' or *feng shui* of Chinese geomancy. Goldsworthy has emphasized his notions of 'energy' in nature by 'drawing' around stones. The continuous lines could be associated with the notions of 'aura' or the astral plane of Western occultism, the envelope of supernatural energy that surrounds objects and animals. The 'aura' or astral plane is another manifestation of primæval animism, associated with the concepts of *mana* and charisma.

As with Richard Long, one of Andy Goldsworthy's main visual motifs is the circle, whether as a globe made of leaves, slate or snow, or a cone or cairn (often built from slate or snow), or circles from leaves half-frosted or stone rubbed with red powder, or circles cut into snow or leaves. The circle is 'such a fundamental form, one can never get away from it altogether' says Goldsworthy,[38] though his circles are usually deliberately slightly irregular (he draws them by hand and eye) – he avoids the connotations of traditional symbolism.[39] There are many 'negative' circles, made by the surrounding material.

The 'feminine' quality of this primary circular symbol has already been mentioned. It sounds too obvious to say that Andy Goldsworthy's circles, globes, cones and rings should have 'feminine', maternal connotations, but it is precisely in this sort of simple world of equivalents and responses that Goldsworthy operates. The simplicity of the structures, such as a circle, cannot be improved upon, but no matter how 'natural' the circle is as a shape, it always looks humanmade in Goldsworthy's art. His circles of white leaves in amongst dark leaves (1981, Yorkshire) always stand out from the surroundings. The viewer is always aware that a human has made those marks, or arranged the leaves in that way.

The globe made from oak leaves (1985), for instance, is typical of Andy Goldsworthy's melding of the 'natural' and the human. Yes, the viewer has perhaps seen oak leaves many times, or any sort of leaves. Yes, the viewer has probably admired the multi-coloured leaves of Autumn. But Goldsworthy's sphere of leaves in the forest is not an object the viewer might expect to come across on a walk. The oak leaf globe asserts itself instantly as *art*, as a humanmade artifact. Yet how right these globes of ice, snow, slate and leaves can appear. The simplicity of the structure (the circle) makes these sculptures seem curiously 'obvious' and 'natural'. Like a really good pop song or film, one wonders: *why haven't they been made before?*

Andy Goldsworthy's snowball and rain shadow prints were another way of exploring transience in the natural world. Like Yves Klein's *Anthropometries*, or Richard Long's textwork account of walks, the shadows and prints were records of far more intriguing events that occurred elsewhere, during the artwork's manufacture. Goldsworthy's series of body prints (begun in the 1980s, and continuing to the present) directly recall Klein's body paintings. Goldsworthy laid down on the ground when it was raining or snowing: the result was the outlines of his body left upon the ground. The title for these works (reproduced in various Goldsworthy books) is: *Lay down as it started raining or snowing/ waited until the ground became wet or covered before getting up*. Goldsworthy 'prints' himself onto the ground negatively, his body covers the dry earth, while around his body the earth (usually stones) is darkened by the rain. Goldsworthy has also 'printed' his shadow on frosty ground in the early morning.40

Yves Klein exhibited a gallery full of empty space – *Le Vide* (void) – and Andy Goldsworthy made his own version of Klein's non-sculpture in his *Hard earth*. The Conceptualism and New Realism of Klein and his contemporaries (Beuys, Nauman, Manzoni, Burgin, Ono) seems far removed from Goldsworthy's land art. Yet Goldsworthy cites Klein's dramatic (but faked) leap into the air as a powerful example of catching a moment in time: '[t]his amazing tension in the moment of suspense! It's like he's been there for ever, or he's gone in a moment. It's like one of my throws'.41

Andy Goldsworthy has said that he is really working with time. 'If I had to describe in one word what I do, I'd say I work with *time*'.42 Although it seems, at first glance, to be all about space, about particular spaces and how materials react with certain locations, time is an important element in Goldsworthy's art. The mystery of time, and the relentless, unstoppable, implacable, unforgiving force of it. Goldsworthy can be expected to explore more collaborations, such as live performance, dance, maybe video or installations and the like. But the core, the spiritual heart, the essence of his art, will continue to be his work within the landscape – and mainly on his own, and mainly in South-West Scotland.

CHRIS DRURY

Born in 1948 (in Sri Lanka) and educated at Camberwell School of Art in London in the late Sixties, Chris Drury belongs to the generation of Michael Heizer, Alice Aycock, Mary Miss, David Nash, Hamish Fulton and Richard Long (all of whom were born between 1944 and 1946). Drury began to make land art in the mid-Seventies; he had started out, like Donald Judd and so many sculptors and land artists (i.e., just about everybody), with figurative sculpture. Among the artists that Drury admired were Roger Ackling and Constantin Brancusi (Drury said he found Joseph Beuys 'immensely irritating' and 'too self-obsessed' [2002, 91]).

Chris Drury's art shares some affinities with Richard Long's: spirituality; working directly with the hands; the same forms (circles and spirals, though Drury employs many more vortexes and spirals than Long, as well as baskets, globes, shelters and cairns); simple materials gathered from the Earth: stones, wood, snow, mud, clay (Drury, like Long, doesn't use complexly manufactured materials); and similar territories: Japan, Italy, the US and Scotland and Ireland (Eire was a favourite place for both Drury and Long). (Long has travelled too far more countries than Drury, than most land artists – few land artists are as well-travelled as Long).

One of Chris Drury's concerns was human history, the relation between people and the land: his artworks re-use dew ponds and stone walls, draw attention to tumuli by building domes over them, and alter maps, one of the most elegant manifestations of human history. *A Dense History of Place* (1996) was one of Drury's map works which combined maps with written text (a common motif in land and Conceptual art, and Richard Long's art). Dense lines of text spread outwards in a circular pattern from an area near the coast in Sussex depicted in an Ordnance Survey map, an area which has many personal associations for Drury. Richard Long has also featured his home town of Bristol in many walks and works, as well as the Rivers Avon and Severn. The environs of Bristol are the starting-point or goal of many Long walks. (For instance, *Dusty To Muddy To Windy* (1993) was yet another walk over very familiar terrain for Richard Long: Bristol to Truro in Cornwall. A textwork, *Dusty To Muddy To Windy,* described the kind of walk Long has been making for decades: 'familiar roads... over the Mendips... the Somerset levels... into Devon... Dartmoor in view' and so on.)

Other aspects of Chris Drury's art include: the use of materials such as animal bones, antlers, horns, and feathers (Richard Long occasionally uses animal bones to make circles), the basket weaving, the spherical 'baskets' like pots, the kayaks, and the cloud chambers. Drury is much more inclined than many a land artist to use in his sculpture material from animals, such as whale bones, or reindeer antlers, or ram's horns, or elk bones, or gull's feathers, or cow dung. In the *Adharc* pieces (1991-92), Drury took the form of a ram's horn and multiplied it in peat and bronze. Drury affirms the community aspect of his art more than many land artists (including Morris, Holt, Oppenheim and Christo), and the spiritual dimension (he speaks of meditation and the Buddhist void, for instance).

A key sculpture in Chris Drury's *œuvre* (perhaps *the* key sculpture, because it led to a new cycle of work) was his *Medicine Wheel* (made in 1983), a calendar work which collected 365 found objects strung on bamboo stalks mounted around the edge of plant papers and a mushroom spore at the centre. Drury wrote his diary in lines spreading outwards from the centre (a recurring motif in his work). Among the objects were hen feathers, wheat, runner beans, snail shells, pebbles, twigs, bark, berries, acorns, flowers, seeds, fish bones, grass, grapefruit, cherry blossom, hawthorn, crab, mussels, sheep bone, mistletoe, seaweed, cork, walnuts, quinces, rabbit skin, figs, and a cat's skull. The *Medicine Wheel* inspired many new forms in Drury's art:

> out of that came different categories of work. It started me off on making shelters and baskets, and then the shelters led to cloud chambers, and the baskets and the large, woven works I've made outside led me to the dewpond works. I've made woven maps, weaving ideas of landscape. And then there are the found objects.[1]

Like many land artists and sculptors, Chris Drury has made many works near his home in Lewes, Sussex (like Andy Goldsworthy in Penpont, Nash in Blaenau-Ffestiniog and Long in Bristol and the South-West).[2] Drury stated that his work was not self-referential, that it referred to things outside of itself. (One of Drury's criticisms of Joseph Beuys was that his work was too self-obsessed). However, there was plenty of self-referentiality in Drury's art: the *Medicine Wheels*, for example, comprised diary entries for every day of the year. Another work also heavy with thousands of closely written words, *A Dense History of Place*, was full of autobiographical associations. The emphasis on cataloguing also had a biographical element, as did the penchant for works linked to Drury's homeground of Lewes in Sussex. Then there's the emphasis on community projects, where the artist interacts with a local community. Those personal interactions, which Drury cherishes, also contain a strong biographical element.

Basket weaving is one of Chris Drury's passions, and he has created many forms using weaving, including a large open dome from hazel branches (*Cuckoo Dome*, 1992), kayak forms (*Kayak Bundles,* 1994), globular forms (*Basket For the Forest Deer*, 1987), and small vessels (*Basket For the Trees*, 1988, *Hollow Vessel*, 1989). Many of Drury's baskets are recognisable traditional baskets: *Five Sisters* (1994), *Basket For the Moment Between Life and Death* (1985) and *Dream Basket* (1985). In *Basket For the Crows* (1986), the distinctive black crow feathers are employed to weave a basket, placed on the floor, with a long row of feathers suspended above it.

Linked with the basket woven pieces are the small bundles of found objects (such as *Cholla Bundles* [199], *Beaver Sticks* [1991], and *Stick Bundle* [1992]). *Seven Sisters Bundles* (1994), for instance, comprises objects found at the famous Sussex Seven Sisters chalk cliffs (driftwood, flint, chalk and fishing twine). The bundles, for Chris Drury, were 'talismans of time and place, souvenirs, made simply at a campsite, or alternatively created at a later date as an act of remembering' (1998, 58).

Some of Chris Drury's vessels have been woven from willow (1994), or bamboo (1997), some have been covered with cow dung (1992), and some have been made with turf (1991). Some of Drury's wall drawings, using river mud (*River Vortex*, 1998), recall Richard Long's mud wall drawings. Another favourite form of Drury's is the globe set on the ground. Drury has created spheres from pine cones (1984), deer bones and deer scats (*Four Spheres,* 1984), and bamboo, ginkgo, vines, moss and seeds (*Shimanto River Spheres*, 1997, Japan). In *Bound Oak* (1990), made in Sherwood Forest, Drury wrapped a rope of grass around an old oak tree.

Chris Drury's art tended to be interconnected: the baskets and woven vessels were linked to the woven maps, and the woven globes, and also some of the larger shelters. The dew ponds were patterned after baskets.

> On occasion I have taken a basket weave, enlarged it, and turned it upside down to act as a shelter or as a valve between inner and outer... basket to shelter, shelter to basket... A web of interconnections links all these works. (1998, 22-23)

One of Chris Drury's most striking sculptures was *Stone Whirlpool* (1996), built from river stones arranged into a spiral in a Japanese river (in Okawa-mura), near a waterfall. It was one of Drury's works which explored vortexes and spirals. An associated piece which took on currents of energy was *Edge of Chaos* (2000), a large paper work covered with handwritten texts describing the world's ocean currents and winds. One of Drury's largest vortex sculptures was *Heart of Reeds* (2000).

Chris Drury has reclaimed and reworked dew ponds, mainly in Sussex (*Basket*

Dewpond [1997 and 1999]), some of which are quite ancient. In these shallow dips in the landscape Drury has fashioned his favourite motifs of spirals and vortexes from grass and snow. *Snow Vortex* (1999) was a labyrinth with paths dug out of snow on Firle Downs in Sussex. Drury has also made a dry stone vortex maze and a 'wave garden'. (Drury has his favourite motifs: the mushroom gill form, the dome, and the spiral or vortex, which recur in so many sculptures.)

Boats, kayaks and 'vessels' are another recurring form in Chris Drury's art. Some of the vessels are enormous cannibalized stone walls (such as *Long Vessel*, 1995) or heaps of stones, willow and reeds woven on top of them (such as *Shelter Vessel*, 1988, made in County Galway). Some of the vessels are basket woven (such as *Connemara Vessels*, 1988). *Air Vessel* (1994), woven from willow, is one of Drury's most intriguing sculptures: in the form of a kayak, a skeletal form of woven twigs, it was exhibited hanging in space in the gallery, evoking all sorts of associations (with boats as flying transports, or the rich symbolism of flight, or shamanic flight). For Drury, *Air Vessel* was about journeying, the 'moments of exhilaration on mountains where I have experienced a feeling akin to flying'.[3] (Richard Long has spoken of the adrenalin high of standing on a mountaintop). Some of the shelters, Drury said, were 'like overturned boats and denote journey, movement' (1998, 20).

Chris Drury has treated his cairns in different ways: many of the stone cairns have had fires lit inside them, such as *Midsummer Fire Cairn* (1989), *Falling Water Fire Cairn* (1997, Norway), *Fire Cairn* (1993, Ireland), *Fire Mountain Cairn* (1996, Japan), and *Fire Cairn* (1989, Colorado). Some cairns have been enclosed with basket weaving, such as *Basket Cairn* (1991) and *Covered Cairn* (1993, Denmark). Drury's stone cairns are usually erected in wilderness or spectacular scenery.[4] For Drury, the cairns are about commemorating a particular moment in a special place: 'they're just saying, 'this is an extraordinary place'. Grab a few rocks, put them up before the moment's gone and photograph it' (2002, 79). If the shelters were the stopping-places on a journey, the cairns were the 'markers of highpoints/ moments of exhilaration along the way' (1998, 58).

Another favourite Chris Drury motif is the shelter: low, squat structures, some like teepees or witches' hats, some like prehistoric beehive huts. The shelters were often made from stone (but also in chalk, turf, ice, wood, plants and coal. Some of these materials, such as turf, coal and chalk, are unexpected, and give Drury's shelters a very particular quality). The shelters are usually (but not always) constructed at human scale. That is, in the correct scale for someone to enter them. *Beara Shelter*

(1995), in West Cork, Ireland, was a squat, square, stone structure, with views of the sea and Bulls Rock. 'The intention was to provide a space for being and contemplation' (1998, 20). Some of the shelters, such as *Shelter For the Winds That Blow From Siberia*, made near Drury's home in Lewes in 1986, have a distinctly Goldsworthyan flavour: blocks of ice mounted on a hazel frame, looking like an igloo. *Shelter For the Northern Glaciers* (1988) was constructed in the spectacular coastal setting of Seiland island, in Norway, surrounded by snow-capped mountains. Geoffrey Harris has also constructed wooden shelters in forests (*Hollow Spruce*, 1988).

Some of the shelters, as with the cairns, have had fires lit inside them (*Shelter For Dreaming*, 1985). Some of the shelters are open structures, without a covering (rather like a frame tent before the canvas is pulled on top). Others are a frame which's wrapped with ice, or turf, or reeds (such as *Shelter For Herbs and Healing*, 1986). *Tree Mountain Shelter* (1994, Italy) was a stone cairn enclosed with a cone of hazel branches. *Turf Chamber* (1992) comprised sections of turf laid on top of a hazel branch frame. *Wave Chamber* (1996) was constructed beside a flooded valley in Northumberland, and contained a mirror and lens in a steel periscope mounted atop the structure so that the image of the waves could be projected inside, onto the floor.

Chris Drury's shelters have all sorts of connotations, stretching back thousands of years (shelters must have been one of the first structures that humans ever built – shelter being one of the primal human needs). 'Shelter is a basic human need and a manifestation of human presence' remarked Drury (1998, 20). Drury's shelters have obvious affinities (with Celtic and Bronze Age huts and houses in Britain, for example), but they are also about 'organic' forms, forms which repeat endlessly, and geometrically, like crystals. They are stopping and resting places, and also enclosing spaces. 'I like the way this interior space draws you inside yourself, enclosing, protecting, just as mountains pull you outside yourself, pushing mind and body beyond their usual confines' said Drury (ibid.).

The shelters are also about the landscapes in which they are constructed, like land art in general. They tend to be built in rural or wilderness zones, and are the only structures of that kind in the area (they stand out as artworks, not as part of the agricultural machinery, for instance). The shelters are thus also free-standing sculptures, artworks which draw attention to themselves. The shelters are also about land art concerns, such as the tensions between what's inside and what's outside, between the humanmade structure and a 'natural' context (the landscape), about the relation between form and function, æsthetics and use. The shelters draw attention to the landscape around them.

One of Chris Drury's shelters, *Covered Tumulus* (1997), took on the theme of human history directly, and the sense of revealing what's there: Drury built a dome of hazel branches over a prehistoric mound on the South Downs in Sussex. The *Hut of the Shadow* (1997) was sited in North Uist in the Scottish Western Isles with the local community in mind. In *Covered Cairn* (1993), made at TICKON in Denmark, Drury placed a hazel and willow twig frame dome over a stone cairn, an approach that combined the Druryan motif of the open, woven frame with the stone cairn created by balancing rocks atop each other. 'The woven dome is a division between outside and in,' commented Drury, 'which nevertheless allows a transition from one to the other, a free flow of inner to outer. The experience inside it is different from the experience outside' (1998, 80).

One of Chris Drury's more unusual shelters was *Mind Wave* (1996), made in the Botanic Gardens in Copenhagen: Drury combined a couple of his favourite forms: the mushroom-shaped text drawing, and the dome. In *Mind Wave*, Drury opted to adapt a geodesic dome greenhouse, which he painted blue and scratched the words 'mind' and 'wave' in the paint, spreading outwards from the centre of the dome, in the pattern of the gills of a mushroom.

Some of Chris Drury's most appealing sculptures are 'cloud chambers', developments of his shelter form: these are basically circular stone or wooden shelters with holes and mirrors in the roof which act as lenses and reflectors. In these *camera obscuras*, the spectator can observe the sky above projected onto the floor below. The cloud chambers (constructed in many areas) articulate classic land art concerns: the dialectic between inner and outer, indoor and outdoor, stillness and movement, nature and culture.5 The cloud chambers are 'still, silent, meditative and mysterious places' Chris Drury wrote on his website.

Some of Chris Drury's larger works, such as *Vortex* (an enormous hollow cone of woven hazel and willow made at Lewes Castle in 1994), have affinities with artists such as Tony Cragg or Richard Deacon. Another large work, *Heart of Reeds* (2000), was a proposal for a spiral vortex on five acres of reclaimed land in Lewes, Sussex.

A later development of Chris Drury's art was to see the (human) body as 'landscape', to explore the processes of the body, and the relationships between the body and the Earth. Manifestations of this development in Drury's interests were the Lewes *Heart of Reeds* project (which was based on the human heart), *Heart River* (1999), a pattern on paper from a cross-section of the heart, and the various works

Drury has made in conjunction with hospitals (such as *Rhythms of the Heart*, 2000, created in Hastings). In these works, Drury has explored the flow of blood and water in the body, wave patterns from echocardiograms, and the formations in rocks, trees and the landscape.

For Chris Drury, there wasn't a separation between humans and nature, no 'us and them' (or, rather, 'us and it'): nature was all around, inside as well as outside: '[w]e ourselves are nature… '[w]e're a part of nature'.[6] Drury was interested in exploring the relation between inside and outside, nature and culture, and how 'nature is really culture' (2002, 76). For Drury, the natural world could never be 'natural', on its own, completely distinct from humanity – at least as far as humans were concerned. The natural world was always totally enculturated. In other words, if humans were looking at nature, they could only ever see nature in human terms.

> When you're out in the countryside, culture, or our view of nature, determines how you see what's in front of you. So you never see a thing as it is, you always see it in the way that you've been programmed to see it. And you can't get away from that, ever… We are nature, we have to touch nature, we touch it every single second of the day, we breathe it.[7]

Chris Drury said he went out into the countryside (into the 'natural' world) to make art because it was inspirational, it was away from telephones, people, cars, etc, and it was different from humanmade environments (like cities). Also, work made outside tended to be less self-conscious (2002, 72). A work being 'site-specific' was important for Drury: it was about the place, the uses of the place, the history of the place, and the people who lived in the place. 'It's made there, it's made out of the material that's there and it's made by people who live there. All those elements come into it and it has to find its place with the landscape but also within the culture relative to what those people are' (2002, 73).

Chris Drury saw the spaces he made that people entered as 'meditative spaces'. They were direct experiences. The cloud chambers, for example, were 'very still, meditative places' where visitors would not sit and think but sit and experience the place directly. The effect the cloud chambers had depended upon the person. They worked best when they encouraged the viewer to sit still for a moment and reflect (2002, 76). The idea of the *Beara Shelter* was 'a space for being and contemplation' (1998, 20).

One of the developments of 1960s land art was to put the artist *inside* the art. In the traditional manner of painting the landscape, the artist was viewing the landscape from a distance, standing back; but 'since the 1960s artists have been putting them-selves into it' Drury observed (2002, 76). For Drury, the photograph is a poor substitute for the work itself. Drury said he had taken photographs of ephemeral works (such as the cairns), but was more interested in working 'with people in the real world' (ib., 81).

Unlike some of his British contemporaries (Long, Fulton), Chris Drury encouraged people to visit the sites of his works. He published a website and postcards with instructions on how to find them. 'In no way could that work communicate itself through a photograph because it's an experience, and nothing you could bring to a gallery would get anywhere near what the thing is about' (2002, 81). In this respect, Drury has more in common with American earth artists, such as Dennis Oppenheim or Robert Smithson, who exalted site and location.

Going out and walking or making work from time to time is important for Chris Drury – especially if he hasn't done any travelling or walking for a while. 'I'm really fortunate to be invited to extraordinary places to go and make work' (ib., 79). However, it wasn't the object itself that was the really valuable aspect of travelling or working on commissions for Drury, but the process and experience of making it, interacting with people, living in particular environments. 'The main thing you bring back is how the experience has changed you inside' (ibid.). So some of the pieces Drury makes are not about specific places or times, but 'the whole activity of being out there in those places'.

> In a sense you can't not be a conceptual artist these days [said Drury], because you have to think about the world and if you don't you're not contributing to the debate in any useful way. But at the same time, in order to make art that's really interesting you have to stop thinking. (2002, 90)

Chris Drury said he didn't think of himself as really fitting into the land art or art and nature genre. 'As soon as you say 'art and nature', it makes people think of fiddling about with sticks, which is really not what I'm interested in' (2002, 90). Although labelled as a land artist, Drury preferred to see himself as an artist who 'explores nature and culture, inner and outer'.[8] There was no division between art, nature and humanity, for Drury: the artist – and art – was always part of nature ('there is no division between man, art and nature').[9] Drury did not think of himself, either, as the kind of artist who had something to express, who wished to make statements about issues or the world. 'Personally I have nothing to communicate, consciously or unconsciously; the work simply reflects the moving from moment to moment in the world as it is, and so it is nature itself that communicates' (ibid.). In this view, Drury saw himself as a shamanic translator of nature and the world, a creative interface between the world and the viewer.

As well as shamanism, critics have also linked Chris Drury's art to Buddhism (as with Long's art). Rather than an 'creator' of art, or an 'expresser' of emotions or statements or views, then, Drury would be seen as a 'reflector' of nature and the world, someone who does not 'create' art but reflects what is already in the world and in nature (and in himself and in other people). In this view, Drury's output is a manifestation of his being-in-the-world, so to speak. It's an art of ontology, of beingness, of being in the moment, of reflecting the moment (or the passing of moments), rather than the traditional (Western) view of art as being about personal expression, about crises of subjectivity, about angst and suffering, about visionary creativity, and all the rest of the Freudian, Nietzschean, psychological baggage. It's not an art of putting a personal stamp on the world (such as making the big earthworks gestures in the American desert), or promoting ego and self (and celebrity and fame), or advertizing a set of philosophical or ideological views. 'Making art, for me, is never the means of finding insight. It is rather the reflection of a growing consciousness'. Drury spoke in Zen Buddhist terms of his artistic process: 'I go to 'outer nature', which is thoughtless, void, in order to see the whole. From the void comes insight, which makes art'. [10]

HAMISH FULTON

One British artist, more than any other, is closest to Richard Long and his walk-based art and art of walking, and that's Hamish Fulton. A fellow student at St Martin's art school on the vocational sculpture course, Fulton was a vital influence in the early development of Long's art. For Fulton, as for Long, the walk is central to the artwork. If there is no walk, there is no work: 'no walk, no work', as Fulton put it, 'First the walk second the artwork' Fulton asserted.[1] Most of his walks have been made alone, Fulton said (though Fulton has also walked in groups, which Long hasn't really done, such as with C.A.S.K. in Japan). But not every walk needed to be be made into a work of art. They were sufficient unto themselves.[2] On the other hand, Fulton said he had to walk to be able to make a work of art. The artwork came out of the work, and if he didn't walk, there couldn't be any art.

There's a social link between Fulton and Long too: they are good friends, and have embarked on a number of walks together (eleven walks, between 1972 and 1990). Hamish Fulton called his walks with Long 'the walks of a lifetime' (2002). It's interesting to compare the different ways that the artists responded to the walks they made together. The walks became inspirations for some of the key works in the *œuvres* of both artists.

Of fellow walking artist Hamish Fulton, Richard Long commented:

> We are very good friends, we have a great deal of respect for each other's work and get on well together. We are old friends and have the same sense of humour. In many ways we are very similar – we are both artists, both like walking and camping, but having said that, we are very different artists. When we are on a walk we are both making completely individual work along the way – the collaboration is the walking. (1994b)

Like Richard Long, Hamish Fulton has his favourite walks and territories, where he has made many walks: the Pilgrims' Way in England, the Cairngorms in Scotland, Japan, and the Himalayas. Both Fulton and Long feature celestial events, such as full moons and solstices, and Fulton, for instance, has a walk entitled *Starting On the Day of the June Full Moon, Ending On the Night of the Summer Solstice* (1995), which could easily be a Long walk and work. Both do coast-to-coast walks, and classic hiker walks. Both have walkworks which record the sounds heard on their walks. Both are nuts about the Orient – Tibet, Japan, China – and the poetry, customs and religion of those regions. Both tend to walk in wilderness or non-urban places (and only feature that type of terrain in their works). Both assert the primacy of The Walk above everything else, including all of the secondary material that comes afterwards, including art.

Both Richard Long and Fulton have conducted walkworks without sleeping, such as walking through a day and a night without sleep. Fulton, though, has gone much further than Long in this regard, and has tested himself by walking for long distances without sleep (such as his walk along the Pilgrims' Way in Southern England between December 21st and 23rd, in 1991, a 125 mile continuous walk without sleep. Or his *Seven Walk Without Sleep* (the *Winter Solstice Full Moon* walk of 1991 being one of them). Fulton likes to toy with the hallucinations and altered states that sleep deprivation brings (i.e., it can be a walk along a familiar route, but it's a completely different experience because the artist-walker's gone without sleep).)

Many of Hamish Fulton's artworks are very similar to Richard Long's – textworks, photoworks, photographs of mountain tops or hillsides or country lanes or lakes or snowfields. And both Fulton and Long opt for irregular snaking lines on gallery walls to indicate the routes they undertook. And they both quote words in Japanese and Chinese ideograms. Like Long's textworks, Fulton photoworks and textworks recall concrete or visual poetry, word sculpture, *haiku,* diaries and journals, and Conceptual art.

Hamish Fulton's art differs from Richard Long's in terms of the appearance of the textworks and wall works. Fulton loves to set text in a variety of typefaces, so that his exhibitions and books look a little like a typographer has gone nuts. While Long usually sticks to trusty old Gill Sans, Fulton happily indulges in shadowed capitals, white out of black, vertical type, extra bold fonts. Fulton, like Barbara Kruger, also loves very large and very bold (and coloured) lettering (such as in *Sweet Grass Hills* [1999], and *Warm Dead Bird* [1999]). (Fulton did not, though, make the wall works in his exhibitions himself. Unlike Long with his handmade mud drawings, Fulton gave the job of putting up his texts and photoworks to others.)

Both Hamish Fulton and Richard Long employ short phrases which aim to capture some of the experience or remind the viewer of something of their walks. In a seven day walk in Scotland, Fulton fills a work with lines and lines of descriptions of the walk which recall many of Long's works: 'sound of the small stream / pale grey pale blue yellow sky in the late afternoon / small herd of deer one rubbing a branch stop look turn and run'. In a 1987 walkwork made in Mexico, Fulton writes: 'shooting star – dark night – grey morning – snowflakes – snow covered ground' and so on. Short phrases which, like Long's, sometimes evoke a *haiku* approach to the evoking the experience of the walk (*less* may be *more*, but Fulton certainly likes to fill some of his walkworks with hundreds of words). While Long counts hours or days or miles, Fulton has sometimes counted footsteps as a way of measuring a walk (as in *Counting 6234 Barefoot Paces* [1994-97], or the barefoot paces counted in Kent between 1999 and 2001).

Hamish Fulton had more a philosophical and ascetic view of walking-as-art than Richard Long.[3] Walking was not, Fulton asserted, for recreation or leisure or for studying nature, or for taking photographs or making sculptures along the way.

It is about an attempt at being 'broken down' mentally and physically – with the *desire* to 'flow inside' a rhythm of walking – to experience a temporary state of euphoria, a blending of my mind with the outside world of nature.[4]

Despite the monk-like austerity, Hamish Fulton also said he loved walking, and 'lived for it. I compare everything to my walks. I've enjoyed all the walks and some were more challenging than others, therefore more rewarding' (2002, 108).

As well as the numerous similarities between the art of Hamish Fulton and Richard Long, there are plenty of key differences: no sculptures in Fulton's work, like Long's stone, bone, wood, slate and mud circles, rows, lines or ellipses, on the wall or the floor. No sculptures made out of doors on walks and photographed. No water splashes or waterlines. No lines made by kicking away stones or flattening grass. No marks made by sleeping places or tents. No fingerprint marks on pieces of wood or hand-made Korean paper. No walks within imaginary circles or along imaginary lines. No mapworks (or very few). No walks carrying stones (or throwing stones, or adding them to cairns).

As with Richard Long, Hamish Fulton rarely included images of people in his art, but his art 'should not be thought of as anti-people' (1995). Instead, Fulton's photographs are of wildernesses (mountains, lakes, forests, fields and country lanes). Fulton separated the walk from the artwork. 'The artwork cannot represent the experience of a walk', Fulton affirmed (1995). The walk was always elsewhere, always only for the walker-artist. 'The *location* of the walk is not in the gallery – and the walk itself is a past event'.[5] Aspects of the work could remind the artist of making the work, but could not communicate the experience of the work to the viewer. 'The texts are facts for the walker and fiction for everyone else' (1995). The artworks, instead, were pointers towards the experience of the walk, reminders perhaps, or dim correlations. Fulton hoped that the viewer 'will create a feeling, an impression in his or her own mind based on whatever my art can provide' (2002, 108). Hamish Fulton said he preferred experiences to objects (2002, 108). For Fulton, 'an object cannot compete with an experience' (2002, 27). Some artists, however, did not separate the two: since the 1960s, the object *is* the experience, and the experience *is* the object.

Hamish Fulton said he preferred to walk rather than sit in a train or plane or car. Travelling (sitting) was of 'little interest' to him (1995). And when he embarked on a walk, Fulton said he walked directly from his home, rather than use transport. The walk was the thing, always. 'I am an artist who walks, not a walker who makes art' Fulton said (1995); this is also Long's stance. Although he walks to make art, Long definitely isn't a walker who also makes art. Fulton complained that he seemed to spend more time on organizing exhibitions, on admin and paperwork, than walking (1995). And, like Long, Fulton said that his walks were not performances.

Hamish Fulton's artistic inspirations came from mountaineering and the exploits of mountaineers such as Reinhold Messner, Peter Boardman and Doug Scott (Fulton, like Richard Long, has travelled many times in mountain regions, but neither would call themselves professional climbers; Fulton has climbed some high peaks, but says he's an 'arm-chair mountaineer'). It was the mind-set that mountaineering created in the individual that interested Fulton (some mountaineers have written in spiritual terms of their experiences). Fulton had been impressed by Doug Scott's light, independent ascent of Kangchenjunga in 1979 (Scott had helped to pioneer the newer, lighter climbs, instead of the big funded expeditions involving hundreds of people). 'The story of [Scott's] ascent of Kangchenjunga in 1979 became for me a symbol for combining a lightness of touch with a genuinely great experience – two qualities I strive for myself, but not without considerable difficulty', Fulton explained (2002, 110).

Another influence was American Indian culture (Hamish Fulton had visited the sites of Sioux, Cheyenne and Plains Indians in the late 1960s). Yet another was ecology and ecologists (Fulton voiced ecological concerns more often than Long, and is a more politicized artist). Fulton also drew on pilgrims and pilgrimages (he has walked a number of pilgrim routes, including Pilgrims' Way, near his home in Canterbury in Kent). Tibetan religious art, *haiku* poetry from Japan (Santoka Teneda and Basho), and 'the walking peoples of the world from all periods of history' were also cited by the artist (1995).

Among artists, Hamish Fulton has referred to Marina Abramovic, Nancy Wilson, Roger Ackling and Richard Long as influences. He also cited *Monsters From the Deep* (1997), a CD by Lawrence Weiner, Bruce Nauman's video *Good Boy Bad Boy* (1985), and native cultures as some of the art he admired (such as the Huichol of Mexico). The Marathon Monks of Mount Hiel (Tendai Buddhist monks in Japan) were also inspirations for Fulton (in particular their repeat walks, walking around a hill for seven years until they had travelled the same distance as the circumference of the Earth).

In "Old Muddy", Hamish Fulton ruminated on working and walking with Richard Long. In the course of the short piece (published in Walking *In Circles* for the 1991 retrospective), Fulton referenced Chuang-tzu, the *Tao Te Ching*, Shakespeare, Dostoievsky, Santoka Teneda (the Japanese *haiku* poet), Bob Dylan, and the Nazca Lines.

Hamish Fulton resisted being categorized as an artist related to the British

Romantic tradition or landscape tradition. He wanted to work, like Richard Long, in an international mode, and not be tied down to the provincial British view of landscape art. He said he was not part of the outdoor sculpture tradition, either. He also preferred, like Richard Long, to walk in landscapes wilder and more extreme than those found in dear old Blighty. Fulton said he respected and was a devotee of countryside walking, but he needed extreme conditions too, like the Himalayas or Alaska. Fulton was happy that his work had 'never been fashionable', that he had survived so long in the art world, and that he could continue to make a variety of work (2002, 107).

The typical Hamish Fulton artwork is a large black-and-white photograph in a frame with a short piece of text in capitals underneath (the look of Fulton's text and photo pieces recalls Richard Long's art closer than anyone else's, except perhaps Dennis Oppenheim). Fulton's works include *Rock Fall Echo Dust* (1988), recording a walk made on Baffin Island; *The Crossing Place of Two Walks at Ringdom Gompa* (1984), *Grims Ditch* (1969-70), *Rock Path, Switzerland* (1986), *Night Changing Shapes* (1991) and *Gazing At the Horizon Line, Sky Horizon Ground* (Australia, 1982). Some of Fulton's works consist only of text in capitals painted on a wall in a gallery: *No Talking For Seven Days* (1993) and *Rock Fall Echo Dust* (1988).

In King's Wood, near Challock in Kent (a modest but appealing woodland sculpture park), Hamish Fulton walked back and forth along the same route for seven days. The results were published in a book (*Walking Through*, 1999). Like Richard Long, Fulton has published books about particular walking trips, and the books can be counted as artworks in themselves. As well as wallworks and photo and textworks, Fulton also produced postcards (the postcards were a part of his art as much as the larger works).

Like many British land artists, Hamish Fulton didn't want to make massive and long-lasting marks on the landscape. It was, rather, absolutely the opposite. Fulton said his art was not aggressive or technological: 'I do not directly re-arrange, remove, sell and not return, dig into, wrap or cut up with loud machinery any elements of the natural environment' Fulton asserted, clearly having various well-known land artists in mind (1995). Fulton was acutely conscious of the ecological aspects of his work. It was ironic, for instance, that putting on an exhibition could actually do more damage to the environment in terms of pollution (such as jet travel and transportation) than if the artist had stayed at home and conserved energy.

OTHER LAND ARTISTS IN BRITAIN AND EUROPE

Other British and European land and site artists of Richard Long's generation whose art has some affinity with Long's art include Graham Moore whose works include three circles of mown grass, entitled *Herbe Garden* (1989, Christchurch Park). This work echoed Long's early turf circles. Gwen Heney made a 30 metre long snake out of bricks at the Garden Festival Wales show (1992). Also at Garden Festival Wales was Mick Petts' *Mother Earth*, created out of a huge pile of slag which was required to be disguised. Valerie Pragnelli made a spiral from rocks in a stream (*Langslie Spiral*, Milepoint). Ron Haselden produced a dance of lights, called *Fete* (1992), out of strings of lights hung from a group of willow trees. One of the largest of contemporary garden and landscape design projects was Giuliano Gori's Parco di Celle.

Richard Harris has produced a wall sculpture, *Dry Stone Passage* (1982). Harris wrote: 'I want the sculpture to become a living and working part of the existing environment'.[1] Harris made a *Willow Walk* (1990), a walk lined with willow branches. Harris's works at Grizedale included *Cliff Structure* (1978), slate slabs set on split oak, and *Quarry Structure* (1977), a 'bridge' of slate and oak sticks. British sculptor Paul Russell Cooper produced *Two Circles in a Stone Bridge*. This is a large dry stone work at Portland in Dorset (1983). Two circles were created with the stones, one 'positive', the other 'negative': the 'negative' circle was a large hole like an archway. Other works by Cooper include *Quincunx*, a series of five globes in concrete set in an open space at Rufford Country Park (near Newark, 1983). The globes sit open partially to display something different in each globe: water, rocks, burning detritus from the garden and a sundial. Cooper's *Quincunx* is based on natural forms – in this case, five-petalled plants.

Michael Dan Archer's *Observatory* (1994) recalled Robert Morris's *Observatory*: it was basically a low circular embankment, the kind seen in Iron Age hillforts or in some Bronze Age stone circles in the United Kingdom (Archer's *Observatory* in particular recalled Avebury stone circle). A stone shaped like a post and lintel (as at Stonehenge) marked the entrance, and two broken circular stones did for benches in the centre of *Observatory*.

Patricia Leighton reworked the earth at the side of the M8 motorway, turning it into a series of *Sawtooth Ramps*. Julia Barton created *A Rural Landmark: Viewing Platform* (1994) in Yorkshire stone at Kirklees Way: the circular platform was cut into a hillside, backed by a low wall and clad in stone. There were no signs to indicate what to look at, as in municipal viewing sites (the sort of tourist brass discs found on hilltops that state '25 miles to Hay Bluff').

Peter Randall-Page, one of the most appealing of contemporary sculptors in Albion (certainly one of the most accomplished of the members of the Royal Society of British Sculptors), created an interaction between modern sculpture and mediæval architecture when he sited some of his boulders made from Finnish glacial granite at Wenlock Priory in rural Shropshire (the outerlying counties of the Midlands aren't really know for cutting edge sculpture). *Boulders and Banner Boulders: Secret Life I, II, III, IV* (1994) contained sculptures that were split open like gigantic seeds. Randall-Page's sculptures were suitably monumental (and abstract) for the architectural space of the ruined Priory.

At Grizedale Forest, Helen Stylianides produced a tree sculpture that looked like a tree with the branches cut off, about five feet from the trunk. A tree with no leaves, but stumps for branches (*Tree Sculpture*, 1984). Collins made a forty foot diameter steel ring that was set, vertically, next to a tree. The enormous ring, *Ting*, was entangled in the branches: the aim was that the circle of steel could not be seen as a whole, in one view, but only glimpsed in parts through the leaves. Alyson Brien fashioned *A Curve Around a Lime Tree* (1987) which looked like a low fence of stripped wood. Eric Geddes bent two young trees over and tied them to a central tree, so they formed a semi-circular arch, with the tree in the centre standing upright.

In the Forest of Dean sculpture park a number of interesting commissions took place in the late 1980s, works which offer a parallel to Richard Long's form of land art. Yvette Martin's *Four Seasons* was an environmental, 'land' sculpture. The first work, *Spring* (1986), was an oval-shaped pond with copper coloured water, a marshy space surrounded by webs of twigs and branches. It was a womb-like space, with a sense of being closed-in.[2] The branches on the trees growing on the bank of the small pond were bent down to add to the feeling of enclosure. Martin's *Spring* was the sort of space novelists such as Thomas Hardy and John Cowper Powys would like, for secluded pools recur in their fictions (Rushy Pond in *The Return of the Native*, and the haunting Lenty Pond in Powys's great novel of nature mysticism, *Wolf Solent*). Like other land artists, Yvette Martin spoke in terms of 'growth cycles', the 'cycle of life from conception, emergence, growth, reproduction, maturity, decay and death' (ib., 75). The pond or pool is a recurring favourite in land art (it's found in Chris Drury, Patricia Johanson, Mary Miss, James Turrell, Evelyn Zimmerman and Jim Sanborn, among many others).

The most exciting sculpture in the Forest of Dean at this time was Cornelia Parker's *Hanging Fire*, a large ring of iron hung 25 or so feet above the forest floor. Parker created a ring of iron flames, which were rusted overnight in salt water. They hung upside down from the ring. Parker wanted to portray the idea of a perpetual flame, a 'flame that would perpetually burn because it was cast in iron' (ib., 89). Hanging sculptures, as Alexander Calder showed time after time, are usually intriguing, and Parker's *Hanging Fire*, though made of heavy materials, floated in the trees. She also wanted to incorporate the notion of a 'circle or fairy ring', and a crown, and to use iron because iron was mined in the Forest of Dean.

Cornelia Parker's most famous work was probably *Cold Dark Matter: An Exploded View* (1991), an installation of a garden shed that Parker had blown up by army experts, exhibiting the debris hung from wires in the gallery (it became a favourite at London's Tate Modern). Parker's installation concerned cosmological themes of opposites, inhaling and exhaling, centripetal and centrifugal motion.

Peter Hutchinson was born in England (in 1930), but spent most of his artistic career in the US (based in Massachusetts). He collaborated with Dennis Oppenheim on a series of underwater works: fruit, vegetables and bread were packed in plastic bags and suspended from a fishing line in the West Indies (1969). Hutchinson also planted flowers in the sand underwater, and made a dam from sand bags in Tobago (*Underwater Dam,* 1969). Along the rim of a volcano (Paricutin, 1970), Hutchinson sited a 76 metre line of white bread wrapped in plastic. Hutchinson recorded the growth of mould and decomposition. Later works include *Ice Sandwich* (1994), a Brancusi-like tower of slabs of wood interlaced with blocks of ice, and 'thrown ropes' of flowers planted in the ground in the shape of a rope that Hutchinson threw (1996). Hutchinson preferred works that combined his love of horticulture, science, art and botany.[3]

Nicholas Pope is an artist whose works recall Barbara Hepworth's and Stephen Cox's – in particular Pope's outdoor works, such as *The Arch* (1985). Made from oak, the arch is large (18 feet long). It is the arch itself that fascinates Pope, for the arch is such an elegant structure, as anyone who has seen ancient Roman architecture (such as the Pont du Gard or Colosseum) can appreciate. Pope's *Arch* was dovetailed and pegged together, made from two young trees and one mature tree. Pope was consciously trying to make a work with oak, not just with any wood. 'I wanted to make an oak-wood arch not an arch made from wood.'[4]

Like Carl Andre, Nicholas Pope has placed large stones in an urban environment (Richard Long has sometimes installed boulders outdoors in cities [for instance, in

Hemisphere Circle, installed outside the Tokyo Forum, in 1996]). Pope's *Three Wilderness Stones* (1980, Southampton) and *Five Amorphous Shapes* are huge boulders of Forest of Dean stone in humanmade environments. Pope's stones spread out across parkland or the forecourts of modern business complexes, bringing the individual, irregular forms of nature into the angular, linear environment of the city.

Like Barbara Hepworth, Constantin Brancusi and Richard Long, Pope was fascinated by stones. David Nash made a large wooden boulder, while Anthony Gormley (b. 1950) emulated a large granite glacial boulder in 1981. Each of Gormley's *Two Stones* is nine feet high, one made of granite, the other of bronze. Set beside an artificial lake in Kent, the 'natural' granite stone was already contextualized as a work of art by its placement in such a setting, just as Carl Andre's boulders on the city street (*Stone Field*) are made into art by their context (ditto with Andre's infamous bricks).

Another sculpture venture in British Isles, the New Milestones Project in Dorset, set up by Common Ground, threw out some accomplished works. Such as Simon Thomas's *Seed Forms* (1988), oak shapes placed on the Dorsetshire downs; or Peter Randall-Page's *Wayside Carving* (1988), a large spiralling cone in blue Purbeck marble, a response to Dorset's richness in fossils. Nigel Lloyd's *Red Deer Wallow* (1983, Grizedale) was a horse-shoe-shaped stone wall enclosure. Keir Smith's works at Grizedale included *The Realm of Taurus*, linking the constellations of stars with animals in enclosures. Gabriel Orozco worked with snowballs – in *Planets of the Volcano* (1992) he placed small snowballs on top of some posts near Popocatepetl volcano. In Anish Kapoor's *Void Field* (1990), each of twenty large pieces of sandstone had small holes bored in the top, which were painted black inside.

Chris Jenning's *Vault* (1992) reacted to the Museum of Installation's space by filling it with curving metal rods which connected the walls and floor together. Bill Viola brought a whole tree into the Newport Harbor Art Museum in California for his *Theatre of Memory* (1985), the branches were hung with bells blown by electric fans. The tinkling tree faced a giant video image of hissing static.

Recalling Wolfgang Laib's pollen floor-pieces, Shelagh Wakely covered the marble floor of the British School at Rome with a layer of tumeric spice (*Curcuma sul Travertino*, 1991). Anthony Gormley covered the entire area of a gallery floor in his *Field* installation (1991) with over 35,000 small humanoid figures. Giovanni Anselmo used stone like painted canvases, mounting thin slabs of granite on a Paris gallery wall like paintings (*Meeting of Two Works*, 1990).

Some installation artists used liquid to cover the floor area: in Glen Onwin's alchemical installations in Halifax (1991), water, wax and black brine were poured into a large concrete pool. Richard Wilson's *20/50* (1987) was a steel pool of sump oil with a walkway in the middle of it. Per Barclay also used pools of oil: in *Old Boathouse* (1990) an oil pool was set in a Norwegian boat-house beside the sea; in *The Jaguar's Cage* (1991), made at Turin Zoo, a large oil pool was set behind bars. Eve Laramee spread a rectangular mound of cobalt glass on the gallery floor in her *Requiem For a Blue Fluid* (1991). Rasheed Araeen spoofed Richard Long's art in his 1988 London installation: a Longian floor circle was made with empty wine bottles, and a Long-like row was made with bones (hilarious: no; pointless: yes).

Sjoerd Buisman constructed a floating mound of willow sticks on a wooden frame in the moat of the Old Castle at Jeemstede (Netherlands, 1995-98). In 1975 Buisman knotted a willow tree stem which the tree absorbed into itself as it grew (*Knotted Willow Branch*). In 1991 Buisman constructed an 'arch' of lime trees (at Haarlemmer-hout, Netherlands), which formed a low curve along a road. Using petals and berries, some of Nils Udo's sculptures are uncannily like Andy Goldsworthy's use of the same materials. Udo has, for instance, pressed berries into the bark of an old tree, just as Goldsworthy has done with leaves and sand.

Nikolaj Recke planted a field of clover in a gallery (1999) covering the whole floor in a carpet of green plants. Although the result recalled land art gestures such as Walter de Maria's *Earth Room*, the aim, according to Recke, was to explore the folklore of four-leaf clovers. In Guiseppe Penone's *To Breathe Shade* (1997-99), a human shape made from bronze bay leaves was installed in five bay trees, and his *Skins of Leaves* (2000) was a 'skin' of bronze leaves in humanoid form.

Part Two

5

Richard Long:

The Art of Walking

A story current at the time [1967] told of Caro confronted by an arrangement of twigs in the exhibition hall of the St. Martin's sculpture department. A conversation ensued. Caro: "What's this?" Long: "It's one part of a two-part sculpture." Caro: "So show me the other half." Long: "It's on top of Ben Nevis." Caro: "So how can I assess it when I can't see all of it?"

Charles Harrison[1]

I like simple, emotional, quiet, vigorous art....

Richard Long[2]

RICHARD LONG: ARTISTIC BIOGRAPHY

The central fact and act of Richard Long's art is walking. His work is founded on the art of walking, the act of walking, the actuality of walking, and on walking as art, as act, as experience. His walks become 'artwalks', artwalks which become artworks. He makes art-walk-works. For Richard Long, (art)walking is (art)working. As he walks he works. Art-walking and art-working become interchangeable. 'I have met with but one or two persons in the course of my life who understood the art of Walking, that is, of taking walks – who had a genius, so to speak, for *sauntering*' wrote Henry David Thoreau.1

Much of Richard Long's art consists of measuring walks, mapping walks, planning walks and executing walks. Memories of walks, dreams of walks... walks in the past, in history. Later and earlier walks in the same landscapes: Dartmoor, Somerset, Ireland, Scotland, Italy, Mexico, India. Real walks, but also artwalks. Walks along imaginary circles or lines. Walks between celestial occurrences such as sunrises or eclipses or solstices. Routes planned and mapped in the studio then carried out in the real world. Walks carrying stones, throwing stones, dropping stones, piling stones. Splashing water. Photographing campsites or mountaintops. Walks in forests and deserts and plains and villages and cities and leafy country lanes. Walks in which lots happens and walks in which nothing much happens. Walks in which hardly anyone is encountered. Walks executed mainly alone, but sometimes with others. Occasional walks with other artists, or critics, or friends. Walks which produce many sculptures along the way and walks which produce only a few words in a frame. Walks which don't produce any work at all. Favourite walks, favourite routes, favourite places, favourite terrain.

Walks that always work (there are no failed walks in Richard Long's art – Long has been walking for too many years to have a bad time walking... he doesn't seem bothered much by the harsh elements, and rarely mentions things that go wrong). But not all walks produce artworks: unseen walks are as important as the exhibited walks. However, not all artists exhibit their failures, and there could have been many failed walkworks (though this is unlikely).

Walks in all seasons and all weathers. Walks through the night. Continuous walks. Slow walks and rapid walks. Meandering walks. Short walks. Long walks.

Richard Long was born June 2, 1945, Bristol, UK. He's of the same generation of land artists such as Alan Sonfist, Charles Simonds, Michael Heizer, William Furlong, Alice Aycock, Mary Miss, Bruce McLean and David Nash, all born between 1944 and 1945. Long studied at the West of England College of Art in Bristol (1962-65) and the famous St Martin's School of Art (1966-68). Long said he used to go on treks with his father – youth hostelling, hitchhiking and cycling (Long's father was a teacher; his parents had met at a rambling club [SS, 307]). Long still lives in Bristol, and is very active, travelling the world, making art, and having exhibitions.

In 1967 Richard Long made his first important walkwork, *A Line Made By Walking*. Long's first one-man show was in 1968 at Konrad Fischer in Düsseldorf, when he was 23 (success came quite early to the artist). Like most land artists, Long makes indoor (gallery) works and outdoor works (not intended for public consumption – at least when they are made). He also produces art books, which are not typical exhibition catalogues, but artworks in their own right, usually with textworks, photoworks, and sometimes map works (he publishes limited edition artists' books too).

Among the influences one can discern in Richard Long's art (*haiku* poetry, Zen Buddhism, Shinto, British Romantic culture, Lawrence Weiner, Yves Klein, Hamish Fulton, Constantin Brancusi, Carl Andre, Joseph Beuys), there is also Jackson Pollock. Long acknowledged the influence of Pollock in making his mud drawings: 'Jackson Pollock has always been an iconic and legendary modernist for my generation, and for me he is also authentically primitive in some ways' (1995a). Long cited John Cage as another inspiration (he had seen Cage give a lecture in central London while at St Martin's).

Richard Long has had one-man shows at most of the major Western galleries, including the Whitechapel Art Gallery in London (1971, 1977), Oxford's MOMA (1971 and 1979), Museum of Modern Art, New York (1972), Scottish National Gallery, Edinburgh (1974, 1991), Venice Biennale (1976), Arnolfini in Bristol (1976, 1983, 1990), Kunstahlle, Berne (1977), National Gallery of Victoria, Australia (1977), Fogg Art Museum, Cambridge, MA (1980), National Gallery of Canada, Ottawa (1982), Konsthall, Malmö (1985), Stedelijk, Amsterdam (1973), Musée Rath, Geneva (1987), Stedelijk, Eindhoven (1979), Guggenheim, New York (1986), Tate Gallery, London (1990), Tate, Liverpool (1991), Pompidou Centre, Paris (1991), Städtische Galerie im Städel, Frankfurt (1991), Musée Départmental d'Art Contemporain, Rochechouart (1990), La Jolla Museum of Contemporary Art (1989), Henry Moore Sculpture Trust Studio (1989), Centre National d'Art Contemporain de Grenoble (1987), Hayward Gallery, London (1991), Philadelphia Museum of Art (1994), Sao Paolo Biennale (1994), Museum of Contemporary Art, Sydney (1994), Setagaya Art Museum, Tokyo (1996), National Modern Art Museum, Kyoto (1996), Contemporary Arts Museum, Houston (1996), Modern Art Museum, Fort Worth (1996), Henry Moore Institute, Leeds (1997), Bristol City Museum (1997), Yorkshire Sculpture Park (1998), Guggenheim Museum, Bilbao (2000), Trento (2000), Milwaukee Art Museum (2001), Tate Gallery, St Ives (2002), Stommein Synagoge (2004), Lismore (2006), Stockholm (2007), New York (2007), Edinburgh (2007), Glaurus (2008), Nice (2008) and Tate Britain (2009). Long has often exhibited alongside Carl Andre, an artist he admires a lot (in 1974, 1976, 1979, 1980, 1991), as well as Lawrence Weiner.

Richard Long has had many one-man shows at his UK art dealer, Anthony d'Offay Gallery in London, including 1979, 1980, 1981, 1983, 1984, 1985, 1986, 1988, 1990, 1993, 1995, 1998 and 2000. Some of the Anthony d'Offay shows have produced some of Long's best art books (*Mountains and Waters*, 1992, *Sixteen Works*, 1984, *Five, Six, Pick Up Sticks*, 1980, *Old World New World*, 1988, *Kicking Stones,* 1990 and *River Avon Book*, 1979). Sadly, d'Offay is no longer in business as a gallery. Long also had many one-man shows at his US art dealer, Sperone Westwater in New York: 1976, 1980, 1981, 1982, 1984, 1986, 1989, 1991, 1994, 1997, 2000 and 2004.

Richard Long's shows at Konrad Fischer in Düsseldorf (one of Long's earliest and most important supporters) include 1968, 1969, 1970, 1973, 1974, 1976, 1978, 1980, 1983, 1984, 1988, 1990, 1992, 1994, 1995, 2000 and 2008. Long also has had many one-man shows at Jean Bernier gallery in Athens (1980, 1984, 1987, 1989, 1992 and 1999). Galerie Tshudi, Glarus in Switzerland was another regular art dealer for Long: 1990, 1991, 1993, 1996, 1998, 2000, 2002, 2005, 2006 and 2008. Then there was Antonio Tucci Rosso gallery in Turin: 1983, 1986, 1989, 1971, 1991, 1994 and 1998.

Richard Long's other one-man shows at commercial art galleries include Paris, 1969, Krefeld, 1969, Milan, 1969, Mönchengladbach, 1970, Dwan Gallery, New York, 1970, Amsterdam, 1971, Turin, 1971, Lissom Gallery, London, 1973, 1974, 1976 and 1979, Antwerp, 1973, John Weber, NYC, 1974, Amsterdam, 1975, Antwerp, 1975, Paris, 1975, Basel, 1975, Plymouth, 1975, Rome, 1976, Antwerp, 1976, Tokyo, 1976, Basel, 1977, Sydney, 1977, Paris, 1978, Amsterdam, 1978, Leeds, 1978, Zurich, 1978, Hamburg, 1978, Zurich, 1979, Basel, 1979, Londonderry, 1979, Southampton, 1979, Tokyo, 1979, Amsterdam, 1980, Edinburgh, 1981, Toronto, 1981, Bordeaux, 1981, Amsterdam, 1982, Paris, 1982, Venice, 1982, Toronto, 1983, Tokyo, 1983, Coracle Press, 1984, Paris, 1984, Kilkenny, 1984, Londonderry, 1984, Basel, 1985, Kendal, 1985, Milan, 1985, Madrid, 1986, Paris, 1986, Pori (Finland), 1986, Liverpool, 1987, Chicago, 1987, Aachen, 1988, St Gallen (Switzerland), 1989, Bristol, 1989, Chagny, 1989, Santa Monica, 1990, Stockholm, 1990, Santa Monica, 1991, Santa Fe, 1991, Barcelona, 1992, New York, 1993, Seoul, 1993, Düsseldorf, 1994, New York, 1994, Rome, 1994, Orkney, 1994, Santa Fe, 1995, Huesca, 1995, Reykjavik, 1995, San Francisco, 1995, Bolzano, 1996, Exeter, 1996, Duisburg, 1997, St Andrews, 1997, Naoshima, 1997, Palermo, 1997, Zugspitze, 1998, Hanover, 1999, Braga (Portugal), 1999, Cleves, 1999, Venice, 2000, New York, 2000, Bristol, 2000, New York, 2000, Leuk,

2000, Paris, 2001, Cleves, 2001, Porto, 2001, Venice, 2002, Salisbury, 2002, Rome, 2003, London, 2003, Portugal, 2004, Seoul, 2004, Glaurus, 2005, San Francisco, 2006 and London, 2006.

Some of Richard Long's group shows include the *Earth Art* exhibition at the White Museum at Cornell University in 1969 (an important land art show), the Conceptual art show *Information* at MOMA in Gotham in 1970, the Guggenheim International in 1971, Documenta 5 at Kassel in 1972, a show with Carl Andre, Daniel Buren, Victor Burgin, Gerhard Richter and Gilbert & George in Brussels in 1974, another show with Andre (and Le Va) in Washington in 1976, *Probing the Earth: Contemporary Land Projects* at the Hirshhorn in Washington 1977 (another important land art exhibition, which travelled to La Jolla and Seattle), *Sculpture/ Nature* in Bordeaux in 1978, the Hayward Annual in 1979, a sculpture show in Berne in 1979 (with Matisse, Andre, Judd, Giacometti and Flavin), a show with Ryman, Dibbets and Andre in Humlebæck in 1980, *Natur-Skulptur* in Stuttgart in 1981, *Objekt, Skulptur, Installation* in Hamburg in 1982, Documenta 7 in 1982, *The British Show,* which travelled to Perth, Sydney and Brisbane in 1985, *Landscape: Place, Nature, Material* at Kettle's Yard in Cambridge in 1986, *The Unpainted Landscape* (1987) which travelled around Scotland, *British Art in the 20th Century* at the Royal Academy in 1987, *A Quiet Revolution: British Sculpture Since 1965* in Chicago and San Francisco in 1987, *Starlit Waters*, another British sculpture show, at Liverpool's Tate in 1988, a show with Judd and Gudmundsson in Reykjavik in 1988, *Magiciens de la Terre* in Paris in 1989, *Von der Natur in der Kunst* in Vienna in 1990, a show with Lawrence Weiner and On Kawara in Paris in 1990, a show with Hamish Fulton in Madrid in 1991, a group show with Andre and Ellsworth Kelly in 1991 in London, a show with Richard Serra, Wolfgang Laib and Weiner at Collioure in 1992, *Gravity and Grace* at the Hayward in 1993, *About Landscape* at Otterlo in 1993, *Donald Judd and His Artist Friends* in Vienna in 1995, *Sculpture in the Close* at Jesus College, Cambridge, in 1996, *Land Marks* in New York in 1998, *Live In Your Head: Concept and Experiment in Britain, 1965-75* at the Whitechapel in 1999, *Paysages* in Amiens in 2001, another Conceptual art show, at the Stedelijk Museum in Amsterdam in 2002, a room at the Tate Modern (London) in 2004, the Irish Museum of Modern Art in 2004, three works at the Royal Academy Summer show in 2004, a group show of British modernists (Moore, Hepworth, Caro, King and Flanagan) in Otterlo in 2004, and another show in Otterlo in 2004, *Openasia (East Meets West)* in Venice in 2004, and Eindhoven's Abbemuseum (installation art) in 2004. Long has contributed to a few shows at the publicly-funded art gallery in Bristol, Arnolfini, the nearest upscale 'white cube' gallery to his home in Bristol. He has also exhibited at an even more local show, at Failand village hall (in 2000).

The biggest collections of Richard's Long's work available to the public are, as one would expect, in the United States and Europe (in Europe: mainly France, Germany, the Netherlands and the UK). There are examples too in Japan, Canada and Australia. Long has work permanently on display in many museums and institutions, including Donald Judd's Marfa site, Tokyo International Forum plaza, Jesus College in Cambridge, and museums in Bordeaux, Bristol, Edinburgh, Duisburg, Mannheim, Rivoli, San Francisco, Seattle and Beirut.

Richard Long hasn't nearly so many works in sculpture parks in the UK as many other sculptors (whether British or international). Many of the major British sculptors have works in the sculpture parks of Albion (Yorkshire Sculpture Park, Forest of Dean Sculpture Park, Sculpture at Goodwood, Grizedale Forest, and King's Wood, Challock), and around the world. Long has exhibited at Goodwood, and East Wintersloe, Roche Court, in the UK. Long prefers to donate or sell works to indoor museums and galleries, rather than outdoor sculpture parks. In the New World, Long's British contemporaries have many more works in sculpture parks and sculpture gardens than Long does (such as Andy Goldsworthy, David Nash, Anthony Caro, William Tucker and Barry Flanagan).

There is a *Richard Long Newsletter*, edited by Gerard Vermeulen, in Nijmegen. (This is the best resource for Richard Long material on the internet:

<http://www.therichardlongnewsletter.org>

Richard Long also has his own site, like many artists:

<http://www.richardlong.org>

The three important, must-have Richard Long books are: *Richard Long* (1986), *Walking in Circles* (1992) and *Walking the Line* (2002). In the second rank of Longania would be books such as *A Walk Across England* (1997), *A Moving World,* (2002), *Mirage* (1998), *Spanish Stones* (1999), *Dialog* with Jivya Soma Mashe (2003), and Long's Anthony d'Offay books: *River Avon Book* (1979), *Five, Six, Pick Up Sticks* (1980), *Sixteen Works* (1984), *Old World New World* (1988), *Kicking Stones* (1990), *Mountains and Water* (1992) and *Walking, Mud, Stones* (1995).

There are many published interviews which are useful (they are listed in the bibliography and the list of abbreviations). If I had to nominate one interview with the artist, it would be the two pamphlets *Richard Long: In Conversation* (1985-86) from MW

Press in Holland. As this may not be widely available, the three main Richard Long books noted above are the best place to start.

The 1991 Hayward show was one of Richard Long's most important in his home country, and featured many stone circles, including *Cornwall Circle, Thames Circle, Planet Circle* and *Summer Circle*, a spiral (*A Line the Length of a Straight Walk From the Bottom To the Top of Silbury Hill*, 1970) and mud wall drawings (*River Avon Mud Circle*).

Long's shows with Jivya Soma Mashe, a traditional Indian artist of the Warli tribe, was a curious collaboration – they were very different artists, from different cultures. Long travelled to India to meet Mashe and to make art, some of which was featured in the exhibitions in Europe (there were also tie-in books).

In some of his more recent shows, Richard Long has taken to producing smaller works on plywood and paper (designed to be portable and sellable). At Sperone Westwater in 2004, for instance, Long installed mud drawings on wood, as well as his usual bigger sculpture (a stone floor-standing ellipse [*13th Street Ellipse*, 2004], and paths on the floor of pieces of wood set end-to-end, very much in the Carl Andre manner. The mud drawings, in the familiar Long forms, were smaller than usual: blocky spirals, open circles, but they also recalled paintings, in particular Minimal works of the 1960s, such as Robert Ryman and Brice Marden. For the 2003 *Hand Made* show at Galleria Lorcan O'Neill Roma, Long produced mud wall drawings (*Untitled*, 2003) on plywood.

Winning the Turner Prize in 1989 was probably the highpoint for Richard Long in terms of media exposure in his homeland (although the premier arts prize in the UK has an even higher media profile now than it had in 1989). Long has been awarded a number of other prizes and awards (including a doctorate from the University of Bristol in 1995, the Chevalier dans l'Ordre des Arts et des Lettres in 1990, the Wilhelm Lehmbruck-Preis in 1996, and the Kunstpreis Aachen in 1988).

Richard Long also produces artists' books, signed editions and limited editions of his books. *Being in the Moment*, for example, comes in an edition of 60 (from PARC Editions, Holland), with screenprints and offset prints, signed by the artist, and retails at 4,000 Euros. The artist's book *Walking and Sleeping* is published by Ivory Press (London) in an edition of 58, with a price tag of £18,000. 16 copies feature hand paintings by the artist; price: £38,000. Long had produced artists' books from the start of his career: in 1970 he made *Along a River Bank*, a small book (4 by 8 inches) published an edition of 300 (by Art & Project).

Stones along the Way (1999) was a series of 12 etchings, each image comprising a thin line, roughly circular or elliptical, traced onto grey paper, with distances printed on each print: 572 miles, 846 miles (apparently records of walks). Richard Long publishes limited edition prints too. For instance: *Limestone Drawing One and Two* and *Slate Drawing One and Two* is a portfolio edition of four screenprints (in an edition of 40, published by Ridinghouse Editions, London), price: £3,500. A limited edition screen-print (200 copies), signed by the artist, was produced by Tate Gallery, St Ives, to coincide with its *A Moving World* show in 2002 (retail: £255, plus postage & packing). There are Richard Long postcards sets and posters, too. In terms of work sold in commercial galleries, a typical price for a Richard Long textwork in 2000 (being sold at Anthony d'Offay gallery in London) was £20,000.

Richard Long hasn't been as prominent a fixture on television or radio as many artists. Certainly, British artists like David Hockney, Richard Hamilton or Sean Scully are far more likely to crop up on a TV arts documentary than the much more reclusive Richard Long. The YBAs and Brit-art crowd are of course media-hungry: Damien Hirst, Tracey Emin, Sarah Lucas, Mark Wallinger, the Chapman brothers. They'd appear on TV even if it was to discuss the price of teabags. Long is the opposite of that kind of celebrity artist, art as celebrity, celebrity as art, the post-Warholian cult of celebrity.

There have been a few TV programmes about Richard Long, including BBC's *Omnibus*, and one or two independent films about the artist, such as Philip Haas's *Stones and Flies: Richard Long in the Sahara*, made in 1988, or Denny Long's *Four Mud Works* (1984), and short films such as *A Round of Desert Flowers* (1987). Audio Arts produced a conversation between Long and William Furlong (1985).

Richard Long is associated with the American land, Minimal, Process, Conceptual and postmodern artists (such as Lawrence Weiner, Michael Heizer, Walter de Maria, Dennis Oppenheim, Nancy Holt, Mary Miss, Alice Aycock, Judy Pfaff, Donald Judd, Robert Smithson, Eva Hesse, Richard Serra, Tony Smith, Robert Morris, Jackie Winsor, Sol LeWitt, and especially Carl Andre), and with European Arte Povera and Minimal/ Conceptual artists (Hans Haacke, Christo, Jannis Kounellis, Lucio Fontana, Alberto Burri, Piero Manzoni, Daniel Buren, Giovanni Anselmo, Mario Merz and Jan Dibbets). Other key names one might link with Richard Long include John Cage, Jackson Pollock, Joseph Beuys, Yves Klein, Constantin Brancusi, Isamu Noguchi, Mel Ramsden, Joseph Kosuth, Bruce Nauman, Barnett Newman, Anthony Caro and Henry Moore.

Contemporary students of Richard Long's at St Martin's art school included Gilbert & George, Bruce McLean, Barry Flanagan and fellow artist-walker, Hamish Fulton. Long is also associated, at various times, by various critics, with other British sculptors such as Tony Cragg, David Nash, Richard Deacon, Shirazeh Houshiary, Ian Hamilton Finlay, Michael Craig-Martin, Nicholas Pope, Peter Randall-Page, Stephen Cox, Bill Woodrow, Anish Kapoor, Hamish Fulton, Alison Wilding, Richard Wentworth, Boyd Webb and the Art & Language group. These sculptors are sometimes grouped together as the 'New British Sculptors' or 'the New Sculpture' (but every few years or season there's a *new* New Something or other). The 'Young British Artists' (Hirst, Emin, Wallinger, Lucas, Chapman), for instance, are well past their sell-by-date, and into their forties.

Key exhibitions of the 'new (British) sculpture' included *The New Generation* (Whitechapel Art Gallery, 1965), *The New Art* (Hayward, 1972), *Objects & Sculpture* (ICA/ Arnolfini, 1981), *British Sculpture in the 20th Century* (Whitechapel, 1981), *Figures and Objects* (Southampton, 1983), *New Art* (Tate, 1983), *The British Art Show* (Arts Council, 1984), *The British Show* (Australia, 1985), *The Poetic Object* (Dublin, 1985), *Entre el Objeto* (Madrid, 1986), *A Quiet Revolution: British Sculpture Since 1965* (Chicago, 1987), *About Landscape* (Otterlo, 1993), *Gravity and Grace* (Hayward, 1993), *Land Marks* (New York, 1998), *Live In Your Head: Concept and Experiment in Britain, 1965-75* (Whitechapel, 1999) and *Paysages* (Amiens, 2001). Long contributed to many of these shows. (*The New Art* in '72, for instance, showed Long, Gilbert & George, Fulton, Craig-Martin, Flanagan, Burgin and Art & Language, among others).

Richard Long employed Minimal forms throughout his artistic career: the circles, lines, rows, ellipses and arcs are very much Minimal forms. The materials Long used drew on Arte Povera (mud, stone, wood, bark, bones, grass). The art of the walk, which Long perfected to become the ultimate artist-as-walker (drifter, nomad, traveller), was based on Conceptual and Process lines: the *idea* of the walk was critical. Long walked in imaginary circles or straight lines (sometimes he meandered, or walked slow, but usually quite fast). He followed routes planned beforehand on maps. The walk itself was the sculpture, the artwork. The work could be as long as the walk. The emphasis was on making the walk itself, the experience of actually walking.

Richard Long appears as a late British Romantic landscape artist, someone who fuses Sixties Conceptualism with 1800s pantheism; he's something of a High Modernist and a postmodernist Conceptualist. He has been described a 'traveller, explorer, pilgrim, shaman, magician, peripatetic poet, hill-walker' as well as an artist.[1] He says it is not enough for him to have an idea or concept: he has to make it (RC, 23). That separates him from some of the more ascetic Conceptualists for whom art doesn't necessarily have to be made. The stone circles of Richard Long espouse the sensuality and beauty of the post-Romantic and modernist art object (as in sculpture by Rodin, Picasso, Maillol, Moore, Kollwitz), while his photographs, mapworks and textworks exhibit the cool, philosophic distantiation and ideations of Process, serial, ABC, Conceptual and Minimal art. The mud and stone and terracotta works are real, sensual objects, which satisfy the modernist critics who exalt the art object (Long likes to provide real, physical sculptures at his exhibitions). The text and photographic pieces, hoever, 'feed the imagination', as Long put it;2 'they are the distillation of experience'. But they are only understandable (assimilable), like television shows or traffic signals, by a heavily enculturated imagination. The text pieces are linguistic structures, dependent for their effect on what the viewer brings to them.

Richard Long's art mixes postwar/ contemporary and Romantic æsthetics. For Anne Seymour, Long 'has not only penetrated more deeply into the world of natural landscape than anyone since Turner, he has taken abstract art with him, creating a new art which allows all parties to retain their full identities' (OW, 54). Mary Rose Beaumont also places Long within a British Romantic tradition. This was a tendency of art criticism of the 1980s, as espoused by fine art gurus such as Peter Fuller and Robert Rosenblum. There was much talk in the 1980s of the New Romantics/ Neo-Romantics/ New Ruralists/ New Arcadians, and so on. Whether High Modernism or postmodernism, Classical or Romantic, Long's art is certainly a romance with the natural world, but always in an ecologically-friendly and Postminimal fashion. Long lives in Bristol, where the pagan/ New Age/ hippy influence is very prominent, and in all points South and West of Bristol (and Long employs many the sites sacred to pagans, New Agers, witches, hippies and tourists in his walks and works).

Richard Long often revisits places many times, Dartmoor being the most obvious case. Dartmoor's a large area of South-West England, but even after a few walks one would soon begin to repeat and revisit places and routes (Dartmoor's 365 miles square). As well as the journeys that Long repeats, he has also revisited particular artworks he'd made years before (which could be the route of an earlier walk, a crossing-place, or a stone cross). In *Dartmoor Time* (1995), a text piece, for instance, Long noted how he passed 'a pile of stones placed sixteen years ago'. If one was able to layer Long's walks in Dartmoor on top of each other, on a map, there would be lines and routes everywhere: Dartmoor is a patch of land that Long has traversed many,

many times over the course of his art and walking career.

Richard Long has tended to concentrate on favourite sites for making walkworks (most walkers have their special places). The Longian territories include America, Scotland, England, Ireland, Italy, Portugal, Tanzania, Turkey, Holland, Japan, Lappland, Nepal, India, the Sahara, Argentina, Malawi, Bolivia, Ecuador, Canada, Korea, Finland, Mongolia, Mexico, Patagonia, Iceland and Peru. That's a pretty big number of territories for anyone to visit, let alone an artist (artists often being poor). But Long hasn't made walkworks absolutely everywhere on the planet. On the European mainland, for instance, Long hasn't made as much art as one would expect in Switzerland, Norway, Finland, Denmark or Sweden, Belgium, Spain, the former Yugoslavia, Hungary, Austria, Germany, Romania, Bulgaria, Albania, Turkey, the Czech Republic and Greece. Many of those countries contain landscapes Long favours.

Ireland was a very important country for Richard Long, in particular the West of Ireland, County Clare, the stony deserts of the Burren. Long liked the climate, the people, the music: '[i]t is one of the great countries in the world' (1994b). Long discovered Ireland first when he went there, he said (1994b), after being thrown out of Bristol art college in 1964.

Most land artists have their preferred spots (like the Americans with the New Mexico, Nevada, Arizona and California deserts). Richard Long has tended to make art in far more countries than many land artists. For instance, Long has walked in Korea, Malawi, Zambia, Kenya, Tanzania, Ecuador and Bolivia, which are not the usual stops on the land art circuit. One of the reasons must be that Richard Long's art does not require huge resources, materials, trucks and helpers: it is made mainly by one person using only the items necessary for a walk. The larger pieces of land art require large sums of capital, easy access, transport, materials, and many assistants. Another reason is that Long's art is not backed by big corporations or patrons. The economics of it are quite different from the art of the Christos or big public commissions. Long undertakes many private commissions, like many artists (land or otherwise), but most of his art is not public or corporate.

Like Ana Mendieta and Hamish Fulton, Richard Long uses his hands and feet to make his art, not an array of machines and tools. No motorcycles, snowmobiles, jets, planes, steam machines, chainsaws, cranes, diggers, tractors, dynamite, tankers, scaffolding or trucks (but transport must be provided for the stones Long uses from nearby quarries for his indoor stone sculptures). The aim is to be unobtrusive, 'invisible', in tune with the Earth. So Long acts like many environmentally-conscious walkers and trekkers: he covers his tracks, does not leave behind trash, does not harm nature. So fierce is the 'right on', politically correct eco-friendly tendency of some walkers and campers, they worry about leaving even a footprint in grass as they pass by. Hamish Fulton declines to make any mark on the world as he moves through it, except footprints. 'The natural environment was not built by man and for this reason it is to me deeply mysterious and religious'.3 Fulton doesn't want to buy it, own it, sell it, build on it, alter it, deface it, exploit it or ruin it (Long does not go as far as the more austere Fulton, who can make Tibetan Buddhist monks look like cigar-chomping industrial capitalists. Long does use parts of the Earth, and does buy and sell the Earth: his mud drawings, his stone rows and circles, his works on paper and wood).

Richard Long has tended to avoid featuring himself in the flesh in his art; although his art is full of all sorts of embodiments of the artist, Long does not include portraits of himself. In a book like *Walking the Line* (2002), although photographs of Long were included, they were over-the-shoulder angles, or pictures of his hands making artworks (such as the fingerprint sculptures), without showing the face in close-up. Richard Long appears in his art like glimpses, a vague presence; it's not that he's just stepped out of the frame – he was never anywhere near it in the first place. It's very different from the long history of artists who included self-portraits as one of their major themes (Rembrandt van Rijn, Max Beckmann, Egon Schiele and Vincent van Gogh).

In the mega-visual postmodern world, even complete unknowns can become celebrities, but many fans of Richard Long's art probably have no idea what the artist looks like. Andy Warhol, David Hockney, Salvador Dali and Barbara Hepworth are familiar faces, but not Long's. For those who haven't seen Long, here's a description by Mark Irving of Long at age 59: 'impressive with his tall rangy frame, close-cropped hair, piercing eyes and straggling eyebrows, he looks half-purposeful evangelist and half-wild countryman' (2003a).

It's the same with television, radio, the internet, magazines, newspapers and Richard Long's own books. Few of them feature headshots of the artist. During the making of a BBC TV documentary in 2004 (*Art and the Sixties*), Long permitted the film crew to shoot only his feet (on a visit to the site on an early Long work of the 1960s). Later in the show Long relented, and agreed to be interviewed in the usual manner (i.e., a medium close-up on his face in a room responding to questions). Long has been interviewed many times over the course of his career, though; he's just averse to personal appearances in the visual or electronic media.

Richard Long is not a performance artist, but there is an element of performance art about his work. He always performs privately. If he makes a mud wall drawing in a gallery, or builds a stone oval or circle in a public space, it is always before the exhibition opens, never during it. The construction of a Richard Long stone circle is never a performance in public in itself. It's the same with the artwalks: they are always made by the artist on his own, without witnesses or spectators. Very occasionally Long embarks on walk(work)s with other people (most famously, his walks with fellow artist-as-walker Hamish Fulton: they walked in Peru, Nepal, Alaska, Mexico, Lappland, India and Spain). The time and place and performance of the walk exist in a quite different time and place and context from their consumption by spectators as artworks, Long maintained.

But Richard Long's art was developed at the same time that performance art was a big thing on the art scene (in the 1960s and 1970s), and some of the theories and ethics of performance art (and body art) also apply to Long's art. For instance, responding to an environment, letting an artwork be shaped by an environment. Allowing for spontaneity, chance, and the unpredictable. Creating work based on simple concepts. Repeating an action many times. Including sound in a work. Performing random/ arbitrary actions (such as throwing stones). All of these (there are plenty more to consider) are part of the philosophy and methodology of performance art, and they are also part of Richard Long's art. (In a performance piece in Amalfi in 1968, for the *Third International Exhibition of Figurative Art*, Long shook hands with twenty or so people in the town square. That was an early work, a specifically performance piece. Long hasn't undertaken many similar performances since).

The tone of Richard Long's art tends towards the laidback, the mellow, the chilled; although he doesn't have the long hair, beard, jeans and West Coast colours, Long's art comes across as hippyish. The ideals, politics and worldview chime with those of the Woodstock generation (and the retinue of hippy stereotypes: the stoner, the drifter, the music fan). Anger, anxiety, pain, self-doubt, lust, aggression, neurosis, or psychic torment are not really a part of Richard Long's art. His art is not the haunted torture of Vincent van Gogh or Edvard Munch, or the flamboyance, narcissism and self-publicizing of Salvador Dali or Andy Warhol, or fiercely feminist body art of Ana Mendieta or Karen Finley, or the stridently ideological combat of Barbara Kruger or Hans Haacke, or the ironic, fey discoursing on the postmodern condition of Jeff Koons or Robert Rauschenberg, or the crazy performances of Stuart Brisley or Annie Sprinkle, or the *avant garde* poses of media favourites Yoko Ono or Matthew Barney.

A LINE MADE BY WALKING, A 2 1/2 MILE WALK SCULPTURE AND OTHER EARLY WORKS

Richard Long's 1967 walkwork *A Line Made By Walking* is routinely cited in art critic-ism as Long's first major work, but let's use another early piece to illustrate Long's æsthetics. In *A 2 1/2 Mile Walk Sculpture* (1969), made when Long was 24, the artist documented how he walked along parallel 55 yard lines four times. The first time, he walked 32 times back and forth, travelling a mile; the second time, 24 times, going 3/4 mile, the third time, 16 times (= 1/2 mile), and the fourth time, 8 times (= 1/4 mile). As well as the text explaining the walk sculpture, there was a photograph of the grass and lines Long walked, and a diagram of the lines.

This work contains all of the key elements of Richard Long's art: there's a photo-graph, written text, and a diagram. Each of those three media are vital in Long's *œuvre*. The work was exhibited as a wall piece. It originated with a performance, made by the artist, alone, with no witnesses (although not in the wilderness spots he became famous for – India, Peru, Iceland, the Sahara. Even though it's not Ladakh, it's still on grass, without people, houses, roads, factories, telephone lines, trash, etc, cluttering up the picture). It was not made in (or for) an art gallery. It was not a commissioned piece (the idea for the walkwork came from the artist, not from anyone else), or funded (it was not paid for any anyone, and the artist owned the work). It was not part of an artists' collective. It did not have manifestos attached to it, or political aims. It was Conceptual: the work was planned beforehand, then executed. The artist knew he was going to document the walk in some way – it would require at least the text, to explain what the artist did; a photograph was probably considered too before the walk was made (Long had his camera with him, and film in it); the diagram may have been an idea that came after the walk. It was partly about the artist's relationship with nature. It involved measurement, time, distance, speed, and direction, all ingredients which Long would experiment with throughout his artistic career. It was Process or serial art: it involved repetition (and meant repeating a simple action). It was composed of small units which were added together to form a larger unit. The materials derived from Arte Povera (grass). It did not 'add' anything to nature (it was not an object; but it did leave the mark of flattened grass). It had a simple geometry and form: straight lines. The written text described the action of the work, including precise accounts of distances and times (with numbers prominent). The photo was a fairly straightforward documentation of the location of the work, and the action of the work (the grass rubbed flat), but the artist was left out of the picture. The walkwork took place during daylight (as most of Richard Long's walks do). The photo, text and diagram is all that is left of the work: the actual walk took place at some former time (which Long usually includes in the documentation of his walks). The walk had to come first, before the photos, textworks and diagrams; Long didn't create the documentation then walk the walk. The exact location of the walk is not included. And the work was primarily a *walk*: the walking was the single most important aspect of the work: walking is the experience upon which all of Long's art is founded.

A Line Made by Walking (1967) was one of Richard Long's early walkworks, which was a short line made on grass and daisies. How did Long make it? By walking repeatedly over the same area, back and forth. This work had all the hallmarks of the Long walkwork, as discussed in relation to *A 2 1/2 Mile Walk Sculpture*: a definite intention, clarity of image/ geometry/ form, a countryside setting (well, grass and trees at least – it was near London, not in the wilder zones Long later visited), a sense of process and formalism, the direct touch of humanity and nature, the sense of time and impermanence, the relation with nature, and the relation between conception and execution.

Ben Nevis Hitch-hike (1967) was the first of Richard Long's recognizable walking works: in it, Long hitch-hiked to Ben Nevis mountain (in Scotland, and back to London, over 6 days. It was a map, text and photo work. Early on in his walking career, Long established the idea of basing walkworks on different types of walking: straight walking, meandering walking, circular walking, and so on (in *A Ten Mile Walk*, for instance [1968], Long 10 miles in a straight line).

In 1994, Richard Long looked back at the *Line Made By Walking* and remarked: 'I definitely had a sense that what I was doing was really important and I had a terrific conviction and belief that it was interesting' (1994b). In 2003, Long acknowledged that *A Line Made By Walking* was 'an utter *Arte Povera* work – it's made with nothing and is yet something' (2003a).

For critic Irving Sandler, *A Line Made By Walking* was Richard Long's 'prototypical, perhaps consummate, piece':

It had all the components of his later outdoor work: an underlying concept; a minimal form; a substance found in nature that reverted back to nature after the piece was completed; and photographic and/ or other documentation. (1996, 82-83)

Of *A Line Made By Walking*, Tony Godfrey remarked that it was a performance piece, which anyone could do (democratic), which was recorded in a photograph (the photo could be exhibited – and sold), it existed outside the commercial gallery system, it was Conceptual (based on a single idea), and was ecologically sound (didn't have a damaging impact on the landscape).

Artist Jeff Wall related *A Line Made By Walking* to Barnett Newman's

notion of the establishment of a 'Here' in the void of a primæval terrain. It is simultaneously agriculture, religion, urbanism and theatre, an intervention in a lonely, picturesque spot which becomes a setting completed artistically by the gesture and the photograph for which the gesture was enacted. (1995)

Although the photograph of *A Line Made By Walking* was documentation or reportage, Wall maintained, it also moved 'in precisely the opposite direction, towards a completely designed pictorial method, an introverted masquerade that plays games with the inherited æsthetic proclivities of art-photography-as-reportage' (ib.).

In the late 1960s Long photographed some concentric plastic stripes in a variety of settings (such as a beach in Ireland in 1967). The works recalled Dutch artist Jan Dibbets' plays with perspective in the landscape (such as *Perspective Corrections*, 1968). Long made sculptures by cutting into grass (*Turf Circle*, 1966 and 1969). In 1964 he created a Goldsworthyan sculpture on the hills near Bristol: the track a snowball made as he rolled it along (*Snowball Track*. Talking about artists being 'child-like' – it's a favourite thing for children and adults to do with snowballs). On a beach in Somerset Long constructed an open square from pebbles (1968). On a beach in Cornwall he fashioned a spiral from seaweed (1970). A square spiral was created with his boot heel in 1970 (Long later made a boot heel line in 1997 in Argentina). Cross-shaped sculptures included one submerged in the shallows of Little Pigeon River in Tennessee (1970); a cross on grass and daisies (1968); a cross made by walking on wet sand at half-tide (Ireland, 1971); and a very large, wide cross comprising pine needles in London (1971).

RICHARD LONG: THE ART OF THE WALK

Afoot and light-hearted I take to the open road,
Healthy, free, the world before me.

Walt Whitman, 'Song of the Open Road'

It is worth remembering that Richard Long's art comes out of the tough, fitness cult-ure of professional and dedicated walkers. The ethos and practices of the professional hiker and trekker informs much of his art. The professional walker aims to go, for a start, where there are very few people.[1] This is not a Sunday afternoon stroll along the cliffs after a pub lunch with five pints of real ale. This is hiking in wilderness country for days on end, carrying everything one needs (however, Long's art is not about adventure and adrenalin activities or extreme sports: he's not going to make a blurred photowork taken on a bungee jump over a gorge in Oz, or a textwork based on some rad skateboarding in Detroit. Canoeing, cycling and walking and occasionally a bit of mountain climbing are more the order of the day).

The professional walker typically has a good pair of boots, which become like old friends, fully waterproof clothes, a backpack, a compass, a map, food, clothing, water bottle, hat, walking stick, rope, sleeping bag, stove, flashlight and a tent, as well as other useful items. Many of these things feature in Richard Long's art – one sees the rucksack or tent in his photographs; the compass is used for walking in straight lines; water is tipped out of his water bottle to create sculptures that dry in the sun; and that all-important walker's tool, the map, is the subject of many works.

On his walking trips Richard Long said the tools he took with him for making art included leather gloves, a collapsible water bottle, and string (for drawing circles). For the walks in wildernesses, Long carries heavier gear, including heavier boots, fuel, a stove, camping gear, and all of his food. Sometimes he uses wood for fires, if there's any around. For the walks made on roads, or near towns or villages, Long travels lighter, buying provisions along the way, often staying in bed and breakfasts and hotels. A watch or clock is essential, too: Long is always logging exactly how long he walks for, and some walks, such as *North and South* (1991), are based around walking in one direction for a certain time, then changing direction. In other walkworks, Long walks for sixty minutes then stops (as in *Hoggar Hour,* or *A Sixty Minute Circle Walk on Dartmoor*, 1984).

Richard Long travels quite a bit, and has visited many countries to make his art or exhibit it. However, Long maintains that he is not a nomad, and is not constantly on the move. He always returns to Bristol, to his home, and to see his family, and do everyday, ordinary things, like shopping or gardening. Being at home is a way of recharging, too, so the artist has more energy and enthusiasm for future walks and works (1994b).

Richard Long's art suggests folklore and phrases to do with walking, some of which Long uses: 'walking the walk', 'walking it off', 'walking the dog', 'going for a walk', 'walking in circles', 'walking a line', 'walk alone', 'leaving no trace', 'leave nothing behind', 'travelling light', 'travelling is better than arriving', 'travelling without moving', 'like a rolling stone', 'free as the road', 'the open road', and so on.

And plenty of poets and thinkers have written of walking and the open road: 'I love roads', wrote Edward Thomas, 'The goddesses that dwell / Far along them invisible / Are my favourite gods' ('Roads'; Thomas is a poet with a deep love of England, and travel, like Richard Long); 'free as the road' (George Herbert); 'he that rolleth a stone, it will return upon him' (*Proverbs*, 26: 27); 'the stone that is rolling can gather no moss' (Thomas Tusser); 'the road goes ever on and on' (J.R.R. Tolkien); 'to travel hopefully is a better thing than to arrive' (Robert Louis Stevenson).

Quite a few of Richard Long's walks (especially the later ones, such as *Heaven and Earth,* 2001) explore the notion of magnetic North (the compass is often mentioned, being one of the walker's chief tools). In *Natural Forces* (2002), Long writes of walking 'along magnetic force by compass'. In *A Walk of Thirteen Days in the Swiss Alps* (2000) he writes of 'turning around all points of the compass countless times'. Magnetic North is one of those invisible concepts to do with cartography that's bound to fascinate the boy scout in Long (the idea that submerged magnetic rocks hundreds or thousands of miles away can affect a tiny compass needle, and also guide a traveller even in an inhospitable and featureless wilderness).

In *Avon To Avon To Avon* (2001), Richard Long walked from one River Avon to another (a walk which could take place all over Britain, 'avon' being another word for river). Long limited himself to the River Avons flowing in Wiltshire, Warwickshire and Hampshire. In *A Highland Walk* (1988) the usual short phrases of the experience of the 244 mile walk, and things encountered on the 14 day walk, were printed in a pattern roughly corresponding to (or suggestive of) the actual route Long undertook. In *Hoggar Hour* Long listed his experience of walking for 60 minutes in the Sahara ('rock / yes / thinking / burnt / flies / boots / horizon').

Twelve Hours, Twelve Summits, made in Scotland in 1983, was a classic kind of professional walker work, a list of the summits Richard Long achieved over 5 days in the Highlands. Long has undertaken many classic routes favoured by hikers: coast to coast walks, walks around the tors of Devon, the Foss Way, the Ridgeway, and even Land's End to John O'Groats (that's *the* classic route across the British mainland, 900 some miles which remains very popular). Many ramblers will be undertaking those classic walks right now. (Little ol' Britain may not have New York to L.A., or across the Sahara, or the Silk Road through Central Asia, or the Great Wall of China, or coast to coast via the Amazon basin, but it sure as rock cakes has Land's End to John O'Groats. It may not be base camp to the summits of Everest or K2, but it's a good walk).

Water Way Walk (1989) was one of Richard Long's more complex textworks, recording a walk of 152 miles in England and Wales, and the many streams, drains, ditches and rivers encountered along the way. The text piece (printed in *Walking In Circles*) lays out the names of the rivers and streams in a pattern loosely approximating to Long's journey (and the work is complicated by Long printing the words in different sizes – i.e., 'River Severn' and 'River Wye', being big rivers for a tiny island like England, are printed large, while 'Ditch' and 'Stream', which don't have names, are printed very small).

From Tree To Tree (1986) was a textwork of a walk made in Avon, listing the trees Richard Long encountered and how far along the walk he saw them:

OAK 9 MILES
SCOTS PINE 15 MILES
HAWTHORN 22 MILES
WILLOW 29 MILES (WC, 13)

Plenty of Richard Long's walks record pretty mundane, everyday events. *To Build a Fire,* made in Tierra del Fuego in 1997, registers nothing more amazing than building a fire at each campsite along a six day walk (Tierra del Fuego may be amazing, but building a fire isn't). *The Space of Time* (1999) simply records the number of days between two circular artworks, one made in Ecuador in 1998, the other in Greece in 1999 (Long likes to find ways of joining two separate walkworks together). In *Dry Walk* (1989), Long records he walked 113 miles between two rainfalls. In four walks on Dartmoor (*Distance and Time, Time and Distance*, 2000), Long simply lists how far he walked and how long he walked for on each day (that's the most basic Richard Long walkwork: how many miles, and how many hours).

In *Five Walks* (1993) the number 30 is the foundation: it comprised a walk of 30 miles, a walk over 30 crossroads, a walk lasting 30 hours, a walk passing 30 farmhouses, and a walk seeing 30 blackbirds. The number five is the star of another walk: five stones, five rivers, five tors, five bogs, five days. In *Up and Down* (1997) Long produced a classic walkers' artwork: a record of the summits encountered on a 7 day walk in Eire:

FROM LECKAVREA MOUNTAIN 2174 FT.
TO LETTERBRECKAUN 2193 FT.
TO BENBAUN 2395 FT.
TO BENCOLLAGHDUFF 2290 FT.

The list of peaks and heights might appear in a walker's notebook after a hiking vacation in the hills.

Many of Richard Long's walkworks are illustrated with landscape photographs of the terrain traversed, and don't feature art objects such as stone circles or rows or waterlines. Instead, there are photos of clouds, mountains, forests, lakes, rivers, boulders, snow and trees: *An Eight Day Walk in Adamello* (2000), *An Eight Day Walk In the Rimrock Area of the Mojave Desert* (1994), *Wet Weather Walking* (1993), *Crossing the Duzon* (1992) and *A Southward Walk of of 220 Miles In 14 Days Across the Middle of Iceland* (1994).

While the photos of rows, lines, crosses, cairns, ellipses and circles attest to a recognizable art object made along the way of the walk, the works without these productions emphasize that the walk itself is the artwork (as in *The High Plains* [1974], a photowork of a walk in Canada). These photographs are not holiday snapshots, though, but they do serve a very similar function: they state *I was there*. The spectator is invited to interpret these photos as a record of the artist actually walking in those landscapes. Vacation photos have the same purpose. Buying postcards or mementos is not enough: tourists and holiday makers take their *own* photos or videos of places they visit, to personalise it. And tourists and visitors typically compose photos where they are standing in front of some monument, view or landmark, again to emphasize their presence at the site. That's not too far from Richard Long's photographs of his walkworks: note how many times Long includes mountains in the background, which say 'Andes' or 'Alps' or 'High Sierra'. Or parts of a desert which say 'Gobi desert' or 'Sahara desert'.

A Walk Across England was a walk from the West coast (in Devon) to the East coast (in East Anglia), with the results published in a book (1997). Long was commissioned to produce the work by Children's Library Press of California. The work contained the usual images in Long's art: country lanes, wide views of hills and fields, streams, gates, bridges, cows, a white horse, boats, clouds, and a windmill. So far, so expected, so Longian.

But there were photographs in *A Walk Across England* not usually found in Richard Long's art, and many of these pictures featured smaller details of the landscape, such as: a dead fox, a snail, a red postbox, street signs, a dead tree, a church clock, a railway crossing, cow shit, bird shit, flowers, puddles, a horse chestnut leaf, crops, a railway station, a dead badger, railway lines, canals, a wooden stile, sunbathers by a river, trucks, canal locks, a pub sign, tree roots, a goat, a ladybird, a phone box, boundary signs, a brick wall, poppies, urine, a pothole, a rock, a canoeist, a feather, apples, pigs and horses. There were also traces of Long himself: his shadow on the road, his boots, his socks, his bare feet in a river, his rucksack, and his campsite. The semi-documentary approach Long took in *A Walk Across England* recalled the work of British photographers such as Martin Parr (Long's book *Dialog* has a similar look).

Different kinds of walking are sometimes valorized in Richard Long's work: meandering walking, fast walking, slow walking (but not strolling or sauntering), straight walking and walking in circles. Also, walking while kicking stones and walking while making lines in the dirt with a boot heel. Judging by the amount of terrain covered in the times stated in his walkworks, Long must usually walk fairly fast, in the region of 3 or 4 m.p.h.

Sometimes animals appear in Richard Long's walkworks and textworks, such as the dog sitting beside the stone circle in *Leaving the Stones* (1995, Norway), the raven on a cairn in *Walk of Seven Cairns* (1992), the moorhens in *Mountains and Waters* (1992), cows in *Dusty To Muddy To Windy* (1993), horses on the Mongolia trip (1996), and monkeys in *A Walk In a Green Forest* (1997).

During his career as the world's premier artist-as-walker, Richard Long would have encountered thousands of animals. In many parts of the world they're a constant presence (even in tame, stuffy, cold, damp Britain, sheep, goats, cows, horses, dogs, chickens, insects, birds and fish are everywhere).

For Richard Long, walking itself is the primary act of his art. Walking is mainly what he does, as an artist. His talent, he says, is to be able to walk. Walking clears the mind, it is a process and experience of simplification and purification. 'I will try to have in my work only what is necessary to it' Carl Andre said (1984). Walking purges the soul, Long says, it forces the self to concentrate on simple things such as air, sky, earth, rock.

> Like art itself, it [walking] is like a focus. It gets rid of a lot of things and you can actually concentrate. So getting myself into these solitary days of repetitive walking or in empty landscapes is just a certain way of emptying out or simplifying my life, just for those few days or weeks, into a fairly simple but concentrated activity which, as you say, is really quite different from the way that people normally live their lives, which is very complicated. So my art is a simplification. (RC, 23)

For Richard Long, as for many people, walking is a way of simplifying life, of cutting through the clutter. When walking, one moves into a different space, a space set quite apart from the rest of life. The time of walking is not the everyday, day-in-day-out time of the working world. It is not the profane, boring time of working at a check-out in a supermarket, or slaving away in some factory in Korea, South Africa, Denmark or Bolivia. Walking takes one right away from that sort of everyday time, into a non-profane time and space. Walking in fact sacralizes space and time. As the walk takes places, sacred time is re-instated.

Walking therefore has a religious or philosophical dimension, which sounds odd only if terms such as religion or art sound odd to the ear. In walking, in travelling, in holidays or other escapes and adventures, people put themselves back together. Walking in wildernesses, people say, is invigorating and refreshing: walking returns people to themselves, and of course renews their contact with nature (inner nature as well as outer). These things can sound stupid, pompous, pretentious – 'renewing one's contact with nature'. But one can't avoid nature in the wilderness everywhere– it surrounds the self entirely. Plus, the walker is also nature themselves.

> I do the things that have a deep meaning for me. I have the most sublime or pro-found feelings when I am walking, or touching materials in natural places. That is what I've decided to do and that is what I am showing you in my art. (RC, 224)

The sculptures that Long made on his walks are a response to the walk (or part of the walk), or an embodiment of the walk, or an eruption of an aspect of the walk. Long said that the sculptures he made on walks were a kind of celebration of the experience of being in particular place at a particular time, a little like celebrating a moment with a poem or a song (1995a). The sculptures also arose spontaneously, they were not planned in advance (2004b). All sorts of things could inspire the artist to make a sculpture in a landscape – something he hasn't seen before, or a particular alignment of forms in the landscape, or a nice flat piece of rock for a water-pour work. Chris Drury said that the cairns he constructed then took down in particular places were about a positive, celebratory response to a moment in time and space.2

The continuity that Richard Long sees between the idea and the walk, between gallery art and art made under the sky, echoes the precepts of Western magic, where the realms of inner and outer are unified, summed up in that key phrase in magic, 'as above, so below'. Magicians imagine that the outer and inner worlds are connected, even that they are the same. Thus, what occurs within the magician occurs in the outer world too. Psychoanalysis sees magicians as less mature than, say, religionists, because they have confused ego boundaries: the magician's self extends beyond her/ his body to the world outside, and the magician imagines the world revolves around herself in some ways.3 Magicians are fixed at an earlier stage of oral-anal adaption, to use the terminology of psychoanalysis. John Cowper Powys was quite aware of this; in his *Autobiography* he says that children are like magicians, because they are in touch with their 'inner life' (27f). As Powys writes, children's games are serious, and magic-al:

> But the great point is that the thrilling moments of happiness with a child are *secret and magical* and come from a level of reality which is completely different from *a level of reality* of grown-up people. (28)

People who are not psychologists or anthropological behaviourists do not speak of anal or oral immaturity: instead, they might see magicians and artists as simply acting at times like children. Which is fine. The sense of play is especially important for Richard Long, as it is for many (most? all?) artists. Defining the qualities of his sculpture, Long says the child and the adult cannot be separated, so that

> all the sensibilities that energize you as a child sort of flow through. And being an artist that means you can use them. So when newspapers derogatorily talk about my work as being sort of playing, like making mud pies or skimming stones across rivers or damming streams – all these childhood pursuits that people leave behind – I say "great!" I don't deny that I'm doing all the same stuff. (WC, 14)

The sense of play is something apparent in every Richard Long art book, every Richard Long exhibition, and every Richard Long walk. Only an artist with a keen sense of child-like play could produce a work called *Two Stones* which is a four day 122 mile walk across the North of England based on nothing more complicated than being a stone's throw from the two seas, Irish and North Seas (featured in *Mountains and Waters*). Another work, made in the Sahara, consisted of the artist clapping two stones together a thousand times (*Two Sahara Stones*, 1988). For many folks, that wouldn't count as anything anywhere near art. It might count as something that could be fun to do, if you like that sort of thing. But for anyone who knows anything about perform-ance art, action art or Conceptual art, it's quite familiar.

> Richard Long [wrote P. Rodaway] builds his art from walking across the landscape, from an intimate sensual experience with space and the materials of his environment and forms his 'sculptures' in pattern with the landscape, its structure and material substance...[4]

Richard Long himself is not quite 'in' his art, though, as are, say, Gilbert & George or performance artists such as Kate Bornstein, Hermann Nitsch or Annie Sprinkle. Despite this, adoring fans such as Anne Seymour go so far as to state '[t]here is also a sense in which the artist not only walks the path or the line, but is the path itself' (WC, 9). Eh? It's true to say that Long's walks are his art, but not that the artist himself 'is' the path. Here Anne Seymour makes the old mistake of humanist/ modernist criticism, by conflating artist and art, the sculptor with his sculpture.[5] No, Long's art is, finally, 'art'. It's not him, the artist is always 'elsewhere' (and Long always asserts that, and his art does too).

Richard Long said on his website that his

> intention was to make a new art which was also a new way of walking: walking as art. Each walk followed my own unique, formal route, for an original reason, which was different from other categories of walking, like travelling. Each walk, though not by definition conceptual, realised a particular idea. Thus walking – as art – provided an ideal means for me to explore relationships between time, distance, geography and measurement.

Long's æsthetics emphasize simplicity, purity, practicality, physicality, actuality and subjectivity. He iterates the simple gesture or structure or idea: if it's too complex, the artwork won't work. The practical aspect of handling materials is always crucial in art. As with Constantin Brancusi, purity is always uppermost in Long's theory of art. The physical and actual nature of his sculptures is what's important. And subjectivity, as in late 18th century Romanticism, rules all – so that, as Donald Judd said, para-phrasing Marcel Duchamp, 'if someone thinks it's art, then it's art'.

In Richard Long's sculpture, the subjective dimension is prime. He exalts the personal, the intuitive, the emotional: '[m]y art is about my senses, my instinct, my own scale and my own physical commitment.'[6] These are some artistic statements of Long's which typify his æsthetics:

> I like the simplicity of walking, the simplicity of stones...
> I like sensibility without technique...
> I choose lines and circles because they do the job...
> My work is about my senses, my instinct, my own scale and my own physical commitment...
> My work is simple and practical. I may choose rolling moorland to make a straight ten mile walk because that is the best place to make such a work, and I know such places well. (in RL, 236)

In *Walden*, Henry David Thoreau exhorts '[s]implicitly, simplicity, simplicity!... Simplify, simplify'.[7] Walking for Richard Long was a way of dealing with the things that sculpture or art deals with but in a way which was not bound up in the rules and genres and formal aspects of traditional sculpture. It allowed Long to step outside of art history, perhaps. Or to bend the rules a bit. Or to rewrite some of the rules.

> Walking as a medium enabled me to bring a big increase in scale and space (distance) into a work of art. Time could become a fourth dimension. Walking can express many different ideas. For example, I have used riverbeds on Dartmoor as footpaths; I have carried stones in my pocket for many miles to make sculptures about movement, transference and relocation. I can use it as a simple human measure of time, like walking across a country, or from one planetary event to another, or from one shower of rain to the next. (2004b)

Richard Long summed up his art with some words in a May 25, 1997 lecture in Japan:

REALITY
TIME
MEMORY
SLEEPING
COUNTING
LANGUAGE
BOOTS

SOLITUDE
MAPS
MUSIC
TENT
HUMOUR
DISTANCE
INTUITION
EXPERIENCE
CHANCE
LOVE (WL, 147)

Denying it or hinting at it, Richard Long's sculpture is definitely 'religious'/ 'mystical'/ 'spiritual'. Walking itself is sacred; making art is sacred; the allusions to stone rings are religious; circles themselves are religious; the awe with which viewers regard the sculpture has a religious aspect, and so on. Not all of Long's works are circles – there are always the lines. Long continued to make lines in the shape of a cross from time to time, such as in *Two Places* (Bolivia, 1972), where a small cross was made on marshland in a pile of stalks. Another cross was built in Iceland from some stones (*Stopping Place Stones*, 1974), or in the Sahara (*Crossing Marks*, 1988).

The crosses are very much like geometric marks 'drawn' onto the landscape, as if to mark a place. Most of the single straight lines are short, like the crosses, such as *Walking Without Travelling* (Sahara, 1988). Occasionally, Long makes a square zigzag line: short right angles are marked upon bare soil, as in *Campfire Ash* (Bolivia, 1972 – most of these works are from *Mountains and Waters*). Another zigzag line sculpture, in Antwerp in 1973, extends outwards to take over the gallery: each Long sculpture is made for a particular space, and expands to consume the gallery floor. The zigzag lines recall the Peruvian Nazca animals and symbols drawn on the lava plain (Long had walked along one of the desert lines in 1972: he also made sculptures which employed symbols such as the puma, condor, falcon, moon, sun and rain). For his 2004 show at Mario Sequeira, Long built *Five Paths* (2004), with a wavy line space between meandering rows of stones. Long has his visual motifs which he returns to time and again, like most artists (circles, lines, rows, and, lately, ellipses and arcs).

Richard Long spoke warmly of Carl Andre and Lawrence Weiner, important Sixties Minimal, Postminimal and Conceptual artists (IC 2, 24). He has exhibited a number of times with both Andre and Weiner. The links between Long and Carl Andre include an emphasis on place; seriality and repetition; simple geometric forms; an emphasis on the experience of making the artwork; nature; the use of unadorned, untreated materials; floor-standing sculptures without pedestals; and objects used as things-in-themselves with don't refer to things outside themselves.

It is significant, too, that Long felt he was working on his own in Britain when he started out (in terms of being an artist making the kind of work he did). But when he stepped out of Britain he realized there was 'a whole new world of ideas going on'. Richard Long notes, perhaps wryly, that '[t]here was an immediate interest and understanding of my work as soon as I stepped outside England' (IC 1, 17). Although Long lives in England and makes many pieces in the British Isles, he has always been very much an international artist, and has exhibited internationally far more than in his home country (perhaps his art was understood best first outside the UK). Long himself declines being described as a Conceptual artist ('[m]y work is real, not illusory or conceptual. It's about real stones, real time, real actions' [RL, 236]). He speaks sympathetically of Arte Povera, the use of 'simple, modest means and procedures' (GL, 6).

Some commentators have negated the tendency to view Richard Long in Romantic terms. 'Richard Long's landscape is… as modern (in feeling) as the city of Bristol from which he sets out for a walk' claimed R.H. Fuchs, one of Long's supporters (1986, 43). Long, Fuchs says, tries to play down 'as much as he can the romantic/ Romantic, poetic connotations' of his locations (ib.). Yet, surely wildernesses such as Dartmoor, Mexico, Nepal, Canada and Lappland, where Long makes his art, have been inscribed with connotations of Romanticism. They are places now described in terms of 'spirit' and 'soul', spaces that in contemporary romantic, nostalgic culture imbue the observer with a sense of infinity, solitude, pantheism, awe, eternity and all the rest of the Romantic æsthetic portfolio. 'A walk is also the means of discovering places in which to make sculpture in 'remote' areas, places of nature, places of great power and contemplation' says Richard Long, speaking in Romantic terms of his walks (RL, 236). The starting points and the end points of the *Four Walks* (1977) sound like a list of destinations a landscape painter might make for a 1790s Grand Tour of Britain: the source of the River Severn, Snowdon, Chesil Beach, Sherwood Forest and Carantouhil peak.

In a walk such as *Straight Miles and Meandering Miles* (1985), Long walked some 'straight miles' along the way, between Land's End and Bristol. As expected, these 'straight miles' were walked in wilderness or countryside or 'Romantic' locations, such as Bodmin Moor, Exmoor and the Mendip Hills (those were places where swooning Romantics swanned around 200 years ago, as they do now – except that Romantics these days are called Goths, neo-pagans, hippies, ramblers, poets and artists).

There are plenty of built-up areas along between Bristol and Land's End that Long could have walked through when he made *Straight Miles and Meandering Miles*, but chose not include in his work: parts of Street, Taunton, Exeter, Plymouth, St Austell, Truro, Redruth, Cambourne and Penzance aren't particular picturesque. Anyone who has visited those places and many others in the Western hemisphere will know that apart from being surrounded by luscious countryside and wild moors, there are service stations, motorways, out-of-town retail parks (with their multiplex cinemas, supermarkets, household, gardening and electronic stores, Burger King, Pizza Hut, KFC and McDonald's), shopping malls (Gap, Boots, Woolworth's, Virgin), warehouses, car pounds, junk yards, hospitals, clinics, cemeteries, factories, power stations, office blocks, electricity substations and poles, telephone exchanges and call centres, ring roads and by-passes, highways, railways, train stations, gasometers, police stations, trash heaps, landfills, water and sewage processing plants, housing estates, tower blocks, and heavy industry. Not far from Richard Long's beloved Dartmoor, for instance, a huge area of Plymouth is taken up by industry, military barracks and naval dockyards.

Although he may downplay the Romantic associations with the art made in or about landscape, Long describes landscape in romantic, emotional terms. He reacts to landscape directly, facing it straight on, as is apparent in all his interviews and writings. He speaks of the need for transcribing landscapes purely and clearly. So, for instance, Long's photographs are simply taken, without too much trickery, and they are printed in a straightforward manner (although the emphasis on 'simplicity' doesn't do away with the many philosophical and technical complications of photography itself).[6] At the same time, Long speaks of 'places of great power and contemplation', terms which William Wordsworth might have used a hundred and fifty years before Long, or Henry Vaughan, the Metaphysical poet born on the Welsh borders, before that. Robert Rosenblum wrote:

> An artist I would think of as still perpetuating an older unbroken tradition of Romanticism is Richard Long who really doesn't have the irony of the 1980s, but he's been doing this for a longtime. If I had to have a candidate for somebody who perpetuated the imagery, the feelings, the emotions of someone like Constable or Wordsworth, I'd vote for him... He is somebody who really continues those endless

magical communions with nature by talking, touching, feeling and accumulating. I find this very direct in terms of his experience and really very moving as a kind of endangered species, but it still works with him. I think he is the last of his race.[8]

Stressing the Romantic heritage and tradition of Richard Long's art though, only makes up part of the picture. Like other artists of the 1960s (whether Pop, Conceptual, Minimal, Process, ABC, Arte Povera, body, action, performance or other art), Long suppresses notions of poetry and Romanticism, as if that interpretation is too limiting, too much to do with art history, and too traditional and conventional. 'My art is not urban, nor is it romantic' Long claimed (RL, 236). Looking at *A Line in Iceland* (1982), a line of boulders Long built in a wilderness space and shot against a brooding sky and a backdrop of snowbound mountains, one can see the affinities with the High Romanticism of William Wordsworth's poeticizing of the Lake District, J.M.W. Turner and his watercolours of Snowdonia or the Alps, or John Ruskin and his evocation of the sublime.[9]

The poetry of Friedrich Hölderlin is one of the supreme manifestations of the Romantic sublime. His 'Unter den Alpen Gesungen' ('Sung Beneath the Alps') is a poetic correlation of Richard Long in his more sublime, expansive mode (it's poetry which has equivalents in the epic landscapes of German Romantic painters like Caspar David Friedrich or Philipp Otto Runge):

So mit den Himmlischen allein zu seyn, und
Geht verüber das Licht, und Strom und Wind, und
Zeit eilt hin zum Ort, vor ihnen ein stetes
            Auge zu haben,

Seeliger weiß und wünsch' ich nichts, so lange
Nicht auch mich, wie die Weide, fort die Fluth nimmt,
Daß wohl aufgehoben, schlafend dahin ich
            Muß in den Woogen;

Aber es bleibt daheim gern, wer in treuem
Busen Göttliches hält, und frei will ich, so
Lang ich darf, eich all', ihr Sprachen des Himmels!
            Deuten und singen.[10]

True, *Red Slate Circle* (1980) in the Fogg Art Museum in Cambridge (MA), or *Sandstone Spiral* (1983) in the National Gallery of Canada, or the *Puget Sound Driftwood Circle* (1996) in Houston, or *Forte de Vinadio Circle* (Italy, 2001), or *13th Street Ellipse* (2004, NYC) are set on museum floors, in the clean, sparse gallery environment, and look Minimal and sophisticated and not obviously 'Romantic'. What concerns Richard Long is that '[e]ach work is appropriate to its place and context', and the wilderness works and the museum pieces are 'equal and complementary'. What counts, Long says, is the feelings that the work, whether inside or outside, arouses: 'my ambition is basically with the emotional power of the work, in both idea and image' (SF). Walking, nature and the landscape are at the heart of Long's work (GL, 8), but Long knows, as any professional artist must know, that the art world conducts its business indoors (and in cities – and the international art scene where Long works and trades is concentrated in a few major cities). The art may be 'natural' or about the natural landscape, but the art world in which artists operate is distinctly urban, sophisticated, wealthy, highly educated and high culture. The *content* of Long's art is walking in the natural world, but the *context* is as urban as Keith Haring, Jean-Michel Basquiat, Frank Gehry or anonymous graffiti artists tagging the New York subway.

The slate, stick, wood and footprint circles of Richard Long look like late 20th century artworks, not 'Romantic', but Minimal, Conceptual and Arte Povera, like Carl Andre's copper and zinc plate squares or Donald Judd's Plexiglas and steel stacks and boxes. They have a coolness and clarity that one associates with Dan Flavin's fluorescent tubes, Anne Truitt's rectilinear slabs, Tony Smith's cubes and the white open boxes of Sol LeWitt. Long's stone circles make sense to the viewer partly because of a grounding in the discourses of contemporary art. Without assimilating the circularity of signs that flow around contemporary art, the spectator might not know how to make full sense of Long's circles. True, the circle as a shape has been around for eons, but only in the contemporary era have circles been made out of bits of the landscape, in galleries and in landscape settings in this particular way.

> I think circles have belonged in some way or other to all peoples at all times [remarked Long]. They are universal and timeless, like the image of a human hand. For me, that is part of their emotional power, although there is nothing symbolic or mystical in my work. They are also easy to make. (1995a)

Take Richard Long's *Tarahumara Circle* (Mexico, 1987): it's what seems at first to be a simple shape. But it's not 'simple'. It's a 'negative circle', a circle made into a circle by the ring of rocks around it (like *Walking a Circle In Ladakh*, 1984). The line of rocks marks out the circle, but not evenly. Some of the rocks are piled deeper on one side of the circle. Hardly anyone will have seen this circle intact, in its situation, so it's known only from a photograph. The seemingly straightforward approach of Long's photography has made a few æsthetic decisions, which shape the viewer's perception of this artwork. For instance, the viewer sees the stone circle in the centre of the frame, in the lower third, in the sort of classical composition that was taught in the fine art academies of yore. Behind the circle the trees and hills of Mexico are glimpsed. Richard Long's photograph thus 'captures' the stone ring amidst the Mexican landscape, placing it firmly within a wilderness landscape. The setting is impressive and it is meant to be. With its wooded slopes and hills receding into the blue haze, the photograph is worthy of the ærial effects described by Leonardo da Vinci in his treatise of Renaissance painting. The composition of *Tarahumara Circle*, the more one studies it, becomes increasingly 'classical' and carefully controlled: there are even two small trees either side of the stone circle, in the foreground, framing the circle, a compositional device favoured by Turner, Girtin, Cotman and other late 18th century landscapists.

So *Tarahumara Circle* is actually a complex cultural artefact. The elements in *Tarahumara Circle* that could be called 'natural' or 'organic' (the landscape setting, the material used for the circle) are actually the last aspects of the work to be considered:. Sure, for the artist, they may be the most important, but they're just one component in a highly sophisticated manifestation of 'high culture'.

Although the photographs and textworks in Long's output were part of a recording or documentary process, Long said he would not want his art to be entirely about documentation. That would appear too 'second hand'. He also had to make something; hence the indoor sculptures (2004b). That way, Long could present both aspects of his art – the faraway places in the photographs, and real artwork on the floor or walls of the gallery.

Richard Long says he has conceived particular walks precisely so he can document them in a textwork (1995a). In other words, the walk may come first, the walk may be primary, but while walking Long is also making art, and walks have been planned so they will fit into the format Long has developed for his textworks. It's an important point, because it indicates that sometimes something does come before The Walk, and that is The Idea. The Walk may be absolutely primary, and absolutely the foundation of Richard Long's art, but occasionally The Idea is as significant.

Richard Long's Summer 1993 show at Anthony d'Offay in London was typical of his kind of art exhibition: in the three galleries of his UK dealer, Long showed a mix of sculptures and text/ map/ photographic works. In no. 23 Dering Street, London, Long exhibited a number of framed works, mostly of text, though there were also maps and titles of these works explains much of Long's typical preoccupations: *Mount Whitney Stone Circle, Orkney Stones, Old Year New Year Walk, Watershed* and *Walking a Circle on Hoy*. These works, from 1992 and 1993, contain the usual Longian obsessions (for instance, walking between two rivers, the Avon and the Thames, in *Watershed*, 1992). Other titles indicate the spiritual nature of Long's work: *Dorset Song Lines* (1991), for example, explicitly relates to the Australian aborigine 'songlines', and with ley lines in Britain of folklorists and occultists. The notion of Aboriginal 'songlines' is taken up by Richard Long in a number of works. Only in a few works, though, does Long directly refer to this notion of the leyline/ song line/ *feng shui* (dragon lines). In *Dorset Song Lines*, a textwork referring to a 7 day walk, Long draws in thick black ink the squiggly lines of his journey through the landscape, an artwork that is halfway between map-making and graphic art. Underneath each line Long prints the names of Dorset's sites, which are familiar as some of the places beloved of Thomas Hardy and his Wessex: Weymouth, Swanage, Cerne Abbas, Milton, Puddletown and Lyme Regis.

Upstairs at d'Offay's no. 23 Dering Street, Richard Long produced one of those circles for which he has become famous: *Midsummer Circles* was a slate circle (1993) over five metres in diameter: the definitive Long form. At no. 9 Dering Street, Long displayed a series of works on paper which were distinctly Oriental in content and appearance. They were calligraphic swirls and splodges of mud and ink on handmade paper, Japanese paper and Korean paper. All these works on paper were titled *Untitled*, which is *the* archetypal title for any 20th/ 21st century work of art. Some works, such as *Untitled* (1993) were described as 'Korean mud on Korean paper'. Other works, such as *Untitled* (1992), were billed as 'River Avon mud on Japanese paper'. The combination of the two elements: mud from near Long's home in Bristol and Japanese paper, is typical of Long's fusion of Eastern and Western culture.

At Anthony d'Offay's no. 21 Dering Street gallery in 1993 were the familiar large-scale Richard Long works: a huge spiral made from terracotta bricks, and a wall painted black and smeared with terracotta. *Footprint Spiral* affirmed the primacy of the body, of feet, of feet walking on the Earth. Each brick was a small unit with the imprint of Long's foot embedded in it. As with the stones in the lines or circles, each brick formed a chain in *Footprint Spiral*, creating a spiral. Walking is simply one step followed by another, and *Footprint Spiral* affirmed the significance of walking, the simplicity and beauty of it.

Untitled (1993) was a large area of liquid terracotta smeared or thrown at a wall. This work could only have occurred after the drip paintings of Jackson Pollock and the furls and curtains of Morris Louis's huge poured canvases. The splashes and smears of the ochre-hued terracotta on the black wall created a sculpture which absorbed the æsthetics of both painting and sculpture. Long's terracotta-smeared wall had affinities with 1960s painting, with installation art and performance art of the 1970s (Michael Craig-Martin and Andy Goldsworthy have produced flat, mobile wall-drawings). It was not quite an 'installation', though the wall and its terracotta covering were specially prepared. It was not a 'performance', because Long had smeared on the terracotta at some earlier time, although the visitor to the gallery could see the splashes on the other walls, and on the floor. It was not, either, a 'painting' in the usual sense of paint on canvas. Nor was it truly sculpture, for it was essentially two-dimensional, a relief perhaps (or, more accurately, just a 'thing'). It was a thin layer of liquid over black paint, not really exhibiting enough volumetrics to be a 'sculpture' in the traditional sense. What mattered about the terracotta splashes, then? It was, perhaps, the actual look and feel and atmosphere of the liquid. For, as in Morris Louis's unfurled and curtain paintings, where the acrylic paint was poured directly onto unprimed cotton duck, Richard Long applied the terracotta directly. The result is an immediate, tactile work. It is simply terracotta on a wall, like Carl Andre's bricks and metal slabs are just those things in themselves. This is, of course, the foundation of Long's art, this fusion of simplicity and complexity, thereness and otherness, inside and outside, nature and art.

THE HUMAN TOUCH

Richard Long uses his life in his works. His walks are what he does much of the time, and these walks become his works.[1] To produce all those sculptures, have all those exhibitions around the world, and embark on those walks (plus preparation, admin, transport, accommodation, flights, etc) takes a lot of time and effort (and he must really enjoy it). There is an æsthetic and philosophical continuity between Long's life and his art. 'My art is the essence of my experience, not a representation of it' Long says (RL, 236). All art, though, is representation, isn't it (among other things)? Long tries to underline notions of essence, where art is always, if nothing else, a form of representation.

> I can use words and they can give me different possibilities than I would get from using a camera [says Long]. So, taking photographs does a certain type of job, records one moment, makes an image. And words do a different job. They can usually record the whole idea of a walk, maybe much better... (IC 1, 7)

Of course, artists have often (if not always) used their life in one way or another in their art. Pierre Bonnard painted his wife in the bath and produced those incandescent late paintings. Vincent Van Gogh painted friends and acquaintances. Auguste Rodin made love to the models he used for his sculptures. Egon Schiele drew his lover. And so on. Discussing the 1982 textwork *A Three Day Bicycle Ride* –

BIRTHPLACE   BRIDGE   THE FAST YEARS
1977 CROSSING PLACE   FOSS WAY   CHALK VALLEY
FELLOW TRAVELLERS ON THE SAME ROAD   FLINT SOURCE
FRIEND

– which used many autobiographical elements[1] (Silbury Hill, the Fossway, Bristol, his birthplace, etc), Richard Long said: '[t]ime, distance, memory, history, and what the land is made of, places you meet, strangers you meet, the friends you stay with, it is actually a very dense work' (IC 1, 21).

True, the experience of making this work might have been very dense for Richard Long,[2] but for the viewer? True, Long may have put together many elements to make a rich work of art, but what does the viewer actually see? The viewer sees a few words printed in capitals in a book or on a piece of framed paper. For the viewer, the text piece may be nothing more than semantics, a semiotic game, arcane wordplay. The viewer has to *imagine* the whole artwork, build it up. The viewer has to put the walk back together, from those few words Long has supplied. For the artist, these words are an abbreviated notebook form with key words to remind her/ him of certain experiences. For the viewer, the experiences are vastly different. The single word 'family' in *A Three Day Bicycle Ride* Long glosses as '[a]nd 'family', well, I cycled back home' (IC 1, 21). But for the viewer, the word 'family' might mean anything and everything. Like 'love' or 'art' or 'world', 'family' is one of the broadest, most general words in the language.

In the textwork made on the Mendip Hills, near Richard Long's home, one finds a vertical list of words: 'turf/ gorse/ trees/ field/ trees/ field'.3 These are simple words which aim to communicate some aspect of the walk. There is so much to experience in a walk, though (in any walk) that Long's notebook form of art must inevitably be extremely reductive. These words read like a stream of consciousness text, or the utterances of someone lifting up their eyes from their feet every few seconds to speak in a dull monotone into a tape recorder, Samuel Beckett-style: 'hillside/ swift/ scrub/ bush/ scrub/ bush'.

So all those things that Richard Long himself experiences – '[t]ime, distance, memory, history' etc – are open to any interpretation. Anyone who's been on a walk knows that there are many, many elements to it. One might list temperature of the body, heartbeat, pulse, sweat, cramp, aching, rubbing, blisters, movement, feel of wind, cloud, rain, water and sun on the body, and a host of other experiences to do with the body; then there is the way the body reacts to the environment; the things seen, heard, smelt, touched; then the mind thinks about the immediate and long-term past and future; people seen; and so on. To list all these in a short textwork is impossible. Poets know the 'inarticulate' nature of words. Simply, one cannot 'capture' a walk in words. And only the very, very greatest writers – such as John Cowper Powys, or Arthur Rimbaud, or Friedrich Hölderlin (great walker-poets) – have come anywhere near describing in words the sensual experiences of walking. Richard Long, who is not a poet of the stature or talent of Powys or Rimbaud or Hölderlin (now that would be an incredible combination), is not as adept at communicating the experience of a walk.

Why, then, is Richard Long's work so popular? It must be that before he made the text pieces he made very sensual works to which people could relate instantly. Long's (relative) fame or popularity must stem (partly) from his stone and slate circles and rows, which people can see and touch and discuss. If Long had never made a stone circle or line or mud wall, would he be as popular as he is today? That is, has a painter or sculptor become successful simply by sending words to a typesetter to be printed and framed and put on gallery walls? It's an interesting question. Imagine a sculptor who produces no objects, no images, no visual material and no photographs of works made outside the gallery. The ultimate post-Conceptual, Postminimal, post-perform-ance, postmodern, post-everything artist. Who doesn't exist, of course. Even the most exquisitely post-Conceptual artist must produce something, even if they produce nothing. As Yves Klein found out, even exhibiting a galery with 'nothing' inside it is something. (It's still too early to see if these Conceptual and post-Conceptual artists will stand the test of time like, say, the ancient Athenian sculptor Praxiletes, who was sculpting statuary between 375 and 330 BC).

Of course, Richard Long was making the textworks *as well as* the slate rings and mud walls. Even Conceptual artists such as Gilbert & George had actual objects people could see. They might have been 'living sculptures', but they also made colourful, easy-to-digest (if mundane) works. There are few artists, it seems, who have become famous merely by manipulating and exhibiting words in frames. And the other important factor explaining Long's success is his use of the Great Outdoors, the wilderness landscape which is so dear to Anglo-American-European art audiences (Long's photos depict gorgeous wild zones in Bolivia, Iceland, Scotland, the Sahara, Nepal). In stinking, sweltering, freezing, abysmally grey and drab cities, Long's works suggest wide open spaces, vast cloudscapes, cycles of growth and decay long obliterated from the Western city. Long commented in 1994 that 'for preference I'm attracted to the empty wilderness places... Through choice I'm not an urban artist – my work is about being in the natural world. Most of the world's surface is still open landscapes' (1994b). It's not that he doesn't travel through built-up areas, of course. 'The map works and also many of the road walks take me through towns and villages because that is where I can buy food, or find a bed and breakfast, find shops' (1994b).

In using walking, Long employs one of the most basic of all human activities, and dance, theatre, and some sports, derive in part from walking.[4] 'Walking is the most primitive, the most immediate, the most corporeal medium for human transport-ation'.[5] And Michel de Certeau saw walking as comparable with speaking: for him, walking, like the speech act, realizes space and place, and sets up relations between form of movement and enunciation.[6] In de Certeau's system, Long is 'speaking' as he walks: clearly, for Long, walking and making art are part of the same thing.

In Richard Long's art, there is often no 'exterior' object, such as a painting or a sculpture, there is The Walk itself. At the same time, the area bounded by The Walk or Cycle Ride can be regarded as the sculptural object. When Long started to make walks as art, he could encompass huge areas and incorporate them into art. Discussing the changes in art, Richard Long said:

I could make a piece of art which was ten miles long. I could also make a sculpture which surrounded an area of 2401 square miles. All I have to do to make that was just to cycle around the countryside and leave it as a sculpture. (IC 1, 16)

The spectator knows about the Long walks from the maps, text and photos. So, as he walks, Long is making art. It is not quite the same as with Joseph Beuys, Hermann Nitsch or Gilbert & George, who were performing, who were 'living sculptures'. Long's absence from his photos and texts is part of his ecologically-friendly, non-destructive stance. 'I consider my landscape sculptures inhabit the rich territory between two ideological positions, namely that of making 'monuments' or, conversely, of 'leaving only footprints'' Richard Long remarked (WL, 68). The walks, though, are not a 'performance'.[7] The walk is not 'performing' something, a performance *of* something, a representation, a reference to something outside of itself. It's not an illusion of space or place, a 3-D illusion, in the post-Renaissance manner of most traditional art in the West. It is about movement in space, a lived experience.[8] The walk is the walk. To call it art is also to call it life, in Long's view. The two things are continuous. 'My work has become a simple metaphor of life' he says.[9] The central thing to grasp with Richard Long's art, as also with other land artists, such as Heizer, de Maria, Nash, Fulton, Aycock and Holt, is the essence of their work, the mythic centre, which may be an idea, an essence, a structure or an experience. For Long, doing the walk itself is pleasurable:

spending a day walking across the moors following the compass point… which is a very enjoyable way to spend the day. But it was also enjoyable because of the fact that I knew I was making a very original, a unique and dynamic work of art which had a new scale to it, which was a sculpture which was invisible and in many other ways was interesting as art. So, for me, it is a domination of things, as I said in my statement, *common means given the simple twist of art*. My work is about ideas and actions, it is a balance of the mental and physical. A good work like the Exmoor walk should be a fantastic idea and also fantastic to actually do. Everything comes together at the right moment. (IC 1, 16)

The walk is also a physical, energetic thing to do. For Richard Long, walking as art is more 'heroic' than painting (though plenty of painters might disagree with him):

[the walk] takes a lot of work, it demands a lot of energy and time. If I have the idea to walk a thousand miles it's great to have the idea but I also have got to do it, I want to do it. That is what I mean by commitment. Doing a walk is far more physical than making some 'heroic' easel painting. (IC 2, 5)

The walk *Hours, Miles,* for instance, when Long walked 82 miles in 24 hours and 24 miles in 82 hours, was about the two walks, one balancing the other, not just the effort and heroism of walking 82 miles in 24 hours. The idea was to explore a 'kind of symmetrical inversion or balance, between difficulty and ease, because the other half of that work was to walk 24 miles in 82 hours' (2004b). As the *Tao Te Ching* put it, 'the difficult and the easy complement each other' (II).

Like Hamish Fulton, Bruce Chatwin and Chris Drury, Richard Long has travelled to some wild places in pursuit of interesting spaces: Lappland, Africa, Australia, Peru, Alaska and the Himalayas. It's easy to see Long's art as simply pure Romanticism, a 'back to the land' art that utterly ignores political, societal, ideological, racial, economic and gender issues. True. Long's art is not concerned with the urban world of issues and daily news at all. It doesn't address political movements, revolutions, entertainment, celebrity gossip, wars, famines, floods, pollution, scientific break-throughs, baseball, charity events, advertizing, pop music, royalty, terrorists, prison riots, crime syndicates, industries, air crashes or assassinations. You won't find Long's art discussing the price of oil, the Superbowl, or stocks and shares, or unions and strikes, or corporate mergers, meltdowns and takeovers. And it looks odd to see Long's work in galleries in cities, to see the stones in a setting quite different from the wildernesses. Rather, Long's sculpture comes across as deeply poetic, personal, subjective and romantic. It is *all* about a response to nature, about getting into connection with nature,[10] as with Chris Drury and David Nash. On his website Richard Long says he has been exploring 'some of the variables of transience, permanence, visibility or recognition'.

> In a way art demands an act of faith from the viewer as well [writes Long], like we accept Carl Andre's bricks as art as well as bricks, or my stones being art as well as stones. Especially when working in a wilderness, art for me is a personal and not a social experience and must be understood like that. (IC 2, 6)

RICHARD LONG'S EASTERN TURN

A journey of a thousand miles
Starts from beneath one's feet.

Tao Te Ching (LXIV)

Richard Long has sometimes made direct use of Far Eastern visual culture in his art: he has produced calligraphic art on Japanese and Korean paper, quoted from the *I Ching* (a favourite text), and based art around Chinese and Japanese ideograms and symbols (in a way, Long may be making his own, Westernized version of the *I Ching*, his own *Book of Changes*). A typical example would be Long's mud wall drawing *Heaven and Earth* (Glarus, 2002). Long has used the trigrams from the *I Ching* as the basis for work, such as the trigrams for mountain, heaven and earth (or the floor-piece *Following Thunder Tranquillity*, 2001, which reproduced the hexagrams from black bricks). Long said he liked the idea that the Chinese ideograms were partly language and partly graphic or abstract images, but they also had a meaning. Long was also attracted to the meaning of the *I Ching* trigrams: 'the symbols have really strong, epic, classic meanings like Wind, Tranquillity, Transience, Change, which give them a power and a strength' (SS, 309).

The eight *pa kua* (trigrams) of the *I Ching* are built from short lines (*yin*) and long lines (*yang*). The trigrams represent water, mountains, earth, thunder, fire, vapour, heaven and wind. Consider *Heaven* and *Earth* (2002): Richard Long has fashioned two wall drawings in mud on a black backing: for *Heaven*, Long built up six long lines of mud, while for *Earth*, there were twelve short lines.

The Chinese Taoist mystic, Chuang-tzu (the 'Groucho Marx of Taoism' as Lawrence Durrell called him), wrote: '[l]eap into the boundless and make it your home.'[1] This statement perfectly describes an artist's act of faith and risk, which is so essential for good artistic creations. As Søren Kirkegaard said, without risk, life is not worth living. Again, these Existentialist and Taoist notions of risk and leaping into the boundless are perfectly in tune with 1960s land art, 'expanded field' sculpture and Richard Long's art.

> I have read a few bits and pieces of [Samuel] Beckett's work [related Long]... he does use things like country lanes and bicycles and stones and doing nothing... like an incredible minimal view of life, which is very attractive and powerful. So I think there are some similarities, in the same way there are similarities with Zen Buddhism. It is just a sort of coincidental, human... we all live in the same world. It

would be maybe very surprising if you could not find parallels with the work of other artists or other religions. (IC 2, 7)

In another place, Long spoke about Japan:

I do feel very close to the spirit of many of their points of view. Zen is quite pure and philosophical, it's close to art, and the Japanese religion, Shinto, is based on nature, and nature is universal. Nature belongs to every culture. (1994b)

Comparisons can be made between the shrines and temples in Shinto religion and some of Long's art; the notion of *kami*, fundamental to Shinto, also chimes with Long's art (*kami* is a vague term which can indicate anything awe-inspiring, including living and inanimate things). Shinto shrines with their abodes of *kami* are typically situated in forests and mountains, surrounded by trees and rocks (mountains, tree and boulders may themselves be objects of worship). Long's stone circles are also obviously reminiscent of *mandalas*, the magic circles of Eastern religion (which are forms of *yantras.* The idea of the *mandala* was famously later taken up by C.G. Jung).

The great philosophers of the Far East, some mythical, some historical, provide numerous points of contact with art since the 1950s: Mencius (371-289 BC), Confucius (551-479 BC), Chuang-tzu (*c.* 369-286 BC), Lao-tzu (6th century BC), author of the *Tao Te Ching,* Bodhidharma (c. 470-543), one of the founders of Zen Buddhism, the Zen Buddhist monk Hui-Neng (638-713), Zen masters Fa-yen (885-958), Lin-chi (10th century), Hui Hai (8th century AD), known as the 'great Pearl', and Chao-chou (778-897), Kuo Hsiang (d. 312), Japanese Zen master Dogen (1200-53), author of the *Shebogenzo,* Shoichi Kokushi (1202-80), Tao-hsin (580-651), Tao-Sheng (*c.* 360-434), Hui Shih (4th century BC), and Tibetan mystic Jetsun Milarepa (1052-1135). Richard Long has referred to some of these sages and mystics, and aspects of their philosophies have clearly influenced his art (consciously and unconsciously).

The great books of Far Eastern mysticism – *Tibetan Book of the Dead, Chuang-tzu,* the *I Ching* (*Book of Changes*) and the *Tao Te Ching* – have many correspondences with Richard Long's art. In some cases, he has drawn on them directly to create artworks.

Among Western mystics and philosophers, one could cite, in connection with Long, Heraclitus (everything's in flux), Empedocles, Paracelsus, Meister Eckhart, Jan van Ruysbroeck, Plato, various Neoplatonists (such as Philo and Plotinus – Platonism and Neoplatonism is everywhere in Western philosophy), and William Blake. Maybe some theosophy, some Quietism, some alchemy definitely, and all sorts of bits of occultism and hermetic philosophy. Pantheism (or nature mysticism) is there in abundance, of course. American Indian spirituality is a big influence too, as well as Australian aborigine religion, with their profound reverence for the land.

Clearly, Richard Long's encounter with Oriental mysticism in the Sixties was profound and has proved long-lasting. There are far fewer references in his art, for instance, to Catholicism (the Mass, say, or sin and repentance), or Anglicanism, or Protestantism, or Calvinism, or Judaism, or the *Qabbalah*, or Zorasterianism. The repressive notions of Western religion – guilt, sin, the Fall, body-hatred – seem to be absent from Long's art (however, the fundamental utopian theme of Christianity is still there. Christianity is haunted by the idea of paradise, some earlier Eden or 'pure land', before the Fall of Man). Note that, although he must have walked beside Western churches, cathedrals and cemeteries thousands of times, Long's art doesn't employ much Christian iconography at all (those early crosses, for instance, were Minimal X's, not references to the Crucifixion).

And when it comes to Eastern religion, Richard Long's art tends towards the Far East, rather than Islam, Sufism, Christianity and Judaism in the Near East, or the religions of India: Hinduism, Jainism and Sikhism. It's far more likely to find references to the *I Ching* in Long's art than the great books of Indian mysticism (the *Upanishads,* the *Bhagavad Gita*). At times it can seem as if Long were creating his own form of the religions of the East: walking as yoga, walking as *zazen* (Zen Buddhist meditation), walking as *tantra*, walking as 'the Way' ('Tao').

CRITICS OF RICHARD LONG'S ART

Richard Long's art polarizes critics and art consumers. People tend to love him or loathe him. For fans, Long's a New Age, eco-friendly mystic, making cool, Conceptual art that doesn't harm the environment. It's art that has a refreshing simplicity and clarity. And it reminds them how beautiful the world is, how complex and multi-layered its landscapes and processes are. Herman de Vries said he liked the work of Long 'very much', in particular his 'feeling for poetry'.[1] Long's supporters include Rudi Fuchs, Anne Seymour, Robert Rosenblum, John Haldane, John Beardsley, Anne Dyson,

Mel Gooding, Colin Renfrew and Hamish Fulton (and many curators and gallery owners, such as Konrad Fischer, Anthony d'Offay, Jean Bernier and Gian Enzo Sperone). Detractors include Peter Fuller, Jonathan Jones, David Sylvester, Rasheed Araeen and David Lee.

For sceptical critics, Richard Long's output is pretentious, shallow, repetitive, unoriginal, arrogant, conservative, apolitical and spiritually bankrupt. Modernist critics moan that there's no object to grasp in Long's art – for them it's a series of empty Conceptual gestures. Postmodernist fans can admire how Long plays the art market, trouncing conventional views of the art object. For Long, a sculpture can be two hundred and thirty miles long if he wishes. If a sculptor wants to make a 'real', physical object 230 miles long, s/he has to have a lot of money (like Christo with his *Running Fence*). Long, however, retorts that his 230 mile long sculpture really is a physical thing: he walked those 230 miles, physically. He might record sensual aspects of the walk: wind direction, incidents along the way, weather, etc. So, 'conceptual' though it seems, Long's sculptures are 'real', physical objects. A walk, after all, is one of the most physical, and fundamental, activities for humans.

Critics of Richard Long's art concentrate on the same things they find lacking in land art in general: its avoidance of political or 'important' or problematic issues, such as AIDS, poverty, 'Third World' debt, globalization, sexuality, gender inequality, colonialism, war, terrorism, and so on. They dislike its romanticizing and spiritualizing of the natural world; its conservatism; its nostalgia; its escapism; its self-indulgence; its élitism; its repetition and lack of imagination (many critics have called Long's art repetitive); its lack of formal experimentation (Long just does the same thing over and over, critics carp); and its over-simplification of its subjects. Tony Godfrey, describing *A Line Made By Walking*, said that Richard Long's art could be seen as political: '

> In so far as Long was positing the possibility of being in nature, not just seeing it, but *being* in it, he is also making a political statement. We can escape from alienation and false consciousness: by a wilful act we can be wholly in the world – reconnected' (1998, 130)

Of course, all art, and all artistic activity, is always (at least) political or ideological. But for nay-sayers, Richard Long's art doesn't engage directly (or obviously) in political issues, and appears to be avoiding them.

Richard Long acknowledged that his art could be seen as repetitious, because walking is endless repetition, and because the forms he employed were repetitious.

But: although his forms were repetitions, Long said his sculptures were also about the infinite variety of the cosmos, so that every footprint, every mud or water splash, every individual work of art was individual and unlike any other in its precise forms and details. 'I could make a million stone circles and they'd all be different' (2004b).

For the negative critics, Richard Long's art and land art in general is a romantic retreat into escapist, nostalgic fantasies about nature, with nothing to say about the anxieties, problems and challenges of living in the contemporary, 21st century world. It's hippy-dippy art that panders to the Western middle class's nostalgia for nature, seen from the perspective of neurotic city dwellers who hanker for the peace and quiet of the countryside. It's also an art that flatters and assuages the bourgeoisie's liberal guilt over wrecking the natural world with its ceaseless, unstoppable and vast consumption and pollution. It's an art that doesn't seem to say much about the particular world critics valorize – a late capitalist, technological, post-industrial, consumer society.

For critics like Jonathan Jones, British land art is hopelessly detached from 'real life'. Jones claimed that Andy Goldsworthy's art 'says nothing about the violence, hypocrisy and waste of our relationship to nature and is about as radical as the Body Shop'. While the United States of America had big, romantic works of land art, such as Robert Smithson's *Spiral Jetty* or Walter de Maria's *Lightning Field*, which were authentic attempts to grapple with the sublime in the natural world, Britain had tree huggers and Goldsworthy's 'twee arrangements of twigs and stones' (2001).

Oddly, critic David Sylvester claimed that Long has had too much adulation:

> He has too many admirers. A quarter of a century has passed since he began to gain an international reputation at about the time he left art school, and this reputation has steadily grown upwards and outwards. Mounting stacks of books, catalogues and articles have ensured that his very particular, ascetic, ritualistic methods and their mystique have become common knowledge.

Can an artist become *too* popular? The downside of popularity is perhaps queuing for four hours to see a Claude Monet show at the Met or trying to peer over people layered five deep in front of Leonardo da Vinci's drawings at the National Museum of Art, Osaka. Richard Long hasn't reached this point of superstardom yet. *Very* few living artists have. To be an artist superstar, you have to be dead (preferably a genius dying young, like Mozart, Arthur Rimbaud or Vincent van Gogh).

Peter Fuller, who advocated a distinctly *British* form of modern painting, saw spiritual bankruptcy in land art. Of Richard Long, one of Fuller's targets, Fuller intoned:

It is, I believe, a tragedy that consideration was given to inviting an artist such as Richard Long to create a piece within Lincoln Cathedral. His work, for me, is symptomatic of the loss of both the æsthetic and the spiritual dimensions of art. He shows little trace of imagination, of skill, of the transformation of materials. Seen in contrast to the greatest achievements of the British tradition in art, Long's relationship to the world of nature is simply regressive. His work is sentimental and fetishistic... claims that his work is worthy of 'spiritual' attention are preposterous...[2]

One sees clearly Fuller's outrage that Richard Long might sully the building beloved of John Ruskin, Nikolaus Pevsner and D.H. Lawrence, one of the finest English cathedrals. But surely Fuller is missing the point with Long, who is clearly as mystical, as in awe, as deep in his feeling for nature as Fuller's cherished Brit artists, Cecil Collins, Henry Moore, J.M.W. Turner or Patrick Heron.

One wonders what happens when Richard Long bumps into members of the public while making his walks and works. Sometimes artists can encounter suspicion or hostility when working outside their studios. Imagine Richard Long's walking in some wilderness somewhere in South-West England, and meets an inquisitive soul. The following conversation might be heard by the surrounding rocks and bushes.

(Do not read this if you are a big fan of Richard Long's work):

SCENE: EXTERIOR. SOMEWHERE IN ENGLAND. DAY.

Inquirer (sporting a heavy West Country accent): 'Allo there.
The Artist (who may have affinities with Richard Long): Hello.
Inquirer: Noice day, innit?
Artist: Yes.
Inquirer: What, out for a walk, then?
Artist: Yep.
Inquirer: Do a lot of walking, do yer?
Artist: You could say that.
Inquirer: Be noice to just walk for a livin', wouldn't it?
Artist: Well, actually...
Inquirer: What you doin' wi' that stone?
Artist: [*lifting up the stone in his hand*] Well, I'm carrying it.
Inquirer: Oh.
Artist: Yes, I'm carrying it from the Dorset coast to Weston-Super-Mare.
Inquirer: *Really?* Why?
Artist: It's a coast to coast walk, English Channel to Bristol Channel. It's what I do.
Inquirer: You carry stones around? Just that?
Artist: Yes.

Inquirer:	Blimey! Anything else?
Artist:	Yes. I make lines in the snow, or circles out of rocks. Or I splatter mud on walls. But mostly I walk.
Inquirer:	Walk?
Artist:	Yes.
Inquirer:	What, you *walk* for a living?
Artist:	Yes.
Inquirer:	And make money out of it?
Artist:	Yes.
Inquirer:	Lots?
Artist:	Sometimes.
Inquirer:	Money just from walking? How's that? Are you sponsored, loike, by a charity? Is it some benefit for cancer research thing?
Artist:	No, I finance it all myself (but there is the gallery's percentage, materials, transport, agents, flights, hotels, frames, film, printing, …) Oh, and sometimes commissions. And sometimes there's public funding. Oh, and the limited edition prints, and artists' books, and posters, and so on.
Inquirer:	Wow. But… [*ponders slowly*] how do you get paid, then? How do they – your bosses – *know* you've done your walk, eh?
Artist:	Sometimes I write about it. Sometimes I take photos.
Inquirer:	Ah, yes, I see the camera. Nikkormat; nice camera. Then what?
Artist:	Then I show the pictures in a gallery.
Inquirer:	Oh God, you're an *artist!* You should've said. That explains *everything*. Must be goin'. 'Bye.

[*Inquirer exits rapidly*]

6

Circles, Lines, Rows, Splashes and Other Forms in Richard Long's Art

There are a lot of things theoretical and intellectual to say about lines and circles, but I think the very fact that they are images that don't belong to me and, in fact, are shared by everyone because they have existed throughout history, actually makes them more powerful than if I was inventing my own idiosyncratic, particular Richard Long-type images. I think it cuts out a lot of personal unwanted æsthetic paraphernalia.

Richard Long (RC, 22)

STONE CIRCLES

The reasons for making a work are many says Richard Long, ranging from time, measurement and mileage to an idea, or a line:

A walk, and place, can be chosen for any reason. For no reason (or on a "hunch"), or to follow an idea, or in a place I know, or in a place I don't know, to complete a time, or to complete a mileage, to go from place to place, or to walk in one place, to cross a country (to "measure" it by footsteps), from sea to sea, or border to border, to follow a river, to follow a straight line. (SF)
The closer one looks at Richard's Long's circles, the more one finds differences

between them. The unifying principle behind them is a circle set flat on the gallery floor or outdoors. Beyond that, there are many variations. The slate circle, which seems to be a Richard Long standard, is not simply a circle full of slate, evenly packed or spread through the area of the circle. The size and shape of each slab of slate varies. Although he favours long oblong chunks of slate, the pieces vary in size and shape: some are triangular in cross section, and short; others are long and rectangular in cross section (the stones in the gallery sculptures usually come from quarries). Some of the slate circles consist of pieces of slate grouped tightly together (such as *Slate Circle* [1979], or *Cornwall Slate Circle* [Bordeaux, 1981], or *Berlin Circle* [1996], or *Bilbao Circle* [2000]); others, such as *Slate Circle* (Amsterdam, 1980) are open circles, with a lot of space between each piece. *Stick Circle* (also Amsterdam, 1980) is another open circle, comprising short (one foot long or so) sticks (other open stick circles include *Black River Circle* [2000] and *Dead Wood Circle* [2001]).

Red Slate Ring (1986) was installed for the 1986 show at the Guggenheim Museum: pieces of slate of a roughly similar size were overlaid to produce a wide open circle, each piece of slate covering the ones below so that no part of the floor showed through. *Stone Lake* (1988) was a large solid circle of stone slabs made in a field of long grass in Schloss Crottorf. *Chisos Circle* (1990) was a medium-sized open circle drawn in the stones in Texas. For the Haunch of Venison show (2003), Long produced irregular, curved rows of stones (*Cornwall State Lines*, 2003), and a *Norfolk Ellipse* (2003).

A 1994 circle, *Merrivale Circle*, shown at Anthony d'Offay, London, is an open ring about thirteen feet in diameter made from Dartmoor granite. The stones are not touching, and the circle is full of light. The openness and relaxed stance of the circle is emphasized by the pale hue the granite. Although each block of stone is weighty, *Merrivale Circle* is not as heavy or opaque as some of Long's other circles (such as the slate circles which're dark toned, filling up the gallery floor with grey and black shapes). In *Circle of Memory Sticks* (1996, made at Richard Long's German art gallery), a collection of short, neatly cut sticks were arranged in an open circle, each stick pointing towards the centre of the circle.

Other stone circle forms by Richard Long include concentric circles. A series of three circles is often favoured by Long (a group of three circles was employed in prehistoric earthworks, such as the Hurlers, on Bodmin Moor, a landscape that boasts at least thirteen stone circles). Three concentric stone circles include *Napoli Circles* (1984), *Midsummer Circles* (1993), and *Little Tejunga Canyon Stone Circles* (Los

Angeles, 1984). *Turf Circles* (1988, Cambridge) comprised concentric circles made using cuts in the grass.

Unlike the stone circles of Nancy Holt or Robert Smithson, Long's concentric circles (like all his stone circles), are constructed from small stones, stones that can fairly easily be carried. These are stones that could be found in the landscape, by hand, not carved out of the earth (the outdoor works are constructed from existing stones; but although the art gallery rings use stones from quarries, Long still opts for small-sized stones). In contrast to the bigger, more bombastic earthworks, such as those by American land artists, Long's circles are distinctly 'human-scale', in the sense that each stone in the circles relates to the human touch, the human hand. One feels one can pick the stones in Richard Long's circles: they are friendly artworks, not domineering. They do not overpower the viewer, but entice the viewer with notions of presence, the natural world, the texture and feel of materials.1 Among the more ambitious concentric stone circles are *Six Slate Circles* (London, 1982), which consists of about 103 stones, and *Six Stone Circles* (England, 1981). Long has also produced flattened concentric circles, such as *White Foot Circles* (1986, Finland).

Some of Richard Long's circles are open at the centre (such as *Helsinki Circle* [1983], or the large open stone circle in the Gobi desert [*Nomad Circle,* 1996]), a shape also favoured in Richard Long's wall circle drawings created with River Avon mud. The open centre circles allow for a larger circle to be constructed using the same quantity of materials. Most of Long's circles are between 4 and 6 metres in diameter: Long likes to make his circles fill up a space (if it's an indoor circle). There is room to walk round the edges of the circle, but also the room is not allowed to dominate the circle. The circle must not be overwhelmed by the gallery space; rather, the circle must assert its own presence in the gallery.

Some of Richard Long's circles are very large – such as the *Red Slate Circle* (Boston, 1980), which is over nine metres in diameter, *Lightning Fire Wood Circle* (1981), which is 8.8 metres wide and *Bushwood Circle* (Melbourne, 1977), which is also nine metres wide. 1982's *Ring of Stones* in Ottawa was an open circle 10.68 metres in diameter.

Pine Tree Bark Circle (1985) is a solid circle, not one of Long's largest, but it dominates the gallery. The slabs of bark, mostly two or three feet long, offer many points of interest for the eye. Each chunk of bark is individual, with its own shape and size, just as in the Orkney 1994 Bob Dylan stone sculpture, where the stones are untreated, made to stand as they are. The circle shape gives the bark a formal unity, while the textures of the pine bark make the sculpture very varied. The wood circles are quite different from the stone or mud circles. The way Long uses wood is to break it up into similar sizes, but to leave the shapes of the pieces of wood alone. So there are irregular edges and points, bits which stick out, as in *Circle in Africa* (1978). This latter is a large open circle made with sticks of wood from the small trees which surround the sculpture in its archetypal Longian wilderness setting.

Some circles in the landscape are created by Richard Long taking away snow (or drawing in the snow) in open circles, so the the ground underneath shows through, as in *Early Summer Circle* (1997), *Shirakami Circle* (1997), *Sunrise Circle* (1998) and *Walking a Circle By the Beagle Channel* (1997), or the snow is cleared away around a closed circle, as in *Tierra del Fuego Circle* (1997) and *Throwing Snow Into a Circle* (1991), or stamped out by the act of walking in a circle (as in *Footprint Circle* [1989, Italy]).

Brough of Birsay Circle (Orkney, 1994) is a large open circle which relies on plants and their blooming in Summer to make it work. Like his late 1960s lines and crosses made by walking, for this work Long has walked in a large circle on a field of flowers. The plants have been pressed flat, leaving a circular mark. In essence, *Brough of Birsay Circle* is no different from the walk sculptures the artist was creating 25 years previously. There is no sense of progression in *Brough of Birsay Circle* compared to the earlier works, no addition, and nothing new. It's the same countryside setting, the same wide shot encompassing the work (taken, as usual, during the daytime), the same notion of grass (and flowers, here) being pressed flat as a trace of the artist's boots, act of walking and route, and it's the same sort of fundamental geometric shape. But that's part of the charm of Long's art: there is, really, no attempt at development or progression. Long really does follow the maxims of Donald Judd and Jasper Johns of doing one thing, then another... and another. Long adds new shapes sometimes, or coloured stones, or alters the paper backing of wall drawings from black to white, but it's all really the same sort of art he's been making for decades.

The largest of circles in Richard Long's art are of course the circular walks he undertakes, which could be many miles in diameter. Some of these find their way onto maps (they begin as circles on maps before they're walked), and some are suggested through words in textworks. These are 'imaginary' circles but no less significant than the tactile stone circles. It's the same with science: the largest scientific experiment in the world is not the particle accelerator buried underground in Switzerland, it's the astronomical observations which use radio telescopes on either side of the Earth to correlate data. The diameter of the planet is the size of the experiment. The telescope is as large as the Earth. There are even larger astronomic experiments: the journeys to Mars and Venus and Jupiter, for instance, or the grand tours of the Solar System of the Voyager spacecraft. But even larger than these million-mile space voyages are the radio telescope investigations, which cross interstellar space at the speed of light. Conceptually, then, humans have made experiments – or art – that stretch away from Earth at light speed. That is, if radio waves have been beamed into the cosmos for, say, ninety years, then the extent of the human touch in the universe is something like 5.3×10^{14}, or 530,000,000,000,000 miles (a concept explored in the 1997 film *Contact*, and beautifully spoofed in *The Simpsons*). It is a reach that is expanding 186,000 miles every second.

Only occasionally has Long ventured into using the spiral, the form of the most famous piece of land, Robert Smithson's *Spiral Jetty*. Richard Long's spiral works include *Along a Four Day Walk In Norway* (1973), *Sandstone Spiral* (Toronto, 1983), and *Rhône Valley Stones Spiral* (Switzerland, 2000). *Whirlwind Spiral* (1988) was made in the Sahara, producing a close-knit white spiral form. The spiral is a shape many land artists progress towards after exploring the circle.

In a 1996 Tokyo circle (*Hemisphere Circle*), one of Richard Long's permanent installations, comprised of large boulders set in a circle, each rock is level underneath, so it is laid flush with the ground. Long sometimes creates rows or groups of circles, such as *Tierra Del Fuego Circle, Santa Cruz Circle* and *Bhubut Circle* (all 1997), *Hogwallow Flat Circle, Stony Man Circle* and *Hazeltop Circle* (all 1993), or *A Line of Circles* (Milwaukee Art Museum, 2001). *Continents Circles* was a group of five large slate circles installed in Barcelona in 1992. The groups and rows of circles are a way of fitting the circle shape into long, narrow galleries. Plenty of art galleries are not 'white cubes', but lengthy rectangular interiors (sometimes they're a bunch of rooms knocked together, and often they're buildings converted from other uses, such as industry). The long rectilinear spaces (sometimes 50 or more yards long) are not the ideal space for Long's sculptures. Hence he often produces lines of stones for those spaces (or more lately ellipses), or mud drawings. But situating one normal-sized circle next to another, in a series, is another method of dealing with galleries which're more like narrow corridors.

A broken circle occasionally appears in Richard Long's *œuvre*, as in *Earth Circle* (Porto, 2001), a stone floor circle split apart down the centre, or *Heaven and Earth Circle* (Glarus, 2002). The broken circle didn't have any hidden meaning, Long asserted. It was 'just another way of doing a circle'. It was just a bunch of stones. 'Stones are what they are... With symbolism there's a fixed meaning. All good art is open-ended' (SS, 310). Long said he had the idea for the broken circle by coming across one on a walk, seeing a path or track made through a patch of land on a hillside (SS, 309).

One or two of Richard Long's stone circles are small: *Circle of Standing Stones* (1983) is 26 stones arranged in a circle of a half metre in diameter, *Cornwall Slate Circle* (1982) is 34 stones in a 2 metre circle, and *Standing Stone Circle* (1982) is 36 stones in a similar size circle. The small stone circles are often made of standing stones, and many of the outdoor circles are of this type (*Evening Camp Stones,* 1995, for instance). Long's use of standing stones, rather than ones laid flat, echoes prehistoric stone circles – for instance, the Scottish stone circle *Stones and Stac Pollaidh* (1981), or *Sincho-lagua Summit Shadow Stones* (1998).

Richard Long's small stone circles are intimate works compared to the broad, large pieces. In Britain there are a number of small stone circles which produce similar atmospheres of human-scale and intimacy (such as the small circles on the ridges of hills in Dorset). 'I like simple, emotional, quiet, vigorous art' remarked Long.24 While the large circles in the galleries of Western cities spoke of polished, upmarket art, the small, 1.5 metre stone circles evoked small wayside shrines. The large gallery circles are planned and organized sometimes months in advance, but still look spontaneous. Long's small outdoor stone circles, though, are direct and immediate responses to a landscape, a moment, an atmosphere, a feeling.

Richard Long has also used animal bones for circle sculptures (as in *Mojave Bone Circle*, 1995). In Ecuador (in 1998) Long placed bones in the direction of his walk. Bricks with footprints on them formed the basis of *Footprint Spiral* (1993). Driftwood was another favourite material for floor-based sculptures (in *Sea Mills Driftwood Circle* [1996], *River Avon Driftwood Circle* [1978 and 1996], *River Avon Driftwood Line* [1977], *Puget Sound Driftwood Circle* [1996], and *A Circle in Alaska* [1977]). Bark was also employed in many solid circles: *Pine Tree Bark Circle* (1985), *Bark Circle* (1993, Paris), and *Bark Circle* (1994, Australia).

In the late Nineties, Richard Long started to fashion floor-based stone circles using different coloured stones: black, white, purple, green, and blue rocks. Each circle comprised coloured stones which were grouped together in single colour. Thus, in *Black White Green Pink Purple Circle* (1998, Galerie Tschudi, Glarus), about half the circle is green stone, a sixth segment is white, a smaller chevron-shaped part is black, a slightly larger zigzag section is pink stone, with purple placed along a third of the circumference. This was also the form of *Black White Blue Purple Circle* (1998, Glarus), and the circles installed at Museum Kurhaus, Kleve (2001). *Mohawk* (2002, Florida) was an ellipse made from white and grey stones, the grey placed in a wide zigzag through the middle. At *OPENASIA 2004: The East Meets the West*, Long showed a *Blue Sky Circle* (2002) comprising different coloured stones.

As one can see from the above examples of Richard Long's stone circles, Long has probably made more circles in land art than any other artist. It's hard to think of any artist who has created more circles out of stone, wood, snow, mud and slate than Richard Long.

New shapes appeared in Richard Long's floor-standing sculptures in the 1990s: solid ellipses (as in *Spring Ellipse* [Salisbury, 1999], *Basalt Ellipse* [2001, Kleve], *Cornwall Slate Ellipse* [New York, 2000], *Trento Ellipse* [Trento, 2000], and *White Quartz Ellipse* [New York, 2000]); open ellipses (as in *Periphery Stones* [1999], *Antibes Ellipse* [Antibes, 1999], *Porfido Ellipse* and *Red Mud Ellipse*, Italy, 1998), and a wheel (as in *Circle of Life*, 1997. This latter sculpture is reminiscent in shape of a Swedish prehistoric stone circle, at Sola, Nerike).

And in the wall and mud drawings, Richard Long developed new forms: the arc (*Glarus Arc* [Glarus, 1996], *Gulf of Mexico Arc* [Houston, 1996], *River Avon Mud Arc* [Bilbao, 2000], and *Fast Hand Mud Arc* [Athens, 1999]); the open ellipse (*River Avon Mud Ellipse* [London, 2000]), and the demi-circle (*From One To Another* [Houston, 1996], or *Seminole* [2004], a half-circle shown at Seminole, Florida). One of the largest of the upside-down arcs was made at the new Guggenheim museum in Bilbao (2000).

Richard Long also created mud drawings on the gallery floor (as in *Sicilian Mud Hand Circle*, 1997). 'Mud Walls' were also a favourite form, a rectangular block of white or brown or red spread high up on the wall, and allowed to drip down the rest of the wall below: *Muddy Water Wall* (Glarus, 1993), *Muddy Water Line* (Rome, 1994), *Setagaya Mud Line* (Tokyo, 1996), *Waterfall Line* (London, 2000), and *White Water Lines* (Hanover, 1999). Some were muddy splash marks (as in *Muddy Water Falls*, 1984). Sometimes Long opted for the visual device of alternating a block of one colour of mud with another, as in *River Avon Mud and China Clay Wall* (2001) and *Red and Grey Mud Wall* (Italy, 1994). These were rarer, because Long prefers a single colour or material for most of his indoor sculptures.

In his 2004 show at the Kukje Gallery, Richard Long made mud works on handmade paper, which were mounted to the wall, as well as stone circles and spirals (*Spring*

Spiral, Monkey Spiral and *Magpie Circles* [all 2004]). Another new development was finger-printing on objects such as flat, round stones or small pieces of oak or driftwood. For the fingerprint sculptures, Long elected to use the geometric forms he'd developed over his career: circles, concentric circles, spirals, lines and ovals: *2000 Fingerprints* (Los Angeles, 2000), *Fingerprint Stone* (New York, 2000), *River Avon Mud On African Mud*, *River Avon* and *Mud* (Switzerland, 2000). To print on the stone or wood, Long used china clay or his beloved River Avon mud, and placed the fingerprints beside each other, in rows.

STONES

A sculpture may be moved, dispersed, carried. Stones can be used as markers of time or distance, or exist as parts of a huge, yet anonymous, sculpture. On a mountain walk a sculpture could be made above the clouds, perhaps in a remote region, bringing an imaginative freedom about how, or where, art can be made in the world.

Richard Long[1]

Stones are *very* important in Richard Long's art (and that's an under-statement). No other contemporary sculptor has made stones, boulders and pebbles so central to their art. They are kicked, thrown, picked up, put down, carried, written on and stacked. 'A walk is an event in space-time, and I may carry, scatter, concentrate or place stones, or exchange their places along a walk, as required. My stones are like sub-atomic particles in the space of the World' Long said in 2001 (WL, 69). Some stones are kicked into a row (as in *A Line In Bolivia*, 1981), or thrown into a line or a circle (as in Morocco in 1979). Sometimes Long throws stones. In *Two Stones* (1991), a walkwork across the North of England, the walk was a stone's throw from the Irish Sea and North Sea. *Skimming Stones Across the Rio Grande* (1990), which was made in Texas, comprised a photograph of the river, a cow, distant hills, and part of Long's tent. In *A Line of 164 Stones* (1974), Long placed a stone on the roadside after every mile, creating a 164 mile long sculpture. In *Stones Added To a Field Circle* (1999), Long added his stones to an existing open circle. In *All Ireland Stones* (1995), a 12 day walk from the South to North coast (ending up at the Giant's Causeway), 32 stones are formed into a line 'randomly spaced along a walking line of 382 miles'. In *Wind Stones* (1985) Richard Long turned 207 stones to point into the wind in Lappland. 'There are millions of stones in the world, and when I make a sculpture, all I do is just take a few of those stones and bring them together and put them in a circle and show you' Long explained (WC, 45).

Sometimes Long writes on the stones and follows the instructions for walking on the pebbles as he draws them from a bag (in two very Conceptual works, made in Dartmoor in 1998: *From Uncertainty To Certainty* and *Walks of Chance*). In *Walks of Chance*, Long wrote a word on each stone and followed the instructions as he drew out the stones one by one (the words included 'North', 'South', 'Straight', 'Fast' and 'Meandering'). For instance, in *From Uncertainty To Certainty*, Richard Long pulled the ten pebbles out of a bag one by one, at random, at indeterminate intervals, puts the pebble on the ground, and follows the instructions on the pebble. The procedure is repeated until all of the pebbles have been used up. The instructions include:

FIRST PEBBLE WALKING EAST
SECOND PEBBLE WALKING STRAIGHT
THIRD PEBBLE SLOW WALKING
FOURTH PEBBLE WALKING DOWN (WC, 151)

From Uncertainty To Certainty, Richard Long explained, 'uses language, stones, chance, walking and Dartmoor'. One can see too that this work required a certain amount of preparation: it was not a spontaneous walk which was written up later as a textwork. It required the artist to collect the pebbles, decide what to write on them, then write and put them in a bag.

In *Time Flowing and Time Repeating* (1999), a walk in the maritime Alps (Villanova to St-Étienne-de-Tinée), Richard Long built columns of stones on the mountain passes. Sometimes he carries a stone a certain distance or a certain time, puts it down and picks up another one, as in *Stone Walk* (1984), *Walking Stones* (1995), and *Heavier, Slower, Shorter, Lighter, Faster, Longer* (1982, England). *Walking Stones*, Long explained, was a walkwork in which '[e]ach day I carried a different stone in my pocket. From stone to stone, from day to day. So the work was called *Walking Stones* and it was eleven days and eleven stones' (WC, 147). Sometimes Long carries a stone from one coast to another (as in *Crossing Stones*, 1987, a walk between the North Sea at Aldeburgh and the Irish Sea at Aberystwyth). 'My work is another agent of change and placement. And walking is simple; stones are common and practical' (WC, 69). Sometimes Long rolls them down a hill, as in *Ten Stones* (Iceland, 1994). (This was also a crossing place walk, between walks made – and stones rolled – in 1974 and 1994). In *Stones Steps Days* (1985), Long combines stones with footsteps, days and the cardinal points:

FIRST DAY A STONE MOVED ONE STEP WEST
SECOND DAY THE STONE MOVED TWO STEPS NORTH
THIRD DAY THE STONE MOVED THREE STEPS EAST
FOURTH DAY THE STONE MOVED FOUR STEPS SOUTH
FIFTH DAY THE STONE MOVED FIVE STEPS WEST[1]

Sometimes he makes a line of stones in water, as in *Europe Asia Stones* (1989), made at the Bosphorus in Turkey. Sometimes he counts the stones and boulders, as in *Granite Stepping-Stone Circle,* a circular walkwork in Dartmoor in 1980 ('passing over 409 rock slabs and boulders'). Sometimes Richard Long exchanges stones in certain places, after a certain duration, as in *An Exchange of Stones At a Place For a Time On Dartmoor* (1997). The description of the walkwork reminds the viewer of the enigmatic behaviour of the artist:

BRINGING A STONE FROM TIERRA DEL FUEGO
PLACING IT ON SADDLE TOR FOR THE DURATION OF A
THREE DAY WALK AROUND DARTMOOR
AND REMOVING IT AT THE END OF THE WALK TO BE
DROPPED INTO THE RIVER AVON IN BRISTOL (WC, 56)

Richard Long related this walk to particle physics, his stones as analogies of sub-atomic particles (WC, 69). What Long has actually done for this walkwork is: carry a stone from his home in Bristol, put it on a tor in Dartmoor, walked for three days, then came back and collected the stone, travelled back to Bristol and dropped it into the Avon. To an observer, it would seem as if Long were engaged in actions that appear like obscure rituals.

Sometimes he throws stones into every river or stream he comes across, as in *Splashing Around a Circle* (1997). This was a four day walk around an imaginary circle 41 miles across in Wiltshire, on Salisbury Plain and the Marlborough Downs. It was a textwork, which described the actions performed, and a circular textwork, with the words 'SPLASH' written around the circle at irregular intervals, to indicate where Richard Long had thrown stones into rivers and brooks on his walk.

Or he carries a stone from one river to the next, as in *Dartmoor Riverbed Stones* (1991). In this walk around the edge of Richard Long's sacred ground (Dartmoor), Long carried stones between Dartmoor's many rivers and streams: from the River Dart to Holy Brook, from Holy Brook to River Mardle, from River Mardle to Dean Burn, and so on. Or he places 1449 stones on a cairn at 1449 feet above sea level (again on Dartmoor, in 1979), or 82 stones at 82 feet above seal level (in *Footstones*, 1979).

Sometimes Richard Long places stones by the road on each day of a walk, as in *Portuguese Stones* (2001). The textwork of this walk is a simple numerical progression ('one stone in Monção, two stones in Braga, three stones near Lixa, four stones near Cinfães', and so on [WC, 66]). Sometimes Long moves a certain number of stones (ninety stones were moved 'each one step' along the route, North, South, East and West, in *Dartmoor Stones*, 1992). 'My work is a balance between the reality of seeing real stones, and then a photograph of perhaps a stone circle made many thousands of miles away' (WL, 147). This is a stony text piece, 1996's *Dolomite Stones*:

STONES DROPPED INTO A CHASM
STONES PLACED IN A CIRCLE
STONES JAMMED INTO FISSURES
STONES THROWN TO HIT A ROCK
STONES SKIMMED ACROSS A SMALL LAKE[2]

A 1998 walk across the British Isles, from the Southernmost point, the Lizard in Cornwall, to Dunnet Head in Scotland, the Northernmost point, was entitled *A Line of 33 Stones, A Walk of 33 Days*, because Richard Long put a stone down in the road on each of the 33 days of the walk. The stones were there to mark and measure Britain, Long explained, to measure the speed and distance and the route of Long's walk (WL, 69). Each of the stones represented a day's walking along the 1,030 miles that Long traversed. 'Each stone has its geological history, yet perhaps momentarily, conceptually, symbolically or privately becomes 'something else' as well' Long remarked (WL, 69).

Cairns are markers along the way which walkers encounter. Richard Long sometimes photographs them, writes about them, or creates his own cairns: as in *Walk of Seven Cairns* (1992), a four day walk in the Brecon mountains and Fforest Fawr in South Wales, where Long built cairns in 'a windy place' or 'after a roll of thunder'; and *Road of Three Cairns* (1992), where he built three cairns on a 586 mile walk from Bordeaux to Turin. Sometimes Long adds to the cairns, piling up stones, as in *Stones On a Cairn,* in Dartmoor (1992, fashioned into a roughly circular form.

Stones are small, portable, and come from the Earth. All very obvious attributes, but vital ones. Unlike plants, grass or trees, stones don't fade away. They are intimately connected to the ground where they're found. They don't decay and die on you like flowers or plants when you pick them, so using stones in art can tie in nicely to an eco-friendly ideology. They're small and easy to carry (vitally important for a walking artist). And they're free. And there's a plentiful supply. And they can be found in almost any territory. And stones also have links with Oriental mysticism (such as Zen Buddhist gardens), and they are one of the fundamental elements that Eastern religion is always talking about (such as the clouds, the wind, the sky, the Earth, water, the sea, pools, rivers, mountains, trees and stones).

Stones always photograph nicely (especially in black-and-white, which Richard Long favours many times over colour photography; it enhances the surface texture of stones). For these, and other reasons, one can see why stones would feature so prominently in the art of Richard Long. 'In my sculptures, a stone is a stone, and I also use other raw materials like dust, water and mud, only to show their own innate natures' Long said in 2001 (WL, 69).

Richard Long could be said to have a 'sacred' relationship with particular objects – stones, mud, water – which is often exactly like the shamanic, animistic relationship of ancient peoples. It's the artist's *relationship* with particular things and places that's as important as the stones or places in themselves. 'Sacred stones or trees are not adored in their natural capacity', Mircea Eliade wrote in *Myths, Dreams and Mysteries,* 'but only because they are *hierophanies*, because they "show forth" something which is no longer mineral or vegetable but *sacred* – "wholly other"' (125). (*Hierophany* for Eliade means 'the act of manifestation of the sacred'). Long's reverence for stones is only surpassed in modern sculpture by perhaps Constantin Brancusi.

One is reminded again of old John Cowper Powys, the visionary novelist, who, on his morning walks, used to kiss certain stones and trees. In upstate New York in the 1930s, Powys went out walking every day and said his prayers and invocations to particular natural objects. He gave his beloved things names: there was the 'Dead Tree', the 'Skian Gates' (some stones), the 'Prometheus Stone', the 'Perdita Stone', 'the Flotsam', 'the Jetsam', the 'Unknown Stone', the '*Other* Unknown Stone', the 'Noble Wreck', the '*other* Apple Tree', the 'Thorn Bush' and the 'Sea Coal'.[3] One doubts if many land artists kneel down and kiss the soil as they say their prayers, as John Cowper Powys did (although I bet a few land artists have literally kissed the ground. Pope John Paul made this act famous), but land art is very much about this loving, spiritual relation with the natural world.

Like John Cowper Powys, like the Romantic poets, like the archaic shaman, Australian aborigines and 'primitive' peoples, land artists sometimes develop an intimate relation with the landscape. Very likely Richard Long has favourite spots, such as familiar prehistoric standing stones, or oak trees he's watched grow over the years, or a favourite crossing place over a stream, or a particular viewpoint on a hillside overlooking the West Country. Even small stones or bushes can become familiar to a walker over oft-trod routes. And one place in particular has come to act as Long's spiritual home: Dartmoor.

LINES AND ROWS

Everywhere the human 'touch' is present in Richard Long's sculpture, as in all sculpture. The shapes might be 'organic' – circles, spirals, zigzags – but the appearance of Long's sculpture in their wilderness settings is always of some sophisticated (not archaic) human gesture at work. Long's work has not changed that much since the late 1960s, when he found and developed his way of working. Critic Penelope Curtis commented: '[h]is way of working over the last two decades has been unusually consistent' (136). Still one finds circles, lines and spirals in his work, thirty years and more after his first works. Presumably circles and rows will remain in Long's repertoire right up until the end, until the last artwork. (There has to be a final work, a Last Walk, some time or other. It would entirely fitting if it was a circle or a line).

Ancient lines, paths and straight roads of ritual or spiritual significance are found in many places. Even little old Blighty has its lines and rows of stone (like the Avebury Avenue) and earthwork cursuses (such as the Dorset Cursus). There are over 60 stone rows on Dartmoor (such as at Merrivale). Then there is the Pilgrims' Way, Offa's Dyke, the Ridgeway, the Foss Way; these are mediæval and prehistoric routes (there are numerous others). And their modern, thoroughly secular equivalents in the long distance paths of Britain: the South-West Coast Path, the Pennine Way, Cotswold Way, Hadrian's Wall, Cumbrian Way, West Highland Way, Pembrokeshire Coast Path, Norfolk Coast Path, the South Downs Way, and Land's End to John O'Groats.[1] Long has walked on many of these straight and crooked paths and lines, and on most of the official long distance paths.

But the most impressive ancient straight lines are in the Americas (Richard Long has also visited some of them): the Nazca lines in Peru, the straight roads at La Quemada, Mexico, the *sacbeob* of the Mayans in Central America, the Miwok Indian forty-mile straight lines in the high sierras of California, the Anasazi lines in New Mexico (the 'Chaco Roads'; some 400 miles of straight roads have been found by archæologists), the Taironas' paths in Colombia, and the tracks in Bolivia, built by the Indians of the altiplano.

The early Long pieces, from 1965 to the early 1970s, contained many more spirals than he makes now. One finds spiral works in Arizona (1970), in *A Sculpture Left By the Tide* (Cornwall, 1970), at Oxford (1971) and in *A Line the Length of a Straight Walk From the Bottom to the Top of Glastonbury Tor* (1974). Zigzags appear too, but much less frequently than the lines and circles (in *Inca Rock Camp-Fire Ash*, 1972, for instance). Rows also feature in the early pieces, as in *Stone Rows* (London, 1977).

The rows are really lines – Long calls them lines. *A Line in Ireland* (1974) is a short pile of flat rocks in a line, while *A Line in Australia* (1977) is a wider line, more like a row of red rocks (RL, 54-55). *A Line in Scotland* (1981) is a row of small flattish rocks that were stood on end at Cul Mór, like a row of prehistoric standing stones. In *Ash Line* and *Bushfire Line* (both 1994, Australia), Long dropped wood ash in a short line in a forest. In Yorkshire in 1977, as in Bolivia in 1981, Long cleared a space each side of the line as he picked up rocks (RL, 124, 126). The opposite of this line is the 'negative' line, made by leaving a path through a tangle of rocks, as in *A Line in California* (1982).

Some of Richard Long's lines are chunky, closely-packed structures, which possess a different, more intense internal architecture, such as *Athens Slate Line* (1984), *Stone Line* (1981, Zurich), *Chalk Line* (Eindhoven, 1979), *Flint Line* (1983, London), *Dublin*

Line (1984), *Carrara Line* (Milan, 1985)*, Crossing Place* (1985, Bristol), and the huge sculptures, *Line of Lake Stones* (1984, Turin), *Stone Line* (1977, Sydney), *Cornwall Slate Line* (1990, Paris), and *Footpath Line* (1999, Spain).

Long's lines or rows are, typically, photographed end-on. This viewpoint emphasizes the direction of the line, the relation of the direction of the line to the horizon, and the sense of motion, of 'walking the line'. And also the stupendous backdrop which's often situated at the end of the line. The *Line in the Himalayas* (1975), for example, is seen from one end: the other end points up the slope, towards the mountains and the sky beyond (other angles on this work don't have quite the same effect). In *A Line In Scotland* (1981) mountains recede behind the line of rocks. In *Snow Stones* (2002) the misty, snowy Alps form the backdrop. *Cloud Mountain Stones* (2001) frames the mountains of Oregon behind the widely-spaced row of stones.

Photographing the line end-on encourages the eye to run along the line, to follow the line to its destination – somewhere on the horizon – or, in the case of *A Line in the Himalayas* – right up into the Tibetan sky or void (the *Tibetan Book of the Dead* speaks of the 'Clear Light of the Void'). The skyward direction of this particular line is wholly appropriate – the Himalayas are called the 'roof of the world'. Mountain climbers have said it's exhilarating standing on Everest, knowing there is nothing else on Earth higher than that point. Long's *A Line in the Himalayas* emphasizes the sense of ascension, flight and transcendence, the archetypal motifs of religion and shamanism. One recalls the asceticism and talk of emptiness of Tibetan Buddhist mystics such as Mila Repa, of the 'clear light of the void' in the *Tibetan Book of the Dead*, of the harsh light and fabulous, transparent air of the Himalayas.

Talking about Tibetan Buddhism, the void, and the 'roof of the world' no doubt romanticizes Richard Long's *A Line in the Himalayas*. But the compositions encourage this reading. Another line or row of stones that echoes *A Line in the Himalayas* was made on Mount Fuji (*A Line in Japan*, 1979). Again, the line of stones is photographed from one end, the lower end, so the line stretches up the mountain, into the mist. Like the Himalayan line, the Mount Fuji line emphasizes the sense of the infinite, the religious/ Romantic reaching up into the heavens. The photographs of the other rows of stones mentioned above (*A Line In Scotland, Cloud Mountain Stones,* and *Snow Stones*) do the same thing.

In galleries, Richard Long's lines are often wide rows of sticks which directly recall Tony Cragg's spreads of found (sometimes painted) objects. *Somerset Willow Line* (1979), like *192 Pieces of Wood* (Switzerland, 1975) and *Forêt du Porge Line* (Bordeaux, 1981), is a large row of widely-spaced sticks, plenty of room between each stick on a gallery floor. These rows re-order the irregularity of nature, shaping the odd lengths and volumes of the branches into a humanmade, geometric structure. These row/ line sculptures inevitably codify and control the natural world. The actual materials used – wood, slate, pine needles – seem less important than the geometric (human) shapes the sculptor makes with them. The lines are partly about time and process, of moving from one place to another, the significance of moving along a line, which is following a predetermined structure. The line takes the viewer from one place to another, yet it looks roughly the same at each point along it. The line, like the walk itself, is different yet the same. Each stage along the line offers a new viewpoint, a new way of looking at the landscape. Yet each stage of the stone or wood line or row looks roughly like the last stage. The beginning and the end of the line thus becomes crucial: and, significantly, Long emphasizes the beginning of the line by choosing to take the photograph beside it. The end of the line is also emphasized: it stretches away into the distance, sometimes lost in mist, sometimes pointing towards a mountainous background, and sometimes pointing up to the heavens.

COLOUR IN RICHARD LONG'S ART

Note how Richard Long sticks very often to black-and-white photography, even when colour photography is easily attainable, technically, and cheap too (and, since the 1980s, large colour prints have become *de rigueur* for any artist or photographer). The preference for black-and-white photography gives Long's photographs the aura of classic photography, in line with the great photographers from the history of photography. Long's photographs can be read as part of the long tradition of landscape photography, then, the canon which includes Ansel Adams, Edward Weston, Paul Strand, Walker Evans and Bill Brandt. There's no suggestion, though, that Long's photographs come anywhere near the sublime heights of those photographers. He is no Ansel Adams or Alfred Stieglitz (and I don't think he would put himself in their class). But photography is absolutely vital to Long's art. Rather, he is one of those artists who is also a photographer: like David Hockney, Andy Warhol, Robert Rauschenberg or Man Ray.

Note how Richard Long tends to avoid colour in his art (and especially rich colours). His text pieces are nearly always typeset in large Gill Sans lettering on white paper. Occasionally, Long allows himself red type (usually for the titles of the works). Very rarely brown, or green, or blue (again mainly for the titles). (Hamish Fulton, for instance, employs all sorts of colours and fonts). But the black-and-white with occasional red colours in Long's art gives the textworks (and the photos) a very Minimal look (which also evokes Chinese calligraphy). Compare with contemporary artists of Long's, such as Donald Judd or John McCracken, who happily took up car spray paint, lacquer, and Plexiglas in pinks, reds, yellows, blues and greens.

Most of Richard Long's photos are in black-and-white, but there are plenty that do use full colour. Even so, the colour photographs, partly because they are of landscapes, partly because of the way Long frames and selects them, tend to use blues, greens, browns, whites and greys. Deeper or more saturated colours are usually avoided in Long's art (look at any magazine newsstand or billboard: saturated colours are easy to achieve). Long's stone sculptures inevitably tend towards black, grey and brown (although, more recently, Long has employed different colours, such as pink, purple, blue and green).

J.M.W. Turner knew the impact and beauty of the colour red. Turner's artistic rival, John Constable, recounted an incident where he, Constable, had painted his famous river scene which he though would be the star of the show at London's Royal Academy. Not to be outdone, Turner came in when Constable was away and added a smudge of red to his otherwise grey seascape. The red blob was intended to be a buoy, and it lifted up Turner's painting a few notches. Constable was enraged.

Richard Long has based walkworks around colours. In *Red Walk* (1986), Long recorded the items he encountered which were red: an apple, a sunset, a rose, a shoe. In *White Light Walk* (1987, Avon), Long recorded the colours of things he met along the way, the colours making up the rainbow of light (red leaves, orange sun, yellow parsnips, etc).

The colour red really stands out. In the historical Japanese Zen garden, colours are carefully orchestrated, so that a single leaf can set off a vast acreage of predominantly green or ochre. In the Oriental garden, notions of *feng shui* and *yin* and *yang* control how a landscape is shaped by humans. In the system of *feng shui*, the elements of a garden or a building must be in harmony with natural forces of air, water and earth. Get it wrong and one messes up the creation. The Zen or Taoist harmonizing approach is very much that of land art. Land artists can be seen as an ecological artists, artists committed to ecological issues. Robert Rosenblum wrote:

> There's a German artist Wolfgang Laib who does something of this sort too. He spends a lot of time in the woods gathering such things as pollen and collecting it and forming minimal geometric patterns out of gossamer and natural materials such as honey or dust of various kinds. It is some kind of ecological last gasp of communion with some pure beautiful stuff of nature. I guess this attitude is expiring even though it may, as in the case of Richard Long, still produce some marvellous artists.[1]

Chinese gardens were designed by balancing the principles of *yin* (feminine) and *yang* (masculine), water and mountain. Land artists re-organize the landscape, building mountains, digging holes, creating pools, as in *feng shui*. Land art, including some of Richard Long's art, can be seen as a kind of modern *feng shui*, a Westerner's way of harmonizing the *yin* and *yang* elements (being in harmony with the world is often evoked in Long's interviews).

Oriental gardens were asymmetrical – in that single non-formal element they differ greatly from Western formal gardens with their patterns, squares, crosses, parallel paths, and mathematically exact *parterres*. Oriental gardens were founded on stone, sand, water, flowers, moss and trees (compare with the materials Richard Long favours: water, grass, stone). If sand was used, it could evoke water by being raked into wave-like shapes. Stones could be mountains, but also, via abstraction, other natural forms. In the 'dry garden' of Zen Buddhism (the *karesanui*), stone could be water, or cascades. Stones were valued highly for gardens, and were bought and sold. Many kinds of stone were used in Oriental gardens, including schist, volcanic rock, granite, limestone, slate and jasper.

Perhaps the most famous of the Japanese Zen gardens is at Ryoanji, Kyoto. It is a must-see for anyone interested in land art (along with James Turrell's *Roden Crater,* Michael Heizer's *Double Negative*, Robert Smithson's *Spiral Jetty* and Donald Judd's Marfa site). Ryoanji garden was constructed in the 1480s. It is 30 by 70 feet with white gravel raked parallel to the longer side. There are 15 rocks placed in it, and a verandah surrounds it. The Ryoanji garden is garden design reduced to its simplest elements, an ultimate manifestation of reduction and purification. There are no trees, flowers or plants in the garden. In Long's art there is a similar emphasis on keeping forms as they appear in nature, on contemplation, on valuing objects such as stones as sacred in their own right, with nothing needing to be added to them. Long has spoken of the famous Kyoto garden:

> I have always been impressed by the ancient rock gardens of Kyoto. For me, they are sublime pieces of contemplation, where the world is represented harmoniously by deep thinking, simple materials, space, and peace of mind. And, I like the idea of *ma*. There are some parallels between Japanese art and my work, because nature is our common condition. Also, I think a desire for simplicity and order is a part of human nature (1995a).

Contemplation was clearly a key purpose of the Oriental garden. 'Contemplation gardens' were meant to be consumed from one viewpoint (from the noble's house, for example). The 'contemplation garden' was often a 'dry garden', with various islands in its midst having particular meanings.

TOUCH, PERFORMANCE, REPETITION

Richard Long makes circles again and again, and it in these repetitions, as with Minimal, Process and serial art, that the insights of his art are to be found. Although Long's work is 'repetitive', it is in this very repetition that his art flourishes. On the one hand, each walk is just another walk, whether in Dartmoor or Nepal, Bolivia or Lappland. On the other hand, look closer, and the viewer sees that every walk is different. The light's different, the weather changes, the ground changes, the route changes, the duration changes, so many things change. And the walker changes too, *during* they walk, as well as between each walk. So a walk, whether Richard Long does it or anyone does it, is always different. Using the terminology of Eastern philosophy, each walk is always different, but always the same. Each walk repeats the first ever walk. Each walk is part of one walk (the One Walk, one might say).

Richard Long sprinkles snow in a circle, or smears mud, often from the River Avon near his home in England, in huge circles or arcs or lines on walls, or he makes marks on grass using his feet, or he dips his feet in white paint and makes footprint circles and lines. The use of hands, feet, the body, mud, soil, stones, snow and sand chime with many land artists' practical methods. Land artists, as David Nash insisted, like to get right in there when making their art.

I like the idea [Long said] that I can make a show anywhere by just going down to the river taking a few handfuls of mud... and literally get on a plane and go anywhere and make a big show with the mud from my bag. (IC 1, 12)

Richard Long's art ethic – *have mud, will travel* – fits in with the notion of a pared-down, simplified, 'essential' æsthetic that was current in the 1960s and 1970s (one wonders how often Long's had to unpack his bags at airport customs: 'what's in the bag, sir?' 'Mud.' 'Uh-huh. Dave, call security'). The great thing is not so much that Long can splatter mud on a wall and call it art (he does the former, not the latter), but that people around the world accept mud splattered on a wall as art.

In the early days, if I was doing a mud circle in New York, I would take a plastic bag of mud from the Avon. One part of my work is the practical aspect – it is possible to take a big handful of mud from the Avon on the plane to New York, mix it with a bucket of water when I get there and make a huge work in New York with my River Avon mud. (1994b)

(Richard Long – one of the success stories of the British art school system (along with David Hockney, Patrick Caulfield, Peter Blake, Barry Flanagan and Shirazeh Houshiary) – knows only too well from his days at St Martin's School of Art that he is lucky to be able to travel the world with a bit of Avon mud in his bag, and have gallery audiences lap it up, because for every major (successful) artist there are thousands of students pouring out of the art colleges each year. And these art students are often producing work just as rich and challenging as that of Long, Blake, Houshiary, Hockney and Flanagan.)

The sense of touch, of gesture and of sensuality is crucial in Richard Long's art of 'circles', 'lines', 'cairns' and routes. 'It's the touching and the meaning of the touching that matters' says Long (OW, 59). Long likes the idea of touching something where people have been or where they will be, of 'touching' history and the future (if it's possible to 'touch' history or the future). Thus, he will brush leaves and stones off a path with a stick (in Nepal in 1983). Not when the people are there, watching him. No, Long is not interested in 'performing' in front of people. He is interested, though, in 'touching' people – directly yet indirectly (all artists want to have some kind of effect on their audience. Otherwise, why bother to reach an audience?).

The idea of this sculpture 'was that the sculpture was absolutely on the line of people's everyday walking' (IC, 2, 14). Richard Long wants to connect with people, but not directly, not by performing to or with them. Long likes the invisibility of the artist, so that his photographs look as if the artist has just stepped around the edge of the frame, is just out of shot. Long's paths have *just* been walked on, *just* been brushed with a stick, *just* been splashed with water. The photographs record a unpremeditated creative act, but do not show the artist doing it. (There are very few published records of Long making his art, in photography, film, TV or written accounts).

Often the 'touch' in the art of Richard Long is the foot. The touch of the feet on grass, rock, soil, sand, water, mud, paper, wood, stone. The walk itself is an artistic 'statement' in Richard Long's work. The walk is a mark, a gesture, an interaction of artist and 'material', the material being the world. 'My talent as an artist is to walk across a moor, or place a stone on the ground' Long says modestly (in RL, 236). If that's Richard Long's only talent, then, perhaps anyone could become a much celebrated land artist? If all it takes is to walk over Dartmoor, the Glarnish Massif (Switzerland), the Sahara, Bolivia, or North India a few times (perhaps picking up a stone, perhaps not) then everyone could have major retrospectives at the Guggenheim or Hayward. If walking makes one a celebrated artist, then anyone can be a celebrated artist. Except this is not the case. Long is in fact a clever manipulator of expectation and perception, shaping his artistic discourse to fit in with the changing times, like most successful artists, whether they are Andy Warhol, David Bowie or Federico Fellini. Long's art has stayed pretty much the same over the course of his artistic career since the mid Sixties, but notice too how he has subtly shifted the way it's presented, carefully altering the framing, the content and marketing so it fits in with the continually changing cultural climate.

Sometimes Richard Long will make a line of stones, or a line of water, or a circle of stones. But always he sticks to simple geometric shapes, the line or the circle (and sometimes the cross and ellipse). The circle speaks so directly and concisely of nature and organic growth. No other shape, it seems, can so swiftly connote nature. Perhaps only the gentle curve − seen in the ridges of hills, or the branches of trees, is more 'organic' and 'natural'. When Long puts his circles into urban galleries, which are nearly always, like most buildings, rectangular, he creates, instantly, a natural, organic presence in the gallery space. At the same time, though, these large circles are also 'unnatural', in the sense that one rarely finds such near-perfect circles in the landscape. So a stone or wood circle built by Long will always stand out, very distinctly, from the surrounding landscape. The stone or wood circle always speaks of 'humanity', even while it is 'natural', and a shape found everywhere in nature. (Note that Long draws out his circles using string, so they are nearly always very accurate circles. But then he often deliberately roughens up the circumference slightly, by allowing stones to be placed on the gallery floor or ground over the line, or letting his mud handprints smear across the line.)

The line or row in Richard Long's *œuvre* more directly relates to humanity – in the sense that although straight lines do exist naturally, they are much rarer than the circle. The line in Long's art relates more obviously to movement, to walking, to distance, to direction, and to time. While the circle connotes cyclical time, time coming back to its starting point (endlessness, and everything is ultimately the same), the straight line speaks of a segment of time (and space), of time with a definite beginning and end, of time being started and stopped, time being measured. A work like *A Walk of Flux* (1999) celebrates movement and change (sticks floating, thunder clouds, tides, water pouring), as does *Half-Tide* (1971), an early work, an 'X' inscribed on the beach in Bertraghboy Bay in Ireland with stones and seaweed.

The indoor lines and rows of stone fit much easier into a gallery space, and Richard Long always relates the size and shape of his stone lines to the space where they are shown. The *Line of Lake Stones* in Turin (1984) is large because the space is large (nearly 22 metres long). *Bordeaux Slate Line* (1985) is over 42 metres long. The line or a cross of lines is as far as Long goes in the direction of 'human' geometric shapes. He does not employ the triangle, for instance, the pentagon or other complex geometric shapes (as so many postwar and contemporary artists have done). Although these may be found in nature (in crystals most spectacularly), Long keeps to the simplicity of lines and circles (with later variations, such as the oval, the broken circle and the demi-circle).

In *Walking a Line Through Leaves* (1993), made in Korea, dead leaves were kicked aside, to form a clear line (but it's not a perfect straight line, it bends slightly, reacting to the terrain and the leaves). In Scotland (1991) Richard Long walked over burnt heather to create a short line. Sometimes snow is heaped into circles and lines, or rubbed out, as in *Along the Way* (1992), made in Japan, and *Throwing Snow Into a Circle* (1991). In this sculpture (created during a 7 day walk in Switzerland), Long picked up snow and threw it onto some grass (where snow had melted away). The result resembled Long's stone rings, where small units are gathered to form a geometric shape. *Dustlines* (1995), in El Camino Real, New Mexico, used kicked up dust to create a line.

White River Line (1994), installed at the São Paolo Bienal, was a large floor sculpture made with splashes of white in a tightly-knit serpentine form. The long, narrow sculpture stretched across the gallery floor in close curved thick lines. It was a continuous snaking line within a rectilinear form (the unbroken line suggested the flow of a river, but also a walk. The line could have been followed on the floor on foot, like a turf maze).

In another riverwork, *The Rivers of France* (1993, Paris), Long drew the courses of rivers on the floor in thick white lines. It certainly wasn't an accurate map of the rivers, and had no sense of distance, scale, terrain, or tributaries. Rather, *The Rivers of France* at the Arc-Musée d'Art Moderne de la Ville de Paris offered only a vague suggestion of the courses the rivers took. In *Atlantic Lava Line* (1995, Iceland) Long placed stones on the gallery floor in snaking loops.

Some of Richard Long's walkworks concern clouds (a section of *Walking the Line* is given over to them). Cloud works included: *A Cloudy Walk*, a walk across Scotland in 1978, coast to coast; *In the Cloud* (1991) was a walk across Scotland with three-quarters of an hour spent inside the clouds while traversing Ben Macdui (the highest point on the walk); *Cloud Circle* was a stone circle built on a hillside in the Tyrol in 1996 (the photowork reveals a cloud drifting behind the sculpture); and there have also been Dartmoor walks following clouds. Clouds crop up in many textworks, such as *Planes of Vision* (1983), part of a list of things encountered on a walk: 'rocks', 'trees', 'cloud', 'sky' and so on.

In *A Cloudless Walk* (1996), Richard Long walked in France under blue skies and decided to halt the walk when he saw the first cloud. Of *A Cloudless Walk*, Long remarked in 1997 that '[t]he walk started at a very solid geographic place, and ended, by chance, with an ephemeral phenomenon like a cloud. One of the things I like about walking is that just the simple and very normal act of days of walking can carry quite interesting ideas' (WL, 147). To anyone not versed in Long's kind of art, stopping a walk when you see a cloud might seem nuts. Stopping when it rains, or blows up a storm, or snows, maybe, but a cloud?!

TIME AND HISTORY

There is a historical and human dimension to Richard Long's walks, because he is always aware (and persuades the viewer to be aware) of the personal and social history of a place, even when it is a wilderness. 'A walk is just one more layer,' Long says, 'a mark laid upon the thousands of other layers of human and geographic history on the surface of the land.'1 Long talks in terms of walking as a kind of palimpsest, where one layer is written upon the next (a notion central to Lawrence Durrell's *The Alexandria Quartet,* where no view is privileged over any other, but everything is relational). Long is conscious of re-activating history as he walks through landscapes. Some of his walks are founded on archæological and historical principles.

Take, for instance, the *Windmill Hill to Coalbrookdale* walk of 1979, where Richard Long travelled from two centres of human 'industry': Windmill Hill is where the inhabitants were the first 'to make permanent changes in the landscape', Long tells the viewer. Ironbridge and Coalbrookdale, as the place name implies, was 'the birthplace of the Industrial Revolution'. These walks of Long's require much imagination and background knowledge on the part of the viewer: s/he has to recreate the significance of the Windmill Hill people, or the Industrial Revolution. When one visits Windmill Hill, or other sites on the Wiltshire Plain, there is not much to see (compared, say, to Aztec temples or the Colosseum in Rome). One has to recreate the past in the mind (as so often in Britain). Similarly, when one goes to a city like Alexandria in Egypt, which has a history far more exotic and extraordinary than most places in Britain (only London could compete with Alexandria), there is hardly anything to see. Pompey's Pillar, a few catacombs, a Roman theatre, and not much else. No sign of the marvellous Library of Alexandria, or the Temple of Serapis, or Cleopatra's Palace, or Alexander the Great's Tomb.

Richard Long's historical walks and works, then, trade on people's capacity to imagine and dream. Even at Ironbridge, a relatively recent historical site, where things haven't had much time to disappear under mounds of soil, there is not much to see. There's the famous bridge, of course (not as big as it looks in pictures), some old houses, railway tracks in the road from factories, but not much else. Instead, Coalbrookdale is now a 'heritage' site; it has been made-over by fervent 1980s Thatcherite heritage mentality. It is full of museums of one sort or another (museums of industrial archæology, of rivers, of engineering, etc). Although it is but two hundred years old, Coalbrookdale requires museums and the 'heritage industry' to explain the place to the visitor. Even something as in-your-face and hard to ignore in the landscape as heavy industry seems to disappear rapidly, so that industrial sites soon slip into the post-industrial decay that Robert Smithson so loved to explore.

Richard Long's works, too, require the viewer to know (and yet not know) exactly where the stones or sticks he deploys in his sculptures were gathered from: the place, time, season, weather, etc. All these things Long reckons are important, and so he includes them in the captions and texts that go with his works. Indeed, sometimes, these captions and texts *are* the works themselves.

> Give me the clear blue sky above my head, and the green turf beneath my feet, a winding road before me, and a three hours' march to dinner – and then to thinking! (William Hazlitt)

Richard Long is aware of walking into his *own history*. As he walks in Dartmoor, for instance (moving into the very familiar 'Dartmoor Time'), he goes over ground he walked on years ago. Year after year of walks. Dartmoor is 'full of memories' for Long. 'More and more I keep intersecting my own past walks, all across England. There is no way I can go down to Dartmoor now and not be aware of what I've done there before. It's full of memories' (WC, 104). There's a desire here to visit Dartmoor again as if for the first time. As if there could be, once again (like a First Dartmoor Visit), a First Walk. But there never can, of course, be a First Walk again.

England has become crisscrossed with Richard Long works and walks, so that Long can 'perceive the same place (England) at different times, from different directions and from artistically different points of view' (RL, 105). A map of Britain with all of Long's walks drawn on it from the mid-1960s onwards in different coloured inks would be a mass of squiggly, interconnecting and overlapping lines. (But then, if many people sketched out all of the journeys they'd made in adulthood on a map it could well look similar).

Mircea Eliade, the 'historian of religions' whose thoughts chime with Long's at many points, spoke eloquently of this nostalgia of revisiting old places. For Eliade, though, it is a joyful nostalgia, in which one meets one's former selves. Eliade spoke of the continuity of one's life which re-emerges when one revisits places of one's earlier life: '[i]t is a comforting experience: you feel you haven't lost all that time, wasted your life. Everything is still there...'[2] (A lost, fondly remembered childhood lurks behind Richard Long's art, which's linked, in the classic nostalgic fashion of the religionist or poet, to an earlier period of history).

Richard Long's art often evokes the past, and for the poet, this layering of one's own life is not a burden but a richness. Eliade wrote of 'reactivating' former experiences when travelling. It is a kind of temporal narcissism, a self-love within time:

> ...the fact that, when visiting Venice, for example, I am reliving that time of my first trips to Venice. One rediscovers the whole past in space: a street, a church, a tree. Suddenly time past has been regained. That is one of the things that make travelling such an enrichment of the self, of one's own experience. One finds oneself again, one can communicate with the person one was fifteen, twenty, years before. One meets him, one meets oneself, one meets one's time, one's historical moment, of twenty years ago.[3]

Richard Long in interviews expresses the doubt that the artist can 'start afresh' each time s/he makes a work (the desire for a First Ever Walk). The artist is conscious of having already made many poems/ songs/ dances/ paintings/ sculptures. This is the challenge for the artist, though: to make each work as if for the first time over the years. This is what everyone has to face: to wake up to another day, to the whole round of life starting again, every day. The anxieties, pains, joys, impossibilities, idiocies, boredoms and chores of each day. What art can do, and what Long's art can do, is to exalt certain moments of life, to make certain aspects special again. The best art refreshes life (among other things). It renews the sense of life. And for some artists it becomes a life on its own: the art *is* the life. Not a 'substitute' life, André Gide might say, but rather the life the artist has chosen (or it has chosen for them).

An essential ingredient of the impact of Richard Long's walks is that they have a history, that Long has been undertaking his walks for many years. Without that history, the viewer might find it harder to accept that the walks were even made in the first place, as Stephen Bann noted.[4] Certainly it's a significant element in Long's art, the sense of layers of history and memory, both personal and social ('travelling is almost like talking with men of other centuries' wrote René Descartes).[5] In some territories, Long is walking upon many layers of previous art and earlier walks. The South-West of England (and Dartmoor in particular), and the Scottish highlands, for instance, are thick with layers of Richard Long walks. Sometimes Long acknowledges earlier artwork-walks in his exhibitions and books. So when Long sets out to walk in Dartmoor or Scotland again, he's going over terrain that he has walked over many, many times. 'I have done so many walks in England – it is really my landscape, my home turf. I think accumulated experience is really great, and that too becomes part of the art' (1994b).

So there's nothing *new* in Richard Long's art: a walk made in the 2000s or 2010s would very likely be not a lot different from one made in 1999 or 1994 or 1986 or 1978 or 1973. In this sense, Richard Long is very like the Conceptual, serial and Process artists of the 1960s and 1970s, such as Donald Judd and Carl Andre, who do 'one thing then another', whose artworks are not grounded in liberal, humanist notions of 'development' and 'progression', of something getting refined or improved, but of simply repeating very similar forms and methods and processes.

> My work is just another layer on the surface of the world that has been shared by all these different generations, so it's really about continuity [Long opined]. But it's also about new ideas about time and space and walking. (2004b)

Richard Long acknowledged that, after decades of making art, repetition was more common, that it was impossible to walk in certain landscapes without being aware of his artistic history. 'Repetition can reinforce significance', however, Long reckoned (2004b). There could be a new kind of value or significance from the accumulation of one walk on top of another.

So if Richard Long makes a walkwork right now, or next year, or in five years' time, or twenty years' time (if he can still walk), it will very likely be a walk of a certain number of miles, a certain number of hours or days, and probably over wilderness terrain, and probably walked alone. And it will probably be recorded (embodied, manifested, expressed) with a photograph, or maybe some short phrases framed on a large piece of paper on a wall, or in a book. Maybe some stones will be picked up, carried, put down, thrown or piled up. Or maybe not. Maybe a stone circle will be constructed and photographed. Maybe water will be splashed over rocks. Or not.

7

Idea/ Text/ Desire: Textworks

THE IDEA AND THE TEXT

Art possesses nature and yet does not possess nature: something always remains elusive. What's there, in nature, is no longer there in the artwork. As David Reason noted of Hamish Fulton's work, and this applies to Richard Long's text pieces: '[i]n the work, everything derives from what cannot be shown and shared – walking and camping in close relationship to a specific patch of the natural world.'[1] The viewer does not experience the real subject of the work, which is the walk, the camping, the experiences the artist had. Instead, the viewer has to place herself or himself into the role played by the artist, as she or he walks in the landscape (it's impossible to reach the experience of the walker-artist, so the spectator has to drawn on her/ his own experiences. It's the same when a novelist writes: 'a man sat on a wooden chair'; the reader has to put that image and reality together for themselves, drawing on their own lives). The text pieces can be seen then as sophisticated forms of holiday snaps, those little coloured slips of plastic, pixels and photochemicals which record two weeks' escape from labour. Mementoes; memorials; mnemonics.

Richard Long's art is always an art of memory (as well as everything else).

Richard Long's textworks do not 'describe' the landscape, in the usual manner.

Short phrases, and sometimes single words (as in Hamish Fulton's work) stand in for (a description of) the landscape. Reminders or hints of the experience of walking (living, breathing, camping) in the landscape. Long's textworks do not claim 'this is the world', but record tiny parts of the world seen from a particular subjective perspective on a particular day in a particular season and frame of mind. The particularity of each work is emphasized by Long's placing of the time and place in the final sentence of each text piece (everything is meticulously recorded). Sometimes, as with the art of Fulton and Chris Drury, a distinct date is mentioned; at other times, just the year. The duration of each walk is also critical: thus the viewer can get an idea of when and where the walk took place, and how much mileage was covered in a certain amount of time.

Instead of trying to depict or describe nature, then, Richard Long's art (like Hamish Fulton's) may be about the impossibility of representing landscape in art. At the same time (here's the paradox again), both Long and Fulton (and other land artists) are consciously making art in or about the landscape. Even though the impossibility of the project is stressed, they are still making art. That is, still indulging in a particular kind of Western, bourgeois, intellectual, creative activity.

Richard Long's textworks are set in Gill Sans, a popular typeface (the artist roughs out the textworks in pen and pencil on ruled lines to be set by the printer). Eric Gill's sans serif font is admired for its stylish simplicity: it is, like Helvetica, an unfussy typeface which typographers and designers admire for its clarity, its economy and its all-round usefulness. It is not a typeface that pulls any tricks, that is fiddly or precious or self-conscious (unlike many display, fancy or joke fonts). Gill Sans is also, like the London Underground fount from which it's partially derived, distinctly 'modern' looking ('modern' in the sense of modernist – early 20th century).

Richard Long's intention with the text pieces is to be as simple and unadorned as possible: the typesetting and design is not intended to draw attention to itself as design (but of course it can't help doing that). Similarly, with his photographs, Long uses the same 35mm Nikkormat camera and lens: '[t]here is always the emphasis on the art and not really on the technique. It should look good but it should not look designed or special' (IC, 1, 18). The idea is to be artless, undesigned, unprecious.

Hamish Fulton, Long's contemporary (he was born a year later than Long), who's has been a companion of Long's on many journeys and walks (and works), commented that his 'work is about the experience of walking.' This could be Long talking here. Fulton continued: '[t]he framed artwork is about a state of mind – it cannot convey the experience of the walk.' This is true also of Richard Long's works (and is the inescapable melancholy of art; that art is always 'after the fact'; that it always comes afterwards, or last; that it can never replace what occurred, or desire, or what was lost).

What counts in Hamish Fulton's work may be the communication of a particular state of mind (in Zen Buddhist fashion). The reduction to one or two words, like Chinese or Japanese *haiku* or a modernist poem by Gertrude Stein or Ezra Pound, plus the clean design of Fulton's text works, plus the lack of extra æsthetic paraphernalia, attest to his desire for clarity of communication. Fulton's *Seven Days (Whistling Elk): a seven day walk in the Rocky Mountains of Alberta Canada* (1978) is similar to Long's text and photoworks: a large black-and-white photograph (of pieces of wood on soil, it seems to be) is set above a caption which is also the title of the work. Another Fulton artwork is a text piece, just like one of Long's text pieces: four words are printed in capitals in red and black: 'ROCK/ FALL/ ECHO/ DUST'. When it comes to typography, however, Fulton is far wilder than Richard Long, and much more experimental.

Have a look at this:

A LINE OF GROUND 226 MILES LONG

ROAD COAL TIP ROAD ROMAN MOUNTAIN ROAD ROAD WOODLAND RIVERBED ROAD STONY TRACK ROAD MUD TRACK ROAD GRASS LANE ROAD PEBBLE RIDGE ROAD BARE ROCK LANE ROAD SLURRY ROAD

This is a 1908 Welsh work by Richard Long, with no picture, no map, no funny little arrows dotted around to indicate wind direction, no 'SPLASHES', no squiggly lines for routes or rivers, and no reference to anything other than itself. It's not a painting *of* something, a sculpture *of* something (a place, perhaps, or a walk), or an object brought back from the making of the work. This textwork is simply these words (reproduced in *Richard Long* [1986, 164]).

At the same time, Richard Long's textworks have all sorts of possible readings. He chooses particular words, often seemingly plain words (*road, lane, rock, mud*), or words used in simple phrases and clauses (*a line of ground, the lark in the morning, ashes blowing in the wind, 120 miles in 4 days*). The vocabulary Long employs – *night, place, clouds, ground, sea, river, grass* – is simple and direct, with few embellishments (one might call it 'plain English', an unadorned vernacular that prefers words with roots in Anglo-Saxon rather than Latin or Romance languages).

Nevertheless, Long's textworks echo concrete, modernist and visual poetry or typewriter or graphic art at many points. In *Mountains and Waters* (1992) there are works with distinctly 'poetic' titles: *November Sunshine, A Spring Walk, In the Cloud, Dorset Song Lines, Walking Up Cedar Creek, Dartmoor Stones and Mind Rock*. Long also uses descriptive words which are usually the province of poetry: for instance, a textwork from Nepal (1983) reads like cut-up poetry, a poem with verbs and pronouns excised:

GREAT HIMALAYAN TIME A LINE OF MOMENTS MY FATHER STARLIT SNOW HUMAN TIME FROZEN BOOTS[2]

The observer needs to insert their own phrases into this *haiku*-like shorthand: '[I'm remembering] my father... [walking in] starlit snow... [this could be called] human time... [I have] frozen boots', and so on. There are some lovely phrases of Richard Long's in textworks like this: 'great Himalayan time' for instance, or 'a line of moments'. But the really explosive phrase is: 'my father'. It suddenly turns the textwork documenting a walk into something personal and emotional.

While we're referencing *haiku* poetry, this is a good moment to illustrate the form with a classic example (from Basho):

A branch shorn of leaves
A raven perching on it –
This Autumn evening.

Another textwork, one of Long's most poetic, the title piece of *Mountains and Waters,* employs techniques such as different coloured text; variable sized text; indented text; and white space.

One of the most obvious comparisons with Richard Long's textworks (chosen from the long history of visual poetry) is the poetry of Gertrude Stein, the feisty and startling American poet who lived in Paris, was a guru to many an aspiring artist, and who wrote *avant garde* poetry way before James Joyce and T.S. Eliot. Two of Stein's celebrated pieces, 'Patriarchal Poetry' and 'Lifting Belly', employ repetition, like Long's poems, but in a highly controlled, stylized manner. Though some people have found

Gertrude Stein's poetry difficult to read, a chore to wade through, it forms the foundation for 20th century concrete/ visual poetry, of which Long's text pieces are a part. It always repays a little effort. This is from Stein's 'Lifting Belly' (a gorgeous, highly erotic lesbian pæan):

Kiss my lips. She did.
Kiss my lips again she did.
Kiss my lips over and over and over again she did.
I have feathers.
Gentle fishes.
Do you think about apricots. We find them very beautiful. It is not alone their color it is their seeds that charm us. We find it a change.
Lifting belly is so strange...
Lifting belly is so kind.
Lifting belly fattily.
Doesn't that astonish you.
You did want me.
Say it again.
Strawberry.
Lifting beside belly.
Lifting kindly belly.
Sing to me I say.
Some are wives not heroes.
Lifting belly merely.
Sing to me I say.
Lifting belly. A reflection.
Lifting belly adjoins more prizes.[3]

There are plenty of other poets in the modernist/ cut-up/ concrete/ visual mode (Stéphane Mallarmé, Kusano Shimpei, Paul van Ostaijen, Tristan Tzara), but Stein provides a suitable illustration (as well as being one of the best).

Richard Long also utilizes quotations from pop music, from artists such as Bob Dylan, John Barleycorn, Johnny Cash (in *Reflections In Little Pigeon River, Great Smokey Mountains, Tennessee*, 1970), and country singer Nanci Griffith. His 1994 work in Orkney had a verse from a Bob Dylan song printed with it which ended: '[b]ut we still ain't going nowhere'.[4] The Johnny Cash song which accompanies the photo work *Reflections in the Little Pigeon River, Great Smokey Mountains, Tennessee* ends: '[b]ecause you're mine / I walk the line' (in *Old World, New World*, 56).

Music, Long feels, is another way of dealing with the emotions of a work. It expresses something in a work which words and photographs cannot (IC, 2, 15). Music is something important for Long – he refers to it a number of times in his works (it is one of the phrases he used to sum up his work in his 1997 Japan lecture). The kind of music Richard Long uses in his art is generally American, country and western or folk or soft rock. Long's favourite time and place in music would probably be the late 1960s in America.

In 1994, Richard Long commented: 'I couldn't imagine life without music. I think it is really a fantastically emotional feel-good kind of art form' (1994b). When he visited art schools to give lectures and slide shows, Long said he used to play a piece of music to accompany just one slide, so the students had to look at one image for the duration of the song. (Andy Goldsworthy recalled a visit from Long to his art college in Northern Britain in the 1970s: how Long played Country and Western music during his 'lecture', but refused to answer questions from the students.)

But the one piece of music that always got the most rapt attention, where you could almost hear a pin drop, was Roisin Dubhn, the slow air played on a tin whistle, with people looking at the circle in Ireland. That was always the most moving piece in the slide show. (1994b)

Roisin Dubh ('a slow air') was cited in the photowork *A Thousand Stones* (1974).

Sometimes, in a text piece, Richard Long will record the wind direction with a series of arrows – as in *Wind Line Walk* (1992) or *Wind Line* (1986) (The wind's a sound that accompanies so many walks). Long's first wind walk work, he recalled, was *Wind Line*, made on Dartmoor:

that was very much to do with the fact that not only does the wind blow from a prevailing part of the sky, but it also reflects the shape of the land... I very much liked the idea that in a subtle way the wind line was also reflecting the shape of the land. (WC, 66)

In *Circle of Autumn Winds* (1994), made (where else?) on Dartmoor, Richard Long recorded the direction of the wind during a 46 mile walk inside one of his imaginary circles. Wind is a huge physical presence on many walks in any territory (and certainly is almost constant blowing in places like Dartmoor). For a walker, in the open landscape, it's impossible to get away from the wind. But the little black arrows dotted about the place in Long's textworks seems fairly arbitrary and pointless, having little to do with the reality, force, sound, sensuality, speed or direction of wind blowing. Stephen Bann has commented that some of Long's works can be a little confusing. Of *Hundred Mile Walk*, made in Ireland, Bann wondered if the 100 miles also included miles up and down hills, or detours for fording rivers, or if it meant out and back (1994b). The mileage in Long's walkworks, presumably, means the no. of miles walked once the walk started, and doesn't count the mileage to the start of the walk, from the hotel, the town, the airport, or Long's home in Bristol.

Any number of poets have produced more evocative writing about walking than Richard Long's text pieces – Shelley, Goethe, Dante, Shakespeare, Lawrence – but Long is no poet. Writers such as John Cowper Powys or Thomas Hardy are much more successful than Long at evoking with words the beauty of the West Country. Take this passage from Powys' ecstatic novel *Wolf Solent*:

> In one warm inrushing wave the fragrance of the whole West-country seemed to flow through him as he came forth. Sap-sweet emanations from the leafy recesses of all the Dorset woods on that side of High Stoy seemed to mingle at that moment with the rank, grassy breath of all the meadow-lands of Somerset. The iron railings in front of that row of meagre, nondescript houses opened upon the airy confluence of two vast provinces of leafiness and sunshine – to the right Melbury Bub, with its orchards and dairies; to the left Glastonbury Tor, with its pastures and fens – while the umbrageous 'auras' of these two regions, blending together in the air above the roofs of Blacksod, merged into yet a third essence, an essence sweeter than either – the very soul of the whole wide land lying between the English Channel and the Bristol Channel. (226)

Richard Long's text pieces are not poems, but they do, like poems, aim to transmit some of the experience of walking, or some idea of walking. The maps, photographs and texts are 'second hand' works, Long remarked (GL, 8). Though they're not poems, Long's text pieces employ many of the formal aspects of poetry (repetition, rhymes, alliteration, visuals, sounds, and so on). First comes the walk, Long says, then the art made from the walk. Other people may make walks, but, Long says, 'what makes me an artist is the art I make from the walks' (IC 2, 19).

In an article on sculpture in the Forest of Dean, David Lee spoofs Richard Long's textworks, calling them 'certain fashionable but pretentious word sequences which nowadays masquerade as art'.[5] David Lee wanders around the Forest of Dean in the following manner:

MOSSY TREE STUMP
CORNED BEEF SANDWICH
RIBENA

It's easy to parody Richard Long's textworks. But Long's text pieces, though, are not 'pretentious', as David Lee attests: Long is not 'pretending' to produce art, he *is* producing art. Long has, too, written notes just like Lee's spoof: his diary entries (such as in *Walking the Line*, 144) record cups of tea and coffee, orange juice, cereals, bread and cheese, soup, scrambled eggs, and bars of chocolate. For instance, this is day 13 from a diary entry in *Walking the Line*, describing a walk (*A Line of 33 Stones, A Walk of 33 Days*, 1998) in Richard Long's beloved West Country:

Watery dawn. Good sleep. Bounty. Into Melton Mowbray: 1. Bank 2. Paper 3. Breakfast, full monty by market. Out on small road north. Post back map No. 2 from first village. Mixed skies. Dry tent at 12, stop on village green, ring Mum. Next village, Kit-Kat, Lilt, ring B from place with closed pub. On straight (down off high land now) to Granby. Look around for pub, very obscure, closed, but Irish lady opens up, makes a cheese sandwich. (WL, 64)

Nearly two weeks later, on day 26 of a 1,030 mile walk, now up in Scotland, Long records similar everyday aspects of his walk:

Lady a bit late for 7.30. Bran flakes. Gear up immediately in pouring rain with Dutch (?) cyclist in doorway. Straight, to Crieff. Buy map in info place. On 2 hours in pouring rain, first stop, an Inn. Coffee pot, with hot milk – 80p! On down, then up Sma 'Glen, over river, then up. Coffee rebounds… bit of diarrhoea behind rock. Next stop a tea room at junction with small road to glen. Great thick veg. soup and tea-cake. Chat to Eng. proprietor about walkers. (WL, 64)

In *All Ireland Walk* (1995), Richard Long registers 'mince beef and onion pie… sharing a pot of tea at a garage… a coffee in a flooded bar'. Some of the text pieces involve simple descriptions of acts that are vivid and easy to grasp. For instance, Long often moves a stone, or carries a stone then drops it. In the text pieces *A Moved Line in Japan* (1983 [In RL, 210]) and *A Moved Line* (1983), the whole line moves, or is constructed from short movements, each of which constitutes a 'moving line' when imagined together:

PICKING UP CARRYING PLACING
ONE THING TO ANOTHER
ALONG A STRAIGHT 22 MILE WALK

MOSS TO WOOL

WOOL TO ROOT
ROOT TO PEAT
PEAT TO SHEEP'S HORN
SHEEP'S HORN TO STONE
STONE TO LICHEN
LICHEN TO TOADSTOOL
TOADSTOOL TO BONE

To make a 'line' out of these acts needs the force of human imagination. Such artworks require culturally sophisticated people to make sense of them (and spectators steeped in contemporary Western art). 'The photos and texts etc feed the imagination, the sculptures (in a gallery) feed the senses' is one of Long's mantras.[6] To some observers in the landscape, watching Long pick up beech nuts or feathers or frogs or toadstools and carry them to another object found on the ground, it might seem that he was mad. An alien, observing Long from a flying saucer, might not be able to make any sense of the land artist working away in Dartmoor (though a child might). For culturally sophisticated people, which is everyone on Earth (all cultures make art, use language, etc), Long's acts would make more sense. To those who know something of contemporary Western art, Long's travels through the landscape make some sense (even if they hate them). Long, though, works on his own. People are used to seeing television crews around the world, and other media folk who use tape recorders, cameras, laptops or notepads. The land artist, though, doesn't go around with a film crew (well, sometimes they do): s/he often works in the landscape without machines or tools.

Richard Long's activities would make sense, perhaps, if the casual onlooker saw the camera. In photographing the artworks made outdoors, the artworks are valorized, memorialized, mythicized. Just as some commentators joke that nothing is 'real' until it has been videotaped, land art may require the mythicizing process of photography to become 'real'. In a heavily mediatized cyber-tech-info world, maybe building a cairn with stones wouldn't make sense to an outsider, but taking a photo or video tape of it afterwards might.

The textwork *A Seven Day Circle of Ground* (1984) is a large circle in which words are placed spatially to suggest where the artist was at various times (*A Circle of Middays* is a related walkwork conducted in 1997). In capitals the word 'MIDDAY' is placed inside the circle. There are seven 'midday' points, showing where Long was at noon on each of the seven days during the random walking. This in itself is a bizarre idea, a little like a map an army general might use, to plot the positions of a roving battalion (although without a grid, references, cardinal points, contours, buildings and measurements, it's meaningless).

Richard Long has written in italic some of the geographical aspects of the circle of land: 'Quickbeam Hill', 'Avon Head', 'Ditsworthy Warren', and so on. *A Seven Day Circle of Ground* is thus halfway between a text work and a map work, and requires the imagination to make sense of it. The clue to the work's interpretation is in its title: the word 'imaginary': 'seven days walking within an imaginary circle 5 1/2 miles wide'. *A Seven Day Circle of Ground* does nothing more, it seems, that plot in an abstract space the artist's physical position at certain times of the day. Apart from the words denoting topographical features, such as 'Erme Plains' or 'Stall Moor', there is no other attempt at the usual elements of cartography (contours, for instance, which are so important for the walker, or streams, or bogs, or paths, or boundaries, or rights of way). Long abstracts just the key features of this landscape, features that he might know well (Avon Head, for instance), and sets them afloat in white space.

How does one walk in a circle over miles? The very notion is intriguing (or baffling, or just silly), just as walking in a straight line is perplexing (though perhaps a little more understandable. There are many ancient straight roads, for instance. A straight road suggests purpose, function, movement, progression). It's one thing keeping to a straight line, by following a compass or map reading. It's another thing to follow a circle with a radius of a few miles, a route which requires constant checking and realignments (a circular route doesn't suggest an obvious function). There's an indiff-erent arbitrariness about Long walking in an imaginary circle which could either appear to the spectator as haunting or dumb. Either this is cool Conceptual art which has a compelling physical equivalent or embodiment in the real world (i.e., Long actually does walk in imaginary circles), or it's just idiotic.

Whether presented as a map (*Low Water Circle Walk*, 1980) or text (*A 2 1/2 Day Walk In the Scottish Highlands* [1979]or *A Circle of Middays* [1997]), the circular walks are designed as fascinating artworks. While some people might organize a circular route in a town (bank to post office, then to the fruit stall then home), Richard Long makes the circular walk a matter of Conceptualism and geometry. The casual circular walk of everyday life (once along the boardwalk and back through the town/ once round the junk yard/ skirting the town centre to avoid the militia's machine guns and drug dealers), becomes in Long's art a living sculpture founded on 'universal and common' principles. 'My work has become a simple metaphor of life… I am content with the vocabulary of universal and common means,' writes Long: 'walking, placing, stones, sticks, water, circles, lines, days, nights, roads.'[7] In *Concentric Days* (1996), Long walked (meandered) within five concentric circles a few miles wide in the Cairngorms.

Early Morning Senses Island Walk (1982) is a poetic record of the sensory input of a walk on the Isles of Scilly, a group of islands 28 miles off Cornwall. Just as Long likes to record how far he travels in a certain amount of time, the recording of sensory details is quite in tune with the project of communicating the experience of the walk. Listing the things that he felt or tasted or touched might be enough for Long, as a sculptor, but for a poet it is probably not enough. A Georges Seferis or Osip Mandelstam would have to do much more with the sensory data. In Long's pared-down, Postminimal or Arte Povera art, though, the simple printing of information ('distant surf roar', 'pebble maze', 'warmth', 'blackberry', 'earth lane') has a richness about it (or it does if the reader or viewer can supply the rest).

In *Rain Drumming On the Tent* (1997), another sensory work, Richard Long recorded the sounds he heard during a seven day walkwork in Ireland. *Sound Line* (1990) documented the sounds Long heard on a walk (with Hamish Fulton) in Spain over 21 days (622 miles): geese, skylarks, dogs, buzzards, surf, fires. Rain and water are the subject of some walks: *Rain Miles* (1989) recorded the number of miles walked in the rain in (inevitably) Ireland ('174 to 175 miles / 170 to 171 miles'). *The Wet Road* (1990) documented the number of hours spent walking on a road wet with rain during a North-South walk across France.

Ten Mile Places (1986) was a walkwork in the West Country, a list of short phrases describing things the artist encountered during (the making of) the walk:

A SINGING SKYLARK TWO SHEEPDOGS
A FLAT DRY EMPTY STRAIGHT ROAD (WC, 48)

Of Richard Long's many walks – *A Ten Mile Walk, A 24 Hour Walk, A Day's Walk on Honshu, On Midsummer's Day, A 100 Mile Walk, Early Morning Senses Island Walk, Four Walks, A Line of Ground 226 Miles Long, A Four Day Walk* – one of the longest has been *A Thousand Miles, A Thousand Hours*, made in the Summer of 1974. This is a textwork and a drawing: of a large square spiral. Long explained that the walk took in the whole of central England, so that the whole of central England became part of the walkwork. *A Thousand Miles, A Thousand Hours* had an appealing simplicity about it, spiralling over central England: it was about the 'geometry of time and distance' (RL, 103).

Some Richard Long walks have rules of space (a 22 mile walk, for instance), while others use time as the framework (like *Hours, Miles*, 1996). Some walks last one hour, such as *A Sixty Minute Circle Walk on Dartmoor* (1984). This is a textwork of a circular walk. In a circle 60 single words are printed. How did Long make it? Did he write the words every minute, i.e., walk for a minute than write 'slant' on a pad; walk for another minute and write 'squint', a minute later another word: 'sheep'. Long explains:

> I have no idea how many words I write. It is only at the end of the day that I realize that I have got maybe twenty lines. I don't have a fixed number to start with or whatever. I let the work happen. (IC 2, 11)

It's possible to write poetry while walking – actually walking, not stopping to sit down for a few minutes. It works best in a certain frame of mind – relaxed, open. This relaxed openness does seem to be Richard Long's basic frame of mind while walking (and other walkers have recorded similar feelings). In the 1983 Nepal visit, he writes of being 'happy alert balanced'.[8]

One of the important tasks on any walk is to find a good campsite. It has to be out of the wind, somewhere sheltered, and preferrably near fresh water and firewood. Note that Richard Long camps in wild spots, usually – or at least, places away from cities, towns, villages. Or that's the impression the viewer gains from his photographs and text pieces (Long may quietly excise pylons, telephone wires, restaurant signs and high-ways from his photos). Long is not, for instance, part of the culture of holiday makers, campers, tourers and tourists who travel around with RVs, trailers, camper vans and caravans. Somehow, one can't imagine Richard Long setting up his tent in a municipal campsite, with its little shop or office, its kids' playgrounds, washrooms, toilets and maybe a swimming pool. No, Long's campsites are strictly no star, open-air affairs, in a forest somewhere, or a hollow in the hills, and not in the *Rough Guide, Lonely Planet* or *Fodor's* guidebook, or the handbooks of travel and camping clubs.

Richard Long has put sleeping places and campsites in his walkworks. He's even recorded the spots where he pissed during a walk (on a 96 mile walk from Dawlish to Bristol: *Urinating Places Line*, 1993). It's bizarre, when you think about it. Next thing he'll be doing a *Defecation Walk*: places he's shat in. Well, Piero Manzoni canned his own excrement, didn't he? And those wall drawings Long does with smearings of brown mud, the sceptical onlooker could call them shit. (Actually, Long has used fæces: *Herd Droppings*, made in Mongolia in 1996, is an open circle which uses what appears to be excrement).

Richard Long often photographs his campsites without the tent, recording the marks on the ground his tent has made: in *Light Snow in the Night* (1993) and *Breaking Camp, Moving On*. In Korea (*Stony Ground*, 1993), Long records that the stones he used to secure his tent were left behind in the shape of the tent. The photos register the grass pressed flat, or the remnants of snow, or the shadow of dry ground; the pictures have a similar function to the images of grass or heather trodden flat by the act of walking. A trace of human presence (but not a lasting trace). *Sleeping Mark* and *Sleeping Place Mark* (1990) were further instances of the marks made by Long's tents and sleeping places. 'Leave no trace' is a maxim followed by Long (and Fulton). 'One who excels in travelling leaves no wheel tracks', said Lao-tzu (XXVII).

Richard Long has often based walks around celestial events, such as sunrise and sunset, or full moons, or lunar eclipses. The lunar eclipse was the focus of a 1996 walk (*Walking To a Lunar Eclipse*). *Midwinter Night's Walk* (1999) was made by the light of the full moon at the Winter solstice. Another lunar event – the tide – was the subject of *Tide Walk* (1992), a continuous walk of 'two and a half tides relative to the walker' (Long said that the walk was about measuring time and distance using the moon, which controls the tides: 'that walk was very much about relativity… It was like measuring the walk with two different clocks' [SS, 308]). In *Highland Time* (2002) Long noted that during the walk the Earth had travelled 5,740,000 miles in its orbit around the sun.

In *Phenomena*, a walk made in Richard Long's home county of Avon in 2002, Long referred to high tides, the Spring equinox, sunrise and moonrise. *High Tide To High Tide* (1992) was a walk between the tides on two rivers, the Medway and the Severn. The solar eclipse of Summer, 1999, was another celestial event that was the basis of a walk (*Walking To a Solar Eclipse*), as Long walked from Stonehenge (of course) to Cornwall.

In *Speed of the Sound of Loneliness* (1998), made on Dartmoor, Richard Long related the time and distance and circularity of his artwalk with the rotation of the Earth, the Earth's orbit around the sun, and the Solar System's orbit around the galaxy. There's something child-like about this listing of big astronomical figures. It's like children who write their addresses with every possible line added to it:

Joanna Wilson
Apt. #8,
1575, South Ellis Avenue,
Chicago,
Illinois,
60637,
U.S.A.,
World,
Solar System,
Milky Way,
Universe

Yep, and in the time it's taken me to write that address the Earth has spun 10,743·109 miles further around the sun. And the Solar System's span a few more million miles along in the spiral arm of the galaxy. And the Milky Way has drifted a fraction of a light year closer to the Virgo cluster of galaxies.

The measurement of most of Richard Long's walks is by days – that is, by solar time. The tidal walks are controlled by the moon, by lunar time (1994b). As Mircea Eliade noted, the moon is the symbol *par excellence* of 'the flow, passage, waxing and waning, birth, death and rebirth, in short the cosmic rhythms, the eternal becoming of things, Time'.[9]

Some of Richard Long's walks are about how far he walked in a single day, either from sunrise to sunset, or continuously, for 24 hours, such as in *Hours, Miles* (1996), or a 24 hour continuous walk on Dartmoor (in *Dartmoor Time*, 1995). In 1994 he walked for 59 miles between sunrise and sunset on Midsummer Day. In *Old Year New Year Walk* (1993) he walked for twelve hours at the close of 1992 and for twelve hours at the beginning of 1993. The concept of this walk was repeated (inevitably) at the millennium: *Walking From One Millennium To Another* (1999-2000), a walk which ended up (inevitably) at Glastonbury Tor.

Rivers are often the basis or starting-point for Richard Long walkworks. In the river walk, *Mud Walk* (1987), Long walked from the mouth of the River Avon to the source of the River Mersey, throwing some mud from the Avon into the Thames, the Severn, the Trent and the Mersey rivers along the way. In *A Cloudless Walk* (1995), Long walked along the course of the River Loire from its mouth (stopping when he saw the first cloud). In *Muddy Water Walk* (1996), Long walked from his favourite river (the River Avon) to Devon, keeping the Bristol Channel in view along the way. Long walked between two bridges (in Bristol and London) in *Watershed* (1992). *Mississippi Waterline Walking Line* (1988) was a photowork of the shoreline and the imprints of

Long's boots in the sand. In *Rio Grande Canyon Stones* (1993) Richard Long threw stones into the rivers in Colorado and New Mexico (a photograph peppered with the superimposed word 'splash' apparently marked where the stones fell into the water). *Stone Water Sound* (1990) recorded the sound of splashes in water in the rivers encountered along the journey of a walk in Wales. In *Water Walk* (1999) Long carried water from one river to another. *River Po Line* (2001) was a serpentine line on the ground which looked back to Long's first land artworks.

In *Four Days and Four Circles* (1994), Richard Long walked within four imaginary circles, drawn on a map of Dartmoor. Long walked for eight hours within the area circumscribed by the map circle, each circle being bigger over the four days of the art-walk. In *A Circle of Middays* (1997), Long walked around Southern England within an imaginary circle 63 miles across. The Monadhliath mountains of Scotland was the site of *No Where* (1993), a 131 mile walk crisscrossing the terrain within an imaginary circle (the 'circle' was a few miles in diameter).

Richard Long walks in time as much as space (so does anyone who walks – or lives). His works emphasize the temporal, historical dimension: for instance, Long will pick up a stone, carry it for a mile then drop it, or spend a certain length of time building a sculpture before moving on. 'A walk marks time with an accumulation of footsteps. It defines the form of the land. Walking the roads and paths is to trace a portrait of the country'.[10] Sometimes Long set out on a walk carrying a stone he picked up from a previous walk (as in *The Same Thing At a Different Time At a Different Place*, 1997).

North and South, made in Blighty and Cymru in 1991, is a truly strange walk: according to the textwork, Richard Long walked for 8 hours along the same road. On the 1st day he walked for 8 hours, North (from Chepstow to Saddlebow Hill). But on the 2nd day he walked for 7 hours North and 1 hour South (from Saddlebow Hill to near Leominster). On the 3rd day he walked for 6 hours North, and 2 hours South. And so on. There's a mathematical system there, which recalls Sol LeWitt, and a wilful arbitrariness which reminds one of Jan Dibbets or Hans Haacke.

WALL DRAWINGS AND HANDPRINTS

Richard Long works with his hands – touches of the hand not to be seen, perhaps, in the walks or the lines of stones amidst rocky valleys – but seen in those circles, lines and ovals of mud smeared on gallery walls, the handprints on the floor and walls, and the fingerprints on bits of wood. (It's not so easy to smear mud on walls with one's feet – although Long has made 'feet' sculptures by making an impression of his foot in terracotta – *Footprint Spiral*, 1993). Some of Long's mud circles allow the handprint to be seen on its own, without being smeared, as in *Kilkenny Circles, Mud Hand Circles* (New York, 1984), *River Avon Mud Hand Circles* (Dublin, 1984), the Rome *Muddy Water Circles* (1994), and *Rhône Valley Mud Hand Circles* (2000). *White Mud Hand Circle* (1996, Tokyo) was a handprint circle made on the floor (against a black backing). *White Hand Spiral* (1990) comprised white handprints on black paint on a wall.

Keeping the handprint intact directly echoes primal gestures such as the Egyptian use of the palm of the hand to ward off the 'Evil Eye'. The hand on its own is a talisman, seen today in Egyptian taxis, swinging from the mirror. Richard Long's *River Avon Mud Hand Circles* (1984 and 2000) directly recall the cosmological visions of ancient and mediæval times, where the earth was seen in astronomical diagrams at the centre of a series of interconnecting circles or levels of existence.

The mud hand and fingerprint circles underline Richard Long's insistence of making art without machines or tools. The physical manufacture of this area of Long's art consists of his hands only. The mud is usually allowed to drip (especially in the lines and rows of mud), and to splash onto other walls. Other mud circles smooth all the mud together, as in *River Avon Mud Circles* (Paris, 1982 and Malmo, 1985) and *Cuckoo Circles* (1987), so that only the short strokes made by the fingers are apparent. These short strokes of the fingers make the mud circles look like the floor circles made with sticks. The short groups of strokes echo Jasper Johns' late paintings, which consist of small crosshatched brushstrokes.

In Richard Long's mud circles, the small, human-size unit (the handprint, the finger stroke) is gathered together to make up a large artwork. As in Long's walks, which are one step followed by another, Long's mud circles are one touch of the hand followed by another. Long's works are always clusters of small units. Each stone, handprint, stick or step goes towards constituting the whole. The totality is manifestly clear: the circle is *the* symbol of psychic, cosmic totality and unity. But each of Long's totalities consists of small fragments (the interrelationship of the macro- and the micro-cosmic, the one in the many, the many in the One). For Oriental mystics, each breath one takes is linked together, to form the basis of one's life. Similarly, in Richard Long's art, a single stone can be added to another to form an artwork.

The eroticism of such mud-smeared works is obvious, as is the sensuality of rites such as mud dancing, where people smother themselves with mud for its healing properties (and today, echoing mud rituals, women – nude, of course – mud wrestle in pornography). The forms themselves, though – circles, lines, ovals, spirals, cairns – are not, Richard Long maintains, the key point of his work. The forms are 'universal', they are forms which don't 'belong' to anyone, which sets Long free to explore other aspects of the work.1 'The creation of my art is not in the common forms – circles, lines – I use, but the places I choose to put them in.'2 Long uses stones because they are simultaneously common and unique; they exist everywhere ('stones are stones' he says), but each one has its own characteristics. Context is absolutely crucial in land art. It is the *place,* not the circle or line, that 'makes' the work. The location is the poetry of the work, not the circle, oval or the line. The circle, oval or line of stones must be sensitive to the place, otherwise it won't work.

Yet Richard Long's lines are not 'organic', like his circles. The stone circles look right on the earth, maybe because so many objects in the natural realm are circles or transcribe circles in their orbits (planets, stars, atoms, electrons, cells, eyes, mouths, etc). The straight line, though, looks instantly odd. The line of a path bends slightly, and the ancient tracks which Long walks on (such as the Foss Way in 1977) are not absolutely straight, but veer and swerve with the lay of the land. The lines that Long walks along, though, are quite different. They are (usually) utterly straight, whether walked in reality or drawn on a map.

Of course, when Richard Long draws on a map, he uses a ruler or straight edge, so he can easily create a near-perfect straight line, just as the Minimal artists produced pin-sharp straight lines (Sol LeWitt in his wall drawings, Robert Morris with his rect-angular solids, Isamu Noguchi with his *Red Cube*). Long, though, could not walk in a purely straight line across uneven ground, could he? Isn't it a physical impossibility? He follows his compass, reads the map carefully and walks in a straight line. But it is, as in so much of Conceptual Art, the *idea* of the straight line walk that is important. One knows that the actual walk in a straight line outdoors may be fraught with problems, but in the mind, all things can reach perfection. In theory, at least. The idea of 'perfection' disturbs some people, because, they say, 'nothing can be perfect'. But an *idea* can be 'perfect'. Similarly with other absolutes, such as infinity. Though astrophysicists state that infinity is an 'impossible' concept, one can still use the *idea* of infinity. Ditto eternity, timelessness, nothingness, imagelessness, all those notions of Buddhism, Hinduism, Taoism and Oriental mysticism which entered the art world in the 1950s and 1960s.

'Purity' is perhaps a better term than perfection, and artists of all ages have been concerned with purity, not just the Minimal artists or Conceptualists (though a term like 'purity' is as philosophically and ideologically problematic as 'perfection'). One can see in Richard Long's *œuvre*, though, a craving for artistic purity (a purity which an artist can conceive of and works towards, which is not the same as the purity of the philosopher or the ideologue). Towards 'pure forms', such as lines and circles, and for the 'pure' work of art. Long says: 'for me art is the possibility to do something pure and focused and simple in a chaotic world' (IC 2, 19).

It is the *purity* of the straight line that fascinates Richard Long. The actual line he makes in his walks may be wobbly, as satellite tracking or mapping might prove. But the purity of the straight line walk is the thing. The *conceptual* dimensions of the shape of the line are crucial for Long. Thus, he made a spiral line in a gallery in Amsterdam which was 'the length of a straight walk from the bottom to the top of the Glastonbury Tor', and another spiral line sculpture was entitled *A Line the Length of a Straight Walk From the Bottom to the Top of Silbury Hill*. The idea of the line being the same length as the walk to these sacred sites is the important thing. It suggests a connection that is both physical (a walked line, a path walked on) and spiritual or conceptual. This is Long's ideal artistic response: something that is both physical and conceptual, both matter and spirit.

In the gallery, confronted by the spirals, the viewer has to make the conceptual connection between what s/he sees in front of them, and the place to which Long refers to in the title. The spirals make more sense when one knows that they refer to Glastonbury or Silbury (and even more, perhaps, if the viewer knows Glastonbury and Silbury well, or has visited them, or has even walked the same walks, walks which visitors undertake most every day of the year). The titles of Long's works are crucial, because without them the piles of stones, the slate lines, the spirals, could come from anywhere. And Richard Long doesn't want that response. It's very important that his works arise from *particular* places. Those stones on the gallery floor are not from simply *anywhere*, but from somewhere in particular (and they're exhibited somewhere in particular too). As Long says, the 'creation' in his art stems from context and places, not from using circles or lines.[3]

The titles of Richard Long's works nearly always have the name of a place in them, so the works are sited firmly within (the context of) a certain place. *Little Tejunga Stone Circles, Napoli Circles, Kilkenny Circles, Crossing Place of 2 Somerset Walks, Bordeaux Slate Line, Walking a Circle in Peru, Trento Ellipse, Tennessee Stone Ring* – these titles make it clear that Long is dealing with particular places: the look, atmosphere, texture, lighting, colour, tone, shape, pattern, sound, taste, smell, touch, history and psychology of specific places.

Although Richard Long celebrates particular places, he likes to keep the locations a secret,[3] as if knowing about his locations, the public would somehow lessen their impact, or disturb them (Long's interventions in the landscape are his own; the public is not invited to share in their construction). Besides, Long's works do not last: only works such as the cairns that walkers use to mark a path, to which Long added some stones, will last. The other pieces fade into anonymity, or melt away to nothing. At the same time, (nearly all) Long's works exist somewhere, as all material artworks exist somewhere, in one form or another.[4]

There is a random aspect to Richard Long's art, an ad lib, arbitrary quality, a sense of the spontaneous. Minimal and Conceptual artists often spoke of not wanting to be too clever, to manipulate things. Robert Barry wrote: 'I try not to manipulate reality. What will happen, will happen. Let things be themselves.'[5] In his instructions for *Slate Circle*, which consists of 214 chunks of Welsh slate in a circle 6.60m in diameter, Long writes:

> First, the perimeter of the circle is marked out lightly on the floor (e.g. in pencil). The circle is then filled in stone by stone in a haphazard pattern. Each stone is placed on its longest, flattest, most stable side, not touching another stone. The stones are chosen at random. There is an even density of stones throughout the sculpture, and a fairly even distribution of sizes and lengths amongst the stones. All the stones should be used.[6]

Long's sculptures, then, have a random, intuitive aspect in keeping with Long's Conceptual stance. Despite his fastidiousness (in his recording of time, measurements and geography), Long lets his sculptures be constructed any which way, but within a loose structure (the pencil-marked circle on the gallery floor). One could equally argue, though, that Richard Long's instructions to museum curators are extremely exact. A curator and assistants installing the work should get something close to the one Long originally built. Long maybe doesn't want a stone circle being constructed which doesn't look like a Richard Long artwork.

There is nothing *special* about Richard Long's choice of location: it could be anywhere on the planet, because he regards the whole planet as a single space. 'My art is about working in the wide world, wherever, on the surface of the earth' he says (FS, 236). His lines and circles, he implies, could occur anywhere. This is not true, though, for Long is very careful about his selection of potential art sites. He makes sure the places have the right atmosphere, background, foreground objects, etc. Although his walks take him in all manner of directions, which conform to a mathematical or geometric formulation, although he includes much spontaneity in his walks, he also makes sure the locations are right. He reacts to places, like any place-sensitive artist. 'I must have a strong feeling' says Long (1986, 2, 21). Sometimes the feeling is so strong, or the 'place is so good' that Long doesn't make any art there.

RICHARD LONG'S BOOKS

Richard Long produces lavish, full-colour books to go with his exhibitions (or rather, his art dealers and publishers do). The coffee table art books and limited edition artists' books reach a market that couldn't get to the exhibition. They act as a substitute for, and a parallel of, the art exhibition. They are expensive books, often with a tiny amount of text in them, consisting mainly of colour photographs of land art. (Although Long may wish to be ideologically anti-capitalist and pro-ecology, colour art books cost plenty to manufacture, and they are probably not all made from sustainable materials. And Long has produced lots of them. So Long has contributed plenty towards deforestation just like everyone else).

Richard Long's 1988 *Old World New World* is typical of the art books that the artist publishes: a landscape-format colour hardback book, with twenty artworks illustrated, as well as photos of Dartmoor, Sniougoutse La and Bolivia (the Anthony d'Offay books are probably the best series in the Richard Long canon). Some of the artworks in *Old World New World* are Conceptual text pieces, such as *Pitching the Tent* (1987, France), which prints two words ('first night', 'second night') in different directions, because this shows, Long says, 'the direction of my tent and my sleeping place each night along a ten day winter walk in the Dauphine Alps' (and don't say you don't care one bit which way his tent was facing during his walk). Here is the typical Long artwork: Conceptual text made out of biography. What one gets in the Richard Long art book is a strange mixture of photography and concrete poetry, a use of graphical text more usually associated with 'concrete' or 'visual' poets.

The text piece *Ten Days Walking and Sleeping on Natural Ground* (1986) is one of Richard Long's most complex textworks: it consists of phrases and lines of words printed in a scattered, 'random' fashion within a circle. It is the lingual equivalent of Long's circles made of slate or sticks. The phrases themselves are the familiar ones taken from a Richard Long walk, those phrases which are usually printed in a vertical column with no punctuation. Here, in *Ten Days Walking and Sleeping on Natural Ground*, the phrases – as usual set typographically in Gill Sans capitals – create a visual poetry record of the Long walk: 'deer tracks... the line of a day's walk the arc of the sun... following a desire... dawn chorus... stepping-stones milestones... bone... frogs... raven... drumming rain... mist all day... scent of heather' (OW, 23). *Ten Days Walking and Sleeping on Natural Ground* offers, though, a contradiction in terminology. What does 'natural ground' mean? Does the artist mean ground that hasn't had a human mark placed upon it? Does he mean ground that is not built over, that is not a city, a road, a gas station, a trash heap or some other human edifice? When he walks on 'natural ground', what is the opposite? '*Un*natural ground'? Anyhow, the 'natural ground' walked on in *Ten Days Walking and Sleeping on Natural Ground* is not 'natural': it (Scotland) is crossed with the memories of human feet, it bears the marks of campfires and campsites, of animals husbanded, of people altering the landscape in small ways (walls, fences, tracks, paths, posts, gates, etc). Also, the area is thoroughly mapped, measured, quantified, and the artist makes use of maps in this very work: even as he walks 'on natural ground' he 'follows a map' (OW, 23). Also, a great many of the 'natural' features of the landscape are named by humans (in traditional magic there's a link between naming something and controlling it). The artist logs these names in a single column of text, which is itself another artwork:

RIVER FEHSIE
ALLT A'CHAORAINN
SCARSOCH BHEAG
CNAPAN GARBH

BYNACK BURN
BRAIGH COIRE CAOCHAN NAN LAOGH
CARN GREANNACH (OW, 22)

Though he employs photographs of 'natural ground' or wildernesses in his work, Richard Long revels in the names given to the natural land in his artworks. A large part of the 'poetry' of Long's works derives from the poetry of place-names: Carn Ealar, Sierra Tarahumara, Hangingstone Hill, Aldeburgh, Lamayuru, Twyn Tal-y-Cefn. There is nothing 'natural' about a place-name: it has essentially nothing to do with the place except the fact that humans have associated the name with the place. There is plenty that's not very 'natural' about Long's wildernesses or 'natural grounds', to be pedantically semantic, unless humans making art is 'natural'.

See the 1984 Welsh Marches walk, in which the evocative names of the Welsh borderlands are cited: 'Hay Bluff to Tympa, Tympa to Y Das, Y Das to Gist Wen'.[1]

You can tell from many of my works, especially the text works, that place names play a really important part. I think the way places are named affects the way we know places. It's like language, how we talk about things is part of our understanding of the world. (1994b)

This part of Britain is particularly beautiful, a true wilderness. Central Wales is one of the least populated areas of the UK (unlike on Dartmoor, you really can be miles from the nearest human). The mountains are magnificent. The Welsh place names are poetic, but they resonate more poignantly if one knows something of the rocky, windswept landscape of Wales. (One can assume that Richard Long will never make a walkwork in somewhere like Disneyland, or the Beverly Center shopping mall, highly artificial, intensely commodified spaces). (For J.R.R. Tolkien, a philologist who found the sound and look of words magical, the Welsh language had a mystical appeal, attracting the writer from a young age when he saw it painted on some coal trucks. Welsh formed one of the key components in Tolkien's invented languages, such as elvish).

Perusing 1992's book and show *Mountains and Waters*, one finds another textwork, entitled *November Sunshine*. In Blighty, the two words 'November' and 'sunshine' are a contradiction in terms. The work is a textual record of the amount of time Richard Long spent in sunshine, 'walking with my shadow'. The result is that, on the second day of the walk, there was six and a quarter hours of sunshine. But this was lucky, for the fourth day revealed 'no sun', while the fifth day had only a quarter of an hour of sunshine and shadows. *November Sunshine* wasn't a failure as a work of art, however. Long was not attempting to walk in sunshine as much as possible, as the Sunday afternoon stroller might have done. Long's walks and works can never be 'rained off'. He doesn't care if it rains, snows, shines or blows. His aim is simply to record his walk, sun or no sun.

In holding a Richard Long art book, then, one holds a Richard Long work of art. The text in the exhibition catalogues and books is exactly that of the large prints and paper works, seen on the gallery walls. In the case of *Ten Days Walking*, the text is coloured brown, to evoke landscape perhaps. Long's works, like Hamish Fulton's, are a little different when seen on a gallery wall instead of a book, but not much different. The context is the biggest difference: the upmarket art gallery is quite a different space from a private home, a bus, a plane. It's true that the scale of the gallery text pieces is different from that of the art books, that one cannot handle the works (unless you're buying), that the works are seen in frames, on a vertical wall, during the gallery's opening hours, in a particular location in a city, and so on. But these differences are not that important, finally. What counts is the idea of the experience that is trying to be communicated.

Richard Long said he didn't have people in his photographs because he has chosen to make art 'about lines and stones and walking'. The social aspect of his work was separate. People were important for hospitality, help finding the way, or for food, Long acknowledged, but 'it's just that people are not the subject of my work' (WL, 146).

One sees Richard Long's rucksack propped up against walls, or his canoe drawn up on the bank of the River Severn,[2] or his tent in some romantic wilderness (as in the photographs of *Campsite Stones*, 1985, or *Sleeping Circle*, 1987). Long himself seldom appears in the photos of his walks. In *Old World New World*, though, he mentions 'friends' once or twice, indicating people he meets on his walks (or people he's walking with). And there are some photographs of two rucksacks leaning against a shrine in India, Mexico, and in other wildernesses (Long walked in India with Hamish Fulton in 1984, and in Mexico with Fulton in 1987). It's understandable that, of any item, the rucksack should appear in Long's photos, for the rucksack is one of the walker's totems, vital source of his/ her food and shelter, where the maps, spare shoes, sleeping mat, tent, poles, clothes, water-bottle, etc, are stored (in *Four Walks of Known and Unknown Factors* [2000] Long writes that he carried a hundredweight).

Anne Seymour says that Richard Long 'sets out upon his journey... *only* with a length of string for making, pencil, notebook and camera for recording things perceived, map and compass for finding the way, gloves for lifting rocks, a water bottle for making water drawings, and a pair of well-worn boots' (WC, 15, my italics). Seymour implies that Long travels lightly: yes, but walkers also carry a lot of items too. They travel lightly but prepared. And the water bottle is not primarily for 'making water-drawings', as Seymour asserts, it is for drinking. It is perhaps the most important item a walker has.

The rucksack is the walker's placenta, an object s/he depends on. These shots of the rucksacks in India and Mexico speak very much of human presence, although the figures of Long and Fulton are deliberately absent (again, they seem to have just stepped around the edge of the frame. In Fulton's books, though, one can see the photos of Fulton taken on these trips of Richard Long). They also speak of the manufacture of the photograph and of the artwork the photograph records, which is the walk. The shots of the rucksacks say, yes, we were here, right here; they acknowledge the presence of the walker within the landscape in a direct, personal manner, quite different from the rarefied, Conceptual aspects of the lines of stones or the snow rubbed out in a circle.3

8

From Photography to Installations

The personal details of each sculpture in land art are important, and artists catalogue themselves and their works meticulously. It is curious to visit a Richard Long exhibition and be confronted by lots of large pieces of paper with Long's documentation of his 'walks' or 'sculptures' printed on them (walks as sculptures, sculpture as walks). (Curious, but no different from a Dennis Oppenheim, Robert Smithson or Lawrence Weiner exhibition.) 'My photographs and captions are facts which bring the appropriate accessibility to the spirit of these remote or otherwise unrecognisable works' said Richard Long (RL, 236).

Typical is Long's *Three Moors Three Circles* of 1982, an archetypal Long artwork – a walk in his beloved Southwest terrain, in three of the main moors in the region (Dartmoor, Bodmin Moor and Exmoor). The whole artwork is a large piece of paper (one can buy it framed or unframed if one likes). There are three concentric rings of words, printed in red, which read: *Three miles on Exmoor, two miles on Dartmoor, one mile on Bodmin Moor.* The words are printed in circles clearly to indicate a number of things – the walk itself, on the earth, in circles, and stone circles, and circles in general, as symbols and as Long's primary motif. The next line, also in red, is the title: *Three Moors, Three Circles.* The next line of type, in black, reads: *A 108 mile walk from Bodmin Moor, to Dartmoor, to Exmoor, walking around three circles along the way.* The next three lines read: *Liskeard to Porlock, Richard Long, England 1982.* That's it. That's the whole artwork, a cursory, matter-of-fact description of the walk. The words being a certain size, or colour, or in a particular frame, 'is all about how they look like' revealed Richard Long (IC 2, 19). The words on the paper, though, have little if anything to do with the actual experience of walking on England's wild moors, with their sudden rainfalls out of nowhere, their amazingly impenetrable mists, their seemingly vast marshes, and their occasional utter solitude.

HEAVIER   SLOWER   SHORTER
LIGHTER   FASTER   LONGER

A FOUR DAY WALK IN ENGLAND
PICKING A STONE UP EACH DAY AND CARRYING IT.
A FOUR DAY WALK IN WALES
SETTING DOWN ONE OF THE STONES EACH DAY[1]

Everyone's experience of walking in wildernesses is different. Most people would be aware of things such as a vast sense of space; of no human habitation or marks for miles (or less marks than a city or a theme park); the presence of the weather; the ever-changing nature of the weather; the attributes of the landscape; the myriad sounds of the natural world, as well as silence; the rhythm of walking; awareness of one's body (feet, thirst, hunger, breathing), and so on and on.

What one misses in Richard Long's representations of his walks is the silence, the ever-present stillness and silence behind, in and over the landscape. True, on windy days (of which there are many in the Southwest of Great Britain) one cannot say the world is 'silent'. But there is often an immense sense of silence, or near-silence (like a giant ear listening), which adds to the sense of solitude. This is what people hanker after when they speak of 'getting away from it all', 'walking it off' by 'going for a walk'. Contemporary life in the Western, 'First' World can be very noisy. In favourite Richard Long places, such as Nepal, Ladakh, Lappland, Iceland, Mexico and Dartmoor, one can escape that technological, mediatized, late capitalist environment, and drink in the (near) silence.

In Albion, one can walk for miles in the counties of the South-West (Wiltshire, Devon, Somerset, Cornwall and Dorset) and not see anyone at all. In these places, one is aware of the faint susurrus of the wind: this is one primal reality that's missing in Richard Long's works. Yet the faint sound of the wind about the ears is such a prominent element of a walk.2 J. Hull has written poetically of the significance of a gently blowing breeze for blind people: it 'brings into life all the sounds in [the] environment.'3 The sound of the wind can liven up acoustic space, setting alight the 'bodyscape', the body's awareness and its relationship to its surroundings. Air, apparently invisible, apparently just 'empty' space, is the stuff that connects people with the world, the stuff that's takes up all of that 'empty' space between the individual and everything else.

To be dumb and obvious for a moment here: perhaps Richard Long should move into multi-media and interactive presentations of his walks? Perhaps he ought to have the sound of recorded atmospherics and wind in the gallery. Nautical museums, like the wonderful one that used to be in Penzance, have the sound of the sea playing through loud speakers. The incessant sound of the waves helps to create the all-pervading environment of the sea in the museum. Perhaps Long ought to try bringing more of the multi-sensory experience of a walk into the gallery space, something more than textworks, photoworks, wall drawings and circular sculptures. Perhaps he ought to encourage someone to spend a proportion of the next exhibition budget on employing some museum designers and curators to create a multi-media *Walk Show* installation. Sounds tacky and silly, and the kind of so-obvious solution a naïve young art student might come up with? Of course it is. But isn't having a framed Ordnance Survey map on a wall and presenting it as an artwork and record of a walk tacky and a little silly? (One knows it doesn't cost much to produce a map work: eight bucks for the map, 150 for the frame, a few cents for the pen to mark on the map). The stone circles 'cost' nothing, it seems, like the River Avon mud (forget transportation from the quarry, admin, overheads, and accommodation for the moment). Richard Long's main materials for his sculpture seem to be 'free' – the walk itself seems to be 'free'. Seen in one way, Long's works can strike the viewer as 'cheap', tacky and pretentious. Mr Average might wander into a Richard Long show and exclaim, *it's just a few stones on the floor, innit? Jeez, anyone could do that!* This was the furore that Carl Andre's bricks generated in the dim and distant days of mid-1970s Britain (when something as innocuous, quaint and humorous as punk rock could cause outrage and a 'moral panic'). Bricks on the floor? Bought by a public museum (the Tate Gallery in London) for six thousand bucks?

So Richard Long's works can appear extremely tawdry, 'low budget' and affected. Unlike Carl Andre, though, Long doesn't 'risk' everything on the socio-cultural context of a gallery. As his sculptures relate to walks, they always have a solid, straightforward, no-nonsense element. No one can argue with the importance of walking. Walking is not namby-pambying around with a paintbrush and canvas like a Sunday afternoon amateur painter. It's not twee arrangements of twigs and flowers. No, walking is good, solid, dependable work. It's only when walking is portrayed as 'art' that the problems occur. (If Long had started out thirty years later, and launched his artistic career in reality TV mode in the late 1990s, rendering his walks in the form of video documentaries, rather than as textworks or stone sculptures, his notion of turning walks into art might well have been accepted wholesale).

Richard Long's bits of paper are word games which only hint at the reality of walking in wildernesses. They are Conceptual, semiotic games which point towards the powerful nature of Long's 'landscape of the soul'. The 'reality' of Long's work is clearly 'out there', in the world, in the landscape. Yet much of his art is conceptual, fictive, images, representations of representations.

> So the walk [Long said]… the idea of the walk just exists in the words or a photograph, or as I said before, the idea exists to be remade whenever I want to remake it. The works themselves disappear but the idea goes on forever. (1986, 1, 9)

There is much ambivalence in Richard Long's importing of 'natural' forms and materials into the urban space of the art gallery. The walks themselves are the reality of his art. Everything else is secondary, something for the punters and art critics, something, perhaps, to do on cold Winter evenings in Bristol in between walks and travels to wildernesses.

One can see how the text pieces, of all Richard Long's works, would be a favourite with the artist. The textworks Long sees as simply another artform, no better or worse than photographs, walking, or mud circles (like many Conceptual, Process and Postminimal artists, Long doesn't privilege any particular form his art takes: it's always all part of the same thing. And it's unified by the artist himself and his experience). The text pieces, however, can actually describe (or try to describe) acts in walking which photgraphs cannot evoke. For instance, some of Long's sculptures consist of stones being picked up and put down. One might see a photograph of a stony landscape, but without a caption saying that the artist walked, say, twenty miles picking up a stone and carrying it for a mile before putting it down and picking up another, one wouldn't know exactly what had happened in the work. The text pieces enable descriptions of events or concepts which don't necessarily occur in the photographs.

Richard Long's atmospheric 35mm photographs of Dartmoor are powerful on their own, but without a caption saying 'Dartmoor, 1987', one wouldn't know that the photograph was Dartmoor. After all, Long is careful to ensure that very few signs of humanity are seen in his photographs. So one wilderness photograph can be interchangeable with another. The artist can recognize this or that place, Dartmoor or rural Japan, say, but the viewer needs the text captions to make the connections (certain landscapes, like Mount Fuji, or the Tibetan mountains, are more recognizable). In one sense, the locations Long walks in (makes art in) are anonymous, or vague, and could be in any of fifty different countries. On the other hand, it is crucial to know that one of Long's most haunting images, *Mountain Lake Powder Snow* (1985) was made in Lappland.

Some of Richard Long's works are photographs of places where a stone was picked up then put down. There is a photo, for instance, of a rocky hillside in County Kerry, Ireland, in mist. Just that: no artwork on display, no stone circle, no line of turf pressed down by Long's boots. Just a hillside of stones and grass. The title of this piece is *Throwing a Stone Around MacGillycuddy's Reeks*. The text then explains the artwork: 'Starting from where I found it, I threw a stone, walked to the landing place and from there threw it forward again' (RL, 53). So Long follows the trajectory of a stone. These moving stone works exist in a strange relation with the viewer, who sees merely a photo, all very nicely shot and framed, of an Irish hillside, a Lappland moor, a path in Nepal.

There's no image, for instance, of the artist picking up or dropping the stone, as many performance or body artists would include (and plenty body artists would find an excuse to take their clothes off too). No image, even, of the stone itself, but a wide shot of the landscape in which the act occurred. Richard Long's photography is not photo-journalism, then: it seldom depicts something in the act of happening. Any reporter and photographer sent to cover a Richard Long stone walkwork in progress would go for one thing first: a photo of the artist in the act of making the work, picking up, throwing, kicking or skimming stones. Instead, Long's photographs have the dis-embodied emptiness which Zen Buddhist monks would approve of.

Other photo pieces of Richard Long's include *The Crossing Place of 2 Somerset Walks,* one of my favourite Long photoworks. The location is Long's heartland, the South West of Albion, and the black-and-white picture reveals a crossroads of two metalled country roads. Black and white cows in the background happily munch grass in a meadow, and there's one of those old country signposts, on the left of the frame, one of those signs with the lettering in black, the white sign edged in black. The sign gives the mileage: 'Stawell 1', 'Moorlinch 1' (these are hamlets near the A39, halfway between Street and Bridgwater).

It's a photograph of a typical country scene, but not much else. Indeed, many people would not look at it twice, as there's nothing much 'happening' in it. Further, there is no 'centre' to the photograph, no person or action or event to hold interest. It's not a picture that would maintain the attention of a newspaper audience, unless the caption anchored the photograph to some great event, such as: 'This crossroads is half a mile from the site where Queen Victoria launched the first spacecraft' (unlikely but not impossible), or, even more sensationalist: 'This is the place where mad axeman Jeff Blumenfeld buried his last victim after ritually abusing her assisted by a coven of witches and ten naked A-list celebrities' (slightly less improbable).

Richard Long's photograph in *The Crossing Place of 2 Somerset Walks,* though, has nothing immediately arresting about it. That's why I like it: it has the blankness and ordinariness of Nowhere-In-Particular (yet it so pointedly captures as aspect of rural Britain). It looks like the sort of picture art students take as they wander about aimlessly with a camera. Or perhaps someone has fired off the last couple of frames, to use up the film, after stopping to phone their analyst/ mother/ husband/ lawyer/ trainer in a layby. Long's photograph, however, is firmly anchored in Conceptual art, because the caption says:

THE CROSSING PLACE OF 2 SOMERSET WALKS

A 40 MILE SOUTHWARD WALK FROM THE AVON BORDER TO THE DORSET BORDER
A 76 MILE EASTWARD WALK FROM THE DEVON BORDER TO THE WILTSHIRE BORDER

ENGLAND 1977

The photograph, it turns out, is about walking, the experience of a walk. 'A figure walking down his road, making his mark.'[4] The photograph that accompanies the walk *A Hundred Tors In a Hundred Hours* is simpler: it's a photograph of a tor (Combestone Tor); just the rocks themselves, no one else's in the picture. Underneath the photograph is a list of the 100 clumps of Dartmoor rock that Long visited during his walk (Yes Tor, Black Tor, Shelstone Tor, Sourton Tor, and so on [RL, 93]).

Note that almost all of Richard Long's photographs are taken during the daytime (with twilight and occasional dawn shots too). Nighttime photography doesn't seem to be something Long has ventured into, even though many of his walkworks take place at night (Long will sometimes walk through a day and into the night). Night photography requires different technicalities (a tripod is fairly essential, fast film, additional lighting). While some sculptors have produced pieces which're meant to be viewed at night (Andy Goldsworthy, James Turrell, Nancy Holt), Long tends to consign nighttime art to his textworks. In an early work (1970), conducted on Dartmoor (naturally), Long walked throughout the night, guided by his compass, along the same straight line, over six consecutive nights, documenting the time it took him each night.

The relationship between titles and the documentation and artworks is precarious in land art, because the photography, the documentation and the title and description of the artwork is often all that remains of it. Richard Long's cairns or lines made by flattening grass will soon be lost. Stuart Morris wrote:

> Richard Long's records of travel challenged fundamental availability to perception, showing temporary arrangements of on-site materials as [a] reminder of some transient human presence.[5]

Christo says his art is 'about displacement. Basically even today I am a displaced person. And this is why I make art that does not last. Of course, it will stay for ever in the minds of people.'[6] Christo here espouses the fundamental Romanticism in land art: that it will live on in the memories of people. Or Lawrence Weiner's notion that once a sculpture is inside someone's head as an idea or experience it was impossible to get it out.

This is how the art of contemporary (postmodern) artists such as Richard Long, Yves Klein, Andy Warhol, Joseph Beuys and Carl Andre differs from traditional Western art. They use the *actual object*, a process begun by Marcel Duchamp with his *Urinal, Bicycle Wheel* and *Bottle Rack* and developed by Kurt Schwitters. Instead of using a replica or imitation or image of a rock or piece of wood, Long uses the rock and wood themselves. The confusions of this relationship between reality and illusion, object and image, life and art in Long's art are compounded by his use of photography, which instantly renders everything an image, a mode of representation, a simulation, a copy, subject to all the strictures and structures of art and representation. The photographs in Long's art are plainly *not* the object in itself, but a representation of it, which is very different, and much more complicated.

The land artist has to face up to the fact that most people know about her/ his art from photographs. Most people who know of Richard Long have *not* seen a Richard Long exhibition; have *not* seen his art in its outdoor environment; have *not* seen the sculptor making a work. They have bought the books, or seen photos of his art in magazines and books. For the punter who consumes art in books and printed material (or on TV or radio or the internet) the 'real' art object doesn't need to exist: what counts is the representation of it in digital, electronic and printed media. But this would upset a realist/ sensualist (i.e., a modernist) like Long, who still enshrines the sculpted object. Yet that is how much art is consumed. Punters have bought the books, seen the photos in magazines and that, for them, is Richard Long's art. Thus, the *photographs* of Long's sculptures are *already* 'so real' that they have, for the consumer, replaced the art itself. In an age of simulcra (Jean Baudrillard), the simulcra not the art predominates. The photographs are incomplete on their own, as artworks: they require the spectator to create the rest of the artwork by using their imagination and memory, the cultural response, by remembering what it was like to be on a mountain, or in a forest, or on a walk. To recall what it was like to be a child, touching stones or snow or ice.[7]

The viewer, then, supplies the 'reality', the 'real' experience, the effect, which the photographs suggest but cannot complete. This could be another reason for the continuing popularity of land art: that land art leaves some part of the sculptures incomplete, and the viewer can supply the rest from their many memories of the real world (because the viewer *likes* to do a bit of work of deciphering and interpreting. Also, the viewer is given just enough decoding to do, but not too much – getting the balance right is critical). A kind of art of interactivity, fed by nature photography. It's also a not insignificant fact that by the time the photographs are published or exhibited in a gallery, most of Long's sculptures have already ceased to exist (they've been blown away, collapsed, eroded, dissolved, dismantled, etc).

Of course, art consumers would probably like to know that the stones *really were* placed in a circle on a Nepalese mountainside, or that Richard Long really *did* walk through the Shirakami mountains in Japan in 1997 when he made *A Walk In a Green Forest*. It's probably essential, in fact, for many spectators to think that Long really made those works. But Yves Klein faked his *Leap* (which enhanced it), and invited people to see an empty gallery. In the age of art impresarios and art 'terrorists' (such as Yves Klein, Andy Warhol, Claes Oldenburg, Jeff Koons, Bruce Nauman, Piero Manzoni, Gilbert & George, the KLF), when artworks are only known through radio, TV, the web and the press, Richard Long could have faked everything. (There are numerous techniques to fake still images – not just with computers, digital manipulation and Photoshop, but older methods such as montage, airbrushing and printing separate negatives. Consider masters of photographic superimposition such as Oscar Rejlander, Henry Peach Robinson, Alexander Rodchenko, Max Ernst or John Heartfield).

9

'A Place of Regeneration': Dartmoor

For me Dartmoor is a place of regeneration, knowledge, history and continuity.

Richard Long[1]

I can't analyze why it is mysterious, why it is beautiful to walk across Dartmoor in a straight line all day, but it is. And because it is beautiful for me to do that, it is good enough for me to make it into art.

Richard Long[2]

Dartmoor is Richard Long's main 'landscape of the soul' (although the area around Bristol would also contend for that title, with possibly parts of rural Scotland as a runner-up). Dartmoor re-appears in one guise or another in most of Long's exhibitions and books. The names of particular places begin to take on a holy aspect, part of a personal litany: Great Gnat's Head, West Dart River, Longford Tor, River Tavy, Grimspound, Great Miss Tor, and so on. In a textwork such as *A Straight Northward Walk Across Dartmoor* (1979), the inventory of beloved sites (East Dart River, White-horse Hill, Naker's Hill) is interspersed with Long's familiar shorthand phrases, listed in a vertical format: 'cairn', 'bracken', 'red lake'.[3] In one show and book, *Mountains and*

Water, Dartmoor is the site or a component of many of the artworks: *Dartmoor Riverbed Stones, Dart, Tamar, Exe, Two Straight Twelve Mile Walks on Dartmoor, Great Gnat's Head, Tide Walk, Dartmoor Stones* and *Muddy Boots Walk.* Any retrospective book or exhibition of Long's is bound to feature a good proportion of Dartmoor works. This is from *Mirage* (1998):

A FOUR DAY WALK ON DARTMOOR

EITHER SLOW WALKING
OR MEANDERING WALKING
OR STRAIGHT WALKING
OR FAST WALKING

Richard Long enjoys Dartmoor for its very abstractness: it is a landscape with seemingly few 'human' marks on it (allowing artists plenty of leeway to imagine whatever they like).

> I also like moorland. Dartmoor can be wonderful. It has very flat hills. It is like an abstract landscape, which is very suitable for making a straight walk. I can walk in a straight line in this very beautiful, empty, flat place... (IC, 2, 14)

Long does simple things in his art. He goes for walks. He does the same thing over and over again: following circular or straight lines on maps and as indicated by his compass. Relying on the compass reading or a line on a map prepared beforehand creates a very simple structure (which can be tough to follow), and frees the artist up for an exploration of other aspects of a walk (Long is still mapreading while he's walking pre-planned routes). The flatness and abstraction of the Dartmoor terrain is particularly suited, Long says, to a straight line walk. In mountainous regions, straight line walks are impractical (even for shaman who can fly), so each walk is defined by its location:

each walk fits the place. I can do straight line on Dartmoor and I can do a footpath walk in Nepal. Another thing to say about the straight line is, I can do them whatever the weather. If the mist comes down I can just look at the compass. I cannot see where I am going but I can still make a walk. (IC, 2, 14)

Although it seems 'flat', Dartmoor is quite high above sea level – high for Britain, that is. The peaks in the North of Dartmoor are over 2,000 feet; the mean elevation of Dartmoor proper is 1,200 feet. As one stands on the High Moors and look outwards, one sees just how elevated it is, how the lowland in the distance is gently rolling green pastures, while the moors slope upwards by 500 or 600 feet.

The amount of history (or 'heritage', to use that very 1980s word) in, on and around Dartmoor is impressive. It is a landscape, for a start, which has changed little since it was formed some 280 million years ago. It is part of the tract of granite that runs from Devon through Cornwall to the Scilly Isles. Dartmoor has a deep sense of prehistory, and of ancient life (humans have lived here for around 7,000 years – Dartmoor was above the deeply wooded areas which covered much of England. It also had water in abundance, rocks aplenty for building materials, areas to farm and keep animals, and other factors). There are many human artefacts on Dartmoor – hut circles, cairns, stone circles, stone rows (60 plus), old tracks, old settlements, walls, as well as gorges, bogs, clay pits, quarries, cairns and clapper bridges. At Merrivale, for instance, there is a dense group of hut circles, stone rows, settlements, standing stones, disused tin workings, quarries and cairns. These centuries of human history and human marks on the landscape form an important element of Richard Long's art. Always he emphasizes the sense of travelling over ground that many people before him have trod upon; in Dartmoor, one is made aware of this 7,000 year historical dimension continually.

There's just enough within the landscape to hold the eye in Dartmoor, yet not too much that the walker can't let their imaginations run wild. It's easy to imagine Dartmoor being used as film location requiring no set dressing at all for a battle between a Roman legion and a band of Celts or Saxons; a group of mediæval knights galloping on horseback; King Lear in the storm on the heath; and the wide expanses of low hills are perfect for a Napoleonic conflict, where every section of the forces is visible from the upper slopes.

In fact, as movies go, Dartmoor has been the setting for precisely some of those historical periods, including *Revolution*, the 1985 flop about the American Civil War, which shot at Deancombe Valley, and nearby Kington and Bigbury bay. For *Knights of* the *Round Table* (1953), a classic Hollywood Arthurian romp with Robert Taylor, Ava Gardner and Mel Ferrer, a castle was built at Haytor Vale. The softer, tamer landscapes to the South of Dartmoor have been used far more than the more inaccessible highlands (*Sense and Sensibility* [1995], for instance, one of the best of the heritage costume dramas, shot as Saltram House and the Flete Estate, both towards Plymouth, and the church at Berry Pomeroy in the beautiful South Hams district of Devon).

Plenty of artists have lived in Dartmoor or visited it to make art: J.M.W. Turner, Thomas Girtin, Edward Lear, Edward Burra, John Skeaping, and Graham Ovenden.[5] Long's contemporary, sculptor Peter Randall-Page, lives on Dartmoor (at Drewsteignton). Alan Lee, the fantasy illustrator who contributed immensely to *The Lord of the Rings* films, lives – like fellow illustrator Brian Froud – at Chagford.

One part of Dartmoor Richard Long keeps returning to: the heads of the rivers Tamar, Exe, East Dart, West Dart, Tavy and others. This is the Northern and wildest part of the moor, the part where soldiers are trained, and where there are a number of Ministry of Defence firing ranges (Okehampton Range, Merrivale Range, Willsworthy Range). This part of Dartmoor has 'DANGER AREA' printed in red over it on the map (visitors are discouraged or forbidden to pass – the military has taken over huge chunks of the British Isles, including some of the loveliest, wildest and most interesting regions, such as Dartmoor, Wales and Dorset).

The landscape of this part of Dartmoor is 'bleak', in the traditional, *Wuthering Heights* sense (i.e., the classic Dartmoorscape). It appears featureless to someone used to a densely-layered cultural space, like a city. Of course, there *are* features: stone walls and fences, which are built all over Dartmoor, including up very steep inclines; observation posts; cairns; streams; pools; Dartmoor letterboxes; paths and tracks; heather; bracken; peat; Dartmoor ponies; tors; sheepfolds; and rocks *everywhere*. The sources of the rivers themselves are simply little pools in among the long grass and bogs (the visitor expecting more will be disappointed by the river sources).

Two Walks was an early Long Dartmoor walkwork (1972), a map-and-photo-work (i.e., the work comprised part of a map of Dartmoor, and a small photograph of a stone cross where two walks met (near the main road, the B3212, one of the most spectacular roads in England, which runs across the centre of Dartmoor).

Richard Long's *A Walk On Dartmoor* (2001) is a photographic work which embodies the appealing absence of Dartmoor's terrain: it consists of a colour plate of the classic Dartmoorscape: bare, grassy hills receding to the horizon, a blue sky, and a couple of birds on the wing. It's the area around the East Dart River, Wistman's Wood and

Sittaford Tor (Wistman's Wood is a terrifically atmospheric spot of stunted oaks and mossy boulders North of Two Bridges, perfect for an encounter with fairies out of Grimms' fairy tales). In a way, the picture in *A Walk On Dartmoor* says everything and nothing. The emptiness is precisely the fullness (in the 'less is more' manner of Eastern mysticism).

The text opposite the image in the *Walking the Line* book (2002) is also cryptically spare (with a palindromic quality):

RIVER TO WOOD
WOOD TO TOR
TOR TO RIVER
RIVER TO TOR
TOR TO WOOD
WOOD TO RIVER[4]

Dartmoor has its own very commanding atmosphere, look and feeling. Britain is a very crowded little island, but in parts of Dartmoor it can feel very wild and isolated. With the wind and rain whipping around, it can seem to go on for miles. But it's not that big at all. And in any part of Dartmoor the visitor can't ever be more than a few miles from the nearest human being. There are plenty of regions more remote than Dartmoor in Britain (central Wales or the Scottish highlands or Southern Ireland, for instance), but Dartmoor creates an unforgettable impression.

At the heart of Dartmoor is a black hole of pain: Dartmoor Prison, situated in the grim town of Princetown, the biggest settlement on the high moors. French and Americans were held here (during and after the Napoleonic wars); hundreds perished on the moors. There are now around 700 prisoners.

Dartmoor is all contradiction: although the stereotype image of Dartmoor is of wild, harsh moorland, it is in fact carefully managed, and human marks are all over it. Even in the most remote spots there are manifestations of humanity. The stone walls, for instance, run everywhere, and must have taken months or years to construct. Although it seems to stretch on forever, it is not that big: Dartmoor National Park is 23 miles East to West and 24 miles North to South. It comprises only 365 square miles. The granite tableland itself is some 300 square miles. For Britain, that's a sizable portion of land; in many another territory, it's a backyard.

Even after a few visits to Dartmoor all of the main villages, roads and landmarks become familiar, so for Richard Long, who's been using Dartmoor as his backdoor studio for decades, they must be intimately known: Ashburton, Dartmeet, Princetown, Two Bridges, Postbridge, Moretonhampstead, Tavistock, Buckfastleigh, Holne, Scorriton, Castle Drogo, Merrivale, Okehampton, Grimspound, Widecombe-in-the-Moor. The tors themselves are a wonderful creation of nature for easy navigation. Each one is a sculpture (like Dartmoor itself), as Barbara Hepworth said of the moors in Northern Britain, and each one is individual: Rough Tor, Hound Tor, Vixen Tor, Sheep's Tor, Combestone Tor, Yes Tor. You couldn't plan a series of landmarks for a sculpture trail better than the outcrops of weathered granite atop each hill.

What fascinates Richard Long about this sort of moorland may be its purity: it is a place of the source of the rivers: this chimes with the Conceptual artist's project of going to extremes with a process or idea, reaching the essence or source. Thus, once the artist as walker has found a river, one of her/ his automatic inclinations is to follow it to its source (one sees groups of waterproof-clad walkers doing just that in Dartmoor). It is an ancient desire, made most famous, perhaps, in the quest for the source of the Nile in the early modern era (and it's part of the frontier and exploration spirit, once immortalized in the deeds of explorers, mariners and adventurers, but now dubbed the aggressive expansionist acts of capitalism, exploitation and imperialism). Though no river in the South West (or in all of Britain) has quite the same sense of grandeur and history of the River Nile (though the Thames is packed with history), these little Dartmoor rivers (Dart, Tamar, Exe, Tavy), have their own atmosphere and poetry (indeed, the Dart becomes a grand river when it reaches Dartmouth and, in its way, I'd say the River Dart's as beautiful and spectacular along its winding route as any of the great rivers of the world. And walking beside Dartmoor's rivers and streams is as enriching as anywhere else. Richard Long has encompassed the River Dart in a classic (and poetic) fashion in 1999's *Continuum Walk*, where he carried water culled from the mouth of the river to its source on Dartmoor).

Thus, in that flat grass and peat moorland (as in the *Dart, Tamar, Exe* walk in *Mountains and Water*), Richard Long takes an idea to its extreme, following the river to its source, in a landscape already hypnotically abstract. Another work in the same 1992 exhibition, *Dartmoor Riverbed Stones*, links together a host of the little rivers and streams of Dartmoor: River Mardle, River Tavy, River Plym, River Okement and River Teign. These are the rivers and brooks which Long has known for decades. Walkers have to love these little streams (or at least deal with them), for they have to be forded one way or another (easy on the high moors in the North, where the rivers are fairly small, but trickier further South as they widen towards the sea). One of the specialities of Dartmoor (which saves leaps and lunges) are the clapper bridges and the stepping stones, which appear in Long's artworks. The heavy granite boulders which do for stepping stones and the great clapper bridges fit in so well with Dartmoor's rugged, stony landscape. The reddened, iron ore rivers are the source, too, of much of the life of the moors themselves, as well as providing washing water and (if careful) drinking water for the walker.

Far from being a quiet place Dartmoor is noisy – there is the wind, for a start, sometimes whipping around the face and body, creating all manner of sounds. There are the birds – exquisite skylarks in late Spring, for instance, and buzzards and kestrels. There are sheep, Dartmoor ponies, horses, cows, rabbits and other animals. And there is the rain (and plenty of it). And water everywhere – the many chattering streams, the bogs and the pools. Walking right next to one of the larger rivers, for example, can be extremely loud – the boulders in the rivers create an insistent white noise.

Certainly Dartmoor is wet – one of the wettest places in Britain. At the highest peaks, the annual rainfall is over 100 inches. That's two and a half metres of rain. (True, that's not much compared to Cherrapunji, Meghalaya in India, where 1,041 inches fell between August 1, 1860 and July 31, 1861. Or the highest average annual rainfall (467 inches), at Mawsynram, Meghalaya in India.)

Water is draining off the granite plateau of Dartmoor all the time – there are many springs and streams. This constant presence of water in Dartmoor becomes a key part of Richard Long's walks, as it does for any walker on the moors. When it rains in Dartmoor, it can really rain. It doesn't matter which way the wind is blowing. Even so-called 'sunny' days in Dartmoor are often a brief moment of sunshine followed by clouds, then rain. If one looks at Long's Dartmoor photographs, they are by no means sunny and bright, but often murky and misty (see the photograph that goes with 'Great Gnat's Head', a 1992 walk, in *Mountains and Waters*).

Every footstep in Dartmoor is (or seems to be) waterlogged, every step is upon water, or mud, or peat, or boggy ground (for a hard granite outcrop, Dartmoor is a very squashy, moist place). The water and rainfall is one thing that's striking about Dartmoor, and appears in most of Long's Dartmoor works. The other thing is its height. One thinks of a plateau as something level and low, but Dartmoor has peaks well over

500 metres, which again makes it comparable with mountainous Wales or Scotland. Indeed, the highest town in Britain is in Dartmoor: the dour prison community of Princetown (where, in the swish Dartmoor National Park Information Centre one can see a Richard Long textwork, in amongst the displays of Dartmoor's history, geology and topography).

10

Walking as Ecstasy

I must go walk the woods so wild
And wander here and there.

Sir Thomas Wyatt1

Richard Long does sometimes speak in poetic, religious terms of his art – 'art should be a religious experience' he says,2 but he also reminds viewers: 'I am not a religious traveller' (SF). Although his sculptures alter the world – no physical *object* can avoid altering the world – he maintains (like a Taoist or Zen follower) that he takes his cue from the landscape, instead of imposing on it 'from outside', as it were: 'I use the world as I find it'.3 Bill Woodrow, a contemporary of Long's, also 'uses' the world as he finds it.4

Richard Long's views have something in common with Zen Buddhism, Taoism, Shinto, American Indian religion, Australian aboriginal 'dreaming', archaic shamanism and Western magic.5 It's not intentional, the Long-Zen connection, and Long is flattered that people find it in his work (FC VI, 18). However, a piece such as 'Mind Rock', in which, during an 11 day walk, the artist bears 'a rock in mind', is given a Zen connotation: first the walk occurs in Japan; it links notions of 'mind' (contemplation) and reality (the rock) in a Zen meditation or *zazen* fashion; and it is a textwork seen next to a photograph that evokes the Japanese Zen gardens (in *Mountains and Waters*). The sculpture and the place are one, in a mystical relationship, as Richard Long points out in his writings:

> The material and the idea are of the place; sculpture and place are one, the same. The place is as far as the eye can see from the sculpture. The place for a sculpture is found by walking. Some works are a succession of particular places along a walk, e.g. *Milestones*. In this work, the walking, the places and the stones all have equal importance.[6]

When he walks, Richard Long has remarked, as so many walkers have said, '[w]hile I am in the landscape... I am in a very good state of mind' (IC 1, 5). The Cornish poet Peter Redgrove told me in 1994 that 'the ideal state for everyday going about is the first stage of orgasmic arousal'.[7] It's typical of Peter Redgrove to eroticize the artist's state of being aware, of being-in-the-world, to sexualize the artist's creativity (he's really just talking about the heightened state of consciousness necessary for making art, or just good living). A religionist or mystic might talk about being in a slight trance, or prayer, or a mild form of spiritual contemplation. Walking as meditation. Or therapy. Or yoga. Or tantra. Or the aboriginal Dreaming.

'Ecstasy' can seem too strong a word for it, but it is ecstasy. It is 'walking' in the Taoist sense; that is, walking as another name for feeling ecstatic. 'A journey in the wilderness becomes a fantastic focus of concentration. I can get totally absorbed in the place and totally absorbed in my work' Long said (IC 1, 14).

The very activity of walking releases chemicals in the brain and body that promote pleasure.[8] Joggers, sports and physical fitness enthusiasts get hooked on them sometimes. 'I think the sexual energy or the energy of creativity or the adrenalin energy you get from being on a mountain, sometimes they are all very close' Richard Long remarked (IC 2, 22). The physical action of walking is soothing, contemplative, sensual. Hamish Fulton spoke of the meditative benefits of walking, how it reduces the 'constant chatter in the head' and promotes 'meditative moments' (2002). Since time immemorial people have 'walked off' their problems; infants can be calmed by walking; and many artists and philosophers were famous for their walks: Arthur Schopenhauer and Immaneul Kant took twilit walks; Thomas Hardy tramped through Dorset; William Wordsworth and Samuel Taylor Coleridge walked in the Lake District; some writers were known as 'supertramps'; Henry Miller was in ecstasy simply by walking around the backstreets of New York and Paris (as eloquently described in trilogies of the *Tropic of Cancer* and *The Rosy Crucifixion*). 'Walking itself has a cultural history, from Pilgrims to the wandering Japanese poets, the English Romantics and contemporary long-distance walkers' said Long (WL, 68).

One thinks of the great walker poets and artists. Friedrich Hölderlin, for instance, the visionary German Romantic poet, and his long hikes through Western Europe between tutoring posts (the artist struggling to support himself by teaching). And that fateful last lengthy trek of Hölderlin's, from Germany, over the Alps, to Bordeaux in January, 1804, which he walked alone. And after it, Hölderlin's mental disturbance approached all too swiftly (also brought on by the death of his beloved, Susette Gonthard, an unattainable married woman). Hölderlin's is an incredible life story: after writing some of the most sublime poetry ever as a young man (much of it in the High Romantic mode: 'Hyperion's Song of Fate', 'The Poet's Courage', 'To Diotima', 'The Blind Singer'), Hölderlin spent the rest of life (some forty years) mentally ill, cared for by a carpenter, Ernst Zimmer, in the 'tower' at Zimmer's house in Tübingen (until Hölderlin's death in 1843).

John Cowper Powys's walks have already been cited here – the daily (morning and afternoon) walks, intricately ritualized, which Powys undertook without fail in all weathers in upstate New York, rural Dorset (in Dorchester and East Chaldon) and finally, for the last thirty years of his life, in grim, mountainous and remote North Wales (in Corwen and Blaenau-Ffestiniog).

Or the incredible restlessness and rebellion of French poet-genius Arthur Rimbaud: always running away from home as a teenager (to Paris and Brussels), and being dragged back home to Charleville, the increasingly desperate drifter existence across Europe (London, Stuttgart, walking to Wütrtenberg, then Switzerland, then Italy, the Cyclades, Marseilles, Scandinavia, Hamburg, Antwerp), the fraught affair with Paul Verlaine, joining the Dutch army then deserting, and winding up in Aden and Abyssinia, a profoundly bored businessman (and possible gun-runner and slave trader). Rimbaud always had to be in movement. A life of disenchantment, disaffection, alienation, wandering, debauchery, and intense self-loathing. Oh – and he composed, between the ages of 16 and 19, perhaps the best poetry ever written.

This's from *A Season In Hell*:

Je dus voyager, distraire les enchantments assemblés sur mon cerveau. Sur la mer, que j'aimais comme si elle eût dû me laver d'une souillure, je voyais se lever la croix consolatrice. J'avais été damné par l'arc-en-ciel. Le Bonheur était ma fatalité, mon remords, mon ver: ma vie serait toujours trop immense pour être dévouée à la force et à la beauté. ("Delirium II: Alchemy of the Word")[10]

Stephen Bann remarked that an artist who makes art by systematically walking through the countryside will seem archaic and even quaint in a few decades, just as the boy scout movement of the 1930s seems intriguing and slightly sinister.

Just as a person on foot in a rich American suburb is a focus of immediate suspicion, it is conceivable that a person who walks all over roads, lanes and double tracks may soon appear eccentric, if the public pressure protecting rights of way is not maintained. (1994b).

Of course, in many territories walking will not die out for some time. Hun-dreds of millions of people don't have cars, or transport, or even access to transport.

For my part [said Robert Louis Stevenson] I travel not to go anywhere, but *to go*. I travel for travel's sake. The great affair is to *move*.[11]

Bruce Chatwin made walking and nomadic existence his central theme – in his life as in his art (as with Richard Long). Chatwin wrote of nomads and caravans; the nomadic existence of ancient peoples; the Bedouin; of mediæval quests; church pilgrimages; and the ritual aspects of migration.[12] Chatwin asserted that 'we should perhaps allow nature an appetitive drive for movement in the widest sense. The act of journeying contributes towards a sense of physical and mental well-being...' (ib., 221). Tibetan sherpas, Chatwin commented – and this could apply to Richard Long – were

compulsive travellers; and in Sherpa-country every track is marked with cairns and prayer-flags, reminding you that Man's real home is not a house, but the Road, and that life itself is a journey to be walked on foot. (ib., 273)

The Australian aborigines' cult of mythic 'dreamtime' is an affinity often cited here with Richard Long's art: walking plays a central role in both (and Long has walked in some of the landscapes sacred to the Australian aborigines). The dream journeys of the aborigines traverse a spiritualized landscape. As James Cowan put it, the 'sacred journey' was imbued at each stage 'with sacred significance', and in the dreaming, when the aborigine enters the dreamworld, 'the land is transformed into a meta-physical landscape saturated with significance' (1989).

To travel the world so often making walks and works, Richard Long must *really* love walking (*really, really* love walking). There are plenty of easier, sedentary ways of living (or earning money). As well as being somewhat compulsive or obsessive (like many artists), Long must also simply really like to walk. He's the ultimate artist as drifter, as nomad, as wanderer, as traveller, as rolling stone (he's made references to rolling stones in his art).13

Having done a little bit of walking in wildernesses myself, I know that one is continually aware when walking of things like the light (direction, intensity, clarity, colour, tone, contrast, etc); the sun; the sky and clouds; the wind (the sound, the direction, the power, the chill factor); the quality of the ground (smooth, rough, stony, soft); difficult terrain ahead (marshes, hills, gulleys, cliffs); the horizon; landmarks; other people (including walkers); animals; sounds (aircraft, animals, traffic, people); the air temperature; what the weather's doing; the time; distance travelled so far; distance to go; time out and time back; the route (including detours); the next halt (where and when); when to break for lunch (and where); finding a place to camp; thirst and hunger; and how much food and water is left. So it's no surprise that Richard Richard Long's art continually refers to many of these elements of a walk – they are the fundamental stuff of his art.

In an interview, Long compared being in the landscape to the notion of Zen Buddhist *satori*, the 'hereness' and 'nowness' of mystical experience:

> A walk can often be the means of stripping away many things; it can be the spectacular embodiment of the Zen idea of the "here and now". To be alone for a few days in a wilderness is the simplest, best way to be in a one-to-one relationship with a place.14

Richard Long evokes having the *participation mystique* with the Earth, with places and atmospheres and organic materials, that the archaic peoples of the world had (and have). It is a pre-institutionalized, pre-pagan and pantheistic rapport with the world, deliberately eschewing dogma, doctrine and manifestos. It is also part, as many commentators have noted, of a British Romantic tradition, that feeling for nature found in Blake, Turner, Byron, Shelley and Constable.15

The archaic shaman is the ancestor of the artist as ecstatic (the shaman is the progenitor of all these interrelated types: poets, artists, musicians, saints, mystics, ascetics and philosophers). The shaman, Mircea Eliade wrote,

> is above all the specialist in ecstasy. It is owing to his capacity for ecstasies – that is, because he is able, at will, to pass out of his body and undertake mystical journeys through all the cosmic regions – that the shaman is a healer, and a director of souls as well as a mystic and visionary.16

Again, it's not being suggested here that Richard Long is a shaman (or a latter-day incarnation of a shaman). He doesn't dance with drums, speak to animals, commune with spirits, master fire, undertake mystic journeys, fly through the air, descend to Hell or ascend to Heaven, heal people and shepherd souls to other worlds (at least, I don't think he does. Maybe he has a secret shamanic practice in Bristol – there are a few such enterprises in the area). Rather, many of the elements of shamanism can be discerned in Long's art: the ecstatic walking (walking as trance, walking as meditation, walking as yoga, walking as healing, walking as shamanic flight), the wilderness landscapes, the utopian project (the nostalgia for paradise), the communing with the natural world, the totemic animals, and the sacred stones and objects.

The stone circles and the cairns that Richard Long builds have obvious links to the World Tree or *axis mundi* or centre of the world of shamanism.15 And it's maybe no coincidence that Long has walked in many regions which are known for shamanism: such as Lappland, South-West America, Mongolia, Peru and rural Japan. (And Long is part of an increasing interest from the 1960s onwards in shamanism, in Eliade's writing, Grey Owl, Black Elk, John Neihardt, Carlos Casteneda and Don Juan, etc).

What one sees of Richard Long himself suggests a relatively easy and enjoyable life of wandering about, camping, travelling. 'Behind my work is the idea that I have seized an opportunity, won a fantastic freedom, to make art, to lay down abstract ideas, in some of the great places of the world' (RL, 74). Maybe making artwalks is for Long dull, arduous, uninspiring and deadening work, as making art is for some artists, or as work is for those who hate labour. Maybe artwalking is tough, difficult and tedious for Long, like so many jobs are. Somehow, it doesn't seem that way. Long appears to be having a good time.

Lawrence Durrell said a similar thing about Blanco, one of the famous tramps of Provence. The Provençal tramps have no special attitude or religion, Durrell said. Blanco's 'attitude to choice… seems to me exactly the same ecstasy that an artist has *vis-à-vis* his empty canvas or his empty sheet of paper. Because your choice is limitless'.17

The pleasure of travel abounds in Richard Long's art: his walks are always partly about the *jouissance* of walking.

So even with storms or bogs or blisters or tiredness, the way I can make my work is intensely pleasurable and satisfying. Even in the more modest ambience of a road walk, the labyrinth of country roads, the inns, the Bed & Breakfasts, the fabric of country life is still an enjoyable part of making the work and, although not spec- ifically the subject of it, it is implicit in the idea of the work and the place of it. (RL,

74)

Richard Long's art is not angst-ridden, like Vincent van Gogh's or Mark Rothko's; it is not the product of despair and alienation; Long is not a melancholic, obsessive artist like Leonardo da Vinci. He is, in fact, *happy*, a terrible state of affairs for an artist. Happy! Yes: Long is not an artist whose art springs from the depths of rage or sorrow, like some of Amedeo Modigliani's art or Georges Rouault's art seems to. He's not about to rush out into a field and cut off his ear (van Gogh) or shoot himself in his studio (Rothko).

> ...usually I am happy and relaxed [remarked Long]. I would say that the way I make my work is from the things that give me pleasure and the materials that I like using – my work doesn't come from a kind of *angst* or discontent. (RC, 23)

The result of this balanced, relaxed approach to art is that the artworks are the expressions of a celebration of certain places. Richard Long noted:

> A sculpture in a landscape, when it really happens well in a good way, is like a celebration of place and my feelings of me being there and having the right idea at the right time and everything coming together in a good way.

So important are walks for Richard Long, that he regards them as life-nourishing experiences, an essential part of his life:

> After a good walk, yes. After 8 days of seeing almost no people (no talking), long sleeps, deep dreaming, brilliant campsites, sharpened senses, new experiences, new knowledge, getting fit – I always have the feeling of being a slightly changed person after a walk than I was before it. (SF)

The great Chinese sage, Chuang-tzu, wrote: '[i]t is easy to keep from walking, the hard thing is to walk without touching the ground.'[18] Chuang-tzu's paradoxical sentence is typical of Eastern philosophy, where things are simultaneously this and not-this, as in the Zen *koan* or Hinduism's definition of Atman or Brahma. In Taoism, walking itself is a holy activity. 'To 'wander' is the Taoist code word for becoming ecstatic.'[19]

Richard Long is not wholly a walker-artist in the manner of ancient Chinese sages or Japanese wanderer-poets. There are some aspects of the ascetic philosophy of Lao-tzu or the *I Ching* which Long doesn't take up. For instance, the notion of meditation, of 'travelling without moving', the shamanic journeying (in spirit, not in body): one of the most illuminating passages in the *Tao Te Ching* speaks about the benefits of being stationary:

> Without stirring abroad
> One can know the whole world;
> Without looking out of the window
> One can see the way of heaven.
> The further one goes
> The less one knows. (XLVII)

Hélène Cixous, the French feminist, in *Three Steps On the Ladder of Writing* (1993), discussed the connections between walking and creativity which chime with Richard Long's poetry of walking. Cixous eloquently likened the poetic act (or creation, or writing) to movement, in particular walking, to pleasure and sex – to the body in action:

> Walking, dancing, pleasure: these accompany the poetic act. I wonder what kind of poet doesn't wear out their shoes, writes with their head. The true poet is a traveller. Poetry is about travelling on foot and all its substitutes, all forms of transportation.

The poet, reckoned Cixous, creates in motion, writes as s/he moves, moves as s/he writes. Creation, dreaming, movement and art are entwined.

> So perhaps dreaming and writing do have to do with traversing the forest, journeying through the world, using all the available means of transport, using your own body as a form of transport.

The walks take place during the day (usually), but at night the walker is also travelling – in dreaming (like shamanic flight). Hélène Cixous continues (and again, keep in mind Richard Long traversing the world):

> ...we have to walk, to use our whole body to enable the world to become flesh, exactly as this happens in our dreams. In dreams and writing our body is alive: we either use the whole of it or, depending on the dream, a part. We must embark on a body-to-body journey in order to discover the body.

It's in keeping with Cixous' philosophy of embodiment that she should emphasize the body's part in this *jouissance* of creativity. The world can become flesh (lived) only through the body for Cixous. The body can never finally be erased, and Richard Long's art has always been an art of embodiment, of being in the moment physically as well as mentally or spiritually. An art of doing as well as being. Being as movement. Rhythm. Steps. A walk.

Finally, Cixous writes:

> In order to go to the School of Dreams, something must be displaced, starting with the bed. One has to get going. This is what writing is, starting off. It has to do with activity and passivity. This does not mean one will get there. Writing is not arriving; most of the time it's *not arriving*. One must go on foot, with the body. One has to go away, leave the self. How far must one not arrive in order to write, how far must one wander and wear out and have pleasure? One must walk as far as the night. One's own night. Walking through the self toward the dark.[20]

Richard Long's final act would likely be a walk – a Last Walk into the Dark.

Illustrations

On the following pages:
• Some classic landscape painters.
• Images of prehistoric sites in the U.K.
• Images of places linked to Richard Long's art, including Dartmoor in England.

On the following pages are some landscapes linked
to the art of Richard Long, beginning with Dartmoor, England

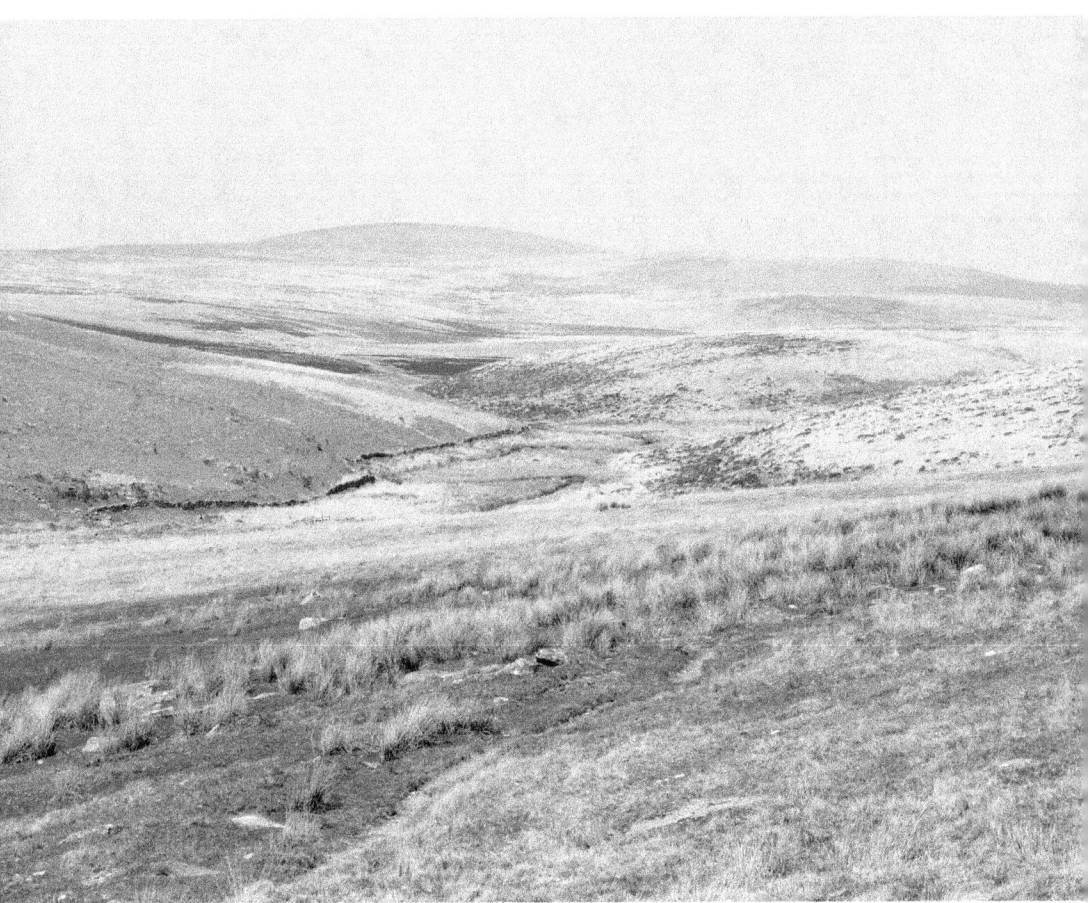

Near Sittaford Tor and Fernworthy Forest, Dartmoor

The Grey Wethers Stone Circle, Dartmoor

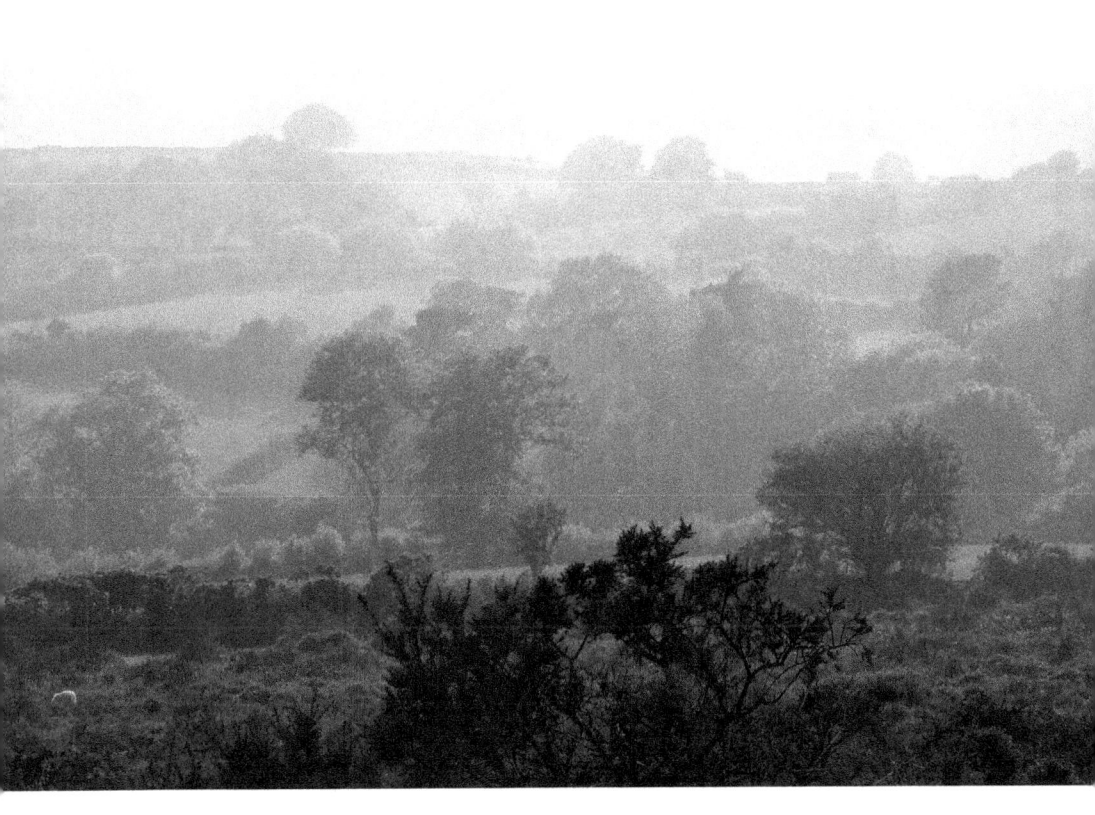

Near Newbridge, Dartmoor

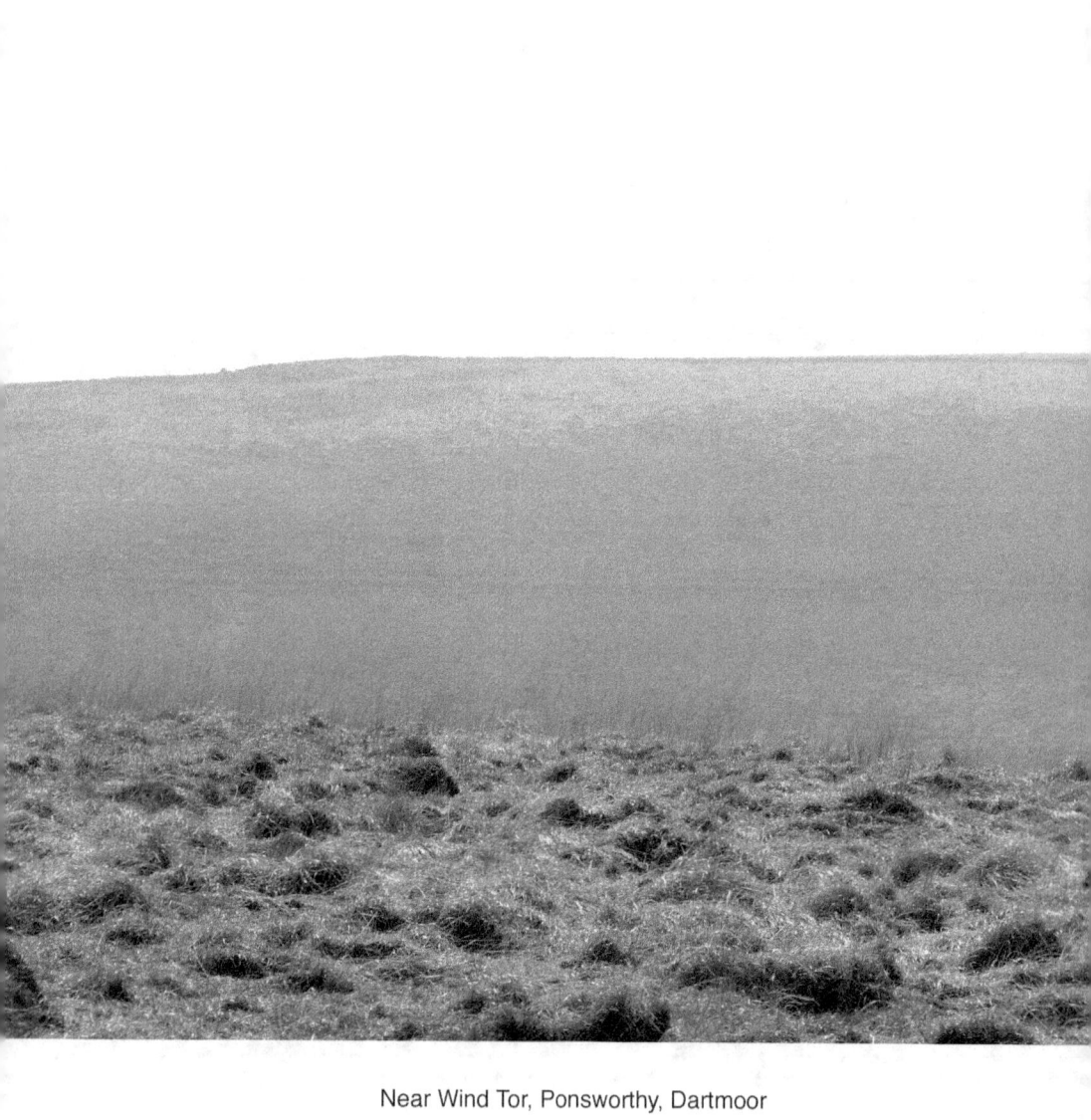

Near Wind Tor, Ponsworthy, Dartmoor

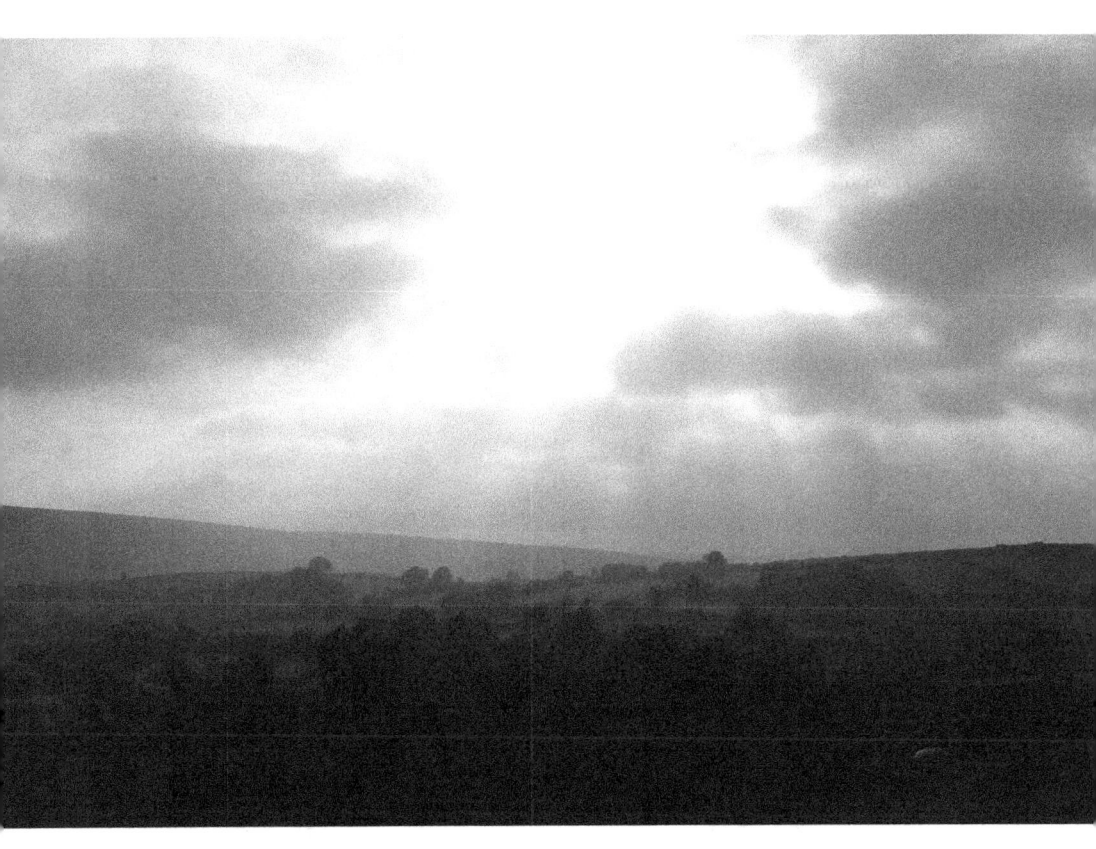

Near Ponsworthy in Dartmoor

Near Ponsworthy, Dartmoor, England

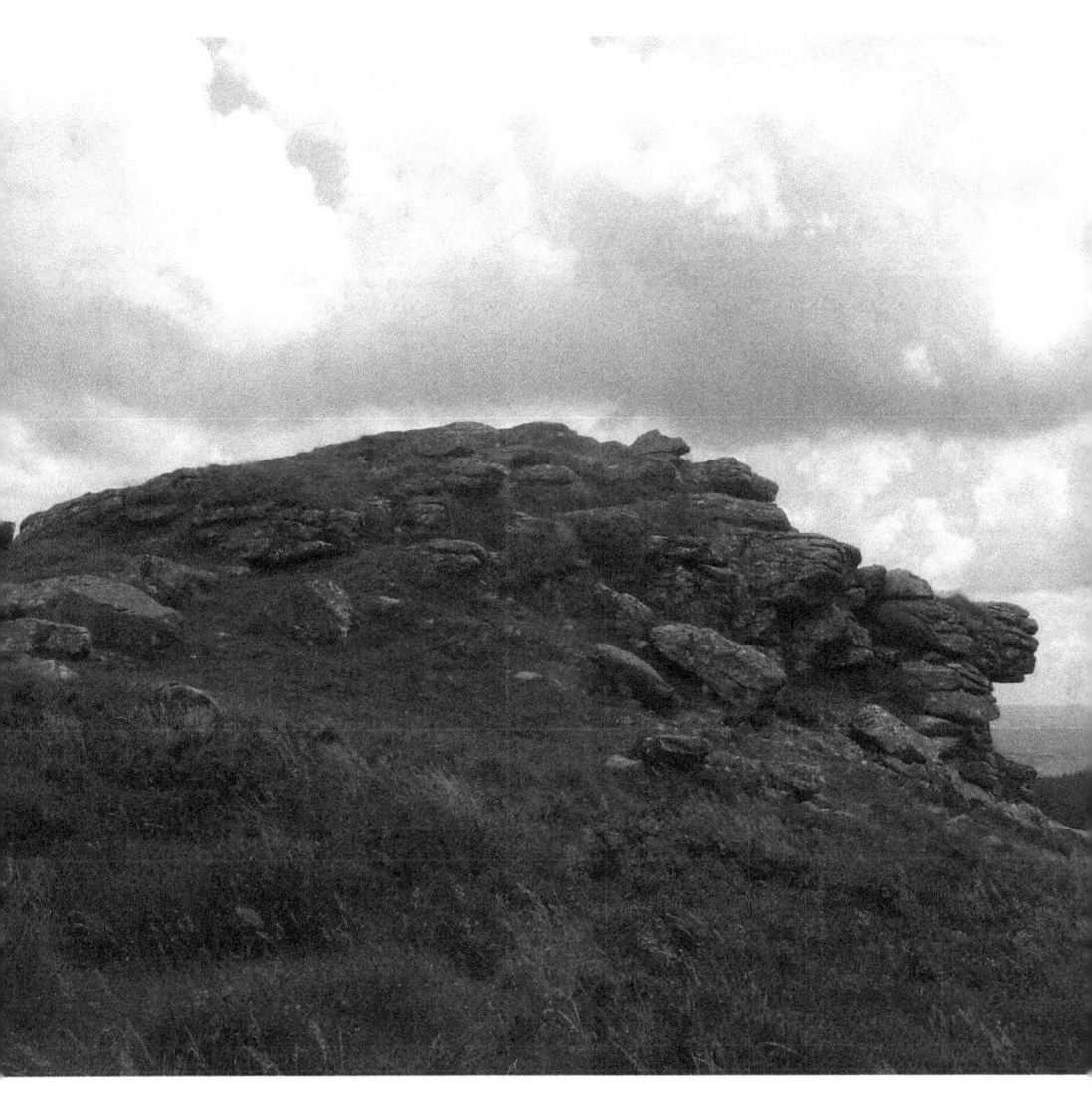

One of Dartmoor's many tors

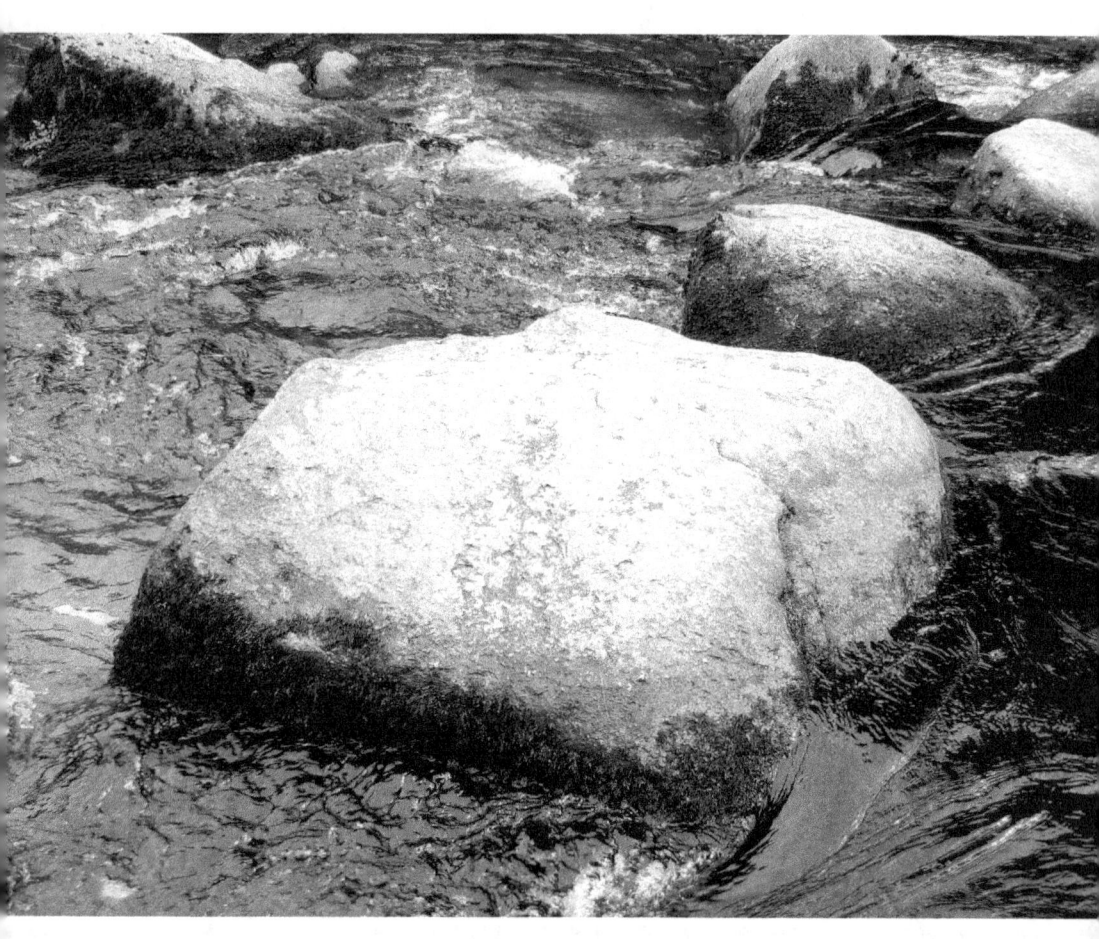

River Dart, near Dartmeet, Dartmoor

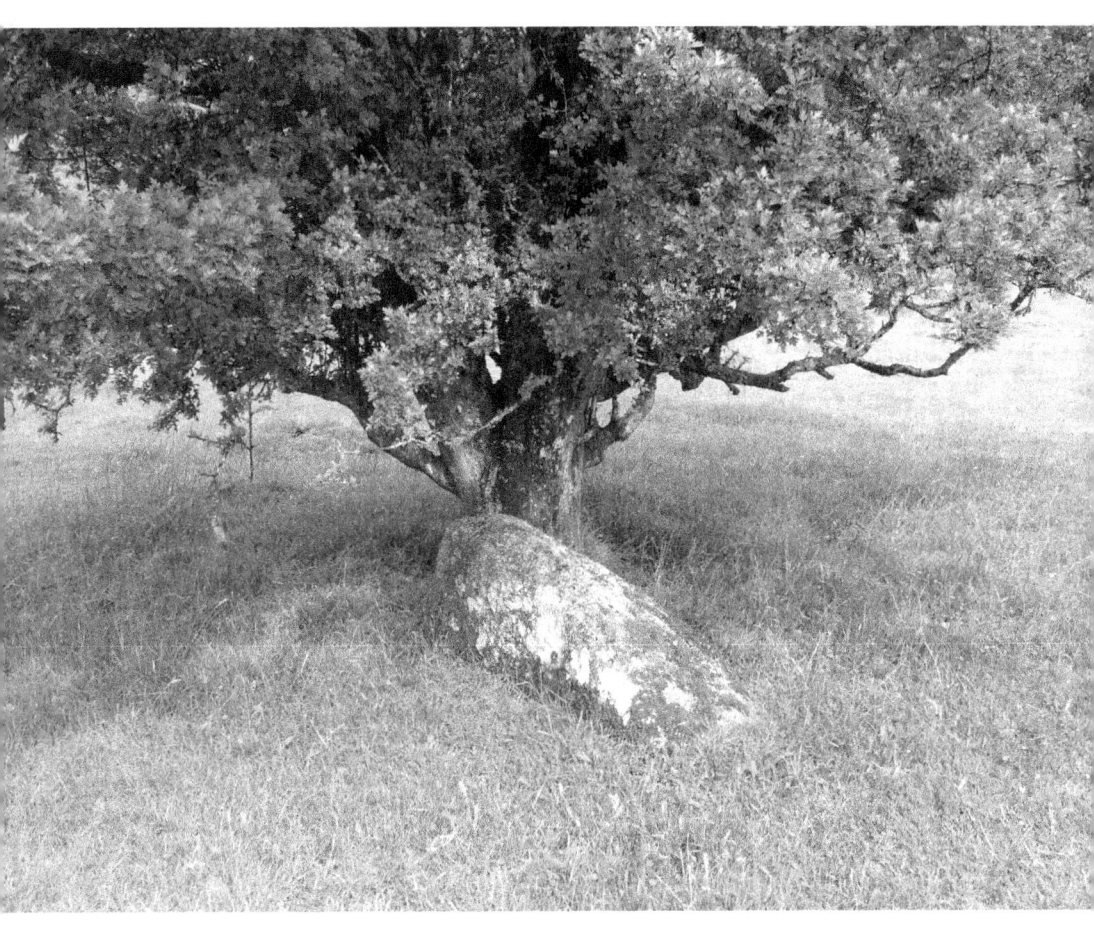

A classic image of England: an oak tree, a granite boulder, and a grassy field.
Near Newbridge, Dartmoor

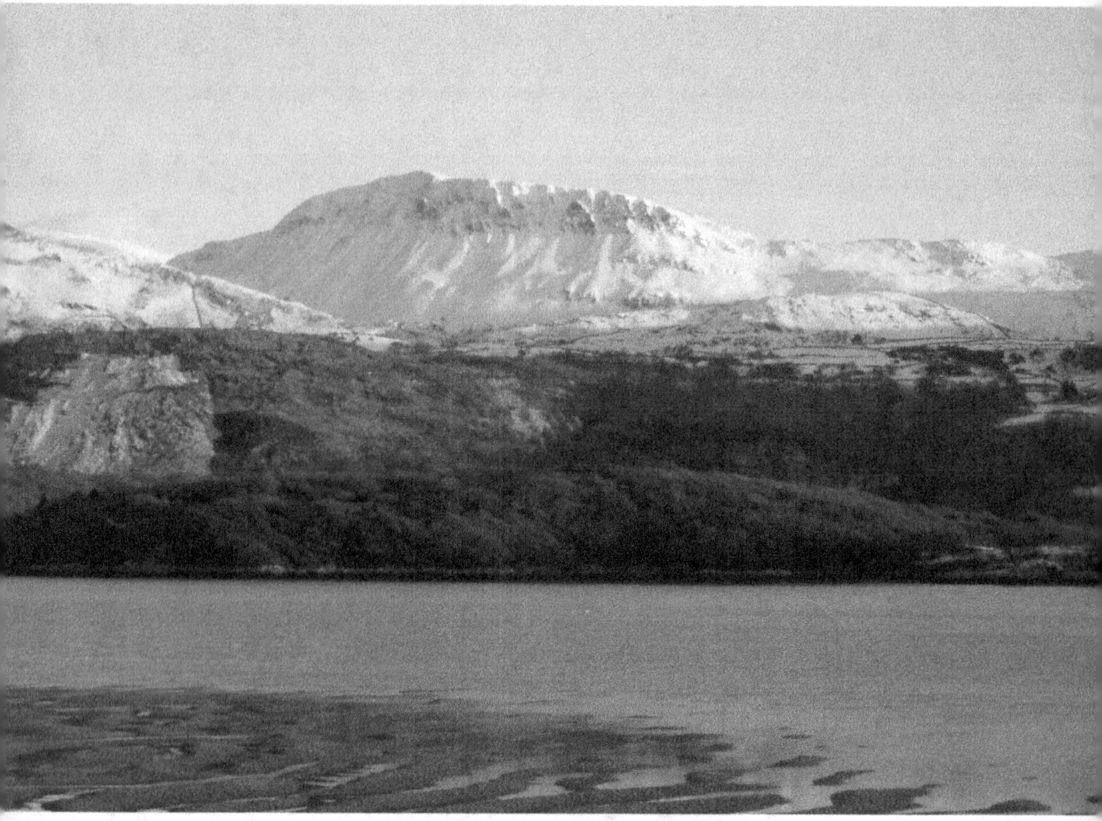

Cader Idris, Snowdonia Mountains, North Wales

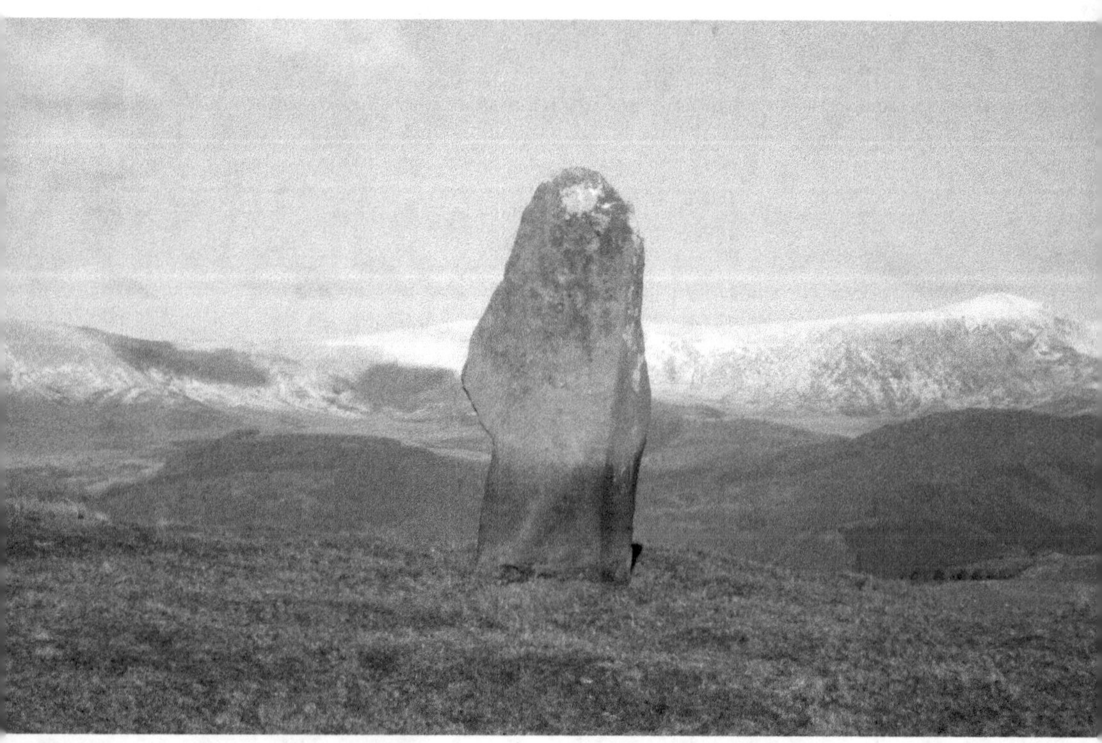

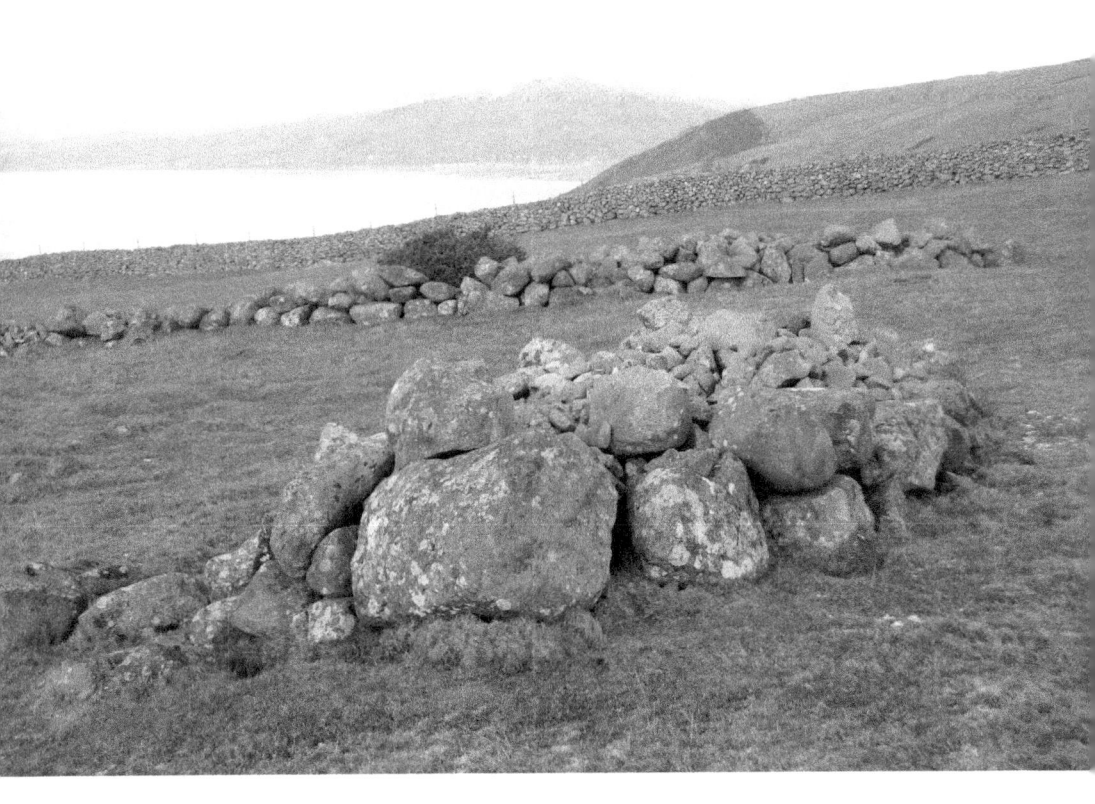

Stone cairn in Snowdonia, North Wales

Dorset Coastal Path

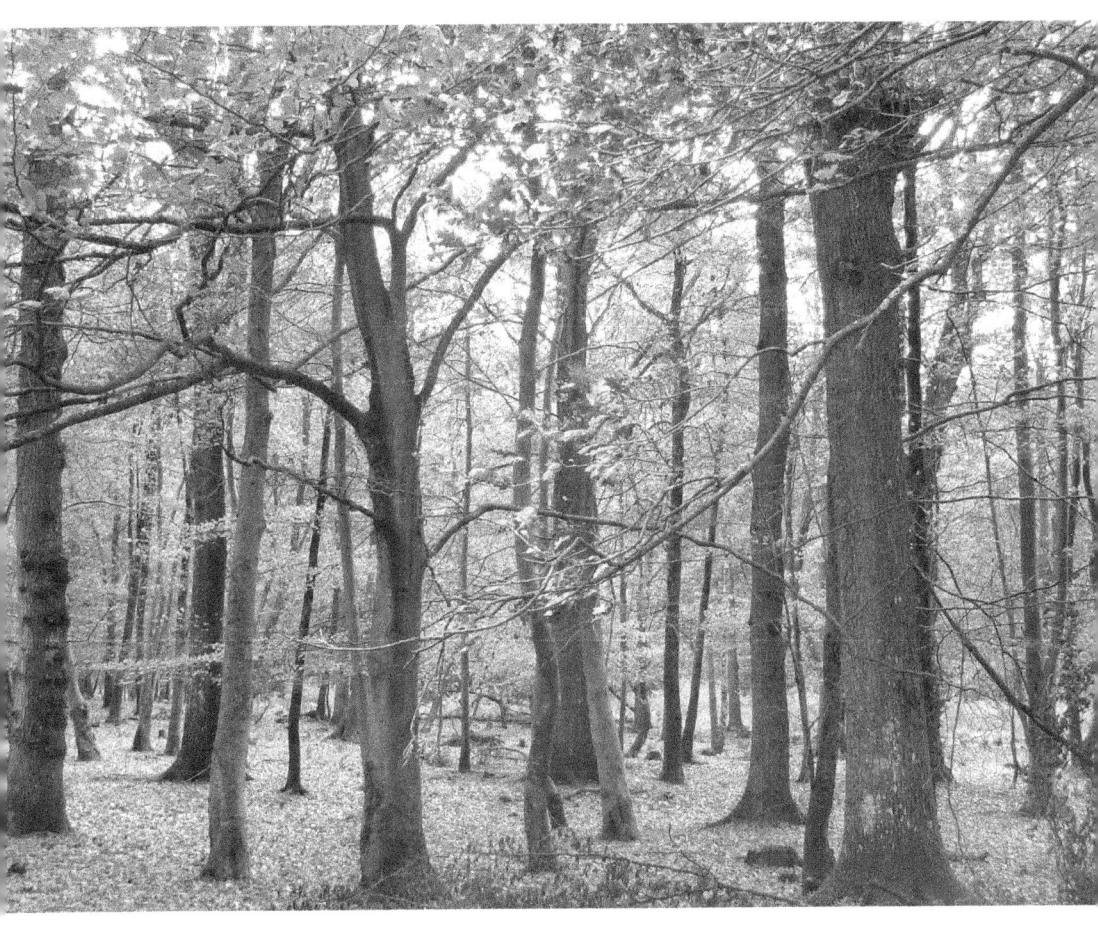

New Forest, Hampshire

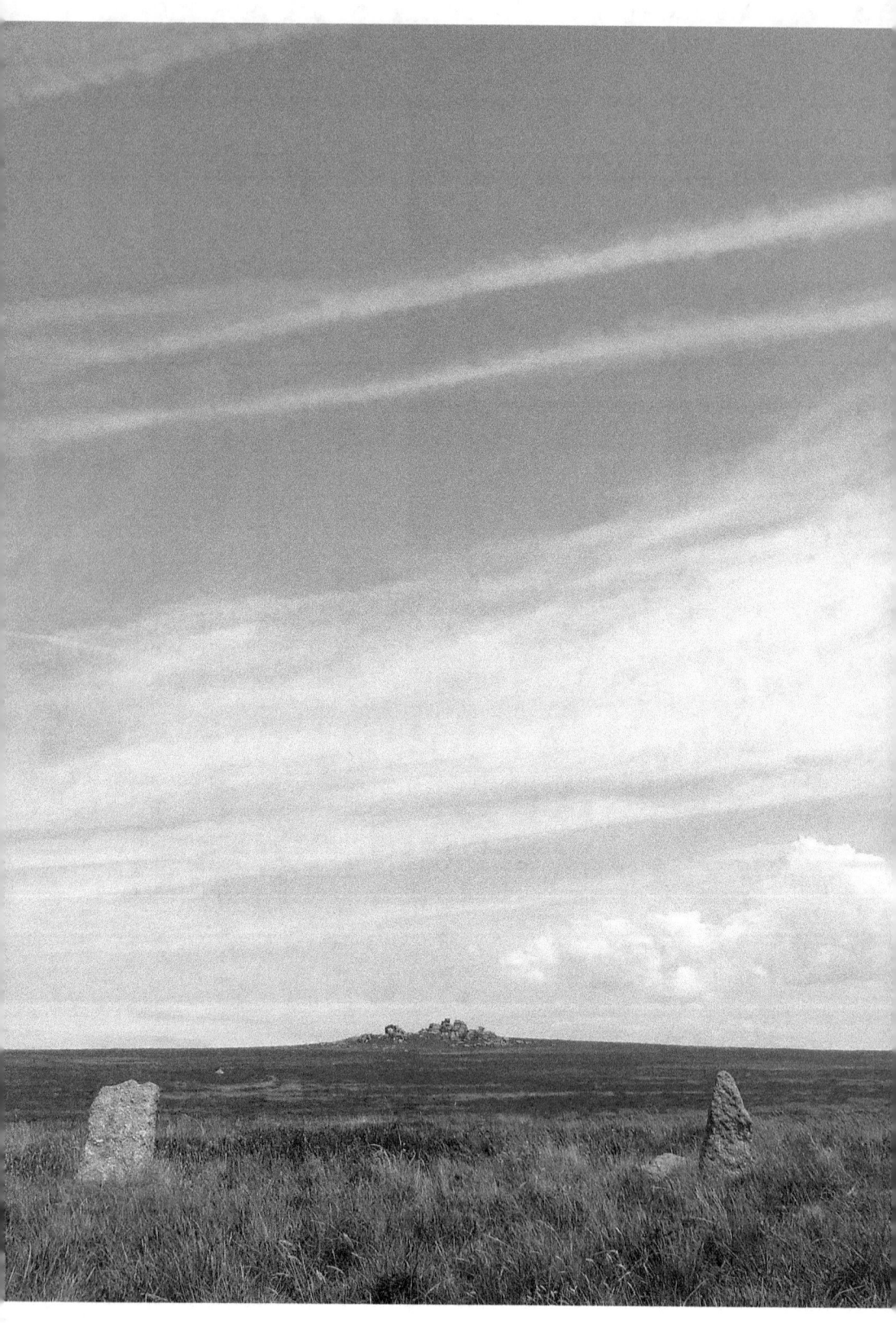

Carn Kenidjack in West Cornwall

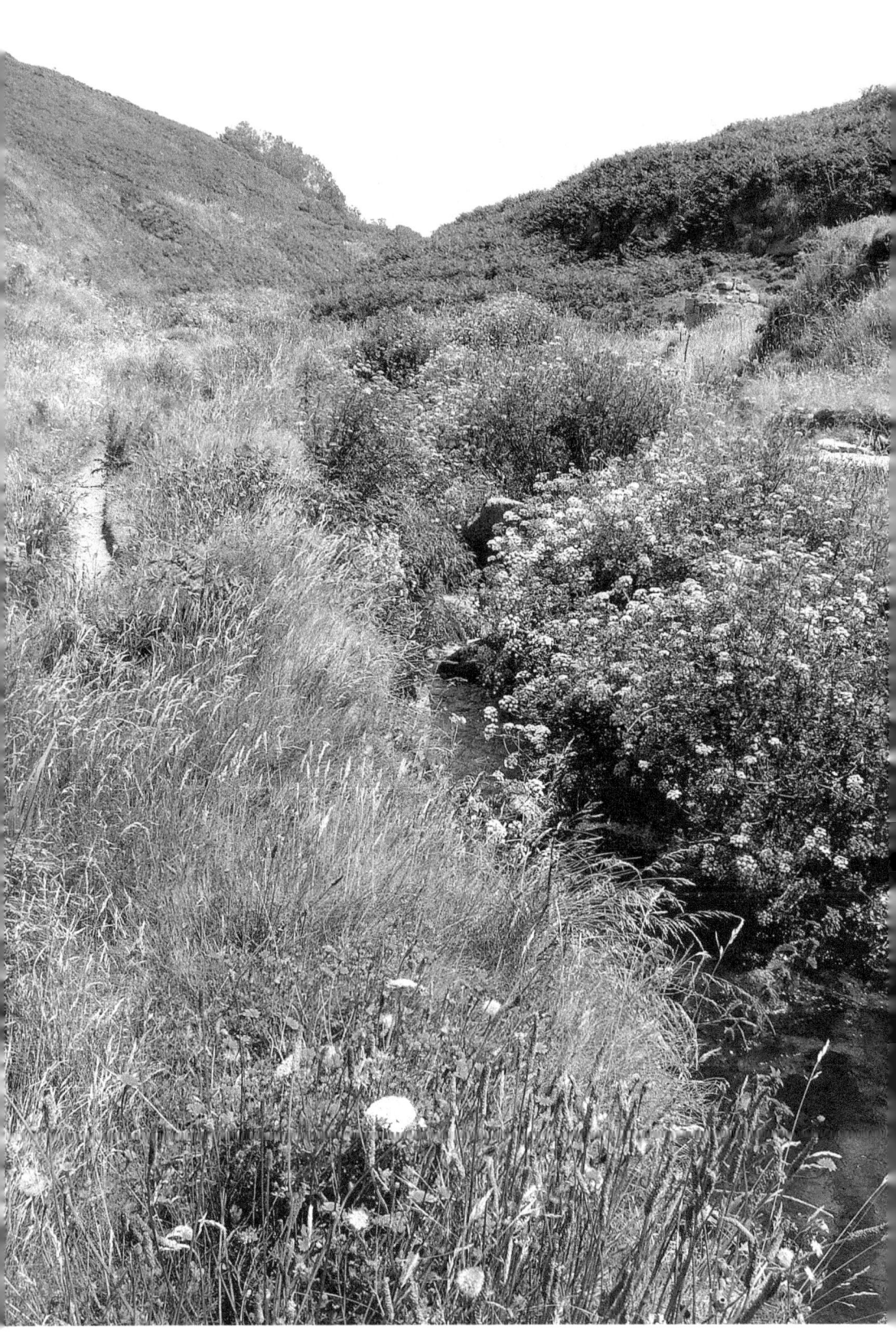

Kenidjack Valley, West Penwith, Cornwall

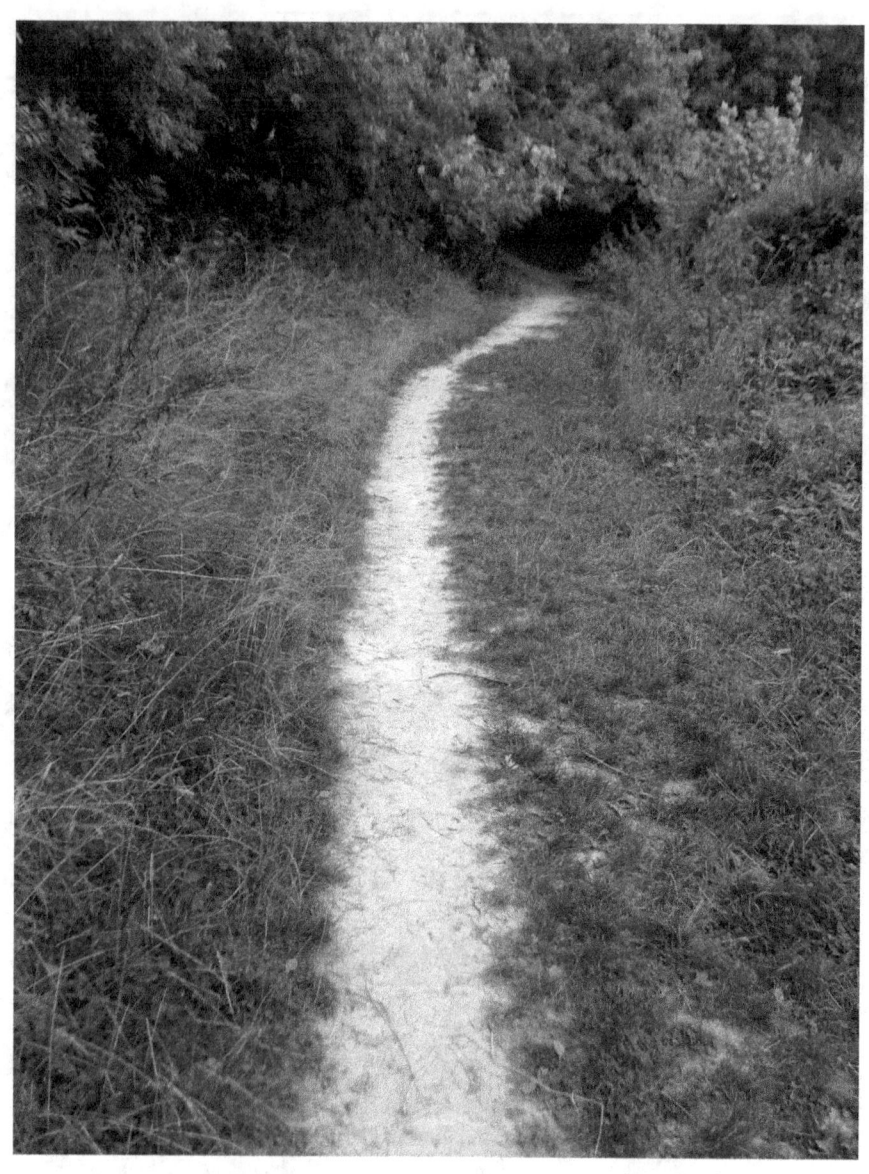

Path at Coldrum Stones, Kent, England.

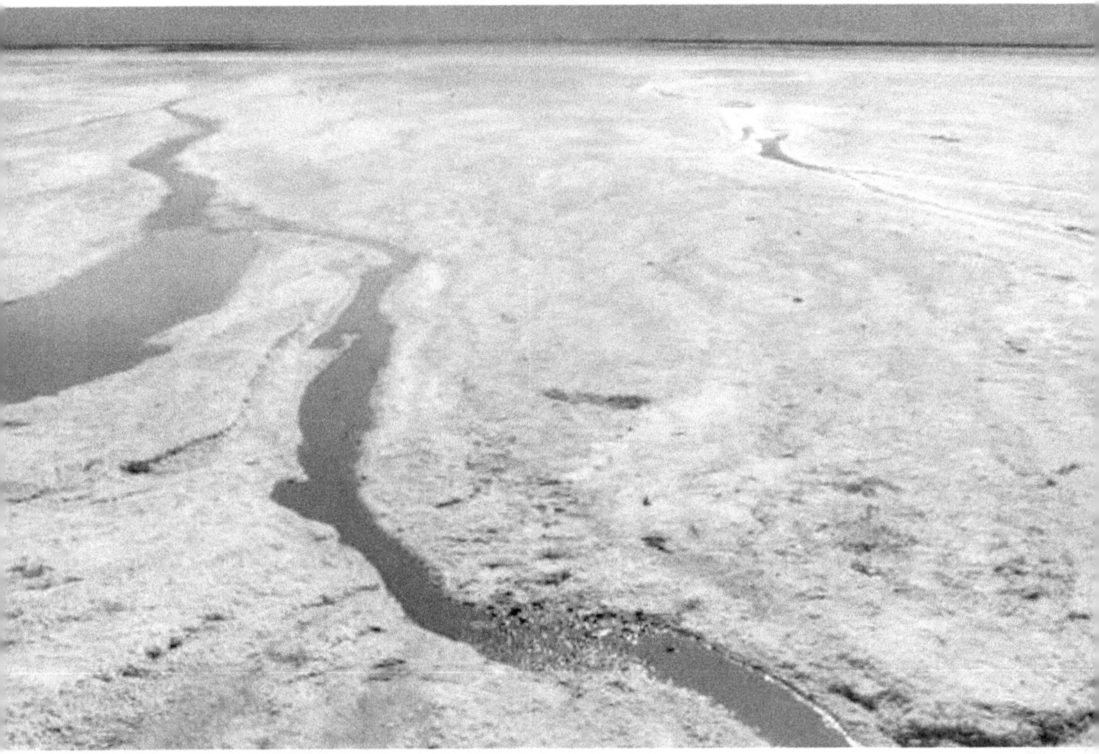

The Californian desert: Zabriskie Point (below),
and salt flats at Death Valley (above).

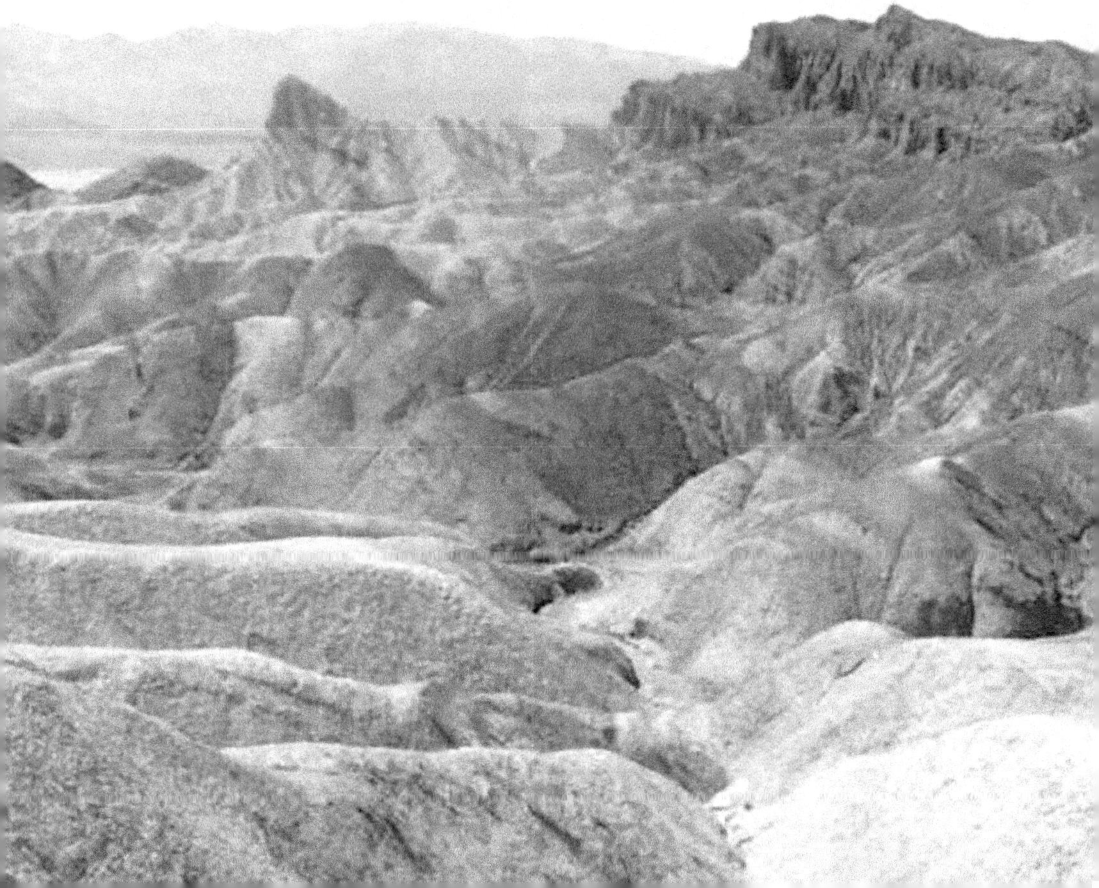

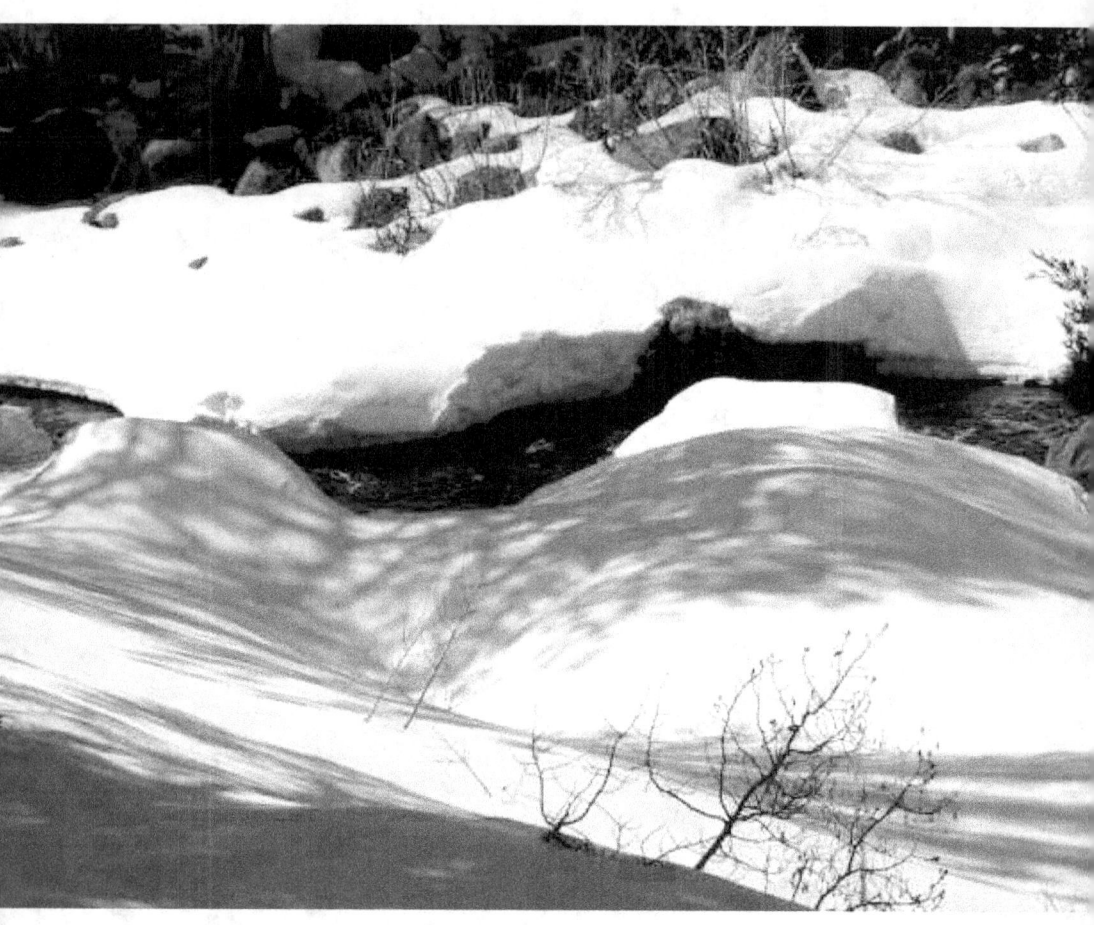

High Sierras, California

New Mexico

Some examples of the landscape painting tradition,
on this page and the following pages,
beginning with Britain's greatest artist, J.M.W. Turner

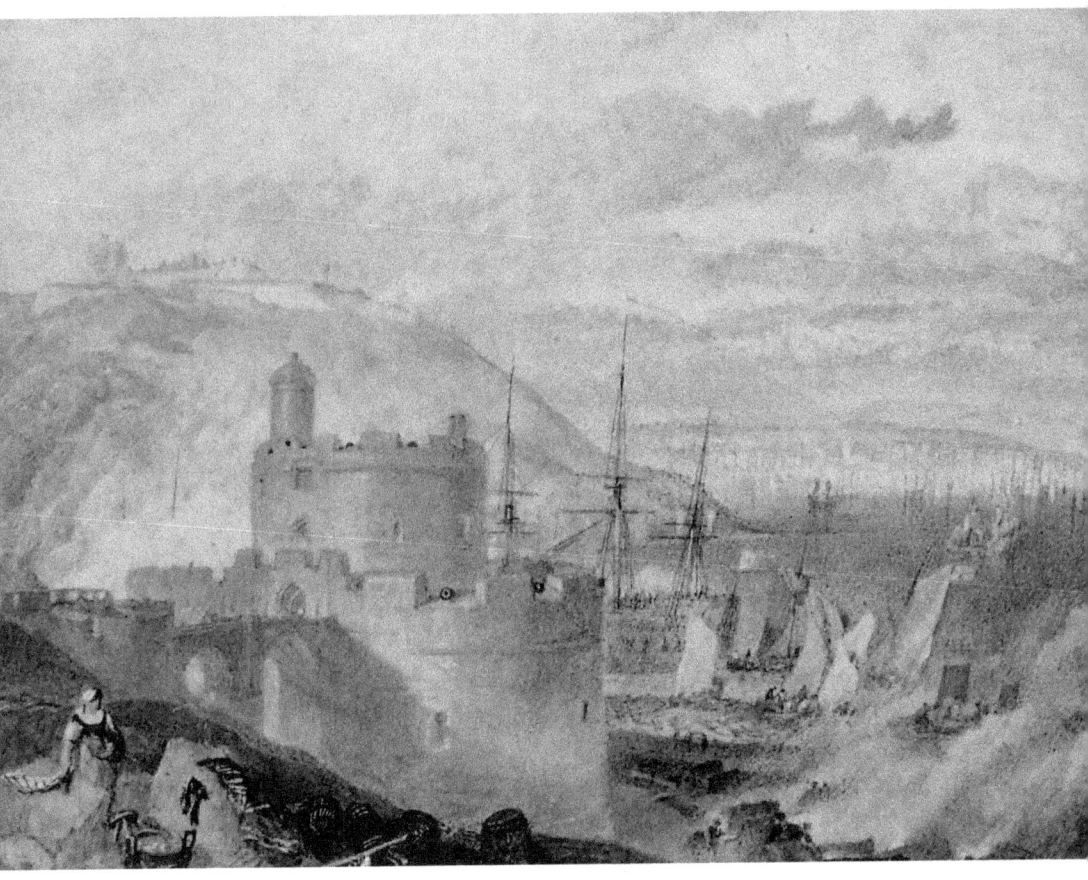

J.M.W. Turner, Falmouth, c. 1825, private collection

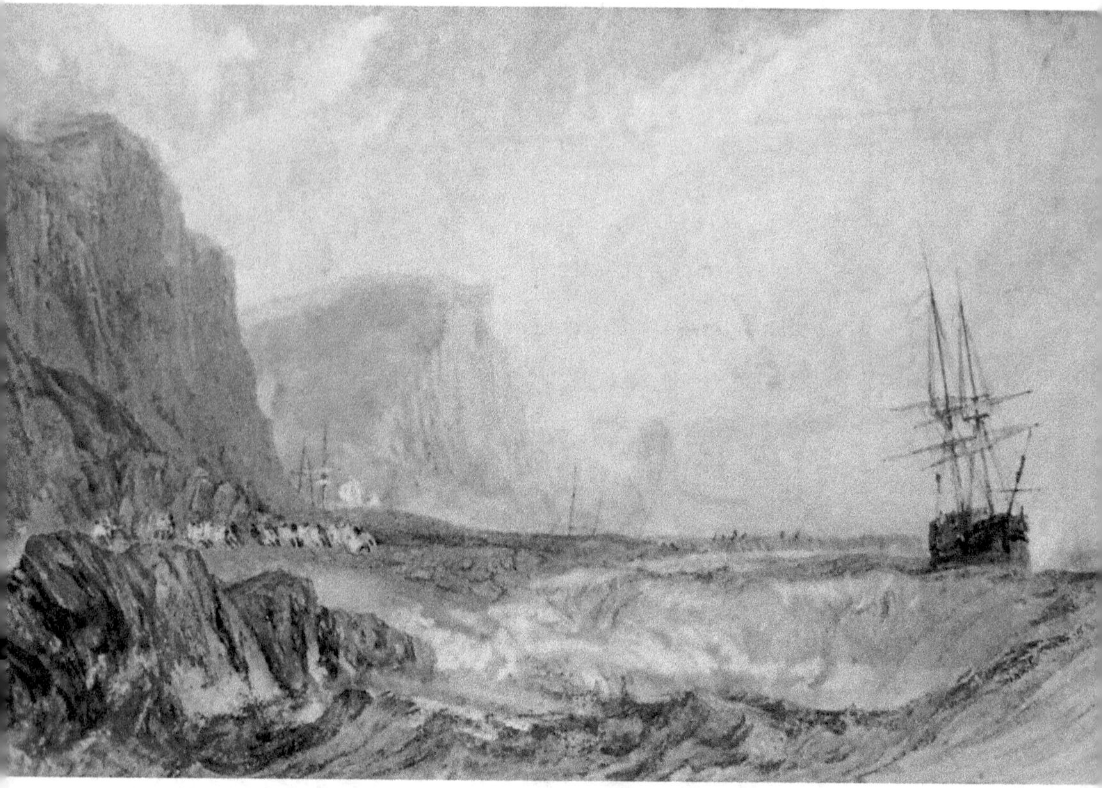

J.M.W. Turner, Bridport, Dorset (above). Folkestone, Kent (below).

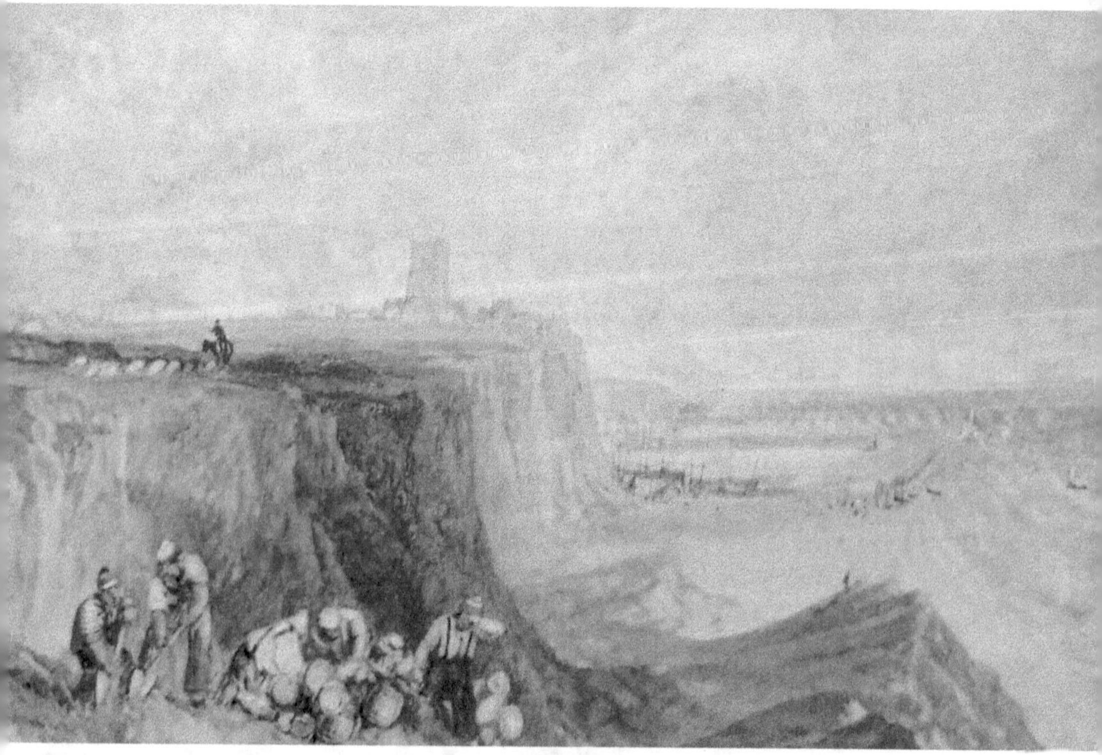

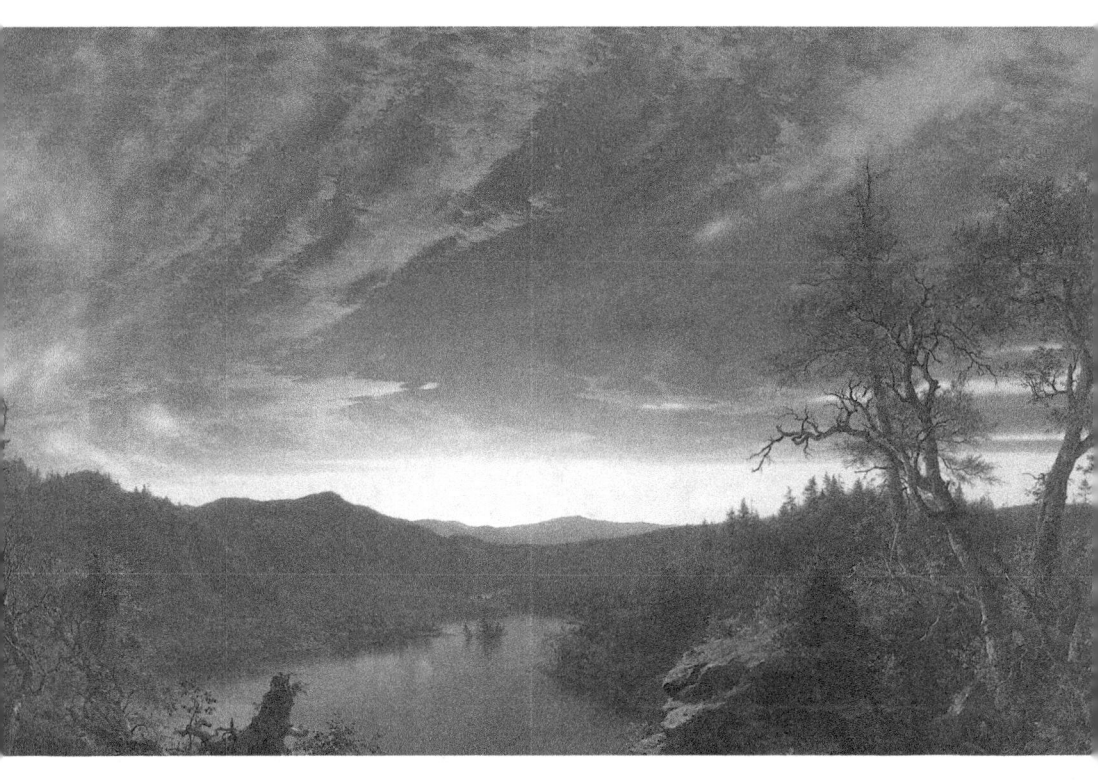

Frederic Edwin Church, Twilight In the Wildnerness, 1860,
Cleveland Museum of Art

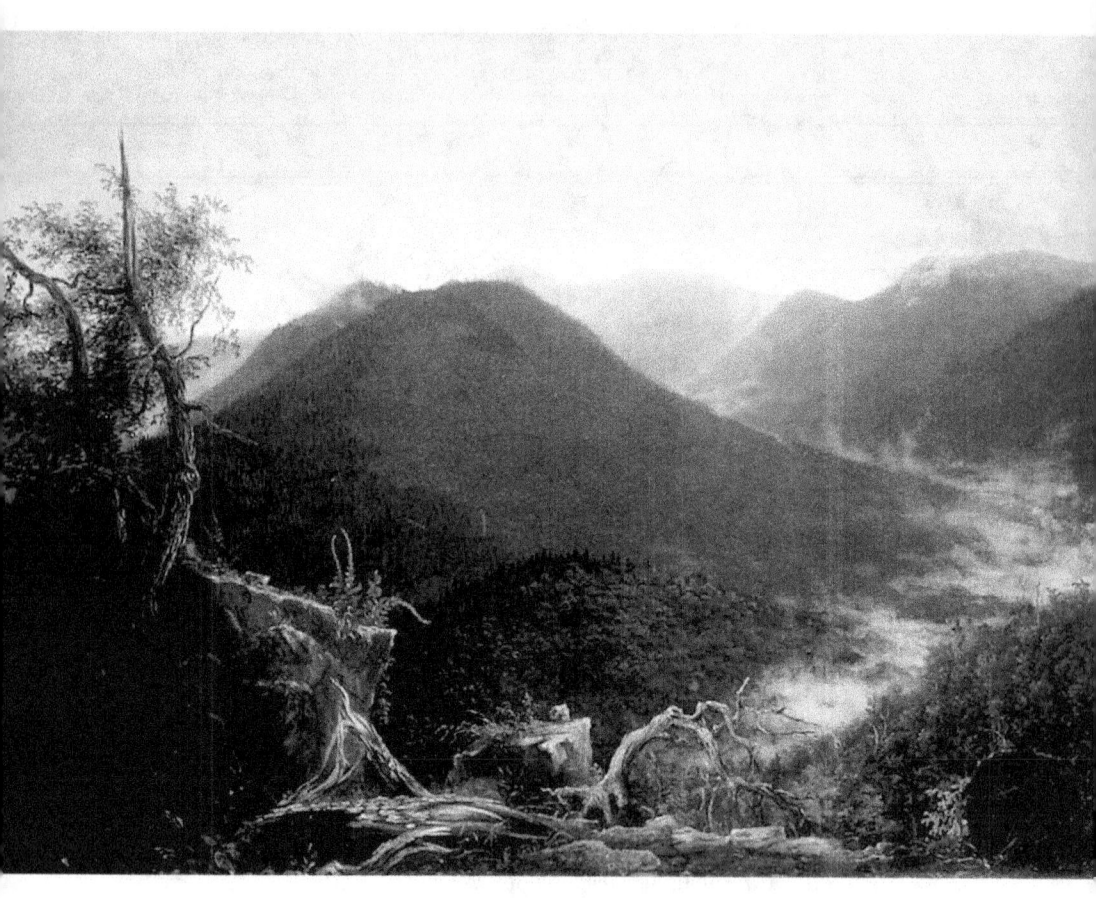

Thomas Cole, Sunrise In the Catskill Mountains, 1826

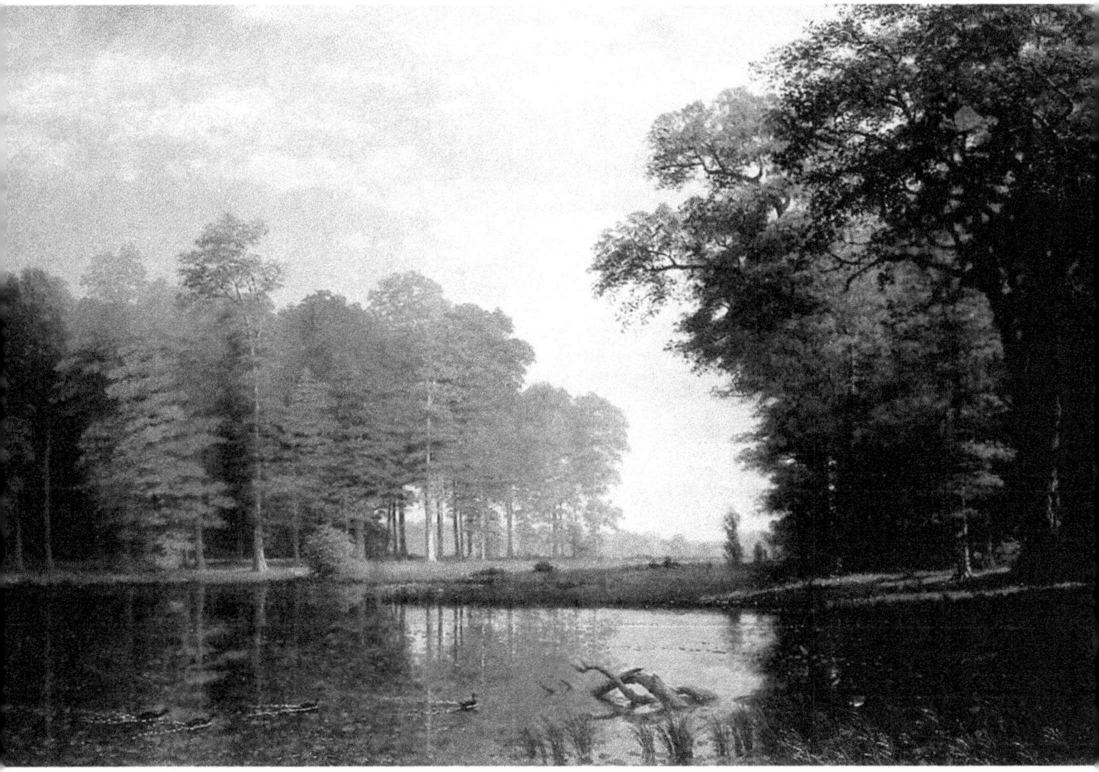

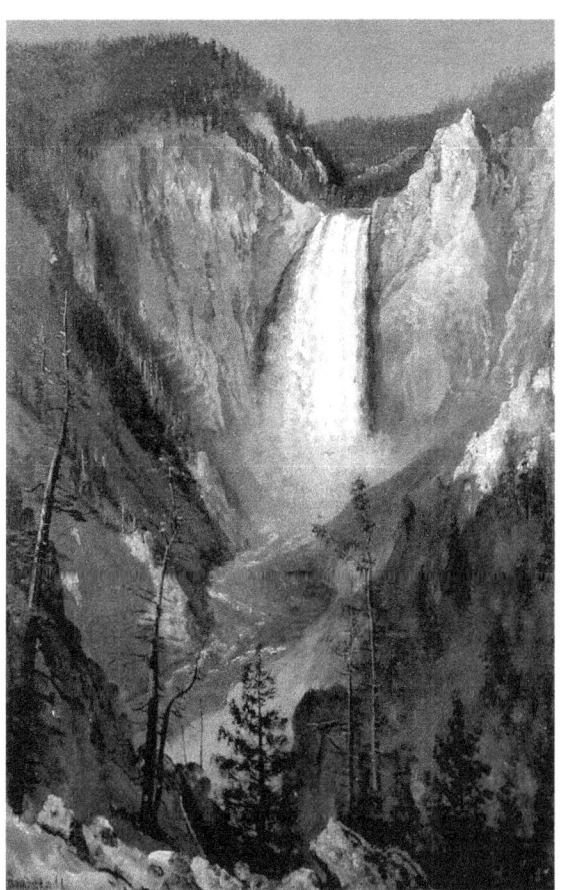

Albert Bierstadt,
Autumn Woods (above), and
Lower Yellowstone Falls (left).

Some prehistoric monuments linked to Richard Long's art,
this page and the following pages

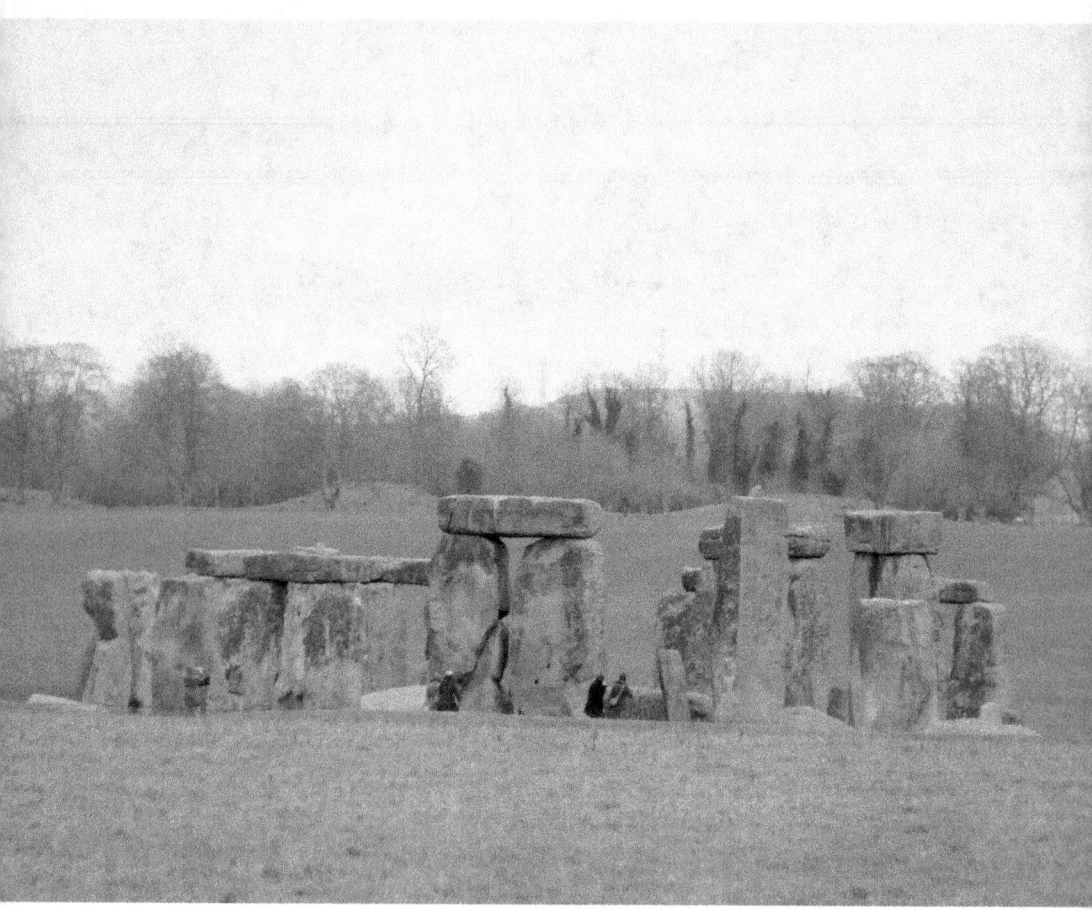

Stonehenge, Wiltshire

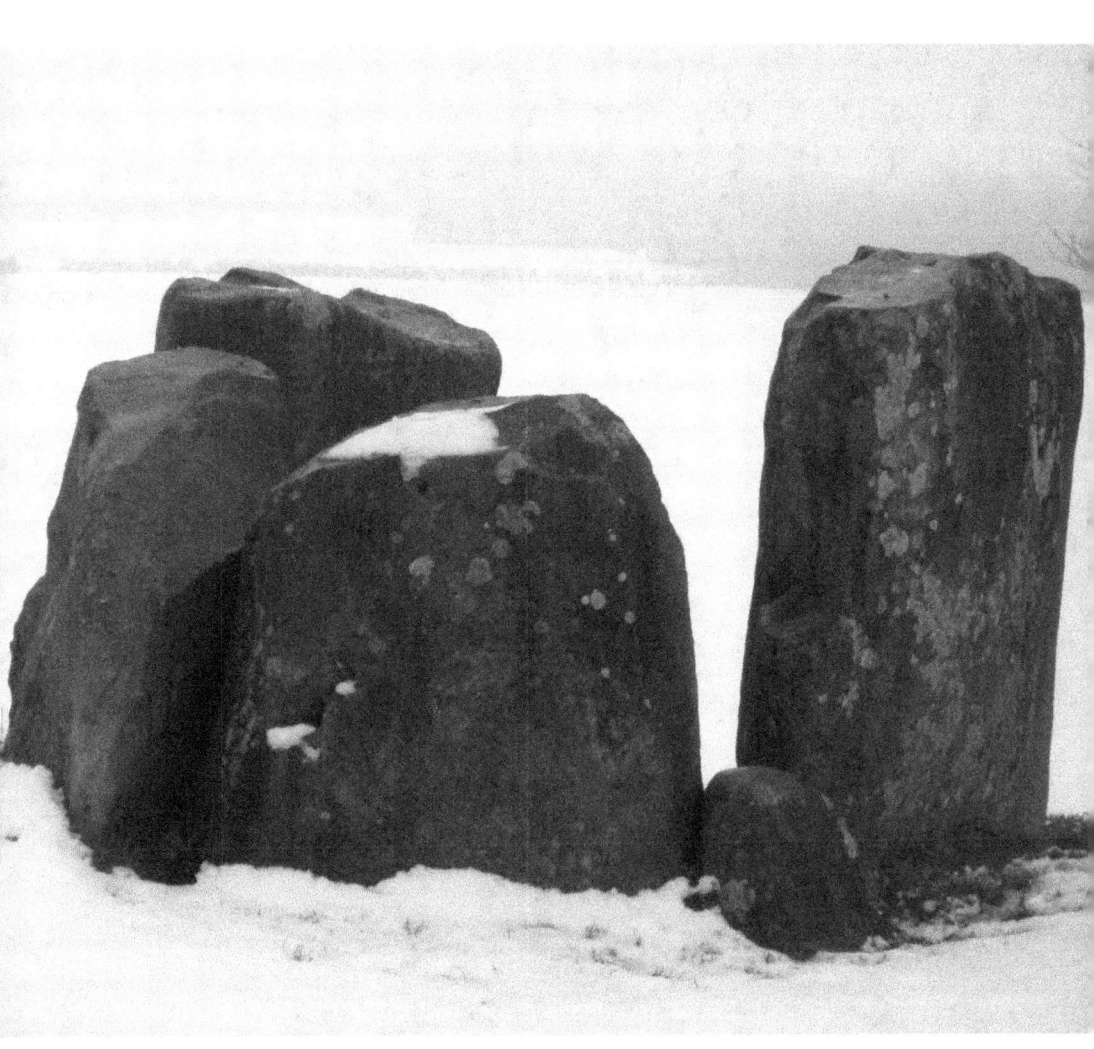

Coldrum Stones, Kent

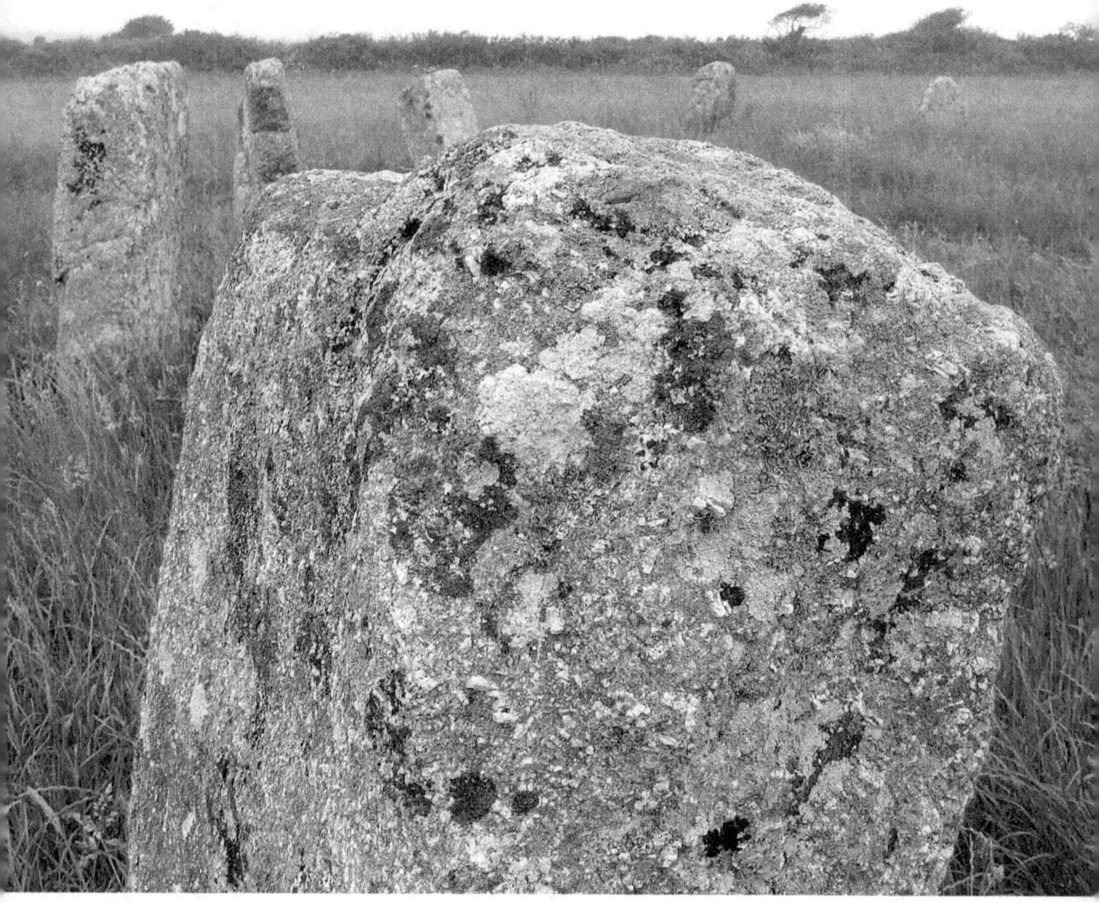

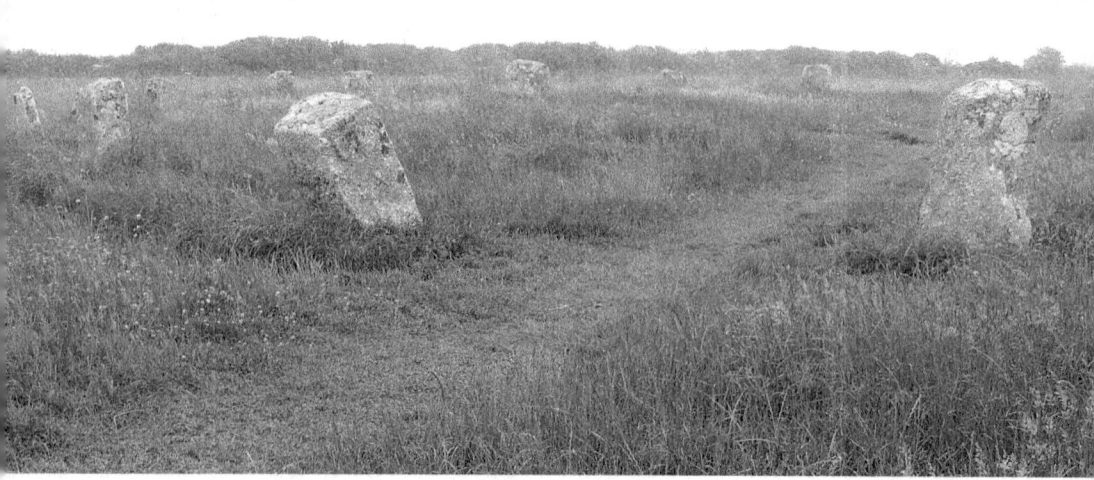

Merry Maidens Stone Circle, St Buryan, Cornwall

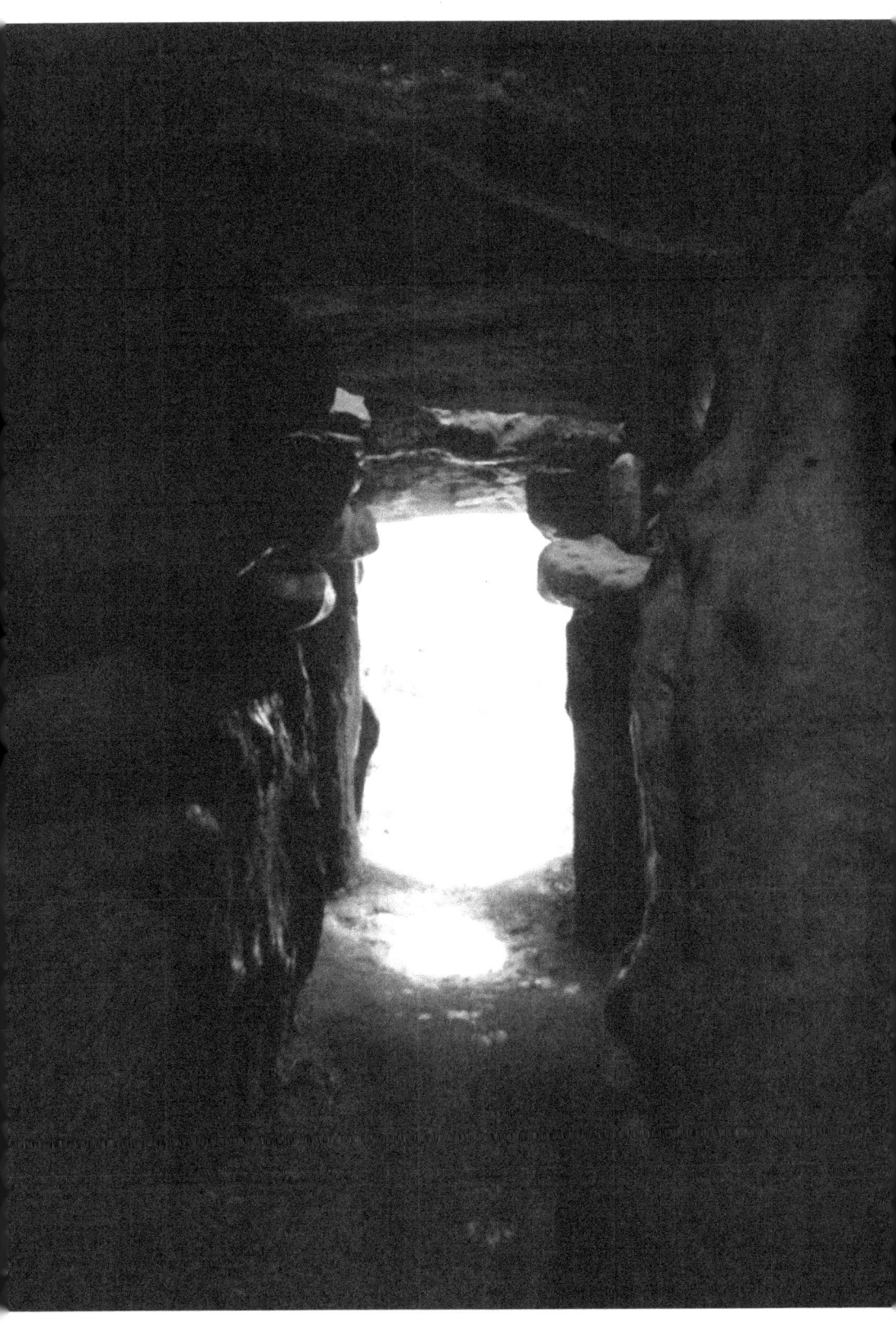

West Kennet Long Barrow, Wiltshire, England

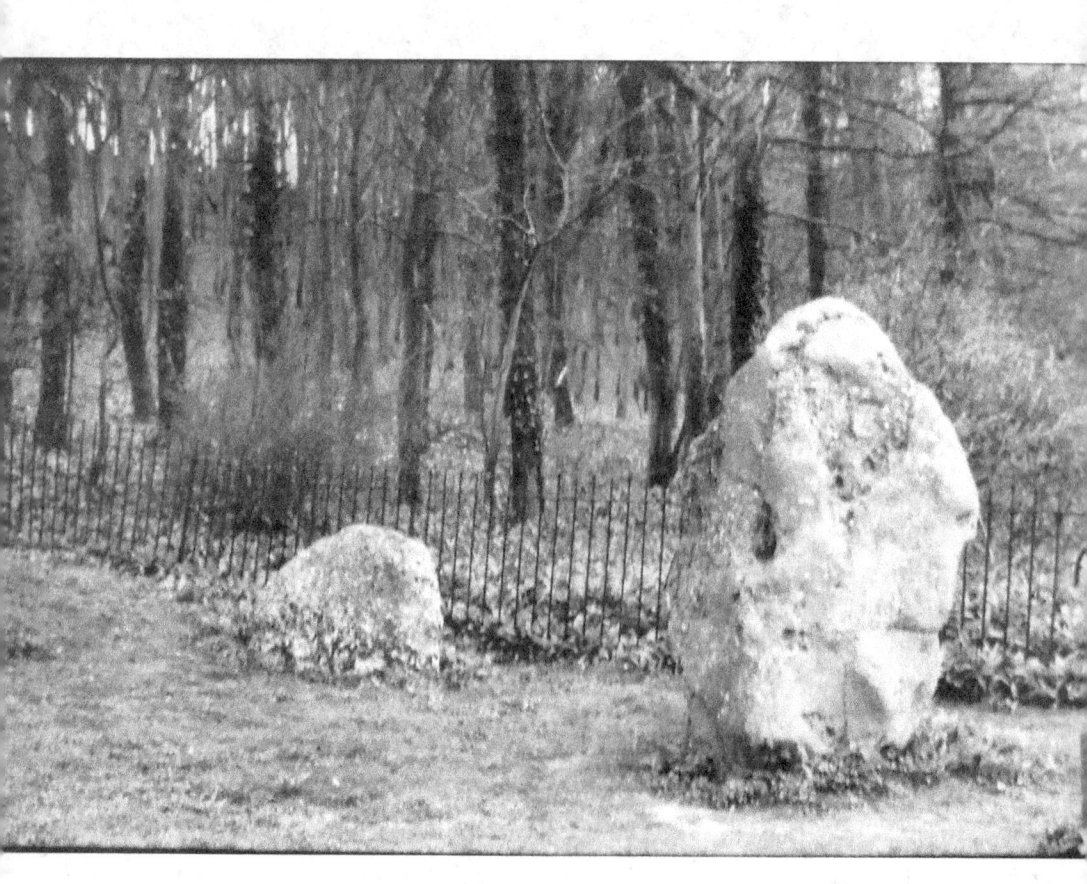

Winterbourne Abbas Stone Ring, Dorset

Notes

List of Works

Bibliography

Notes

INTRODUCTION

1. W. Malpas, *Andy Goldsworthy: Touching Nature*, Crescent Moon, 1995, 2005; *Richard Long: The Art of Walking*, Crescent Moon, 1995, 1998; *The Art of Andy Goldsworthy*, Crescent Moon, 1998, 2004.

1 • SCULPTURE IN THE CONTEMPORARY ERA

1. R. Krauss, 1979.

THE SCULPTURE OF ARROGANCE

1. D. Judd, 1975, 200f.
2. Mark Rothko wrote of his intentions with regard to scale thus:

> I paint very large pictures... The reason I paint them... is precisely because I want to be very intimate and human. To paint a small picture is to place yourself outside your experience, to look upon an experience as a stereopticon view or with a reducing glass. However you paint the larger picture, you are in it. It isn't something you command. (1951, in D. Waldman, 1978)

3. "Donald Judd", *New York Times*, Apl 1, 1977, C20.
4. L. Lippard, 1968, 42.
5. See L. Anderson, 1973; *Mary Miss: Interior Works*, Bell Gallery, University of Rhode Island, Autumn, 1981.
6. See N. Holt, 1975 and 1977; T. Castle, 1982.
7. See D. Judd: *Complete Writings*; W. Agee, 1975, 40-49; P. Carlson, "Donald Judd's Equivocal Objects", *Art in America*, Jan, 1984, 114-8; D. Kuspitt, 1985; B. Haskell, 1988; B. Smith, 1975.
8. See L. Lippard, 1972a; G. Baro, 1967, 27-31; E. Greene: "Morphology of Tony Smith's Work", *Artforum*, April, 1974, 54-59.
9. See I. Licht, 1968, 50-57; W. Wilson: "Dan Flavin: Fiat Lux", *Art News*, Jan, 1970, 48-51; J. Burnham, 1969, 48-55.
10. See R.E. Krauss, 1972, 38-43; D. Crimp: "Richard Serra: Sculpture Exceeded", *October*, Fall, 1981, 67-78.
11. See K. Baker, 1980, 88-94; D. Waldman, 1970, 60-62, 75-79; P. Tuchman, 1978, 29-33; E. Develing, 1969.

KINETIC SCULPTURE

1. This is not to say that pre-20th century or traditional sculpture is 'immobile': far from it. Take Giovanni da Bologna's *Mercury*, for instance: as the winged messenger of mythology, a static depiction of Mercury or Hermes would be a mistake, and da Bologna's statue is full of movement. Bernini's *David* is similarly kinetic: the man's body is twisting, ready for battle, ready to carry out one of the most celebrated acts of murder in the history of art.
2. Jean Tinguely: *Hommage à New York*, 1960, mixed media, motorized, Sculpture Garden of the Museum of Modern Art, New York.
3. Daniel Wheeler described Tinguely's monster machine:

> Few of these particular "events' ever took place, owing to immediate and chronic breakdown, which almost invariably happened in Tinguely's Metamatic performances, but all kinds of other wonders did come to pass, which, being, unexpected, struck Tinguely as far superior to anything he had programed. (D.

Wheeler, 1991, 239-240)

SUGARMAN, NOGUCHI, POMODORO, SAMARAS

1. Quoted in D. Waldman, 1966, 56.

BARNETT NEWMAN AND ALEXANDER CALDER

1. N. Kricke, *Space Sculpture*, 1958-59, Municipality, Leverkusen, Germany.
2. See H. Rosenberg, 1975; L. Alloway, "The Stations of the Cross and the Subjects of the Artist", in *Barnett Newman: The Stations of the Cross: Lama Sabacthani*, Guggenheim Museum, New York, NY, 1966; E.C. Goossen, "The Philosophic Line of B. Newman", *Art News*, Summer, 1958.

LESS IS MORE: ARTE POVERA

1. J. Kounellis, in W. Sharp, 1972.

HYPERREALIST SCULPTURE

1. J. De Andrea, quoted in A. Le Normand-Romain *et al*, *Sculpture: The Adventure of Modern Sculpture in the Nineteenth and Twentieth Centuries*, Skira, Geneva, 1986, 241.
2. E. Lucie-Smith, *Sculpture Since 1945*, 33.

CONSTANTIN BRANCUSI AND LAND ART

1. H. Moore, in *The Listener*, 1937, quoted in H. Chipp, 595.
2. B. Flanagan, quoted in the catalogue of *Entre el Objeto y la Imagen: Escultura britanica contemporanea*, Palacio de Velasquez, Madrid, 1986, 233.
3. A. Goldsworthy, *Réfuges d'art*, 85.

JASPER JOHNS AND LAND ART

1. Quoted in M. Crichton, *Jasper Johns*, Thames & Hudson, London, 1977, 21.
2. J. Johns, quoted in M. Crichton, 28.
3. J. Johns, quoted in D. Wheeler, 134-5.
4. S. LeWitt, quoted in F. Colpitt, 63.

THE WORLD OF MINIMAL AND POSTMINIMAL ART

1. S. Gablik: "Minimalism", in N. Stangos, ed. *Concepts of Modern Art*, Thames & Hudson, London, 1981, 245.
2. B. Rose, 1964, 41.
3. R. Morris, 1966, in G. Battock, 1995, 224.
4. R. Morris, 1966, 20-23. See also: P. Patton, "Robert Morris and the Fire Next Time", *Art News,* 82, 10, Dec, 1983.
5. See I. Sandler, *American Art*, 245f; L. Lippard, 1966b, 62; R. Morris: "Notes on Sculpture", op.cit.; K. McShine, 1966; R. Lund: "Why Isn't Minimal Art Boring?", *Journal of Aesthetics and Art Criticism*, 45, 2, Winter, 1986, 195-7.
6. P. Fuller, 1993, xxxv,
7. L. Lippard, 1966a, 50.
8. A. Warhol, in K. Stiles, 340.
9. D. Judd: "Questions to Stella and Judd", in G. Battock, 1995, 159.
10. J. Mellow: "New York Letter", *Art International*, April 20, 1966, 89.

11. B. Rose: "Looking at American Sculpture", 34.
12. H. Kramer: "Display of Judd Art Defines an Attitude", *The New York Times*, May 14, 1971, D48.
13. B. Haskell, *Donald Judd*, 72.
14. In K. McShine, 1966.
15. R. Mangold, in F. Colpitt, 121.
16. D. Judd: "Specific Objects", in G. de Vries, 1974, 128.
17. Rosalind Krauss wrote:

The art of [Rodin and Brancusi] represented a relocation of the point of origin of the body's meaning – from its inner core to its surface – a radical act of decentring that would include the space to which the body appeared and the time of its appearing. What I have been arguing is that the sculpture of our time continues this project of decentring through a vocabulary of form that is radically abstract. The abstractness of Minimalism makes it less easy to recognize the human body in those works and therefore less easy to project ourselves into the space of that sculpture with all of our settled prejudices left intact. Yet our bodies and our experience of our bodies continue to be the subject of this sculpture – even when a work is made of several hundred tons of earth. (1977, 279)

18. R. Morris: "Notes on Sculpture", part 3, 29.
19. R. Rosenblum: "Notes on Sol LeWitt", 1978, 15-16.
20. See C. Huber: *Robert Ryman*, Kunsthalle, Basel; N. Grimes: "Robert Ryman's White Magic", *Art News*, Summer 1968, 86-92; C. Ratcliff, 1986, 92-97.
21. Agnes Martin, quoted in P. Schjedahl, 26.
22. Quoted in D. Wheeler, 1991, 207.
23. See A. Wooster: "Sol LeWitt's Expanding Grid", *Art in America*, 68, 5, May, 1980, 143-7.
24. S. LeWitt: "Paragraphs on Conceptual Art", *Art Language*, May, 1969. See *Sol LeWitt*, Gemeentemuseum, The Hague 1970; L. Lippard, 1967b; R. Smith: "Sol LeWitt", *Artforum*, Jan, 1975; A. Wooster, 1980.
25. D. Oppenheim, 1992.

THE ART OF SPACE AND LIGHT

1. Quoted in J. Butterfield, 161.

2 • SCULPTURE AND GENDER

1. B. Hepworth, quoted in A.M. Hammacher, 1968, 99.

EROTICISM IN SCULPTURE

1. K. Bloomert & Charles W. Moore, *Body, Memory and Architecture*, New Haven, CT, 1977, 34; see also J. Gibson.
2. P. Redgrove: *The Man Named East and other new poems*, Routledge & Kegan Paul, London, 1985.
3. There is eroticism in Tony Cragg's steel vessels, or Anne and Patrick Poirier's long, elegant *Archæological Model*, or Jannis Kounellis' *Cotton Sculpture*, a mass of cotton stuffed into a large steel container – a sculpture of contrasts between the softness of the cotton and the rigidity of the steel, or Jackie Winsor's *Burnt Piece*, a 3 ft cube made of concrete, wire and burnt wood. Tony Cragg has spoken of having 'an erotic response to the external world', something which, it seems, all artists have, or have to have, to be truly 'great' artists (quoted in D. Wheeler, 1991, 324).

See also T. Neff, 1967; B. Jones, 1977, 16; L. Ponti, 50-51; I. Lamaitre, 1985, 7-11; G. Celant, 40-46.

WOMEN SCULPTORS

1. Other artists who have worked in postmodern, feminist modes include Cindy Sherman, Mary Kelly, Marie Yates, Yve Lomax, Martha Rosler, Sutapa Biswas, Mitra Tabrizian, Zarina Bhimji, Mona Hatoum, Lubaina Himid, Barbara Kruger, Jenny Holzer, Rose Garrard, Susan Hiller, Nancy Spero, Rosa Lee and Rachel Whiteread.
2. See B. Barrette: *Eva Hesse's Sculpture*: Catalogue Raissonné, New York, 1989; R. Krauss, 1979; C. Nemser, 1973, 12-13.
3. C. Nemser, 1970, 62.
4. A. Chave, in H. Cooper, ed. *Eva Hesse*, Yale University Press, New Haven, CT, 1992, 100f.
5. In L. Lippard, 1976.
6. Quoted in L. Lippard, ib., 6.
7. J D. Wheeler, 1991, 323.
8. See M. Roustayi: "Getting Under the Skin: Rebecca Horn's Sensibility Machines", *Arts*, May, 1989, 58-68; M. Kimmelman: "A Sculptural Circus of Whips and Suspense", *New York Times*, Sept 23, 1988, C29.
9. In A. Hammacher, op.cit., 98.
10. B. Hepworth, in W. Forma, 1965.
11. See H. Gresty: *Bare*, Newlyn Art Gallery, Newlyn, 1993.
12. See L. Cooke, *Alison Wilding*, Arts Council, 1985; L. Biggs, 1986; W. Beckett, 116; T. Neff, 43-45.
13. A. Wilding, quoted in W. Beckett, 116.
14. A. Wilding, quoted in T. Neff, 45.
15. S. Houshiary, quoted in *Entre el Objeto y la Imagen: Escultura britanica contemporanea*, Palacio de Velasquez, Madrid, 1986, 235.
16. See D. Bourdon, 1987; J.-Y. Mock, 1980.
17. See A. Berman: "Nancy Graves", *Art News*, Feb, 1986, 57-64; D.B. Balken and L. Nochlin: *Nancy Graves: Painting, Sculpture, Drawing, 1980-85,* Vassar College Art Gallery, Poughkeepsie, 1986; E.A. Carmean *et al: The Sculpture of Nancy Graves*, Fort Worth, TX, 1987; A. Collins and B. Collins: "The Sum of the Parts [Nancy Graves]", *Art in America*, 1988, 113-8; L. Cathcart: *Nancy Graves: A Survey 1969-1980*, Albright-Knox Gallery, Buffalo, NY, catalogue, 1981.
18. D. Wheeler, 1991, 303.
19. D. Wheeler, 1991, 285.
20. C. King: "Feminist Arts", in F. Bonner *et al*, eds, 185.

CONTEMPORARY SCULPTURE AND THE BODY

1. C. Andre, 1978, 31.
2. See D. de Menil *et al: Yves Klein: 1958-62: A Retrospective*, Institute for the Arts, Rice University, Houston, TX, 1982.
3. In K. Stiles, 755.
4. G. Brus, in *Günter Brus*, Whitechapel Gallery, London, 1980.
5. L. Tickner: "Body Politic", op.cit., 239. This's not a satisfying comparison of Tickner's, because the *Venus of Urbino* is an artwork, not a flesh-and-blood, 'real' person.
6. L. Tickner, "Body Politic", op cit , 239
7. See C. Schneemann: *Interior Scroll*, 1975; *More Than Meat Joy: Complete Performance Works and Selected Writings*, ed. B. MacPherson, Documentext, New York, NY, 1979.
8. C. Carr: "Unspeakable Practices, Unnatural Acts", *Village Voice*, June 24, 1986.

9. See A. Adler: "Dangerous Woman: Karen Finley", *Chicago Reader*, Oct 26, 1990; C. Schuler: "Spectator Response and Comprehensions: The Problems of Karen Finley's *Constant State of Desire*", *The Drama Review*, Spring, 1990; C. Barnes: "Finley's Fury", *New York Post*, July 24, 1990; T. Page: "Karen Finley's Tantrum, Amid Chocolate", *New York Newsday*, July 24, 1990.

10. M. Duffy: *Cutting the Ties that Bind*, 1987; *Stories of a Body*, 1990; see H. Robinson: "The Subtle Abyss: Sexuality and Body Image in Contemporary Feminist Art", unpublished dissertation, RCA, 1987; M. Duffy: "Cutting the Ties that Bind", *Feminist Art News*, 2:10, 1989, 6-7; M. Duffy: "Redressing the Balance", *Feminist Art News*, 3:8, 1991.

11. J. Spence and T. Sheard: *Narratives of Disease*; see J. Spence: *Putting Myself in the Picture: A Political, Personal and Photographic Autobiography*, Camden Press, London, 1986; P. Holland *et al*, eds. *Photography/ Politics: Two*, Commedia, London, 1986; D. Grigsby: "Dilemmas of Visibility: Contemporary Women Artists' Representations of Female Bodies", *Michigan Quarterly Review*, XXIX: 4, Autumn, 1990, 584-618.

12. C. Elwes: "Floating femininity: a look at performance art by women", in S. Kent & J. Morreau, eds: *Women's Images of Men*, Pandora Press, London, 1985, 172.

13. C. Elwes, ib., 182.

14. Quoted in L. Lippard, 219; see also I. Lippard: "Dinner Party", *Art in America*, Apl, 1980, 122.

15. *Rosarium Philosophorum*, quoted in A.T. Mann, *Sacred Architecture*, Element Books, Shaftesbury, Dorset, 1993, 87.

16. Land art labyrinths can be regarded as part of the resurgence of interest in mazes which occurred in the 1980s (aligned, as ever, with green/ ecological/ occult/ New Age trends). Mazes were commissioned for country houses, zoos and theme parks. A maze was seen as one more feature for visitors to enjoy: apart from the country mansion or palace or museum interior and formal gardens, the public could visit a maze, and perhaps a children's playground. Some mazes were set beside adventure playgrounds, emphasizing the sense of play, rather than ritual. At country houses such as Ragley Hall in Staffordshire (UK), the maze was part of the children's playground, and was conceived as something of a gym or assault course: there were walkways and bridges over some of the passages in the brick maze, which were climbed via ropes and ladders. Probably the most famous maze in Britain is at Hampton Court. Maize mazes were also cut from crops in July and August.
1991 was 'The Year of the Maze' (largely orchestrated by maze designer Adrian Fisher of Minotaur Designs). Some modern mazes were conceived as part of civic architecture, such as the Bristol Water Maze, which took its design from a roof boss in nearby St Mary Redcliffe church. Some pavement mazes were made as part of new parks or new shopping centres (such as at Worksop). An underground maze was constructed at Leeds Castle in Kent. Old turf and hedge mazes were re-cut and restored (Fisher, 1991). At Symonds Yat in Herefordshire the Jubilee Maze was made in 1977 by the brothers Lindsay and Edward Heyes. The way out of the maze led to a small Maze Museum, where the history of mazes was told via simple displays. The Symonds Yat Jubilee maze made a leisure outing of the maze: the maze is the centrepiece of the visit. This is unusual: mazes are more often add-ons to the theme park or country house.
The maze is a very satisfying motif or design: it is self-contained, like other geometric patterns; it can use almost any perimeter shape, from circles and squares to 'organic' shapes; it offers opportunities for games and play; it can be a visual device, for decorating floors or walls, or one of the main features of a garden; and it carries a sizable slice of symbolism, religion, paganism and history. The symbolism and history of the labyrinth can be happily ignored in favour of simply enjoying solving a maze. Unlike sacred sites such as churches and stone circles, which are loaded with religious significance, and generally demand some religious or

intellectual response from the visitor, the maze can be consumed simply as an interesting structure. One doesn't need to know about mythology (such as Theseus and the Minotaur in the Greek myth) or religion (such as the ritual aspect in Christianity of walking a maze) to appreciate a maze.

3 • SPIRIT AND MATTER: LAND ART

SPIRIT OF PLACE

1. In M. Elvy, 1994, 35.
2. In B. Redhead, 24-25.
3. In B. Redhead, 22.
4. In M. Elvy, 1994, 38.
5. S. Ross, 1993, 161.
6. S. Ross, 1990, 23.
7. S. Bann, in M. Mosser & G. Teyssot, eds., *The History of Garden Design*, Thames & Hudson, London, 1991, 495.
8. R. Smithson, paraphrased by Lucy Lippard (1983).

ART AND LIFE

1. J. Campbell, *The Power of Myth,* 118.
2. J. Campbell, ib., 230.
3. On the 'pollen path', see J. Campbell, *The Power of Myth*, 230; on Australian 'dreamtime' see P. Devereux: *The Dreamtime Earth and Avebury's Open Secrets*, Gothic Image, Glastonbury, 1992, 7-12.
4. Alfred Watkins published *The Old Straight Track* and his theory of 'leys' in 1925.
5. See J. Cowan, 1989; B. Chatwin, *The Songlines*, Picador, London, 1988; L. Levy-Bruhl, *Primitive Mythology,* University of Queensland Press, 1983.
6. Rilke wrote in the *Sonnets to Orpheus*: 'Gesang ist Dasein. Für ein Gott ein Leichtes. / Wann aber *sind* wir?' ('Song is Being. It's easy for a god. But when shall we *be*?').
7. B. Flanagan, in G. Baro, 1969.
8. J. Turrell, 1987.
9. G. Celant, 1969.
10. P. Redgrove, letter to the author, Mch 5, 1993.
11. J.C. Powys, 1930, 104.
12. From *The Countess of Pembroke's Arcadia,* in G. Miller, ed. *Poems of the Elizabethan Age*, Methuen, London, 1977, 215.
13. R. Herrick, *Selected Poems*, ed. M.K. Pace, Crescent Moon, 1998.

SPIRIT OF PLACE IN LITERATURE

1. In *The Big Supposer*, ed. M. Alyn, Grove Press, New York, NY, 1974, 90.
2. L. Durrell, *Nunquam*, Faber, London, 1970, 211.
3. L. Durrell, *Justine*, Faber, London, 1963, 156.
4. In ib., 36.
5. L.W. Market: "Symbolic Geography: D.H. Lawrence and Lawrence Durrell", in M. Cartwright, ed: *On Miracle Ground: Proceedings From the First National Lawrence Durrell Conference/ Deus Loci: The Lawrence Durrell Newsletter,* V, 1, Autumn, 1981, 90f.
6. L. Durrell, *Justine*, 100.
7. L. Durrell, 1971, 156.

THE ALCHEMY OF MATTER

1. "David Smith Makes a Sculpture", 1951, in D. Smith, 149.
2. *Nature*, 1836, in H. Hugo, 386-7.
3. W. Goethe: *The Sorrows of Young Werther,* tr. M. Hulse, Penguin, London, 1989, 44.
4. C. Hussey, *The Picturesque*, Putnam's, New York, 1927. E. Burke wrote: '[t]he passion caused by the great and sublime in *nature*, when those causes operate most powerfully, is astonishment: and astonishment is that state of the soul in which all its motions are suspended, with some degree of horror'. (E. Burke, in *The Philosophy of Edmund Burke*, University of Michigan Press, Ann Arbor, 1967, 256.)
5. C. Greenberg: "Abstract, Representational, and so forth", in 1961, 133.
6. R. Long, Sante Fe interview.
7. J.C. Powys, 1967, 168-9.
8. J.C. Powys, 1955, 926.
9. J.C. Powys, 1937, 353.
10. M. Eliade: "The Sacred and the Modern Artist", *Criterion*, 4, 1965, and in M. Eliade, 1988.
11. W. Laib, in A. Benjamin, 91.

THE ECONOMICS OF LAND ART

1. A. Henri, *Total Art*, 81-82.
2. Richard Long, quoted in S. Gablik: *Has Modernism Failed?*, Thames & Hudson, London, 1984, 44.
3. 'I make art in the capitalist system which in itself is a political statement (selling art for the next walk)', remarked Hamish Fulton (1995).
4. In A. Haden-Guest, 40.
5. Isn't famine relief a better alternative? Perhaps one could make famine relief/ earthquake relief/ medical supply/ housing, and other 'charity' and 'aid' projects, an art event? Perhaps if Christo spent $26 million on providing food for the needy instead of wrapping a building in Berlin in a bit of plastic, people would not be so angry?
6. If Christo's artworks cost a lot, this is chickenfeed next to scientific and military experiments, which cost billions of dollars. The *Large Hadron Collider, for instance*, will cost $1.5 billion. Just one nuclear submarine costs the same amount. In the mid-1980s, 1,000,000 dollars per minute were spent on the arms industry (1982 figures). That's $16,500 per second.

THE OBJECT IN LAND ART AND MINIMAL ART

1. On Minimalism, see M. Tuchman, 1967; F. Tuten: "American Sculpture of the Sixties", *Arts Magazine*, 41, 7, May, 1967; I. Sandler, *Concrete Expressionism*, Loeb Student Center, New York University, NY, 1965; R. Wollheim: "Minimal Art", *Arts Magazine*, 39, 4, Jan, 1965; D. Mayhall, 1979; R. Krauss, 1973; B. Reise, 1969; P. Tuchman, 1988.
2. See C. Robins, 1966; M. Fried: "Art and Objecthood", 1967.
3. B. Rose: "ABC Art", 1965, 66.
4. M. Bochner: "Systematic", 1966, 40.
5. F. Stella: "The Pratt Lecture", 1960, in B. Richardson, *Frank Stella: The Black Paintings*, Baltimore Museum of Art, Baltimore, MD, 1976, 78.
6. W. Tucker, 1969, 12-13.

LAND ART AND CONCEPTUAL ART

1. A noteworthy exhibition of Conceptual art was held at the Kunsthalle in Bern, curated by Harald Szeemann: *When Attitudes Become Form* (1969); some key land artists

were involved: Richard Long walked in the mountains and recorded his walk in a gallery statement; Walter de Maria installed a telephone, with a message beside it saying the visitor could talk to him; Jannis Kounellis put bags of grain on a stairway; Michael Heizer created *Berne Depression*, smashing the pavement near the Kunsthalle with a wrecking ball; Joseph Beuys smeared fat along the walls.

2. "Mel Bochner on Malevich", 1974, 62.
3. R. Serra, in *Richard Serra, Interviews,* Hudson River Museum, New York, NY, 1980, 37.
4. D. Oppenheim, in 1992.
5. L. Weiner, in E. Lucie-Smith, 1987, 117.
6. R. Long, 1985, 2, 24.

MAPS

1.R. Long, IC 1, 6.
2. B. Redhead, 54.
3. R. Long, quoted in B. Redhead, 54.
4. Quoted in B. Redhead, 48.
5. F. Colpitt, 60.

LAND ART AND PHOTOGRAPHY

1. S. Mills: "Special Kaye [Tony Kaye]", *Sunday Times Magazine*, June 12, 1994, 55.
2. D. Smith, *c.* 1953-54, in D. Smith, 158.
3. E. Hesse, in *Eva Hesse*, Guggenheim Museum, New York, NY, 1972.
4. J. Dibbets, 1970.
5. R. Long, Santa Fe interview.
6. R. Long, in W. Malpas, 1995.
7. R. Long, 1985, 1, 1.
8. K. Schwitters, quoted in F. Roh, *German Art in the Twentieth Century*, Thames & Hudson, London, 1968, 133.
9. Jasper Johns, quoted in D. Sylvester, op. cit., 15-16.
10. R. Smithson, in C. Robins, 1984, 78.

INTERIOR AND EXTERIOR ART

1. Robert Smithson reckoned that a 'work of art when placed in a gallery loses its charge and becomes a portable object or surface disengaged from the outside world' (*Selected Writings*, 132).
2. D. Oppenheim, 1992.
3. D. Nash, in A. McPherson, 30.
4. In M. Heizer, 1970.
5. D. Nash, in B. Nemitz, 98.
6. L. Weiner, in *Avalanche*, Spring, 1972, 67.

LAND ART AND CHANGE

1. J. Beuys, in *Documenta 7*, 2, Documenta, Kassel, 1982.
2. R. Long, FC VI, in WC, 16. 'Time passes, a place remains. A walk moves through life, it is physical but afterwards invisible. A sculpture is still, a stopping place, visible' (R. Long, WF).
3. See J. Burnham, 1971.
4. Quoted in G. Baro, 1969, 122; see C. Harrison, 1968, 266-8; J. Kirshner, "Barry Flanagan", *Artforum*, 23, 10, Summer, 1985, 112.

LAND ART AS RELIGION

1. M. Basho, *The Narrow Road to the Deep North and Other Travel Sketches*, tr. N. Yuasa, Penguin, London, 1966, 33.
2. M. Ueda: *Matsuo Basho*, Twayne, New York, NY, 1970, 167.
3. C. Andre, in *Carl Andre: Sculpture*, 1984.
4. M. Heizer, 1970.
5. J. White, 67-69.
6. R. Long, 1985, part 1, 14.
7. R. Long, 1985, part 2, 22.
8. M. Eliade: "Sacred Architecture and Symbolism", in *Eliade*, ed. C. Tacou, L'Herne, Paris, 1978, and in M. Eliade, 1988, 107.
9. M. Fried, "Art And Objecthood", 1967, in G. Battock, 1995, 28.
10. M. Eliade, 1984, 185.
11. John Beardsley says Long's works are like 'physical traces of some sort of private ritual' (1977, 52).
12. M. Eliade, "Sacred Architecture and Symbolism", in M. Eliade, 1988, 107.
13. M. Eliade, 1988, 107.

STONE CIRCLES (LAND ART AND PREHISTORIC ART)

1. J. Campbell, in *An Open Life*, 105-6.
2. As Mircea Eliade explained:

> the most representative mystical experience of the archaic societies, that of shamanism, betrays the *Nostalgia for Paradise,* the desire to recover the state of freedom and beatitude before "the Fall", the will to restore communication between Earth and Heaven; in a word, to abolish all the changes made in the very structure of the Cosmos and in the human mode of being by that primordial disruption. The shaman's ecstasy restores a great deal of the paradisiac condition: it renews the friendship with the animals; by his *flight* or ascension, the shaman reconnects Earth with Heaven; up there, in Heaven, he once more meets the God of Heaven face to face and speaks directly to him, as man sometimes did *in illo tempore.* (1975, 66)

3. See M. Berger, 1989.
4. Quoted in L. Lippard, 1967c, 26.
5. R. Long, letter to the author, in W. Malpas, 1995.
6. The allusions to prehistory would be quite different if Long had stuck a picture of the Cerne Giant next to himself instead of the Wilmington Man. The interpretation might be different, for the Cerne Giant has the biggest phallus in prehistoric (or any) art (at least in the UK).
7. R. Long, 1972, in *Fragments of a Conversation I-VI*, in *Walking in Circles*, 38.

TREES

1. D.H. Lawrence, in M. Elvy, 74.
2. Writers on the symbolic and religious aspects of trees include Mircea Eliade (*Patterns of Comparative Religion*), Robert Graves (*The White Goddess*), James G. Frazer (*The Golden Bough*), and J.R.R. Tolkien, among others.
3. See R. Parker, 1987, 316; L. Lippard, 1976, 203.
4. Film director John Boorman's phrase, talking about J.R.R. Tolkien in a BBC documentary (2001) on the author.

LIVING PLANTS

1. J. Koons, in A. Muthesiues, ed. *Jeff Koons*, Cologne, 1992.

LAND ART AND CONTEMPORARY SCULPTURE IN BRITAIN

1. A. Caro, in L. Alloway, 1961, 1.
2. W. Tucker, 1969, 13.
3. A. Caro, op. cit.
4. D. Lee: "Wimbledon Sculpture", in G. Hughes, ed: *Arts Review Yearbook 1989,* 25.
5. P. Fuller: "Likely Prospects: A British Art Questionnaire", *Artscribe*, 50, Jan, 1985, 27-28; "Onward Christian Soldiers", *Artscribe*, 52, July, 1985.
6. P. Fuller: "Black cloud over the Hayward", *Art Monthly*, 70, Oct, 1983; "Lee Grandjean and Glynn Williams", *Art Monthly*, 51, Nov, 1981.
7. This is often the way certain pop groups are criticized: 'they can't play their own instruments' pundits often carp. But *it doesn't matter* If a pop musician can or can't play, writes their own material or not: what counts, in the postmodern era, is the text itself, the effect, the experience. What counts is the song, the sound, the image.
8. T. Cragg, in E. Lucie-Smith, 1987, 130.
9. K. Blacker, in P. de Monchaux, 1983, 94.
10. See T. Neff, 1987; B. Jones, 1977; L. Ponti, 1980; I. Lamaitre, 1985; G. Celant, 1981.
11. Tony Cragg, quoted in D. Wheeler, 1991, 324.
12. S. Reynolds: "New Pop and Its Aftermath", *Monitor*, 4, 1985.
13. See R. Carr: "Another Sex Pistols Record (turns out to be the future of rock & roll", *New Musical Express*, July 2, 1977.

THE BRITISH LANDSCAPE TRADITION

1. R. Long, interview, April, 1985 (IC 2, 9).
2. R. Rosenblum, quoted in "Romanticism and Retrospective: An Interview with Robert Rosenblum", in A. Papadakis, *The New Romantics*, 7.
3. C. Andre, quoted in A. Causey, 1977, 126.
4. Long talks about doing things which have a 'deep meaning' for him; he says he has 'the most sublime or profound feelings' when he walks: this is the language of the sublime artist, from the Romantics (Wordsworth, Keats, Turner) to the Abstract Expressionists (Newman, Rothko, Still).
5. R. Long: 'I think if I only worked outdoors it could perhaps be seen as romantic escapism' (RC, 20).
6. T. Hughes, 1969, 79-80.

4 • LAND ARTISTS IN BRITAIN, EUROPE AND AMERICA

ROBERT SMITHSON

1. In C. Robins, 78.
2. R. Hobbs, 12.
3. J.G. Ballard, in R. Smithson, 1997.
4. Smithson labelled pre-existing sites land artworks, non-sites, such as the pipes, boxes and walkways of an industrial zone in *Monuments of Passaic* (1967)
5. J.G. Ballard, in R. Smithson, 1997.
6. R. Smithson, "A Sedimentation of the Mind: Earth Projects", in *Selected Writings,* 85.
7. R. Smithson, "Discussion with Heizer, Oppenheim, Smithson", *Avalanche*, 1970, and in E. Johnson, 1982, 182.
8. C. Robins, 1984, 82.

9. In L. Lippard, 1973, 88.
10. See M. Gimbutas, *The Language of the Goddess*, Thames & Hudson, London, 1989.
11. R. Smithson: "The Spiral Jetty", unpublished MS, quoted in R. Krauss, 282. See R. Hobbs, 1981.
12. I. Sandler, 1990, 60.
13. *Selected Writings*, 37.
14. J. Coplans: "Robert Smithson: The Amarillo Ramp", in R. Hobbs, 53.

CARL ANDRE

1. C. Andre, quoted in D. Bourdon: "The Razed Sites of Carl Andre", in G. Battock, 1995, 103.
2. In ib., 104.
3. L. Lippard, 1973, 157.
4. C. Andre, in *Carl Andre: Sculpture*, 1984.
5. L. Lippard, 1965, 58.
6. C. Andre, 1970, 61.
7. In ib., 107.
8. G. Evans, 1969, 62.
9. D. Bourdon, 1978, 56. See M. Bochner, 1967, 39-43.
10. D. Bourdon, in G. Battock, 1995, 107.
11. R. Krauss, 1977, 271f.
12. M. Bochner, in G. Battock, 1995, 94.
13. C. Andre, in L. Lippard, 1970, 7.
14. Carl Andre, *Joint*, 1968, 183 units, each 14 x 18 x 36 in, installation at Windham College, Putney, Vermont.
15. C. Andre, quoted in D. Bourdon, in G. Battock, 1995, 108.
16. T. Smith, quoted in M. Fried, 1967, in G. Battock, 1995, 131.
17. David Lee said that 'Andre repeats one thing in each piece; Smithson repeats one thing but increases its size' (1967, 44).

DENNIS OPPENHEIM

1. In D. Oppenheim, 1992.
2. L. Lippard, 1983, 52.
3. In M. Heizer, 1970.
4. D. Oppenheim, in M. Heizer, 1970.
5. In D. Oppenheim, 1978.

ROBERT MORRIS

1. Critic John Perreault wrote of Morris:

> Robert Morris is the genius of negative presence and the perversity of odd proportions that are subliminal in their aggressiveness. Works of art can in some sense be defined as those man-made objects that are designed solely to call attention to themselves. In this age of bombast, chatter, and random activity, that which does not move and that which is silent is often that which compels our attention and stimulates our awareness most effectively. Donald Judd, too, appears to have this "anti-art," pro-silence bias, and his works, although scrupulously elegant, are a well-formulated attack on "artistic" cliché. (J. Perreault, 1995, 259.)

2. R. Morris, quoted in M. Fried, 1967, in G. Battock, 1995, 126.
3. M. Friedman, 1966, 23.
4. D. Factor, "Los Angeles", *Artforum*, 4, 9, May, 1966, 13.

5. In M. Compton, 1971, 16.
6. R. Morris, "Notes on Sculpture", 4, 51.
7. In D. Wheeler, 1991, 221.
8. B. Rose, 1965.
9. D. Sylvester, 1996, 243.
10. Robert Morris preferred not to give titles to many of his works. He said:

> I think that the reason I don't title them is that I don't think the work is about allusions. And I think titles always are. And I think the work is very much about that thing there in space, quite literally. And titles seem to me to have some allusion to what the thing isn't, and that's why I avoid titles. (In M. Compton, 1971, 19)

MICHAEL HEIZER

1. For some this was a gigantic 'violation' of the planet, in ecological/ green terms. See A. Sonfist, 1983; J. Deardsley, 1984. Sol LeWitt was sceptical of enormity: '[i]t it's so big that you can't really comprehend it except by its emotive force then I don't want it' (in F. Colpitt, 77). And Robert Morris wrote that 'beyond a certain size the object can overwhelm and the gigantic scale becomes the loaded term' (1966, 21).
2. See J. Brown, 1984; G. Müller, "Michael Heizer", *Arts Magazine*, Dec, 1969, 42-45.
3. In H. Smagula, 1983, 286.
4. M. Heizer, in J. Bell: "Positive and Negative", *Arts Magazine*, Nov, 1974, 55.
5. R. Hughes, 1997, 571.
6. M. Heizer, 1970.
7. R. Hughes, 1991, 386.

JAMES TURRELL

1. Dia Foundation, the McArthur Foundation, the National Endowment for the Arts, the Lannan Foundation, the Canon Company, the Bohen Foundation, the Martin Bucksbaum Family Foundation, Count Guiseppe Panza di Buimo, Dr Pentti Kouri, Jean Stein, plus other donors.
2. J. Turrell, in A. Benjamin, 47.
3. J. Turrell, 1987.
4. W. Furlong, in M. Gooding, 2002, 81.

NANCY HOLT

1. N. Holt, "Sun Tunnels", 1977, 34.
2. In T. Castle, 1982, 88.
3. See N. Holt, 1975, 1977; T. Castle, 1982.
4. C. Robins, 1984, 10.
5. M. Eliade, 1975, 64.

ALICE AYCOCK

1. H. Risatti, "The Sculpture of Alice Aycock", *Woman's Art Journal*, Summer, 1985, 37.
2. A. Aycock, quoted in E. Johnson, 1982, 223.
3. R. Smith, 1975, 68.
4. A. Aycock, quoted in N. Rosen: "A Sense of Place: Five American Artists", *International Sculpture*, Merriewold West, 1975.
5. E. Johnson, 1982, 221.
6. A. Aycock, 1977.

MARY MISS

1. Mary Miss attended the University of California at Santa Barbara, took sculpture at Colorado College, and graduated in 1966 from UC. Miss subsequently studied at the Rhinehardt School of Sculpture at the Maryland Art Institute until 1968.
2. R. Onoratio, 1978, 32. See also R. Onoratio, 1979; K. Linker, "Mary Miss", *Mary Miss*, ICA, 1983.
3. See L. Anderson, 1973; M. Miss, 1981.

WALTER DE MARIA

1. De Maria proposed another shaft, *Olympic Mountain Project* (1970) – never made – which would have been 400 feet deep and three feet wide.
2. Quoted in H. Smagula, 289.
3. R. Smith, 1978, 104.
4. H. Rosenberg, 1972, 36.
5. K. Baker, 1988, 125-7.
6. See D. Bourdon, 1968, 39-43, 72; M. Winton, "Sculptures That Blow Away", *Ark*, Spring, 1970, 18-19; R. Smith, 1978, 102-5.
7. W. de Maria, 1980.
8. Art critic Kenneth Baker related de Maria's *Lightning Field* to issues of philosophy and politics:

   The piece also serves as an instrument for intensifying one's grasp of the beauty of the earth... The *Lightning Field* acquaints the visitor with the possibility that beauty may be the only conscionable and feasible refuge from history. That is, the apprehension of reality as everywhere radiant with its being may be the only bearable consciousness of life that does not entail repressing awareness of the horrors of our time. Beauty in this sense is just what the *Lightning Field* makes available... (1988, 127)

9. See P. Redgrove, *The Black Goddess and the Sixth Sense*, Bloomsbury, London, 1987; *The Cyclopean Mistress*, Bloodaxe, Newcastle, 1993. In many poems, Peter Redgrove wrote of the sensualism of nature, thunderstorms being particular favourite natural phenomena.
10. H. Smagula, 290. De Maria himself thought that a lightning strike is a 'false climax' to the work, which really needs to be seen over a period of time to appreciate its qualities.
11. Incredible as Walter de Maria's *Lightning Field* is, or Christo's wrapped coasts and islands, far stranger and wilder are the constructions of modern science. The gigantic particle accelerators, for instance, where quarks, strangeness and charms are examined, are truly mind-boggling structures. 'Only by battering streams of other particles together in giant underground accelerators has it been possible to generate the energies necessary to create these elusive entities,' wrote Robin McKie ("Why we are so positive", *The Observer*, May 1, 1994).
   There are plans to produce a Large Hadron Collider, using the existing 26 mile tunnel deep underground in Switzerland. These particle accelerators go far beyond most land art in creating sheer astonishment. Not the least amazing aspect about these circular tunnels is that they are so large, using gigantic machines set in caverns. The ironic thing is that such massive scientific equipment is being used to explore... the tiniest, invisible objects, the most mysterious things in the New Physics: atoms, quarks, strangeness, charms, Higgs' bosons, neutrons and protons. If Christo's artworks cost a lot – 26 million dollars or whatever – this is chickenfeed to scientific and military experiments, which cost billions of dollars. The Large Hadron Collider, for instance, will cost $1.5 billion.

SOME OTHER AMERICAN LAND ARTISTS

1. G. Matta-Clark, "Interview With *Avalanche*", *Avalanche*, Dec, 1974.
2. See L. Lippard, 1983, 49.
3. T. Murak. in B. Nemitz, 94.
4. D. Hollis, in B. Oakes, ed. *Sculpting the Environment*, Van Nostrand Reinhold, New York, NY, 1995, 107.

CHRISTO

1. J. Marck, 1969.
2. Christo, quoted in E. Johnson, 1982, 198.
3. See W. Spies, *The Running Fence Project, Christo*, Abrams, New York, NY, 1977.
4. Christo, in A. Haden-Guest, 40.

HANS HAACKE

1. H. Haacke, in J. Burnham, 1967.
2. H. Haacke, in ib.

DAVID NASH

1. See A. McPherson, 1978; H. Adams, 1979; D. Nash, 1980.
2. H. Adams, 1979, 46-47.
3. D. Nash, *Sea Hearth*, 1981, Isle of Bute, Scotland, *Wood Stove*, 1979, Maentwrog, Wales, *Slate Stove*, 1981, Blaenau Ffestiniog, Wales, *Snow Stove*, 1982, Kotoku, Japan.
4. At the University of Colorado, 1991.
5. D. Nash, in K. Martin, 1990, 66.
6. H. de Vries, in M. Gooding, 2002, 69.
7. D. Nash, *Fletched Over Ash Dome*, planted 1979, Caen-y-Coed, Maentwrog, Wales.
8. David Nash explained:

   Earlier, I used sawmill wood, regular standard units; later, greenwood, fresh from the tree; now the tree itself. The more I look at the tree, the more I see the tree; it's space and location, its volume and structure, its engineering and balance. More than that, I see the uniqueness of each simple tree, and beyond that still I see it as a great emblem of life. A potent vibrant tower, a whirling prayer wheel of natural energy.

ANDY GOLDSWORTHY

1. Many of the big names in British sculpture have exhibited works at Goodwood, including Elisabeth Frink, David Mach, Phillip King, David Nash, Eduardo Paolozzi, Bill Woodrow, Tony Cragg, Ian Hamilton Finlay, Stephen Dilworth, Anthony Caro and Anthony Gormley.
2. A. Goldsworthy, *Time*, 82.
3. A. Goldsworthy, *Time*, 193.
4. J. Dibbets, in D. Ashton, ed. *20th Century Artists on Art*, Pantheon, New York, NY, 1985, 174.
5. A. Goldsworthy, in A. Causey, 1980.
6. A. Goldsworthy, in *Aspects*, 1986.
7. A. Goldsworthy, ib., *Hand To Earth*, 165.
8. A. Goldsworthy, *Sheepfolds*, 17.
9. Interview with T. Friedman, *Third Ear*, June, 1989 in *Hand To Earth*, 166.

10. Another link is nature-man Mellors in *Lady Chatterley's Lover* (1928), the no-nonsense outdoor man who is in fact a New Man, painfully sensitive and alive. The D.H. Lawrence connection with Andy Goldsworthy is emphasized by Goldsworthy himself: in *Stone* he quoted from Lawrence's *The Rainbow* (1915), one of those euphoric, ithyphallic passages about the ecstasy of consummation in an arch. Lawrence's intensely poetic novel about three generations of a Midlands family (his 'Brangwen-saga') is a strident inrush of energy into Goldsworthy's otherwise pedestrian prose in *Stone*. Goldsworthy's own pontifications can be banal (it's more effective perhaps to use quotes from Locke and Lawrence, as he does in *Stone*).

11. A. Goldsworthy, *Stone*, 21.

12. R. Long, letter to the author, in W. Malpas, 1995.

13. K. Carter: "*Stone*", *New Welsh Review*, 27, Winter, 1994-95, 100.

14. A. Goldsworthy, *Wall*, 68-69.

15. A. Goldsworthy, *Réfuges d'Art*, 85.

16. 'My strongest work is so rooted in place that it cannot be separated from where it is made' Goldsworthy wrote in *Stone* (6).

17. A. Goldsworthy, *Hand To Earth*, 167.

18. In A. Papadakis, 1991, 250.

19. In J. Beardsley, 1984, 134.

20. A. Goldsworthy, *Midsummer Snowballs*, 31.

21. A. Goldsworthy, quoted in *Andy Goldsworthy*.

22. A. Goldsworthy, interview, Dec 9, 1987, in *Hand To Earth*, 163.

23. 'Urban living has always tended to produce a sentimental view of nature' wrote John Berger (*The White Bird: Writings by John Berger*, London, 1988, 7).

24. 'Nature for me is the clearest path to discover – *uncluttered by personalities* or associations – *it just is*' says Goldsworthy in a telling statement (my emphasis, sketchbook no. 19, 1988, *Hand To Earth*, 150).

25. A. Goldsworthy, *Midsummer Snowballs*, 33.

26. A. Goldsworthy, *Time*, 112.

27. A. Goldsworthy, *Andy Goldsworthy*, Viking, London, 1990, no page numbers; and in N. Hedges, 67; *Hand To Earth*, 160-1.

28. A. Causey: "Environmental Sculptures", in *Hand To Earth*, 128.

29. 'Some works have qualities of snaking but are not snakes. The form is shaped through a similar response to environment' (*Andy Goldsworthy*).

30. A. Goldsworthy, *Réfuges d'Art*, 113.

31. In R. Davies, 1984, 151.

32. A. Goldsworthy, *Hand To Earth*, 163.

33. A. Goldsworthy, unpublished notes, 1988, in *Hand To Earth*, 134-5.

34. A. Goldsworthy, *Réfuges d'Art*, 89.

35. 1987, *Hand To Earth*, 147.

36. There were six different variants of sheepfolds in the project; cairn folds (pinfolds), boulder folds, drove arch folds (folds restored for the *Arch* project), restored folds, touchstone folds, which have works built into the walls, and the ephemeral pieces made on the Coleridge walk route. The sheepfolds containing cairns were built near the Nine Standards in Cumbria, rock formations which have long fascinated Goldsworthy.

37. In 1994's *Herd of Arches* in London, Goldsworthy had fitted together masses of small slabs of stone, with tiny pebbles and wafer-thin stones wedged in, to hold the arch tightly together. Roger Partridge has made an arch out of stone (1983, private collection) which recalls Goldsworthy's *Herd of Arches*. Alan Sonfist's *Rock Monument of Rocky Mountains*, very much an ancestor of Goldsworthy's arches, was made in 1971.

38. Goldsworthy was pleased to have cracked creating sculptures under the harsh, bright sun of South France. One of his methods was to submerge stones in the River Bès (which he had tried once or twice before). 'I like the way that the water confuses

the form of the stones, so you forget the stone and all you see is the colour' Goldsworthy commented (*Réfuges d'Art*, 111).

Part of Goldsworthy's Digne works were the three *Sentinels* – very large stone cairns which marked the walking route in the three valleys. Another important commission was the five *Water Cairns*, built at the Réserve Géologique on the route to the car lot. Also part of the Digne projects was the clay wall (*River of Earth*, 1999) constructed in the museum in Digne and filmed, to form a backdrop for Régine Chopinot and the Ballet Atlantique and their *Danse du Temps* (2000).

39. Goldsworthy has made rain, frost and shadow prints at the Royal Museum of Scotland, at Cornell University, Central Park, Yorkshire, Cumbria, Holland, Japan, Angers (France), Australia, Denmark and Ciudad Real (Spain).
40. A. Goldsworthy, *Hand To Earth*, 19.
41. A. Goldsworthy, *Winter Harvest*; *Hand To Earth*, 162.
42. A. Goldsworthy, quoted in M. Church. For Goldsworthy, moments are intense precisely because they are only momentary: *pace* his icicle spiral sculpture of 1996, Goldsworthy said that 'intensity can only be shown for a short time. In fact, the moment is intense only because it lasts for a short time, and it would be wrong for such an intensity to last longer than that' (*Wood*, 10). In fact, it's difficult for the spectator, let alone the artist, to sustain that kind of æsthetic intensity.
43. A. Goldsworthy, in M. Church; and *Stone*, 120.

CHRIS DRURY

1. C. Drury, 2002, 91.
2. Drury's works in Sussex include *Vortex* (Lewes Castle), *Cuckoo Dome*, *Beehive Shelter* (Goodwood), *Holding Light* (Brighton), *Guardian Shelter* (Sheffield Forest), *Chalk Chamber* (a barn in Sussex), *Rhythms of the Heart* (Hastings), *Heart of Reeds* (Lewes), Towner Art Gallery, Eastbourne, *Seven Sisters Bundles* (near Eastbourne), and the dewponds up on the Sussex downs.
3. C. Drury, 2002, 72, 76.
4. Norway (1988), New Mexico (1993), De Lank River, Cornwall (1990), Lappland (1988), Wester Ross, Scotland (1992), Kintail, Scotland (1994), Ladakh (1997) and Colorado (1989).
5. Drury's cloud chambers include *Coppice Cloud Chamber* (1998, Kent), *Cloud Chamber* (Piccadilly, London, 1993), *Cloud Chamber* (1994, Aberdeen), *Eden Cloud Chamber* (2002, Cornwall), *Reed Chamber* (2002, Arundel), *Cedar Log Sky Chamber* (1996, Japan), *Hut of the Shadow* (1997, Western Isles), *Clohan Cloud Chamber* (1992, Dublin), *Cloud Chamber* (1990, Belgium), *Cloud Chamber For the Trees and Sky* (2003, North Carolina) and *Wicklow Cloud Chamber* (1990, Glencree, Ireland).
6. C. Drury, 2002, 76, 84.
7. C. Drury, 2002, 90.
8. Statement, on C. Drury's website.
9. C. Drury, in 1998, 6.
10. C. Drury, 1998, 7.

HAMISH FULTON

1. H. Fulton, in D. Beal, 2000.
2. H. Fulton, 1995.
3. Michael Archer, comparing the art of Long and Fulton, reckoned that Fulton 'offers possibilities', while Long 'designates' Long's art was 'intentional in ways which Fulton's is not', and 'Fulton's art is conceptual in ways which Long's is not' (Archer, 1991).
4. H. Fulton, in 1999.
5. H. Fulton, in M. Auping, 1990.

OTHER LAND ARTISTS IN BRITAIN AND EUROPE

1. R. Martin, 31.
2. B. Nemitz, 78.
3. N. Pope, quoted in W. Strachan, 70.
4. R. Harris, quoted in D. Petherbridge, "Public commissions and the new concerns in sculpture", in P. de Monchaux, 1983, 136.
5. In W. Strachan, 179.
6. See R. Parker, 1987, 316; L. Lippard, 1976, 203.

5 • RICHARD LONG: THE ART OF WALKING

1. C. Harrison, in T. Neff, 32.
2. R. Long, FS, in RL, 236.

RICHARD LONG: ARTISTIC BIOGRAPHY

1. H. Thoreau. in *Walking*, 1861, in *The Portable Thoreau*, ed. C. Bode, Viking, New York, NY, 1980, 592.
2. A. Seymour: "Walking in Circles", 1.
3. Richard Long, letter to the author, July 11, 1994.
4. H. Fulton, in M. Auping, 1982.

RICHARD LONG: THE ART OF THE WALK

1. 'It always amazes me that I can go down to Dartmoor for a walk, and even though it's a relatively small place and in the middle of a crowded island, I can still spend a whole day walking without seeing anyone' (Long, FC VI, 16).
2. Kate Blacker, discussing Richard Long, Ian Hamilton Finlay and Willats, remarked:

> I don't think Long... *reversed* anything. They just weren't concerned with the same things as their predecessors were. Long went to St Martin's and was introduced to a very strict set of self-perpetuating rules. He seems to have spent no time considering what [Anthony] Caro or [Philip] King had to say. Instead he placed himself in another British tradition: that of landscape. Regardless of the format of how to display the sculpture, he was the first British artist to bring landscape indoors. It's no longer a framed picture, a window onto the landscape, as it was in Constable or the Norfolk School. He brings the sense of scale, the whole sensibility of that tradition, into three dimensions. (K. Blacker, in P. de Monchaux, 1983, 92).

3. See Weston La Barre: *The Ghost Dance*, Allen & Unwin, London, 1972.
4. P. Rodaway, 3.
5. Anne Seymour makes many critical mistakes, too numerous to list. For instance, she says 'there is nothing mystical or religious about Long's work' (Seymour, WC, 12). Then she goes on to note the yogic states of consciousness in his work; the sense of meditation, Zen Buddhism, C.G. Jung, etc.
6. Richard Long: '[e]ven though it is necessary to get a good photograph, the photographs should be as simple as possible... the photographs have got to be fairly simple and straightforward, so that the feeling of the work somehow accurately comes through.' (RC, 24.)
7. H. Thoreau, in H. Hugo, 471.
8. R. Rosenblum, in A. Papadakis, 10.
9. 'Working out there in nature, then, Long is a performer in the open-air theatre of the sublime' (David Sylvester).

10. Hölderlin's poems translates thus:

Being alone with heavenly powers, and when the
Light begins to pass by, and swiftly river,
Wind and time seek out the place, with a constant
    Eye then to face them –

Nothing more blessed I know, nor want, as long as
Not like willows me too the flood sweeps on, and
Well looked after, sleeping, down I must travel,
    Waves for my bedding;

Gladly, though, he will stay at home who harbours
Things divine in his heart; and you, all heaven's
Languages, freely, as long as I may, I'll
    Sing and interpret.

(F. Hölderlin, *Hölderlin's Songs of Light: Selected Poems*, tr. M. Hamburger, Crescent Moon, 2003, 30-33.)

THE HUMAN TOUCH

1. 'My work is really a self-portrait, in all ways' (Long, GL, 6).
2. R. Long, WAF, in RL, 236.
3. In RL, 196: for the complete work, see illustration.
4. See D. Charles: "Flux de marche avec pietinement", *Traverses*, 14-15, 1979, 81-92.
5. S. Hosokawa: "The Walkman Effect", in R. Middleton & D. Horn, eds. *Popular Music 4: Performers and Audiences*, Cambridge University Press, New York, NY, 1984, 175.
6. M. de Certeau: *L'Invention du quotidien*, Paris, 1980, 180.
7. '[The walk] is never a performance. It is usually a very private, quiet activity. I am happy to make it in solitude' (Long, RC, 20).
8. Jean-Francçois Augoyard: *Pas a Pas. Essai sur le cheminement quotidien en milieu urbain*, Paris, 1979; C. Norberg-Schultz: *Existence, Space and Architecture*, London 1971.
9. In D. Sylvester.
10. R. Long, in WAF in RL, 236.
11. 'Nature is the source of my work' (Long, GL, 5).

RICHARD LONG'S EASTERN TURN

1. 5. Chuang-tzu, *Basic Writings*, 44.

CRITICS OF RICHARD LONG ART

1. In M. Gooding, 2002, 70.
2. P. Fuller, 1993, xxxvi-xxxvii.

6 • CIRCLES, LINES, ROWS, SPLASHES AND OTHER FORMS

STONE CIRCLES

1. 'The beauty of Long's work is that it is what you see, and that what you see is all is needed to bring you to a stop and as you look to make you feel that time has stopped, and to fill you with a sense of well-being and completeness' wrote David

Sylvester.
2. In RL, 236.

STONES

1. R. Long, website, 2000.
2. Printed in *Richard Long: Walking the Line*, 45.
3. In *Richard Long: Walking the Line*, 46.
4. J.C. Powys: *Petrushka and the Dancer: The Diaries of John Cowper Powys, 1929-1939*, Carcanet/ Alyscamps, 1995, 98, 136.

LINES AND ROWS

1. These modern paths were created by (and in association with) organizations such as the Countryside Commission, the Ramblers' Association, local councils and the National Parks.

COLOUR IN RICHARD LONG'S ART

1. R. Rosenblum, 1988, 11.

TIME AND HISTORY

1. R. Long, quoted in D. Wheeler, 264.
2. M. Eliade, 1984, 186.
3. M. Eliade, 1984, 101.
4. S. Bann, 1994b.
5. R. Descartes, *Le Discours de la méthode*.

7 • IDEA/ TEXT/ DESIRE: TEXTWORKS

THE IDEA AND THE TEXT

1. D. Reason: "Echo and Reflections", in S. Bann, 1991, 169.
2. Quoted in RL, 201.
3. G. Stein, in J. Rothenberg & P. Joris, eds. *Poems For the Millennium*, University of California Press, Berkeley, CA, 1995
4. R. Long, Orkney, 1994.
5. D. Lee: "Sculpture Outside: The Forest of Dean Sculpture Project", in G. Hughes, 1989, 22.
6. Richard Long, letter to the author, July 11, 1994.
7. R. Long, WAF, 1980, in RL, 236.
8. R. Long, in RL, 201.
9. M. Eliade, "Shadows In Archaic Religions", in 1988, 4.
10. R. Long, RC, 23.

WALL DRAWINGS AND HANDPRINTS

1. R. Long, in FS in RL, 236.
2. R. Long, FS in RL, 236.
3. '...the work comes from one person being on his own in nature and the spirit of the work is about that one to one relationship. If many people came to that place it would destroy the spirit of that place' (IC 1, 1; also RL, 133-4).
4. If an artwork's made of molecules, it'll still be on the planet, somewhere (this is a

sci-fi fantasy wish about the base matter of alchemy, or maybe it's sheer desperation). Thus, works the art lover would yearn to see, such as Michelangelo's lost *Leda,* the half million volumes of the Great Library of Alexandria, Simone Martini's portrait of Francesco Petrarch's beloved Laura, or the Hanging Gardens of Babylon, must still be on Earth somewhere, even if they're just bits of dust.

5. R. Barry, in U. Meyer, 1972, 35.
6. R. Long, quoted in RL, 135.

RICHARD LONG'S BOOKS

1. R. Long, 'Stone Walk', OW, 12.
2. R. Long: *A journey of the same length as the River Avon/ an 84 mile canoe journey down the River Severn,* 1977.
3. Other objects the walker treasures or relies on include boots, maps, the water bottle, and the tent. One would suspect that a seasoned walker like Long would have all sorts of other items he's incorporated over the years: a Walkman or radio, for instance, vitamins or pills, perhaps, or a gas stove.

8 • FROM PHOTOGRAPHY TO INSTALLATIONS

1. 1982, in RL, 193.
2. Wind is 'an elemental part of nature, it's often part of a walk, it's part of the energy of the world' (Long, GL, 8). Ted Hughes says that poets often write their best poems when they deal with elemental forces such as wind.
3. J. Hull, *Touching the Rock: An Experience of Blindness,* SPCK Publications, London, 1990, 12.
4. R. Long, in WAF, RL, 236.
5. S. Morris: "A Rhetoric of Silence: Redefinitions of Sculpture in the 1960s and 1970s", in S. Nairne, 198.
6. Christo, quoted in A. Haden-Guest, 40.
7. A. Goldsworthy, *Stone,* 120.

9 • 'A PLACE OF REGENERATION': DARTMOOR

1. R. Long, quoted in G. Greig, 1991.
2. Quoted, in B. Redhead, 48.
3. In RL, 148.
4. See B. Le Messurier, 2002.
5. In *Walking the Line,* 304.

10 • WALKING AS ECSTASY

1. T. Wyatt, in M. Elvy, 6.
2. Quoted in D. Wheeler, 1991, 264.
3. R. Long, in L. Cooke, 1983, 20-21; R. Fuchs, 1974, 172-3.
4. Woodrow trawls the world for materials with which to make sculptures:

My choice of objects is dictated, I think in the first instance by what is available, what I come across in the streets, on dumps... What I find more interesting about the work, is that these items are material for me that is found in my environments...
(B. Woodrow, quoted in *Objects and Sculpture,* Institute of Contemporary Arts, London, 1981, 37.)

5. See A. Seymour: "El Estanque de Basho – una nueva perspectiva", in 1986.
6. R. Long, quoted in E. Lucie-Smith, 1987, 121.
7. P. Redgrove, letter to the author, Apl 20, 1994.
8. R. Long, interview with R. Cork, in D. Sylvester.
9. See B. Chatwin, *What Am I Doing Here*, Picador, London, 220f.
10. Arthur Rimbaud, *A Season In Hell*, tr. A. Jary, Crescent Moon, 1998. The translation reads:

I had to travel, to divert the enchantments that crowded over my brain. On the sea, which I loved as if it were washing away a stain, I saw the consoling cross rise. I had been damned by the rainbow. Happiness was my misfortune, my remorse, my worm: my life would be always too huge to be devoted to strength and beauty. (40-41)

11. R.L. Stevenson, *Travels With a Donkey*. My italics.
12. J. Beardsley, 1984, 42.
13. R. Long, SF. In another interview, though, Long states: '[m]y work is completely independent from all the mystical ideas which were prevalent in the sixties' (1985, 2, 8). 'I wouldn't make any claims to be mystical' (FC VI, 17).
14. See A. Seymour, op.cit.; S. Gablik, op.cit. Lynne Cooke writes that

by the early 1970s, Long's work had become increasingly interpreted in terms of an atavistic archetypal content, with the artist assuming the mantle of spiritual wanderer. Allusions to a rural, pastoral tradition, often couched in a language of almost Georgian naivete, were gradually replaced by a more universal statement, one in which the concept of the timeless, unchanging order of nature was preeminent. Referring to prehistoric artifacts, like menhirs and leylines, introduced a megalithic symbolism and an engagement with cosmic forces fully in keeping with the way in which the stone sculptures in the gallery or the photographs of stone and stick circles and lines in remote, untouched sites postulated not a linear, historical sense of time but chthonic time, the time of the earth's functioning. All evidence of contemporary, and especially of urban, existence was therefore eliminated. By establishing this ahistorical temporality, and by eliciting a symbolic order from chaos and formlessness through the imposition of pure geometric forms, Long was felt to have posited an alternative to modern man's sense of alienation. The grandeur and monumentality in works such as *Slate Circle* or the photo-sculpture *Stones in the Sierra Nevada, Spain* attest to the shift in his work from a pastoral mood and a concern with the *genius loci* in which a harmonious unity between man and nature is intimated... to a heroic statement centred on the notion of a sacred site or a site with mystical meaning, a *locus consecratus*. (1987, 40).

15. M. Eliade, 1975, 61.
16. M. Eliade, 1975, 64.
17. Lawrence Durrell, 1971. Writer-drifter Philip O'Connor remarked that after walking in England he experienced 'an incomparable feeling... as though one were a prayer winding along a road; the feeling is definitely religious' (P. O'Connor, *Britain In the Sixties: Vagrancy*, Penguin, London, 1963).
18. Chuang-tzu, 54.
19. W. Johnson, *Riding the Ox Home*, 52.
20. Hélène Cixous: *Three Steps on the Ladder of Writing*, Columbia University Press, New York, NY, 1993, 64-65.

List of Works

RICHARD LONG

Circle in Alaska, driftwood on the Arctic Circle, Bering Strait 1977; *Untitled*, 1987, mud on paper, Anthony d'Offay Gallery, London; *Avon Mud Circle*, 1986, installation, Guggenheim Museum, New York; *Five, six, pick up sticks/ Seven, eight, lay them straight*, 1980, Anthony d'Offay Gallery, September, 1980; *Connemara Sculpture*, 1971, Ireland, photography, text and drawing, 66 x 83cm, private collection, Italy; *Red Slate Circle*, 1980, 914cm diam, Fogg Art Museum, Cambridge, MA; *Sandstone Spiral*, 1983, 154 stones, 373cm diam, National Gallery of Canada, Ottawa; *Pine Tree Bark Circle*, 1985, diam. 460cm, collection: FRAC Rhone-Alpes, Lyon; *Six Day Walk over all Roads, Lanes and Double Tracks Inside a Six Mile Wide Circle Centred on the Giant of Cerne Abbas*, 1975, photograph & map, 36 x 53.5cm and 72.5 x 73.5cm, Tate Gallery, London.

OTHERS

Carl Andre: *Lead Piece (144 Lead Plates)*, overall 75 x 144.8 x 145.5in, Museum of Modern Art, New York; *Last Ladder*, 1959, wood, 214 x 6 x 15.6cm, Tate Gallery, London; *Cedar Piece*, 1959/64, 68.7 x 36.3in, Öffentliche Kunstammlung Basel.

Alice Aycock: *One Thousand and One Nights in the Mansion of Bliss*, 1983, mixed media, private collection; *The Miraculous Machine in the Garden (Tower of the Winds)*, 1983, mixed media, 16ft high, private collection.

Hans Bellmer: *La Poupée,* 1936, painted bronze, 16.8in high, Musée National d'Art Moderne, Paris.

Gianlorenzo Bernini: *David*, 1623, Galleria Borghese, Rome.

Joseph Beuys: *Lightning*, 1982-85, bronze, Anthony d'Offay Gallery, London.

Giovanni da Bologna: *Mercury*, 1564, Museo Nazionale, Florence.

Louise Bourgeois: *Nature Study,* 1984, bronze, 30 x 19 x 15in, Serpentine Gallery, London.

Constantin Brancusi: *Endless Column*, 1918, 80 x 9.8 x 9.8in, Museum of Modern Art, New York.

Reg Butler: *Girl on Red Base*, 1968-72, painted bronze, 32 x 43 x 63.5in, Pierre Matisse Gallery, New York.

Alexander Calder: *Red Flock, c.* 1949, hanging mobile, metal, 2.8 x 5.5ft, Phillips Collection, Washington, DC; *Thirteen Spines*, 1940, sheet steel, rods, wire and aluminium, 84 in, Wallraf-Richartz Museum, Cologne.

Canova: *Hercules and Lichas*, 1812-15, marble, 138in high, Gallery of Modern Art, Rome.

Benvenuto Cellini: *Perseus with the Head of Medusa*, 1554, bronze, Loggia dei Lanzi, Florence.

John Chamberlain: *Toy*, 1961, welded auto parts and plastic, 4 x 3.1 x 2.6ft, Art Institute, Chicago; *Wagon I*, 1963-64, painted steel, 308.6 x 162.6 x 224.8cm, National Gallery of Scotland.

Christo: *Surrounded Islands, Biscoyne Bay, Greater Miami*, 1980-83, 6 million square feet of polypropylene fabric; *Valley Curtain*, synthetic fabric, 417m long, 1970-72, Grand Canyon, Colorado; *Running Fence*, 1972-76, steel poles, steel cables, woven nylon, 18ft high, 24.5 miles long, Sonoma & Marin Counties, CA.

Tony Cragg: *Instinctive Reactions*, 1987, cast steel, 8 x 21 x 15ft, Lisson Gallery, London; *New Stones*, 1982, Marian Goodman Gallery, New York.

Richard Deacon: *Turning a Blind Eye No.2*, 1984-85, High Museum of Art, Atlanta,

Georgia.

Edgar Degas: *Dancer Putting On Her Stocking*, bronze, 17in high, Metropolitan Museum of Art, New York.

John De Andrea: *Reclining Woman*, 1970, life-size, David Bermant Collection; *Couple*, 1971, acrylic on polyester and hair, man 5.7ft high, woman 5.1ft high, Musée d'Art Moderne, Paris.

Anthony Donaldson: *Girl Sculpture "Red 'n' Gold"*, 1970, 75 x 448cm, Rowan Gallery, London.

Donatello: *David, c.* 1440-42, bronze, Museo Nazionale, Florence.

Chris Drury: *River Vortex*, 1998; *Air Vessel*, 1994; *Wave Chamber*, 1996, Northumberland;*Basket Dewpond,* 1997, 1999, Sussex.

Marcel Duchamp: *Bottle Rack*, 1914, readymade, galvanized iron, 25.5in, Galleria Schwarz, Milan; *Rotorelief (Revolving Glass)*, 1920, three strips of painted glass on metal frame, 4 x 6ft, Yale University Art Gallery, New Haven, CT.

Mary Beth Edelson: *Great Goddess Series*, 1975, collection: the artist; *Blood Mysteries*, 1973, drawing, 91 x 57 in, collection: the artist.

Helen Escobedo: *Snake,* 1980-81, painted steel, 49ft high, National University of Mexico Cultural Centre.

Barry Flanagan: *Soprano*, 1981, bronze, 80 x 66 x 57cm, Arts Council of Great Britain.

Dan Flavin: *Untitled (to the "innovator" of Wheeling Peachblow)*, 1968, 96.5 x 96.5 x 5.7in, Museum of Modern Art, New York; *Untitled*, 1976, pink, blue, green fluorescent light, 96in high, Saatchi Collection, London.

Naum Gabo: *Kinetic Construction*, 1920, metal rod with electric vibrator, 24.2in high, Tate Gallery, London.

Henri Gaudier-Brzeska: *Red Stone Dancer*, 1914, waxed stone, 33.5in high, Tate Gallery, London.

Alberto Giacometti: *Spoon Woman*, 1926, bronze, 57.2in high, Kunsthaus, Zurich.

Andy Goldsworthy: *Japanese maple leaves stitched together to make a floating chain*, November 21, 1987, Ouchiyama-mura, Japan; *Slate Stack*, 1988, Scaur Water Valley, Penpont, Dumfriesshire, Scotland; *Circular stalks in a lake*, April 29, 1987, Yorkshire Sculpture Park; *Dandelion Flowers*, May 1, 1987, Yorkshire Sculpture Park, West Bretton; *Oak Globe*, September 15, 1985, branches and oak leaves, Jenny Noble's Gill, Dumfriesshire; *Slits cut into frozen snow*, February 12, 1988, Blencathra, Cumbria; *Touching North*, April 24, 1989, North Pole; *Touching North*, Fabian Carlsson Gallery, London 1989; *Leadgate and Lambton Earthworks*, 1989, County Durham; *Herd of Arches*, stone, 1994, London.

Nancy Graves: *Zaga*, 1983, cast bronze with polychrome chemical patination, 6' x 4'1" x 2'8", Nelson-Atkins Museum of Art, Kansas City; *Cantileve*, 1983, bronze with polychrome patina, 99 x 67 x 55in, M. Knoedler & Co, New York.

Red Grooms & Mimi Gross: *The City of Chicago*, 1967, mixed media, *c.* 12 x 25 x 25ft, Art Institute of Chicago.

Duane Hanson: *The Tourists*, 1970, polyester resin, polychrome glass fibre, National Gallery of Scotland, Edinburgh; *Bunny*, 1970, fibreglass, life-size, O.K. Harris Gallery, New York.

Tim Head: *State of the Art*, 1984, colour photograph, 183 x 274cm, collection: the artist.

Michael Heizer: *Double Negative*, 1969-70, 1,500 x 50 x 42 feet, Mormon Mesa, Nevada; *Displaced, Replaced Mass*, 1969, Silver Springs, Nevada.

Barbara Hepworth: *Porthmeor: Sea Form*, 1958, bronze, 30.5in high, Hirshhorn Museum and Sculpture Garden, Washington, DC; *Pendour*, 1947, painted wood, 10 x 27in, Hirshhorn Museum and Sculpture Garden, Washington, DC; *Forms in Movement*, 1956, Barbara Hepworth Museum and Sculpture Garden, St Ives, Cornwall; *Two Forms*, 1937, marble, 26in high, private collection.

Eva Hesse: *Contingent*, 1969, reinforced fibreglass and latex over cheesecloth, each of 8 units, 9.5-14 x 3-4ft, Australian National Gallery, Canberra; *Aught,* 1968, double sheets of latex rubber, polyethylene plastic inside, 4 units, each 78in high, collection: the artist; *Ice Piece*, 1969, fibreglass and wire, 62 x 1in, Xavier Fourcade Gallery, New York.

Nancy Holt: *Stone Enclosure: Rock Rings*, 1977-78, hand-quarried schist, outer ring 40 feet, inner ring 2 feet across, ring walls 10 feet high, Western Washington University, Bellingham; *Sun Tunnels*, 1973-76, concrete, each pipe 18 ft long, 9ft high, Great Basin Desert, near Lucin, Utah; *Dark Star Park*, 1979-84, concrete, steel, water, earth, 0.67 of an acre, Rosslyn, Virginia.

Rebecca Horn; *Ballet of the Woodpecker*, 1986-87, room installation with mirrors, small hammers and a painting machine, 330 x 230cm (4 mirrors), 330 x 125cm (4 mirrors), Eric Franck Gallery, Geneva; *Peacock Machine*, 1982, installation at Documenta 7, Kassel.

Valerie Jaudon: *Caile*, 1985, oil on canvas, 48 x 40in, Sidney James Gallery, New York.

Philip Johnson; *Untitled*, 1971, hot-rolled steel, outer circle: min. height 24in, max. height 32.8in, radius 90in, Guggenheim Museum, New York.

Donald Judd: *Untitled*, 1970, copper, 5 x 69 x 8.8in, private collection; *Untitled*, 1969, steel with blue Plexiglas, ten units, each 9 x 40.3 x 31.2in, at 9.2in intervals, Norton Simon Museum of Art, Pasadena, CA;*Untitled*, 1978, brass, 10 units, 6 x 27 x 224in, Indiana University Art Museum, Bloomington, IN; *Untitled*, 1969, brass and red fluorescent Plexiglas, 10 units, 6.2 x 24 x 27in, Hirshhorn Museum and Sculpture Garden, Washington, DC; *Untitled*, 1971, concrete, min. height 36 in, max. height 48in, external radius 150 in, private collection; *Untitled*, 1968, ten units, each 9 x 40in x 31in, height 14'3", Nelson A. Rockefeller Empire State Plaza Art Collection, New York.

Allan Kaprow: *Fluids*, 1967. Pasadena, California.

Lila Katzen: *Guardian*, 1979, bronze, 35 x 15 x 3ft, private collection, Saudi Collection.

Edward Kienholz: *Back Seat of a '38 Dodge*, 1964, the Kleiner Foundation, Los Angeles.

Philip King: *Call*, 1967, fibreglass and painted steel, two pieces each 14.5 x 0.5 x 0.5ft, two pieces each 5 x 6 x 3 ft, Juda Rowan Gallery, London; *Genghis Khan*, 1963, fibreglass and plastic with steel support, 41 x 56.5 x 34.5in, Tate Gallery, London.

Ernst Kirchner: *Standing Nude*, 1908-12, wood, painted yellow, 35.5in, Stedelijk Museum, Amsterdam.

Joyce Kozloff: *New England Decorative Arts*, 1985, tile mural, 8 x 83 feet overall, Harvard Square subway station, Cambridge, MA.

Jannis Kounellis: *Cotton Sculpture*, 1967, steel and cotton, 3.9 x 3.9 x 4.9ft, collection: the artist.

Norbert Kricke: *Space Sculpture*, 1958-59, stainless steel, 9.4 ft high, Municipality Leverkusen, Germany.

Anish Kapoor: *Half*, 1984, polystyrene, cement, earth, acrylic medium and pigment, 5.6 x 3.1in, Barbara Gladstone Gallery, New York; *Six Secret Objects*, 1983, mixed media, 115 x 425 x 60cm, Lissom Gallery, London.

Gaston Lachaise: *Standing Woman*, 1912-27, bronze, 70in high, Whitney Museum of American Art, New York.

Wolfgang Laib: *Hazelnut Pollen*, Dokumenta 8, Kassel.

Sol LeWitt: *Untitled Cube*, 1968, 15.5 x 15.5 x 15.5in, Whitney Museum of Art, New York; *Open Modular Cube*, 1966, painted aluminium, 5ft cube, Art Gallery, Ontario.

Len Lye: *The Loop*, 1963, stainless steel, 60 x 6in, Art Institute, Chicago; *Fountain II*, 1959, steel, motorized, 7.5 ft high, Howard Wise Gallery, New York.

Aristide Maillol: *Desire*, 1903-05, lead relief, Musée Nationale d'Art Moderne, Paris.

Paul Manship: *Dancer and Gazelles*, 1916, bronze, 32.2in high, Smithsonian Institute, Washington, DC.

Agnes Martin: *Night Sea*, 1963, oil and gold leaf on canvas, 72 x 72in, Saatchi Collection, London; *Drift of Summer*, 1965, acrylic and graphite on canvas, 72 x 72in,

Saatchi Collection, London; *Mountain II*, 1966, oil and pencil on canvas, 72 x 72in, collection: R. Solomon, New York.

John McCracken: *Untitled*, 1967, fibreglass and lacquer, 7.9 x 1.2 x 0.1 ft, Saatchi Collection, London.

Mary Miss: *Field Rotation*, 1981, wood, steel, gravel, earth, 5-acre site, central well 60 ft square and 7 feet deep, Governors' University, Park Forest South, Illinois.

Henry Moore: *Reclining Figure*, 1945-46, elmwood, 75in long, collection: Humana Corp, Louisville; *Three Piece Reclining Figure: Draped*, 1975, bronze, 14ft 8in long, Henry Moore Foundation.

Robert Morris: *Observatory*, 1971, earth, grass, wood, steel, granite, diameter *c.* 300 feet, Oosterlijk Flevoland, Holland; *Labyrinth*, 1974, painted masonite, plywood & two-by-fours, 96 x 360in, Institute of Contemporary Art, University of Pennsylvania, Philadelphia, PA.

Elie Nadelman: *Dancer, c.* 1918, painted wood, 28.5in high, Robert Isaacson Gallery, New York.

David Nash: *Fletched Over Ash Dome*, 1977/9, Caeny-Coed, Maentwrog, Wales; *Sea Hearth*, 1981, Isle of Bute, Scotland; *Slate Stove*, 1988, Blaenau Ffestiniog, Wales; *Wood Stove*, 1979, Maentwrog, Wales; *Snow Stove*, 1982, Kotoku, Japan; *Wooden Boulder*, 1978, oak, Maentwrog, Wales.

Louise Nevelson: *Royal Tide IV*, 1960, wood, 1 x 14ft, Ludwig Museum, Cologne; *Sky Cathedral – Moon Garden Plus One*, 1957-60, black painted wood, 9.1 x 10.1 x 1.6ft, collection: A. & M. Glimcher, New York.

Barnett Newman: *Broken Obelisk*, 1963-67, Cor-Ten steel, 26 ft high, Institute of Religion and Human Development, Houston, TX.

Isamu Noguchi: *Red Cube*, 1969, painted welded steel and aluminium, 28 ft high, 140, Broadway, New York.

Dennis Oppenheim: *Annual Rings*, 1968, 150 x 200 feet, Fort Kent, Maine and Clair, New Brunswick, NJ; *Branded Mountain*, 1969, 30ft diameter, San Pablo, California.

Roger Partridge: *Arch*, 1983, Portland stone, 77 x 91.5 x 20cm, private collection.

Beverly Pepper: *Sand Dunes*, 1985, Mylar over wood, approximately 100 feet long, temporary installation for the Atlantic Center for the Arts, New Smyrna Beach, Florida.

Picasso: *Bust of a Woman,* 1932, bronze, 25.1in high, estate of the artist.

Anne & Patrick Poirier: *Archæological Model*, 1986, Bath International Festival.

Gio Pomodoro: *Tensione*, 1959, black fibreglass, 5.9 x 4.2 x 1.9 ft, David Anderson Gallery, Buffalo, CO.

George Rickey: *Peristyle III*, 1966, stainless steel, 40.5 x 102.5 x 60.2in, Corcoran Gallery of Art, Washington, DC.

Robert Ryman: *Department*, 1981, oil on aluminium, 60 x 60in, collection: Rhona J. Hoffman, Chicago, IL.

Lucas Samaras: *Book 4*, 1962, 5.5 x 8.8 x 11.5in, Museum of Modern Art, New York.

Niki de Sant-Phalle: *Black Venus*, 1967, painted polyester, 110 x 35 x 24in, Whitney Museum of Art, New York; *Pink Childbirth*, 1964, painted relief, 86.24in high, Moderner Muséet, Stockholm; *Un Ensemble de "Les Nanas"*, 1965, Archives Galerie Alexandre Iolas, New York.

Miriam Schapiro: *Heartland*, 1985, acrylic, fabric and glitter on canvas, 7.1 x 7.8ft, Bernice Steinbaum Gallery, New York.

Kurt Schwitters: *Picture*, 1925, Sammlung Janlet, Brussels.

Tim Scott: *Quinquereme,* 1966, Tate Gallery, London.

Richard Serra: *Clara-Clara*, 1983, Cor-Ten steel, installation, Jardin des Tuileries, Paris; *Prop*, 1968, 96in high, sheet 60 x 60in, Whitney Museum of Art, New York.

David Smith: *Cubi XXVII*, 1965, stainless steel, 9.2ft high, Guggenheim Museum, New York.

Tony Smith: *Die*, 1962, 72 x 72 x 72in, Paula Cooper Gallery, New York.

Robert Smithson: *Spiral Jetty*, 1969-70, rock, salt crystal and earth, 1,500 feet long, Great Salt Lake, Utah; *Closed Mirror Square*, 1969, rock salt, mirrors and glass, Blum

Helman Gallery, New York; *Amarillo Ramp*, 1973, red sandstone shale, 1800in diameter, estate of the artist; *Floor Piece*, 1964, 17 x 17 x 288in, Green Gallery, New York, 1964.

Frank Stella: *Ophir*, 1960-61, copper oil paint on canvas, 250.2 x 210.2cm, private collection.

Sylvia Stone: *Crystal Palace*, 1971-72, Plexiglas, 6.5 x 14 x 16ft, Andre Emmerich Gallery, New York.

George Sugarman: *Bardana*, 1962-63, polychromed woof, 8 x 12 x 5.1ft, Galerie Renee Ziegler, Zurich.

James Turrell: *Roden Crater*, 1977-, Flagstaff, Arizona; *Space That Sees*, 1992, Jerusalem; *Heavy Water*, 1992, Poitier, France; *Razor,* 1991, London.

Andrea del Verrocchio: *David, c.* 1475, bronze, Museo Nazionale, Florence.

Andy Warhol: *Clouds*, 1966, Leo Castelli Gallery, New York.

Lawrence Weiner: *Billowing Clouds...,* 1986, 86.2 x 17.5 in, Anthony d'Offay Gallery, London.

Alison Wilding: *Bare*, 1989-90, Newlyn Art Gallery, Cornwall; *Into the Dark*, 1986, limewood, lead and pigment, Newlyn Art Gallery; *Hemlock III*, 1986, lime, hemlock, lead, beeswax, pigment, Karsten Schubert; *Blueblack,* 1984, lime & elm woods, wax, lead, 36 x 28 x 49cm, collection: the artist.

Jackie Winsor: *Burnt Piece*, 1977-78, concrete, wire and burnt wood, 36in cube, Paula Cooper Gallery, New Yor; *Installation*, 1982, mixed media, Paula Cooper Gallery, New York.

Bill Woodrow: *Winter Jacket*, 1986, mixed media, collection: Anne MacDonald Walker, San Francisco; *English Heritage – Humpty Fucking Dumpty*, 1987, vaulting box and mixed media, Tate Gallery, London.

Bibliography

RICHARD LONG

Richard Long, Städtisches Musem, Mönchengladbach, 1970
Two Sheepdogs Cross In and Out of the Passing Shadows, Lissom Gallery, London, 1971
From Along a Riverbank, Art & Project, Amsterdam, 1971
John Barleycorn, Stedelijk Museum, Amsterdam, 1973
South America, Konrad Fischer, Düsseldorf, 1973
From Around a Lake, Art & Project, Art & Project, Amsterdam, 1973
Inca Rock Campfire Ash, Scottish National Gallery, Edinburgh, 1974
The North Woods, Whitechapel Art Gallery, London, 1977
A Hundred Stones, Kunsthalle, Bern, 1977
A Straight Hundred Mile Walk In Australia, John Kaldor Project 6, 1977
Rivers and Stones, Newlyn Art Gallery, Cornwall, 1978
Sydamerika, Kalejdoskop, Lund, Sweden, 1978
Aggie Weston's No 16, Coracle Press, London, 1979
River Avon Book, Anthony d'Offay Gallery, London, 1979
Richard Long, Stedelijk Van Abbesmuseum, Eindhoven, 1979
A Walk Past Standing Stones, Coracle Press, London, 1980
Five, Six, Pick Up Sticks, Anthony d'Offay, London, 1980
Twelve Works, London, 1979-1981, Coracle Press, 1981
Richard Long, CAPC Musée d'Art Contemporain, Bordeaux, 1981
Selected Works, National Gallery of Canada, Ottawa, 1982
Mexico, Stedelijk Van Abbesmuseum, Eindhoven, 1982
"Correspondence: Richard Long Replies To a Critic", *Art Monthly*, July, 1983
Touchstones, Arnolfini, Bristol, 1983
Fango, Pietri, Legni, Galleria Tucci Russo, Turin, 1983
Countless Stones, Stedelijk Van Abbemuseum, Eindhoven, 1983
Planes of Vision, Ottenhausen Verlag, Aachen, 1983
River Avon Mud Works, Orchard Gallery, Londonderry, 1984
Postcards, 1968-1982, CAPC Musée d'art Contemporain de Bordeaux, 1984
Sixteen Works, Anthony d'Offay Gallery, London, 1984
Richard Long, Century Cultural Foundation, Tokyo, 1984
Mud Hand Prints, Coracle Press, London, 1984
Richard Long, Fonds Regional d'Art contemporain Aquitaine, 1985
Il Luogo Buono, Padiglione d'Arte Contemporanea, Milan, 1985
Lines of Time, Stichting Edy de Wilde Lezing/ Openbaar Kunstbezit, Amsterdam, 1985
Richard Long: In Conversation, Parts 1 & 2, MW Press, Noordwijk, Holland, 1985-86
Muddy Water Falls, MW Press, Noordwijk, Holland, 1986
Richard Long, text by R. Fuchs, Thames & Hudson, London, 1986
Out of the Wind, Donald Young Gallery, Chicago, IL, 1987
Dust Dobros Desert Flowers, Lapis Press, Venice, 1987
Stone Water Miles, Musée Rath, Geneva, 1987
Old World New World, Anthony d'Offay, London, 1988
Angel Flying Too Close To the Ground, Kunstverein St Gallen, 1989
Richard Long, Magasin 3, Stockholm, Sweden, 1990
Kicking Stones, Anthony d'Offay Gallery, London, 1990
Surf Roar, Museum of Contemporary Art, San Diego, CA, 1990
Sur La Route, Musée départmental de Rochechouart, 1990
Nile, Papers of River Muds, Lapis Press, Los Angeles, CA, 1990
Labyrinth, Frankfurt, 1991
Richard Long: Walking in Circles, Hayward Gallery/ Thames & Hudson, London, 1992
An Interview With Richard Long by R. Cork, in *Waking in Circles*
Fragments of a Conversation I-VI, in *Walking in Circles*
Mountains and Water, Anthony d'Offay, London, 1992

River to River, Musée d'Art Moderne de la Ville de Paris, 1993
An Interview with Richard Long, Neery Melkonian, Center for Contemporary Arts, Santa
    Fe, New Mexico, 1993-94
Interview with G. Lobacheff, 1994a
No Where, interview with C. Kirkpatrick, Piers Arts Centre, Orkney, 1994b
Richard Long, British Council, London, 1994
Richard Long, Kunstsammlung Nordhrhein-Westfalen, Düsseldorf, 1994
Richard Long, Palazzo delle Esposizione, Rome, 1994
Books, Prints, New York Public Library, New York, NY, 1994
"Question For Richard Long", interview with Yuko Hasegawa, 1995a
Walking, Mud, Stones, Anthony d'Offay, London, 1995b
Dolomite Stones, AR/ Ge Kunst, Bolzano, 1996
Circles, Cycles, Mud, Contemporary Arts Museum, Houston, TX, 1996
Dartmoor Time, Spacex Gallery, Exeter, Devon, 1996
From Time to Time, DAP, 1997
Richard Long, Hatje Cantz, Stuttgart, 1997
A Walk Across England, Thames & Hudson, London, 1997
A Road From the Past To the Future, J. Haldane, Crawford Arts Centre, St Andrews, 1997
Wind Circle, Memory Sticks, Wilhelm Lehmbruck Museum, Duisburg, 1997
Interview with M. Codognato, 1997; in *Mirage*, 1998
Mirage, Phaidon, London, 1998
Every Grain of Sand, Kunstverein Hannover, Hanover, 1999
Being In the Moment, Museum Kurhaus Kleve, Cleves, 1999
Being in the Moment, PARC, Lent, 1999
Spanish Stones, Édiciones Polígrafa, Barcelona, 1999
Selected Walks, 1979-1996, Morning Star Press, 1999
Statement on the Richard Long website, 2000
Richard Long in Leuk, Stiftung Schloss Leuk, 2000
Adamello Walk, Museo d'Arte Moderne, Trento, 2000
Midday, Museum Kurhaus Kleve, Cleves, 2001
Walking and Sleeping, Ivory Press, London
A Moving World, Tate Publishing, London, 2002
Walking the Line, Thames and Hudson, London, 2002
Interview with D. Hooker, *Stepping Stones*, in *Richard Long: Walking the Line*
"I am just passing through the world", *Financial Times*, July 9, 2003a
Dialog, with J. Mashe, Museum kunst palast, Düsseldorf, 2003
Dialog, with J. Mashe, Padiglione d'Arte Contemporanea, Milan, 2003
Here and Now and Then, Haunch of Venison, London, 2003
Floating Time, Akita City, Japan, May, 2004a
"Still walking, after all these years", *The Art Newspaper*, July, 2004b
Richard Long at Kukje Gallery, Kukje Gallery, Seoul, 2004
The Music of Stones, Synagoge Stommeln, Stommeln, 2004
Richard Long: An Encounter, Buson Museum of Modern Art, 2004
Richard Long, Galeria Máno Sequeira, Braga, 2005

OTHERS

H. Adams. "The Woodman", *Art and Artists*, 13, Apl, 1979

S. Adams & A. Robins, eds. *Gendering Landscape Art*, Manchester University Press, Manchester, 2000

W.C. Agee. *Don Judd*, Whitney Museum of American Art, New York, NY, 1968

—. "Unit, Series, Site: A Judd Lexicon", *Art in America*, May, 1975

—. *The Sculpture of Donald Judd*, Art Museum of South Texas, Corpus Christi, TX, 1977

L. Alloway. "Interview with Anthony Caro", *Gazette*, 1, 1961

—. "Robert Smithson", *Artforum*, 11, Nov, 1972

—. "Site Inspection", *Artforum*, Oct, 1976

P. Allison *et al. Beyond the Minimal*, Architectural Association Publications, London, 1998

W. Andersen. *American Sculpture in Process, 1930/, 1970*, New York Graphics Society, Boston, MA, 1975

L. Anderson: "Mary Miss", *Artforum*, Nov, 1973

C. Andre. "Frank Stella: Preface to Stripe Painting", in D.C. Miller, ed. *Sixteen Americans*, Museum of Modern Art, New York, NY, 1959.

—. "An Interview with Carl Andre", P. Tuchman, *Artforum*, 8, 10, June, 1970

—. *Carl Andre, Sculpture, 1958-1974*, Kunsthalle, Bern, 1975

—. "Object vs Phenomenon", *Sculpture Today*, The International Sculpture Center, Toronto, 1978

—. *Carl Andre: Sculpture*, State University of New York Press, Albany, NY, 1984

—. *Stichomythia, 12 Dialogues 1962-63*, Whitechapel Art Gallery, London

—. *Carl Andre: works on land*, Exhibitions International, 2001

J. Andrews. *The Sculpture of David Nash*, Lund Humphries, London, 1999

M. Andrews. *Landscape and Western Art*, Oxford Paperbacks, Oxford, 1999

E. de Antonio & M. Tuchman. *Painters Painting*, Abbeville Press, New York, NY, 1984

M. Archer. "A Walk In the Endless Summer From Duncansby Head To The Place of the Camel Dropping", *Art Monthly*, Sept, 1991

—. *Art Since 1960*, Thames & Hudson, London, 1997

M. Auping. *Common Ground*, John & Mable Ringling Museum of Art, Sarasota, 1982

—. "Hamish Fulton", *Art in America*, 71, Feb, 1983

—. "Tracking Fulton", in H. Fulton, 1990

A. Aycock. "Work", "Maze", 1975, in A. Sondheim, 1977

E. Baker: "Judd the Obscure", *Art News*, 67, 2, 1968

K. Baker. "Andre in Retrospect", *Art in America*, Apl, 1980a

—. "Reckoning with Notation: The Drawings of Pollock, Newman, and Louis", *Artforum*, 18, 10, Summer, 1980b

—. *Minimalism: Art of Circumstance*, Abbeville, New York, NY, 1988

S. Bann & W. Allen, eds. *Interpreting Contemporary Art*, Reaktion Books, London, 1991

—. "Shrines, Gardens, Utopias", *New Literary History*, 24, 4, Autumn, 1994a

—. "The Map As Index of the Real: Land Art and the Authentication of Travel", *Imago Mundi*, 46, British Library, London, 1994b

G. Baro. "Toward Speculation in Pure Form", *Art International*, Summer, 1967

—. "American Sculpture", *Studio International*, 172, 896, 1968

—. "Sculpture made visible: Barry Flanagan in discussion with Gene Baro", *Studio International*, 178, 915, Oct, 1969

D. Batchelor. *Minimalism*, Tate Publishing, London, 1997

G. Battock, ed. *Idea Art*, Dutton, New York, NY, 1973

—. ed. *Minimal Art: A Critical Anthology*, University of California Press, Berkeley, CA, 1995

G. Beal. "Richard Long: "the simplicity of walking, the simplicity of stones"", in T. Neff, 1987

—. ed. *Art In the Landscape*, Chinati Foundation, Texas, 2000
J. Beardsley. *Probing the Earth: Contemporary Land Projects,* Smithsonian Press, Washington, 1977
—. *Art in Public Spaces*, Partners For Liveable Places, Washington, DC, 1981
—. *Earthworks and Beyond: Contemporary Art in the Landscape*, Abbeville Press, New York, NY, 1984/ 1998
M.R. Beaumont. "Romantic Sculpture", in A. Papadakis, 1988
—. "Andy Goldsworthy", *Arts Review*, July 14, 1989
A. Benjamin, ed. *Installation Art, Art & Design*, 30, 1993
N. Bennett, ed. *The British Art Show: Old Allegiances and New Directions, 1979-1984*, Arts Council/ Orbis, London, 1984
M. Berger. *Labyrinths: Robert Morris, Minimalism, and the 1960s*, Harper & Row, New York, NY, 1989
—. *Minimal Politics*, University of Maryland, Fine Arts Gallery
F. Berthier. *Reading Zen in the Rocks: The Japanese Dry Landscape Garden*, University of Chicago Press, Chicago, IL, 2000
L. Biggs. "Richard Long", *Arnolfini Review*, Apl, 1983
—. *Between Object and Image*, British Council, 1986
M. Bochner. "Art in Process – Structures", *Arts Magazine*, 40, 9, 1966
—. "Primary Structures", *Arts*, June, 1966
—. "Systematic", *Arts Magazine*, 41, 1, Nov, 1966
—. "Serial Art Systems: Solipsism", *Arts Magazine*, 41, 8, Summer, 1967
—. "Mel Bochner on Malevich", interview with J. Coplans, *Artforum*, June, 1974
S. Boettger. *Earthworks*, University of California Press, Berkeley, CA, 2002
D. Bourdon. "Walter de Maria: The Singular Experience", *Art International*, Dec 20, 1968
—. *Carl Andre: Sculpture, 1959-1977*, Jaap Rietman, New York, NY, 1978
—. *et al. Niki de Sant-Phalle: Fantastic Vision*, Nassau County Musem of Fine Art, Rosyln, NY, 1987
—. *Designing the Earth*, Abrams, New York, NY, 1995
J. Bradley. *Richard Long*, National Gallery of Canada, Ottawa, 1982
D. Brown. "While Out Walking", *Times Literary Supplement*, July 5, 1991
J. Brown *et al. Michael Heizer: Sculpture in Reverse*, see M. Heizer, 1984
—. ed. *Occluding Front: James Turrell*, Lapis Press, Larkspur Landing, CA, 1985
J. Burnham. *Beyond Modern Sculpture*, George Braziller, New York, NY, 1968
—. "A Dan Flavin Retrospective in Ottawa", *Artforum*, 8, 4, Dec, 1969
—. "Haacke's Cancelled Show at the Guggenheim", *Artforum*, June, 1971
J. Butterfield. *The Art of Light and Space*, Abbeville Press, New York, NY, 1993
J. Campbell. *The Power of Myth*, with B. Moyers, ed. B.S. Flowers, Doubleday, New York, NY, 1988
—. *The Hero With a Thousand Faces,* Paladin, London, 1988
—. *An Open Life*, Larson Publications, New York, NY, 1988
—. *The Hero's Journey: Joseph Campbell On his Life and Work,* ed. P. Cousineau, Harper & Row, San Francisco, CA, 1990
M. P. Carroll. *The Cult of the Virgin Mary*, Princeton University Press, Princeton, NJ, 1986
T. Castle: "Nancy Holt, Siteseer", *Art in America*, Mch, 1982
A. Causey. "Space and Time in British Land Art", *Studio International*, 193, 98, Feb, 1977
—. *Nature as Material: An Exhibition of Sculpture and Photographs Purchased For the Arts Council Collection,* Arts Council, London, 1980
—. "Environmental Sculptures", in A. Goldsworthy, *Hand to Earth* 1990
—. *Sculpture Since 1945*, Oxford University Press, Oxford, 1998
G. Celant. "Tony Cragg and Industrial Platonism", *Artforum*, 20, 3, Nov, 1981
—. *Dennis Oppenheim*, Edizioni Charta Srl, 1997
A. Chave: "Minimalism and the Rhetoric of Power", *Arts*, Jan, 1990

H.B. Chipp, ed. *Theories of Modern Art,* University Press of California, LA, CA, 1968
Chuang-tzu. *Basic Writings*, tr. B. Watson, Columbia University Press, New York, NY
M. Church. "A shower of stones, a flash in the river", *Sunday Telegraph*, Apl 10, 1994
M. Codognato. Interview with R. Long, 1997; in *Mirage*, 1998
M. Cohen. "Richard Long", review, April 15, 2000
F. Colpitt. *Minimal Art: The Critical Perspective,* University of Washington Press, Seattle, WA, 1990
M. Compton & D. Sylvester. *Robert Morris*, Tate Gallery, London, 1971
—. *Some Notes on the Work of Richard Long*, British Council, London, 1976
L. Cooke. "Richard Long replies to a critic", *Art Monthly*, 68, July, 1983
—. "Between Image and Object: The "New British Sculpture"", in T. Neff, 1987
J. Coplans. "Serial Imagery", *Artforum*, 7, 2, Oct, 1968
—. *Donald Judd*, Pasadena Art Museum, CA, 1971
—. "Robert Smithson", *Artforum,* Apl, 1974
D. Cosgrove, ed. *Mappings*, London, 1999
J. Cowan. *The Mysteries of the Dream-Time*, Prism Press, 1989
P. Crowther, ed. *The Contemporary Sublime, Art & Design,* 40, 1995
P. Curtis. *Modern British Sculpture from the Collection*, Tate Gallery, Liverpool, 1988
A. Davies. "Richard Long and Hamish Fulton", *Art Monthly*, 25, Apl, 1979
H. Davies *et al. Blurring the Boundaries: Installation Art 1969-1996*, Museum of Contemporary Art, San Diego, CA, 1997
R. Davies & T. Knipe, eds. *A Sense of Place. Sculpture in Landscape*, London, 1984
W. de Maria. "The Lightning Field", *Artforum*, 18, 8, Apl, 1980
P. de Monchaux *et al*, eds. *The Sculpture Show*, Arts Council of Great Britain, London, 1983
N. de Oliveira *et al. Installation Art*, Thames & Hudson, London, 1994
—. *et al*, eds. *Installation Art in the New Millennium*, Thames & Hudson, London, 2003
E. Develing. *Carl Andre*, Gemeentenmeuseum, The Hague, 1969
—. & L. Lippard. *Minimal Art*, Stadtische Kunsthalle, Dusseldorf, 1969
C. Drury. *Silent Spaces*, Thames & Hudson, London, 1998
L. Durrell. *Spirit of Place*, Faber, London, 1971
A. Dyson. *Richard Long: Sao Paulo Biennial 1994,* The British Council, 1994
J.C. Eade, ed. *Projecting the Landscape*, Humanities Research Centre, Canberra, 1987
M. Eliade. *Patterns in Comparative Religion*, Sheed & Ward, London, 1958
—. *Shamanism: Archaic Techniques of Ecstasy*, Princeton University Press, Princeton, NJ, 1972
—. *Myths, Dreams and Mysteries*, Harper & Row, New York, NY, 1975
—. *From Primitives to Zen: A Sourcebook*, Collins, London, 1977
—. *A History of Religious Ideas*, I, Collins, London, 1979
—. *Ordeal by Labyrinth*, University of Chicago Press, Chicago, IL, 1984
—.*Symbolism, the Sacred and the Arts*, Crossroad, New York, NY, 1988
M. Elvy, ed. *The Crescent Moon Book of Nature Poetry*, Crescent Moon, 1994
G. Evans. "Sculpture and Reality", *Studio International*, 177, 908, Feb, 1969
J. Fineberg. "Robert Morris Looking Back", *Arts Magazine*, 55, 1, 1980
—. *Art Since 1940: Strategies of Being*, Laurence King, London, 2000
A. Fisher & J. Saward. *The British Maze Guide*, Minotaur Designs, London, 1991
—. & D. Kingham. *Mazes*, Shire Publications, London, 1991
J. Fisher. "Richard Long", *Aspects*, 14, Spring, 1981
S. Foley. *Unitary Forms: Minimal Structures by Carl Andre, Donald Judd, John McCracken, Tony Smith*, Museum of Modern Art, San Francisco, CA, 1970
N. Foote. "Long Walks", *Artforum*, 18, 10, Summer, 1980
W. Forma. *Five British Sculptors*, New York, NY, 1965
M. Fried. "Shape as Form: Frank Stella's New Paintings", *Artforum*, 5, 3, Nov, 1966
—. "Art and Objecthood", *Artforum*, 5, Summer, 1967
M. Friedman. "Robert Morris: Polemics and Cubes", *Art International*, 10, 10, Dec, 1966

—. *14 Sculptors*, Walker Art Center, Minneapolis, MN, 1969
D. Friis-Hansen. *Circles, Cycles, Mud*, Contemporary Arts Museum, 1996
E. Fry. *Alice Aycock*, University of South Florida Art Galleries, Tampa, FL, 1981
—. "The Poetic Machines of Alice Aycock", *Portfolio*, Nov, 1981
—. *et al. Robert Morris*, Museum of Contemporary Art, Chicago, IL, 1986
R.H. Fuchs. "Memories of Passing: A Note on Richard Long", *Studio International*, 187, 965, Apl, 1974
—. *Richard Long*, text by R. Fuchs, Thames & Hudson, London, 1986
P. Fuller. Black cloud over the Hayward", *Art Monthly*, 70, Oct, 1983
—. "Likely Prospects: A British Art Questionnaire", *Artscribe*, 50, Jan, 1985
—. "Onward Christian Soldiers", *Artscribe*, 52, July, 1985
—. *Peter Fuller's Modern Painters: Reflections on British Art*, ed. J. McDonald, Methuen, London, 1993
H. Fulton. *Hamish Fulton: Selected Walks, 1969-89*, Albright-Knox Art Gallery, Buffalo, New York, NY, 1990
. *Richard Long*, Thames & Hudson, London, 1991
—. *One Hundred Walks*, Haags Gemeetemuseum, The Hague, 1991
—. "Into a Walk Into Nature", *Thirty One Horrors*, Lenbachhaus, Munich, 1995
—. *Walking Artist*, Annely Juda, London, 1998
—. *Walking Through*, Stour Valley Art Project, Challock, Kent, 1999
—. *Wild Life*, Pocketbooks, Edinburgh, 2000
—. *Walking Artist*, Richter Verlag, Düsseldorf, 2001
—. "Specific Places and Particular Events", in B. Tufnell, 2002
L. Geddes-Brown. "The Long March of Richard Long", *Sunday Times*, March 27, 1983
J. Gibson. *The Senses Considered as a Perceptual System*, Houghton Mifflin, Boston, MA, 1966
J. Giovannini. *Mary Miss*, Architectural Association, London, 1987
T. Godfrey. *Conceptual Art*, Phaidon, London, 1998
R. Goldberg. *Performance: Live Art Since the 60s*, Thames & Hudson, London, 1998
A. Goldstein, ed. *Reconsidering the Object of Art: 1965-1975*, Museum of Contemporary Art, L.A., CA, 1995
A. Goldsworthy & J. Fowles. *Winter Harvest*, Scottish Arts Council, 1987
—. *Touching North*, Fabian Carlsson, London, 1989
—. *Snowballs in Summer Installation*, Old Museum of Transport, Glasgow, 1989
—. *Andy Goldsworthy*, Viking, London, 1990
—. *Hand to Earth: Andy Goldsworthy, Sculpture, 1976-1990*, Henry Moore Centre for Sculpture, Leeds, Yorkshire, 1990
—. *Stone*, Viking, London, 1994
—. *Wood*, Viking, London, 1996
—. *Sheepfolds*, Michael Hue-Williams Gallery, London, 1996
—. *Andy Goldsworthy: A Collaboration With Nature*, Abrams, NY, 1996
—. *Hand to Earth: Andy Goldsworthy Sculpture,* T. Friedman, Thames and Hudson, London, 1997 & 2004
—. *Arch*, with D. Craig, Thames & Hudson, London, 1999
—. *Wall,* intr. K. Baker, Thames & Hudson, London, 2000
—. *Time,* Thames & Hudson, London, 2000
—. *Midsummer Snowballs*, intr. J. Collins, Abrams, New York, NY, 2001
—. *Andy Goldsworthy – Réfuges D'Art,* Editions Artha, 2002
—. *Passage,* Thames & Hudson, London, 2004
—. *Enclosure*, Thames & Hudson, London, 2007
M. Golding. "Thoughts on Richard Long", *Modern Painters*, 3, 1, Spring, 1990
—. & W. Furlong. *Song of the Earth,* Thames and Hudson, London, 2002
A. Gopnik. "Basic Stuff: Robert Smithson, Myth, Science and Primitivism", *Art Magazine*, Mch, 1983
B. Graziani. "Robert Smithson's Picturable Situation", *Critical Inquiry*, 20, 3, Spring,

1994
C. Greenberg. *Art and Culture,* Beacon Press, Boston, MA, 1961
G. Greig. "Circular Tours In the Name of Art", *Sunday Times,* June 16, 1991
A. Haden-Guest. "The King of Wrap", *The Sunday Times Magazine,* Jan, 1994
J. Haldane. *A Road From the Past To the Future,* Crawford Arts Centre, St Andrews, 1997
—. "Images After the Fact", *Modern Painters,* 11, 3, Fall, 1998
—. "Back To the Land", *Art Monthly,* June, 1999
A.M. Hammacher. *The Sculpture of Barbara Hepworth,* Abrams, New York, NY, 1968
C. Harrison. "Barry Flanagan's sculpture", *Studio International,* 175, 900, May, 1968
—. "Richard Long", *Studio International,* 183, 940, Jan, 1972
B. Haskell. *BLAM! The Explosion of Pop, Minimalism, and Performance, 1958-64,* Whitney Museum of American Art, New York, NY, 1984
—. *Donald Judd,* Whitney Museum of American Art, New York, NY, 1988
L. Hegyi. *Arte Povera, Minimal Art, Concept Art,* Art Data, 1995
M. Heizer, D. Oppenheim & R. Smithson. "Discussion", *Avalanche,* 1, Autumn, 1970
—. *Sculpture in Reverse,* Museum of Contemporary Art, Los Angeles, 1984
A. Henri. *Environments and Happenings,* Thames & Hudson, London, 1974
—. *Total Art,* Praeger, New York, NY, 1974
Galerie Max Hetzler. *Carl Andre, Gunther Forg, Hubert Kiecol, Richard Long, Meuser, Reinhard Mucha, Bruce Nauman and Ulrich Ruckreim,* Cologne, 1985
G. Hilty. *Recent British Sculpture,* Arts Council, London, 1993
R. Hobbs. *Robert Smithson: Sculpture,* Cornell University Press, Ithaca, NY, 1981
—. "Earthworks", *Art Journal,* 42, Fall, 1982
N. Hodges ed. *Art and the Natural Environment, Art & Design,* 36, 1994
—. ed. *The Contemporary Sublime, Art & Design,* 40, 1995
N. Holt. "Amarillo Ramp", *Avalanche,* Fall, 1973
—. "Hydra's Head", *Arts Magazine,* Jan, 1975
—. "Sun Tunnels", *Artforum,* Apl, 1977
S. Hubbard, intr. *Sculpture At Goodwood: A Vision For 21st Century British Sculpture,* Sculpture At Goodwood, Sussex, 2002
R. Hughes. *Nothing If Not Critical: Selected Essays on Art and Artists,* Collins Harvill, London, 1990
—. *The Shock of the New,* Thames & Hudson, London, 1991
—. *American Visions: The Epic History of Art In America,* Knopf, New York, NY, 1997
T. Hughes. *Poetry in the Making,* Faber, London, 1969
H.E. Hugo, ed. *The Portable Romantic Reader,* Viking Press, New York, NY, 1957
S. Hunter, ed. *An American Renaissance: Painting and Sculpture Since 1940,* Abbeville Press, New York, NY, 1986
—. *American Art of the 20th Century,* Thames & Hudson, London, 1973
L. Iizawa. "Earth work", *Studio Voice,* Mch, 1988
G. Jeppson. *Richard Long,* Harvard College, Cambridge, MA, 1980
E.H. Johnson. *Modern Art and the Object,* Harper & Row, New York, NY, 1976
—. ed. *American Artist on Art,* Harper & Row, New York, NY, 1965
B. Jones. "A New Wave in Sculpture: A survey of recent work by ten younger sculptors", *Artscribe,* 8, Sept, 1977
J. Jones, *The Guardian,* Mch 4, 2000
D. Judd. "Frank Stella", *Arts Magazine,* 36, Sept, 1962
—. "In the Galleries", *Arts Magazine,* 37, 10, Sept, 1963
—. "Local History", *Arts Yearbook 7,* 1964
—. "Black, White and Gray", *Arts Magazine,* 38, 6, Mch, 1964
—. "Specific Objects", *Arts Yearbook,* 8, Art Digest, New York, NY, 1965
—. "Barnett Newman", *Studio International,* 179, 919, Feb, 1970
—. *Complete Writings, 1959-1975,* Nova Scotia College of Art and Design, Halifax, Canada, 1975
—. *Complete Writings, 1975-1986,* Van Abbemuseum, Netherlands, 1987

E. Juncosa. "Landscape as experience", *Lapiz*, 61 Oct, 1989
J. Kastner, ed. *Land and Environmental Art,* Phaidon, London, 1998
P. King *et al.* "Colour in Sculpture", *Studio International*, 177, 907, 1969
C. Knight: *Art of the Sixties and Seventies: The Panza Collection*, Rizzoli, New York, NY, 1987
N. Konstam: *Sculpture: The Art and the Practice*, Collins 1984
R.E. Krauss. "Richard Serra: Sculpture Redrawn", *Artforum*, May, 1972
—. "Sense and Sensibility: Reflection on Post '60s Sculpture", *Artforum*, 12, Nov, 1973
—. *Passages in Modern Sculpture,* Thames & Hudson, London, 1977
—. "Sculpture in the Expanded Field", *October*, 8, Spring, 1979
—. *Eva Hesse*, Whitechapel Art Gallery, London, 1979
—. *et al. Robert Morris*, Abrams, New York, NY, 1994
Z. Kraus, ed. *From Nature to Art, From Art to Nature*, Venice Biennale, Milan, 1978
D. Kuspitt. "Sol LeWitt", *Art in America*, 63, 5, 1975
—. "Robert Smithson's Drunken Boat", *Arts Magazine*, Oct, 1981
—. "Aycock's Dream Houses", *Art in America*, Sept, 1985
—. "Donald Judd", *Artforum*, 23, 5, Feb, 1985
I. Lamaitre: "Interview with Tony Cragg", *Artefactum*, 2, Dec, 1985
B. Laws. "Where Art and Nature Meet", *The Telegraph Weekly*, 12 Nov, 1988
D. Lee. "Opinion: Richard Long and Hamish Fulton", *Arts Review*, July 26, 1991
A. Legg, ed. *Sol LeWitt*, Museum of Modern Art, New York, NY, 1978
B. Le Messurier. *Dartmoor Artists*, Halsgrove, Tiverton, Devon, 2002
P. Leider. "Literalism and Abstraction: Frank Stella's Retrospective at the Modern", *Artforum*, 8, Apl, 1970
—. "For Robert Smithson", *Art in America*, Nov, 1973
—. *Stella Since 1970*, Fort Worth Art Museum, TX, 1978
K. Levin. "Robert Smithson", *Art News*, Sept, 1982
—. "Reflections on Robert Smithson's *Spiral Jetty"*, *Arts Magazine*, May, 1978
F. Licht. *Sculpture, 19th and 20th Centuries*, Michael Joseph, London, 1967
—. "Dan Flavin", *Artscanada*, Dec, 1968
I. Licht. "Dan Flavin", *Artscanada*, Dec, 1968
L. Lippard. "New York Letter: Apl-June, 1965", *Art International*, 9, 6, 1965
—. "New York Letter: Recent Sculpture as Escape", *Art International*, Feb, 1966a
—. "An Impure Situation", *Art International*, 20 May, 1966b
—. *Ad Reinhardt*, Jewish Museum, New York, NY, 1966c
—. "The Silent Art", *Art in America*, 55, 1, Jan-Feb, 1967a
—. "Sol LeWitt: Non-Visual Structures", *Artforum*, Apl, 1967b
—. "Tony Smith", *Art International*, Summer, 1967c
—. "Rebelliously Romantic?", *New York Times*, June 4, 1967d
—. "Escalataion in Washington", *Art International*, 12, 1, Jan, 1968
—. ed. *Surrealists on Art*, Prentice-Hall, Englewood Cliffs, NJ, 1970
—. *Tony Smith*, Thames & Hudson, London, 1972a
—. *Grids*, Philadelphia Institute of Contemporary Art, PA, 1972b
—. *Six Years: The Dematerialization of the Art Object from 1966 to 1972*, Praeger, New York, NY, 1973
—. *From the Center: feminist essays on women's art*, Dutton, New York, NY, 1976
—. *Eva Hesse*, New York University Press, New York, NY, 1976
—. "Complexities: Architectural Sculpture in Nature", *Art in America*, Feb, 1979
—. "Dinner Party", *Art in America*, Apl, 1980
—. *Ad Reinhardt*, Abrams, New York, NY, 1981
—. *Overlay: Contemporary Art and the Art of Prehistory*, Pantheon, New York, NY, 1983
G. Lobacheff. Interview with Richard Long, 1994; in *Mirage*, 1998
E. Lucie-Smith. *Sculpture Since 1945*, Phaidon, London, 1987
N. Lynton. introduction to *Tony Cragg*, Fifth Triennale India, British Council, 1982
—. *David Nash: Sculpture, 1971-90*, Serpentine Gallery, London, 1990

W. Malpas. *Andy Goldsworthy: Touching Nature*, Crescent Moon, 1998/ 2004
—. *Land Art*, Crescent Moon, 1996/ 2004
B. Marcelis. "Richard Long: Beaute et ambiguite du Land Art", *Domus*, 601, Dec, 1979
J. van der Marck. *Wrapped Museum*, Museum of Contemporary Art, Chicago, IL, 1969
M. Marmer. "James Turrell", *Art in America*, 69, May, 1981
R. Martin. *The Sculpted Forest: Sculpture in the Forest of Dean*, Redcliff, Bristol, 1990
D. Mayhall: *The Minimal Tradition*, The Aldrich Museum of Contemporary Art, Ridgefield, CT, 1979
D. Macmillan. "David Nash: Brancusi Joins the Garden Gang", *Art Monthly*, 65, Apl, 1983
D. Marzona & E. Carlini. *Minimal Art*, Taschen, Cologne, 2004
A. McPherson. "David Nash: interviewed by Allan McPherson", *Artscribe*, 12, June, 1978
K. McShine. *Primary Structures*, Jewish Museum, New York, NY, 1966
—. *Information*, Museum of Modern Art, New York, NY, 1970
—. *An International Survey of Recent Painting and Sculpture*, MOMA, New York, NY, 1984
J. Meyer, ed. *Minimalism*, Phaidon, London, 2000
U. Meyer. *Conceptual Art*, Dutton, New York, NY, 1972
M. Miss. *Mary Miss: Interior Works*, Bell Gallery, University of Rhode Island, Autumn, 1981
J.-Y. Mock. *Niki de Sant-Phalle: Exposition Retrospective*, CGP, 1980
R.C. Morgan. "Richard Long's Poststructural Encounters", *Arts*, 61, 6, Feb, 1987
—. *Art Into Ideas*, Cambridge, 1996
J. Morland. *New Milestones: Sculpture, Community and the Land*, Common Ground, London, 1988
H. Morphy & M. Boles, eds. *Art from the Land*, University of Washington Press, 2000
R. Morris. "Notes on Sculpture", *Artforum,* Feb, 1966, Oct, 1966, June, 1967, Apl, 1969
—. "Aligned with Nazca", *Artforum*, Oct, 1975
—. *Robert Morris: Mirror Works, 1961-1978*, Leo Castelli Gallery, New York, NY, 1979
—. *et al. Earthworks*, Seattle Art Museum, Seattle, WA, 1979
—. "American Quartet", *Art in America*, Dec, 1981
—. *Selected Works*, Contemporary Arts Museum, Houston, TX, 1981
—. *Continuous Project Altered Daily*, MIT Press, Cambridge, MA, 1993
S. Nairne & N. Serota. *British Sculpture in the Twentieth Century*, Whitechapel Art Gallery, London, 1981
D. Nash. *Fletched Over Ash*, AIR Gallery, 1978
—. "David Nash", *Aspects*, 10, Spring, 1980
—. *Stoves and Hearths*, Duke Street Gallery, London, 1982
T.A. Neff, ed. *A Quiet Revolution: British Sculpture Since 1965*, Thames & Hudson, London, 1987
B. Nemitz. *Trans Plant: Living Vegetation in Contemporary Art*, Hatje Cantz, Stuttgart, 2000
C. Nemser. "An interview with Eva Hesse", *Artforum*, May, 1970
—. "My Memories of Eva Hesse", *Feminist Art Journal*, Winter, 1973
M. Newman. "New Sculpture in Britain", *Art in America*, Sept, 1982
M. Nixon. *Eva Hesse*, MIT Press, Cambridge, MA, 2002
P. Noever. *Donald Judd: Architecture*, Hatje Cantz, Stuttgart, 2003
I. Noguchi. *A Sculptor's World,* Harper & Row, New York, NY, 1968
R. Onoratio. *Mary Miss – Perimeters/ Pavilions/ Decoys*, Nassau County Museum, 1979
P. Osborne, ed. *Conceptual Art*, Phaidon, London, 2002
A.C. Papadakis, ed. *British and American Art: The Uneasy Dialectic, Art & Design*, 3, 9/1, Academy Group, London, 1987
—. ed. *Abstract Art and the Rediscovery of the Spiritual, Art & Design*, 3, 5/6, Academy Group, London, 1987

—. ed. *The New Romantics*, Art & Design, 4, 11/12, Academy Group, London, 1988

—. *et al,* eds. *New Art*, Academy Group, London, 1991

R. Parker & G. Pollock. *Old Mistresses: Women, Art an Ideology*, Routledge & Kegan Paul, London, 1981

J. Perrone. "Seeing Through Boxes", *Artforum*, 15, Nov, 1976

R. Pincus-Witten. *Postminimalism*, Out of London Press, New York, NY, 1977

—. *Entries: Maximalism*, Out of London Press, London, 1983

—. *Post-Minimalism into Maximalism*, UMI Research Press, Ann Arbor, MI, 1987

J.-M. Poinsot. "Richard Long: construire le paysage", *Art Press*, 53, Nov, 1981

G. Pollock: *Vision and Difference: femininity, feminism and histories of art*, Routledge, London, 1988

L. Ponti: "Tony Cragg", *Domus*, 611, Nov, 1980

J.C. Powys. *In Defence of Sensuality*, Gollancz, London, 1930

—. *Maiden Castle,* Cassell, London, 1937

—. *A Glastonbury Romance*, Macdonald, London, 1955

—. *Wolf Solent*, Penguin, London, 1964

—. *Autobiography*, Macdonald, London, 1967

S. Prokopoff. *A Romantic Minimalism*, Institute of Contemporary Art, Philadelphia, PA, 1967

J. Prown *et al. Discovered Lands, Invented Pasts*, Yale University Press, New Haven, CT, 1992

C. Ratcliff. *In the Realm of the Monochrome*, Renaissance Society, University of Chicago, Chicago, IL, 1979

—. "The Compleat Smithson", *Art in America*, Jan, 1980

—. "Robert Ryman Making Distinctions", *Art in America*, June, 1986

—. *Out of the Box*, Allworth Press, London, 2001

S. Rainbird. "Crossing Places: Some Notes on the Works of Richard Long", in *Walking in Circles*

B. Redhead. *The Inspiration of Landscape: Artists in National Parks*, Phaidon, Oxford, 1989

W. Reh & C. Steenbergen. *Architecture and Landscape,* Prestel Publishing, 1996

C. Robins. "Object, Structure or Sculpture: Where Are We?", *Arts Magazine*, 40, 9, 1966

—. "Empty Paintings", *SoHo Weekly News*, Apl 22, 1976

—. *The Pluralist Era: American Art, 1968-1981*, Harper & Row, New York, NY, 1984

P. Rodaway. *Sensuous Geographies*, Routledge, London, 1994

W. Romey. "The artist as geographer: Richard Long's Earth Art", *Professional Geographer*, 39, 4, 1987

A. Rorimer. *New Art in the 60s and 70s*, Thames & Hudson, London, 2001

B. Rose. "New York Letter", *Art International*, Feb 15, 1964

—. "ABC Art", *Art in America*, 53, 5, Nov, 1965

—. Looking at American Sculpture", *Artforum*, 3, Feb, 1965

—. *A New Aesthetic*, Washington Gallery of Modern Art, Washington, DC, 1967

H. Rosenberg. *The De-Definition of Art*, Horizon Press, New York, NY, 1972

—. *Art on the Edge*, Macmillan, London, 1975

R. Rosenblum. "Notes on Sol LeWitt", in Legg, 1978

—. *Modern Painting and the Northern Romantic Tradition*, Thames & Hudson, London, 1978

—. "Romanticism and Retrospective: An Interview with Robert Rosenblum", in A. Papadakis, 1988

S. Ross. "Gardens, earthworks, and environmental art", in S. Kemal, 1993

—. *What Gardens Mean*, University of Chicago Press, Chicago, IL, 1998

M. Ryan, ed. *Gravity and Grace: The Changing Condition of Sculpture, 1965-1975*, Hayward Gallery, London, 1993

A. Saalfield. *Mary Miss*, Fogg Art Museum, Cambridge, MA, 1980

I. Sandler. *American Art of the 1960s,* Harper & Row, New York, NY, 1988

—. *Art of the Postmodern Era: From the 1960s to the Early 1990s*, HarperCollins, London, 1997

D. Schaff. "British Art Now, at the Guggenheim and Beyond", *Art International*, March, 1980

P. Schjeldahl. *Art in Our Time: The Saatchi Collection*, Lund Humphries, London, 1984

A. Seymour. *The New Art*, Hayward Gallery, London, 1972

—: "Walking in Circles", in R. Long, *Walking in Circles*

—. "El Estanque de Basho - una nueva perspectiva", in *Piedras Richard Long*, Ministerio de Cultura, Direccion general de Bellas Artes y Archivos and the British Council, 1986

—. "Old World New World", in R. Long, *Old World New World*

E. Shanes: *Constantin Brancusi*, Abbeville, New York, NY, 1989

G. Shapiro. *Earthworks: Robert Smithson and After Babel*, University of California Press, Berkeley, CA, 1995

W. Sharp *et al. Earth Art*, Andrew Dickson White Museum of Art, Cornell University, Ithaca, NY, 1969

—. "Structure ad Sensibility", *Avalanche*, 5, Summer, 1972

P. Sims. *From Minimalism to Expressionism*, New York, NY, 1963

N. Sinden. "Interview: Art in Nature: Andy Goldsworthy", *Resurgence*, 129, Aug, 1988

H. J. Smagula. *Currents: Contemporary Directions in the Visual Arts*, Prentice-Hall, Englewood Cliffs, NJ, 1983

B. Smith. *Fluorescent Light, etc, from Dan Flavin*, National Gallery of Canada, Ottawa, 1969

—. *Donald Judd*, National Gallery of Canada, Ottawa, 1975

D. Smith. *Sculpture and Drawings*, ed. J. Merkert, Prestel-Verlag, Munich, 1986

R. Smith. "Sol LeWitt", *Artforum*, Jan, 1975

—. "Review", *Artforum*, Dec, 1975

—. "De Maria: Elements", *Art in America*, May, 1978

R. Smithson. "Entropy and the New Monuments", *Artforum*, 4, 10, June, 1966

—. "Incidents of Mirror-Travel in the Yucatan", *Artforum*, Sept, 1967

—. The Monuments of Passaic", *Artforum*, Dec, 1967

—. "Toward the Development of an Air Terminal Site", *Artforum*, Summer, 1967

—. "A Museum of Language in the Vicinity of Art", *Art International*, 12, 3, Mch, 1968

—. *The Writings of Robert Smithson*, ed. N. Holt, New York University Press, New York, NY, 1979

—. *Robert Smithson*, ed. J. Flam, University of California Press, Berkeley, CA, 1996

T. Sokolowski *et al. Robert Morris*, New York University Press, New York, NY, 1989

A. Sondheim, ed. *Post-Movement Art in America*, Dutton, New York, NY, 1977

A. Sonfist, ed. *Art in the Land: A Critical Anthology of Environmental Art*, Dutton, New York, NY, 1983

F. Stella. *Working Space*, Harvard University Press, Cambridge, MA, 1986

N. Stewart. "Richard Long, Lines of Thought: A Conversation with Nick Stewart", *Circa*, Nov, 1984

K. Stiles & P. Selz, eds. *Theories & Documents of Contemporary Art: A Sourcebook of Artists' Writings*, University of California Press, Berkeley, CA, 1996

W.J. Strachan. *Open Air Sculpture in Britain*, Zwemmer, London, 1984

E. Suderburg, ed. *Space, Site, Intervention*, University of Minnesota Press, Minneapolis, MN, 2000

D. Sylvester. "Interview", *Jasper Johns Drawings*, Museum of Modern Art, Oxford, 1974

—. *About Modern Art*, Chatto & Windus, London, 1996

Tao Te Ching, Lao-tzu, tr. D.C. Lau, Penguin, London, 1963

G. Tiberghien. *Land Art*, Art Data, London, 1995

S. Tillim. "Earthworks and the New Picturesque", *Artforum*, Dec, 1968

E. Tsai. *Robert Smithson Unearthed*, Columbia University Press, New York, NY, 1991

M. Tuchman. *American Sculpture of the Sixties*, Los Angeles County Museum of Art, Los

Angeles, CA, 1967

—. *The Spiritual in Art: Abstract Painting 1880-1985*, Los Angeles County Museum of Art/ Abbeville Press, New York, NY, 1986

P. Tuchman. "Interview With Robert Ryman", *Artforum*, May, 1971

—. "Minimalism and Critical Response", *Artforum*, 15, 9, May, 1977

—. "Background of a Minimalist: Carl Andre", *Artforum*, Mch, 1978

—. "Minimalism", *Three Decades: The Oliver-Hoffmann Collection*, Museum of Contemporary Art, Chicago, IL, 1988

M. Tucker. *Robert Morris*, New York, NY, 1970

W. Tucker. "An Essay on Sculpture", *Studio International*, 177, 907, Jan, 1969

—. *The Language of Sculpture*, Thames & Hudson, London, 1974

B. Tufnell & A. Wilson. *Hamish Fulton: Walking Journey*, Tate Publishing, London, 2002

G. de Vries, ed. *On Art: Artists' Writings on the Changed Notion of Art After, 1965*, Cologne, 1974

A.M. Wagner. *Three Artists (Three Women): Modernism and the Art of Hesse, Krasner and O'Keeffe*, University of California Press, Berkeley, CA, 1996

D. Waldman. "Samaras", *Art News*, Oct, 1966

—. *Carl Andre*, Guggenheim Museum, New York, NY, 1970

—. "Holding the Floor", *Art News*, Oct, 1970

—. *Mark Rothko*, Thames & Hudson, London, 1978

J. Wall. "'Marks of Indifference': Aspects of Photography In, Or As, Conceptual Art", in A. Goldstein, 1995

U. Weilacher *et al. Between Landscape Architecture and Land Art*, Birkhauser Verlag AG, 1999

L. Weiner. *Lawrence Weiner, Works,* Anatol AV und Filmproduktion Hamburg, 1977

D. Wheeler. *Art Since Mid-Century: 1945 to the Present*, Thames & Hudson, London, 1991

O. Wick *et al. James Turrell*, Turske & Turske Gallery, Zurich, 1990

A. Wildermuth. *Richard Long*, Galerie Buchmann, Basel, 1985

R. Williams. *After Modern Sculpture: Art in the United States and Europe 1965-70*, Manchester University Press, Manchester, 2000

C. van Winkel. "The Crooked Path, Patterns of Kinetic Energy", *Parkett*, 33, 1992

R. Wittkower. *Sculpture: Process and Principles*, Harper & Row, New York, NY, 1977

G. Woods *et al*, eds. *Art Without Boundaries*, Thames & Hudson, London, 1972

du Zeitschrift für kultur, *Walking Into Existence*, no. 756, 2005

L. Zelevansky. "Richard Long", *Art News*, 83, 8, Oct, 1984

WEBSITES

Robert Smithson <www.robertsmithson.com>
Walter de Maria <www.lightningfield.org>
Christo <www.christojeanneclaude.net>
James Turrell <www.rodencrater.org>
Mary Miss <www.marymiss.com>
Hamish Fulton <www.hamish-fulton.com>
Chris Drury <www.chrisdrury.co.uk>
Donald Judd <www.chinati.org>
Andy Goldsworthy, Sheepfolds site: <www.sheepfolds.org>
Andy Goldsworthy, *Rivers and Tides* DVD <www.skyline.uk.com/riversandtides>
Richard Long <www.richardlong.org>
Richard Long Newsletter <therichardlongnewsletter.org>

Earthworks <www.earthworks.org>
The Artists: <www.the-artists.org>
Sculpture at Goodwood, CASS: <www.sculpture.org.uk>
Crescent Moon Publishing: <www.crescentmoon.org.uk>

www.ingramcontent.com/pod-product-compliance
Lightning Source LLC
Chambersburg PA
CBHW072011230526
45468CB00021B/1182